The New Chess Player

Le Nouveau Joueur d'Échecs

Der neue Schachspieler

De Nieuwe Schaakspeler

Den nye Schackspelaren

Il Nuovo Giocatore di Scacchi

El Nuevo Ajedrecista

Новый Шахматист

4

1978

D

PITMAN

PITMAN PUBLISHING LIMITED
39 Parker Street, London WC2B 5PB

Associated Companies
Copp Clark Limited, Toronto
Fearon-Pitman Publishers Inc., Belmont, California
Pitman Publishing New Zealand Ltd., Wellington
Pitman Publishing Pty Ltd., Melbourne

Distributed in Italy by
Edizioni Scolastiche APE SpA
Via Tanaro 14, 20128 Milano

First published in Great Britain 1979

Printed and bound in England by
Billing & Son Ltd., Guildford

ISBN 0 273 01288 6

Contents

Contributors 5
Journals/Bulletins 5
Novelties 6
Combinations 6

Theory 7
Tournaments/Matches 37

1 b3 — Larsen 52
1 c4 c5 — English 52
1 c4 e5 57
1 c4 ♘f6 61
1 d4 — Queen's Pawn 64
1 d4 d5 2 c4 dxc4 — QGA 68
1 d4 d5 2 c4 c6 — Slav 69
1 d4 d5 d4 e6 — QGD 71
Catalan 79
1 d4 f5 — Dutch 81
Benoni 81
Nimzo-Indian 87
Bogoljubow Indian 93
Queens Indian 93
Grunfeld 98
King's Indian 103
Sicilian
  2 c3 111
  2 ♘c3/2 d3 113
  3 ♗b5 114
  5...e5 116
  4...g6 123
  Najdorf 130
  Sozin 130
  Boleslavsky 130
  Richter-Rauzer 131
  Scheveningen 132
  Dragon 134
  4 ♕xd4 135
  2...e6, 4...a6 — Kan 136
  2...e6, 4...♘c6 — Taimanov 138
  2...e6, 4...♘f6 — Paulsen 139
  2...♘f6 142
Caro-Kann 142
1 e4 e5 2 ♘c3 — Vienna 145
Spanish 146
1 e4 e5 2 ♘f3 ♘c6 3 ♗c4 155
Scotch 156
1 e4 e6 — French 157
1 e4 ♘f6 — Alekhine 166
1 e4 g6 — Pric 168
1 ♘f3 179
1 f4 185
1 g3 185

Games Index 187

+ = white stands slightly better les blancs ont jeu un peu meilleur Weiss steht etwas besser wit staat er iets beter voor vit står något bättre il bianco sta un po' meglio el blanco está algo mejor белые стоят немного лучше

= + black stands slightly better les noirs ont jeu un peu meilleur Schwarz steht etwas besser zwart staat er iets beter voor svart står något bättre il nero sta un po' meglio el negro está algo mejor черные стояат немного лучше

± white has the upper hand les blancs ont le meilleur jeu Weiss steht besser wit staat beter vit står bättre il bianco sta meglio el blanco está mejor белые стоят лучше

∓ black has the upper hand les noirs ont le meilleur jeu Schwarz steht besser zwart staat beter svart står bättre il nero sta meglio el negro está mejor черные стоят лучше

+ − white has a decisive advantage les blancs ont un avantage décisif Weiss hat entscheidenden vorteil wit heeft een beslissend voordeel vit har avgörande fördel il bianco è in vantaggio decisivo el blanco tiene una ventaja decisiva белые имеют решающее преимущество

− + black has a decisive advantage les noirs ont un avantage décisif Schwarz hat entscheidenden vorteil zwart heeft een beslissend voordeel svart har avgörande fördel il nero è in vantaggio decisivo el negro tiene una ventaja decisiva черные имеют решающее преимущество

= the game is even le jeu est égal das Spiel ist ausgeglichen de stellingen zÿn gelÿkwaardig spelet är jamnt giuoco pari el juego está equilibrado игра равна

≈ approximately equal plus où moins égal ungefähr gleich ongeveer gelÿkwaardig narmelsevis jämnt piu o meno eguale más o menos igual приблизительно равно

∝ the position is unclear le jeu est incertain das Spiel ist unklar de posities zÿn onduidelÿk ställningen är oklar il giuoco è poco chiaro la posición no es clara неясная позиция

! a very good move un tres bon coup ein sehr guter Zug een zeer goede zet ett bra drag una buona mossa una jugada muy buena очень хороший ход

!! an excellent move un excellent coup ein ausgezeichneter Zug een uitstekende zet ett utmärkt drag una mossa ottima una jugada excelente отличный ход

? a mistake un coup faible ein schwacher Zug een fout ett dåligt drag una mossa debole una mala jugada плохой ход

?? a blunder une grave erreur ein grober Fehler een ernstige fout ett grovt fel un grave errore un gran error грубая ошибка

!? a move deserving attention un coup qui mérite l'attention ein beachtenswerter Zug een zet die de aandacht verdient ett drag som fortjäner uppmärksamhet una mossa degna di considerazione una jugada que merece atención ход, заслуживающий внимания

?! a dubious move un coup d'une valeur douteuse ein Zug von zweifelhaftem wert een dubieuze zet ett tvivelaktigt drag una mossa dubbia una jugada de dudoso valor ход, имеющий сомнительную ценность

Δ with the idea . . . avec l'idée . . . mit der Idee . . . met het idee om . . . med idén . . . con l'idea . . . con idea . . . с идеей...

N a novelty une innovation eine Neuerung een nieuwtje en nyhet un'innovazione una novedad новинка

Contributors

Name	Title
A. Adorjan	GM
B. Balogh	
G. Botterill	IM
W. Browne	GM
V. Ciocaltea	IM
A. Filipowicz	IM
D. Friedgood	
F. Gheorghiu	GM
T. Ghitescu	IM
A. Gipslis	GM
E. Gufeld	GM
E. Haag	IM
P. Hardicsay	
K. Honfi	IM
R. Hubner	GM
G. Iskov	IM
A. Kapengut	
H. Kasparov	
B. Larsen	GM
T. Lemachko	
J.-C. Letzelter	
B. Malich	GM
R. Maric	IM
S. Mechkarov	
E. Mednis	IM
A. Miles	GM
O. Neikirch	
J. Nunn	GM
L. Ochoa	
E. Paoli	IM
H. Pfleger	GM
L. Polugaevsky	GM
N. Povah	IM
J. Pribyl	IM
C. Pritchett	IM
K. Pytel	IM
D. Sahovic	GM
S. Samarian	
W. Schmidt	GM
M. Sher	
G. Sosonko	GM
J. Speelman	IM
A. Suetin	GM
S. Taulbut	IM
M. Tseitlin	IM
S. Webb	IM
H. Westerinen	GM

Journals

Ajedrez, British Chess Magazine, Butlleti D'Escacs, Ceskoslovensky Sach, Chess, Chess Bulletin (Canada), Chess in Australia, Chess Life and Review, Deutsche Schachblatter, Deutsche Schachzeitung, Europe Echecs, Fernschach, Jaque, Jaque Mate, Le Courrier Des Echecs, L'Italia Scacchistica, Magyar Sakkelet, Modern Chess Theory, Revista Romana de Sah, Rochade, Sahovski Glasnik, Scacco, Schaakbulletin, Schach, Schach-Echo, Schack nytt, Schakend Nederland, Shahmat, Shakhmatna Mis'l, Skakbladet, South African Chessplayer, Suomen Shakki, Szachy, Tidskrift for Schack, 64 **Шахматы Шахматный Бюллетень Шахматы в СССР**

Bulletins

1977: Stary Smokovec

1978: Bogota, BRD Final, British Final, Chiburdanidze-Gaprindashvili, Decin, IBM 1, IBM 2, Italy Final, Karpov-Korchnoi, Kiev, London, Lublin, Netherlands Final, Polanica Zdroj, Slupsk, Tilburg, Vienna Final, Vilnius, Warsaw, Wroclaw.

Novelties

No.	White	Black
10	Hodos	Gofstein
42	Pribyl	Peev
60	Barczay	Lukacs
81	Miles	Botterill
98	Korchnoi	Karpov
99	Vaiser	Zilberstein
114	Martin	J.Fernandez
116	Miles	Spassky
123	Smejkal	Boll
127	Kozlov	Mishuchkov
148	Martin	Botterill
162	Regan	Adorjan
173	Kapengut	Kim
191	Artishevsky	Fridman
193	Silva	Ochoa
199	Kapengut	Juferov
205	Kapengut	Tseshkovsky
210	J.Fernandez	Csom
219	Kasparov	Gufeld
227	Borngasser	Miles
234	Mednis	Malich
239	Mednis	J.Fernandez
247	Liu Wen Che	Ciocaltea
253	Maric	Weill
263	Karpov	Korchnoi
266	Padevsky	Honfi
269	Kapengut	Beljavsky
271	Astapov	Kolker
286	Diez del Corral	Portisch
306	Martin	J.Fernandez
313	Liu Wen Che	Donner
349	Gofstein	Buturin

Combinations

No.	White	Black
3	Djindjihashvili	Ribli
17	Speelman	Ree
33	Ftacnik	Romanishin
35	Nikolaevsky	Bronstein
40	Pribyl	Hazai
54	Polugaevsky	Pfleger
60	Barczay	Lukacs
62	Timman	Nikolac
75	Sosonko	Schneider
78	Pytel	Hjartarsson
107	Cooper	Petrosian
119	Beljavsky	Petrosian
120	Buturin	Chechelian
123	Smejkal	Boll
139	Rashkovsky	Gufeld
147	Botterill	Whiteley
157	Speelman	Biyiasas
159	P.Littlewood	Speelman
169	Filguth	Panchenko
187	Wedberg	Bouaziz
190	Kolker	Bigeldin
194	Sampouw	Ghitescu
214	Chiburdanidze	Gaprindashvili
236	Pokojowczyk	Sznapik
246	Radulov	Makropoulos
264	Karpov	Korchnoi
268	Adorjan	Radio Listeners
280	M.Tseitlin	Vladimirov
300	Nicevski	Vilela
306	Martin	J.Fernandez
309	Kasparov	Palatnik
313	Liu Wen Che	Donner
324	Raitza	Thormann
327	Sax	Donner
331	Pribyl	Swic
345	Jansa	Adorjan
347	Schurade	Thormann

Theory

English

1 c4 ♘f6 1...c5 2 ♘f3 ♘f6 3 ♘c3

a) 3...e6 4 g3 d5 5 cxd5 ♘xd5 6 ♗g2 ♘c6 7 0-0 ♗e7 8 d4 0-0 9 ♘xd5 exd5 10 dxc5 (10 ♗e3 ♗f6 11 dxc5 ♗xb2 12 ♖b1 ♗f6 13 ♘e1! d4 14 ♗f4 ♕a5 15 ♘d3 ♕xa2 16 ♗d6 ♖e8 17 ♘f4 ♗f5 18 ♖xb7± Portisch-Keres, Petropolis 1973) 10...♗xc5 11 b3 ♗f5 12 ♗b2 ♖e8 13 ♖c1 ♕d6 14 e3 ♖ad8 =+ Adamski-Lerner, Kiev 1978;

b) 3...d5 4 cxd5 ♘xd5 5 g3 g6 6 ♗g2 ♗g7 7 0-0 0-0 8 ♘xd5 ♕xd5 9 d3 ♘c6 10 a3 (10 ♗e3 ♗d7 11 ♕d2 ♕d6 12 ♗h6 ♖ac8 13 a3 b6= Larsen-Miles, London 1977) 10...b6 11 ♖b1 ♗b7 12 b4 ♕a2! 13 ♗e3 ♘d4 14 ♗xd4 cxd4 15 ♖a1 ♕d5∓ Ribli-Miles, Amsterdam 1978

2 ♘c3 e5

a) 2...e6 3 ♘f3 ♗b4 4 ♕c2 c5 5 a3 ♗a5 6 e3 0-0 7 ♘a4 d6 8 ♖b1 ♘c6 9 ♗e2 e5 10 0-0 ♕e7 11 d3 a6 12 ♘c3 ♗xc3 13 ♕xc3 b5= L.Garcia-Cuartas, Bogata 1978; 3...d5

b) 2...e6 3 e4 c5 4 e5 ♘g8 5 ♘f3 (5 d4 cxd4 6 ♕xd4 ♘c6 7 ♕e4 d6 8 ♘f3 dxe5 9 ♘xe5 ♘f6!? 10 ♘xc6 ♕b6 N 11 ♕f3 bxc6 12 ♗e2 ♗b7 13 0-0 += Korchnoi-Karpov (29) 1978) 5...♘c6 6 d4 cxd4 7 ♘xd4 ♘xe5 8 ♘db5 f6 9 ♗f4 a6 10 ♘d6+ ♗xd6 11 ♕xd6 ♘f7 12 ♕a3 b6 13 ♗e2 ♗b7 14 0-0 ♘e7 15 ♖fd1 ♗c6 16 ♘a4 ♖a7∝ Adorjan-Hort, Amsterdam 1978

c) 2...e6 3 e4 d5 4 e5 d4 5 exf6 dxc3 6 bxc3 ♕xf6 7 d4 e5!? N (7...♘d7 8 ♘f3 h6 9 ♗d3 ♕d8 10 ♕e2 ♗e7 11 0-0 0-0 12 c5 ♘f6 13 ♘e5 ♗d7 14 f4 b6 15 c6± L.Garcia-Cuellar, Bogata 1978) 8 ♕e2 ♘c6 9 f4 e4 10 ♕xe4+ ♗e7 11 ♗d3 ♗g4 12 ♘f3 ♗xf3 13 ♕xf3 0-0-0∝ Povah-Flear, England 1978

3 ♘f3

3 g3 ♗b4 4 ♕b3 ♘c6 5 ♘d5 ♗c5 6 e3 0-0 7 ♗g2 ♘xd5 8 cxd5 ♘e7 9 ♘e2 d6 10 0-0 c6= Korchnoi-Karpov (25) 1978

3...♘c6 4 e3

a) 4 g3 g6 5 ♗g2 ♗g7 6 0-0 0-0 7 d3 d6 8 a3 a5 9 ♖b1 ♘d4 10 ♘d2 c6 11 e3 ♘f5 12 ♘f3 ♖e8 13 e4 ♘d4 14 ♘xd4 exd4 15 ♘e2 += Reshevsky-Lebredo, Vilnius 1978

b) 4 e4 ♗c5 5 ♘xe5 ♘xe5 6 d4 ♗b4 7 dxe5 ♘xe4 8 ♕d4 ♘xc3 9 bxc3 ♗e7 10 ♗d3 N d6 11 ♗f4 dxe5 12 ♗xe5 0-0 13 0-0-0 ♗d6 14 ♖he1 ♗e6 15 ♖e3 += Bukal-Jasnikowski, Wroclaw 1978;

c) 4 d4 exd4 5 ♘xd4 ♗b4 (5...♗c5 6 ♘c2 [6 ♘xc6! bxc6 7 g3 +=] 6... 0-0 7 g3 ♖e8 8 ♗g2 a5 9 0-0 h6 10 b3 d6 11 ♗e3 ♗xe3 12 ♘xe3 ♘e5= Deze-Akvist, Wroclaw 1978) 6 ♗g5 ♗xc3+ (6...h6 7 ♗h4 ♗xc3+ 8 bxc3 d6 9 f3 ♘e5 10 ♕c2!? N [10 e4 ♘g6 11 ♗f2 0-0 12 ♕d2 c6 13 ♗e2 d5!= Tal-Dvoretsky, USSR 1976] 10...0-0 11 e3 ♖e8 12 ♗e2 c5! 13 ♘f5 ♘g6 14 ♗f2 ♗xf5 15 ♕xf5 ♕a5 16 ♕c2 d5! 17 0-0 dxc4 18 ♗xc4 ♘e5 19 ♗e2 ♘d5 20 ♖ac1 c4!∓ Cederlind-Horton, Corres 1978) 7 bxc3 ♘e5

8 f4! ♘g6 9 g3 h6 10 ♗xf6 ♕xf6 11 ♗g2 d6 12 ♖b1 0-0 13 0-0 c6 14 e4 ♖d8 15 ♕h5± Hernandez-Cuellar, Bogata 1978

4...♗b4

4...♕e7!? N 5 d4 exd4 6 ♘xd4 g6 7 ♘db5 d6 8 ♘d5 ♘xd5 9 cxd5 ♘e5 10 f4 ♘g4 11 ♗e2 ♘f6 12 ♕a4! ♔d8 13 ♘xa7 ♕e4 14 ♕xe4 ♘xe4 15 ♘xc8± Timman-Romanishin, Amsterdam 1978

5 ♕c2 0-0 6 ♘d5 ♖e8

6...h6!? 7 a3 ♗e7 8 ♗d3 d6 9 ♘xf6+ ♗xf6 10 ♗e4 ♗e6 11 b4 ♕e7 12 ♗b2 a5 13 b5 ♘d8 14 0-0 c6?! 15 bxc6 bxc6 16 c5!± Adamski-Paoli, Lublin 1978

7 ♕f5 d6 8 ♘xf6+ gxf6?

8...♕xf6 9 ♕xf6 += Keene-Ljubojevic, Moscow 1977

9 ♕h5 e4

9...d5 10 a3 ♗f8 11 d4 ♗e6 12 ♗d3 e4 13 ♗c2 ♘e7 14 ♘d2 f5?! 15 cxd5 ♕xd5 16 f3 ♕c6? 17 ♘xe4!! +− Goodman-Nunn, London 1978

10 a3 exf3 11 axb4 ♘xb4 12 ♖a4 ♖e5 13 ♕xf3 ♘c2+ 14 ♔d1 ♗d7 15 ♖a2 ♘b4 16 ♖a3 c5 17 d4 ♖g5∝ Lerner-Romanishin, Kiev 1978

Owen

1 d4 b6 2 c4 e6 3 e4

3 ♘c3 ♗b7

a) 4 e4 ♗b4 5 ♗d3 f5 6 ♕h5+!? g6 7 ♕e2 ♘f6 8 e5?! ♗xg2 9 exf6 ♕xf6 10 ♗f4 ♘c6 11 0-0-0 ♗xh1∓ Knott-Speelman, British Final 1978;

b) 4 a3 ♘f6 5 d5 b5 (5...exd5 6 cxd5 c6 7 g3 ♘xd5 8 ♘xd5 cxd5 9 ♗g2 ♕f6 10 ♘h3 ♘a6= Lukacs-Regan, Budapest 1978) 6 e4 bxc4 (6...b4 7 axb4 ♗xb4 8 ♗d3 exd5 9 cxd5 ♕e7 10 ♕e2 0-0 11 ♘f3 ♖e8 12 0-0!? ♗xc3 13 bxc3 ♗xd5 14 ♖e1 ♗xe4 15 ♗g5∝ Mohring-Espig, Eggesin 1978) 7 ♗xc4 exd5 8 exd5 ♗c5? (8...♗e7) 9 b4 ♗e7 10 ♘f3 0-0 11 0-0± Farago-Bednarski, Polanica Zdroj 1978

3...♗b7 4 ♗d3

4 ♘c3 ♗b4 5 f3 ♕h4+ 6 g3 ♕h5 7 ♗d2 f5 8 exf5 ♕xf5 9 ♘b5 ♗xd2+ 10 ♕xd2 ♘a6 11 0-0-0 ♘e7 12 ♗d3 ♕f6 13 ♘h3!? ♕xf3 14 ♘g5 ♕h5 15 ♖hf1∝ Ree-Miles, Amsterdam 1978

4...f5!? 5 exf5! ♗xg2 6 ♕h5+ g6 7 fxg6 ♗g7 8 gxh7+ ♔f8 9 ♘e2!! N

9...♗xh1 10 ♗g5 ♘f6 11 ♕h4 ♘c6 12 ♘f4 ♔f7 13 ♗g6+ ♔e7 14 ♘h5 ±/+− Browne-Miles, Tilburg 1978

1 d4 ♘f6 2 ♗g5

1 d4 ♘f6 2 ♗g5 ♘e4

a) 2...c5 3 d5 ♘e4 (3...♕b6 4 ♘c3! ♕xb2 5 ♗d2 ♕b6 6 e4 d6 7 f4 e5 8 fxe5 dxe5 9 ♘f3 ♗d6 10 ♗c4 ♕d8?! 11 0-0 ♗g4 12 ♕e1! ♘bd7 13 ♘h4± Pribyl-Hazai, Varna 1978) 4 ♗f4 ♕b6 5 ♗c1!? (5 ♕c1 g5! 6 ♗e5 f6 7 ♗g3 ♗g7 8 c3 f5 9 e3 0-0 10 ♘d2 ♘xg3 11 hxg3 ♕f6 12 ♕c2 d6 13 ♘gf3 e5∓ Van der Sterren-Jusupov, IBM 2 1978) 5...e6 6 f3 ♘f6 7 dxe6 fxe6 8 e4 ♘c6 9 ♘c3 ♗e7 10 f4 0-0! 11 e5 ♘d5 12 ♘xd5 exd5 13 ♕xd5+ ♔h8∓ Bohm-Jusupov, IBM 1978;

b) 2...d6 3 ♗xf6 exf6 4 e3 g6 5 ♗d3 f5 6 ♘d2 ♗g7 7 ♕f3 0-0 8 ♘e2 ♘d7 9 ♘f4 ♘f6 10 h4 h5 11 0-0-0 d5 12 ♕e2 ♕d6 =+ Barle-Gligoric, Ljubljana 1975

c) 2...g6!? 3 ♗xf6 exf6 4 e3 f5 N (4...♗g7 5 ♘e2 b6 6 ♘f4 d5 7 h4 h5 8 c4 dxc4 9 ♗xc4 ♗b7 10 ♘c3 ♗h6 11 ♗xf7+! +− Vaganian-Botterill, Hastings 1974/75) 5 ♘f3 d6 6 g3 ♘d7 7 c4 ♗g7 8 ♘bc3 ♘f6 9 ♗g2 0-0 10 0-0 a5 11 ♕c2 ♖e8 12 ♖fd1± Tseitlin-Schmidt, Polanica 1978

3 ♝h4

3 ♗f4 c5 (3...♘c6 4 ♘f3 e6 5 ♘bd2 d5 6 ♘xe4 dxe4 7 ♘e5 ♗d6 8 e3 0-0 9 ♗g3 += Hort-Planinc, Ljubljana 1975) 4 f3 ♕a5+! 5 c3 ♘f6 6 d5 d6 7 e4 g6 8 ♕d2 ♗g7 =+ Alburt-Dorfman, USSR Final 1977

3...c5 4 f3

4 d5 ♕b6 5 b3 g5 6 ♗g3 ♕h6! Δ ♘xg3

4...♛a5+

a) 4...g5 5 fxe4 gxh4 6 e3 e6? (6...♗h6 7 ♔f2! cxd4! 8 exd4 ♕b6 9 ♘c3 e6 10 ♘f3 ♘c6 11 ♗e2 d6 12 ♖f1 ♔e7! Levin) 7 ♘d2 ♘c6 8 c3 ♗h6 9 ♘c4 d5 10 ♕h5 ♗g7 11 ♘d2 cxd4 12 exd4 dxe4 13 ♘xe4 0-0 14 ♘f3± Palatnik-Adamski, Kiev 1978;

b) 4...♘f6 5 dxc5 e6 6 b4 a5 7 e4 ♗e7 8 c3 axb4 9 cxb4 ♘xe4?! 10 ♗xe7 ♕xe7 11 fxe4 ♕h4+ 12 g3 ♕xe4+ 13 ♔f2 ♕xb4 14 ♘f3± Pribyl-Adamski, Lodz 1978

5 c3 ♞f6 6 d5 d6 7 e4 g6 8 ♞a3

8 ♗xf6!?

8...♝g7 9 ♞c4 ♛c7 10 a4 0-0 11 ♝e2 ♞bd7 12 ♞g3 ♞b6 13 f4 += Pribyl-Helmers, Lodz 1978

Q.G.A.

1 d4 d5 2 c4 dxc4 3 ♞f3

3 e4 e5 4 ♘f3 ♗b4+ (4...exd4 5 ♗xc4 ♗b4+ 6 ♗d2 ♗xd2+ 7 ♘bxd2 c5 8 ♕a4+ ♘d7 9 b4 ♘e7= Inkiov-Radulov, Bulgaria 1977) 5 ♘c3 exd4 6 ♘xd4 N (6 ♕xd4 ♕xd4 7 ♘xd4 ♘f6 8 f3 ♗d7 9 ♗xc4 ♘c6 10 ♘xc6 ♗xc6 11 ♗g5 += Gulko-Ribli, Niksic 1978) 6...♕e7 7 ♗xc4! ♕xe4+?! 8 ♔f1 ♗xc3 9 bxc3 ♗e6 10 ♕b3 ♗xc4 11 ♕xc4 ♘c6 12 ♗g5 ♕g6 13 ♖e1+ +− Alburt-Romanishin, Kiev 1978

3...♞f6 4 e3

a) 4 ♕a4+ ♘bd7?! 5 ♘c3 e6 6 e4 a6 (6...c5 7 d5 exd5 8 e5 d4 9 exf6 dxc3 10 ♗xc4 gxf6 11 0-0 cxb2 12 ♗xb2 ♗e7 13 ♖ad1! 0-0 14 ♗b5 ♕b6 15 ♗xd7 ♕xb2 16 ♗xc8 ♖axc8 17 ♖db1 ♕c3 18 ♖fe1 Δ ♖e3!± Knezevic-

Mesing, Jugoslavia 1976) 7 ♗xc4 c6 8 ♕c2 c5 9 dxc5 ♗xc5 10 0-0 ♕c7 11 ♕e2 ♘g4 12 ♗b3 h5?! (12...0-0 +=) 13 ♗d2 ♘de5 14 ♘xe5 ♕xe5 15 g3 ♗d4 16 ♗f4 ♕a5 17 ♖ad1± Knezevic-Romanishin, Kiev 1978;

b) 4 ♘c3 a6 5 e4 b5 6 e5 ♘d5 7 a4 ♘xc3 8 bxc3 c6 9 axb5 cxb5 10 ♘g5 f6 11 ♕f3 ♖a7 12 e6 ♗b7 13 ♕f4 ♕c8 14 ♗e3 (14 ♘f7 ♖g8 15 ♗e3 ♖a8 16 ♕g4 g6 17 ♕h3∞ Dementiev-Tichonski, USSR 1967; 14 d5!? N ♗xd5 15 ♗e3 ♖a8 16 ♕f5 ♕c6 17 0-0-0 g6 18 ♕xd5 ♕xd5 19 ♖xd5 fxg5 20 ♖c5 +- Webb-Bernard, Warsaw 1978) 14...♗d5 15 ♕f5 ♕b7 N (15...♕c6 16 ♘xh7 ♔d8!∓ Polugaevsky-Gurgenidze, USSR Final 1967) 16 ♘f6 g6 17 ♕h3 ♖g8 18 ♕xh7± Ligterink-Van der Sterren, Amsterdam 2 1978

4...♝g4 5 ♝xc4 e6 6 ♞c3

6 h3 ♗h5 7 ♘c3 (7 g4 ♗g6 8 ♘e5 ♘bd7 9 ♘xg6 hxg6 10 ♕f3 c5 11 0-0 cxd4 12 exd4 ♗e7 13 ♘c3 ♘b6 14 ♗b5+ ♔f8 15 ♗e3 += Hort-Miles, Amsterdam 1978) 7...a6 8 0-0 ♘c6 (8...c5 9 ♗e2 ♘c6 10 ♘e5 ♗xe2 11 ♕xe2 ♖c8 12 ♘xc6 ♖xc6 13 ♖d1 cxd4= Browne-Romanishin, Amsterdam 1978) 9 ♗e2 ♗d6 10 b3 0-0 11 ♗b2 ♕e7 12 ♘d2 ♗g6= Tukmakov-Lebredo, Vilnius 1978

6...♞bd7

6...a6 7 h3 ♗h5 8 ♗e2 ♘c6 9 0-0 ♗d6 10 b3 0-0 11 ♗b2 ♕e8 12 ♘e5 ♗xe2 13 ♘xe2 ♖d8 14 ♘xc6 ♕xc6= Lerner-Beljavsky, Kiev 1978

7 0-0 ♝d6 8 h3 ♝h5 9 e4 e5 10 ♝e2 0-0 11 dxe5 ♞xe5

12 ♞d4 ♝xe2

a) 12...♗c5!? 13 ♘b3 ♕xd1 14 ♗xd1 ♗b6 15 a4! += Portisch-Miles, Lone Pine 1978;

b) 12...♗g6?! 13 ♗g5 ♖e8? 14 ♘db5± Portisch-Spassky (8) 1977

13 ♛xe2 ♞g6 14 ♜d1?!

14 ♗g5!?; 14 ♘f5 ♗e5 15 f4 +=

14...♛c8 15 ♝g5 ♝e5 16 ♛e3 ♞h5 17 ♛f3 += Portisch-Miles, Tilburg 1978

Tarrasch

1 d4 d5 2 c4 e6 3 ♞c3 c5 4 cxd5 exd5 5 ♞f3 ♞c6 6 g3 ♞f6 7 ♝g2 ♝e7 8 0-0 0-0 9 ♝g5

a) 9 dxc5 ♗xc5 10 ♗g5 d4 11 ♗xf6 ♕xf6 12 ♘d5 ♕d8 13 ♘d2 ♖e8 14 ♖c1 ♗f8 N (14...♗d6 15 ♘b3 ♗e5 16 ♘c5 ♖b8 17 ♕a4 += Timman-Ivkov, Geneva 1977) 15 ♘b3 ♗g4 16 ♖e1 ♖e5 17 ♘f4 ♗b4 18 ♘d2 d3 19 ♘xd3

♗xe2 20 ♖xe2 ♕xd3 21 ♗e4!± Timman-Gligoric, Bugojno 1978;
b) 9 ♗e3 c4 10 ♘e5 ♗e6 11 ♖c1 ♕a5 12 ♕d2 ♕a6 13 ♗g5 ♖ad8 14 f4 += Gurgenidze-Gonsior, Hradec Kralove 1977/78

9...cxd4

9...♗e6 10 dxc5 ♗xc5 11 ♗xf6 ♕xf6 12 ♘xd5 ♕xb2 13 ♘c7 ♖ad8 14 ♕c1 ♕xc1 15 ♖axc1 ♗e7 N (15...♗b6 16 ♘xe6 fxe6 17 ♖c4 ♘d4 18 ♘xd4 ♖xd4 19 ♖xd4 ♗xd4 20 ♗xb7± Alburt-Meduna, Decin 1977) 16 ♘xe6 fxe6 17 ♖c4 ♗f6 18 ♖b1 ♖d7 19 h4 += Ftacnik-Minev, Bucharest 1978

10 ♘xd4 h6

11 ♗e3 ♖e8

a) 11...♘g4?! N 12 ♘xd5! ♘xe3 13 fxe3 ♗g5 14 ♕b3! ♘e7 (14...♗g4!?) 15 ♖ad1 ♘xd5 16 ♗xd5 ♗xe3+ 17 ♔g2 ♗xd4 Panno-Garcia, Bogata 1978, 18 ♖xf7! ♖xf7 19 ♗xf7+ ♔f8 20 e3 ♕e7 21 ♖xd4±;
b) 11...♗g4 12 ♕a4 ♕d7 13 ♖fd1 ♗h3 14 ♗h1 ♖fd8 15 ♘b3 ♕f5 16 ♘a5! N ♘xa5 17 ♕xa5 b6 18 ♕b5 ♖d7∝ Ljubojevic-Marjanovic, Jugoslavia 1978

12 ♘xc6

12 ♖c1 ♗f8 13 ♘xc6 bxc6 14 ♘a4 ♘g4!? N (14...♗d7 15 ♗c5 ♗xc5 16 ♘xc5 ♗g4 17 ♖e1 += Ljubojevic-Gligoric, Bugojno 1978) 15 ♗c5 ♗xc5 16 ♘xc5 ♕f6 17 h3 ♘e5 18 e4 += Timman-Gligoric, Niksic 1978

12...bxc6 13 ♕a4 N **♗d7 14 ♕c2 ♕c8 15 ♖fd1 ♗h3** =+ Vadasz-Nunn, Budapest 1978

Q.G.D.

1 d4 d5 2 c4 e6

2...♗f5?! 3 cxd5 ♗xb1 4 ♕a4+ c6 5 ♖xb1 ♕xd5 6 ♘f3 ♘d7 7 ♗d2 ♘b6 8 ♕a5± Farago-Kuligowski, Polanica Zdroj 1978

3 ♘c3 ♘f6 4 ♘f3 ♗e7

a) 4...♗b4 5 ♕a4+ ♘c6 6 e3 ♗d7 7 ♕c2 0-0 8 ♗d2 dxc4 9 ♗xc4 ♗d6 10 e4 e5 11 dxe5 ♘xe5 12 ♘xe5 ♗xe5 13 0-0-0!?∝ Sakharov-Estrin, Lublin 1978)
b) 4...c5 5 cxd5 ♘xd5 6 e4 ♘xc3 7 bxc3 cxd4 8 cxd4 ♘c6 9 ♗c4 (9 ♗e2 ♗b4+ 10 ♗d2 ♗xd2+ N 11 ♕xd2 0-0 12 0-0 b6 13 ♖ac1 ♗b7 14 ♖fd1 ♘a5 15 ♗d3 ♕d6= Balicki-Swierczewski, Wroclaw 1978) 9...b5 10 ♗e2 ♗b4+ N (10...a6 11 0-0 ♗e7 12 ♗b2 ♗f6!= Bagirov-Shamkovich, USSR Final 1972) 11 ♗d2 ♕a5 12 ♖b1 ♗xd2+ 13 ♕xd2 a6 14 ♕xa5 ♘xa5 15 ♔d2± Barczay-Lukacs, Budapest 1978;
c) 4...♘bd7 5 cxd5 exd5 6 ♗g5 c6 7 e3 ♗e7 8 ♗d3 0-0 9 ♕c2 ♖e8 10 0-0 ♘f8 11 ♖ae1 (11 ♗xf6 ♗xf6 12 b4 ♗g4 13 ♘d2 ♖c8 14 ♗f5 ♗xf5 15 ♕xf5 ♕d7 N 16 ♕xd7 ♘xd7 17 a4 += Korchnoi-Karpov (31) 1978) 11... ♘e4 12 ♗xe7 ♕xe7 13 ♗xe4 dxe4 14 ♘d2 f5 15 f3 exf3 16 ♘xf3 ♗e6 17 e4 fxe4 18 ♖xe4 ♕d6 N (18... ♖ad8 19 ♖e5 h6 20 ♘e4 += Marshall-Rubinstein, Moscow 1975) 19 ♖e5 ♘g6 20 ♘e4 ♕b4 21 ♘eg5 ♗c4 22

♖e1 ♖xe5 23 dxe5± ♖f8 24 a3?? ♕xe1+ 0-1 Razuvaev-Sakharov, Lublin 1978

5 ♗f4 0-0 6 e3 c5 7 dxc5 ♗xc5 8 ♕c2 ♘c6 9 ♖d1 ♕a5 10 a3 ♗e7

a) 10...♖d8 11 ♘d2! dxc4 12 ♘xc4 ♖xd1+ 13 ♕xd1 ♕d8 14 ♕xd8+ ♘xd8 15 ♘a4 += Samarian;

b) 10...♖e8!? N 11 ♘d2 e5 12 ♗g5 ♘d4!? 13 ♕b1! ♗f5 14 ♗d3 e4 15 ♗c2 ♘xc2+ 16 ♕xc2± Korchnoi-Karpov (21) 1978

11 ♘d2 e5 12 ♗g5 d4 13 ♘b3 ♕d8

13...♕b6 14 ♗xf6 ♗xf6 15 ♘d5 ♕d8 16 ♗d3 g6 17 exd4 ♘xd4 18 ♘xd4 exd4 19 ♘xf6+ (19 0-0= Forintos-Doroshkevich, Lipetsk 1968) 19... ♕xf6 20 0-0 ♗e6 N (20...♗d7 += Forintos-Smederevac, Wijk aan Zee 1970) 21 ♖fe1 (21 f4! Δ f5) 21... ♖ac8 22 b3 += Korchnoi-Karpov (23) 1978

14 ♗e2 ♘g4

14...h6 N 15 ♗xf6 ♗xf6 16 0-0 ♗e6 17 ♘c5 ♕e7 18 ♘xe6 ♕xe6 19 ♘d5 ♖ad8 Korchnoi-Karpov (9) 1978, 20 e4 ♘e7 21 ♗f3 ♘xd5 22 exd5 +=

Diagram

15 ♗xe7 ♕xe7 16 exd4 ♕h4 17 g3 ♕h3 18 d5 ♘d4 19 ♘xd4 exd4 20

♖xd4 ♖e8 21 ♖e4 ♗d7 22 ♗f1 ♕h5 23 h3! N

23 ♗e2 ♕h3 ½-½ Portisch-Spassky, Havana Olympiad 1966

23...f5

a) 23...♗f5 24 hxg4 ♗xe4 25 gxh5 ♗xc2 26 ♔d2 ±/+−;

b) 23...♘e5 24 ♗e2 ♘f3+ 25 ♔d1

24 ♖e2 ♘e5 25 f4 ♘xc4 26 ♔f2 ♘d6 27 ♗g2± Ree-Kuipers, Netherland Final 1978

Benko Gambit

1 d4 ♘f6 2 c4 c5 3 d5 b5 4 cxb5 a6 5 e3

5 bxa6 ♗xa6 6 ♘c3 g6 7 ♘f3 d6 8 g3 ♘bd7 9 ♗h3 ♘b6 (9...♗g7 10 0-0 0-0 11 ♖e1 h5 12 ♗f4 ♘g4 13 ♖c1 ♕a5 14 ♕d2 ♖ab8 15 b3 ♖fc8= Mikenda-Swoboda, Vienna Final 1978) 10 0-0 ♗g7 11 ♖e1 0-0 12 e4 ♘fd7 13 ♕c2 ♘c4 14 ♗xd7 ♕xd7 15 b3 += Beljavsky-Palatnik, Kiev 1978

5...g6

5...axb5 6 ♗xb5 ♗a6 7 ♗xa6 ♘xa6 8 ♘c3 d6 9 ♘f3 g6 10 0-0 ♗g7 11 e4 0-0 12 ♗f4 (12 ♖e1 ♘b4 13 ♖e2 ♕b6 14 ♗g5 h6 15 ♗h4 g5 16 ♗g3 ♘h5= Farago-Alburt, Kiev 1978) 12... ♖b8 13 ♕d2 ♖b4 14 ♖fe1 ♕b6 15 ♖ab1 += Beljavsky-Damjanovic,

Vilnius 1978

6 ♘c3

6 ♘f3 axb5 7 ♗xb5 ♕a5+ 8 ♘c3 ♘e4 9 ♕b3 ♗g7 10 ♗d2 ♘xd2 11 ♘xd2 0-0∝ De Roode-Van der Sterren, Amsterdam 2 1978

6...d6 7 ♘f3 ♗g7 8 e4 0-0 9 a4 axb5 10 ♗xb5 ♗a6

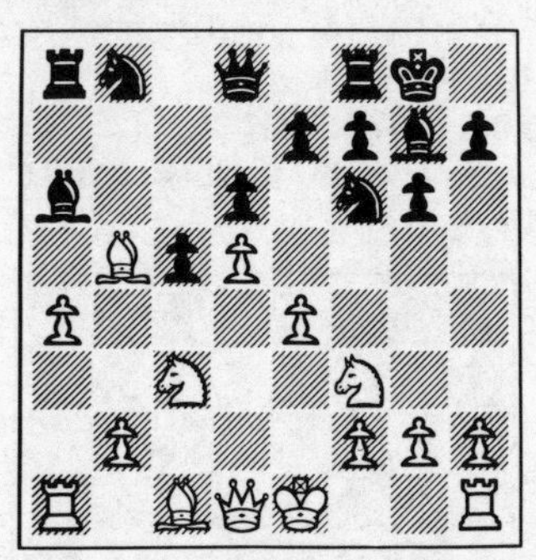

11 ♗g5

a) 11 ♗d2 ♘e8 12 0-0 ♘c7 13 ♕e2 ♘d7 14 h4 ♘b6 15 h5± F.Portisch-Barlov, Belgrade 1975;

b) 11 ♗f4 ♕a5 12 0-0 ♕b4 13 ♕c2 ♗xb5 14 axb5 ♘bd7 15 ♗d2 ♖fb8 ∝/= Farago-Palatnik, Kiev 1978

11...♕a5 12 0-0 ♕b4 13 ♕c2 ♘bd7 14 ♖fe1 ♗xb5 15 ♘xb5 ♕a5 16 ♗d2 ♕b6 17 ♗c3 Δ ♘d2, ♘c4± Balogh-Schinzel, Warsaw 1978

Nimzo-Indian

1 d4 ♘f6 2 c4 e6 3 ♘c3 ♗b4 4 e3

4 f3 c5 5 d5 ♗xc3+ 6 bxc3 ♘h5 7 g3 f5 8 ♘h3 N (8 e4 f4 9 ♗xf4 ♘xf4 10 gxf4 ♕h4+ 11 ♔e2 ♕xf4 12 ♘h3 ♕f6∝ Szabo-Csom, Hungary 1973) 8...♕f6 9 ♗d2 0-0 10 ♗g2 d6 11 0-0 ♕g6 12 e4 += Van der Sterren-Timman, Netherlands Final 1978

Diagram

4...c5

a) 4...b6 5 ♘e2 (5 ♗d3 ♗b7 6 ♘f3 ♘e4?! 7 0-0 [7 ♕c2 f5 8 0-0 ♗xc3 9 bxc3 0-0 10 ♗b2 N c5 11 ♖ad1 d6 12 d5!?∝ Kraidman-Keene, Beersheva 1978] 7...♘xc3 8 bxc3 ♗e7!? N 9 e4 d6 10 ♗e3 ♘d7 11 ♘d2 0-0 12 ♕g4!? ♘f6 13 ♕e2 ♘e8≈ Farago-Romanishin, Kiev 1978) 5... ♗a6 6 ♘g3 (6 a3 ♗xc3+ 7 ♘xc3 d5 8 b3 0-0 9 ♗e2 ♘c6 10 a4 [10 0-0 ♘a5?! 11 ♖b1 c6 N 12 a4 ♕e7 13 ♗d2 ♖fe8 14 ♕e1! += Hort-Lombardy, Reykjavik 1978] 10...dxc4? 11 ♗a3 ♖e8 12 bxc4! N [12 b4 ♘e7 13 0-0? ♘ed5 14 ♖c1 c6 15 ♗f3 b5∓ Evans-Fischer, USA Final 1966] 12...♘a5 13 ♘b5 c6? 14 ♘d6 ♖e7 15 e4!± Kuzmin-Ree, Kiev 1978) 6...♗xc3+ 7 bxc3 d5 8 ♗a3 (8 ♕f3 0-0 9 cxd5 exd5 10 ♗xa6 ♘xa6 11 ♕e2 ♘b8 12 0-0 c5 13 ♗a3 ♕c7 14 f3 += Toth-Cosulich, Italy 1978) 8...♗xc4 9 ♗xc4 dxc4 10 ♕a4+ ♕d7 11 ♕xc4 ♕c6 12 ♕xc6+ ♘xc6 13 ♔e2 0-0-0 14 ♖hc1 ♖d7= Nikolac-Adorjan, Amsterdam 1978;

b) 4...0-0 5 ♗d3 c5 (5...d5 6 ♘f3 ♘c6 7 0-0 a6 8 h3 h6 9 a3 dxc4 10 ♗xc4 ♗d6 11 e4 e5 12 ♗e3 b5 13 ♗a2 += Farago-Knezevic, Kiev 1978; 6 a3 ♗xc3+ 7 bxc3 dxc4 8 ♗xc4 c5 9 ♘e2 ♕c7 10 ♗d3 ♘c6 N [10...

♘bd7 11 0-0 e5 12 e4 cxd4 13 cxd4 exd4 14 f3 += Lein-Platanov, USSR Final 1969] 11 0-0 e5 12 ♕c2 ♗e6 13 ♖b1 ♖ac8 14 ♗f5 ♗xf5 15 ♕xf5 ♖fd8 =+ Reshevsky-Peshina, Vilnius 1978) 6 ♘f3 d5 7 0-0 cxd4 (7...♘c6 8 a3 ♗xc3 9 bxc3 dxc4 10 ♗xc4 ♕c7 11 ♗a2 [11 ♗d3 e5 12 ♕c2 ♖e8 13 dxe5 ♘xe5 14 ♘xe5 ♕xe5 15 f3 ♗e6 16 e4 N c4 17 ♗e2 ♕c5+ 18 ♔h1 ♖ad8 19 a4 a6 20 a5 ♖d7 21 ♕b2 += Webb-Bohlig, Warsaw 1978; 16 ♖e1 ♖ad8 17 ♖b1 ♕d5! 18 ♗b5!? ♗f5!= Gligoric-Olafsson, Bad Lauterberg 1977] 11... e5 12 ♕c2 ♗g4 13 dxe5 ♘xe5 14 ♘e1! N [14 ♘xe5 ♕xe5 15 f3 ♗e6= Simic-Chekhov, Jugoslavia v USSR 1976] 14...♖ad8 15 f3 ♗e6 16 c4 ♕a5 17 ♗b2 += Portisch-Sosonko, Tilburg 1978) 8 exd4 dxc4 9 ♗xc4 b6 10 ♗g5 ♗b7 11 ♖e1 ♘bd7 (11... ♗xc3 12 bxc3 ♘bd7 13 ♗d3 ♖c8 N [13...♕c7 14 c4 ♕d6 15 ♘e5 ♘xe5 16 dxe5 ♕c6 17 ♗f1 ♘e4= Gligoric-Unzicker, Milan 1975] 14 ♖c1 ♕c7 15 ♗h4 ♕c6 16 c4 ♘h5!? 17 d5! ♕c5 18 ♘g5± Portisch-Browne, Tilburg 1978) 12 ♖c1 N ♖c8 13 ♕b3 ♕e7 14 ♗d5! ♗a6 15 ♕a4 ♗xc3 16 bxc3 ♘b8 17 ♗b3 +− Browne-Ljubojevic, Tilburg 1978

5 ♗d3

a) 5 ♘e2 d5 6 a3 ♗xc3+ 7 ♘xc3 cxd4 8 exd4 dxc4 9 ♗xc4 ♘c6 10 ♗e3 0-0 11 0-0 b6 12 ♕d3 (12 ♕f3 ♗b7 13 ♗d3) 12...♗b7 13 ♖ad1 h6 14 f3!? N (14 ♖fe1 ♘e7 15 ♗f4 ♖c8 16 ♗e5 ♘fd5 17 ♘b5 ♗a6 18 a4 += Petrosian-Olafsson, Portoroz 1958; 14 ♗a2 Larsen) 14...♘e7 15 ♗f2 ♘fd5 16 ♗a2 ♘f4 17 ♕d2 ♘fg6 18 ♗b1 ♕d7 19 h4 ♖fd8∝ Korchnoi-Karpov (5) 1978;

b) 5 ♘e2 cxd4 6 exd4 d5 (6...0-0 7 a3 ♗e7 8 g3 d5 9 cxd5 ♘xd5 10 ♗g2 ♘xc3 11 bxc3 ♘c6 12 0-0 ♗d7 13 ♘f4!± Gligoric-Sosonko, Bad Lauterberg 1977) 7 c5 ♘e4 8 ♗d2 ♘xd2 9 ♕xd2 a5!? N (9...♘c6 10 a3 ♗a5 11 b4 ♗c7 12 g3 += Korchnoi-Spassky, USSR Final 1973) 10 a3 ♗xc3 11 ♘xc3 ♗d7 12 ♗d3 a4 13 0-0 0-0 14 f4 g6 Korchnoi-Karpov (3) 1978, 15 g4! ∝/±

5...0-0 6 d5!? N **b5!?**

6...exd5 7 cxd5 ♘xd5 8 ♗xh7+ Δ 8 ♕xd5 +=

7 dxe6 fxe6 8 cxb5 a6!?

8...♗b7 9 ♘f3 d5 10 0-0 ♘bd7 11 ♘e2 ♕e8 12 ♘g3 e5 13 ♗f5 g6 14 ♗h3 a6 15 ♘g5 axb5 16 ♘e6 c4 17 ♗d2 ♗c5!? Korchnoi-Karpov (7) 1978, 18 a4! b4! 19 ♘xc5 ♘xc5 20 ♗xb4 ♕c6 21 ♕c2± Larsen

9 ♘e2 d5 10 0-0 e5 11 a3 axb5 12 ♗xb5 ♗xc3 13 bxc3 ♗a6 14 ♖b1 ♕d6 15 c4 d4 16 ♘g3± Korchnoi-Karpov (17) 1978

Queen's Indian

1 d4 ♘f6 2 c4 e6 3 ♘f3 b6 4 g3

a) 4 ♘c3 ♗b7 5 a3 ♘e4 6 ♘xe4 ♗xe4 7 e3 c5 N (7...♗e7 8 ♗d3 ♗xd3 9 ♕xd3 d5 10 cxd5 ♕xd5= Smyslov-Panno, Palma de Mallorca 1970)

8 d5 exd5 9 cxd5 ♕f6 10 ♗e2 ♕f5 11 0-0!? ♕xd5 12 ♘d2 ♗xg2 13 e4 ♗xe4 14 ♘xe4 ♕xe4 15 ♗f3 ♕g6+ 16 ♔h1 ♘c6 17 ♖g1 ♕d6 ∞/∓ Timman-Ljubojevic, Amsterdam 1978; b) 4 ♗f4 ♗b7 5 e3 ♗e7 (5...♗b4+! 6 ♘fd2!? 0-0 7 ♗d3 d5 8 0-0 c5= Miles-Andersson, Buenos Aires 1978; 5...c5 N 6 d5 exd5 7 ♘c3!? a6 8 cxd5 d6 9 e4 ♕e7 10 ♗e2 ♘bd7 11 ♘d2 b5 12 0-0 ♘e5 13 ♗g3 h5!? 14 ♗h4 ♘g6 15 ♗g5 h4 16 h3 ♕c7 17 ♗xf6 gxf6∞ Miles-Hort, Tilburg 1978) 6 h3 0-0 7 ♘c3 d5 8 cxd5 exd5 (8...♘xd5 9 ♘xd5 ♗xd5 10 ♗d3 ♗b4+ 11 ♔e2 ♗d6 12 ♗xd6 cxd6 13 ♕c2 f5 14 ♗c4 ♗xf3+ 15 gxf3 ♕f6 16 ♖ac1 +=/± Miles-Browne, Amsterdam 1978) 9 ♗d3 c5 10 0-0 ♘c6 11 ♘e5 a6 N (11...c4 12 ♗c2 a6 13 g4! b5 14 g5 ♘e8 15 ♕g4 g6 16 ♖ad1± Miles-Spassky, Montilla 1978) 12 ♕f3 ♖e8 13 ♖ad1 cxd4 14 ♘xc6 ♗xc6 15 exd4 b5 16 a3 ♘e4= Miles-Spassky, Buenos Aires 1978

4...♗b7

a) 4...♗a6 5 ♕a4 ♗e7 6 ♘c3 ♗b7 7 ♗g2 ♘e4 8 ♕c2 ♘xc3 9 ♕xc3 0-0 10 0-0 ♗e4 11 ♘e1 ♗xg2 12 ♘xg2 c6 13 ♗f4 d6= Beljavsky-Gulko, Lvov 1978;

b) 4...♗a6 5 b3 ♗b4+ 6 ♗d2 ♗e7 (6... ♗xd2+ 7 ♕xd2 c6 N [7...0-0 8 ♘c3 d6 9 ♗g2 ♘bd7 10 0-0 c6 11 ♘e1 d5= Kuligowski-Pokojowczyk, Lublin 1976] 8 ♘c3 d5 9 ♘e5 0-0 10 ♗g2 ♘fd7 11 ♘d3 dxc4 12 ♘b4 cxb3 13 ♘xc6 ♘xc6 14 ♗xc6 ♖c8 =+ Browne-Andersson, Amsterdam 1978) 7 ♗g2 (7 ♘c3 c6 8 e4 d5 9 ♕c2 dxe4 10 ♘xe4 ♗b7 11 ♗d3!? ♘bd7 12 0-0-0 ♘xe4 13 ♗xe4 ♘f6 =+ Ribli-Hort, Tilburg 1978) 7...c6 8 0-0 d5 9 ♘c3 0-0 10 cxd5? cxd5 11 a3 ♘c6∓ O'Kelly-Miles, England 1978

5 ♗g2 ♗e7 6 0-0 0-0 7 ♘c3 ♘e4

7...d5 8 ♘e5 ♘bd7? 9 ♕a4 ♘xe5 10 dxe5 ♘e8 11 cxd5 exd5 12 ♘xd5 ♗xd5 13 ♖d1 c6 14 e4 b5 15 ♕c2 ♘c7 16 exd5 cxd5 ∞/± Szul-Sikova, Lublin 1978

8 ♗d2

8 ♕c2 ♘xc3 9 ♕xc3 f5 10 b4!? N a5 11 b5 ♗f6 12 ♗b2 d6 13 ♖fd1 ♘d7 14 ♕d2 ♕e7 15 ♖ac1 ♖ad8 16 a4 += Peev-Grahn, Slupsk 1978

8...f5

a) 8...♗f6 9 ♖c1 c5 10 ♘xe4 ♗xe4 11 ♗c3 ♘c6 12 dxc5 (12 e3 cxd4 13 ♘xd4 ♗xg2 14 ♔xg2 ♗xd4 15 ♗xd4 d5= Petrosian-Portisch 1974) 12...♗xc3 13 ♖xc3 bxc5 14 ♕d2 ♕e7 15 ♖d1 += Adamski-Grahn, Slupsk 1978;

b) 8...d6 9 d5 ♘xd2 10 ♘xd2 e5 11 f4 exf4 12 gxf4 ♗f6 N (12...♘d7 13 ♘f3 ♗f6 14 ♘d4 ♖e8 15 e4 a5∝ Vaganian-Furman, USSR 1971) 13 ♘de4 ♘d7 14 ♕d2 ♗h4 15 ♘g3 f5 16 ♘b5± Adamski-Bachman, Slupsk 1978; 11 e4± Matanovic/Ugrinovic

9 d5 ♝f6 10 ♜c1 ♞a6 11 ♝e1 ♞ac5 12 ♞d4 ♛e7 13 ♞db5 N

13 b4 ♘xc3 14 ♖xc3 ♘e4 15 ♖d3 a6∝ Pietzsch-Bilek, Salgotarjan 1967

13...a6! 14 ♞xc7 ♝xc3 15 ♝xc3 ♜ac8 16 b4 ♜xc7 17 bxc5 ♞xc3 18 d6 ♛f6= Browne-Djindjihashvili, Amsterdam 1978

Grunfeld

1 d4 ♞f6 2 c4 g6 3 ♞c3 d5 4 ♝f4

a) 4 cxd5 ♘xd5 5 e4 ♘xc3 6 bxc3 ♗g7 7 ♗c4 c5 8 ♘e2 0-0 9 0-0 ♘c6 10 ♗e3 ♗g4 (10...cxd4 11 cxd4 ♘a5 12 ♗d3 ♘c6 13 ♗b5 ♗d7 14 ♖b1 N [14 d5 ♗xa1 15 ♕xa1 ♘a5 16 ♗h6 f6 17 ♗xd7 ♕xd7 18 ♗xf8 ♗xf8 19 ♘f4 ± Karpov] 14...e6 15 ♗d3 ♗c8 16 e5 b6 =+ Van der Sterren-Kirov, Amsterdam 2 1978) 11 f3 ♘a5 12 ♗d3 (12 ♗d5 ♗d7 13 ♖b1 ♕c8 14 dxc5 e6 15 ♗b3 ♗b5 16 ♕c2 += Hort-Timman, Niksic 1978) 12...cxd4 13 cxd4 ♗e6 14 d5 ♗xa1 15 ♕xa1 f6 16 ♖b1 ♗d7 17 ♘f4!? N ♕b8 18 ♕c3 b6 19 ♗a6 ♕d6∝ Nikolac-Hort, Amsterdam 1978;

b) 4 ♘f3 ♗g7 5 e3 0-0 6 b4 b6 7 ♕b3 c6!? [7...c5!=] 8 cxd5 cxd5 9 b5 ♗b7 10 ♗b2 ♘bd7 11 ♗e2 ♖c8 12 0-0 += Miles-Ribli, Tilburg 1978;

c) 4 ♘f3 ♗g7 5 ♕b3 dxc4 6 ♕xc4 0-0 7 e4 a6 (7...♘a6 8 ♗e2 c5 9 d5 e6 10 ♗g5 ♕b6 N 11 0-0 exd5 12 exd5 h6 13 ♗f4 ♖e8= Portisch-Uhlmann, Niksic 1978) 8 ♗e2 b5 9 ♕b3 ♗b7 10 e5 ♘d5 (10...♘e4 11 0-0 ♘xc3 12 ♕xc3 ♗d5 13 a4 c6 14 ♘e1 ♘d7= Diesen-Swic, Polanica Zdroj 1978) 11 0-0 ♘xc3 12 ♕xc3 ♘d7 13 ♗f4 ♗d5 14 ♖fc1 c6 15 ♘d2 f6 16 ♗g3 fxe5 17 dxe5 += Petrosian-Gulko, Vilnius 1978;

d) 4 ♘f3 ♗g7 5 ♗g5 ♘e4 6 ♗h4 (6 cxd5 ♘xg5 7 ♘xg5 e6 8 ♕d2 [8 ♘f3 exd5 9 b4!? 0-0 10 e3 c6 11 ♕b3 ♗e6 12 ♗e2 ♕d6= Goodman-Silva, London 1978] 8...exd5 9 ♕e3+ ♔f8 10 ♕f4 ♗f6 11 h4 ♔g7 12 e4 dxe4 13 0-0-0 ♘c6 N [13...h6 14 ♘gxe4 ♗c6 15 d5 ♗f5 16 ♘xf6± Taimanov-Liberzon, Suhumi 1972] 14 ♗c4 ♕d6 15 ♕xd6 cxd6 16 ♘cxe4± Lechtynsky-Gulko, Vilnius 1978) 6... ♘xc3 7 bxc3 dxc4 (7...0-0!? N 8 cxd5 ♕xd5 9 ♗xe7 ♖e8 10 ♗a3 ♗g4 11 e3 ♗xd4!? 12 ♕xd4 ♗xf3 13 gxf3 ♕xf3 14 ♖g1 ♘c6∝ Pojedziniec-Zyla, Wroclaw 1978) 8 ♕a4+ (8 e3 ♗e6 9 ♘d2 N b5 10 a4 c6 11 ♗e2 a6 12 ♗f3 ♖a7 13 0-0 0-0∝ Lehmann-Ftacnik, Kiev 1978) 8...♘d7 9 e3 0-0 10 ♕a3 N (10 ♗xc4 c5 11 ♕a3 ♕c7 12 ♖c1 e5 13 0-0 += Kazilaris-Smyslov, Siegen 1970) 10...♖e8 11 ♗xc4 ♘b6 12 ♗b3 a5 13 ♘g5 e6 14 ♘f3 ♕d6 15 ♕c1 c5 =+ Dorfman-Gulko, Vilnius 1978

4...♗g7 5 e3

a) 5 ♘f3 0-0 6 ♖c1 dxc4 (6...c5 7 dxc5 ♕a5? 8 cxd5 ♘e4 N [8...♖d8 9 ♗d2 ♕xc5 10 e4 ♘g4 11 ♕e2 ♘d7 12 h3± Portisch-Rossetto, Havana 1964] 9 ♗e5 f6 10 ♗d4 ♘xc5 Opl-Beni, Vienna Final 1978, 11 b4! ♕xb4 12 ♖b1 ♕a3 13 ♘d2±) 7 e4 c5 8 dxc5 ♕a5 9 e5 ♖d8 10 ♗d2 ♘g4 11 ♗xc4 ♕xc5 12 ♘e4 ♕b6 13 ♗xf7+ ♔h8 N [13...♔xf7 14 ♖xc8 ♖xc8 15 ♘fg5+ ♔g8 16 ♕xg4 += Borisenko-Tukmakov, USSR 1971] 14 ♗b3 ♗f5 15 0-0 ♘bd7 16 ♕e1± Gliksman-Hansson, Wroclaw 1978;

b) 5 ♘f3 0-0 6 e3 c5 7 dxc5 ♘e4?! (7...♕a5 8 ♖c1 dxc4 [8...♗e6? 9 ♘d4 ♘c6 10 ♘xc6 bxc6 11 ♕a4 ♕xc5 12 b4 ♕b6 13 c5± Kaploon-Ochotnik, Odessa 1976] 9 ♗xc4 ♕xc5 10 ♗b3 ♘c6 11 0-0 ♕a5 12 h3 ♗f5 13 ♕e2 ♘e4 14 ♘xe4 ♗xe4 15 ♘d2 ♗d5= Nevole-Beggi, Wroclaw 1978) 8 ♖c1 ♘xc3 9 bxc3 dxc4!? (9...♕a5 10 cxd5 ♗xc3+ 11 ♘d2 ♗f5? [11...♘d7] 12 e4! ♗xe4 13 ♕b3 Δ ♕c4± Farago-Ftacnik, Kiev 1978) 10 ♕xd8 ♖xd8 11 ♗xc4 ♘d7 12 ♗g5 ♖e8 13 ♗b5 a6 14 ♗a4 h6 15 ♗h4 g5 16 c6 ♘c5!∓ Ribli-Timman, Amsterdam 1978

5...0-0 6 ♕b3 c6

6...c5 7 cxd5 cxd4 8 exd4 ♘bd7 9 ♗e2 ♘b6 10 ♗f3 ♗f5 11 ♖d1 ♕d7 12 h3 h5 13 ♗e5 (13 ♘ge2 ♖fd8 14 d6 exd6 15 0-0 ♖ac8= Dorfman-Tukmakov, Vilnius 1978) 13...♖fd8 14 ♗xf6 ♗xf6 15 ♘ge2 h4 16 0-0 ♖ac8 17 ♖fe1 ♘c4= Gulko-Tukmakov, Vilnius 1978

7 ♘f3 ♕a5 8 ♘d2 ♘bd7 9 ♗e2 ♘h5 10 ♗xh5 dxc4 11 ♘xc4 ♕xh5 12 0-0 b5! N

12...b6 13 ♖fd1 ♗a6 14 a4 e5 15 ♘xe5 ♘xe5 16 dxe5 ♗xe5 17 ♗xe5 ♕xe5 18 a5 += Beljavsky-Ftacnik, Kiev 1978

13 ♘a5 e5 14 ♗g3

14 dxe5 ♘xe5 15 ♗xe5 ♗xe5 16 f4 ♗e6 17 ♕b4 c5! =+ Beljavsky-Gutman, Baku 1977

14...exd4 15 exd4 c5?!

15...b4!? 16 ♕xb4 c5 17 dxc5 ♘xc5 18 ♗d6!? ♘d3∝

16 ♗d6 b4 17 ♗xf8 ♗xf8 18 ♕d5± Inkiov-Witkowski, Lodz 1978

KID

1 d4 ♘f6 2 c4 g6 3 ♘c3 ♗g7 4 e4 d6 5 f4 0-0 6 ♘f3

6 ♗e2 c5 7 d5 b5 8 cxb5 a6 9 bxa6 ♕a5 10 ♕d2!? N (10 ♗f3 ♘xa6 11 ♘e2 ♘b4 12 0-0 ♘d7 13 ♗e3 c4 14 a3 ♘d3 15 b4 cxb3!≈ Dozsa-Gufeld, Marianske Lazne 1962) 10...♗xa6 11 ♗xa6 ♕xa6 12 ♘ge2 ♘bd7 13 0-0 ♖fb8 14 ♕c2 c4∓ Grahn-Pokojowczyk, Slupsk 1978

6...c5 7 d5

7 ♗e2 cxd4 8 ♘xd4 ♘c6 (8...a6 N 9 ♗e3 ♘bd7 10 0-0 e6 11 ♘b3 ♕c7 12 ♕d2 b6 13 ♖ad1 ♘e8 14 f5 += Mikenas-Csom, Vilnius 1978) 9 ♗e3 ♕b6 10 ♘c2 ♕a5 11 0-0 ♘d7 12 ♕d2 N (12 ♗d2 ♕d8 13 ♗f3 ♘c5 14 ♖b1 f5= Uhlmann-Donner, Varna 1962)

12...♘c5 13 e5 ♗f5 14 b4 ♘xb4 15 ♘xb4 ♕xb4 16 ♘d5≈ Mikenas-Lechtynsky, Vilnius 1978

7...e6 8 ♗e2

8 dxe6 ♗xe6 9 ♗d3 ♘c6 (9...♗g4 10 h3 ♗xf3 11 ♕xf3 ♘c6 12 0-0 ♘d7 13 ♗d2 a6 14 ♖ae1 b5!= Kavalek-Byrne, Montilla 1977) 10 f5! ♗d7 11 0-0 ♘b4?! (11...♘g4 12 ♘d5 ♘b4! 13 ♔h1 ♘xd5 14 exd5 ♖e8 =+ Lanka-Gufeld, Jurmala 1978; 11...♘e5 12 ♗g5 ♗c6 13 ♘xe5 dxe5 14 ♘d5 ♗xd5 15 exd5 ♕b6 16 ♕b3± Murei-Kraidman, Beersheba 1978) 12 ♗b1 ♗c6 13 a3 ♘a6 14 ♗g5 ♘c7? 15 ♕d2!± Lombardy-Westerinen, Lone Pine 1978

8...exd5 9 cxd5 ♗g4! 10 0-0 ♘bd7

10...♖e8 11 ♘d2 ♗xe2 12 ♕xe2 a6 13 a4 ♘bd7 14 a5 b5 15 axb6 ♘xb6 =+ Grahn-Schmidt, Slupsk 1978

11 h3 ♗xf3 12 ♗xf3 ♘e8 N

12...♖e8 13 g4 h6 14 h4± Peev-Bohosian, Bulgarian Final 1971

13 a4 ♖b8 14 ♗e3 a6 15 a5 ♘c7 16 ♖a2 ♖e8 17 ♗f2 b5= Bohm-A. Rodriguez, Amsterdam 1978

1 d4 ♘f6 2 c4 g6 3 ♘c3 ♗g7 4 e4 d6 5 ♗e2

5 f3 0-0 6 ♗g5 (6 ♗e3 ♘c6 7 ♘ge2 a6 8 ♕d2 ♖b8 9 h4 h5 10 ♘d5 b5 11 ♘xf6+ exf6 12 g4 f5 13 gxf5 bxc4∓ Razuvaev-Arapovic, Lublin 1978) 6... c5 7 d5 e6 8 ♕d2 exd5 9 ♘xd5 ♗e6 10 ♘e2 ♗xd5 11 cxd5 ♖e8 12 ♘c3 a6 13 a4 += Jusupov-De Roode, Amsterdam 1978

5...0-0 6 ♘f3 e5 7 0-0

7 ♗e3 exd4 8 ♘xd4 ♖e8 9 f3 c6 10 ♕d2 d5 11 exd5 cxd5 12 0-0 dxc4 13 ♗xc4 a6 14 ♖ad1 b5 15 ♗b3 ♗b7 16 ♗h6 (16 a4! +=) 16...♗xh6?! N (16...♕b6 17 ♗xg7 ♔xg7 18 ♕g5 ♘bd7 19 ♔h1 ♖e5= Barden) 17 ♕xh6 ♘bd7 18 ♘e4 ♗d5 19 ♗xd5 ♘xd5 20 ♘d6 ♖e5 21 ♘xf7! +− Christiansen-A.Rodriguez, Amsterdam 1978

7...♘c6 8 d5 ♘e7 9 ♘e1 ♘d7 10 f3 f5 11 g4 ♔h8

11...♘f6 12 ♘d3 c6! (12...c5 13 ♗d2± Ribli-Ciocaltea, Moscow 1977) 13 ♘f2 ♔h8 14 ♗d2 a5 15 a3 ♗d7= Taimanov-Kavalek, Montaill 1977

12 ♘d3 ♘g8 13 ♔h1 a5 14 ♖g1 ♖f7 15 g5 f4 16 ♗f1 ♗f8 17 b3 ♗e7 18 ♘b5! b6!= Vaganian-Uhlmann, Niksic 1978

1 d4 ♘f6 2 c4 g6 3 ♘f3 ♗g7 4 g3 0-0 5 ♗g2 d6 6 0-0 ♘c6 7 ♘c3 a6

7...♖b8 8 d5 ♘a5 9 ♘d2 c5 10 ♕c2 a6 11 b3 b5 12 ♗b2 ♗h6 (12...bxc4

13 bxc4 ♗h6 14 ♘cb1!? ♗g7 15 ♘c3 ♗h6 16 f4! e5 17 dxe6 fxe6 18 ♖b1 += Petrosian-Chiburdanidze, Vilnius 1978) 13 f4 bxc4 14 bxc4 ♗g7 N 15 ♘d1 ♖xb2!? 16 ♘xb2 ♘g4 17 ♖f3 ♗d4+ 18 ♔h1 Kirov-Taulbut, Amsterdam 1978 18...♘f2+∞

8 ♞d5 ♞d7 N

a) 8...♘e4!? 9 ♘e3 f5 10 d5 ♘a5 11 ♘d2 ♘g5∞ Bilek-Liberzon, Venice 1974;

b) 8...♗d7 9 ♘xf6+ (9 e3 ♖b8 10 ♘xf6+ ♗xf6 11 ♘d2 ♗g7 12 b3 e5= Robatsch-Ciocaltea, Havana 1965) 9... ♗xf6 10 ♗h6 ♖e8 11 ♕d2 ♕c8 12 d5 ♘e5 13 ♘xe5 ♗xe5 14 f4 ♗g7= Bilek-Ciocaltea, Szombathely 1966

9 ♝e3 b5!? 10 cxb5 axb5 11 ♜c1 ♝b7

12 ♞xc7! ♛xc7 13 d5 ♞db8 14 dxc6 ♞xc6 15 ♞d4 ♝xd4 16 ♛xd4! ♞xd4 17 ♜xc7± Romanishin-Adorjan, Amsterdam 1978

Sicilian

1 e4 c5 2 ♞f3 ♞c6 3 ♝b5 e6

a) 3...♕b6 4 ♘c3 (4 ♘a3 e6 5 0-0 a6 6 ♗a4 ♕c7 7 c3 b5 8 ♗c2 e5 9 d4 cxd4 10 cxd4 exd4 11 ♘xd4 ♘xd4 12 ♕xd4 += Bohosian-Witkowski, Slupsk 1978) 4...e6 5 0-0 ♘ge7 6 ♖e1 ♘d4 7 a4! (7 ♗c4 ♘ec6 8 d3 d6 9 ♘xd4 cxd4 10 ♘e2 ♘a5 11 c3 += Kudriasov-Korchnoi, USSR 1965) 7... a6 8 ♗c4 ♘g6 9 d3 ♘xf3+ 10 ♕xf3 ♗d6 11 ♕h5 ♕c7 12 ♗e3 0-0 13 a5 ♘f4 14 ♕g4 += Inkiov-Helmers, Lodz 1978;

b) 3...g6 4 0-0 ♗g7 5 ♖e1 (5 ♘c3 ♘f6 6 ♖e1 0-0 7 a4 d6 8 h3 ♘d4 9 ♘xd4 cxd4 10 ♘d5 ♘h5 11 ♗e2 ♘f6 12 ♗c4 ♘d7= Bachmann-Bohosian, Slupsk 1978) 5...♘f6 6 e5 ♘d5 7 b3!? ♘c7 8 ♗xc6 dxc6 9 d3 ♗g4 10 ♘bd2 0-0 11 ♗b2 ♘e6 =+ Kaiszauri-Damjanovic, Vilnius 1978

4 0-0

4 ♗xc6 bxc6 5 0-0 f6?! N 6 ♘h4 ♕e7 7 f4 ♕f7 8 c4 ♘e7 9 d3 ♘g6 10 ♘xg6 ♕xg6 11 e5 d5= Dobosz-Bielczyk, Slupsk 1978

4...♞ge7

4...♘f6 5 ♘c3 ♘d4 6 e5 ♘xb5 7 ♘xb5 ♘d5 8 c4 ♘b4 9 d4 a6 10 ♗g5 ♕b6 11 dxc5 ♗xc5 12 ♘c3 += Speelman-Wade, London 1978

5 c3 a6 6 ♝a4 b5

6...d5!=

7 ♝c2 d5

8 exd5 N

8 e5 h6? 9 d4 ♕c7 Timman-Damjanovic, Banja Luka 1974, 10 ♘bd2±

8...♘xd5 9 d4 ♗b7 10 dxc5 ♗xc5 11 ♘bd2 ♘f6 12 ♕e2 ♕c7 13 ♘e4 ♗e7= Damjanovic-Chiburdanidze, Vilnius 1978

1 e4 c5 2 ♘f3 e6 3 d4 cxd4 4 ♘xd4 a6 5 ♗d3 ♘c6

a) 5...♘f6 6 0-0 (6 c4!? ♗b4+ 7 ♗d2 ♕b6 8 ♗xb4 ♕xb4+ 9 ♕d2 ♕xd2+ 10 ♘xd2 d6 11 0-0 b6= Gasik-Swierczewski, Warsaw 1978) 6...♕c7 7 ♕e2 d6 8 c4 g6 9 ♗e3 ♗g7 10 ♘c3 0-0 11 ♖ac1 b6 N (11...♘c6 12 ♘xc6 bxc6 13 f4 += Karpov-Hubner, Leningrad 1973) 12 f3 ♘bd7 13 b3 ♗b7 14 ♖fd1 ♖ac8 15 ♕d2 += Djindjihashvili-Hubner, Tilburg 1978;

b) 5...♕c7 6 0-0 ♘f6 7 ♔h1 ♗e7 8 f4 d6 9 c4 ♘c6 10 ♘xc6 bxc6 11 ♘c3 e5! =+ Cappello-Mariotti, Italy Final 1978

c) 5...♗c5 6 ♘b3 ♗a7 7 0-0 ♘c6 8 ♕e2 d6 9 ♗e3 ♗xe3 10 ♕xe3 ♘f6 11 c4 0-0 12 ♘c3 ♘e5 13 ♗e2 ♕c7 14 ♖fd1 b6 N (14...♘xc4?! 15 ♗xc4 ♕xc4 16 ♖xd6± Parma-Capelan, Solingen 1968) 15 ♖ac1 ♗b7 16 ♘d2 ♖fd8 17 ♘f3 ♘g6 18 h3 += Kuzmin-Velikov, Kiev 1978

6 ♘xc6 dxc6 7 ♘d2

7 0-0 e5 8 ♘d2 ♗c5?! 9 ♘c4 ♕c7 10 a4 N (10 ♕h5 ♗d4 11 c3 g6 12 ♕f3 ♗a7 13 a4 b5 14 ♘e3± Szabo-Forintos, Hungary 1959) 10...♘e7 11 ♕h5 ♘g6 12 ♔h1 ♗e7 13 g3 Δ f4± Beni-Nehonsky, Vienna Final 1978

Diagram

7...e5 8 ♘c4

8 ♕h5!? ♗d6 9 ♘c4 ♘f6 10 ♘xd6+ ♕xd6 11 ♕e2 += Jansa-Cebalo, S. Palanka 1978

8...♘f6

8...♘e7 9 a4 (9 h4!?) 9...♘g6 10 a5 +=

9 0-0 ♗g4?

9...♗d6 10 f4 0-0 11 fxe5 ♗xe5 12 ♘xe5 ♕d4+ 13 ♔h1 ♕xe5 14 ♗f4!? ♕xb2 15 ♗d6 Δ e5∝

10 ♕e1! ♘d7 11 f4 ♗c5+ 12 ♔h1 exf4 13 ♗xf4 0-0 14 e5!± Adorjan-Miles, Amsterdam 1978

1 e4 c5 2 ♘f3 ♘c6

2...a6 3 ♘c3 b5 4 d4 cxd4 5 ♘xd4 b4!? N 6 ♘d5?! e6 7 ♗c4? exd5 8 ♗xd5 ♖a7 9 0-0 ♘f6 10 ♗g5 d6 11 ♗xf6 ♕xf6 12 f4 ♕d8 ∓/−+ Sznapik-Andersson, Polanica Zdroj 1978

3 d4 cxd4 4 ♘xd4 e6 5 ♘c3 ♕c7

a) 5...a6 6 ♘xc6 bxc6 7 e5 ♕c7 8 ♗f4 g5!? 9 ♗g3 ♖b8 10 ♗d3! h5 11 h3 ♖xb2 12 0-0 g4 13 h4!± Kristiansen-Filipowicz, Roskilde 1978;

b) 5...a6 6 g3 ♘ge7 7 ♘b3 ♘a5 8 ♕h5 b5 (8...♘xb3 9 axb3 ♘c6 10 ♗g5 ♗e7 11 ♗xe7 ♕xe7 12 ♗g2 0-0 13 0-0-0± Timman-Radev, Tbilisi 1971) 9 ♘xa5 ♕xa5 10 ♗g2 (± Taimanov) 10...♗b7 11 0-0 ♘c6 12 ♗f4 ♗e7 13 ♘d5!? exd5 14 exd5 0-0 15 dxc6 ♗xc6 16 c3 += Timman-Andersson, Amsterdam 1978

6 g3

6 ♗e3 a6 7 ♗d3 ♘f6 8 0-0 b5 9 ♘xc6 ♕xc6 10 a3 ♗b7 11 ♕e2 ♗e7 12

f4 h5!? (12...0-0 13 e5 ♘d5 14 ♘xd5 ♕xd5 15 c4 bxc4 16 ♗xc4 += Vogt-Mista, Havirov 1971) 13 e5 ♘g4 14 ♗d4 ♗c5 15 ♗xc5 ♕xc5+ 16 ♔h1 ♕e3= Peshina-Damjanovic, Vilnius 1978

6...a6 7 ♗g2 ♘f6 8 0-0 ♘xd4 9 ♕xd4 ♗c5 10 ♗f4 d6 11 ♕d3 ♘d7 12 ♘a4 e5 13 ♗d2 b5 14 ♘c3?! ♘b6!? N

14...♗b7 15 ♘d5 ♗xd5 16 ♕xd5 0-0 =+ Hubner-Petrosian, Wijk aan Zee 1971; 15 a4!? b4 16 ♘d5 ♗xd5 17 ♕xd5 ♖b8 18 a5!?∝

15 a4?! ♗e6 16 b3 b4 17 a5 ♘d7 18 ♘d5 ♗xd5 19 ♕xd5 += Kwatschewsky-Waller, Vienna Final 1978

1 e4 c5 2 ♘f3 ♘c6 3 d4 cxd4 4 ♘xd4 ♘f6 5 ♘c3 d6 6 ♗c4 e6

a) 6...♗d7 7 ♗b3 a6 8 0-0 g6 9 f3 ♗g7 10 ♗e3 0-0 11 ♕d2 ♖c8 12 ♖ad1 ♘e5 13 ♔h1 ♘c4 14 ♗xc4 ♖xc4 15 ♕e2 b5 16 a4!± Straus-Hubner, Vienna Final 1978;

b) 6...♕b6 7 ♘b3 e6 8 0-0 a6 9 a4! ♗e7 (9...♕c7 10 a5 ♘xa5 11 ♘xa5 b6 12 e5! bxa5 13 exf6 ♕xc4 14 fxg7 ♗xg7 15 ♕xd6± Hladky-Pletanek, Corres 1977) 10 a5 ♕c7 11 ♗e3 ♘b4 12 ♗d3 ♗d7 13 ♗b6 ♕c8 14 f4 e5≈ Damjanovic-Csom, Vilnius 1978

7 ♗e3 ♗e7 8 ♕e2 0-0 9 0-0-0 a6 10 ♗b3 ♕c7 10...♕e8 11 g4!? N (11 ♖hg1 Δ g4 += Gufeld) 11...♘xd4 12 ♗xd4 e5 13 ♗e3 ♗xg4 14 f3 ♗e6 15 ♖hg1 ♔h8∓ De Eccher-Cappello, Italy Final 1978

11 ♖hg1

11 g4 ♘xd4 12 ♖xd4 b5 13 g5 ♘d7 14 ♖g1 ♗b7 15 f4 ♘c5 16 f5± Nunn-Paoli, Lublin 1978

11...♘a5 12 g4 b5 13 g5 ♘xb3+ 14 axb3 ♘d7 15 f4

15 ♖g3 b4 16 ♘f5 exf5 17 ♘d5 ♕d8 18 exf5 ♖e8 19 ♕d3 ♗f8 20 ♘f6+ +− Stean-Schneiderom, Haifa 1976

15...b4

16 ♘f5!

16 ♘a4 ♗b7 17 f5 e5 18 f6 exd4 19 fxe7 ♖fe8 20 ♖xd4 ♖xe7 21 ♖xb4 ♗xe4 =+ Velimirovic-Ivanovic, Jugoslav Final 1978

16...exf5

16...♘c5 17 ♘xe7+ ♕xe7 18 e5! dxe5 19 ♗xc5 ♕xc5 20 ♘e4 ♕a5 21 ♘f6+! +− Goldenberg-Szymczak, Sandomierz 1976

17 ♘d5 ♕d8 18 exf5 ♖e8 19 g6! N

19 f6 ♗f8 20 fxg7 ♗xg7 21 ♘f6+∝ Gutman-Ozolin, USSR 1976

19...fxg6 20 fxg6 h6?!

20...♘f6∝

21 ♕c4 ♔h8 22 ♗d4 ♗f8?

22...♗f6!∝

23 ♘c7± Velimirovic-Ivanovic, Niksic 1978

1 e4 c5 2 ♘f3 d6 3 d4 cxd4 4 ♘xd4 ♘f6 5 ♘c3 e6 6 g4 h6

6...a6 7 g5 ♘fd7 8 ♗e3 (8 f4 ♘c6 9 ♗e3 h6 10 f5 ♘xd4 11 ♕xd4 ♘e5 12 0-0-0 hxg5 13 fxe6 ♗xe6 14 ♘d5+= Beljavsky-Ree, Kiev 1978) 8...b5 9 a3 ♘b6 10 h4 N d5?! 11 exd5 exd5? 12 ♘de2 ♘c4 13 ♕xd5 ♘xe3 14 fxe3 ♖a7 15 ♕xd8+ ♔xd8 16 0-0-0+± Hort-Ree, Amsterdam 1978

7 g5 hxg5 8 ♗xg5 ♘c6 9 ♕d2

9 ♘b3 a6 10 f4 ♕c7 11 ♕e2 ♗e7 12 0-0-0 b5 13 ♗g2 ♗b7= Lanc-Pritchett, Decin 1978

9...a6 10 0-0-0 ♕b6

10...♗d7 11 h4 ♗e7 12 ♖h3 ♘xd4 13 ♕xd4 e5 14 ♕e3 ♗xh3 15 ♗xh3 ♘g8 16 ♘d5 f6 17 ♕c3! fxg5 18 ♘c7+ ♔f7 19 ♕b3+ ♔g6 20 ♗f5+ ♔h6 21 ♕f7 1-0 Pokojowczyk-Adamski, Slupsk 1978

11 ♘b3 ♕c7 12 f4

12 ♗g2 ♗d7 13 f4 0-0-0 14 h4 ♗e7 15 ♗f3 g6 16 ♕f2± Mednis-Fernandez, Budapest 1978

12...b5 13 ♗g2 ♗b7 14 h4

14 ♕e3 b4 15 ♘a4 ♘d7 16 e5!± Razuvaev-Commons, Lublin 1978

14...0-0-0 15 f5 ♔b8 16 fxe6 fxe6 17 ♘d4 ♘xd4 18 ♕xd4 ♗e7 19 ♗h3 += Timman-Ligterink, Netherlands Final 1978

1 e4 c5 2 ♘f3 ♘c6 3 d4 cxd4 4 ♘xd4 ♘f6 5 ♘c3 e5 6 ♘db5 d6 7 ♗g5

7 ♘d5 ♘xd5 8 exd5 ♘e7 9 c3!? ♘f5 (9...♘g6 10 ♕a4 ♗d7 11 ♕b4 ♕b8 12 h4 h5 13 ♕c4± Broza-Brustman, Warsaw 1978) 10 ♕a4 ♗d7 11 g4! ♘h4 12 ♕b4 ♘g6 13 ♗e2 ♕c8 14 h3± Cycling-Broza, Warsaw 1978

7...a6 8 ♗xf6 gxf6 9 ♘a3 b5 10 ♘d5 f5

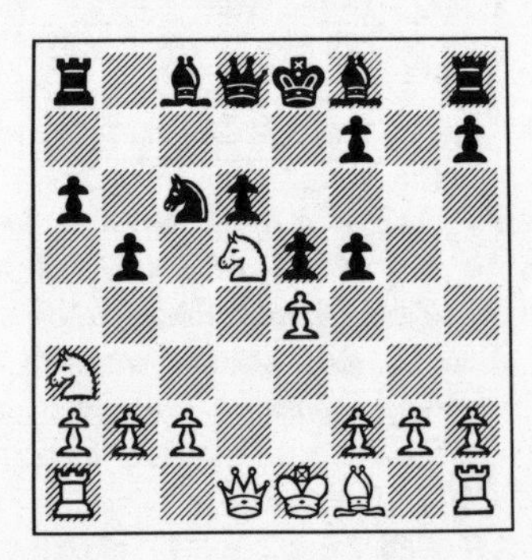

11 ♗xb5!?

a) 11 exf5 ♗xf5 12 ♗d3 e4 13 ♕e2 ♘d4 14 ♕e3 ♗g7 15 f3 ♕h4+ 16 g3 ♘xf3+ 17 ♕xf3 exf3 18 gxh4 ♗xd3 19 cxd3 ♗xb2 20 ♔f2 N (20 ♖d1 ♗xa3 21 ♘c7+ ♔d7 22 ♘xa8 ♖xa8 =+ Joksic-Simic, Jugoslavia 1978) 20... ♗xa1 21 ♖xa1 ♖c8 ∞/∓ Browne-Adorjan, Amsterdam 1978;

b) 11 ♗d3 ♗e6 12 ♕h5 ♗g7 13 c3 0-0 14 exf5 ♗xd5 15 f6 e4 16 fxg7 ♖e8 17 ♗e2 ♖e5 18 ♕h6 ♕g5!? N 19 ♕xg5 ♖xg5 20 0-0 b4 21 ♘c2 bxc3 22 bxc3 ♗e6= Swic-Bielczyk, Polanica Zdroj 1978

11...axb5 12 ♘xb5 ♖a4!?

a) 12...♖b8 13 ♘bc7+ ♔d7 14 ♕h5 ♘d4 15 0-0 ♔c6 16 b4!± Nunn-

Bhend, Buenos Aires 1978;

b) 12...♕g5! N 13 ♘dc7+ ♔d8 14 ♘xa8 ♕xg2 15 ♖f1 ♕xe4+ 16 ♕e2 ♕a4!∓ Honfi-Horvath, Subotica 1978

13 ♘bc7+ ♔d7 14 0-0 ♕g5!?

14...♖xe4 15 ♕h5 ♘e7 16 ♕xf7 ♔c6 17 c4!± Honfi-Piasetski, Subotica 1978

15 c4!? ♖xc4 16 b4∞ Nunn-F.Portisch, Budapest 1978

1 e4 c5 2 ♘f3 d6 3 d4 cxd4 4 ♘xd4 ♘f6 5 ♘c3 a6 6 ♗g5 e6 7 f4 ♕c7

a) 7...♗e7 8 ♕f3 ♕c7 9 0-0-0 ♘bd7 10 ♗d3 h6 11 ♕h3 ♘f8 12 ♘f3 (12 ♗xf6!?) 12...♘g6 13 ♗xf6 ♘xf4 14 ♕g3 ♘xd3+ 15 ♖xd3 ♗xf6 16 e5 dxe5 17 ♘e4 ♕e7 18 ♘d6+ ♔f8 19 ♖f1∞ Trabattoni-Valenti, Italy Final 1978;

b) 7...♕b6 8 ♕d2 ♕xb2 9 ♘b3 ♘c6 10 ♗xf6 gxf6 11 ♘a4 ♕a3 12 ♘b6 ♖b8 13 ♘c4 ♕a4 14 ♔f2 e5 15 ♗d3 exf4 N (15...♗e6 16 ♘b6 ♕b4 17 ♕xb4 ♘xb4 18 f5 ♗d7 19 a3 ♘xd3+ 20 cxd3 ♗c6= Ligterink-Barczay, Wijk aan Zee 1977) 16 ♕xf4 ♘e5 17 ♘b6 ♕c6 18 ♘d5 ♘g4+∞ Fernandez-Nunn, Budapest 1978

8 ♕f3 b5

8...♘bd7 9 0-0-0 b5 10 ♗xb5!? axb5 11 ♘dxb5 (11 e5 ♖a5! 12 ♘dxb5 ♖xb5 13 ♘xb5 ♕b8∞ Minev) 11...♕b6 (11...♕b8 12 e5 ♖a5!∞ Balashov-Polugaevsky, Manilla 1976) 12 e5 ♗b7 13 ♕e2!? dxe5 14 fxe5 ♘d5 15 ♘xd5 ♗xd5 16 ♖xd5! exd5 17 ♘d6+ (17 e6!) 17...♗xd6 18 exd6+ ♔f8 19 ♕e7+ ♔g8 20 ♕xd7 h6! 21 ♖f1 N (21 ♗d2 ♖xa2 Guseynov-Tseitlin, Kronstadt 1975; 21...♖d8! −+) 21...hxg5 ½-½ Pirisi-Schussler, Eeeklo 1978

9 0-0-0 ♗b7 10 ♗d3 ♘bd7 11 ♖he1 0-0-0 12 ♕h3 b4!? N **13 ♘d5?!**

13 ♘a4

13...exd5 14 e5 dxe5 15 fxe5 ♗c5 16 exf6 ♗xd4 17 fxg7 ♗xg7∓ Garcia-Dorfman, Polanica Zdroj 1978

Caro-Kann

1 e4 c6 2 d4

2 ♘c3 d5 3 ♘f3 ♗g4 4 h3 ♗xf3 5 ♕xf3 e6 6 d3 d4?! 7 ♘e2 c5 8 g4 ♘c6 9 ♘g3 g6?! 10 ♗g2 ♗d6 11 0-0± Garcia-Velandia, Bogata 1978

2...d5 3 exd5 cxd5 4 c4

a) 4 c3 ♘c6 5 ♗f4 ♗f5 6 ♘f3 e6 7 ♕b3 ♕c8 8 ♘bd2 ♘f6 9 ♗e2 ♗e7 10 0-0 ♘e4= Larsen-Spassky, San Juan 1969;

b) 4 c3 ♘f6 5 ♘f3 ♗f5 6 ♗b5+ ♘bd7 7 ♘h4 ♗g6 8 ♗f4 e6 9 ♘d2 ♘h5 10 ♘xg6 hxg6= Fischer-Hort, Vinkovci 1968;

c) 4 c3 ♘f6 5 ♘f3 ♘c6 N 6 ♘e5 ♘d7 (6...g6!?) 7 f4 ♕b6 8 ♗d3 g6 9 ♕b3 ♕xb3 10 axb3 f6 11 ♘xc6! bxc6 12 h4!± Straub-Kwatschewsky, Vienna Final 1978;

d) 4 ♗d3 ♘c6 5 c3 ♘f6 6 ♗f4 e6 (6...g6 7 ♘d2 ♗g7 8 ♘gf3 0-0 9 h3 ♗d7 10 0-0 ♖c8 11 ♖e1 ♖e8 12 ♘e5 ♘h5= Messa-Cappello, Italy Final 1978; 6...♗g4 7 ♕b3 ♕c8 8 ♘d2 e6

9 ♘gf3 ♗e7 10 0-0 0-0 11 ♘e5 ♗h5 12 ♖fe1 += Rupeni-Taruffi, Italy Final 1978) 7 ♘d2 ♗d6 8 ♗xd6 ♕xd6 9 ♘gf3 0-0 10 0-0 e5!? 11 dxe5 ♘xe5 12 ♘xe5 ♕xe5 13 ♕c1 += Akvist-Kubien, Wroclaw 1978

4...♞f6

4...♘c6 5 ♘c3 e6 6 ♘f3 ♘f6 7 c5 ♗e7 8 ♗b5 ♗d7 9 0-0 0-0 10 ♖e1 b6 11 ♗xc6 ♗xc6 12 ♘e5! N (12 b4 ♘e4 13 ♘xe4 dxe4 14 ♘e5 ♗d5= Botvinnik) 12...♗e8 13 ♗e3 bxc5 14 dxc5 ♖b8 15 ♖b1 ♕c7 16 ♕d4 += Grabczewski-Kubien, Wroclaw 1978

5 ♞c3 ♞c6

5...e6 6 c5 g6!? N 7 ♗f4 ♘h5 8 ♗e5 f6 9 ♗xb8 ♖xb8 10 ♗b5+ ♗d7 11 ♗xd7+ ♕xd7 12 ♘ge2 ♗h6 13 0-0 += Passerotti-De Eccher, Italy Final 1978

6 cxd5 ♞xd5 7 ♞f3 ♝g4 8 ♛b3 ♝xf3 9 gxf3 e6

9...♘b6 10 ♗e3 e6 11 ♖g1! N (11 0-0-0 ♖c8 12 ♔b1 ♕c7 13 ♘b5 ♕b8 14 ♘xa7 +− Sisniega-Groszpeter, Innsbruck 1977) 11...♖c8 12 ♖d1 g6 13 d5 ♘xd5 14 ♕xb7± Velimirovic-Nikolac, Jugoslav Final 1978

10 ♛xb7 ♞xd4 11 ♝b5+ ♞xb5 12 ♛c6+ ♚e7 13 ♛xb5

13 ♘xb5? ♖b8 14 ♘d4 ♕d7 15 ♗e3 ♖xb2 16 ♕c4 f6 17 ♖d1 ♔f7 18 ♘b3 ♗e7 19 0-0 ♖c8 −+ Zhuravlev-Stecko, USSR 1971

13...♛d7

13...♘xc3 14 ♕b4+ ♔e8 15 ♕xc3 ♖c8 16 ♕b3 ♖b8 17 ♕a4+ ♕d7 18 ♕xd7+ ♔xd7 19 ♗e3 ♗b4+ 20 ♔e2 ♗d6 21 b3 a6 22 ♖hg1 g6 23 ♖gd1 ♖hc8 24 ♖d2 ♖c6 25 ♖ad1 ♖b5 26 ♗f4 e5 27 a4!± Velimirovic-Augustin, Moscow 1977

14 ♛a5 N

14 ♘xd5+ ♕xd5 15 ♕xd5 exd5 16 ♗e3 ♔e6 17 ♖c1 ♗d6= Shiravevic-Bukic, Banya Luka 1976

14...♞xc3 15 bxc3 f6! 16 ♜b1 ♚f7 17 ♛a6 ♝e7 18 ♜b7 ♛d5!= Gaprindashvili-Chiburdanidze (6) 1978

1 e4 c6 2 d4 d5 3 ♞c3 dxe4 4 ♞xe4 ♞f6

4...♗f5 5 ♘g3 ♗g6 6 ♘h3 ♘f6 7 ♘f4 e5 (7...♘bd7 8 ♗c4 e5 9 ♕e2 ♕e7 10 dxe5 ♕xe5 11 ♗e3 ♗b4+ 12 c3 ♗c5= Ljubojevic-Portisch, Tilburg 1978) 8 ♘xg6 hxg6 9 dxe5 ♕a5+ N (9...♕xd1+ 10 ♔xd1 ♘g4 11 ♘e4 ♘xe5 12 ♗e2 f6 13 c3 ♘bd7 14 ♗e3 += Fischer-Foguelman, Buenos Aires 1960) 10 ♗d2 ♕xe5+ 11 ♕e2 ♕xe2+ 12 ♗xe2 ♘bd7 13 0-0-0 ♗c5= Teshkovsky-Bagirov, Lvov 1978

5 ♞xf6+ exf6 6 ♝c4 ♛e7+

6...♘d7!? N 7 ♘e2 ♗d6 8 0-0 0-0 9 ♗f4 ♘b6 10 ♗d3 ♗e6 11 c3 ♘d5 12 ♗xd6 ♕xd6 13 ♕d2 += Karpov-Korchnoi (20) 1978

Diagram

7 ♛e2 ♝e6

7...♗g4 8 ♕xe7+ ♗xe7 9 ♘e2 ♘d7 10 f3 ♗f5 11 ♗b3 0-0 12 ♔f2 ♖fe8= Lerner-Mohring, Stary Smokovec 1977

8 ♝xe6 ♛xe6 9 ♝f4 ♞a6 10 c3 0-0-0

11 ♕xe6+ fxe6 12 0-0-0 N

12 ♘e2 c5 13 ♗e3 ♗d6 14 0-0-0 ♖he8= Gaprindashvili-Andersson, Dortmund 1978

12...c5 13 ♘f3? cxd4 14 ♘xd4? e5 −+ Hodgson-Wade, London 1978

Scandanavian

1 e4 d5 2 exd5 ♘f6

2...♕xd5 3 ♘c3 ♕a5 4 d4 ♘f6 5 ♗c4!? (5 ♘f3 ♗g4 6 h3 ♗xf3 7 ♕xf3±) 5...♗g4? (5...♘c6 6 d5 ♘e5 7 ♗b3 c6 8 ♕e2 ♘ed7 9 ♗d2 cxd5 10 ♘xd5 += Aronin) 6 ♘f3 (6 f3 ♗f5 7 ♘e2 ♘bd7 8 g4 ♗g6 9 h4 h6 10 ♘f4± Kavalek-Larsen, Beverwijk 1967) 6...♘c6 7 ♗b5 e6 8 ♕d3 ♗b4 9 ♘e5!± Baljon-Bohm, Netherlands Final 1978

3 d4

3 c4 c6 4 d4 cxd5 5 ♘c3 g6 6 cxd5 ♗g7 7 ♗b5+ ♘bd7 8 d6 e6 9 ♘f3 a6 10 ♗e2 b5 11 ♕b3 ♕b6 12 0-0 ♗b7 13 ♗f4± Banas-Petran, Stary Smokovec 1977

3...♘xd5

3...g6?! N 4 c4 b5! 5 b3 ♗g7 6 ♘f3 0-0 7 ♗e2 c6 8 dxc6 bxc4 9 bxc4 ♘xc6 10 0-0? (10 ♘c3!±) 10...♘e4! 11 ♗e3 f5! ∞/∓ Linton-Bonner, British Final 1978

4 c4

a) 4 ♘f3 ♗g4 5 h3 ♗h5 6 g4 (6 c4 ♘b6 7 ♕b3! ♗xf3 8 ♕xf3 ♕xd4 9 ♕xb7 e5 10 ♘c3 += Kapengut-Shereshevsky, Minsk 1978) 6...♗g6 7 ♘e5 ♘d7 8 ♘xg6 hxg6 9 c4 N ♘5b6 10 ♗f4 e5!=+ Cuartas-Velandia, Bogota 1978;

b) 4 ♘f3 ♗g4 5 ♗e2 e6 6 h3 ♗h5 7 0-0 ♗e7 8 c4 ♘b6 9 ♗e3 ♘c6 10 ♘bd2 0-0 11 ♖c1 += Van Wijgerden-Christiansen, IBM 2 1978;

c) 4 ♘f3 ♗g4 5 ♗e2 ♘c6 6 0-0 e6 7 c3 ♗d6 8 ♘e5 N (8 ♘bd2 ♘f4 9 ♘e4 ♘xe2+ 10 ♕xe2 0-0= Zinser-Karaklaic, Monte Carlo 1967) 8...♗xe2 9 ♕xe2 ♗xe5 10 dxe5 ♕h4 11 f4 0-0= Sikora-Commons, Lublin 1978

4...♘b6 5 ♘c3

5 ♘f3 ♗g4 6 c5 ♘bd7 7 ♗c4 (7 ♗e2 e6 8 ♕b3 b6 9 ♗e3 ♗e7 10 ♘bd2 0-0 11 0-0 ♘f6= Shamkovich-Rogoff, USA Final 1978) 7...e6 8 h3! (8 ♗e3 b6! 9 ♘c3 Christiansen-Commons, USA Final 1978, 9...c6!∞) 8...♗h5 9 ♗e3 ♘c6 10 ♘c3 ♗e7 11 a3 += Byrne-Rogoff, USA Final 1978

5...e5! 6 dxe5

6 ♗e3 N exd4 7 ♗xd4 ♘c6 8 ♗e3 ♗e6 9 c5 ♘d7 10 ♘a4 ♕h4 11 a3 0-0-0∓ Paoli-Commons, Lublin 1978

6...♕xd1+ 7 ♘xd1 ♘c6 8 f4 ♗e6 9 ♘e3 N

9 b3 0-0-0 10 ♘e3 ♗c5 11 a3 ♖he8 12 ♘f3 f6∓ Treybal-Bogoljubov, Pistyan 1922

9...0-0-0 10 ♘f3 ♗c5 11 ♗e2 ♘b4 12 a3 ♘d3+ 13 ♗xd3 ♖xd3∓ Mrdja-Commons, Lublin 1978

1 e4 e5 2 ♗c4

1 e4 e5 2 ♗c4 ♘f6 3 d3 ♘c6

3...c6 4 ♘f3! ♗e7 N (4...d5 5 ♗b3 ♗d6 6 ♘c3 ♗e6 7 ♗g5 ♕a5 8 0-0 ♘bd7 9 ♖e1 0-0-0 10 exd5 cxd5 11 ♕d2 +=) 5 ♘c3 d6 6 0-0 0-0 7 ♕e2 b5 8 ♗b3 ♘bd7 9 ♗e3 ♘g4 10 d4 ♘xe3 11 ♕xe3 ♕b6 12 a4 b4 13 ♘e2 ♗f6= Sikova-Knezevic, Stary Smokovec 1977

4 ♘c3 ♗c5

a) 4...♘a5 5 ♘ge2 ♘xc4 6 dxc4 ♗e7 7 0-0 d6 8 b3 0-0 9 ♘g3 c6 10 ♗b2 ♕a5 11 ♕e1 ♕c7 12 a4 += Larsen-Portisch (10) 1968;

b) 4...♘a5 5 ♗e3 N ♘xc4 6 dxc4 d6 7 f3 ♗e6 8 ♕d3 ♘d7 9 0-0-0 c6 10 g3 a6 11 a4 ♕a5 12 b3 ♘c5 13 ♕d2 b5∓ Filipowicz-Schinzel, Warsaw 1978

5 ♗g5 h6 6 ♗h4 d6 7 ♘a4 ♗b6

7...a6 8 ♘xc5 dxc5 9 ♘e2 ♕d6 10 ♗b3 g5 11 ♗g3 ♗e6 12 ♗xe6 ♕xe6= Larsen-Letelier, Havana 1967

8 ♘xb6 axb6 9 f3 N

9 ♘e2 ♗e6 10 ♘c3 ♘d4 11 0-0 c6 12 ♕d2 b5 =+ Euwe 13 ♗xe6 fxe6 14 ♗g3 0-015 ♘e2 ♘xe2+ 16 ♕xe2= Larsen-Quinteros, Amsterdam 1964

9...♗e6 10 ♘e2 d5 11 ♗xf6 gxf6 12 exd5 ♗xd5 13 ♘c3 ♗e6 14 ♗xe6 fxe6 15 ♕d2 f5 16 0-0 += Larsen-Spassky, Tilburg 1978

Spanish

1 e4 e5 2 ♘f3 ♘c6 3 ♗b5 f5!? 4 ♘c3

a) 4 exf5 e4 5 ♕e2 ♕e7 6 ♗xc6 dxc6 7 ♘d4 ♕e5 8 ♘f3 ♕e7 9 ♘d4 ♕e5 10 c3 N (10 ♘f3 ♕xf5 11 ♘c3 ♘f6 12 d3 ♗b4∝ Nikolic-Maric, Jugoslavia 1965) 10...♗d6?! 11 ♘a3! ♗xa3 12 bxa3 ♘f6 13 g4 += Mrdj-Lipski, Lublin 1978;

b) 4 d3 fxe4 5 dxe4 ♘f6 6 0-0 (6 ♕e2!? d6 7 ♗g5 ♗g4 8 h3 ♗h5 9 ♘c3 ♗e7 10 0-0-0 0-0 11 g4 ♘xg4? 12 ♗xe7 ♕xe7 13 ♗c4+ ♔h8 14 hxg4 ♗xg4 15 ♖xh7+!! +− Horner-Knox, British Final 1978) 6...d6 7 ♘c3 ♗e7 8 a3?! N (8 ♘d5; 8 ♕d3) 8...♗g4 9 h3 ♗xf3 (9...♗h5) 10 ♕xf3 0-0 11 ♕d3 ♔h8 13 ♗e3 ♘h5 Δ ♗g5= Chiburdanidze-Gaprindashvili (1) 1978

4...♘d4

4...fxe4 5 ♘xe4 ♘f6 6 ♕e2 ♕e7 (6... d5 7 ♘xf6+ gxf6 8 d4 e4 9 ♘h4 ♕e7 10 ♗f4 f5 [10...♗e6!?] 11 g3 ♗g7 12 ♕h5+ ♕f7 13 ♕xf7+ ♔xf7 14 c3± Savon-Parma, Ljubljana 1977) 7 0-0 d5 8 ♘c3 (8 ♘xf6+ gxf6 9 d4 e4 10 ♘d2 ♗d7 11 c4!) 8...e4 9 ♘d4 ♗d7 10 ♗xc6 bxc6 11 d3 c5 12 ♘db5 ♗c6? (12...♗xb5 13 ♘xb5 c6 14 ♘c3 exd3 15 ♕xd3 ♕d7 16 ♖e1+ ♗e7=) 13 ♗g5! d4 14 ♗xf6 gxf6 15 ♘xe4 +− Radulov-Inkiov, Hungary Final 1978

5 exf5

5 ♗c4 c6 6 d3?! (6 0-0! ♘f6 7 ♘xe5!

fxe4 8 ♘f7 ♕e7 9 ♘xh8 d5 10 ♗e2 ♗f5 11 d3 0-0-0 12 ♗e3± Geller-Rodriguez, Las Palmas 1976) 6... ♘xf3+ 7 ♕xf3 ♕f6! 8 ♕e2 f4 9 ♗d2 ♘e7 10 0-0-0 d6 11 f3 ♗d7?! (11... g5!) 12 ♕f2 g5 13 h4 g4∞ Westerinen-Lanka, Jurmala 1978

5...♘xb5 6 ♘xb5 d6

7 ♕e2! N

7 d4 e4 8 ♕e2! ♕e7 9 ♗g5 ♘f6 10 ♘h4 c6 11 ♘c3 d5 12 0-0 += Swic-Bednarski, Polanica 1978

7...♗xf5

7...c6

8 d4 e4 9 ♘g5 ♕d7 10 g4 ♗g6 11 ♘e6! c6

11...♖c8

12 ♘bc7+ ♔e7 13 f4 ♖c8 14 f5 ♗f7 15 ♕xe4± Pokojowczyk-Lipski, Krakow 78

1 e4 e5 2 ♘f3 ♘c6 3 ♗b5 a6 4 ♗a4 d6 5 ♗xc6+

a) 5 c4 ♘f6 6 d4 ♗d7 7 ♘c3 ♗e7 8 0-0 0-0 9 d5 N (9 ♖e1= Rabar) 9... ♘a7 10 ♗xd7 ♕xd7 11 b4 += Valenti-Tatai, Italy Final 1978;

b) 5 c3 f5 6 exf5 ♗xf5 7 0-0 ♗d3 8 ♖e1 ♗e7 9 ♗c2 e4? (9...♗xc2 10 ♕xc2 ♘f6 11 ♘g5 ♕d7= Gipslis-Shianovsky, Baku 1961) 10 ♗xd3 exd3 11 ♖e3 (11 ♕b3 +− Klavin-Zhuravlev, USSR 1961) 11...♘h6 12 ♖xd3 0-0 13 ♖e3 ♘e5 N (13...d5 14 d4± Gasibajarov-Pozarski, USSR 1961) 14 d4 ♘eg4 15 ♖e2± Timoshenko-Trapl, Decin 1978

5...bxc6 6 d4 f6 7 ♗e3

7 ♕d3 a5 8 ♕c4 ♕d7 9 ♗e3 ♗a6 10 ♕a4 ♗b5 11 ♘xb5 cxb5 12 ♕b3 += Roos-Berg, Herzlia 1978

7...♘e7 8 ♘c3 ♘g6 9 ♕d2

9 h4 h5 10 ♕d3 ♗e7 11 0-0-0 ♗d7 12 ♕c4 ♕b8 13 dxe5 fxe5 14 ♕d3 a5 =+ Cosulich-De Eccher, Italy Final 1978

9...♗d7 10 0-0-0 ♗e7 11 h4 h5 12 d5 ♕b8 13 ♖dg1 += Messa-De Eccher, Italy Final 1978

1 e4 e5 2 ♘f3 ♘c6 3 ♗b5 a6 4 ♗a4 ♘f6 5 0-0 ♗e7 6 ♖e1 b5 7 ♗b3 d6 8 c3 0-0 9 d4 ♗g4 10 d5

a) 10 ♗e3 ♘a5 11 dxe5! ♗xf3 12 ♕xf3 dxe5 13 ♗c2 ♘c4 14 ♗c1 c6 N (14...♕c8 15 h3 ♕e6 16 ♗b3 += Kavalek-Forintos, Polanica 1968) 15 b3 ♘b6 16 ♘d2 a5 17 ♘f1 Δ ♘e3, ♘f5± Kasparov-Litvinov, Minsk 1978;

b) 10 ♗e3 d5!? 11 exd5 exd4 12 ♗xd4! ♘xd4 13 cxd4 ♗b4 14 ♘c3 a5 (14...♗xc3 Δ ♘xd5) 15 a3 ♗xc3 16 bxc3 a4 17 ♗a2 ♕d6 18 h3 ♗xf3 19 ♕xf3 ♕xa3 20 ♗c4± Gulko-Geller, Lvov 1978;

c) 10 ♗e3 ♗h5!? 11 h3 ♖e8 12 ♘bd2 ♗f8 13 d5 ♘a5 14 ♗c2 ♖c8 15 b4 ♘b7 Gulko-Romanishin, Lvov 1978, 16 c4!±;

d) 10 ♗e3 exd4 11 cxd4 ♘a5 (11...d5 12 exd5? [12 e5] 12...♘xd5 13 ♘c3 ♘xe3 14 fxe3 ♘a5 15 ♗c2 c5∓ Smyslov-Savon, Lvov 1978) 12 ♗c2 c5 (12...♘c4 13 ♗c1 c5 14 b3 ♘b6 15 ♘bd2 ♖c8!? 16 ♗b2 cxd4 17 h3 ♗h5 18 ♗xd4 N [18 g4 ♗g6 19 ♘xd4

+= Rubtsova-Kushnir, USSR Team Ch 1966] 18...♘bd7! 19 a4 ♘c5 20 axb5 axb5 21 ♕b1 ♗g6 22 ♘h4?! ♘e6 23 ♗e3 d5!∓ Ligterink-Klovan, Jurmala 1978) 13 dxc5 (13 h3 ♗h5!? N 14 dxc5 dxc5 15 ♘bd2 ♘d7 16 ♕c1 ♖e8= Riemsdyk-Smyslov, Sao Paulo 1978) 13...dxc5 14 ♘bd2 ♘c6 15 ♖c1 ♘b4 N (15...♘d7 16 h3 ♗e6 17 ♘b3 a5∞ Gulko-Podgaets, Vilnius 1971) 16 ♗b1 ♖c8 17 h3 ♗e6 18 ♘b3 ♕b6 19 ♘g5 ♖fd8 20 ♕f3 ♘d7 21 e5 += Gulko-Portisch, Niksic 1978

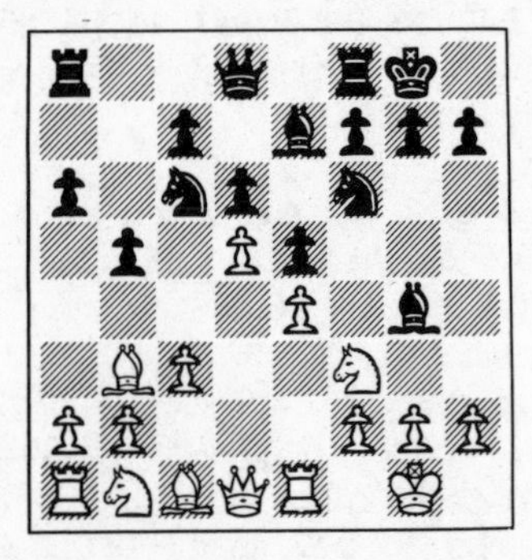

10...♞a5 11 ♝c2 c6

a) 11...♘c4 12 h3 ♗d7 13 a4! ♘b6 14 a5 ♘c8 15 b3 += Sax-Gligoric, Osijek 1978;

b) 11...c5 12 dxc6 ♕c7 13 h3 ♗e6 14 ♘bd2 ♕xc6 15 ♘f1 ♘c4 16 ♘g3 ♖fe8= Ostojic-Ivkov, Jugoslavia Final 1978;

c) 11...c5 12 ♘bd2 ♘e8 13 h3 ♗d7 14 ♘f1 g6 15 ♗h6 ♘g7 16 ♘g3 ♘c4 17 ♕c1 ♘b6= Tseshkovsky-Savon, USSR Final 1977;

d) 11...c5 12 h3 ♗d7 13 ♘xe5 dxe5 14 d6 ♗e6 15 dxe7 ♕xe7 16 ♘d2 ♖fd8 17 ♕f3 c4?! 18 ♘f1 += Timman-Ree, Netherlands Final 1978

12 h3 ♝xf3

a) 12...♗h5 13 dxc6 ♕c7 14 ♘bd2 ♖ad8 15 ♘f1 ♘xc6 16 ♘e3 d5 17 ♘xd5 ♘xd5 18 exd5 f5 19 ♕e2 e4 20 dxc5 ♗xc5∞ Gufeld-Schneider, Jurmala 1978;

b) 12...♗d7 13 ♘xe5 dxe5 14 d6 ♗xd6 (14...c5 15 dxe7 ♕xe7 16 ♘d2 c4 17 ♕f3 ♖e8 18 ♘f1 += Tringov-Kovacevic, Titovo Uzice 1978) 15 ♕xd6 ♘c4 N 16 ♕d1 ♗e6 17 b3 ♘b6 18 ♗g5 ♕xd1= Tseshkovsky-Smyslov, Lvov 1978

13 ♛xf3 cxd5 14 exd5 ♞c4 15 ♞d2 ♞b6 16 ♞f1 ♞bxd5

16...♘e8 17 a4 g6 18 ♗h6 ♘g7 19 axb5 axb5 20 ♗d3 b4!? 21 cxb4 ♖xa1 22 ♖xa1 ♗g5! 23 ♗xg5 ♕xg5 24 ♖a7 ♕f4 25 ♕xf4 (25 ♗e4 ♕xf3 26 ♗xf3 ♖b8 27 ♘e3 += Tal-Gligoric, Bugojno 1978) 25...exf4 26 b5± Adorjan-Gligoric, Osijek 1978

17 ♞g3 ♞c7 18 ♞f5

18 a4 b4 19 ♘f5 ♘e6 20 ♕b7 ♖e8 21 ♕xb4 += Kurajica-Smejkal, Titovo Uzice 1978

18...♞e6 19 ♝b3 ♚h8 20 ♛g3 ♞e8 21 a4 ♝f6 22 ♝d5± Helmers-Luczak, Lodz 1978

1 e4 e5 2 ♞f3 ♞c6 3 ♝b5 a6 4 ♝a4 ♞f6 5 0-0 ♝e7 6 ♜e1 b5 7 ♝b3 d6 8 c3 0-0 9 h3 ♞b8

a) 9...♗b7 10 d4 ♕d7!? 11 ♘bd2

♖ad8 N [11...♖ae8 12 ♘f1 ♗d8 13 ♘g3 h6 14 ♗c2 Δ b3, d5, c4 += Karpov-I.Zaitsev, USSR 1969] 12 d5 ♘b8 13 ♘f1 c6! 14 dxc6 ♗xc6 15 ♘g3 ♕b7! =+ Gutierrez-Geller, Bogota 1978;

b) 9...♕d7 10 d4 ♖e8 11 ♘bd2 ♗f8 12 a3 N (12 d5 ♘e7 13 ♘f1 h6!? Polugaevsky 14 c4 c6 15 dxc6 ♘xc6= Timoshenko-Lanc, Decin 1978) 12... ♘d8 13 ♗c2 g6 14 b4 ♘h5 15 ♗b2 ♘e6 16 ♗d3 += Kuzmin-Smyslov, Lvov 1978;

c) 9...♘d7 10 d4 ♘b6 11 ♘bd2 exd4 12 cxd4 ♘b4 (12...d5 13 e5 ♗f5 14 ♘f1 ♘b4 15 g4 N ♗g6 16 ♘g3 ♘d3 17 ♖e2 ♘c4 18 ♘f5 += Sznapik-Banas, Stary Smokovec 1977) 13 ♘f1 c5 14 a3 ♘c6 15 ♗e3 N ♘a5 16 ♗c2 ♘bc4 17 ♗c1 cxd4 18 b3 d3!= Sznapik-Swic, Lodz 1978;

d) 9...h6 10 d4 ♖e8 11 ♘bd2 ♗f8 12 ♘f1 ♗d7 13 ♘g3 ♘a5 14 ♗c2 ♘c4 15 ♘h2 c5 16 b3 ♘b6 17 f4 cxd4 18 cxd4 ♕c8! 19 ♘f3!? N (19 ♖e2 ♕c3!= Tal-Geller, USSR Final 1977) 19...♗xh3! 20 gxh3 ♕xh3 21 ♘f1 ♖ac8∞ Acosta-Geller, Bogota 1978

10 d4

10 d3 ♘bd7 11 ♘bd2 ♗b7 12 ♘f1 ♘c5 13 ♗c2 a5!? N 14 ♘g3 g6 15 d4 += Garcia-Cuellar, Bogota 1978

10...♘bd7 11 ♘bd2 ♗b7 12 ♗c2 ♖e8 13 ♘f1

13 b3 ♗f8 14 a4 g6 15 ♗b2 c6 16 b4 N (16 ♗d3 ♗g7 17 ♕c2 ♖c8= Korchnoi-Portisch, USSR v World 1970) 16...♘b6 17 a5 ♘bd7 18 ♕b1 ♘h5 =+ Garcia-Panno, Bogota 1978

13...♗f8 14 ♘g3 g6 15 a4 c5 16 d5 ♘b6 17 ♕e2 bxa4 18 ♗xa4 ♘xa4 19 ♖xa4 ♘d7

19...♗c8 20 c4 N ♖b8 21 ♖a2 ♗g7 22 ♗d2 ♖e7 23 ♖b1 ♖eb7= Chiburdanidze-Reshevsky, Vilnius 1978

20 b3 ♗c8 21 ♖a3 ♖b8= Sigurjonsson-Cuellar, Bogota 1978

1 e4 e5 2 ♘f3 ♘c6 3 ♗b5 a6 4 ♗a4 ♘f6 5 0-0 ♘xe4 6 d4 b5 7 ♗b3 d5 8 dxe5

8 ♘xe5 ♘xe5 9 dxe5 ♗b7 10 c3 ♗e7 N 11 ♗e3 c5 12 a4 0-0 13 axb5 axb5 14 ♖xa8 ♗xa8 15 f3?! ♘g5 16 ♗c2 ♕c7 =+ Lawton-Corden, British Final 1978

8...♗e6 9 c3

9 ♕e2 ♗e7 10 ♖d1 0-0 11 c4 bxc4 12 ♗xc4 ♗c5 13 ♗e3 ♗xe3 14 ♕xe3 ♕b8 15 ♗b3 ♘a5 (15...♕b6 16 ♕e2 ♖ad8 17 ♘c3 ♘xc3 18 bxc3 ♘e7 19 ♖ab1 ♕a5 20 c4 Tal-Geller, Budva 1967, 20...dxc4=) 16 ♘e1 ♕b6 N (16...♘xb3 17 axb3 ♕b6 18 ♕xb6 cxb6 19 b4 Δ f3± Hubner-Demarre, Dresden 1960) 17 ♕xb6 cxb6 18 f3 ♘xb3 19 axb3 ♘c5= Karpov-Korchnoi (12) 1978

9...♗c5

9...♘c5 10 ♘bd2 d4 (10...g6?! 11 ♕e2 ♗g7 12 ♘d4! ♘xe5?! 13 f4 ♘c4 14 f5 gxf5 15 ♘xf5 ±/+− Karpov-Korchnoi (8) 1978) 11 ♘g5!? N dxc3 (11...♕xg5 12 ♕f3! ♔d7! 13 ♗d5! ♗xd5 14 ♕xd5+ ♗d6! 15 ♘e4

Qxe5 16 Nxc5+ Kc8 17 Qxe5 Bxe5=) 12 Nxe6 fxe6 13 bxc3 Qd3 14 Nf3 Qxd1 15 Bxd1± Karpov-Korchnoi (10) 1978

10 Nbd2 0-0 11 Bc2 Bf5

11...f5 12 Nb3 Bb6 13 Nfd4 Nxd4 14 Nxd4 Bxd4 15 cxd4 f4 16 f3 Ng3 17 Rf2 Qh4 18 Bd2? (18 Qd3 Rf5 19 Bxf4 Rxf4 20 hxg3 Qxg3 21 Qxh7+ Kf7 22 Qh2!= Keres) 18... Rae8 N (18...Nf5 19 Bxf5 Rxf5 20 Be1 Rh5 21 h3 Qg5 22 Kf1 c5!∓ Ajanski-Sapundiev, Gabrovo 1969) 19 Bb4 Rf7 20 a4! Bc8 21 axb5 Re6 22 bxa6?? (22 h3±) 22...Qxh2+! 0-1 Geller-Garcia, Bogota 1978

12 Nb3 Bg4 13 Nxc5

13 h3!? N Bh5 (13...Bxf3 14 gxf3 Bxf2+ 15 Rxf2 Nxf2 16 Kxf2 Nxe5 17 Be3± Larsen) 14 g4 Bg6 15 Bxe4 N dxe4 16 Nxc5 exf3 17 Bf4 += Karpov-Korchnoi (14) 1978

Diagram

13...Nxc5 14 Re1 d4! N

a) 14...Bh5!? 15 h3 N (15 Bg5 Bxf3 [15...Qd7 16 Be3 Na4! Larsen] 16 Qxf3 Qxg5 17 Qxd5 Rae8!= Korchnoi) 15...Re8 16 Bf4 Ne6= Karpov-Korchnoi (4) 1978;

b) 14...Re8 15 Bf4 Ne6!? Euwe

16 Qd3 N g6 17 Bg3 Bf5 18 Qe2 Ne7 19 Bh4± Arnlind-Haag, corres 1977/78

15 h3 Bh5 16 cxd4

a) 16 g4? d3!

b) 16 b4!? d3 17 Bb1 Bxf3 18 gxf3 Qd5 19 bxc5 Rad8 20 Bf4 Qc4∞

16...Bxf3 17 Qxf3 Nxd4 18 Qc3 Qd5!!= Karpov-Korchnoi (2) 1978

Petroff

1 e4 e5 2 Nf3 Nf6 3 d4

3 Nxe5 d6 4 Nf3 Nxe4

a) 5 d3 Nf6 6 d4 Bf5 7 Bd3 Bxd3 8 Qxd3 c6 9 0-0 Be7 10 Bg5 0-0= Cappello-Toth, Italy Final 1978;

b) 5 Nc3 Nxc3 6 dxc3 Be7 7 Bf4 0-0 N (7...Nc6 8 Qd2 Bg4 9 Be2 0-0 10 0-0-0 Re8 11 Kb1 Bf6= Michell-Tylor, Hastings 1935/36) 8 Qd2 Nd7 9 0-0-0 Nc5 10 Nd4 (10 h3 Re8 11 Bc4 Be6 12 Bxe6 Nxe6 13 Be3 a5 14 h4 a4 15 a3 Qd7∞ Savon-Kochiev, Lvov 1978) 10...Re8 11 f3 Ne6 12 Be3 Nxd4 13 cxd4 Bf6= Sveshnikov-Kochiev, Lvov 1978;

c) 5 d4 d5 6 Bd3 Be7 7 0-0 0-0 (7... Nc6 8 Re1 Bg4 9 c3 f5 10 Qb3 0-0 11 Nbd2 Kh8 12 h3 += Garcia-Szmetan, Bogota 1978) 8 c4 c6 9 Nc3 Nxc3 10 bxc3 dxc4 11 Bxc4 Nd7 12 Re1 Nb6 13 Bd3 Be6 14 a4

+= Mrdja-Paoli, Lublin 1978

3...exd4

a) 3...d5 4 exd5 e4 5 Ne5 Nxd5 6 Bc4 Be6 7 0-0 Be7 8 f3 += Sozin;
b) 3...d5 4 Nxe5 Nxe4 5 Bd3 Bd6 6 Nd2 Ng5 7 Ndf3 Nxf3+ 8 Qxf3 += Shamai-Berg, Herzlia 1978;
c) 3...Nxe4 4 Bd3 d5 5 Nxe5 Nf6 6 0-0 Be7 7 Bg5 N (7 c4 0-0 8 Nc3 dxc4 9 Bxc4± Sozin) 7...0-0 8 c3 Nbd7 9 f4 Ne4 10 Bxe7 Qxe7 11 Nd2 f6 12 Nxd7 Bxd7 13 Re1 += Waller-Glass, Vienna Final 1978;
d) 3...Nxe4 4 Bd3 d5 5 Nxe5 Nd7 6 Nxf7!? Qe7 7 Qe2!? N (7 Nxh8 Nc3+ 8 Kd2 Nxd1 9 Re1 Nxf2 10 Bxh7 Ne4+ 11 Rxe4 dxe4 12 Bg6+ Kd8 13 Nf7+ Ke8 14 Nd6+ Kd8= I.Zaitsev-Karpov, USSR 1966) 7... Kxf7 8 Qh5+ Kf6 9 0-0 Qf7 10 Qh4+ g5?! 11 Bxg5+ Nxg5 12 f4 Ke6 13 fxg5 Qg7 14 Nc3± Gurgenidze-Bellin, Tbilisi 1977
e) 3...Nxe4 4 Bd3 d5 5 Nxe5 Bd6 6 0-0 0-0 7 c4 Nc6 8 Nxc6 (8 cxd5 Nxd4 9 Bxe4 Bxe5 10 Nc3 Bf5 11 Be3 Bxe4 12 Bxd4 Bc2 13 Qd2 Bxd4 14 Qxd4 Re8= Hooper, 15 Rac1 Bg6 16 Qb4!± Bellin) 8...bxc6 9 c5 Be7 10 Nc3 N (10 Nd2 Nxd2 11 Bxd2 Bf6 12 Bc3 a5 13 Bc2 Qd7 14 h3 g6 15 Re1± Geller-Naranja, Palma 1970) 10...f5 11 Ne2 Bf6 12 Qa4 += Rumens-Milner-Barry, British Final 1978

Diagram

4 e5 Ne4 5 Qxd4 d5 6 exd6 Nxd6 7 Bg5!?

a) 7 Bd3 Nc6 8 Qf4 g6 9 0-0 Bg7 10 Re1+ Be6 11 Ng5?! 0-0 12 Nc3 N (12 Nxe6 fxe6 13 Qg4 Qf6!= Hubner-Segal, Dresden 1969) 12...Bf5 13 Nf3 Bxd3 14 cxd3 Nf5= Feustel-Kube, Eggesin 1978;
b) 7 Nc3 Nc6 8 Qf4 g6 9 Bd2 Qe7+ 10 Be2 Be6 11 0-0 N Bg7 12 Rae1 0-0-0= Geller-Smyslov, Lvov 1978

7...f6

7...Nc6

8 Bf4 Qe7+ N

8...Nc6 9 Qa4 +=

9 Be2 Nc6 10 Qa4 g5 11 Bxd6 Qxd6 12 Nc3 Qb4 13 Qb5 Bd7 Romanishin-Smyslov, Lvov 1978, 14 h4!±

King's Gambit

1 e4 e5 2 f4 exf4

a) 2...d6 3 Nf3 Nf6 4 Nc3 Nc6 5 Bb5! Bd7 6 d3 exf4 7 Bxf4 += A.Rabinovich;
b) 2...Nf6!? 3 fxe5 Nxe4 4 Nf3 Ng5 5 d4! Nxf3+ 6 Qxf3 Qh4+ 7 Qf2 Qxf2+ 8 Kxf2 d6! 9 Bf4 Nc6 10 Bb5 Bd7 11 Bxc6 Bxc6 12 exd6 Bxd6 13 Bxd6 cxd6 14 Nc3 +=;
c) 2...Bc5 3 Nf3 d6 4 fxe5 dxe5 5 c3 Nf6 (5...Qe7 6 d4! exd4 7 cxd4 Bb6 8 Nc3 Bg4 9 Qa4+ Nd7 10 Bg5± Lutikov-Lanka, Jurmala 1978) 6 Nxe5! Qe7 7 d4 Bd6 8 Nf3 Nxe4 9 Be2 0-0 10 0-0 c5 11 Nbd2= Charousek-Janowski, Berlin 1897; 11 d5! c4?! 12 Bxc4 Bg4 13 Qc2 Bxf3 14 gxf3! Ng5 15 Qg2±; 11...Bf5 12

♘a3!;

d) 2...d5 3 exd5 (3 ♘f3 dxe4 4 ♘xe5 ♘d7 5 d4 exd3 6 ♘xd3 ♘gf6 7 ♘c3 ♘b6 8 ♗e2 ♗d6 9 0-0 0-0= Lutikov-Nikitin, Tiflis 1959) 3...e4 4 d3 ♘f6 5 dxe4 ♘xe4

1) 6 ♗e3 ♕h4+ 7 g3 ♘xg3 8 ♘f3 ♕e7 9 hxg3 ♕xe3+ 10 ♕e2 ♕xe2+ (10...♗c5 N 11 ♘c3 ♗f5 12 ♕xe3 ♗xe3 13 ♘h4 ♗g4 14 ♗e2 ♗xe2 15 ♔xe2 ♗b6 16 ♘f5 0-0 17 ♘e7+! ♔h8 18 ♖xh7+ +− Roth-Rajna, 1975) 11 ♗xe2 ♗g4 12 ♘c3 ♗b4 13 ♘g5 ♗xe2 14 ♔xe2 ♗xc3 15 bxc3 h6= Spassky-Matanovic, Belgrade 1964;

2) 6 ♗e3 ♗d6! 7 ♘f3 0-0 8 ♗c4 ♘d7 9 0-0 ♖e8 10 ♖e1 ♘ef6 11 ♔h1 ♘g4 12 ♗g1 ♘b6 13 ♗b3 ♗xf4= Bronstein-Unzicker, Moscow 1956;

3) 6 ♘f3 ♗f5 7 ♗e3 c6 8 ♗c4 b5 9 ♗b3 c5 10 d6 c4 11 ♕d5 +− Alekhine-Tarrasch, St. Petersburg 1914;

3) 6 ♘f3 ♗c5 7 ♕e2 ♗f5 8 ♘c3 ♕e7 9 ♗e3 ♘xc3 10 ♗xc5 ♘xe2 11 ♗xe7 ♘xf4 12 ♗a3! ♘xd5 13 0-0-0 c6 14 ♘g5 ♘d7 15 ♗c4 ♗e6 16 ♖he1 += Kuznetsov-Pozhavsky, USSR 1963

3 ♗c4

a) 3 ♘f3 d6 4 ♗c4 h6 5 d4 g5 6 0-0 ♗g7 (6...♘c6!? Larsen) 7 g3 ♘c6 8 gxf4!? N (8 c3 ♗h3 9 gxf4 ♗xf1 10 ♕xf1∞) 8...g4 9 d5 gxf3 10 dxc6 ♕f6! 11 ♗b5? ♕g6+ 12 ♔f2 ♕g2+ 13 ♔e3 ♔f8!∓ Arnason-Larsen, Reykjavik 1978;

b) 3 ♘f3 ♗e7 4 ♘c3 ♗h4+ (4...♘f6 5 e5 ♘g4 6 d4 ♘e3 7 ♗xe3 fxe3 8 ♗c4 d6 9 0-0 0-0 10 ♕d3 ♘c6 11 exd6 Spassky-Holmov, Moscow 1964 11...♗xd6! 12 ♘e4 ♗e7!=) 5 ♔e2 d6 (Euwe) 6 d4 ♗g4 7 ♗xf4 ♘c6 8 ♕d3 (8 h3 ♗xf3+ 9 gxf3 ♕d7 10 ♘d5 0-0-0? 11 ♗g5! ♗xg5 12 h4± Bashina-Katskova, USSR 1969) 8... ♘ge7 N 9 ♔d2 ♗xf3 10 gxf3 ♕d7 11 ♖d1 0-0-0 12 ♔c1 += Planinc-Ivkov, Jugoslavia Final 1978

3...d5

a) 3...f5 4 ♕e2! ♕h4+ (4...fxe4 5 ♕h5+ g6 6 ♕e5+ ♕e7 7 ♕xh8 ♘f6 Pillsbury-Marshall, Vienna 1903, 8 b3! d5 9 ♗a3 c5 10 ♗xc5 ♕xc5 11 ♕xf6 dxc4 12 ♕xf4±) 5 ♔d1 fxe4 6 ♕xe4+ ♗e7 7 ♘f3 ♕h5 8 ♖e1 ♘c6 9 ♗xg8 ♖xg8 10 ♘c3 d6 11 ♘d5 ♗f5 12 ♕c4 ♗xc2+ 13 ♔e2 ♘e5 14 ♕xc7 ♕f7 15 ♕xb7 ♖d8 16 ♔f1 ♗d3+ 17 ♔g1 ♔f8 18 ♘d4± Glazkov;

b) 3...♘e7 4 ♘c3 c6 5 ♘f3 (5 ♕f3 ♘g6 6 d4 ♗b4 7 ♘e2 0-0 8 0-0 ♕f6 9 e5 ♕e7 10 ♗xf4 ♘xf4 11 ♘xf4 d5 12 exd6 ♕xd6 13 ♘fe2 ♗e6 14 ♘e4 ♕e7 15 ♗xe6 ♕xe6 16 ♘f4 ♕e7 17 c3± Planinc-Matanovic, Ljubljana 1969) 5...d5 6 ♗b3! dxe4 7 ♘xe4 ♘d5 Fischer-Minic, Vinkovci 1969, 8 c4! ♘f6 9 ♘xf6+ ♕xf6 10 0-0 ♗e7 11 d4 ♘d7 12 ♕e2! g5 13 ♘xg5 ♕xg5 14 ♗xf4 +− Fischer;

c) 3...♘c6 4 d4 (4 ♘f3! g5 5 d4 Δ 0-0) 4...♘f6 5 e5 d5 6 ♗b3 ♗g4 7 ♕d3 ♘h5 8 ♘h3 Charousek-Chiborin, Budapest 1896; 8...f3!;

d) 3...♕h4+ 4 ♔f1 c6 5 d4 g5 6 ♕f3 ♘f6 7 g3 ♕h5 8 e5 d5 9 ♕xh5 ♘xh5 10 ♗e2 += Zakharchenko-Usachi,

Kiev 1970;

e) 3...♘f6 4 ♘c3 c6! (4...♘c6 5 ♘f3 ♗b4 6 0-0 0-0 7 ♘d5! ♘xe4 8 d4 ♘f6 9 ♘g5 h6 10 ♘xf7 ♖xf7 11 ♘xf6+ gxf6 12 ♕h5 ♕e7 13 ♕g6+ ♔f8 14 ♗xf4 +− Hlusevic-Verhovter, 1974) 5 ♗b3 d5 6 exd5 cxd5 7 d4 ♗d6 8 ♘ge2 0-0 9 0-0 g5 10 ♘xd5 ♘c6 Spielmann-Bogolyubov, Mahrisch-Ostrau 1923, 11 h4! h6 12 hxg5 hxg5 13 ♘ec3 Tartakover

4 exd5!

a) 4 ♗xd5 ♕h4+ 5 ♔f1 g5 6 ♘f3 ♕h5 7 h4 ♗g7 8 ♘c3 c6 9 ♗c4 ♗g4 10 d4 ♘d7 11 ♔f2 ♗xf3 12 gxf3 0-0-0= Lasker-Harujek, Nuremberg 1896;

b) 4 ♗xd5 ♘f6 5 ♘c3 ♗b4 6 ♘f3 ♗xc3! 7 dxc3 c6 8 ♗c4 ♕xd1+ 9 ♔xd1 0-0 10 ♗xf4 ♘xe4 11 ♖e1=

4...♞f6

4...♕h4+ 5 ♔f1 ♗d6 (5...f3 6 ♗b5+! c6 7 ♘xf3± Gheorghiu-Troianescu) 6 ♘f3 ♕h5 7 ♘c3 ♘e7 8 d4 += Blackburne-Schlechter, 1898

5 ♞c3 c6

5...♗d6 6 ♕e2+ ♗e7 7 d4 0-0 8 ♗xf4 (8 ♘f3 c6 9 ♗xf4 cxd5 10 ♗b3! += Bronstein-Klovan, USSR 1974) 8... ♗b4 9 ♘f3 ♘xd5 10 ♗xd5 ♕xd5 11 0-0 ♗xc3 12 bxc3 b6 13 ♕f2 ♗e6 14 ♖fe1 ♘d7 15 ♗xc7 ♕c6 16 ♗f4 ♕xc3 17 ♘g5!± Bronstein

6 d4 cxd5

6...♘xd5 7 ♘xd5 cxd5 8 ♗b5+ ♘c6 9 ♕e2+ ♗e7 10 ♗xf4 0-0 11 0-0-0 ♖e8 12 ♘f3±

7 ♝b5+ ♞c6 8 ♝xf4 ♝d6 9 ♞ge2 0-0 10 0-0 ♝xf4 N

10...♗g4 11 ♕d2 (11 ♗g5 ♗e7 12 ♗a4 ♖c8 13 ♔h1 ♖fe8 =+ Bronstein-Nogeiras, Jurmala 1978) 11...a6 12 ♗d3 ♕c7 13 ♖ae1 ♖ae8 14 ♗h6! ♘e4 15 ♗xe4 dxe4 16 ♘g3 ♗xg3 17 hxg3 ♕d6 18 ♗f4 ♕xd4+ 19 ♕xd4 ♘xd4 20 ♗d6± Lepeshkin-Judovich, USSR

11 ♜xf4 ♝g4 12 ♛d2 ♝xe2?! 13 ♝xe2 ♛b6 14 ♜ad1! ♜ad8 15 ♝d3 ♞e7 16 h3 ♞g6 17 ♜f2 ♜fe8 18 ♝b5!± Δ ♗a4, ♗b3 Bronstein-Tseshkovsky, USSR 1978

French

1 e4 e6 2 d4 d5 3 ♞d2

a) 3 ♘c3 ♗b4 4 ♘e2 dxe4 5 a3 ♗e7 6 ♘xe4 ♘f6 7 ♘2g3 0-0 8 c3 ♘c6 9 f4 b6 10 ♗d3 ♗b7 11 0-0 += Filipowicz-Rajna, Warsaw 1978;

b) 3 e5 c5 4 c3 ♘c6 5 ♘f3 ♕b6 (5... f5 N 6 exf6!? ♘xf6 7 ♗b5 ♗d6 8 ♘e5 0-0! 9 ♗xc6 bxc6 10 0-0 cxd4 11 cxd4 c5∓ Eley-Horner, British Final 1978) 6 ♗d3 cxd4 7 cxd4 ♗d7 8 0-0 ♘xd4 9 ♘xd4 ♕xd4 10 ♘c3 a6 11 ♔h1 (11 ♕e2 ♘e7 12 ♔h1 N ♘c6 13 f4 ♘b4 14 ♖d1 ♘xd3 15 ♖xd3 ♕b6 16 f5∞ Opl-Stoppel, Vienna Final 1978) 11...♕xe5 12 f4!? N (12 ♖e1 ♕d6 13 ♕f3 ♗c6∞) 12...♕d6 13 ♗e3 ♗e7 14 ♕f3 ♗c6 15 ♗d4 ♘f6 16 ♖ae1 g6!∓ Eley-Whiteley, British Final 1978

3...c5

a) 3...♘c6 4 ♗b5!? N ♘f6 5 e5 ♘d7 6 c3 ♗e7 7 f4 ♘cb8 8 ♘e2 b6 9 ♘f3 c6 10 Bd3 g6 11 0-0 += Savon-Lehmann, Kiev 1978;

b) 3...Nf6 4 e5 Nfd7

1) 5 f4 c5 6 c3 Nc6 7 Ndf3 Qb6 (7... cxd4 8 cxd4 h5 9 Bd3 g6 10 Ne2 Nb6 11 Kf2!? Bd7 12 a3 a5 =+ Nicolaiczyk-Reefschlager, BRD Final 1978) 8 g3 (8 Ne2 f6 9 g3 cxd4 10 cxd4 fxe5 11 Bh3?! exd4 12 Bxe6 Nf6 13 Bxc8 Rxc8 =+ Chiburdanidze-Lechtynsky, Vilnius 1978) 8...cxd4 9 cxd4 Bb4+ 10 Kf2 f6 11 Kg2 Nf8 N (11...0-0 12 Bd3 Kh8 13 Ne2 += Gufeld-Hasin, Moscow 1961) 12 Bd3 Bd7 13 Ne2 0-0-0 14 a3 Be7 15 b4 ± Cappello-Spinetti, Italy Final 1978;

2) 5 Ngf3 c5 6 c3 Nc6 7 Bd3 Qb6 8 0-0 cxd4 9 cxd4 Nxd4 10 Nxd4 Qxd4 11 Nf3 Qb6 12 Qc2 h6 13 Bf4 N g5 14 Be3 Bc5 15 Rae1 Bxe3 16 Rxe3 g4∞ Nunn-Mrdja, Lublin 1978;

3) 5 Bd3 c5 6 c3 Nc6 (6...b6 7 Nh3! Ba6 8 Bxa6 Nxa6 9 0-0 Nc7 10 Re1 N [10 Qg4 c4 11 Nf3 Nb8= Pachman] 10...h6 11 Nf4 Qc8 12 c4! += Ivanovic-Andersson, Niksic 1978) 7 Ne2 f6 (7...cxd4 8 cxd4 f6 9 exf6 Nxf6 10 Nf3 Qb6 N [10... Bd6 11 Bf4 0-0 12 Bxd6 Qxd6 13 0-0± Suetin-Portisch, Ljubljana 1973] 11 0-0 [11 Bf4 Qxb2 12 0-0 Be7 13 Rb1 Qa3 14 Ne5 0-0∓ Sznapik-Farago, Polanica Zdroj 1978] Bd6 12 Rb1 0-0 13 b4 a6 14 Bf4 += Kuzmin-Farago, Kiev 1978) 8 exf6 (8 Nf4 Qe7 9 exf6 Qxf6 10 Nf3 Bd6 11 Nh5 +=) 8...Qxf6 9 Nf3 Bd6 N 10 0-0 e5 11 Ng3!? cxd4 12 Nh5 Qe7 13 Bf5 0-0∞ Waller-Nehonsky, Vienna Final 1978

Diagram

4 exd5 exd5 5 Bb5+ Bd7 6 Qe2+ Be7

6...Qe7 7 Bxd7+ Nxd7 8 dxc5 Nxc5 9 Nb3 Qxe2+ 10 Nxe2 Nxb3 11 axb3 Bc5 12 Bd2 Ne7 13 Nf4 0-0 14 0-0 Rfd8 15 Nd3 += Karpov-Korchnoi (16) 1978

7 dxc5 Nf6 8 Nb3

8 Ngf3 0-0 9 0-0 Bxc5 10 Nb3 Re8 11 Qd3 Bb6 12 Bg5 Nc6! 13 a4 h6 14 Bh4 a6 15 Bxc6 Bxc6 16 Nfd4 Re4!∓ Prandstetter-Uhlmann 1977

8...0-0 9 Be3 Re8 10 Nf3 Bxc5!?

10...a6! 11 Bd3!? N (11 Bxd7 Nbxd7 12 0-0 Nxc5 13 Rfe1= Parma-Korchnoi, Moscow 1971) 11...Ba4! 12 Nfd4 Nbd7 13 0-0 Nxc5 14 Nxc5 Bxc5 15 Qf3 Qb6 16 Nf5 Bxe3 17 fxe3 Bd7= Larsen-Portisch, Tilburg 1978

11 Nxc5 Qa5+ 12 Qd2 Qxb5 13 0-0-0 b6?

13...Bg4 14 h3 Bxf3 15 gxf3 b6 Δ Nbd7=

14 Nxd7 Nbxd7 15 Kb1 Ne4!? 16 Qd3 Qxd3 17 Rxd3 += Karpov-Korchnoi (22) 1978

Alekhine

1 e4 Nf6 2 e5

2 Nc3 d5 3 exd5 (3 e5 Nfd7 4 Nxd5 Nxe5 5 Ne3 c5 6 b3!? Nbc6?! 7 Bb2

a6 8 f4 ♘d7 9 ♘f3 ♘f6 10 ♗c4 e6 11 f5!± Planinc-Kovacevic, Jugoslav Final 1978) 3...♘xd5 4 ♘xd5 ♕xd5 5 d4 ♘c6 6 ♘f3 e5 N (6...♗g4 7 ♗e2 0-0-0 8 c3 e5= Alburt-Vasyukov, USSR Final 1967) 7 ♗e3 ♗g4?! (7... exd4 8 ♘xd4 ♗c5=) 8 dxe5 ♗xf3 9 ♕xf3 ♕xf3 10 gxf3 ♘xe5 11 0-0-0 ♗d6 12 ♗b5+!± Peresipkin-Alburt, Kiev 1978

2...♞d5 3 d4 d6 4 ♞f3 g6

a) 4...♘c6 5 c4 ♘b6 6 exd6 exd6 7 h3 ♗e7 8 ♗e2 0-0 9 0-0 ♗f6 10 ♘c3 ♗f5 11 a3 a5 12 b3 d5 13 c5 ♘c8 14 ♗f4± Taulbut-Bohm, Amsterdam 1978;

b) 4...♗g4 5 ♗e2 e6 (5...♘c6 6 exd6 exd6 7 0-0 ♗e7 8 h3 ♗h5 9 c4 ♘b6 10 ♘c3 0-0 11 d5 ♗xf3 12 ♗xf3 ♘e5 13 b3 ♗f6= Chiburdanidze-Mikenas, Vilnius 1978) 6 h3 ♗h5 7 0-0 ♗e7 8 c4 ♘b6 9 ♘c3 0-0 10 ♗e3 d5 11 c5 ♗xf3 12 ♗xf3 (12 gxf3!? ♘c8 13 f4 ♘c6 14 b4 ♗h4 15 b5 ♘a5= Dorfman-Bagirov, USSR 1978) 12... ♘c4 13 ♗f4 ♘c6 14 b3 ♘4a5 15 ♖c1 ♕d7! =+ Beljavsky-Alburt, Kiev 1978

5 ♝c4

5 ♘g5 c6 6 c4 ♘c7 7 ♕f3 f6 8 exf6 exf6 9 ♘e4 f5? 10 ♘ec3 ♘e6? (10... ♗g7) 11 d5 ♘d4 12 ♕e3+ ♕e7 13 ♘a3± Savon-Alburt, Kiev 1978

5...♞b6 6 ♝b3 a5 7 e6! N

7 a4 d5 8 0-0 ♗g7 9 ♗f4 0-0 10 ♘bd2 += Ciocaltea-Ogaard, Reykjavik 1974

7...♝xe6 8 ♝xe6 fxe6 9 ♞g5 ♞c6 10 ♞xe6 ♛d7 11 ♛e2 ♞d8 12 ♞xf8± Lukin-Alburt, USSR 1977

Pirc

1 e4 d6 2 d4 ♞f6 3 ♞c3 g6 4 f4

a) 4 ♗g5 h6 5 ♗h4 ♗g7 6 ♕d2 c6 7 f4 0-0 8 ♗d3 b5 9 ♘f3 b4 10 ♘e2 a5 11 0-0 d5= Romanishin-Pfleger, Amsterdam 1978;

b) 4 ♗g5 ♗g7 5 ♕d2 h6 6 ♗h4 g5 7 ♗g3 ♘h5 8 0-0-0 ♘c6 9 ♗b5!? N ♗d7 (9...♘xg3 10 hxg3 a6 11 ♗xc6 bxc6∞) 10 ♘ge2 e5 11 dxe5 ♘xe5 12 ♘d4 += Perespikin-Ftacnik, Kiev 1978;

c) 4 ♘f3 ♗g7 5 ♗e2 0-0 6 0-0

1) 6...♗g4 7 ♗e3 ♘c6 8 ♕d3!? N e5 9 d5 ♘b4 10 ♕d2 a5 11 h3 (11 ♘e1 Korchnoi) 11...♗d7 12 ♗g5 ♕e8 13 ♘h2 ♔h8 14 a3 ♘a6 15 ♗h6 += Karpov-Korchnoi (18) 1978;

2) 6...c5!? 7 d5 ♘a6 8 ♗f4 ♘c7 9 a4 b6 10 ♖e1 ♗b7 11 ♗c4± Karpov-Korchnoi (32) 1978;

3) 6...a5? N 7 h3 (7 a4 ♘a6 8 ♗e3 ♘b4 9 ♘d2 e5 10 dxe5 dxe5 11 ♗c5 ♖e8 12 ♘c4 ♕xd1 13 ♖axd1 += Sanz-Larsen, Las Palmas 1978) 7...♘a6 8 ♗f4 c6 9 ♕d2 b5 10 e5! dxe5 11 ♘xe5 ♗b7 12 ♗f3 ♕b6 13 a4 ♘b4 14 ♘e2 ♖fd8 15 c3± Stean-Larsen, Las Palmas 1978;

4) 6...c6 7 h3 ♘a6 (7...♕b6?! 8 a3! d5 9 e5 ♘e4 10 ♘xe4 dxe4 11 ♘g5 ♖d8 12 ♗e3 ♕xb2 13 ♗c4 e6 14 ♘xe4 ♗xe5 15 dxe5!! +− Beni-Soluch, Vienna Final 1978) 8 ♖e1 ♘c7 9 a4 b6?! 10 ♗f4 ♗b7 11 ♕d2 ♖e8? 12

♖ad1± Geller-Panno, Bogota 1978

4...♗g7 5 ♘f3 0-0

a) 5...c5 6 ♗b5+ ♗d7 7 e5 ♘g4 8 e6 ♗xb5 9 exf7+ ♔d7 10 ♘g5?! ♘h6?! N (10...h5 11 ♘xb5 ♕a5+ 12 ♘c3 cxd4 13 ♕e2 dxc3∓ Jensen-Keene, The Hague 1967) 11 ♕f3 ♗c4 12 d5 ♘f5 13 ♕e4 ♘d4 14 b3∝ Vokroj-Soluch, Vienna Final 1978;

b) 5...c5 6 dxc5 ♕a5 7 ♗d3 ♕xc5 8 ♕e2 0-0 9 ♗e3 ♕a5 10 0-0 ♗g4 11 ♕f2!? N ♗xf3 12 ♕xf3 ♘c6 13 ♘e2 ♘d7 14 c3? ♘de5! −+ Ljubojevic-Timman, Tilburg 1978

6 ♗e3

a) 6 ♗e2 c5 7 dxc5 ♕a5 8 0-0 ♕xc5+ 9 ♔h1 ♘bd7 10 ♕e1 b6 11 ♗d3 ♗b7 12 ♗e3 ♕c7 13 ♘h4 e5= Sikora-Nunn, Lublin 1978;

b) 6 e5 ♘fd7 7 h4 c5 8 e6 fxe6 9 h5 gxh5 10 ♖xh5!? N (10 dxc5 ♘f6 11 ♗d3 ♘c6 12 a3 h6 =+ Kristiansen-Botterill, Graz 1972) 10...♘f6 11 ♖h4 cxd4 12 ♘xd4 ♘c6 13 ♗e3 ♕b6 14 ♗d3 ♘b4 15 ♕d2 e5 =+ Estrin-Nunn, Lublin 1978

6...c5 7 dxc5 ♕a5 8 ♗d3 ♘g4 9 ♗d2 ♕xc5 10 ♕e2 ♘f6 11 ♗e3

11 a3 ♗g4 12 h3 ♗xf3 13 ♕xf3 ♘c6 14 ♗e3 ♕a5 15 0-0 ♘d7 =+ Balashov-Timman, Bugojno 1978

11...♕a5 12 0-0 ♗g4 13 ♗c4 ♘c6 14 ♗b3 ♘d7 15 ♗d2 ♘d4 16 ♕f2 ♗xf3 17 gxf3 a6∝ Hort-Pfleger, Amsterdam 1978

Malgrat de Mar 20-29.ix.78

				1	2	3	4	5	6	7	8	9	0	
1	Andersson	GM	2545	x	½	1	½	1	1	½	½	1	1	7
2	Tseshkovsky	GM	2550	½	x	1	1	1	0	½	1	1	1	7
3	O.Rodriguez	IM	2485	0	0	x	1	½	1	1	½	½	½	5
4	Cebalo		2450	½	0	0	x	0	1	1	1	½	1	5
5	Vadasz	GM	2505	0	0	½	1	x	1	½	0	1	½	4½
6	O.Castro	IM	2425	0	1	0	0	0	x	½	1	1	1	4½
7	Fraguela	IM	2305	½	½	0	0	½	½	x	½	½	½	3½
8	Debarnot	IM	2425	½	0	½	0	1	0	½	x	½	½	3½
9	Garriga		2400	0	0	½	½	0	0	½	½	x	½	2½
10	Gonzalez-Mestres		2400	0	0	½	0	½	0	½	½	½	x	2½

Category 8 (2449) GM = 6½ IM = 5

Linares 30.xi.-8.xii.78

				1	2	3	4	5	6	7	8	9	0	
1	Eslon	IM	2365	x	½	½	½	½	1	1	1	0	1	6
2	Debarnot	IM	2425	½	x	½	½	1	½	½	½	1	1	6
3	Ochoa		2345	½	½	x	½	½	½	½	½	1	1	5½
4	Martin		2390	½	½	½	x	½	0	½	½	1	1	5
5	Palacios		2335	½	0	½	½	x	½	½	½	1	½	4½
6	Visier		2360	0	½	½	1	½	x	½	½	0	1	4½
7	Medina	IM	2350	0	½	½	½	½	½	x	½	½	1	4½
8	O.Rodriguez	GM	2485	0	½	½	½	½	½	½	x	½	1	4½
9	O.Castro	IM	2425	1	0	0	0	0	1	½	½	x	½	3½
10	Pacheco			0	0	0	0	½	0	0	0	½	x	1

Category 5 (2368) IM = 6

Herculari 3-8.x.78

		1	2	3	4	5	
1	Jugoslavia	x	3	2½	5	6	16½
2	Rumania	3	x	5	4	3½	15½
3	Bulgaria	3½	1	x	3½	5½	13½
4	Greece	1	2	2½	x	2	7½
5	Turkey	0	2½	½	4	x	7

Virovitica 22.ix.-7.x.78

				1	2	3	4	5	6	7	8	9	0	1	2	3	4	
1	Marovic	GM	2455	x	1	½	½	½	½	½	1	½	½	½	1	1	½	8½
2	Smejkal	GM	2555	0	x	1	½	1	½	½	½	½	½	1	½	1	1	8½
3	Nemet	GM	2425	½	0	x	1	½	½	1	½	½	1	1	0	½	1	8
4	Kurajica	GM	2530	½	½	0	x	½	½	½	½	½	1	½	1	1	1	8
5	Plachetka	IM	2465	½	0	½	½	x	½	½	½	½	1	½	1	1	1	8
6	L.Lengyel	GM	2430	½	½	½	½	½	x	½	½	½	½	½	½	1	½	7
7	Bukic	GM	2500	½	½	0	½	½	½	x	½	1	0	1	0	1	1	7
8	Pavicic		2450	0	½	½	½	½	½	½	x	1	½	½	0	1	½	6½
9	Kovacevic	GM	2505	½	½	½	½	½	½	0	0	x	0	½	1	1	1	6½
10	Ostojic	GM	2420	½	½	0	0	0	½	1	½	1	x	0	½	1	1	6½
11	F.Portisch	IM	2450	½	0	0	½	½	½	0	½	½	1	x	½	½	1	6
12	Duckstein	IM	2425	0	½	1	0	0	½	1	1	0	½	½	x	½	½	6
13	Maroja			0	0	½	0	0	0	0	0	0	0	½	½	x	1	2½
14	Zoric			½	0	0	0	0	½	0	½	0	0	0	½	0	x	2

Category 8 (2429)

Odjaci 9-23.x.78

				1	2	3	4	5	6	7	8	9	0	1	2	3	4	
1	Matulovic	GM	2525	x	½	1	½	1	1	½	½	½	1	1	1	1	1	10½
2	Plachetka	IM	2470	½	x	0	1	0	1	1	1	½	1	½	1	1	1	9½
3	Raicevic	GM	2450	0	1	x	½	1	0	½	½	½	½	1	1	1	1	8½
4	Diesen	IM	2440	½	0	½	x	½	½	½	½	½	1	½	1	1	1	8
5	Kirov	GM	2465	0	1	0	½	x	½	½	½	1	½	1	½	1	1	8
6	Rakic		2410	0	0	1	½	½	x	½	½	½	½	1	1	1	1	8
7	F.Portisch	IM	2450	½	0	½	½	½	½	x	½	½	1	1	½	1	1	8
8	Minev	IM	2370	½	0	½	½	½	½	½	x	½	1	½	1	½	1	7½
9	Lengyel	GM	2430	½	½	½	½	0	½	½	½	x	½	½	½	1	1	7
10	Govedarica		2405	0	0	½	0	½	½	0	0	½	x	1	1	1	1	6
11	Cobo	IM	2395	0	½	0	½	0	0	0	½	½	0	x	1	1	1	5
12	Malovic			0	0	0	0	½	0	½	0	½	0	0	x	1	1	3½
13	Konc			0	0	0	0	0	0	0	½	0	0	0	0	x	1	1½
14	D.Markovic			0	0	0	0	0	0	0	0	0	0	0	0	0	x	0
	Buljovcic	IM	2445			0	0		0		½	½		0				–

Category 6 (2386) GM = 9½ IM = 8

Ruma 24.x.-9.xi.78				1	2	3	4	5	6	7	8	9	0	1	2	3	4	5	6	
1	Martinovic	IM	2460	x	½	½	1	½	½	½	1	1	1	½	1	½	1	1	1	11½
2	Spiridonov	IM	2405	½	x	½	½	1	1	½	½	½	1	½	½	1	1	1	1	11
3	Matulovic	GM	2525	½	½	x	½	½	0	½	½	½	½	0	½	1	1	1	1	10½
4	Barczay	GM	2465	0	½	½	x	½	½	½	½	1	½	½	1	1	1	½	1	9½
5	Marjanovic	GM	2450	½	0	½	½	x	½	½	½	0	½	½	1	1	1	1	1	9
6	Lukacs	IM	2460	½	0	1	½	½	x	½	½	½	½	1	½	1	1	1	1	9
7	Doda	IM	2405	½	½	½	½	½	½	x	½	½	1	½	½	½	½	1	1	9
8	P.Orlov		2375	0	½	½	½	½	½	½	x	½	½	½	1	1	½	1	1	9
9	Kirov	GM	2465	0	½	½	0	1	½	½	½	x	½	½	½	½	1	1	1	8½
10	Kovacs	IM	2400	0	0	½	½	½	½	0	½	½	x	1	½	½	1	1	1	8
11	Deze	IM	2395	½	½	1	½	½	0	½	½	½	0	x	0	1	1	1	1	7½
12	Bjelajac	IM	2415	0	½	½	0	0	½	½	0	½	½	1	x	1	½	1	½	7
13	Laketic			½	0	0	0	0	0	½	0	½	½	0	0	x	½	0	½	3
14	Micic			0	0	0	0	0	0	½	½	0	0	0	½	½	x	½	½	3
15	Cernicek			0	0	0	½	0	0	0	0	0	0	0	0	1	½	x	½	2½
16	C.Djukic			0	0	0	0	0	0	0	0	0	0	0	½	½	½	½	x	2

Category 6 (2376) GM = 11 IM = 9

Hungary Final 2-22.xii.78				1	2	3	4	5	6	7	8	9	0	1	2	3	4	5	6	
1	Pinter	IM	2430	x	½	½	½	1	½	½	½	½	1	1	1	½	1	½	1	10½
2	Rigo		2360	½	x	½	0	½	½	½	½	1	½	½	½	1	1	1	1	9½
3	Petran	IM	2400	½	½	x	½	½	½	½	½	½	½	½	½	1	1	1	½	9
4	Farago	GM	2510	½	1	½	x	0	½	½	½	½	½	1	½	½	½	1	1	9
5	Groszpeter		2230	0	½	½	1	x	½	0	½	½	1	1	½	½	1	½	1	9
6	Tompa		2400	½	½	½	½	½	x	1	½	½	1	½	1	½	0	½	½	8½
7	Szekely		2435	½	½	½	½	1	0	x	½	½	½	½	½	½	½	½	1	8
8	Lukacs	IM	2460	½	½	½	½	½	½	½	x	0	0	0	½	1	1	1	1	8
9	Hazai	IM	2455	½	0	½	½	½	½	½	1	x	½	½	½	½	½	½	½	7½
10	Barczay	GM	2465	0	½	½	½	0	0	½	1	½	x	½	1	½	1	½	½	7½
11	Eperjesi		2395	0	½	½	0	0	½	½	1	½	½	x	½	½	½	1	0	6½
12	Orso			0	½	½	½	½	0	½	½	½	0	½	x	½	1	1	0	6½
13	Dely	IM		½	0	0	½	½	½	½	0	½	½	½	½	x	0	½	1	6
14	T.Horvath		2410	0	0	0	½	0	1	½	0	½	0	½	0	1	x	½	1	5½
15	Szell		2435	½	0	0	0	½	½	½	0	½	½	0	0	½	½	x	1	5
16	Kovacs	IM	2400	0	0	½	0	0	½	0	0	½	½	1	1	0	0	0	x	4

Athens 17-29.viii.78

	Name	Title	Rating	1	2	3	4	5	6	7	8	9	0	1	2	Total
1	Rogulj	IM	2420	x	0	½	½	0	1	1	1	1	1	1	1	8
2	Suba	IM	2430	1	x	0	1	½	½	½	½	½	1	1	1	7½
3	Makropoulos		2345	½	1	x	½	1	½	0	½	½	1	½	1	7
4	Bertok	IM	2415	½	0	½	x	1	½	½	1	½	½	½	1	6½
5	Georgiev	IM	2415	1	½	0	0	x	½	½	½	½	1	1	1	6½
6	Radev	IM	2395	0	½	½	½	½	x	1	1	½	0	1	1	6½
7	Ioakimides			0	½	1	½	½	0	x	½	½	0	1	½	5
8	Ipek			0	½	½	0	½	0	½	x	½	1	1	½	5
9	Ungureanu		2410	0	½	½	½	½	½	½	½	x	0	0	1	4½
10	Kokkinos			0	0	0	½	0	1	1	0	1	x	½	0	4
11	Ornithopoulos		2265	0	0	½	½	0	0	0	0	1	½	x	1	3½
12	Suer	IM	2275	0	0	0	0	0	0	½	½	0	1	0	x	2

Category 3 (2310) IM = 8

Helsinki 14-28.ix.78

	Name	Title	Rating	1	2	3	4	5	6	7	8	9	0	1	2	Total
1	Schussler		2365	x	½	½	½	1	1	½	1	1	½	½	½	7½
2	Bilek	GM	2445	½	x	½	½	½	½	1	½	1	1	½	1	7½
3	Sznapik	IM	2430	½	½	x	½	0	0	1	½	1	1	1	1	7
4	Adamski	IM	2470	½	½	½	x	½	½	½	½	½	1	½	1	6½
5	Binham		2340	0	½	1	½	x	1	½	½	0	½	0	1	5½
6	Rantanen	IM	2420	0	½	1	½	0	x	½	½	½	0	1	1	5½
7	Niklasson		2340	½	0	0	½	½	½	x	½	1	1	0	1	5½
8	Kristiansen		2320	0	½	½	½	½	½	½	x	0	½	1	1	5½
9	Pirttimaki			0	0	0	½	1	½	0	1	x	½	1	½	5
10	Kivipelto		2350	½	0	0	0	½	1	0	½	½	x	1	0	4
11	Nikkanen			½	½	0	½	1	0	1	0	0	0	x	0	3½
12	Nykopp		2310	½	0	0	0	0	0	0	0	½	1	1	x	3

Category 4 (2349) IM = 7½

Jugoslavia Final 78

	Name	Title	1	2	3	4	5	6	Total
1	Matanovic	GM	½	½	½	½	1	½	3½
2	Ivkov	GM	½	½	½	½	0	½	2½

Budapest 2 23.x.-7.xi.78			1	2	3	4	5	6	7	8	9	0	1	2	3	4	
1 Nicevski	IM	2400	x	0	½	½	1	0	1	½	1	1	1	½	1	1	9
2 Pal.Petran	IM	2400	1	x	½	0	½	½	½	1	1	1	½	½	½	1	8½
3 Rigo		2360	½	½	x	1	0	1	½	1	0	1	0	1	½	1	8
4 Gliksman	IM	2320	½	1	0	x	½	1	½	0	½	1	½	1	½	1	8
5 Szymczak	IM	2390	0	½	1	½	x	0	½	½	½	½	1	1	1	½	7½
6 Ozsvath		2320	1	½	0	0	1	x	0	½	1	0	1	0	1	1	7
7 Schinzel		2400	0	½	½	½	½	1	x	½	0	½	½	1	½	1	7
8 Ujtelky	IM	2280	½	0	0	1	½	½	½	x	½	½	½	½	1	½	6½
9 Hradetzky		2300	0	0	1	½	½	0	1	½	x	½	½	0	1	1	6½
10 Sapi		2380	0	0	0	0	½	1	½	½	½	x	½	1	1	½	6
11 B.Balogh		2280	0	½	1	½	0	0	½	½	½	½	x	½	0	1	5½
12 Gereben	IM	2270	½	½	0	0	0	1	0	½	1	0	½	x	½	1	5½
13 Perenyi		2295	0	½	½	½	0	0	½	0	0	0	1	½	x	½	4
14 Starosta			0	0	0	0	½	0	0	½	0	½	0	0	½	x	2

Category 4 (2328) IM = 9

Amsterdam 24.xi.-17.xii.78			1	2	3	4	5	6	7	8	9	0	1	2	3	4	5	
1 Miles	GM	2565	x	½	½	½	½	½	1	1	1	1	1	1	1	1	1	11½
2 Timman	GM	2585	½	x	1	½	1	½	1	0	1	1	1	1	1	1	1	11½
3 Stean	GM	2510	½	0	x	½	½	1	1	1	1	1	½	1	1	1	1	11
4 Sosonko	GM	2575	½	½	½	x	½	1	1	½	1	0	1	1	1	1	1	10½
5 Speelman	IM	2410	½	0	½	½	x	½	0	1	1	½	1	½	1	1	1	9
6 Langeweg	IM	2450	½	½	0	0	½	x	½	1	½	1	½	½	0	1	1	7½
7 Sanz		2330	0	0	0	0	1	½	x	1	0	½	1	1	1	½	½	7
8 Bellon	GM	2350	0	1	0	½	0	0	0	x	½	1	1	1	0	1	½	6½
9 Ligterink	IM	2440	0	0	0	0	0	½	1	½	x	1	½	½	1	½	1	6½
10 Rivas			0	0	0	1	½	0	½	0	0	x	0	1	½	½	1	5
11 Meulders			0	0	½	0	0	½	0	0	½	1	x	½	0	½	1	4½
12 Morrison			0	0	0	0	½	½	0	0	½	0	½	x	1	1	½	4½
13 L.Roos			0	0	0	0	0	1	0	1	0	½	1	0	x	0	1	4½
14 Keogh			0	0	0	0	0	0	½	0	½	½	½	0	1	x	1	4
15 Feller		2225	0	0	0	0	0	0	½	½	0	0	0	½	0	0	x	1½

Bulgaria Final 5-20.xii.78

				1	2	3	4	5	6	7	8	9	0	1	2	3	4	
1	Velikov	IM	2430	x	½	½	½	½	½	1	½	½	1	1	½	1	1	9
2	Kirov	GM	2465	½	x	½	½	½	½	½	1	½	1	1	1	1	½	9
3	Donchev		2350	½	½	x	½	½	1	½	0	1	1	½	1	½	1	8½
4	Lukov	IM	2330	½	½	½	x	½	0	½	1	1	1	1	½	½	1	8½
5	Georgiev	IM	2415	½	½	½	½	x	½	1	1	0	½	0	1	1	1	8
6	Spassov	GM	2450	½	½	0	1	½	x	½	0	1	½	½	1	1	1	8
7	Spiridonov	IM	2405	0	½	½	½	0	½	x	1	½	½	½	½	1	1	7
8	Toshkov		2200	½	0	1	0	0	1	0	x	½	0	1	1	½	1	6½
9	Grigorov		2335	½	½	0	0	1	0	½	½	x	½	1	½	½	½	6
10	P.Atanasov		2305	0	0	0	0	½	½	½	1	½	x	½	½	½	½	5
11	Dolmadjan		2350	0	0	½	0	1	½	½	0	0	½	x	½	½	½	4½
12	R.Angelov		2310	½	0	0	½	0	0	½	0	½	½	½	x	½	½	4
13	Pantaleev		2310	0	0	½	½	0	0	0	½	½	½	½	½	x	0	3½
14	Semkov		2355	0	½	0	0	0	0	0	0	½	½	½	½	1	x	3½

Buenos Aires 14.xi.-1.xii.78

				1	2	3	4	5	6	7	8	9	0	1	2	3	4	
1	Andersson	GM	2545	x	½	½	½	½	1	½	½	1	½	½	1	1	1	9
2	Vaganian	GM	2570	½	x	½	½	½	1	1	½	1	½	½	0	1	1	8½
3	Panno	GM	2580	½	½	x	½	½	½	½	1	½	½	1	1	½	1	8½
4	Smyslov	GM	2575	½	½	½	x	½	½	½	½	1	1	½	1	½	1	8½
5	Gheorghiu	GM	2520	½	½	½	½	x	½	½	1	1	½	½	1	½	½	8
6	Browne	GM	2550	0	0	½	½	½	x	1	1	1	½	1	½	½	1	8
7	Najdorf	GM	2525	½	0	½	½	½	0	x	½	½	½	½	½	1	½	6
8	Djindjishashvili	GM	2550	½	½	0	½	0	0	½	x	½	½	½	1	½	1	6
9	Szmetan	IM	2420	0	0	½	0	0	0	½	½	x	1	½	½	1	1	5½
10	Keene	GM	2480	½	½	½	0	½	½	½	½	0	x	½	½	0	½	5
11	Quinteros	GM	2480	½	½	0	½	½	0	½	½	½	½	x	0	1	0	5
12	Chi Ching-Hsuan		2405	0	1	0	0	0	½	½	0	½	½	1	x	½	½	5
13	Garcia Palermo		2385	0	0	½	½	½	½	0	½	0	1	0	½	x	½	4½
14	Torre	GM	2490	0	0	0	0	½	0	½	0	0	½	1	½	½	x	3½

Category 11 GM = 7½ IM = 6

Barcinona 2-11.x.78

				1	2	3	4	5	6	7	8	9	0	
1	O.Rodriguez	IM	2485	x	1	½	½	½	½	½	1	1	1	6½
2	Haik	IM	2425	0	x	1	1	0	½	1	1	1	1	6½
3	Cebalo		2450	½	0	x	½	1	½	1	1	1	1	6½
4	Debarnot	IM	2425	½	0	½	x	1	½	1	½	1	1	6
5	Gonz. Mestres		2400	½	1	0	0	x	½	1	1	1	1	6
6	Eslon	IM	2365	½	½	½	½	½	x	1	½	1	1	6
7	Anguera			½	0	0	0	0	0	x	1	1	1	3½
8	Garcia Conesa		2345	0	0	0	½	0	½	0	x	½	½	2
9	Perdigo			0	0	0	0	0	0	0	½	x	1	1½
10	Pares		2285	0	0	0	0	0	0	0	½	0	x	½

Vinkovci 24.xi.-4.xii.78

			1	2	3	4	5	6	7	8	9	0	
1	Klaric	2340	x	1	1	½	½	1	½	1	1	1	7½
2	Simic	2390	0	x	0	1	1	1	1	1	1	1	7
3	Maslesa	2305	0	1	x	½	½	1	1	½	1	½	6
4	Ledic	2340	½	0	½	x	½	½	1	1	1	1	6
5	Paniagva	(Panama)	½	0	½	½	x	½	1	1	1	1	6
6	Wong Meng Kong	(Sing.)	0	0	0	½	½	x	0	½	1	1	3½
7	Constantinou	(Cyprus)	½	0	0	0	0	1	x	0	½	1	3
8	Henni	(Algeria)	0	0	½	0	0	½	1	x	0	1	3
9	Hatem Bel Kchij??	(Tunis)	0	0	0	0	0	0	½	1	x	½	2
10	Ogundipe	(Nig)	0	0	½	0	0	0	0	0	½	x	1

Il Ciocco 8-15.x.78

		1	2	3	4	5	6	7	
1	Jugoslavia	x	1½	3	3	2	3½	4	17
2	Italy	2½	x	3	1½	3½	2½	3½	16½
3	Germany	1	1	x	2½	3½	3	4	15
4	Switzerland	1	2½	1½	x	2	2½	4	13½
5	Austria	2	½	½	1½	x	2	4	10½
6	France	½	1½	1	2	2	x	3½	10½
7	Luxembourg	0	½	0	0	0	½	x	1

Stip 16.xi.-1.xii.78

				1	2	3	4	5	6	7	8	9	0	1	2	3	4	
1	Smejkal	GM	2555	x	1	½	0	1	1	½	½	1	1	½	1	1	1	10
2	Planinc	GM	2430	0	x	0	1	½	1	½	½	1	1	1	1	1	1	9½
3	Kurajica	GM	2530	½	1	x	1	½	0	1	½	½	½	1	1	1	1	9½
4	Honfi	IM	2420	1	0	0	x	½	½	½	1	½	1	½	1	1	1	8½
5	Vukic	GM	2480	0	½	½	½	x	½	½	1	½	½	1	½	1	1	8
6	Nicevski	IM	2400	0	0	1	½	½	x	½	½	1	½	½	½	½	1	7
7	Szekely	IM	2440	½	½	0	½	½	½	x	½	½	½	½	½	1	½	6½
8	Diesen	IM	2440	½	½	½	0	0	½	½	x	½	1	½	½	½	1	6½
9	Raicevic	GM	2450	0	0	½	½	½	0	½	½	x	0	½	1	1	1	6
10	Nemet	GM	2425	0	0	½	0	½	½	½	0	1	x	½	1	½	½	5½
11	Sydor	IM	2395	½	0	0	½	0	½	½	½	½	½	x	½	½	1	5½
12	Doda	IM	2405	0	0	0	0	½	½	½	½	0	0	½	x	1	1	4½
13	Zaharijev		2300	0	0	0	0	0	½	0	½	0	½	½	0	x	½	2½
14	Golomeov			0	0	0	0	0	0	½	0	0	½	0	0	½	x	1½

Category 7 (2419) GM = 9½ IM = 7½

Pazardjik 28.x.-12.xi.78

				1	2	3	4	5	6	7	8	9	0	1	2	3	4	
1	Merdinian		2315	x	½	½	½	1	½	½	½	1	1	½	½	½	1	8½
2	Eperjesi		2395	½	x	½	½	1	0	½	1	½	1	0	1	1	1	8½
3	Grigorov		2340	½	½	x	½	½	1	½	½	½	½	1	½	1	1	8½
4	Peev	IM	2420	½	½	½	x	½	1	0	½	½	½	1	1	1	1	8½
5	Radev	IM	2395	0	0	½	½	x	½	1	1	½	½	1	½	1	1	8
6	Marszalek		2340	½	1	0	0	½	x	1	½	0	½	1	1	1	1	8
7	Basagic		2400	½	½	½	1	0	0	x	½	½	½	1	1	1	1	8
8	Pokojowczyk	IM	2385	½	0	½	½	0	½	½	x	½	½	1	1	1	1	7½
9	Bohosian	IM	2425	0	½	½	½	½	1	½	½	x	½	½	½	1	½	7
10	Mihaljcisin	IM	2385	0	0	½	½	½	½	½	½	½	x	½	½	1	1	6½
11	Pelitov		2340	½	1	0	0	0	0	0	0	½	½	x	½	1	1	5
12	Mechkarov		2420	½	0	½	0	½	0	0	0	½	½	½	x	½	1	4½
13	Dachev			½	0	0	0	0	0	0	0	0	0	0	½	x	1	2
14	Bariakow			0	0	0	0	0	0	0	0	½	0	0	0	0	x	½

Category 5 (2354) IM = 8½

Novi Sad 2-19.x.78

				1	2	3	4	5	6	7	8	9	0	1	2	3	4	5	6	
1	Geller	GM	2590	x	0	½	1	½	1	1	½	1	1	½	½	½	1	1	1	11
2	Sahovic	IM	2490	1	x	½	1	½	½	½	0	½	½	1	1	½	1	1	1	10½
3	Farago	GM	2510	½	½	x	1	½	½	½	½	0	½	1	1	½	1	1	1	10
4	Vukic	GM	2480	0	0	0	x	½	½	1	1	½	1	½	½	1	1	1	1	9½
5	Martinovic	IM	2460	½	½	½	½	x	½	½	½	½	½	½	0	1	1	1	1	9
6	Barczay	GM	2465	0	½	½	½	½	x	½	1	½	½	½	1	½	½	½	1	8½
7	Planinc	GM	2430	0	½	½	0	½	½	x	½	0	½	1	1	1	1	1	½	8½
8	Nogueiras	IM	2385	½	1	½	0	½	0	½	x	1	½	½	½	1	½	1	0	8
9	Spiridonov	IM	2405	0	½	1	½	½	½	1	0	x	½	½	½	0	½	1	1	8
10	Jansa	GM	2505	0	½	½	0	½	½	½	½	½	x	½	0	1	1	½	1	7½
11	Notaros		2355	½	0	0	½	½	½	0	½	½	½	x	1	1	0	½	½	6½
12	Jovic		2325	½	0	0	½	1	0	0	½	½	1	0	x	½	½	0	1	6
13	Deze	IM	2395	½	½	½	0	0	½	0	0	1	0	0	½	x	1	½	1	6
14	Popovic		2400	0	0	0	0	0	½	0	½	½	0	1	½	0	x	½	1	4½
15	Bjelajac		2415	0	0	0	0	0	½	0	0	0	½	½	1	½	½	x	½	4
16	Stanojevic			0	0	0	0	0	0	½	1	0	0	½	0	0	0	½	x	2½

Category 7 (2425) GM = 10½ IM = 9

Halle 5-21.xi.78

				1	2	3	4	5	6	7	8	9	0	1	2	3	4	
1	Uhlmann	GM	2575	x	½	1	½	½	1	1	0	½	½	1	1	1	½	9
2	Farago	GM	2510	½	x	½	½	½	½	1	1	½	½	½	1	1	1	9
3	Knaak	GM	2520	0	½	x	½	0	½	1	1	1	1	½	1	1	1	9
4	Vogt	GM	2520	½	½	½	x	1	½	0	½	½	1	½	1	1	1	8½
5	Hort	GM	2620	½	½	1	0	x	½	1	½	½	½	½	½	1	1	8
6	Holmov	GM	2550	0	½	½	½	½	x	½	½	1	½	1	1	½	1	8
7	Bonsch	IM	2490	0	0	0	1	0	½	x	1	½	1	1	1	0	½	6½
8	Skrobek	IM	2460	1	0	0	½	½	½	0	x	½	½	½	1	½	½	6
9	Malich	GM	2535	½	½	0	½	½	0	½	½	x	½	½	½	½	1	6
10	Georgadze	GM	2535	½	½	0	0	½	½	0	½	½	x	½	½	½	1	5½
11	Espig	IM	2470	0	½	½	½	½	0	0	½	½	½	x	0	½	½	4½
12	Meduna	IM	2425	0	0	0	0	½	0	0	0	½	½	1	x	1	1	4½
13	J.Fernandez	IM	2370	0	0	0	0	0	½	1	½	½	½	½	0	x	½	4
14	Bohlig		2450	½	0	0	0	0	0	½	½	0	0	½	0	½	x	2½

Category 11 (2502) GM = 7½ IM = 6

Ashkabad 1978		1	2	3	4	5	6	7	8	9	0	1	2	3	4	5	6	7	
1	Tseshkovsky	x	½	1	½	1	½	1	½	½	1	1	½	½	0	1	½	½	10½
2	Tukmakov	½	x	½	½	½	1	½	½	1	½	½	1	1	1	½	½	½	10½
3	Beljavsky	0	½	x	½	½	½	1	1	½	½	½	1	½	1	0	1	1	10
4	Mihalchishin	½	½	½	x	½	½	½	½	½	½	½	1	1	0	1	1	1	10
5	Timoshenko	0	½	½	½	x	½	½	0	1	½	½	1	½	½	1	½	1	9
6	Makarichev	½	0	½	½	½	x	½	½	½	½	1	½	1	½	½	½	1	9
7	Rasuvaev	0	½	0	½	½	½	x	½	½	1	½	1	½	1	½	½	1	9
8	Jusupov	½	½	0	½	1	½	½	x	½	1	½	0	½	1	0	½	½	8
9	Kochiev	½	0	½	½	0	½	½	½	x	0	1	1	1	½	0	½	1	8
10	Sveshnikov	0	½	½	½	½	½	0	0	1	x	½	0	½	1	1	½	1	8
11	Savon	0	½	½	½	½	0	½	½	0	½	x	1	½	½	1	½	½	7½
12	Kupreichik	½	0	0	0	0	½	0	1	0	1	0	x	1	1	½	½	1	7
13	Alburt	½	0	½	0	½	0	½	½	0	½	½	0	x	1	1	1	0	6½
14	Ivanov	1	0	0	1	½	½	0	0	½	0	½	0	0	x	1	½	½	6
15	Gutman	0	½	1	0	0	½	½	1	1	0	0	½	0	0	x	1	0	6
16	Kapengut	½	½	0	0	½	½	½	½	½	½	½	½	0	½	0	x	0	5½
17	Kakageldiev	½	½	0	0	0	0	0	½	0	0	½	0	1	½	1	1	x	5
18	Vaganian			½		½							½			1		½	

46 USSR Final 1978		1	2	3	4	5	6	7	8	9	0	1	2	3	4	5	6	7	8	
1	Tal	x	½	½	½	1	½	½	½	½	½	½	1	½	1	½	½	1	1	11
2	Tseshkovsky	½	x	½	½	1	½	½	½	1	½	0	1	½	1	1	½	1	½	11
3	Polugaevsky	½	½	x	½	½	1	1	½	0	½	½	½	½	½	½	½	1	1	10
4	Georgadze	½	½	½	x	½	½	½	½	½	½	1	½	½	½	1	½	½	½	9½
5	Beljavsky	0	0	½	½	x	½	1	½	0	½	1	½	1	0	½	1	½	1	9
6	Geller	½	½	0	½	½	x	1	0	½	½	½	½	½	1	½	½	½	1	9
7	Romanishin	½	½	0	½	0	0	x	0	½	1	1	½	1	1	½	1	1	0	9
8	Sveshnikov	½	½	½	½	½	1	1	x	½	1	0	0	½	½	½	½	½	½	9
9	Kasparov	½	0	1	½	1	½	½	½	x	½	½	½	0	0	0	½	1	1	8½
10	Bagirov	½	½	½	½	½	½	0	0	½	x	½	½	½	½	½	½	½	1	8
11	Gulko	½	1	½	0	0	½	0	1	½	½	x	½	½	½	½	½	½	½	8
12	Makarichev	0	0	½	½	½	½	½	1	½	½	½	x	½	½	½	½	½	½	8
13	Timoshenko	½	½	½	½	0	½	0	½	1	½	½	½	x	0	½	1	½	½	8
14	Mihalchishin	0	0	½	½	1	0	0	½	1	½	½	½	1	x	½	0	½	½	7½
15	Razuvaev	½	0	½	0	½	½	½	½	1	½	½	½	½	½	x	½	½	0	7½
16	Tukmakov	½	½	½	½	0	½	0	½	½	½	½	½	0	1	½	x	½	½	7½
17	Dorfman	0	0	0	½	½	½	0	½	0	½	½	½	½	½	½	½	x	1	6½
18	Kuzmin	0	½	0	½	0	0	1	½	0	0	½	½	½	½	1	½	0	x	6

Marina Romea 1978

				1	2	3	4	5	6	7	8	9	0	1	
1	Joksic		2405	x	1	½	½	½	½	½	½	1	½	1	6½
2	Karaklaic	IM	2460	0	x	½	1	½	½	½	1	½	1	1	6½
3	Grabczewski	IM	2375	½	½	x	½	½	½	½	½	½	1	1	6
4	Taruffi		2340	½	0	½	x	½	1	½	½	½	1	1	6
5	Padevsky	GM	2455	½	½	½	½	x	½	½	½	½	½	½	5
6	Gliksman	IM	2320	½	½	½	0	½	x	1	½	½	½	½	5
7	Ziembinski		2270	½	½	½	½	½	0	x	½	½	1	½	5
8	Witkowski	IM	2365	½	0	½	½	½	½	½	x	½	½	½	4½
9	Belkadi	IM	2350	0	½	½	½	½	½	½	½	x	0	1	4½
10	Rosino		2295	½	0	0	0	½	½	0	½	1	x	½	3½
11	Magalotti			0	0	0	0	½	½	½	½	0	½	x	2½

Eerbeek 23.xi.6.xii.78

				1	2	3	4	5	6	7	8	9	0	1	2	
1	Nikolac	IM	2495	x	½	½	1	1	½	1	½	1	½	½	1	8
2	Bohm	IM	2410	½	x	0	½	1	1	½	1	½	1	1	½	7½
3	Scheeren			½	1	x	0	½	½	½	1	½	1	½	1	7
4	Bellin	IM	2420	0	½	1	x	0	1	1	½	1	0	0	1	6
5	Baljon		2220	0	0	½	1	x	0	0	½	1	1	1	½	5½
6	Kelecevic	IM	2410	½	0	½	0	1	x	1	½	0	½	½	½	5
7	Taylor		2460	0	½	½	0	1	0	x	1	1	0	1	0	5
8	Trois	IM	2405	½	0	0	½	½	½	0	x	1	1	½	½	5
9	Pribyl	IM	2455	0	½	½	0	0	1	0	0	x	1	½	1	4½
10	v.d. Sterren		2400	½	0	0	1	0	½	1	0	0	x	½	1	4½
11	Borm		2260	½	0	½	1	0	½	0	½	½	½	x	0	4
12	Rogers		2400	0	½	0	0	½	½	1	½	0	0	1	x	4

Category 6 (2377) IM = 7

Prstina 4-18.xi.78

#	Player	Title	Rating	1	2	3	4	5	6	7	8	9	0	1	2	3	4	Score
1	B.Ivanovic	GM	2460	x	½	½	1	½	1	½	½	1	½	1	½	½	1	9
2	Bukal	IM	2410	½	x	½	0	½	½	½	1	½	1	1	1	1	1	9
3	Rogulj	IM	2420	½	½	x	½	½	½	0	½	1	½	1	1	1	1	8½
4	Vlahovic		2250	0	1	½	x	½	½	1	½	0	0	1	1	1	1	8
5	Smederevac	IM	2335	½	½	½	½	x	0	1	½	½	½	½	1	1	1	8
6	Badnarski	IM	2365	0	½	½	½	1	x	½	1	½	½	½	½	½	1	7½
7	Cetkovic		2300	½	½	1	0	0	½	x	0	½	1	½	1	1	1	7½
8	B.Bujupi		2350	½	0	½	½	½	0	1	x	½	½	½	1	1	1	7½
9	Rajna	IM	2410	0	½	0	1	½	½	½	½	x	½	½	½	1	1	7
10	Cobo	IM	2395	½	0	½	1	½	½	0	½	½	x	½	½	½	½	6
11	Pacl		2330	0	0	0	0	½	½	½	½	½	½	x	0	½	1	4½
12	Sadiku			½	0	0	0	0	½	0	0	½	½	1	x	½	½	4
13	Caza			½	0	0	0	0	½	0	0	0	½	½	½	x	0	2½
14	Servinski		2360	0	0	0	0	0	0	0	0	0	½	0	½	1	x	2

Category 4 (2341) IM = 9

Buenos Aires Olympiad x-xi.78 14 Rd SS

(1) Hungary 37, (2) USSR 36 (3) USA 35; (4) BRD 33; (5-6) Israel, Rumania 32½; (7-11) Denmark, Poland, Spain, Switzerland, Canada 32; (12-14) England, Bulgaria, Holland 31½; (15-17) Jugoslavia, Sweden, Argentina 31; (18-21) Cuba, Austria, China, Mexico 30½; (22-23) Finland, Colombia 30; (24-27) Philippines, New Zealand, Indonesia, Brazil 29½; (28-31) Iceland, Chile, Australia, Norway 29; (32) Paraguay 28½; (33-35) Scotland, Venezuela, Syria 28; (36-40) France, Uruguay, Dominican Rep., Sri Lanka, Hong Kong 27½; (41-46) Wales, Peru, Guayana, Japan, Luxembourg, Faroe Islands 27; (47-49) Belgium, Guatemala, Morocco 26½; (50-54) Tunisia, Ecuador, Bolivia, Trinidad & Tobago, Jordan 26; (55) Jamaica 25½; (56-57) Puerto Rico, Malaysia 25; (58-59) Libya, Mauritania 23½; (60) Andorra 22½; (61) US Virgin Islands 22; (62) Bermuda 20½; (63) Zaire 16; (64) Arab Emirates 12½; (65) British Virgin Islands 12½.

Satu Mare 1978

1	Banas		2385	8½
2	Armas		2385	8
3	Kluger	IM	2355	8
4	Bohosian		2425	7½
5	Biriesu		2390	7½
6	I.Szabo		2355	7½
7	Kaposztas		2305	7
8	Ungureanu		2410	7
9	Ilijin		2330	7
10	Basu			7
11	I.Fischer		2405	5½
12	Dobosz		2375	4½
13	Follert			3
14	Muller (Rum)			3

Banick Prievidzi 20.vi.-2.vii.78

1	Gazik		10½
2	Arnaudov	2260	9½
3	Fronczek	2280	8
4	Radojevic	2240	8
5	Franzen	2290	8
6	Babev	2335	8
7	Hardicsay	2355	7½
8	Trikaliotis	2245	7
9	Dobrovolsky		6½
10	Schranz	2300	6½
11	Hanko		4
12	Pacl	2330	4
13	Fabry		2
14	Bugar		1½

US Open Phoenix 12 rds SS

1	Bradford		10½
2	Shamkovich	GM	10
3	Youngworth		10
4	Lindsay		9½
5	Soltis	IM	9½
6	Carlson		9½
7	Odendahl		9½
8	Fedorowicz		9½
9	Tarjan	GM	9
10	Bisguier	GM	9
11	Lein	GM	9

. . . . (400+)

Graz 3-17.ix.78 13 Rd SS
World Junior Final

1	Dolmatov		2495	10½
2	Jusupov	IM	2450	10
3	J.O.Fries-Nielsen		2260	9
4	Bjork			8½
5	Barbero			8½
6	Sisniega		2455	8
7	van der Wiel			8
8	Foisor		2310	7½
9	Ristic			7½
10	Morrison			7½
11	Karolyi		2310	7½
12	Toshkov			7½
13	Cordes			7
14	Seirawan		2455	7
15	Petursson		2350	7
16	Mokry		2310	7
17	Tiller		2305	7
18	Passman			7
19	Plaskett		2410	7
20	Franzoni			7
21	L.Ortega		2350	7
22	Morovic		2275	7
23	Dur		2365	7
24	Pacis			7

. . . . (47)

Bhel ix.78

1	Vasyukov	GM	2555	10
2	Torre	GM	2490	9½
3	Lein	GM	2505	9
4	Shirazi	IM	2285	7
5	Sharif	IM	2380	7
6	R.Rodriguez		2415	7
7	Ravishekar			6½
8	Thipsay		2360	6
9	Bordonada		2360	5
10	Mascarinas		2355	4
11	Hassan			3
12	Ghalib			3
13	Liew			1

Category 5 (2354) GM=9½ IM=8

Biel vii-viii.78 11 Rd SS

1	Partos	IM	2420	8½
2	Bergstroem		2250	8
3	Fahnenschmidt		2350	8
4	Toth	IM	2480	8
5	Karsa		2240	7½
6	Govedarica		2405	7½
7	Rukavina	IM	2435	7½
8	Sahovic	GM	2490	7½
9	Hermann		2425	7½
10	Y.Grunfeld			7½
11	Nemet	IM	2425	7½
12	Wirthensohn	IM	2410	7½
13	Piket			7½
14	Freise			7½
15	Lederman	IM	2405	7
16	Welin			7
17	Prang			7
18	O.Castro	IM	2425	7

Daugavpils 13 rds SS

1	Kasparov			9
2	I.Ivanov		2415	9
3	Kupreichik	IM	2530	8½
4	Mihalchishin	IM	2460	8½
5	Kapengut		2465	8½
6	Panchenko	IM	2495	8½
7	Tseshkovsky	GM	2550	8½
8	Palatnik	IM	2490	8
9	Alburt	GM	2515	8
10	Dolmatov		2495	8
11	Makarichev	GM	2495	8
12	Rashkovsky	IM	2500	8
13	Lerner		2445	8
14	Vorotnikov		2410	7½
15	Kosikov		2395	7½
16	Malanyuk			7½
17	Holmov	GM	2550	7½
18	Averkin	IM	2455	7
19	Gufeld	GM	2525	7
20	Zilberstein		2455	7
21	Katalimov			7
22	Klovan	IM	2490	7
23	Korsunsky			7
24	Lputian			7
25	Suetin	GM	2535	7
26	Faibisovich		2460	7
27	M.?Tseitlin		?	7
28	Juferov		2450	7
29	Arbakov			6½
30	Bronstein	GM	2570	6½
31	Vitolins		2415	6½
32	Vaiser		2385	6½
33	?Vladimirov		2445	6½
34	Gusev		2410	6½
35	Zlotnik		2430	6½
36	Kim			6½
37	Leibovich			6½

. . . . (64)

Bogota 11-31.iii.78

1	Geller	GM	2590	12
2	L.Garcia		2325	10½
3	R.Hernandez	IM	2465	10½
4	Sigurjonsson	GM	2500	9½
5	Guild.Garcia		2365	9½
6	Panno	GM	2580	9
7	Cuartas	IM	2415	8½
8	Guellar	IM	2365	7½
9	Gutierrez	IM	2380	7
10	Guil.Garcia	GM	2535	6½
11	Minaya		2355	6
12	A.Zapata		2355	5½
13	J.Gonzales	IM	2370	5
14	Szmetan	IM	2420	5
15	Velandia		2220	4½
16	Acosta			3½

Category 7 (2409) GM=10½ IM=9

China 31.iii.-16.iv.78

China	6	Malaysia	1
"	5	"	2
"	4½	"	2½
"	4	"	3
"	5	"	2

Val Thorens 22-30.vii.78 9 rds SS

1	Smejkal	GM	2555	8½
2	Ostojic	GM	2420	7½
3	Klaric		2340	7
4	Pytel	IM	2390	7
5	Ghitescu	IM	2450	7
6	Villeneuve		2270	6½
7	Tatai	IM	2455	6½

. . . .

Skien 4-9.viii.78 9 rds SS

1	Sigurjonsson	GM	2500	7½
2	Schussler		2365	7
3	Grunfeld			7
4	Ogaard	IM	2435	7
5	L.A.Schneider	IM	2430	7
6	Westerinen	GM	2450	6½
7	de Firmian		2405	6½
8	Angantysson		2350	6½
9	Ekstrom		2360	6½
10	Rantanen	IM	2420	6
11	Pytel	IM	2390	6
12	Jensen		2230	6
13	Kristinsson		2385	6
14	Balinas	GM	2440	6
15	Andrijevic			6
16	Hjartarson			6
17	J. Benjamin		2330	6

. . . .

Tramandai Zonal 1978

1	Trois		2405	9
2	L.Bronstein		2400	8½
3	van Riemsdyk		2375	8½
4	Emma		2390	8
5	Frias		2400	7
6	Campora		2370	6
7	Segal	IM	2395	5½
8	Hase		2410	5½
9	C.Silva		2405	5½
10	? Gonzalez (Peru)			5
11	Braga			4½
12	Estrada		2205	3
13	Dienavorian		2360	2

Gausdal 11-18.viii.78 9 rds SS

1	Grunfeld			7
2	Wibe	IM	2420	6½
3	Petursson		2350	6
4	Sydor	IM	2395	6
5	Westerinen	GM	2450	6
6	de Firmian		2405	6
7	Schussler		2365	6
8	Sigurjonsson	GM	2500	5½
9	Pytel	IM	2390	5½
10	Wedberg		2370	5½
11	Ekstrom		2360	5½
12	Rantanen	IM	2420	5½
13	L.A.Schneider	IM	2430	5½
14	Rath		2405	5½
15	Wahlbom		2375	5½
16	Goichberg		2530	5½

. . . .

Albufieri 23.xi-18.xii.78

1	Velimirovic	GM	2520	18
2	Ljubojevic	GM	2605	17½
3	Ivkov	GM	2515	17
4	Mariotti	GM	2475	16
5	Tatai	IM	2455	15½
6	Knezevic	GM	2505	15
7	Makropoulos		2345	15
8	Matulovic	GM	2525	14½
9	S.Bouaziz	IM	2365	14
10	Skalkotas		2285	12½
11	F.Silva	IM	2350	12½
12	L.Santos		2255	12
13	Durao	IM	2315	11
14	Toth	IM	2480	11
15	Oney			9½
16	P.Santos			8½
17	Yilmaz			8½
18	Camilierri		2215	6½
19	Najar			5
20	Hmido			5
21	Bagli			5
22	Omuku			3
23	Hadjitafi			½

IM = 15 (Zonal)

1 b3

1 Nurmi-Speelman Mexico 78

1 b3 b6 2 ♝b2 ♝b7 3 e3 e6 4 f4 ♞f6 4...♘h6?! Δ ♘f5, ♗e7-f6 **5 ♞f3 ♝e7 6 ♝e2 0-0 7 0-0 a5 8 ♞c3** 8 a4; 8 a3 **♞a6 9 d4? ♞b4! =+ 10 ♞d2 ♞bd5 11 ♞xd5 exd5** 11...♘xd5!? 12 ♘f3 f5 **12 ♝f3 a4 13 c4 ♝b4! 14 ♜c1 ♜e8 15 ♜e1 axb3 16 axb3 ♜a2** 16...♗xd2 17 ♕xd2 ♘e4 **17 ♝c3 ♝xc3 18 ♜xc3 ♛a8 19 ♜c2**

19...♝c6 19...♖a7!? 20 c5 bxc5 21 ♖xc5; 19...♖a6; 19...♖a5; 19...♖a3; 19...♕a5; 19...♕a3 **20 ♛b1 ♜xc2 21 ♛xc2 ♛a5 22 ♚f2! dxc4 23 ♞xc4** 23 bxc4!? ♗xf3 24 gxf3 ♕h5 25 ♔g2 **♞e4+ 24 ♝xe4 ♝xe4 25 ♞xa5** 25 ♕xe4?? ♕xe1+ **♝xc2 26 ♜c1! ♝e4 27 ♞c4 ♜a8 28 ♞d2 ♜a2 29 ♚e2** 29 ♔e1!? ♖c2 **c6 30 g4 f6 31 ♜c3 h5 32 ♚d1 ♝g2 33 gxh5 f5 34 ♞c4! b5 35 ♞e5 ♝d5 36 ♞xd7 b4 37 ♜d3 ♜xh2 38 ♞c5 ♜h1+ 39 ♚e2 ♜xh5** 39...♔h7 **40 ♜d2 ♜h2+ 41 ♚d1 ♜h1+ 42 ♚c2 ♜e1 43 ♚d3 ♜c1 ½-½** 44 ♖a2 ♗xb3 45 ♘xb3 ♖c3+ 46 ♔d2 ♖xb3 47 ♖c2= **Speelman**

2 Lebredo-Petrosian Vilnius 78

1 b3 d5 2 ♝b2 ♞f6 3 ♞f3 e6 4 e3 ♝e7 5 ♝e2 0-0 6 0-0 c5 7 c4 ♞c6 8 cxd5 8 d4 **♞xd5 9 ♞a3** 9 d4!? ♗f6 Δ 10 ♗a3 cxd4! 11 ♗xf8 dxe3; 9 a3 Δ d3, ♕c2, ♘bd2 **b6 10 ♞c4 ♝b7 11 ♞fe5!? ♞xe5 12 ♞xe5 ♜c8** 12...f6 **13 ♜c1** 13 f4!? **f6 14 ♞f3 e5 =/=+ 15 a3** 15 d3 **e4 16 ♞e1 f5 17 f3 ♚h8 18 fxe4 fxe4 19 ♜xf8+ ♛xf8 20 ♞c2 ♝f6 21 ♝xf6 ♞xf6 22 b4 ♝c6 23 b5** 23 bxc5 ♗a4! 24 cxb6 axb6 25 d4! ∓/−+ **♝d5 24 ♞a1 ♜d8 25 ♝c4 ♝xc4 26 ♜xc4 ♛d6 27 ♞b3 ♛d3! 28 ♛c2 ♛e2 29 h3 ♜f8 30 ♚h2 h6 31 ♞c1 ♛e1 32 d4 ♞g4+ 33 hxg4 ♜f1 0-1 Speelman**

1 c4 c5

3 Djindjihashvili-Ribli IBM 78

1 ♞f3 c5 2 c4 ♞f6 3 ♞c3 e6 4 g3 b6 5 ♝g2 ♝b7 6 0-0 ♝e7 7 b3 7 d4 cxd4 8 ♕xd4 0-0 9 ♗f4 d6 10 ♕d2 ♕c8 11 ♖ac1 ♖d8 12 ♖fd1 ♘bd7 += Romanishin-Guil.Garcia, Leningrad 77 **0-0 8 ♝b2 d6** 8...d5 **9 e3 ♞bd7 10 d4 ♜b8 11 ♛e2** 11 d5 exd5 12 cxd5 a6 13 a4 ♗a8 Δ b5 **♜e8 12 e4 cxd4 13 ♞xd4 a6 14 f4?! ♝f8! 15 e5?! dxe5 16 fxe5**

16...♞xe5!! −+ 17 ♛xe5 ♝d6! 18 ♛e3 18 ♕e2 ♗c5 −+ **e5 19 ♝xb7 exd4 20 ♛f3 ♜e3 21 ♛g2** 21 ♕f2 dxc3 −+ **dxc3 22 ♝c1 ♜e7 23 ♝f3 ♛c7 24**

♚h1 24 ♗g5?? ♕c5+ **h6 25 g4 ♝f4 26 h4 g6 27 ♝xf4** 27 g5 hxg5 28 hxg5 ♘h7 **♛xf4 28 ♛h2** 28 ♗d5 ♕xg4 **♛xh2+ 29 ♚xh2 b5 30 cxb5 axb5 31 b4 ♜c8 32 ♜ac1 ♜c4 33 ♚g3 ♞e4+ 34 ♚g2 ♞d2 35 ♜fe1 ♜xe1 36 ♜xe1 ♜xb4 37 ♜c1 ♜b2 38 ♚g3 ♞xf3 39 ♚xf3 b4 40 a3 bxa3 41 ♜xc3 a2 42 ♜c8+** 42 ♖a3 ♖b3+ **♚g7 43 ♜a8 ♚f6 44 ♜a5 ♚e6 45 ♚e4 ♚d6 46 g5 0-1 Taulbut**

4 Pytel-Keller Biel 78

1 c4 ♞f6 2 ♞c3 c5 3 g3 e6 4 ♞f3 ♞c6 5 ♝g2 a6 6 0-0 ♛c7 7 b3 ♜b8?! 7... d6 8 d4 cxd4 9 ♘xd4 ♗d7 10 ♗b2 ♖c8 11 ♖c1 ♕b8 12 ♘e4!! ♗e7 13 ♘xf6+ ♗xf6 14 ♘xc6 ♗xc6 15 ♗xf6 gxf6 16 ♕d4 ♗xg2 17 ♔xg2 ♔e7 18 ♖c3 h5 19 ♖f3 ♖h6 20 h4 ♖g6 21 e4 ♕c7 22 ♖fd1 ♕c5 22 ♖fd3 ♕xd4 24 ♖xd4 ♖c6 25 c5!!± Pytel-Filipowicz, Poland 72 **8 d4 cxd4 9 ♞xd4 ♝c5 10 ♝e3** 10 ♘c2 b5∞ **♞xd4 11 ♝xd4 b6 12 e4 e5 13 ♝xc5 bxc5 14 ♛d2! 0-0 15 f4 ♝b7** 15...d6 16 fxe5 dxe5 17 ♖xf6 gxf6 18 ♘d5 ♕d8 19 ♕h6 ♖b6 20 ♖f1± **16 fxe5 ♛xe5** 16...♘g4 17 ♕d6 **17 ♜f5 ♛e6 18 ♛f4 d6 19 ♜d1 ♜bd8 20 e5! dxe5 21 ♜xe5 ♜xd1+ 22 ♞xd1 ♛d6 23 ♞c3 ♝xg2 24 ♚xg2 ♞g4?** 24...♕d3 25 ♕f3 ♕d2+ 26 ♖e2±; 24...♖d8!? **25 ♜e2! ♛c6+ 26 ♛f3 +− ♛xf3 27 ♚xf3 ♞f6 28 ♜e5 ♜c8 29 ♞e4 ♞d7 30 ♜d5 ♜c7 31 ♞xc5 ♜xc5 32 ♜xd7 g6 33 ♜d5 ♜c6 34 ♚e4 ♚g7 35 ♚d4 ♚f6 36 c5 ♚e6 37 b4 ♚e7 38 a4 ♜f6 39 b5 axb5 40 axb5 ♜f1 1-0 Pytel**

5 Pytel-Zaschke Graz 78

1 c4 c5 2 ♞c3 g6 3 g3 ♝g7 4 ♝g2 ♞c6 5 b3 d6 6 ♝b2 f5! 7 e3 e5 8 ♞ge2 ♞ge7 9 0-0 0-0 10 a3 ♜b8 11 ♜b1 b6 11...a6! **12 d4 ♛e8?** 12...exd4 13 exd4 ♘xd4 14 ♘xd4 ♗xd4 15 ♘b5 ♗xb2 16 ♖xb2 f4 17 ♖d2 ♘f5 18 ♘xd6 ♘d4!= **13 ♞b5! ♛d7 14 dxc5 dxc5 15 ♛c2 ♝b7 16 ♜fd1 ♛c8 17 ♞d6 ♛c7 18 ♞ec3 a6 19 ♞xb7 ♛xb7 20 ♞d5 ♞xd5 21 cxd5** 21 ♗xd5! **♞d8 22 f4 ♞f7 23 fxe5 ♝xe5? 24 d6 ♛d7 25 b4!± ♜fc8? 26 ♝xe5 ♞xe5 27 bxc5 1-0 Pytel**

6 Tuck-Filipowicz Bagneux 78

1 c4 g6 2 g3 ♝g7 3 ♝g2 c5 4 ♞c3 ♞c6 5 e3 e5 6 ♞ge2 ♞ge7 7 0-0 7 a3 d6 8 ♖b1 0-0!? 9 d3 ♗e6 10 ♘d5 ♖b8 11 b4 b5!= Klaman-Faibisovich 67; 9...a5 10 0-0 ♖b8 11 ♗d2 ♗f5! Danov-Botvinnik 65; 7 b3 d6 8 ♗b2 0-0 9 0-0 a6 10 d3 ♖b8 11 ♕d2 b5 12 ♖fd1 ♕a5∞ Polugaevsky-Bobotsov 66 **0-0 8 a3 ♜b8!?** 8...a6? 9 b4!±; 8...d6! 9 ♖b1 ♗e6! 10 ♘d5 ♗f5! 11 ♘xe7+ ♕xe7 12 d3 e4! Botvinnik **9 ♜b1 a5 10 ♞b5? d5!= 11 d3 ♝e6?!** 11...dxc4 12 dxc4 ♗f5! 13 e4 ♗e6 Δ ♘d4 =+ **12 ♛c2 ♛b6** 12...dxc4 13 dxc4 ♗f5! =+ **12 b3 d4 14 exd4 cxd4 15 ♚h1** 15 f4! **♜bd8 16 b4 axb4 17 axb4 ♝f5!** Δ e4 **18 f3 ♞d5!! 19 ♛b3** 19 cxd5 ♕xb5 20 dxc6 ♗xd3 −+ **♞dxb4 20 ♝a3 ♝xd3 21 ♝xb4 ♝xe2 22 ♜fe1 ♞xb4 23 ♜xe2 ♞a6 −+ 24 ♛d1 ♞c5 25 ♜a2 ♛c6 26 ♜a7 ♜fe8 27 ♜a2 f5 28 ♛f1 e4 29 fxe4 fxe4 30 ♜f2 d3 31 ♜f7 ♜d7 32 ♜f4 ♜dd8 33 ♜f7 ♜f8 34 ♜xf8 ♜xf8 35 ♛e1 b6 36 ♞c3 ♝xc3 37 ♛xc3 ♛f6 38 ♛d2 ♛f2 39 ♛g5 d2 40 ♛d5+ ♚g7 41 ♛e5+ ♛f6 0-1 Filipowicz**

7 Romanishin-Ribli IBM 78

1 ♞f3 c5 2 g3 g6 3 ♝g2 ♝g7 4 c4 ♞c6 5 ♞c3 e6 6 d3 ♞ge7 7 h4!?

7 0-0 d5= **h6 8 h5 g5**

9 ♞xg5!? hxg5 10 ♝xg5 f6! 11 ♝e3 11 ♗d2 (Δ h6, e4, ♕h5) ♘f5! **d6 12 h6 ♝f8 13 g4 ♞e5! 14 f3** 14 g5 ♘f5! **♝d7 15 ♞e4 ♞7g6 16 ♛d2 ♝c6 17 ♞f2 d5!∓ 18 cxd5 exd5 19 ♛c2 d4 20 ♝d2 ♛c7 21 0-0-0 0-0-0 22 g5 fxg5 23 ♝xg5 ♝e7 24 ♝d2 ♚b8 25 ♜dg1 ♜df8** Δ ♘f4 **26 ♝f1 ♞f4 27 ♞e4 c4! 28 ♜g7 cxd3 29 exd3 ♞xf3 30 ♝b4 ♞xd3+ 31 ♝xd3** 31 ♕xd3 ♗xe4+ −+ **♛f4+ 32 ♝d2** 32 ♔b1 ♗xb4 Δ ♗xe4, ♘d2+, ♖xh6 **♞xd2 33 ♛xd2 ♝xe4 34 ♛xf4 ♜xf4 35 ♝xe4 ♜xe4 36 h7 ♝f6 37 ♜g8+** 37 ♖f7 ♖c8+ 38 ♔d1 ♗h8; 38 ♔b1 ♗h8 **♜e8 38 ♜h6 ♝e5 39 ♜hg6 ♜c8+ 40 ♜xc8+ ♚xc8 0-1** 41 ♖h6 ♗f4+; 41 ♖g8+ ♔d7 Δ ♖xh7 **Taulbut**

8 Espig-Csom Vilnius 78

1 ♞f3 c5 2 c4 b6 3 g3 ♝b7 4 ♝g2 ♞f6 5 0-0 e6 5...g6!? **6 ♞c3 a6** 6... ♗e7 7 b3 (7 ♖e1!?) d5!? **7 b3** 7 ♖e1 Δ e4 **d6 8 ♝b2 ♝e7 9 d4** 9 d3 **cxd4 10 ♛xd4 ♞bd7 11 ♜fd1 ♛b8** 11... ♕c7 **12 ♛e3 0-0 13 ♞d4 ♝xg2 14 ♚xg2 ♛b7+** 14...♖c8 **15 ♛f3 ♛xf3+ 16 ♚xf3** 16 ♘xf3 ♖fc8 17 ♘d4 ♖ab8 18 ♖ac1 h6 19 e4 ♘e8 20 f4 +=/± Karpov-Gheorghiu, Moscow 77 **♜fc8 17 h3** 17 ♔g2 Karpov/Gheorghiu **♞c5 18 ♚g2 ♚f8 19 ♜ac1 ♜c7 20 ♞c2** 20 f4!? Δ ♘f3, e4 **♞e8 21 ♝a3 b5!? 22 ♞e3!** 22 cxb5? axb5 23 ♘xb5 ♖b7 24 ♗xc5 ♖xb5 Δ ♖xa2 =+; 24 ♘xd6?? ♗xd6 25 ♖xd6 ♖xa3! **bxc4?!** 22...♖b8 **23 ♞xc4**

23...d5!? 23...♖b8 24 e4 +=/± **24 ♞b6 ♜aa7?** 24...♖d8 25 ♘cxd5!? exd5 26 ♘xd5 ♖cd7 27 ♖xc5 ♗xc5 28 ♗xc5+ ♔g8 ∞/+= **25 ♞cxd5! exd5 26 ♞xd5** Δ ♘xe7 **♞e6 27 ♜xc7! ♞8xc7** 27...♖xc7? 28 ♘xe7 ♖xe7? 29 ♖d7 **28 ♞xe7 +− ♜a8 29 ♞d5+** 29 ♘f5+ **♚e8 30 ♞xc7+ ♞xc7 31 ♜d4 ♞e6 32 ♜c4 ♜d8 33 ♝c1 ♜d5 34 ♜a4 ♜d6 35 ♝e3 ♚d7 36 ♜a5 ♜c6 37 b4 f6 38 a4 ♚d6 39 f4 ♚d7 40 ♚f2 ♚d6 41 f5 +− 1-0 Speelman**

9 Zilberstein-Kapengut USSR 78

1 d4 ♞f6 2 c4 c5 3 ♞f3 cxd4 4 ♞xd4 e5!? 5 ♞b5 d5 6 cxd5 ♝c5!? 7 ♞5c3 0-0 8 e3 e4 9 a3 9 ♘d2 ♗f5 10 ♗e2 ♗b4 11 g4 ♗g6 12 h4 h6 13 ♕b3 ♗xc3 14 bxc3 ♕xd5 15 ♗a3 ♖c8 16 h5 ♗h7∞ Hasin-Karasev, Moscow 77; 10 ♘b3 ♗d6 11 ♗e2 a6 12 ♘d4 ♗g6 13 g4 h6 14 h4 ♘bd7 15 ♗d2 ♘e5 Mariotti-Vaganian, Rome 77 **♞bd7?!** 9...♕e7 10 ♘d2 ♗f5 11 b4 ♗d6 12 ♘c4 ♘bd7 13 ♗b2 a6 13 ♕d4 ♖fe8 15 ♗e2 ♖ad8 16 g4!? ♗xg4

17 ♘xe4 ♕xe4 18 ♕xe4 ♗xb4+ 19 axb4 ♖xe4 20 ♘d6 ♖xb4 21 ♗a3 ♖a4 22 f3 ♘e5! 23 ♘xb7 ♖b8 24 fxg4 ♖xb7 25 0-0 ♘xd5 26 ♖fd1 ♖d7 27 ♗b2 ♖xa1 28 ♖xa1 f6 ½-½ Zilberstein-Gusev, Daugavpils 78 **10 ♞d2 ♜e8 11 ♛c2 ♛e7 12 ♝e2 ♞b6 13 b4 ♝d6 14 ♛b3 ♝f5 15 ♝b2 ♜ac8?!** 15...♖ed8!= **16 ♞b5 ♝b8?!** 16...a6 17 ♘xd6 ♕xd6 18 ♖d1 ♖ed8 **17 d6! ♛d8** 17...♗xd6 18 ♘xa7± **18 ♝d4 ♞fd7 19 a4! ♛g5 20 g4 ♝e6 21 ♛b2?!** 21 ♕b1!± **♞c4 22 ♞xc4 ♝xc4 23 h4** 23 ♘xa7 ♗xa7 24 ♗xa7 ♗xe2 25 ♕xe2 ♘e5 =+ **♛g6 24 g5 ♝xe2 25 ♚xe2 a6∓ 26 ♞c7 ♜ed8 27 ♞d5** 27 ♗c5 ♕h5+ 28 ♔e1 ♘xc5 29 bxc5 ♗xc7 30 dxc7 ♖xc7∓ **♛xd6 28 ♞f4 ♞e5 −+ 29 ♜ac1 ♞f3 30 ♜hd1 ♜xc1 31 ♛xc1 ♛xb4 32 ♛c3 ♛xa4 0-1**
Kapengut

10 Hodos-Gofstein
Daugavpils 78
1 d4 ♞f6 2 c4 c5 3 ♞f3 cxd4 4 ♞xd4 e5!? 5 ♞b5 d5 6 cxd5 ♝c5! 6...♗b4+; 6...♕a5+ **7 ♞5c3** 7 d6! 0-0 8 ♗e3 ♗xe3 9 fxe3 ♘a6 10 ♘1c3 ♗d7 11 ♕d2 ♗xb5 12 ♘xb5 ♘e4 13 ♕d5 ♕a5+ 14 ♘c3 ♘ac5∓ Shvedchikov-M.D.Tseitlin, Lvov 77 **0-0 8 e3 e4 9 ♝e2 ♛e7** 9...♖e8 10 a3 ♘bd7 11 ♘d2 ♘b6 12 0-0 ♘bxd5 13 ♘xd5 ♕xd5 14 b4 ♗b6 15 ♗b2 ♕g5 16 ♔h1 ♘g4 17 ♕a4 ♗f5 18 ♗xg4 ♗xg4 19 b5 ♗e2 20 ♘xe4 ♕xb5 21 ♕xb5 ♗xb5 22 ♘d6 ♗xf1 23 ♘xe8 ♗xg2+∓ Sher-Pukshansky, Frunze 77; 10 0-0 ♗f5 11 ♘d2 a6 12 a3 ♕c7 13 ♘c4 b5 14 d6 ♕c8 15 ♘a5 ♕e6 16 b4 ♗xd6 17 ♗b2 ♘bd7 18 ♘b7 ♗f8 19 ♕d2 ♖ab8 20 ♘a5 ♘e5 =+ Peresipkin-Vaganian, Baku 77 **10 a3 ♜d8 11 b4 ♝d6 12 ♝b2 ♞bd7 13 ♞d2!?** N 13 ♘b5 ♘f8?! 14 ♘xd6 ♖xd6 15 ♘c3 ♗e6 16 ♕b3 ♘xd5 17 ♘xe4! ♖c6 18 ♘c5 ♘xb4 19 ♕xb4 ♕xc5 20 ♗d4 += Saharov-Mochalov, Belcy 77; 13... ♘e5! 14 ♘1c3 ♗g4∝ **♞b6 14 ♛b3 ♝e5 15 ♞c4 ♞xc4 16 ♝xc4 ♝f5 17 ♞b5** 17 0-0? ♗xh2+ 18 ♔xh2 ♘g4+ 19 ♔g3 ♕e5+ 20 f4 exf3+ 21 ♔xf3 ♕xe3 mate; 17 0-0-0 ♖ac8 18 ♔b1 ♕c7? 19 ♘b5; 18...♗xc3 19 ♗xc3 ♘g4 20 ♗e1; 18...♘g4 19 ♖d2 ♕c7 20 h3 ♕xc4 21 ♕xc4 ♖xc4 22 hxg4 ♗xc3 23 ♗xc3 ♗xg4= **♝xb2 18 ♛xb2 ♞xd5 19 ♞d4 ♛e5 20 ♛b3 ♝g6 21 ♝xd5 ♜xd5 22 ♜c1 f5 23 ♜c5 ♝f7 24 ♜xd5 ♝xd5 25 ♛c3 f4! ½-½**
Kapengut

11 Madenbrinck-Pytel Skien 78
1 c4 ♞f6 2 d4 c5 3 ♞f3 cxd4 4 ♞xd4 e6 5 e3 ♞c6 6 ♝e2 d5 7 0-0 ♝d6 8 ♞c3 0-0 9 ♝f3 ♞e5 10 cxd5 ♞xf3+ 10...exd5 11 ♗xd5! **11 ♛xf3 exd5 12 h3** 12 ♘xd5? ♘xd5 13 ♕xd5 ♗h2+ −+ **♝e6 13 e4 ♞xe4**

14 ♞xe4 14 ♘xe6! fxe6 15 ♕g4= **dxe4 15 ♛xe4 ♝d5! =+ 16 ♛g4 ♛f6 17 ♝e3 ♜fe8** 17...♕e5 18 g3 f5 **18 ♛g5 ♛xg5 19 ♝xg5 ♝e5! 20 ♝e3 a6 21 ♜fe1 g6 22 b3 ♜ad8 23 ♜ed1 f5!∓ 24 f3 ♝f6 25 ♝f2 ♜d7 26 ♜d3 ♜ed8 27 ♜ad1 ♝f7 28 ♚f1? f4! 29**

♚e2 g5 30 ♞c2 ♜e8+ 31 ♚f1 ♜xd3 32 ♜xd3 ♝g6 0-1 32 ♖d2 ♗c3; 32 ♖d6 ♗e5 **Pytel**

12 Gurevich-Galahov USSR 78

1 g3 ♞f6 2 ♝g2 c5 3 c4 d5 4 cxd5 ♞xd5 5 ♞c3 ♞c7 6 ♛b3!? ♞c6 7 ♝xc6+ bxc6 8 d3 ♞e6?! 8...e5 **9 ♛a4 ♝d7 10 ♞f3 g6 11 ♝e3 ♝g7 12 ♜c1 ♛b6 13 b3 ♝d4 14 ♛c4 0-0 15 0-0 ♜fd8 16 ♞a4 ♛a5 17 ♜fd1** 17 ♗xd4 cxd4 18 ♘xd4? ♘xd4 19 ♕xd4 ♗h3∓ **♝e8 18 ♞xc5! ♝xe3 19 fxe3 ♞xc5 20 b4! ♛a3 21 bxc5 ♜ab8 22 ♜b1 ♜b5!? 23 ♜xb5 cxb5 24 ♛c2 b4 25 ♛b3 ♛a5 26 ♜c1 ♝a4 27 ♛b2 ♜c8 28 ♛d4 ♝c6 29 ♛c4 e6 30 ♞e5 ♝d5 31 ♛d4 ♛xa2 32 ♞g4 ♛xe2 33 ♞f6+ ♚f8 34 ♞xh7+ ♚g8 35 ♞f6+ ♚f8 36 e4 ♝c6 37 ♞g4! ♚g8** 37...♕xg4 38 ♕h8+ +− **38 ♞h6+ ♚f8 39 ♜f1 +− f5** 39...♖c7 40 ♕h8+ +−; 39... ♗e8 40 ♘xf7 +− **40 ♛f6+ ♚e8 41 ♛xe6+ ♚d8 42 ♛d6+ ♝d7 43 ♞f7+ ♚e8 44 ♞e5 ♛e3+ 45 ♚h1 ♜d8 46 ♛xg6+ ♚e7 47 ♛f7 mate 1-0 Gufeld**

13 S.Garcia-Farago Polanica 78

1 c4 ♞f6 2 ♞c3 c5 3 g3 d5 4 cxd5 ♞xd5 5 ♝g2 e6?! 5...♘c7 **6 ♞xd5** 6 ♘f3 ♘c6 7 0-0 ♗e7 8 ♘xd5 exd5 9 d4 += **exd5 7 ♛b3!?** 7 d4! **♝e6 8 ♛xb7 ♞d7 9 ♞h3** 9 ♘f3 ♗e7 10 0-0 0-0 11 d3 ♗f6 12 ♗f4 g5 13 ♗d6 ♖e8 14 e4 ♕b6 15 ♕xb6 axb6 16 e5± (Filipowicz) ♗g7 17 ♖fe1 h6∓ (Pytel) S.Garcia-Swic, Polanica 78; 9 ♗xd5? ♖b8 10 ♕c6 ♖b6 11 ♕a8 ♖b8= **♞b6 10 ♛a6 ♝d6 11 d3 0-0 12 ♞f4 ♝c8 13 ♛a5 ♝b7 14 0-0 ♛e7** 14...g5 15 ♘h3 h6 16 f4!± **15 h4! ♝xf4 16 ♝xf4 ♛xe2 17 ♛xc5 ♛xb2?** 17...♕xd3 Pytel **18 ♛e7! ♝a6** 18...♘c8 19 ♕c7 ♕b6 20 ♖fc1± **19 ♝e5!± ♛e2** 19...♕c2 20 ♕g5! f6 21 ♗xf6 ♖xf6 22 ♗xd5+ ♔f8 23 ♗xa8 ♘xa8 24 ♖ac1 +− **20 ♛g5! f6 21 ♝xf6 ♜xf6 22 ♝xd5+ ♚f8** 22... ♔h8 23 ♗xa8 ♘xa8 24 ♖ae1 ♕f3 25 ♖e8+ ♖f8 26 ♕e7 ♔g8 27 ♕e6+ ♕f7 28 ♖xf8+ ♔xf8 29 ♕xa6 +− Pytel **23 ♝xa8 ♞xa8 24 ♜ae1 ♛xd3 25 ♜d1 ♛f3 26 ♜d7! g6 27 ♛e5 ♚g8 28 ♛e8+ ♜f8 29 ♛e6+ 1-0 Filipowicz**

14 Adamski-Lerner Kiev 78

1 c4 ♞f6 2 ♞f3 c5 3 ♞c3 e6 4 g3 d5 5 cxd5 ♞xd5 5...exd5 += **6 ♝g2 ♞c6 7 0-0 ♝e7 8 d4 0-0 9 ♞xd5** 9 e4 ♘b6 10 d5 exd5 11 exd5 ♘b4 12 ♘e5 ♗f6 13 f4 ♗f5∞ **exd5 10 dxc5** 10 ♗e3 ♗f6 11 dxc5 ♗xb2 12 ♖b1 ♗f6 13 ♘e1! +=; 10...c4!? **♝xc5 11 b3!?** 11 ♕c2; 11 ♘e1 **♝f5 12 ♝b2 ♜e8 13 ♜c1 ♛d6 14 e3 += ♜ad8 15 ♛d2?** 15 ♘d4 ♗xd4! 16 ♗xd4 ♗e4 **♝b4! 16 ♝c3 ♝a3 17 ♝b2 ♝e4 18 ♜fd1 ♝xb2 19 ♛xb2 ♛e7** Δ ♖d6 **20 ♜d2 ♜d6= 21 ♞d4 h5!** 21...♘e5? 22 ♗xe4 dxe4 23 ♘f5 ♘f3+ 24 ♔g2 +− **22 ♝xe4 ♛xe4 23 ♛a3?** 23 ♘xc6 Δ ♕d4 **♜f6 24 ♞xc6 bxc6 25 ♛a6** 25 ♕xa7 ♕f3 26 ♕d4 ♖e4! −+ **h4∓ 26 ♛f1 ♛f5 27 ♜d4 hxg3 28 hxg3 g5! 29 b4 ♚g7 30 b5 c5! −+** 30...cxb5 31 ♕g2 =+ **31 ♜xc5 ♜xe3** Δ ♖xg3+ **32 ♜cxd5** 32 ♖dxd5 ♖xg3+ 33 ♔h2 ♖h6+ −+; 32 ♖d1!? **♜xg3+ 33 ♚h2 ♛f3! 34 ♜d6 ♜xd6 35 ♜xd6 ♜g4 36 ♛a1+ f6 37 ♜d7+ ♚h6 0-1 Gufeld**

15 Zichichi-Gonsior Italy 78

1 ♞f3 ♞f6 2 c4 c5 3 g3 e6 4 ♝g2 d5 5 0-0 ♞c6 6 d3 ♝e7 7 e3 0-0 8 ♛e2 b6 9 b3 ♝b7 10 ♝b2 ♛c7 11 ♞c3 a6 11...♖ac8! 12 ♘b5 ♕b8 **12 ♜ac1 ♜ad8 13 d4 dxc4 14 bxc4**

♜d7 14...cxd4 15 exd4 ♘xd4? 16 ♘xd4 ♖xd4 17 ♘b5 +− **15 d5!? exd5 16 ♞xd5 ♞xd5 17 cxd5 ♜xd5 18 ♞h4 ♜fd8?!** 18...♘e5 19 f4! ♘d3 20 ♗xd5 ♘xc1 21 ♕g4! +− **19 ♝xd5 ♜xd5 20 ♜fd1 ♛d7** 20...♖xd1+ 21 ♖xd1 ♗xh4 22 ♕g4! **21 e4 ♜xd1+ 22 ♜xd1 ♛e6 23 ♞f5 ♝f8**

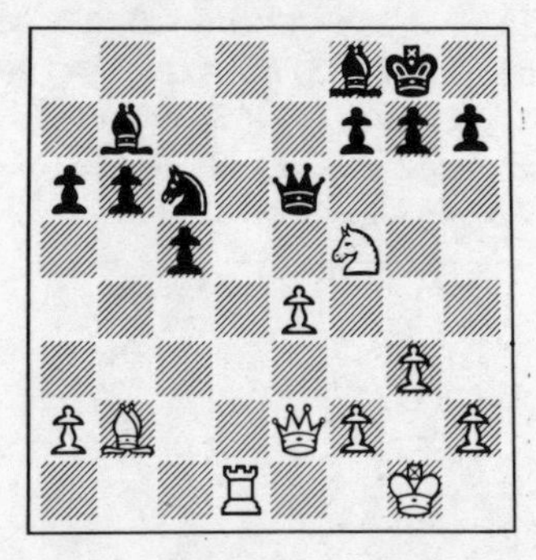

24 ♝xg7!? ♝xg7 25 ♜d7 ♝c8? 25...♕xd7!? 26 ♕g4 ♕d4 27 ♘xd4 ♘xd4! 28 ♕d7 ♗c6 29 ♕d8+ ♗f8 30 ♕xb6 ♗b5 =+ **26 ♛g4 ♛f6 27 e5! 1-0** 27...♘xe5 28 ♖d8+; 27...♕xe5 28 ♘h6+ ♔f8 29 ♖xf7+ **Paoli**

1 c4 e5

16 Pytel-Seret Bagneux 78

1 c4 e5 2 ♞c3 ♞c6 3 ♞f3 f5 4 d4 e4 5 ♞g5 5 ♗g5 **♝b4** 5...♘f6 6 e3 ♗b4 7 ♗d2 ♕e7 8 ♘h3 ♘d8! += Polugaevsky-Balashov, USSR Final 77 **6 ♞h3 ♝xc3+ 7 bxc3 ♞f6 8 e3 0-0** 8...b6 9 ♗a3 ♗a6 10 ♕a4 ♘a5 11 ♗b4!? ♗xc4 12 ♗xc4 ♘xc4 13 ♕b5! a5! += Uhlmann-Karner, Tallinn 77 **9 ♝e2 b6 10 ♛a4 ♛e8 11 c5! bxc5** 11...♗b7!? **12 ♛c4+ ♚h8 13 ♛xc5± d6 14 ♛a3 ♞d5 15 0-0 ♞b6 16 c4 ♛e7 17 ♞f4 a5 18 c5!?** 18 ♗d2! ♗a6 19 ♖fc1± **dxc5 19 dxc5 ♞d7 20 ♝b2 ♞de5** 20...♕xc5? 21 ♗xg7+; 20...♘xc5 21 ♗c4 ♘b4 22 ♘h5 **21 ♜fd1 ♝a6 22 ♝xa6 ♜xa6 23 ♛c3 ♜fd8 24 ♜xd8+ ♛xd8 25 ♞e6 ♛d7 26 ♞d4! ♞xd4 27 ♛xd4 ♛xd4 28 ♝xd4 ♞c6 29 ♝c3 ♞b4 30 a3 ♞d3 31 ♜b1 ♚g8 32 ♜b8+ ♚f7 33 ♜c8 ♜c6 34 ♝xa5 ♚e6 35 ♜xc7 ♜xc5 36 ♜xc5 ♞xc5 37 ♝b6 ♞a4** 37...♘d7 38 ♗d4 g6 39 a4 **38 ♝d4 g6 39 f3 exf3 40 gxf3 ♚d5 41 ♚f2 f4 42 h4 ♚c4 43 ♚e2 fxe3 44 ♚xe3 ♚b3 45 ♚f4 ♚c4 46 ♚e4 1-0 Pytel**

17 Speelman-Ree
Lone Pine 78

1 c4 e5 2 ♞c3 d6 3 ♞f3 3 e3 **f5 4 d4 e4 5 ♝g5!?** 5 ♘g5; 5 ♘d2 **♞f6** 5...♗e7 6 ♗xe7 ♕xe7 7 ♘d2 e3!? 8 fxe3 ♘f6; 7 ♘d5!? **6 ♞d2 ♝e7 7 e3 0-0 8 h4!?** 8 ♗e2 c6 9 0-0 ♘a6 10 f3 exf3 11 ♗xf3 ♘c7 12 ♕b3 ♔h8 13 ♖ae1 c5= Timman-Ligterink, Lone Pine 78 **c6 9 ♝e2 ♞a6 10 a3!?** Δ g4!? **♞c7 11 g4!? d5 12 cxd5 cxd5 13 ♛b3 ♞xg4! 14 ♝xg4** 14 ♗xe7 ♕xe7 15 ♗xg4 fxg4 16 ♘xd5 ♘xd5 17 ♕xd5+ ♗e6 18 ♕xe4 α/∓; 15 ♘xd5? ♘xd5 16 ♕xd5+ ♗e6 17 ♕xe6+ ♕xe6 18 ♗c4 ♕xc4 19 ♘xc4 ♖ac8∓ Δ ♖c2; 14 ♗f4!? ♗xh4 15 ♗xg4 fxg4 16 ♗xc7 ♗xf2+ 17 ♔e2 ♕xc7 18 ♘xd5 ♕f7 19 ♘e7+ ♔h8 20 ♖xh7+! +−; 14...♗e6!?; 14...♘f6!? **♝xg5** 14...fxg4 **15 hxg5 fxg4 16 ♞dxe4 ♝e6** 16...♔h8 17 g6 h6 18 ♘g3∓; 17 ♘f6?! Ree gxf6 18 g6 ♔g7! −+ **17 ♞g3 ♛xg5 18 ♛xb7 ♛e7** 18...♖f7 Δ ♖af8 **19 ♛b3** 19 ♘b5!? **♜ab8 20 ♛c2 g6 =+/∓ 21 ♜c1 ♞b5 22 ♞a4!? ♞xd4!?** 22...♗f7 Δ h5-h4 **23 exd4 ♝d7+ 24 ♚d1!** 24 ♔f1 ♗xa4 25 ♕xa4 ♕e3! 26 ♖c2 ♕xg3 27 ♕d7 ♕d3+!; 24 ♔e2 ♗xa4 25 ♕xa4 ♖xb2 26 ♕d1 ♕e4! Δ ♖e8 −+; 26 ♖c2 ♖b1+ **♜xf2!?**

24...♗xa4 25 ♕xa4 ♖xf2∞; 27...♖xb2 **25 ♛xf2 ♝xa4+ 26 b3 ♜xb3 27 ♜c8+ ♚g7**

28 ♞f5+! 28 ♖xh7+ ♔xh7 29 ♕h2+ ♔g7 **gxf5 29 ♜xh7+ = ♚xh7 30 ♛xf5+ ♚g7 31 ♛xg4+ ♚f6 32 ♛f4+ ♚g6 33 ♛g4+ ♚f6 34 ♛f4+ ½-½ Speelman**

18 Karpov-Korchnoi (26) 78
1 c4 e5 2 ♞c3 d6 3 g3 f5 4 ♝g2 ♞c6 5 d3 ♞f6 6 e3 ♝e7 7 ♞ge2 0-0 8 0-0 ♛e8 9 f4 ♝d8 10 a3 ♜b8 11 b4 ♝e6 12 ♞d5 b5 13 ♝b2 bxc4 14 dxc4 e4 15 ♞xf6+ 16 ♖c1 **♝xf6 16 ♝xf6 ♜xf6 17 ♜c1 a5!** 17...♕f7? 18 c5 **18 b5 ♞d8 19 ♜f2 ♞b7 20 ♝f1 ♞c5 21 ♞c3 ♝f7 22 ♞d5** 22 ♖d2; 22 ♘a4 ♗h5 23 ♕c2 c6 24 ♖d2 ♘d3!; 24 ♘xc5 dxc5 25 ♖d2±; 23...♖e6! (Δ ♘d3) 24 ♘xc5 dxc5 **♝xd5 23 cxd5 ♞d3!?** 23...h6 24 ♖b2 ♔h7 25 ♕d2 ♖a8 26 b6± **24 ♝xd3 exd3 25 ♛xd3 ♛xb5 26 ♛xb5 ♜xb5 27 ♜xc7 ♜f7!** 27...♖xa5? 28 ♖b2! ½-½ 28 ♖c8+ ♖f8 29 ♖xf8+ ♔xf8 30 ♖d2? ♖b3

19 Smejkal-Labarthe
Val Thorens 78
1 c4 e5 2 ♞c3 f5 3 d4 exd4 4 ♛xd4 ♞c6 5 ♛e3+ ♞ce7 5...♕e7 6 ♘d5 **6 g3 ♞f6 7 ♝g2 c6** 7...g6 **8 ♞h3± d5 9 cxd5 cxd5 10 ♛e5! ♛b6 11 ♝e3! ♛xb2 12 ♜b1 ♛a3 13 ♞b5 ♞g4 14 ♛c7! 1-0 Pytel**

20 Vilela-Prandstetter Decin 78
1 c4 e5 2 ♞c3 ♞f6 3 ♞f3 ♞c6 4 d3 d5!? 5 cxd5 ♞xd5 6 e3 += ♝e7 7 ♝e2 0-0 8 a3 ♝e6 9 ♝d2 f5 10 0-0 ♛e8?! 10...♗f6 Δ a5 **11 b4 a6 12 ♛b1!** Δ b5± **♛g6 13 b5 axb5 14 ♛xb5 ♞xc3 15 ♝xc3 e4 16 ♞e5 ♞xe5 17 ♝xe5 exd3 18 ♝xd3 c6 19 ♛xb7 ♝d5 20 ♝g3 ♝xa3 21 ♜fb1**

21...♛e6!? 21...♕e8! Δ ♖f7 **22 h3 c5?** 22...♕e8 **23 ♜b6! ♛f7 24 ♛xf7+ ♜xf7 25 ♝c2!** Δ ♖d6, 25 ♖d6 ♗b3 **g6 26 ♜d6 ♝c4 27 ♝d1!** Δ ♗f3 **♜fa7 28 ♝f3 ♝b4?** 28...♖c8 29 ♗e5; 28...♖e8 29 ♗c6 ±/+− **29 ♜c1 ♜a1 30 ♜dd1! 1-0 Pritchett**

21 Pytel-Ostojic Bagneux 78
1 c4 e5 2 ♞c3 ♞f6 3 ♞f3 ♞c6 4 d4 e4 5 ♞d2 ♝b4 6 e3 0-0 7 ♛c2 ♜e8 8 ♞d5?! d6 9 ♞xb4 ♞xb4 10 ♛c3 a5 11 d5?! c6 12 dxc6 bxc6 13 a3 ♞a6? 13...d5 14 b3? d4! 15 exd4 e3! 16 fxe3 ♖xe3+ 17 ♕xe3 ♘c2+ −+ **14 b3 c5 15 ♝b2 ♞b8 16 ♝e2 ♛e7?** 16...♗f5 17 h3 += **17 ♞xe4!± ♞bd7** 17...♘xe4?? 18 ♕xg7 mate; 17...♕xe4 18 ♗f3 **18 ♜d1!**

♜a6 19 ♞g3 ♝b7 20 0-0 ♜eb8 21 ♝d3 ♛f8 22 ♝c2 h5 23 h3 g6 24 ♝a1 ♛h6 25 f3 △ e4, ♖f2, ♘f1-e3-d5 **d5?! 26 cxd5 ♞xd5 27 ♜xd5 ♝xd5 28 ♛d3 ♜d6 29 e4 h4 30 ♞e2 ♜e8?** 30...♗xb3 31 ♕xd6 ♕e3+ 32 ♔h2 ♗xc2 33 ♕xd7 ♕xe2 34 ♕d6 ♖e8 35 ♕f6 ♔f8 36 ♕xh4! +− **31 exd5 ♞b6 32 ♞c3 f5 33 f4 ♛f8 34 ♛f3 ♛e7 35 ♝d3 a4 36 ♞xa4 c4 37 ♝xc4 ♞xc4 38 bxc4 ♛a7+ 39 c5 1-0 Pytel**

22 Adorjan-Timman
IBM 78

1 c4 e5 2 ♞c3 ♞f6 3 ♞f3 ♞c6 4 e3 ♝b4 5 ♛c2 0-0 6 ♞d5 a5 6...♖e8 7 ♕f5 Keene **7 a3 ♝c5 8 ♞g5** 8 ♗e2= **g6 9 ♞xf6+** 9 h4!? h6 10 h5 hxg5 11 hxg6 e4; 10 ♘xf6+ ♕xf6 11 ♘e4 ♕e7 12 h5 g5 13 ♘xc5 ♕xc5 14 ♕f5 ♔g7! =+ **♛xf6 10 ♞e4 ♛e7 11 ♝e2 d6 12 b3** 12 ♘xc5 dxc5 =+ **♝a7 13 0-0 f5 14 ♞c3 f4 15 ♞d5 ♛g5 16 ♚h1 ♝h3!! 17 gxh3** 17 ♖g1 ♗f5 =+ **f3 18 ♝xf3** 18 ♖g1 fxe2 19 ♗b2 ♕h5 −+ **♜xf3 19 ♛e4 ♜af8! 20 ♛g4 ♛d8 21 ♝b2** 21 ♔g2 ♖3f5 **♜xf2 22 ♚g1 ♜2f5 23 ♜xf5 ♜xf5 24 ♜f1 ♜xf1+ 25 ♚xf1 ♚f7 26 ♚e2 ♞b8! 27 b4 axb4 28 axb4 c6 29 ♞c3 h5 30 ♛f3+?! ♛f6 31 b5 ♛xf3+ 32 ♚xf3 ♞d7 33 ♞e4 ♝b8 34 bxc6 bxc6 35 ♝a3 d5 36 cxd5 cxd5∓ 37 ♞g5+ ♚f6 38 h4 e4+ 39 ♚g2 ♞e5 40 ♝b2 ♚f5 41 h3** 41 ♗xe5 ♗xe5 42 h3 ♗f6 −+; 42 ♘f7 ♗c7 △ ♗a5 −+ **♝c7 42 ♝c3 ♝d6 43 ♚f2 ♞d3+ 44 ♚g2 ♝e7 −+ 45 ♝a5 ♝xg5 46 hxg5 ♚xg5 47 ♚g3** 47 ♗d8+ **h4+ 48 ♚g2 ♚h5 49 ♝d8 g5 50 ♝f6 g4 51 hxg4+ ♚xg4 52 ♝c3 h3+ 53 ♚h2 ♞e1 54 ♚g1 ♚g3! 55 ♝e5+ ♚f3 56 ♚f1 ♞d3 57 ♝c7 ♞b2 0-1 Taulbut**

23 Timman-Romanishin IBM 78

1 c4 e5 2 ♞c3 ♞f6 3 ♞f3 ♞c6 4 e3 ♛e7!? 5 d4 exd4 6 ♞xd4 g6?! 6...♘xd4 7 ♕xd4 += **7 ♞db5 d6** 7...♕d8 8 ♘d5 ♘xd5 9 cxd5 a6 10 dxc6 axb5 11 ♕d4 ♖g8± △ 12 ♕e4+ **8 ♞d5 ♞xd5 9 cxd5 ♞e5** 9...♘d8 10 ♘xa7 △ ♖xa7 11 ♕d4 **10 f4! ♞g4 11 ♝e2 ♞f6 12 ♛a4 ♚d8 13 ♞xa7 ♛e4 14 ♛xe4** 14 ♘c6+ bxc6 15 ♕xa8 ♕xg2 16 ♖f1 ♗g7∝ **♞xe4 15 ♞xc8 ♚xc8 16 ♝d3 ♞c5 17 ♝c2 ♝g7 18 a3 ♜e8 19 ♚e2 ♞a4 20 ♜b1 ♞b6 21 ♜d1 ♜a5 22 ♝b3 f5 23 ♝d2 ♜a8 24 ♝b4 ♚d7 25 ♚f3 ♜e4 26 ♝c2 ♜e7 27 ♝b3 ♜e4 28 ♜d3 ♞c4**

29 ♝xc4 ♜xc4 30 ♜d2 ♜e8 31 b3 ♜ce4 32 ♜d3 h6 33 ♝c3 ♝xc3 34 ♜xc3 c5 35 dxc6+ bxc6 36 b4 g5 37 ♜d1 g4+ 38 ♚f2 ♜8e6 39 h3 h5 40 hxg4 hxg4 41 ♜h1 d5 42 ♜h7+ ♜e7 43 ♜xe7+ ♜xe7 44 b5 cxb5 45 ♜c5 ♚d6 46 ♜xb5 ♜c7 47 ♜b6+ ♚e7 48 ♜b2 ♜c4 49 ♜a2 ♜a4 50 ♜d2 ♜xa3 50...♔e6 51 ♖d3 △ ♔e2-d2-c2-b3 **51 ♜xd5 ♜a2+ 52 ♚g3 ♚f6 53 ♜b5 ♜e2?! 54 ♜e5 ♜e1 55 e4 fxe4 56 ♚xg4 ♜e3 57 ♜f5+ ♚e6 58 ♜a5 ♜e2 59 g3 ♜e3 60 ♜e5+ ♚f6 61 ♚h4 ♜e1 62 g4 ♜h1+ 63 ♚g3 ♜g1+ 64 ♚h3 ♜e1 65 g5+ ♚g6 66 ♜e6+ ♚f7 67 ♜f6+ ♚g7 68 ♚g4 ♜g1+**

69 ♔f5 e3 70 ♖e6 ♖g3 71 ♖e7+ ♔f8 72 ♔f6 ♖f3 73 ♖e4 e2 74 f5 ♖f2 75 g6 1-0 Taulbut

24 Schussler-Lundin Gausdal 78

1 c4 e5 2 ♘c3 ♘c6 3 ♘f3 ♘f6 4 e4!? ♗b4 4...♗c5 5 ♘xe5∝ **5 d3 d6 6 g3** 6 h3 **♗g4 7 h3 ♗xf3 8 ♕xf3 ♘d4 9 ♕d1 c6 10 ♗g2 h5?!** 10...♘d7; 10...a6 Δ b5= **11 0-0 h4 12 g4 ♘e6?!** 12...♘d7 Δ g5, ♘f8-g6-f4 **13 ♘e2 ♗c5 14 ♗d2 a5 15 a3 ♗b6?** 15...♕b6!? **16 ♗c3 ♘d7** 16...♘d4! **17 d4!± ♕f6? 18 c5! ♗a7** 18...dxc5 19 dxe5 ♘xe5? 20 f4 **19 b4 exd4 20 ♘xd4 ♘e5** 20...dxc5? 21 ♘b5 **21 ♘xe6 ♕xe6 22 ♕xd6 ♕xd6 23 cxd6 f6 24 ♔h2 0-0-0 25 f4 ♘c4 26 e5 +− ♖hf8 27 ♗e4 ♘e3 28 ♗f5+ ♔b8 29 ♖f3 ♘d5 30 ♖d1 axb4 31 ♗xb4 fxe5 32 fxe5 ♘xb4 33 axb4 ♗b6 34 e6 ♖de8 35 e7 ♖f6 36 ♔g2!** Δ ♗d7 **1-0 Pytel**

25 Korchnoi-Karpov (27) 78

1 c4 ♘f6 2 ♘c3 e5 3 ♘f3 ♘c6 4 g3 ♗b4 5 ♘d5 ♘xd5 6 cxd5 ♘d4 7 ♘xd4 7 ♘xe5? ♕e7 8 f4 d6 9 ♘d3 ♕e4 **exd4 8 ♕c2 ♕e7** 8...0-0 9 ♕c4 **9 ♗g2** 9 ♕xc7 ♕e4 **♗c5 10 0-0 0-0 11 e3 ♗b6?** 11...d6 **12 a4 dxe3 13 dxe3 a5 14 ♗d2 ♗c5 15 ♗c3 d6 16 ♕d2± b6 17 ♖fe1 ♗d7 18 e4?** 18 b3 **♖fe8 19 ♔h1?** 19 ♗f1! Δ ♗c4 **c6 20 e5 cxd5 21 ♗xd5 ♖ad8 22 ♕f4 ♕f8 23 ♕f3? dxe5 24 ♗xe5 ♗g4! 25 ♕xg4 ♖xd5 26 ♗c3** 26 ♗xg7? ♖xe1+ 27 ♖xe1 ♕xg7 28 ♖e8+ ♗f8 **♖ed8** 26...♖xe1+? 27 ♖xe1 ♗xf2 28 ♖e8! +− **27 ♔g2 ♗d4 28 ♖ac1 g6 29 ♕e2?** 29 ♖ed1!= **♕d6 30 ♗xd4 ♖xd4 31 ♕b5??** 31 b3 ♖d3 32 ♖b1 **♖b4 32 ♖e8+ ♔g7 38 ♖xd8 ♕xd8 34 ♕e2 ♕d5+ 35 f3 ♖xa4 36 ♖c2 ♖d4 37 ♕e3 b5 38 h4 h5 39 ♕e2 a4 40 ♕e3 b4 41 ♖f2 0-1** 41...♖d3

26 Karpov-Korchnoi (6) 78

1 c4 e5 2 ♘c3 ♘f6 3 ♘f3 ♘c6 4 g3 ♗b4 5 ♗g2 0-0 6 0-0 e4 7 ♘e1 ♗xc3 8 dxc3 h6 9 ♘c2 ♖e8 9...b6 10 ♘e3 ♗b7 11 ♘d5 ♘e5 Korchnoi-Karpov (9) 74 **10 ♘e3 d6 11 ♕c2 a5 12 a4 ♕e7 13 ♘d5** 13 f4 exf3 14 exf3 ♕e5 15 ♗d2 ♕c5 16 ♖ae1 ♗e6 17 b3 d5 =+ **♘xd5 14 cxd5 ♘b8 15 ♗e3 ♗f5 16 h3 ♘d7 17 c4 b6 18 ♕c3 ♘c5 19 b3 ♕d7 20 ♔h2 ♖e7 21 ♗d4 f6 22 ♖ac1 ♕e8 23 ♕e3 ½-½** 23...♕h5 24 ♖c3 ♗g4 25 ♖e1 ♖ae8 Δ 26...♘d3 27 exd3 exd3 28 ♕xe7 ♖xe7 29 ♖xe7 d2 −+

27 Korchnoi-Karpov (25) 78

1 c4 ♘f6 2 ♘c3 e5 3 g3 ♗b4 4 ♕b3 ♘c6 5 ♘d5 5 e3 **♗c5 6 e3 0-0 7 ♗g2 ♘xd5 8 exd5 ♘e7 9 ♘e2 d6** 9...c6 **10 0-0 c6 11 d4 exd4 12 exd4 ♗b6 13 ♗g5 ♗d7 14 a4 h6 15 ♗xe7 ♕xe7 16 ♗f3** 16 ♖fe1; 16 a5 ♕xe2 17 axb6 axb6 18 ♕xb6 ♕b5= **♖ab8 17 a5 ♗c7 18 ♕c3** 18 ♖ac1 **♖fc8 19 ♘f4?** 19 a6 ♗b6 20 axb7 ♖xb7 21 dxc6 ♗xc6 22 ♗xc6 ♖bc7= **♗d8 20 ♖fe1 ♕f8 21 ♕b3 ♗g5 22 ♘e2 ♗f6 23 ♖ad1 c5 24 ♗e4 ♕d8 25 ♕a2 ♗g4 26 dxc5 ♖xc5 27 b4 ♖c7 28 ♕b3 ♖bc8 29 f3 ♗d7 30 ♕e3 a6 31 ♗d3 ♗b2 32 ♔g2 ♕f6 33 ♖b1 ♗a4 34 ♘f4 g6 35 ♖e2 ♗c1 36 ♕e4**

Diagram

36...♔f8? 36...♖e8 **37 b5 axb5 38 ♕b4 ♖c5?** 38...♗xf4 **39 ♖xc1?** Zeitnot 39 ♘xg6+ fxg6 40 ♖xc1 ♖xc1 41 ♖e6 ♕g5 42 ♕xd6+ ♔g7 43 ♕d7+ ♔f8 44 ♕d6+ = **♖xc1 40 ♘xg6+!**

Kg7! 41 Ne7 R8c4? 41...Rd8 **42 Bxc4 Rxc4 43 Qxd6!** 43 Qb1? b4 44 Nf5+ Kh8 45 Ne3 Qe5 46 Qe1 Rc3 47 Nd1 Rc2 **Rc3!** 43...Qxd6 44 Nf5+ Kf8 45 Nxd6 +−; 43...Bd1? 44 Qxf6+ Kxf6 45 Ng8+ Kg7 46 Rd2 Bxf3+ 47 Kxf3 Kxg8 48 d6 Rc8 49 Ke4; 46...Ba4 47 d6 b4 48 Nxh6! Bd7 49 Nf5+! **44 f4 Qxd6 45 Nf5+ Kg6 46 Nxd6 Bb3 47 f5+ Kg7 48 Ne8+ Kf8 49 Nf6 Kg7 50 Nh5+ Kf8 51 Nf4 Bc4 52 Re5** 52 Rd2 b4 53 d6 Ke8 54 Nd5 Bxd5+ 55 Rxd5; 52...Ke8! 53 d6 Kd7 54 Nd5? Rd3! **Ra3 53 d6 Ra2+ 54 Kf3 Rd2 55 Re7 Rxd6 56 Rxb7 Ra6 57 Rb6 Rxa5 58 Rxh6 b4 59 Rc6 Bb5 60 Rc1 b3 61 Rb1 Bc4 62 Ke4 Ra2 63 Kd4 Rc2 64 Nd3 Bxd3 65 Kxd3 Rxh2 66 Rxb3 Kg7 67 Ke4 Ra2 68 Kf4 Ra4+ 69 Kg5 Ra5 70 g4 Rc5 71 Kh5 Ra5 72 Rf3 Rb5 73 g5 Rb1 74 f6+ Kh7 75 Rh3 Rg1 76 Rh2 Rg3 77 Rh1 Rg2 78 Ra1 Rh2+ 79 Kg4 Kg6 80 Ra8 Rg2+ ½-½**

1 c4 Nf6

28 Velikov-Savon Kiev 78

1 c4 Nf6 2 Nc3 d5 3 cxd5 Nxd5 4 Nf3 4 g3 **Nxc3** 4...g6 5 e4 Nxc3 6 dxc3! += **5 bxc3 g6 6 g3 Bg7 7 Bg2 0-0 8 0-0 c5 9 Qa4** 9 Rb1 **Bd7 10 Qh4 Bc6= 11 Rb1 e6!** 11...Nd7 12 d4 += **12 Qxd8 Rxd8 13 Bb2** 13 Ba3?! Nd7 **b5! 14 d3 Nd7 15 Nd2! Rac8 16 Ba1 a6** 16...a5!? 17 c4 b4 **17 c4 Bxa1 18 Rxa1 Nb6** 18...b4 19 a3!? **19 Rfc1 Na4** 19... Bxg2!? Δ Kf8 **20 a3 Rc7 21 Nb3 Bxg2 22 Kxg2 Kf8 23 Rc2 Ke7 24 Na5! Rb8 25 Rb1 Rcc8 26 Rb3 Kd6 27 Rc1 Kc7 28 cxb5 Rxb5 29 Rxb5 axb5 30 Rb1 Rb8 31 Kf3 Kb6 32 Nc4+ Ka6 33 Nd6= f6 34 Ke3 Nc3 35 Rc1** 35 Rb3 **Nd5+ 36 Kd2 Kb6 37 Nxb5** 37 Rb1 Kc6 =+ **Kxb5 38 Rb1+ Nb4 39 Kc3 Ra8 ½-½** 40 axb4?! Ra3+ Δ cxb4 =+; 40 Rb3 Ra4 41 d4? cxd4+ 42 Kxd4 Rxa3 −+; 41 axb4

29 Murashko-Semeniuk USSR 78

1 c4 Nf6 2 Nc3 d5 3 cxd5 Nxd5 4 g3 e5!? 4...g6 **5 Bg2 Nb6** 5...Ne7 6 Nf3 Nbc6 7 b4!? a6 8 0-0 g6 9 a4 Bg7 10 Ba3 0-0 11 b5 += Zwaig-Romanishin, Hastings 76/77 **6 Nf3 Nc6 7 0-0 Be7 8 d3** 8 a4?! a5 9 Nb5 0-0 10 d4 exd4 11 Nfxd4 Nxd4 12 Qxd4 Qxd4 18 Nxd4 c6 =+ Demeny-Florian, Hungary 76 **0-0 9 Be3 f5** 9... Be6!? **10 b4!?** 10 Qc1 h6 11 Rd1 Bf6 12 Bc5 Rf7 13 e3 += Panno-Riemsdijk, Fortaleza 75; 10...Kh8 11 Rd1 Bf6 12 d4! exd4 13 Nxd4 Nxd4 14 Bxd4 Bxd4 15 e3 += Pribyl-Kozlov, Stary Smokovec 76 **Bf6 11 Bc5** 11 Qb3+!? Kh8 12 Rac1 += **Re8 12 e4?! Kh8 13 Rc1 Be6∝ 14 a3 Qd7 15 b5 Nd4 16 Nxd4 exd4 17 exf5** 17 Bxb6?! axb6 Δ Rxa3 **dxc3! 18 fxe6 Qxb5 19 Bb4 Na4∓ 20 Rb1** 20 Bxb7 c5! 21 Bxa8 cxb4 −+ **c6 21 Re1 Nb2 22 Qc2 Nxd3 23 Re4 Nxb4! 24 Rbxb4 Qf5 25 Rxb7 Rxe6 26 Qe2 Rxe4 27 Bxe4 Qe5 28 Qc4 Qd6! −+ 29 Rb1 Qxa3 30 Qxc6 Rf8 31 Rd1 Qb4 32**

♜d5? ♛xe4 0-1 33 ♖d8♕e1+ −+ **Gufeld**

30 Karpov-Korchnoi (30) 78

1 c4 ♞f6 2 ♞c3 d5 3 cxd5 ♞xd5 4 g3 g6 5 ♝g2 ♞xc3 6 bxc3 ♝g7 7 ♞f3 0-0 8 0-0 c5 9 ♜b1 ♞c6 10 ♛a4 ♞a5 11 d3 b6 11...♗xc3 12 ♗h6 **12 ♛h4 ♝b7 13 ♝h6 ♝xh6 14 ♛xh6 ♝xf3 15 ♝xf3 ♜c8 16 ♝g2 ♛d7 17 ♜ae1 b5 18 ♜b1 ♜b8 19 ♛e3 ♛d6 20 ♜fd1 a6 21 ♜d2 ♜fc8 22 ♜db2 ♞c6 23 ♛d2** 23 a4? b5 **♞e5 24 ♛f4 ♞d7 25 ♛xd6 exd6 26 ♝h3 ♜d8 27 a4 bxa4 28 ♝xd7 ♜xb2 29 ♜xb2 ♜xd7 30 ♜a2** 30 ♖b8+ ♔g7 31 ♖a8 ♖b7 32 ♖xa6 ♖b3 33 c4 a3 34 ♔g2 ♖b2 **♚f8 31 ♜xa4 ♜a7 32 ♚f1 ♚e7 33 ♚e1 ♚d7 34 ♚d2 h5 35 ♚c2 ♜a8 36 ♜c4 ♚e6 37 h4 ♜b8 38 ♜e4+ ♚d7 39 ♜a4 ♜a8 40 ♜f4 ♚e6 41 ♜c4 ♜a7 ½-½**

31 Korchnoi-Karpov (29) 78

1 c4 ♞f6 2 ♞c3 e6 3 e4 c5 4 e5 ♞g8 5 d4 5 ♘f3 ♘c6 6 d4 cxd4 7 ♘xd4 ♘xe5 Keene-Furman, Bad Lauterberg 77 **cxd4 6 ♛xd4 ♞c6 7 ♛e4 d6 8 ♞f3 dxe5 9 ♞xe5 ♞f6** 9...♗d7 **10 ♞xc6 ♛b6 11 ♛f3 bxc6 12 ♝e2 ♝b7 13 0-0 c5 14 ♛h3** 14 ♕e3 Δ b3, ♗b2 **♝e7 15 ♝f3 0-0 16 b3 ♜fd8 17 ♝e3 ♝c6 18 ♞a4 ♛c7 19 ♝xc6 ♛xc6 20 ♜ad1 ♜ac8 21 ♛g3 ♝d6 22 ♛h4 ♝e7 23 f3 ♚f8 24 ♛f2 ♜xd1 25 ♜xd1 ♛c7 26 ♛g3 ♛xg3 27 hxg3 h5 28 ♚f2 ♚e8 29 ♚e2 g6 30 ♞c3 a6 31 ♞a4 ♜c6 32 ♜h1 ♝d6 33 ♝f2 ♞d7 34 g4!? hxg4 35 ♜h8+ ♚e7 36 fxg4** 36 ♗h4+ g5! **g5 37 ♝e3 f6 38 ♞c3 ♚f7 39 ♜h7+ ♚e8 40 ♞e4 ♝e7 41 ♜h6**

Diagram

41...♚f7 41...a5 42 ♖h8+ ♘f8 43 ♗d2 ♖a6 44 ♗c3 ♔f7 45 ♖h6 ♔g7? 46 ♖xf6! ♗xf6 47 ♗xf6+ ♔g6 48 ♘xc5; 45...♘d7! 46 ♖h7+ ♔e8 47 ♖h8+ ♔f7= **42 ♜h7+ ♚f8 43 ♜h8+ ♚f7 44 ♝d2 ♞f8** 44...♘e5 45 ♘f2 ♖d6? 46 ♗c3 ♘c6 47 ♘e4 ♘d4+ 48 ♔d3 ♖d7 49 ♘xc5 **45 ♜h1 ♚g6 46 ♜d1 f5? 47 ♞f2 ♝d6 48 ♝c3 ♞d7 49 gxf5+ exf5 50 g4! ♞b6** 50...♘e5? 51 ♖xd6+; 50...♘f6 51 ♗xf6 ♔xf6 52 ♖d5; 50...fxg4 51 ♘e4 **51 ♚f3** 51 ♗a5 **♝e7 52 ♝a5 ♜f6 53 ♚g2 fxg4 54 ♞xg4 ♜e6 55 ♚f3 ♝f6 56 ♞xf6 ♜xf6+ 57 ♚g4! ♞c8 58 ♝d8! ♜f4+** 58...♖d6 59 ♖xd6+ ♘xd6 60 ♗xg5 +− ♔f7 61 ♗e3 ♘b7 62 ♔f5 **59 ♚g3 ♜f5** 59...♖d4 60 ♖xd4 cxd4 61 ♔g4 ♘d6 62 ♗xg5 ♘e4 63 ♗f4 **60 a4 ♚f7 61 ♜d3 ♜e5 62 ♚g4 ♚g6** 62...♔e6 63 ♗xg5 ♘e7 64 ♗f4 **63 a5 ♜e4+ 64 ♚f3 ♜f4+** 64...♔f5 65 ♗xg5 ♘a7 66 ♗d2 ♘c6 67 ♗c3 ♘d4+ 68 ♗xd4 cxd4 69 b4 ♖h4; 66 ♖d7! +−; 64...♖e5 65 ♖d7 Δ ♖c7 **65 ♚e3 ♜h4 66 ♜d5 ♜h3+ 67 ♚d2!** 67 ♔e4?! **♜xb3 68 ♜xc5 ♜b8** 68...♘d6? 69 ♖c6 **69 ♜c6+ ♚f5 70 ♜xa6 g4 71 ♜f6+ ♚e4 72 ♝c7!** Δ ♖f4 mate **♜b2+ 73 ♚c3 ♜b7 74 ♝h2 ♜h7 75 ♝b8 ♜b7 76 ♝g3 ♜b1 77 ♜f4+! ♚e3 78 ♜f8 ♞e7 79 a6 1-0** 79...♘c6 80 a7 ♘xa7 81 ♗f2+ +−

32 Pytel-Tiller Gausdal 78
1 c4 Nf6 2 Nf3 e6 3 Nc3 Bb4 4 Qc2 c5 5 a3 Ba5 6 g3 Nc6 7 Bg2 0-0 8 0-0 d6 9 e3 e5 10 d4 exd4 11 exd4 Bg4 11...cxd4 12 Nb5 **12 dxc5 Bxf3 13 Bxf3 Nd4 14 Qd1 dxc5 15 Bg2!± Re8 16 Be3 Ne6 17 Nd5 Bb6 18 b4 Rc8 19 Rc1 cxb4 20 Nxb6 axb6 21 axb4 Qc7 22 Qf3 Rb8 23 Rfd1 Nd7 24 Qd5 Ne5 25 Qb5 Ng4 26 Bxb6 Qe5 27 Qxe5 Nxe5 28 f4 Nc6 29 b5 1-0 Pytel**

33 Ftacnik-Romanishin Kiev 78
1 Nf3 Nf6 2 c4 e6 3 Nc3 Bb4 4 Qc2 c5 4...0-0 5 a3 Bxc3 6 Qxc3 b6 7 g3 Bb7 8 Bg2 d5 Δ dxc4≈ **5 g3** 5 a3 Ba5 6 g3 Nc6 7 Bg2 0-0 8 0-0 Qe7 9 d3 d6 10 Rb1 += Tal-Polugaevsky, USSR 75 **Nc6 6 Bg2 0-0 7 0-0 Qe7 8 e3!** 8 Rd1 Bxc3!? 9 Qxc3 e5 10 d3 h6 11 b3= Vaganian-Romanishin, USSR 75; 8 d3 h6! 9 e4 d6 10 Nh4 Rb8 11 f4 Bd7∝ Hubner-Tal, Biel 76 **d6** 8...Bxc3 9 Qxc3 e5 10 b3 d6 11 Bb2 h6≈ Uhlmann-Balashov, Halle 76; 8...b6!? 9 b3 d6 10 Bb2 Bb7!? **9 b3 h6 10 Bb2 Bd7 11 a3 Ba5 12 d4 += cxd4 13 exd4 Bxc3 14 Bxc3 d5 15 b4 a5** 15...dxc4!? **16 b5 Nd8 17 a4** Δ c5 **dxc4 18 Bb2± Nd5** 18...Rc8 19 Ne5± **19 Ba3 Nb4 20 Qxc4** 20 Bxb4 Qxb4 21 Rab1 Qe7 22 Qxc4 += **Rc8 21 Qb3 e5!?** Δ Ne6 **22 Nxe5 Ne6** 22...Bxe6? 23 d5 **23 Rad1 b6 24 Bxb4 axb4 25 Nxd7 Qxd7 26 Qxb4 Rfd8 27 Bc6 Rxc6 28 bxc6 Qxc6**

Diagram

29 d5! +− Rxd5 30 Qe4 Rc5 31 Qxc6 Rxc6 32 Rc1 Rc5 33 Rxc5 Nxc5 34 Ra1 Kf8 35 f3 Ke7 36 Kf2 Kd6

37 Ke3 Kd5 38 g4 Ke6 39 Ra2 Ke5 40 h4 Ke6 41 f4 Kf6 42 Ra3 Ke6 43 Kd4 1-0 Gufeld

34 Pfleger-Timman IBM 78
1 c4 Nf6 2 Nc3 e6 3 Nf3 Bb4 4 g3 4 Qc2 c5 5 a3 Ba5 6 e3 d5 7 b3 Nc6 8 cxd5 Bxc3 9 Qxc3 Qxd5 10 Bb2 += Smejkal-Govedarica, Vrbas 77 **0-0 5 Bg2 d5 6 cxd5 exd5 7 a3 Be7 8 d4 c6 9 0-0 Bf5= 10 h3 Ne4 11 Ne5 Nd7! 12 Nd3 Re8 13 g4 Bg6 14 Nf4 Bd6 15 Nxg6 hxg6 16 Nxe4 dxe4 17 Qb3 Nb6 18 f4 Qe7**

19 f5!? gxf5 20 Bf4 20 Rxf5 Nd5∓ **Rad8! 21 gxf5** 21 Bxd6 Rxd6 Δ Rxd4; 21 e3 fxg4 22 Rf4 gxh3 23 Rxe4 Re6 −+; 21 Rad1 fxg4 **Bxf4 22 Rxf4 Rxd4 23 f6 Qc5 24 Kh1 e3 25 Rxd4** 25 Rf3 Qc4∓ **Qxd4 26 fxg7 Qc4 27 Qxc4** 27 Qd1 Qh4 Δ

♘d5-f4, ♖d8, ♕f2 **♞xc4 28 ♜d1 ♞d2 29 ♜c1 ♚xg7 30 ♚h2 ♚f6 31 ♜c3 ♚f5 32 b4 ♜e7 33 a4 ♚f4 34 b5 cxb5 35 axb5 f5 36 ♜a3 b6 37 ♝c6 ♜g7 38 ♜a1 ♚e5 39 h4 f4 40 ♚h3 ♞b3 41 ♜a2 0-1** 41...♘d4 −+ **Taulbut**

Queen's Pawn

35 Nikolaevsky-Bronstein USSR 78
1 d4 ♞f6 2 ♞f3 e6 2...b6 **3 g3** 3 ♗g5 **b5!? 4 ♝g2 ♝b7 5 c3** 5 a4 a6?! 6 axb5 axb5 7 ♖xa8 ♗xa8 8 ♕d3 ♗c6 9 ♘bd2 +=; 5...b4; 5 0-0 c5 6 ♗g5! ♗e7 7 c3 ♘a6 8 e3 ♖b8 9 ♘bd2 0-0 10 a3 ♘e4 Petrosian-Portisch, Varese 76 **♝e7 6 a4 b4 7 a5 0-0 8 0-0 c5 9 cxb4 cxb4 10 ♞bd2 d5** 10...a6 11 ♘c4 ♘c6 12 ♘fe5 ♖c8 13 ♘b6 ♖c7 14 ♘xc6 ♗xc6 15 ♗f4 d6 16 ♗xd6 ♖xd6 17 ♕a4± **11 ♞e5 ♞fd7 12 ♞d3! ♝a6 13 ♛a4 ♛c7 14 ♜e1! += ♛b7** 14...♘c6 15 ♘b3 ♕b7 16 ♘bc5 +=

15 e4! ♝xd3 16 exd5 ♝b5! 17 ♛b3 ♞f6! 18 d6 ♝c6 18...♘c6 19 a6 ♕d7 20 dxe7 ♕xe7 21 ♘f3 ♖ad8 22 ♗e3 ♘d5 23 ♗g5 f6 24 ♗h3± **19 a6 ♛d7** 19...♘xa6 20 dxe7 ♖fe8 21 ♘c4± **20 dxe7 ♜c8?!** 20...♖e8 **21 ♞f3 ♝d5 22 ♛xb4 ♞c6 23 ♛a4** 23 ♕b7? ♕e8! 24 ♘e5 ♘xd4 25 ♗xd5 ♘xd5 =+ **♛xe7 24 ♝f4 ♞d7 25 ♜ec1! ♞b6 26 ♛a3 ♛d8 27 ♜c5 h6 28 h4 ♞c4 29 ♛c3 ♝xf3 30 ♛xc4! ♞xd4 31 ♝c7** 31 ♗xf3 ♘xf3+ 32 ♔g2 e5!∝ **♛d7 32 ♝xf3 ♞xf3+ 33 ♚g2 ♞d2! 34 ♛c2** 34 ♖d1? ♕xc7!∓ **♞b3!** 34...♖xc7 35 ♖xc7 ♕d5+ 36 ♔h3 +− **35 ♛xb3 ♜xc7 36 ♜xc7 ♛xc7 37 ♛b7 ♜c8 38 ♜d1** 38 b4! Δ b5± **♛c6+ 39 ♚g1 ♜c7 40 ♜d8+?** Zeitnot 40 ♕b8+ ♔h7 41 b4±; 40...♖c8 41 ♖d8+ ♖xd8 42 ♕xd8+ ♔h7 43 ♕d3+ f5 44 b4 ♕c1+ 45 ♕f1 += **♚h7 41 ♛b4 ♛xa6 42 ♛e4+ f5 43 ♛a8 ♜c1+ 44 ♚g2 ♛c6+ 45 ♛xc6 ♜xc6 46 ♜d7 a6 47 ♜b7 ♚g6 =+ 48 b4! e5 49 b5 axb5 50 ♜xb5 e4 51 ♜e5 ♜c2 52 ♚g1 ♚f6 53 ♜e8 g5 54 hxg5+ ♚xg5 55 ♜g8+ ♚f6 56 ♜f8+ ♚g6 57 ♜e8 ♜c6 58 g4!= fxg4 59 ♜xe4 ♚f5 60 ♜a4 ♜c5 61 ♚g2 h5 62 ♜a8 h4 63 ♜f8+ ♚g5 64 f4+! gxf3+** 64...♔g6 65 ♖g8+ = **65 ♚xf3 ♜f5+ 66 ♜xf5+ ♚xf5 ½-½ Gufeld**

36 Browne-Miles Tillburg 78
1 c4 b6 2 d4 e6 3 e4 ♝b7 4 ♝d3! 4 d5!? **f5!?** 4...♘c6?! 5 ♘f3 ♘b4 6 ♘c3± **5 exf5!!** 5 d5? fxe4 6 ♗xe4 ♕h4 7 ♕e2 ♘f6 8 ♗f3 ♗b4+ 9 ♗d2 ♗xd2+ 10 ♘xd2 0-0 11 dxe6 ♘c6!∓; 5 ♕e2?!; 5 ♘c3?! **♝xg2** 5...♗b4+!? 6 ♔f1! ♘f6 7 ♗g5! 0-0 8 ♘f3 +=; 6 ♘c3? ♗xg2 7 ♕h5+ ♔f8! **6 ♛h5+ g6** 6...♔e7 7 ♕g5+ +− **7 fxg6 ♝g7** 7...♘f6 8 g7+ ♘xh5 9 gxh8♕ ♗xh1 10 ♕xh7 +− **8 gxh7+ ♚f8 9 ♞e2!!** 9 hxg8♕+? ♔xg8 10 ♕g4 ♗xh1 11 ♗g5 ♕e8∓; 10 ♕g6 ♗xh1 11 ♗g5 ♕f8 12 ♘e2 ♕f7∓; 9 ♘f3? ♘f6 10 ♕h4 ♗xh1 11 ♘e5 d6! 12 ♘g6+ ♔f7 =+ **♝xh1 10 ♝g5! ♞f6** 10...♗f6?! **11 ♛h4 ♞c6** 11...d6? 12 ♘f4 +− **12 ♞f4!** 12 ♘d2± **♚f7?** 12...♘xd4!? 13 ♘g6+ ♔e8 14 ♕xd4 ♖xh7 15 ♘e5!

♖h3! 16 ♗g6+ ♔f8 17 ♘c3! d6 18 0-0-0±; 17...c5 18 ♕d6+ ♕e7?? 19 ♘xd7+ +−; 12...e5! 13 ♘g6+ ♔f7 14 dxe5 ♖e8! 15 f4!! d6 16 ♘c3 dxe5 17 0-0-0± **13 ♝g6+ ♚e7 14 ♞h5 ♛f8 15 ♞d2 +− e5** 15...d5 16 0-0-0 ♗e4 17 ♘xe4 dxe4 18 ♘xg7! ♕xg7 19 ♗xe4 +−; 15...♘b8 16 0-0-0 ♗b7 17 ♖e1 +−; 17 d5 +− **16 0-0-0 ♞xd4 17 ♜xh1 ♞e6 18 f4! d6 19 ♞e4 ♞xg5 20 ♛xg5 ♝h6 21 ♛h4! ♝g7 22 fxe5 dxe5 23 ♜f1 ♚d7 24 ♞exf6+ ♝xf6 25 ♞xf6+ ♚c8 26 ♝e4! c6 27 ♛h3+ ♚b7 28 ♝xc6+! 1-0** 28...♔xc6 29 ♕d7+ ♔c5 30 ♕d5+ ♔b4 31 ♕b5 mate; 28...♔a6 29 ♗b5+ ♔a5 30 a3! **Browne**

37 Hardicsay-Malich Budapest 78

1 d4 ♞f6 2 ♞f3 d6 3 c4 ♞bd7 4 ♞c3 e5 5 ♝g5 5 e4 ♗e7 6 ♗e2 0-0 7 0-0 c6 8 ♗e3 a6 9 ♕c2 ♕c7 10 b4± Uhlmann-Espig, DDR 77 **♝e7 6 e3** 6 ♕c2 0-0 7 ♖d1!? **0-0** 6...♘g8 7 ♗xe7 ♘xe7 8 ♗d3 += **7 ♝e2** 7 ♕c2 c6 8 ♗e2 ♘e8 9 ♗xe7 ♕xe7 10 0-0 f5 11 b4 e4 12 ♘d2 ♘df6 13 ♖ab1 d5 14 b5± Knezevic-Ostojic, Jugoslavia 78 **c6 8 0-0 ♞e8 9 ♝xe7 ♛xe7 10 b4 ♞c7** 10...f5!? **11 ♜e1 ♞f6 12 c5!?** 12 ♖b1 **dxc5!** 12...e4 13 cxd6 ♕xd6 14 ♘d2 ♗f5 15 ♕b3 Δ b5 += **13 bxc5?!** 13 dxe5 ♘fd7; 13 dxc5 ♘cd5 14 ♘xd5 ♘xd5 15 a3 ♘c3 16 ♕d6≈; 15...♖d8 16 ♕b3 ♗g4= **exd4 14 exd4 ♛d8?!** 14...♗g4!?= **15 ♛b3 ♜b8 16 h3 ♝e6 17 ♝c4 ♞fd5** 17...♗xc4 18 ♕xc4 ♘fd5= **18 ♞e4! ♞f4 19 ♝xe6 ♞cxe6 20 ♜ad1 b6! 21 ♛e3 ♞d5 22 ♛a3 ♛c7 23 ♞d6 bxc5 24 dxc5 ♞b4 25 ♜e4! a5 26 ♛e3 ♞d5 27 ♜xd5! cxd5 28 ♜xe6 fxe6 29 ♛xe6+ ♚h8 30 ♞e5 d4=** 30...h6 31 ♘g6+ ♔h7 32 ♘xf8+ ♖xf8 33 ♕xd5=; 30...g6 31 ♕xd5! Δ 32 ♘ef7+ ♔g7?? 33 ♕d4+ ♔g8 34 ♕h8 mate **31 ♞ef7+ ♜xf7 32 ♞xf7+ ♚g8 33 ♞g5+ ♚h8 34 ♞f7+ ♚g8 ½-½ Malich**

38 Speelman-Larsen
Lone Pine 78

1 e4 c6 2 c4 e5 2...e6; 2...d5 **3 ♞f3 d6 4 d4 ♝g4!?** 4...♘d7 **5 ♝e2** 5 dxe5? ♗xf3! **♞d7 6 ♞c3 ♝e7 7 0-0 ♞gf6** 7...♗xf3!? 8 ♗xf3 ♗g5 9 ♗g4 += **8 ♜b1 0-0** 8...a5!? **9 ♜e1 ♜e8** 9...♗h5!? **10 ♝e3 ♝h5 11 ♞d2 ♝g6!?** 11...♗xe2 12 ♕xe2 += **12 d5** 12 f4?! exf4 13 ♗xf4 ♗f8 14 ♗f3 c5; 14...d5!? **a6 13 b4 h5!? 14 a4 h4?! 15 h3 ♛c7 16 ♜b3 a5?!** 16...♖b8 17 a5 c5; 17 ♕b1 ♘h5!? **17 b5 cxd5?!** 17...c5 18 ♗g5!? ♘h7? 19 ♗xe7 ♖xe7 20 ♘f3; 18...♕d8 19 ♗xh4; 17...c5 18 b6!?; 17...c6!?; 17...♘e5!? **18 ♞xd5! ♞xd5 19 cxd5 ♜ec8? 20 ♝g4! +−**

20...♜f8 21 ♛c1 ♞c5 21...♖ac8 22 ♕xc7 ♖xc7 23 b6 +−; 21...♕d8 +− **22 ♝xc5 dxc5 23 b6** 23 ♘c4 b6! **♛d8 24 ♞c4 +− ♝xe4 25 ♜xe4 f5 26 ♝xf5** 26 d6 ♗g5 27 ♕d1 fxe5 28 ♕d5+! ♔h8 29 ♘xe5 +− **♜xf5 27 d6 ♝f6 28 ♛d1! ♛d7 29 ♛g4 ♜d8** 29...♕xa4 30 ♖a3 ♕d7 31 ♘e3 **30 ♜b5 ♛c8 31 ♜xa5 ♜f4 32 ♛xc8 ♜xc8**

33 ♜xf4 exf4 34 ♜a7 ♜e8 34...♖b8 35 a5 Δ ♖xb7! **35 ♜xb7 ♚h1 36 ♜e7! 1-0** 36...♗xe7 37 dxe7 ♖xe7 38 a5 +– **Speelman**

39 Platonov-Gofstein USSR 78

1 d4 ♞f6 2 ♞f3 e6 3 ♝g5 c5 3...d5 **4 e3 ♛b6** 4...b6 **5 ♝xf6** 5 ♘bd2! ♕xb2 6 ♗d3 += **gxf6** 5...♕xb2 6 ♗xg7 ♗xg7 7 ♘bd2∞ **6 ♛c1 d5 7 c3 ♞c6 8 ♞bd2 ♝d7 9 ♝e2 ♜c8** 9...0-0-0!? **10 0-0 ♝e7** 10...cxd4 **11 dxc5 ♛xc5 12 e4!± dxe4 13 ♞xe4 ♛d5 14 ♛e3** 14 ♘g3!± **f5 15 ♞ed2?** 15 ♘g3 **e5?** 15...♕c5!? 16 ♕h6 ♗f8= **16 ♝c4 ♛d6**

17 ♝xf7+ 17 ♖ad1 **♚xf7 18 ♞c4 ♛e6 19 ♞fxe5+ ♚g7 20 ♛g3+ ♚f8 21 ♜fe1 ♝e8 22 ♛h3** 22 ♘xc6 ♕xc6 23 ♖xe7 ♖g8!!∓ **♛f6 23 ♜e3 ♞xe5 24 ♞xe5 ♜c7 25 ♜ae1** 25 ♖f3 ♗g6 **♝g6 26 ♛h6+** 26 ♘d3!?∞ **♚g8 27 ♜g3?** 27 ♘d3! ♕g5 28 ♕h3∞ **♝f8∓ 28 ♛f4 ♝d6 29 h4? ♜e7 –+ 30 ♜ge3 ♚g7 31 ♛d4 ♜he8** 31...f4! –+ **32 f4 b6** Zeitnot **33 b4** Zeitnot **♝h5 34 g3 ♝g4 35 ♚h2 h5 36 a3 ♝xe5 37 fxe5 ♛h6 0-1 Gufeld**

40 Pribyl-Hazai Varna 78

1 d4 ♞f6 2 ♝g5!? c5 3 d5 ♛b6 4 ♞c3 ♛xb2 5 ♝d2! ♛b6 6 e4 d6 7 f4 e5 7...g6 **8 fxe5 dxe5 9 ♞f3 ♝d6 10 ♝c4 ♛d8 11 0-0 ♝g4 12 ♛e1 ♞bd7?** 12...♗xf3 **13 ♞h4!± ♞b6 14 ♝b5+ ♚f8** 14...♗d7 15 ♘f5 **15 ♛g3 ♝c8**

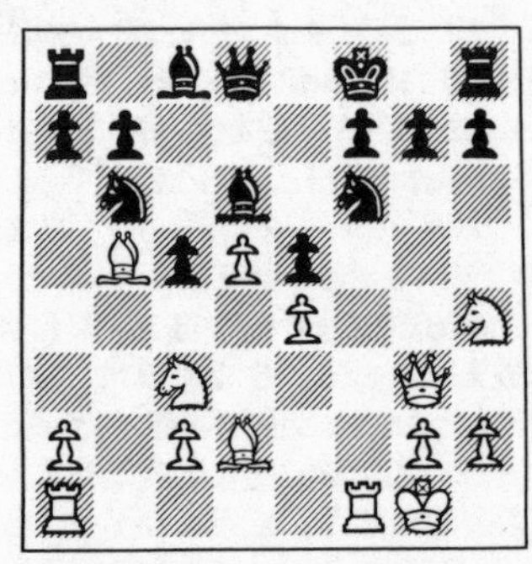

16 ♜xf6! ♝e7 16...♕xf6 17 ♗g5; 16...gxf6 17 ♗h6+ ♔e7 18 ♗g7 ♖g8 19 ♖f1 **17 ♜h6!! a6 18 ♜f1 ♝xh4** 18...axb5 19 ♕g6!! **19 ♜xh4 axb5 20 ♛xe5! ♞c4 21 ♛f4 ♛e7 22 ♝e1 g5 23 ♛f3 ♜a6 24 ♜h5 ♜g6 25 ♞xb5 ♞e5 26 ♛c3 ♚g7 27 h4 ♝g4 28 ♜xg5 f6 29 ♜xg6+ hxg6 30 ♝g3 ♝e2 31 ♜b1 ♞c4 32 ♞c7 ♛xe4 33 ♞e6+ 1-0 Pytel**

41 Shereshevsky-Gufeld USSR 78

1 d4 ♞f6 2 ♝g5 ♞e4 3 ♝h4 c5 4 f3 ♞f6! N 4...g5 5 fxe4 gxh4 6 e3∞ **5 dxc5** 5 d5 ♕b6! Δ ♕b4+ **e6 6 ♝f2 ♛c7 7 ♞c3 ♝xc5 8 ♝xc5 ♛xc5 9 ♛d2** 9 e4 ♕b4!? **d5 10 0-0-0 ♞c6 11 e4** 11 e3!? 0-0 12 f4 **dxe4 12 ♞xe4 ♞xe4 13 fxe4 0-0 14 ♞f3 e5 =+ 15 ♛d6** 15 ♗d3 **♛e3+ 16 ♚b1 ♝e6** 16...♕xe4?! 17 ♖e1 **17 ♝d3 h6 18 ♛a3** 18 ♘xe5? ♖fd8 19 ♕c7 ♕f4 –+ **♜ac8 19 ♜he1 ♛b6 20 b3 ♜fd8 21 ♛b2 ♛c5∓ 22 ♝e2 a6 23 ♜xd8+ ♜xd8 24 ♜d1? ♜xd1+ 25 ♝xd1 ♛e3 –+ 26 ♛a3** 26 ♘xe5 ♕d2 –+ **♛xe4 27 ♛d6 ♛e3 28 ♚b2 g6** 28...e4 29 ♘d2 ♕e1 30 ♘b1! **29 ♛d2** 29 ♕c7 e4 30

♕xb7 exf3 31 ♕xc6 f2 32 ♕xa6 ♕d4+ 33 ♔c1 ♗c4 −+ **♛xd2 30 ♞xd2 f5 31 c4 ♚f7 32 ♚c3 ♚f6 33 b4 e4 34 ♞b3** 34 b5 axb5 35 cxb5 ♘a5 −+ **♚e5 35 ♞c5 ♝c8 36 b5 axb5 37 cxb5 ♞d4 38 b6 ♚d5 39 ♞b3 ♞xb3 40 ♝xb3+ ♚c5 41 ♝f7 g5 42 ♝g6 e3 0-1 Gufeld**

42 Pribyl-Peev Decin 78

1 d4 ♞f6 2 ♝g5 ♞e4 3 ♝h4 c5 4 f3 g5 5 fxe4 gxh4 6 e3 e6 6...♕b6 7 ♘d2!? cxd4 8 exd4 ♕xd4 9 ♕h5 ♕e3+?! 10 ♗e2 ♘c6 11 0-0-0 ♕h6 12 ♖f1 ♕xh5 13 ♗xh5 ♘e5 14 ♘gf3 ♘g6 15 ♘g5 f6 16 ♘xh7 ♔f7 17 ♗xg6+ ♔xg6 18 ♘xf8+± Pribyl-Peev, Varna 78; 6...♗h6 **7 ♞c3** 7 ♘f3; 7 ♘d2! **♝h6 8 ♛h5 ♝xe3 9 ♛xc5 a6!** N 9...d6 10 ♗b5+ ♔f8∝ Gusev-Timoshenko, USSR 78 **10 e5!? d6! 11 exd6** 11 ♕xd6 ♕xd6∓ **♞d7 12 ♛b4?** 12 ♕h5! ♗xd4 13 ♘f3 ♗xc3+ 14 bxc3 ♕f6 15 0-0-0!± **♛f6!? 13 ♞f3 h3! 14 ♞d1?! ♝h6! 15 ♞f2 hxg2 16 ♝xg2 ♜g8 17 ♚f1 b6! 18 ♞g5?** 18 d5 a5 19 ♕d4 ♗a6+ 20 ♘d3 e5 21 ♕e4 0-0-0 22 c4 ♕xd6∝ **a5! 19 ♛c3 ♝a6+ 20 ♚e1 ♛xg5! 0-1** 21 ♗xa8 ♕g1+ 22 ♖xg1 ♖xg1 mate **Pribyl/Pritchett**

43 Sahovic-Speelman
Lone Pine 78

1 d4 ♞f6 2 ♝g5 e6 3 ♞c3 3 e4 **h6 4 ♝h4 d5 5 ♞f3** 5 e4!? **c6** 5...♘bd7 **6 a3!?** 6 ♕d3 **♞bd7 7 ♛d3 ♝e7 8 h3!?** 8 e4!? g5!? 9 ♗g3 dxe4 10 ♘xe4 ♘xe4 11 ♕xe4 f5!? 12 ♕xe6 ♘f6 13 ♕b3!?; 12...♘f8 13 ♕e5!; 12...f4∝ **c5 9 e4 dxe4 10 ♞xe4 ♞xe4 11 ♛xe4** 11 ♗xe7? ♘xf2! **♝xh4 12 ♞xh4** 12 ♕xh4! ♕xh4 13 ♘xh4 cxd4 14 0-0-0 **0-0 13 ♞f3** 13 0-0-0?? ♕a5 Δ ♘f6 −+ **♛a5+! 14 c3 cxd4 15 ♛xd4 e5 16 ♛b4 ♛c7** 16...♕xb4?! 17 axb4 += **17 ♛e7 ♛b6 18 ♛b4 ♛c7 ½-½** 19 ♕e7=; 19 0-0-0!? ♘c5 20 ♖d5 b6 21 ♖xe5∝ **Speelman**

44 Djindjindashvili-Adorjan IBM 78

1 d4 ♞f6 2 c4 g6 3 d5 b5!? 4 cxb5 a6 5 bxa6 5 e3 ♗g7 6 ♘c3 0-0 7 ♘f3 ♗b7 8 ♗e2 axb5 9 ♗xb5 ♘xd5 10 ♘xd5 ♗xd5 11 ♕xd5 c6 12 ♗xc6 ♘xc6 13 0-0 ♕c7∓ Spassov-Ribli, Camaguey 74 **c6 6 dxc6 ♞xc6∝ 7 e3 ♝g7 8 ♞f3 0-0 9 ♝e2** 9 ♘c3 ♕a5 Δ ♘e4 **♝xa6 10 ♝xa6 ♛a5+ 11 ♞c3** 11 ♗d2 ♕xa6∓ **♞e4! 12 0-0 ♞xc3 13 bxc3 ♜xa6 14 ♝d2** 14 ♕xd7 ♖d8 Δ ♕xc3 **♜fa8 15 ♛c2 ♛d5 16 ♜fb1 ♜xa2 17 c4 ♛a5! 18 ♜xa2** 18 ♗xa5? ♖xc2 −+ **♛xa2 19 ♛xa2 ♜xa2 20 ♚f1 g5! 21 ♝e1 g4 22 ♞d4** 22 ♘d2 f5 Δ ♘e5 **♝xd4 23 exd4 ♜c2 24 ♜b7 ♜xc4 25 ♜xd7 ♜xd4 26 ♜xd4** 26 ♖c7 (Δ ♗c3) ♖d6 −+ **♞xd4 27 ♝c3 ♞f5 −+ 28 h3?! g3 29 ♚e2 gxf2 30 ♚xf2 f6 31 ♚f3 ♚f7 32 g4 ♞d6 33 ♝b4 ♚e6 34 ♚f4 ♚d5 35 g5 e5+! 36 ♚g4 f5+ 37 ♚h5 ♞f7 38 g6 hxg6+ 39 ♚xg6 f4 40 h4 f3??** 40...e4! 41 ♔xf7 f3 42 ♗e1 e3 −+; 41 ♗e1 e3 −+ Δ f3, f2 **41 ♝e1 e4 42 ♝f2 ♞e5+ 43 ♚f5 ♞d3 44 ♝e3 f2 45 ♝xf2 ♞xf2 46 h5 e3 47 h6 e2 48 h7 e1♛ 49 h8♛**

49...♛e4+ 50 ♚g5 ♛g2+!? 50...♕g4+!? 51 ♔h6 ♕h4+ 52 ♔g7 ♕g5+ 53 ♔h7 ♕f5+ 54 ♔g7 ♘e4 Δ ♘d6 **51 ♚f4!** 51 ♔h6 ♘g4+ −+; 51 ♔f6 ♘e4+ −+ **♞h3+ 52 ♚e3 ♛f2+ 53 ♚d3 ♞f4+ 54 ♚c3 ♞e2+** 54...♕e3+!? 55 ♔c2 ♕d3+ 56 ♔b2 ♕d2+ ∞ **55 ♚d3 ♞c1+ 56 ♚c3 ♛c5+ 57 ♚d2 ♞b3+ 58 ♚d3 ♛c4+ 59 ♚e3 ♛c1+ 60 ♚f2 ♛f4+ 61 ♚g2 ♞d4 62 ♛a8+ ♚c4 63 ♛a4+ ♚d3 64 ♛a3+ ♚d2 65 ♛b4+ ♚e3 66 ♛a3+ ♚e2 67 ♛b2+ ♚d1 68 ♛b1+ ♚d2 69 ♛b4+ ♚e3 70 ♛a3+ ♞b3 ½-½ Taulbut**

45 Kagan-Kasparov USSR 78

1 d4 ♞f6 2 ♞f3 g6 3 ♝f4 d6 4 e3?! 4 h3 **♞h5! 5 ♝g5 h6 6 ♝h4 g5 7 ♞fd2 ♞g7 8 ♝g3 ♞f5 9 ♝e2 ♞d7 10 c3 ♝g7 11 ♞a3 e6 12 ♞c2 0-0 13 e4 ♞xg3 14 hxg3 c5 15 ♞e3** 15 0-0 b6 =+ **cxd4 16 cxd4 ♝xd4 17 ♞dc4** 17 ♘g4 ♘f6 18 ♘xh6+ ♔g7 19 ♘c4 e5∓ **♝g7** 17...♗xe3?! 18 ♘xe3 ♘f6 19 ♖xh6 ♘xe4 20 ♕d4 ♕a5+ 21 b4 ♕e5 22 ♕xe5 dxe5 23 ♖c1= **18 ♞g4 ♞f6** 18...b5?! 19 ♘xd6 ♗xb2 20 ♘xh6+ ♔g7 21 ♘hf5+ exf5 22 ♘xf5+ ♔g8 23 ♘h6+ = **19 ♞xh6+ ♝xh6 20 ♜xh6 ♚g7 21 ♜h2?!** 21 ♖h1 **d5 22 e5!** 22 exd5 exd5 23 ♘e3 d4 24 ♘c2 ♖e8 25 ♕xd4 ♗g4∓ **dxc4!** 22...♘d7 23 ♕c2 ♖h8 24 ♖xh8 ♔xh8 25 0-0-0 dxc4 26 ♖h1+ ♔g8 27 ♕h7+ ♔f8 28 ♗h5 ♘xe5 29 ♕h8+ ♔e7 30 ♕xe5 ♕d5 31 ♕g7 ♕f5 32 ♕g8 Δ ♗xf7±; 24...♕xh8 25 ♘d6 +=; 22...♘e4 23 ♘d2= **23 exf6+ ♛xf6 24 ♛c2 ♜d8 25 ♛h7+ ♚f8 26 ♛h8+ ♚e7 27 ♛xf6+ ♚xf6 28 ♝xc4 ♝d7?!** 28...b5! 29 ♗e2 b4∓ **29 ♜d1 ♝c6** 29...♖ac8 30 ♗b3 a5∓; 30 ♗e2 =+ **30 f3 ♚e5 31 ♜h7 ♜xd1+ 32 ♚xd1 ♚d4?!** 32...f5 =+ **33 ♝b3 ♚e3 34 ♜xf7 ♜d8+ 35 ♚c1 ♜d2 36 ♝xe6 ♜xg2 37 ♝g4 ♜xg3 38 ♜f5?!** 38 ♖g7= **♜g2 39 b4?** 39 ♖xg5 ♗xf3 40 ♗xf3 ♖xg5 41 ♗xb7 ♖c5+ 42 ♔b1 ♔d2 43 a3 =+ **♚d4! 40 b5 ♝d5 41 a4** 41 ♖xg5 ♗xf3 42 ♗xf3 ♖xg5 43 ♗xb7 ♖c5+ 44 ♔d1 ♖xb5 −+ **♝b3! 42 ♜xg5 ♚c3 0-1 Kasparov**

46 Shereshevsky-Kasparov
USSR 78

1 d4 ♞f6 2 ♞f3 g6 3 ♝f4 ♝g7 4 e3 d6 5 ♝e2 0-0 6 0-0 c5 7 ♞c3!? 7 dxc5? ♘h5 =+; 7 c3 b6= **b6 8 h3 ♞a6!** 8...♗b7 9 d5 += **9 ♜e1** 9 d5 ♘c7 10 e4 b5= **♞c7 10 ♝f1 ♝b7 11 ♝h2 ♞d7 12 a4?!** 12 ♗e2 ♘f6= **♝xf3 13 ♛xf3 cxd4 14 exd4 ♝xd4 15 ♜ad1 ♞e6 16 ♝g3** 16 ♗c4? ♖c8 17 ♗b3 ♖c5∓ **♜c8 17 ♞d5 ♝xb2!** 17...♘f6 18 c3 ♘xd5 19 cxd4 ♘f6 20 d5∞; 17...♖xc2? 18 ♕e4± **18 c3 ♞e5! 19 ♝xe5 dxe5 20 ♜xe5** 20 ♘f6+?! exf6 21 ♖xd8 ♖fxd8∓ **♚g7** 20...♖c5? 21 ♘f6+ exf6 22 ♖xc5!±; 20...♔h8!? **21 ♞f4** 21 ♕e2 ♕d6∓ **♜xc3! 22 ♞xe6+** 22 ♕g4 ♕c8 23 ♖xe6 fxe6 24 ♘xe6+ ♔g8 25 ♘xf8 ♕xg4 =+ **fxe6 23 ♛e2 ♛c7 24 ♜xe6 ♝a3∓ 25 ♛d2 ♜f4! 26 ♜de1** 26 g3 ♖xf2! 27 ♔xf2 ♕xg3+ 28 ♔e2 ♗c5 −+; 27 ♕xf2 ♗c5 28 ♖d4 ♖c2 −+ **♜c2 27 ♛d1 ♛c5! 28 ♜xe7+ ♚h6 29 ♜7e2 ♜xf2 30 ♚h1 ♜fxe2 31 ♝xe2** 31 ♖xe2 ♖c1 32 ♕d2+ ♕g5 33 ♕xg5+ ♔xg5 −+ **♛f2! 32 ♚h2 ♛f4+ 0-1 Kasparov**

1 d4 d5 2 c4 dxc4

47 Grigorian-Kishnev USSR 78

1 c4 ♞f6 2 ♞c3 e6 3 ♞f3 d5 3...b6 **4 d4 dxc4?!** 4...c5; 4...♗e7 **5 e3** 5 e4 += **a6 6 a4 c5 7 ♝xc4 ♞c6 8 0-0**

Be7 9 Qe2 9 Ne5!? 0-0 10 Nxc6 bxc6 11 b3 += **cxd4 10 Rd1 e5!** 10...d3 11 Bxd3 Qc7 12 h3 Δ e4 += **11 exd4 exd4 12 Nxd4 Nxd4 13 Qe3!?** N 13 Qe5 Qd6 14 Qxd6 Bxd6 15 Rxd4 Bc5= **0-0** 13...Ng4 14 Qxd4 Qxd4 15 Rxd4 Bc5 16 Re4+ Δ Re2 += **14 Rxd4 Qb6! 15 a5 Qa7 16 Na4 += Ng4 17 Qf4 Bg5 18 Qe4 Bh4** 18...Bf5!? 19 Qxf5 Qxd4 20 Bxg5 Qxc4 21 Nb6∝ **19 g3 Bf5 20 Qf4 Bf6?!** 20...Bg5! **21 Rd1! += g6 22 Nb6 Rad8 23 Be2 Rxd1+** 23...Be5!? **24 Bxd1 h5?** 24...Qb8 **25 Bxg4 hxg4 26 Nd7 +- Bxd7 27 Qxf6 Kh7 28 Be3 1-0 Gufeld**

48 Miles-Rivas Montilla 78

1 d4 d5 2 c4 dxc4 3 e4!? e5 4 Nf3 exd4 5 Bxc4 Bb4+ 6 Nbd2 Nc6 7 0-0 Be6 8 Bxe6 fxe6 9 Nb3 Nf6? N 9...e5? 10 Nxe5 Nxe5 11 Qh5+ Nf7 12 Qb5+±; 9...Qd7! 10 Nbxd4 Nxd4 11 Qxd4 Qxd4 12 Nxd4 += Taimanov-Peterson, USSR 64 **10 Nfxd4!** 10 e5 Nd5 += **Nxe4** 10...Nxd4 11 Nxd4 Qd7 12 Nxe6!± **11 Qh5+ g6 12 Qg4 Nxd4** 12...Nf6 13 Qxe6+ Qe7 14 Bg5 +-/±; 12...Nf6 13 Qh4!?± **13 Qxe4 Nxb3 14 axb3± Qe7 15 Bh6!** 15 Qxb7 0-0 16 Rxa7± **Bd6!** 15...c6 16 Qe5! Rg8 17 Rfd1 a5 18 Bg5 Qf7 19 Rd4! Be7 20 Rxa5! Rc8 21 Qc7! +- **16 Qxb7** 16 Rfd1 c6 17 Qd4 0-0-0∝ **Kf7 17 Rfd1 Rab8 18 Qf3+ Qf6 19 Rd3 Rhc8 20 Rxa7 Qxf3 21 Rxf3+ Ke8 22 Ra4 Rb5 23 Re4 Re5 24 Rxe5 Bxe5 25 Re3** 25 Rf8+!? **Rd8 26 Kf1 Rd5 27 f4 Bxb2 28 Rxe6+ Kd7 29 Re2 Bf6** 29...Rd1+? 30 Kf2 Bd4+ 31 Kf3 Rd3+ 32 Ke4 **30 Bf8 Rd3** 30...c5!? 31 Ra2 **31 b4 h5 32 g3 h4 33 Kg2 hxg3 34 hxg3 g5 35 fxg5** 35 f5? g4 **Bxg5 36 Re4 Bf6 37 Bc5 Bc3 38 g4** 38 Kh3!? **Bf6 39 Be3 Rd5 40 Kf3 Be7 41 Rc4 Rb5!?** 41...c6 += **42 Bc5 Bg5?!** 42...Bxc5 **43 Ke4±**

43...Ke6 44 Rc2 Rb8 45 Ra2 Be7! 46 Kd4 Bf6+ 47 Kc4 Rg8 48 Rg2 Kd7 49 Be3 Re8 50 Kd3 50 Bd2?! Re4+ **Be7 51 Bd2 Rg8** 51...c5 52 b5 ±/+- **52 g5 Ke6?** 52...Rg6 53 Ke4 Ke6 54 Rg1! Δ Rc1± **53 g6! +- Kf5 54 g7 Ke6 55 Kc4 Kf7 56 Bc3 c6 57 Rf2+ Kg6 58 Bd4! Bh4** 58...Rd8 59 Bc5! Bh4 60 Bf8 Rd4+ 61 Kc3 Kh7 62 Rg2 Kg8 63 Kxd4 +-; 59...Bf6 60 Bf8 Kf7 61 Rxf6+ +-; 60...Bxg7 61 Rg2+ +-; 59...Bxc5 60 Rg2+! Δ Kxc5 +-; 58...Rb8 59 Bc5! +- **59 Rf8 Kh7 60 Rf7** Δ Rc7 **Bg3** 60...Rc8 61 Rf8 +- **61 Kc5 Be1** 61...Rd8 62 g8Q+ Kxg8 63 Rg7+ +- **62 Rf1 Bd2 63 Rd1 Bh6 64 Rh1 Kg6 65 Kxc6 1-0 Miles**

1 d4 d5 2 c4 c6

49 Shestoperov-Koifman
USSR 78

1 d4 d5 2 c4 e6 3 Nc3 c6 4 Nf3 4 e4!? += **dxc4 5 a4 Bb4 6 e3 b5?!** 6...Nf6 7 Bxc4 Nbd7 8 0-0 0-0 9 Qb3! Qe7 10 e4!± **7 Bd2!? a5** 7...Bb7 **8 axb5 Bxc3 9 Bxc3 cxb5 10 b3! +=**

♝b7 11 bxc4 b4 12 ♝b2 ♞f6 13 ♝d3 ♞bd7 14 0-0 0-0 15 ♛c2 ♛c7 16 e4± e5 17 c5 exd4 18 ♝xd4 ♝a6 19 e5! ♝xd3 20 ♛xd3 ♞h5 21 ♞g5 g6 22 e6 +− fxe6 23 ♞xe6 ♞f4 24 ♞xc7 ♞xd3 25 ♞xa8 ♜xa8 26 c6 ♞7c5 27 ♝xc5 ♞xc5 28 ♜fb1! Δ ♖xb4 +− **b3 29 c7 a4** 29...♖c8 30 ♖xa5 ♖xc7 31 ♖b5 +− **30 ♜xb3! ♞xb3 31 ♜d1 1-0 Gufeld**

50 Rashkovsky-Kosikov
USSR 78
1 ♞f3 ♞f6 2 c4 c6 3 d4 d5 4 cxd5 cxd5 5 ♞c3 ♞c6 6 ♝f4 ♝f5 6...e6 7 e3 ♗d6 8 ♗g3 ♘e4 9 ♘xe4 dxe4 10 ♘d2 ♗xg3 11 hxg3 e5 12 dxe5 ♕a5 13 ♕b3!± Petrosian-Kupreichik, USSR 76 **7 e3 e6 8 ♝b5 ♞d7 9 ♛a4 ♛b6** 9...♖c8 10 ♗xc6 ♖xc6 11 0-0 a6 12 ♖fc1 += **10 ♞h4 ♝e4?!** 10... ♗g6 11 ♘xg6 hxg6 12 e4 ♗b4! +=; 12 0-0! ♗e7 13 e4! ♘f6 14 exd5 exd5 15 ♖fe1 ♔f8 16 ♗xc6± **11 ♜c1 ♜c8 12 0-0 a6!?** 12...♗e7 **13 ♝xc6 ♜xc6 14 ♞xe4 dxe4 15 d5!± exd5 16 ♞f5 g6 17 ♞d4 ♜xc1 18 ♜xc1 ♛xb2** 18...♗c5 19 b4 +− **19 ♜c8+ ♚e7 20 ♞b3 g5!?** 20...♗g7 21 ♕b4+ +− **21 ♝xg5+ f6 22 ♛b4+ ♚f7 23 ♛xb7 ♝e7** 23...♔g6 24 ♕xd7 ♔xg5 25 ♕xd5+ +− **24 ♛xd5+ +− ♚g7 25 ♛xd7 ♜xc8 26 ♛xe7+ 1-0 Gufeld**

51 Pfleger-Nikolac IBM 78
1 d4 d5 2 c4 e6 3 ♞c3 ♞f6 4 ♞f3 c6 5 e3 ♞bd7 6 ♝d3 dxc4 7 ♝xc4 b5 8 ♝d3 a6!? 8...♗b7 9 0-0 b4 10 ♘e4 ♗e7 11 ♘xf6+ ♘xf6 12 e4 0-0 13 e5 ♘d7 14 ♕c2 h6 15 ♗h7+ ♔h8 16 ♗e4 ♕b6 17 ♗e3 c5 18 dxc5 ♗xc5 19 ♖ad1! Korchnoi-Polugaevsky (3) 77 **9 a4** 9 e4 c5 10 d5 c4 11 dxe6 fxe6 12 ♗c2 ♕c7 13 ♕e2 += Podgaets-Kupreichik, USSR 75 **♝b7 10 0-0 ♝e7 11 e4! b4 12 e5 bxc3** 12...♘d5 13 ♘e4± **13 exf6 ♞xf6 14 bxc3 c5** 14...0-0 15 ♖b1 ♕c7 16 ♗f4 += **15 ♜b1 ♛c8 16 ♞e5 0-0 17 ♝g5** 17 ♗a3!? **♜a7 18 dxc5 ♜d8** 18...♕xc5 19 ♗xf6 ♗xf6 20 ♘d7 ♕d5 21 ♖xb7 ♖xb7 22 ♘xf8 +=; 19 ♗e3!? **19 ♛e2 h6** 19...♕xc5 20 ♗e3 ♕d5 21 ♘f3 += Δ ♖fd1 **20 c6! ♝xc6 21 ♝e3 ♜a8 22 ♝b6 ♜d6 23 a5** 23 ♗c5 ♗xg2 **♞d5 24 ♛f3 ♝f6 25 ♞xc6 ♛xc6 26 c4 ♞c3** 26...♘xb6 27 ♕xc6 ♖xc6 28 axb6± **27 ♛xc6 ♜xc6 28 c5! ♞xb1 29 ♝e4 ♜ac8 30 ♜xb1 ♝d4 31 ♝xc6 ♜xc6 32 ♚f1 e5 33 ♝a7 ♚h7 34 ♚e2 e4 35 ♜d1 ♝e5 36 ♝b6 ♚g6 37 ♚e3 f5 38 ♜d7 ♚f6 39 ♜a7 ♚e6 40 ♜xa6 ♚d5 41 ♜a8 ♝d4+ 42 ♚f4 ♝xc5 43 ♝xc5 ♚xc5 44 ♜b8 ♜a6 45 ♚xf5 ♜f6+ 46 ♚xe4 ♜xf2 47 a6 ♜a2 48 ♜g8 g5 49 ♜g6 ♜xg2 50 ♜xh6 g4 51 ♚f4 ♜g1 52 ♜g6 ♜g2 53 a7 ♜a2 54 ♜g7 ♜a4+ 55 ♚f5 ♚d6 56 ♜g6+ ♚d5 57 ♜xg4 ♜xa7 58 h4 ♜a8 59 ♜g6 ♜a1 60 ♜g2 ♚d6 61 ♚g6 ♚e7 62 ♚g7 ♜h1 63 ♜g4 ♚e6 64 ♚g6 ♚e7 65 ♜f4 ♜g1+ 66 ♚h7 ♜h1 67 ♚h6 ♜g1 68 h5 ♜g2 69 ♚h7 ♜g1 70 h6 ♚e8?** 70...♖g2 **71 ♜f6 ♜e1 72 ♚g7 ♜e7+ 73 ♚g8 1-0 Taulbut**

52 Gofstein-Filipenko
USSR 78
1 d4 d5 2 c4 c6 3 ♞f3 ♞f6 4 ♞c3 e6 5 e3 ♞bd7 6 ♝d3 dxc4 7 ♝xc4 b5 8 ♝d3 ♝b7 9 e4 9 0-0 a6!? 10 e4 c5 11 d5 c4∞ **b4 10 ♞a4 c5 11 e5 ♞d5 12 0-0** 12 ♘xc5 ♘xc5 13 dxc5 ♗xc5 14 0-0 h6 15 ♘d2 ♘c3 16 ♕c2 ♕d5 17 ♘f3 += **cxd4 13 ♜e1 a6** 13...♕a5 14 ♘xd4 0-0-0 15 ♗g5! +=; 13...♗e7 14 ♘xd4 ♕a5 15 b3!?; 13...g6 14 ♗g5 ♕a5! 15 ♘xd4 a6!= **14 ♞g5!?**

14 Nxd4 g6! **g6** 14...Be7!? 15 Qh5 Bxg5 16 Bxg5 Qa5= **15 Qf3 Qe7 16 h4 h6** 16...Bg7 17 Qg3∝

17 Qg3!? Bc6 18 Nxf7!? Qxf7 19 Bxg6 Bxa4 20 Bxf7+ Kxf7 21 Qf3+ Ke7 22 Qe4 Rg8?! 22...Kd8! ∆ Bc5 **23 Bd2 Bc6 24 Rac1 Rc8 25 Qxd4 += Kd8 26 Re4 h5? 27 Bg5+± Be7 28 Qd2 Bxg5?! 29 hxg5 a5 30 Rh4 Nxe5 31 Rxh5 Ng6 32 Rc4! +− Rg7 33 Qd4 e5** 33...Rd7 34 Rh8+! Nxh8 35 Qxh8+ Kc7 36 Rxc6+ +− **34 Qc5 Kd7 35 Rh6 a4 36 a3 bxa3 37 bxa3 Rc7 38 Qa5 Nge7 39 Qd2 Ng6 40 Rxc6 1-0 Gufeld**

53 Tukmakov-Sveshnikov Lvov 78

1 d4 d5 2 c4 e6 3 Nc3 c6 4 e3 Nf6 5 Nf3 Nbd7 6 Bd3 dxc4 7 Bxc4 b5 8 Bd3 Bb7 9 e4 b4 10 Na4 c5 11 e5 Nd5 12 0-0 cxd4 13 Re1 g6 14 Bg5 Qa5 15 Nd2 Ba6 16 Bxa6 Qxa6 17 Ne4 Bg7 18 Nac5 18 Nd6+ Kf8 19 Qf3 Nxe5 20 Rxe5 Qxd6 **Nxc5 19 Nxc5 Qb5 20 Qxd4 0-0 21 Ne4 Qb6! 22 Qxb6 axb6**

Diagram

23 Nf6+? 23 Nd6 Ra6 24 a4 bxa3 25 bxa3 Rfa8 26 Nb5 Bf8 27 Bc1 Ra5; 26 Bc1 Nb4 **Bxf6 24 Bxf6 Rfc8**

25 Rec1 Kf8 26 g3 Rxc1+ 27 Rxc1 Ke8 28 Ra1 b5 29 Bg5 b3 30 a3 Rc8 31 Rc1 Rc4 32 Kf1 Kd7 33 Bh6 Kc6 34 Ke2 Nb6 35 Kd3 Kd5 36 Rc3 Na4 0-1

1 d4 d5 2 c4 e6

54 Polugaevsky-Pfleger
Buenos Aires 78

1 c4 Nf6 2 Nf3 e6 3 g3 d5 4 Bg2 c5 5 cxd5 exd5 6 d4 Nc6 7 0-0 Be7 8 Nc3 0-0 9 Bg5 c4 Aronin 9...cxd4 10 Nxd4 h6 11 Be3 += **10 Ne5 Be6 11 Nxc6** 11 e3!? Nd7 Polugaevsky-Pfleger, Montilla 74 **bxc6 12 b3 Qa5** 12...cxb3 13 axb3 Qb6 += Ribli-Pfleger, IBM 78 **13 Na4** 13 Qc2 Bb4∝ **Rfd8 14 e3** 14 Qc2!? Rac8 15 Bxf6 Bxf6 16 Nc5 Bxd4 17 Nb7 Qb6 18 Nxd8 Rxd8 19 bxc4 Bxa1 20 cxd5 ½-½ Portisch-Spassky (2) 77 **c5** 14... Rac8 15 Bxf6 Bxf6 16 Nc5 += **15 Bxf6 gxf6 16 dxc5** 16 bxc4 cxd4 17 exd4 Rab8 18 c5 Bd7 =+ **Bxc5 17 Qh5** 17 Nxc5 Qxc5 18 Rfd1 Rac8∝ **Rac8 18 Rfd1 Bf8** 18...Bb4!? **19 Rac1** 19 Be4!? **Qb4** 19...f5 20 Bh3± **20 Bxd5?** 20 Nc3 cxb3 21 Nxd5 Rxc1? 22 Nxf6+ Kg7 23 Qg5+ +−; 21... Rxd5! 22 Bxd5 Rxc1 23 Rxc1 Qb5 24 e4 bxa2 25 Ra1 +−; 23...b2! 24 Rb1 Qc5 25 e4 Qc1+ 26 Qd1 Ba3 27

♗xe6 fxe6 28 ♔g2 Δ ♕d3, f4, ♔h3 +=

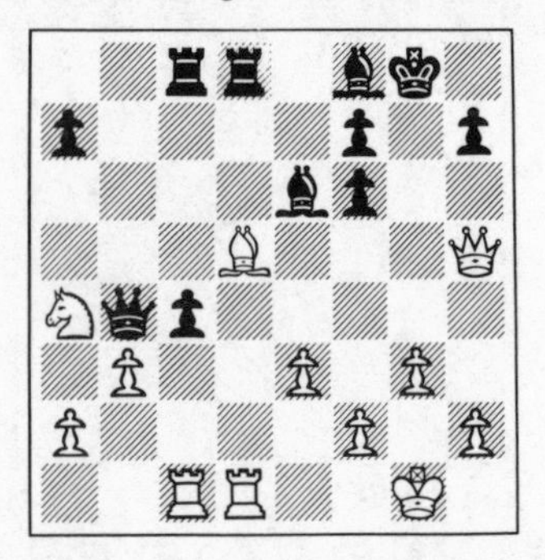

20...♖xd5!∓ 21 ♖xd5 cxb3 22 ♖xc8 ♗xc8 23 axb3? 23 ♕d1! bxa2 24 ♖d4 ♕b1 25 ♘c3; 23...♕xa4 24 axb3 ♕c6 25 ♖d8 f5∓ **♗g4! −+ 24 ♕h4** 24 ♖g5+ fxg5 25 ♕xg5 ♗g7 26 ♕d8+ ♕f8 −+ **♕e1+ 25 ♔g2 ♗e2 26 g4 ♕f1+ 27 ♔g3 ♕g1+ 28 ♔f4 ♕g2 29 ♕xf6 ♕xf2+ 30 ♔e5 ♕xe3+ 31 ♔f5 ♕f3+ 32 ♔e5 ♕e3+ 33 ♔f5 ♗d3+ 34 ♖xd3 ♕xd3+ 35 ♔g5 ♕e3+ 36 ♔h5 ♗e7 0-1 Polugaevsky/Pfleger**

55 Polugaevsky-Day
Buenos Aires 78

1 c4 e6 2 g3 d5 3 ♗g2 c5 4 ♘f3 ♘c6 5 cxd5 exd5 6 d4 ♘f6 7 0-0 ♗e7 8 ♘c3 0-0 9 ♗g5 c4 10 ♘e5 ♗e6 11 ♘xc6 bxc6 12 b3 ♕a5 13 ♘a4 ♖fd8 14 e3! c5 15 ♗xf6 gxf6 16 dxc5 ♗xc5 17 ♕h5 ♗f8? 18 e4!± ♖ab8 18...♗b4 19 exd5 ♗xd5 20 ♕g4+ ♔f8 21 ♗xd5 ♕xd5 22 bxc4± **19 exd5 ♗d7** 19...c3 20 ♘xc3 +− **20 ♘b2! cxb3 21 axb3 ♕b6** 21...♕c3 22 ♖xa7 ♕xb2 23 ♖xd7 +− **22 ♘c4! ♕xb3 23 ♗e4! h6** 23...f5 24 ♘e5! fxe4 25 ♕xf7+ ♔h8 26 ♘xd7 ♖a8 27 ♖xa7! ♖xa7 28 ♕f6+ +−; 26...♕b7 27 ♘e5! Δ ♖xa7 +− **24 ♘e3 ♕b4 25 ♗f5 ♗xf5 26 ♘xf5 ♖b7 27 ♖ad1 ♔h7 28 ♖d4 ♕c5 29 ♖fd1 ♖dd7 30 ♔g2 a5 31 ♕h4! ♖b6 32 ♕e4 ♔h8 33 ♘xh6! +− ♖b4** 33...♗xh6 34 ♕e8+ +− **34 ♘f5 ♖d8 35 ♖xb4 axb4 36 ♖d4 ♗g7 37 ♕g4 ♕f8 38 ♕h5+ ♔g8 39 ♖h4 ♕c5 40 ♕h7+ 1-0 Polugaevsky**

56 Vaganian-Nunn
Buenos Aires 78

1 ♘f3 d5 2 c4 e6 3 g3 c5 4 ♗g2 ♘c6 5 cxd5 exd5 6 d4 ♘f6 7 0-0 ♗e7 8 ♘c3 0-0 9 ♗g5 cxd4 10 ♘xd4 h6 11 ♗e3 ♖e8 11...♗g4 12 ♕a4 ♕d7 13 ♖fd1 ♗h3 14 ♗f3 += **12 ♕a4** 12 ♖c1 ♗f8 13 ♘xc6 bxc6 14 ♘a4 += **♗d7 13 ♖ad1 += ♘b4 14 ♕b3 a5 15 a4** 15 a3?? a4! **♗f8 16 ♘c2!! ♗e6 17 ♗d4± ♘e4 18 ♘xb4 axb4 19 ♘b5 ♕a5 20 ♗xe4! dxe4 21 ♕e3 ♖ac8 22 b3 ♕a6 23 ♖c1! ♗h3 24 ♘c7 ♖xc7 25 ♖xc7 ♗xf1 26 ♔xf1 ♗d6 27 ♖c4 b5 28 axb5 ♕xb5 29 ♗c5! ♗xc5 30 ♖xc5 ♕d7 31 ♔g2 ♖e6 32 ♖c4 ♕d6 33 ♕d4! ♕a6** 33...♕xd4 34 ♖xd4 e3 35 f4 +− **34 ♕d7 e3 35 ♖c7 ♖f6 36 ♕e8+ ♔h7 37 ♕e4+ g6 38 ♕xe3 +− ♕a8+ 39 f3 ♕d5 40 ♕e7 ♖f5 41 ♕xb4 ♕d1 42 ♕c4 1-0 Gipslis**

57 Timman-Gligoric Niksic 78

1 d4 d5 2 c4 e6 3 ♘c3 c5 4 cxd5 exd5 5 ♘f3 ♘c6 6 g3 ♘f6 7 ♗g2 ♗e7 8 0-0 0-0 9 ♗g5 cxd4 9...♗e6; 9...♗g4; 9...c4 **10 ♘xd4 h6 11 ♗e3 ♖e8 12 ♖c1 ♗f8 13 ♘xc6 bxc6 14 ♘a4 ♘g4** 14...♗d7 15 ♗c5 ♗xc5 16 ♘xc5 ♗g4 17 ♖e1 Ljubojevic-Gligoric, Bugojno 78; 15...♘e4 16 ♗xf8 ♔xf8 17 ♖e1± Tukmakov-Balashov, USSR 72 **15 ♗c5 ♗xc5 16 ♘xc5 ♕f6 17 h3 ♘e5 18 e4! ♖b8 19 b3 ♖b5 20 exd5 cxd5 21 ♖e1 g5 22 ♕xd5 ♗b7**

Diagram

23 ♞e4! ♞f3+ 24 ♚h1 ♜xe4 25 ♛xb5 ♞xe1 26 ♛xb7 ♜e2 27 ♛xa7 ♞c2 28 ♚g1 ♞d4 29 ♜f1 ♜b2 Δ ♘e2+ ♘c3 **30 a4 ♜xb3 31 a5 ♚g7 32 ♜d1 ♜b4 33 a6 ♞e2+ 34 ♚h2 ♜b6 35 ♜d7 ♜xa6 36 ♛e3 ♜e6 37 ♛f3 ½-½**

58 Vadasz-Nunn Budapest 78

1 ♞f3 d5 2 c4 e6 3 g3 c5 4 ♝g2 ♞c6 5 0-0 ♞f6 6 cxd5 exd5 7 d4 ♝e7 8 ♞c3 8 dxc5 ♗xc5 9 ♘bd2 0-0 10 ♘b3 ♗b6 11 ♘bd4 ♖e8 12 ♗e3 ♗g4 13 ♘xc6 bxc6 14 ♗d4 ♗xd4 15 ♘xd4 c5 16 ♘f3 ♕b6 ½-½ Miles-Nunn, London 75; 12 b3 ♗g4 13 ♗b2 ♘e4 14 ♘xc6 bxc6 15 ♘e5? ♘xf2! 16 ♖xf2 ♗xf2+ 17 ♔xf2 ♕f6+ 18 ♗f3 ♗xf3 19 exf3 ♖xe5∓ Chandler-Nunn, London 77 **0-0 9 ♝g5 cxd4 10 ♞xd4 h6 11 ♝e3 ♜e8 13 ♞xc6 bxc6 13 ♛a4** 13 ♗d4 ♘h7!? 14 ♘a4 ♘g5 Δ ♗h3, ♘e6 **♝d7 14 ♛c2 ♛c8 15 ♜fd1 ♝h3 16 ♝h1?** 16 ♘a4 ♗xg2 17 ♔xg2 ♕e6 += **♞g4 =+ 17 ♝d2 ♛e6** Δ 18...♗c5 19 ♗e1 ♘e3! **18 ♝e1 ♜ad8 19 e4!** 19 ♗g2? ♗xg2 20 ♔xg2 d4 21 ♘a4 ♕d5+ 22 ♔g1 ♕h5 −+; 21 ♘e4 f5 **♛f6!** 19...d4? 20 ♘e2 Δ ♘f4 **20 exd5?** 20 ♗g2! ♗xg2 21 ♔xg2 d4 22 ♘e2 ♗b4! 23 ♘f4 ♗xe1 24 ♖xe1 ♘e5 Δ d3; 23 ♗xb4 ♕xf2+ 24 ♔h3 ♘e3 −+ **♞e3 21 ♛a4 ♞xd1 22 ♜xd1 cxd5 23 ♞xd5 ♛e6 24 ♝a4** 24 ♘c7 ♕e2; 24 ♘f4 ♖xd1 25 ♕xe8+ ♔h7 −+; 24 ♘xe7+ ♕xe7 25 ♗c3 ♖xd1+ 26 ♕xd1 ♖d8 −+ **♝c5!** −+ Δ ♕e2 **25 ♛c2** 25 ♕c4 ♗xf2+ 26 ♔xf2 ♖xd5 27 ♕xd5 ♕e3 mate **♝b6! 26 ♞xb6** 26 ♗c3 ♕e2 27 ♕xe2 ♖xe2 28 ♗e1 ♖de8 −+ **♛f5! 27 ♜xd8 ♜xd8** 27...♕xc2? 28 ♖xe8+ ♔h7 29 ♗e4+ **0-1** 28 ♕c1 ♕xa5 29 ♘c4 ♕xa2 **Nunn**

59 Kasparov-Begun USSR 78

1 d4 d5 2 c4 e6 3 ♞c3 ♞f6 4 ♞f3 c5 5 cxd5 ♞xd5 6 e3 ♞c6 7 ♝d3 ♝e7 8 0-0 0-0 8...cxd4 9 exd4 0-0 10 ♖e1 += **9 ♞xd5 ♛xd5 10 e4 ♛d8** 10...♕h5 11 dxc5 ♗xc5 12 ♗f4 += **11 dxc5 ♝xc5** 11...♘b4 12 ♗e2 ♗xc5 13 a3 ♘c6 14 b4 ♗d4 15 ♘xd4 ♘xd4 16 ♗b2 ♘xe2+ 17 ♕xe2 += **12 e5 ♝e7 13 ♛e2 ♞b4?!** 13...♘d4 14 ♘xd4 ♕xd4 15 ♖d1 += **14 ♝b1 ♝d7 15 a3 ♞d5 16 ♛e4 g6 17 ♝h6 ♜e8 18 h4 ♛b6 19 h5! f5?** 19...♕xb2 20 ♖a2 ♕b5! 21 ♕g4 ♕a4 22 ♕g3 ♗f8 23 ♗xf8 ♖xf8 24 hxg6? fxg6 25 ♗xg6 ♕f4! =; 24 ♖d2! Δ ♖d4-g4± **20 exf6 ♞xf6 21 ♛e1! ♞xh5 22 ♞e5 ♝b5 23 ♝xg6! ♞f6** 23...hxg6 24 ♕e4 ♗f8 25 ♕xg6+ ♘g7 26 ♘g4! +− **24 ♝xh7+! 1-0** 24...♔xh7 25 ♕b1+ +−; 24...♘xh7 25 ♕e4 +− **Kasparov**

60 Barczay-Lukacs Budapest 78

1 d4 ♞f6 2 c4 e6 3 ♞f3 d5 4 ♞c3 c5 5 cxd5 ♞xd5 6 e4 ♞xc3 7 bxc3 cxd4 8 cxd4 ♞c6 9 ♝c4 b5 10 ♝e2 ♝b4+ 11 ♝d2 ♛a5 12 ♜b1 12 d5 **♝xd2+ 13 ♛xd2 a6 14 ♛xa5 ♞xa5 15 ♚d2!** N 15 ♗d3 ♔e7 16 ♖c1 ♗d7 17 ♔d2 ½-½ Petrosian-Korchnoi, (2) 77 **♚e7?!** 15...♗b7! 16 ♗d3 ♔e7 +=; 16 ♔e3 **16 ♜hc1 ♝d7 17 ♜c5 ♜hc8 18 ♜bc1**

♖xc5 19 ♖xc5 ♖c8 20 ♖xc8 ♗xc8 21 ♔c3!± ♗d7 21...♗b7 22 ♔b4± **22 ♘e5 ♗e8 23 ♘d3 ♘b7 24 e5 a5 25 d5 exd5 26 ♔d4 b4 27 ♘f4 ♗c6 28 ♗f3 a4 29 ♗xd5 ♘a5**

30 ♔c5!! 30 ♗xc6 ♘xc6+ 31 ♔c5 b3 32 axb3 axb3 Δ ♘xe5, ♘d3= **b3 31 axb3 a3 32 b4 ♗xd5 33 ♘xd5+ ♔d7 34 ♘c3 ♘b3+ 35 ♔c4 ♘c1 36 f4! g6! 37 g4 ♘e2?** 37...a2, Δ ♘xa2-c1-e2-f4!= **38 f5! gxf5 39 gxf5 ♘g1 40 b5 ♘f3 41 ♔d5 ♘xh2 42 e6+ fxe6+ 43 fxe6+ ♔c7 44 b6+ 1-0 Haag**

61 Miles-L.Bronstein
Buenos Aires 78

1 d4 d5 2 c4 e6 3 ♘c3 ♘f6 4 cxd5 exd5 5 ♗g5 ♗e7 6 e3 c6 7 ♗d3 ♗g4!? 8 ♘ge2 8 ♕c2 ♘bd7; 8...♗h5!?; 8 ♕b3!?; 8 f3 **♘bd7 9 f3 ♗h5 10 ♘g3 ♗g6 11 ♘f5 ♗xf5 12 ♗xf5 g6 13 ♗c2 ♘h5 14 ♗xe7 ♕xe7 15 ♕e2 += f5!** 15...♕h4+ 16 ♕f2 +=; 15...0-0?! 16 0-0-0±; 15...0-0-0 16 0-0± **16 0-0-0 ♘hf6 17 ♖he1 0-0-0 18 h3** 18 e4!? += **♖he8** 18...h5? 19 e4± **19 g4 fxg4 20 hxg4 ♘b6 21 ♔b1 ♕d6! 22 g5 ♘h5 23 ♕f2 ♕e7?!** 23...♖e7≈ **24 f4 ♘c4 25 ♖e2! ♕b4** 25...♘xe3?? 26 ♖de1 +− **26 ♗d3!** 26 ♗b3 ♘a5 27 ♗c2 ♘c4= **♘xb2 27 ♖xb2 ♕xc3 28 f5! ♘g7 29 fxg6?** 29 f6 ♘e6 30 f7 ♖f8 31 ♕f6±; 29...♘h5!? **hxg6 30 ♗xg6 ♖f8** 30...♖xe3?? 31 ♖b3 +− **31 ♕g3** Δ ♖c1, ♖xc6+ **♕a5 32 ♗d3?!** 32 e4!? +=/± **♕c7 33 ♕g4+** 33 ♕xc7+ **♕d7 24 ♕e2 ♖de8!?** Zeitnot 34...♘f5! =/=+ **35 ♗a6! bxa6!** 35...♕f5+ 36 e4!? ♖xe4 37 ♗d3 ∝/+=; 36 ♔a1!? **36 ♕xa6+ ♔d8 37 ♖b7!** 37 ♖b8+? ♔e7 38 ♖b7 ♖b8 −+ **♕f5+ 38 ♔a1 ♖e7 39 ♖db1!** 39 ♖bb1?? (Δ ♖f1/♕xc6) 39...♕c8! −+ **♖xb7 40 ♕xb7 ♕d7!** 40...♘e6 41 ♕xc6 +−; 40...♕c2 41 ♕b8+ ♔e7 42 ♖b7+ ♔e6 43 ♕e5 mate; 40...♕c8 41 ♕xg7 +− **41 ♕xd7+ ♔xd7 42 ♖b7+ ♔d6 43 ♖xg7 +=/= ♖f1+ =** 43...a5=; 43...♖e8=; 43...♖f3= **44 ♔b2 ♖f2+ 45 ♔c3** 45 ♔b3!? **♖xa2 46 g6 ♖e2 47 ♔d3 ♖g2 48 ♖g8 ♔c7 49 ♔c3 a5 50 ♔b3 ♔b7 ½-½ Miles**

62 Timman-Nikolac IBM 78

1 d4 d5 2 c4 e6 3 ♘c3 ♘f6 4 ♗g5 ♘bd7 5 cxd5 exd5 6 e3 ♗e7 7 ♗d3 ♘f8 7...c6 8 ♕c2 0-0 9 ♘f3 h6 10 ♗h4 ♖e8 11 0-0 ♘e4 12 ♗xe7 ♕xe7 13 b4 += Geller-Durao, Sochi 77 **8 ♕c2 ♘e6 9 ♗h4 g6 10 ♘f3 ♘g7 11 b4 a6** 11...♗xb4?? 12 ♕a4+ **12 0-0 0-0 13 a4 ♘f5** 13...♗xb4?? 14 ♗xf6 **14 ♗g5 ♗e6** 14...h6 15 ♗xf6 ♗xf6 16 ♕b3 ♘e7 += **15 b5 a5 16 ♘e2 ♘g7 17 ♖fc1 ♖c8 18 ♘e5 ♗f5 19 ♘f4 ♕d6** 19...♗xd3 20 ♕xd3 ♘f5 21 ♕b3± **20 ♕b3 ♖fd8**

Diagram

21 ♗xf5 ♘xf5 22 ♘c6! +− ♖d7 22...bxc6 23 ♖xc6 ♕d7 24 ♗xf6 ♗xf6 25 ♖xf6 +− **23 ♘xa5 ♖b8 24 ♗xf6 ♗xf6 25 ♘d3 ♖e7** Δ ♗xd4, ♘xd4 **26 ♕b4 ♕d8 27 ♘b3 ♗g5 28 ♖c2 ♕f8 29 ♘d2 ♕h6 30 ♘f1 ♕h4 31**

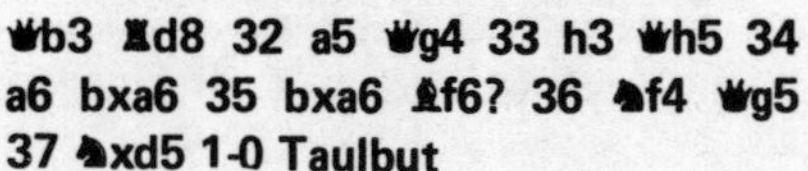
♛b3 ♜d8 32 a5 ♛g4 33 h3 ♛h5 34 a6 bxa6 35 bxa6 ♝f6? 36 ♞f4 ♛g5 37 ♞xd5 1-0 Taulbut

63 Korchnoi-Karpov (31) 78

1 c4 e6 2 ♞c3 d5 3 d4 ♞f6 4 cxd5 exd5 5 ♝g5 ♝e7 6 e3 0-0 7 ♝d3 ♞bd7 8 ♞f3 ♜e8 9 ♛c2 c6 10 0-0 ♞f8 11 ♝xf6 ♝xf6 12 b4 ♝g4 13 ♞d2 ♜c8 14 ♝f5 ♝xf5 15 ♛xf5 ♛d7 16 ♛xd7 ♞xd7 17 a4 ♝e7 18 ♜fb1 ♞f6 19 a5 a6 20 ♞a4 ♝f8 21 ♞c5 ♜e7 22 ♚f1 ♞e8 23 ♚e2 ♞d6 24 ♚d3 ♜ce8 25 ♜e1 g6 26 ♜e2 f6 27 ♜ae1 ♝h6 28 ♞db3 ♝f8 29 ♞d2 ♝h6 30 h3 ♚f7 31 g4 ♝f8 32 f3 ♜d8 33 ♞db3 ♞b5 34 ♜f1 ♝h6 35 f4 ♝f8 36 ♞d2 ♞d6 37 ♜fe1 h6 38 ♜f1 ♜b8 39 ♜a1 ♜be8 40 ♜ae1 ♜b8 40...♖d8 **41 e4!? dxe4+ 42 ♞dxe4 ♞b5 43 ♞c3** 43 f5? gxf5 44 gxf5 ♖d8 45 ♘e6 ♖d5; 45...♖xd4+ 46 ♘xd4 ♖d7 **♜xe2 44 ♜xe2 ♝xc5** 44...♘xc3 45 ♔xc3 ♖e8 46 ♖xe8 ♔xe8 47 d5 cxd5 49 ♔d4 g5!=; 46 ♖b2! ♖e7 48 d5 cxd5 49 ♔d4 **45 bxc5 ♜d8 46 ♞xb5 axb5 47 f5**

Diagram

47...gxf5 47...♖a8 48 fxg6+ (48 ♖a2 h5!) ♔xg6 49 ♖e7 ♖xa5 50 ♖xb7 ♖a3+ 51 ♔e4 ♖xh3 52 ♖b6; 47...g5 **48 gxf5 ♜g8** 48...♖a8 49 ♖a2 ♔e7 50 ♔c3 h5 51 h4 Zugzwang **49 ♚c3 ♜e8?** (1) 49...♖g5 50 ♖e6 ♖xf5 51 a6 bxa6 52 ♖xc6 a5 53 ♖b6 ♖f3+ 54 ♔d2 b4 55 c6 ♔e7!=; 55...♔e6 56 c7 ♔d7 57 ♖c6! ♔c8 58 d5 +−; (2) 49...♖g1 50 a6 bxa6 51 ♖e6 a5 52 ♖xc6 ♖g3+ 53 ♔d2 a4 54 ♖a6 a3 55 d5 b4 56 d6? a7!=; 56 c6! ♔e7 57 c7! +−; (3) 49...♖g3+ 50 ♔b4 ♖d3 51 a6 ♖xd4+ 52 ♔a5 bxa6 53 ♔b6 b4; 51 ♖e4 ♖d1! 52 a6 bxa6 53 ♔a5 ♖a1+ 54 ♔b6 b4= **50 ♜d2! ♜e4** 50...♖e1 51 d5 ♖c1+ 52 ♔b2! ♖xc5 53 dxc6 ♖xc6 54 ♖d7+; 53... bxc6 54 a6 +− **51 ♚b4 ♚e8 52 a6 bxa6 53 ♚a5 ♚d7 54 ♚b6** Δ ♔b7, d5; 54 ♔xa6 ♔c7! **b4 55 d5** 55 ♔b7 b3 56 d5 ♖b4+ **cxd5 56 ♜xd5+ ♚c8 57 ♜d3! a5 58 ♜g3 b3 59 ♚c6 ♚b8 60 ♜xb3+ ♚a7 61 ♜b7+ ♚a6 62 ♜b6+ ♚a7 63 ♚b5 a4 64 ♜xf6 ♜f4 65 ♜xh6 a3 66 ♜a6+ ♚b8 67 ♜xa3 ♜xf5 68 ♜g3 ♜f6 69 ♜g8+ ♚c7 70 ♜g7+ ♚c8 71 ♜h7 1-0**

64 Korchnoi-Karpov (23) 78

1 c4 ♞f6 2 ♞c3 e6 3 ♞f3 d5 4 d4 ♝e7 5 ♝f4 0-0 6 e3 c5 7 dxc5 ♝xc5 8 ♛c2 ♞c6 9 ♜d1 ♛a5 10 a3 ♝e7 10...♖e8 **11 ♞d2 e5 12 ♝g5 d4 13 ♞b3 ♛b6** 13...♕d8 **14 ♝xf6 ♝xf6 15 ♞d5 ♛d8 16 ♝d3 g6** Δ ♗g7 **17 exd4 ♞xd4 18 ♞xd4 exd4 19 ♞xf6+ ♛xf6**

20 0-0 Be6 20...Bd7 Forintos-Smederevac, Wijk aan Zee 70 **21 Rfe1** 21 f4 Bf5 22 Bxf5 gxf5 23 Qb3 Δ Qg3+, Qg5 **Rac8 22 b3 Rfd8 23 Be4 Rc7 24 Qd2 Bg4 25 f3 Be6 26 a4! b6 27 a5 b5!? 28 cxb5 Bxb3 29 Rb1 Bd5** 29...Rc3 30 b6! axb6 31 a6! **30 b6** 30 Bxd5 Rxd5 31 Re8+ Kg7 32 b6 axb6 33 Rxb6 Qg5 **axb6 31 Rxb6 Rc6 32 Rxc6** 32 Bxd5? Rxd5 33 Re8+ Kg7 34 Rbb8 h5 35 Rh8 Qg5! **Bxc6 33 Bd3 Bd7!** Δ Bf5, Bxd3 **34 a6** 34 Ra1 Bf5 35 Bxf5 d3 **Bf5 35 Qf4 Kg7 36 Bxf5 Qxf5 37 Qxf5 gxf5 38 Ra1** 38 Kf2 d3=; 38 a7= **d3 39 Kf2 Re8! 40 Ra2 Re7 41 Rd2** 41 a7 d2 **Re6 ½-½**

65 Korchnoi-Karpov (9) 78

1 c4 Nf6 2 Nc3 e6 3 Nf3 d5 4 d4 Be7 5 Bf4 0-0 6 e3 c5 7 dxc5 Bxc5 8 Qc2 Nc6 9 Rd1 Qa5 10 a3 Be7 11 Nd2 e5 12 Bg5 d4 13 Nb3 Qd8 14 Be2 h6 14...Ng4 Portisch-Spassky, Havana 66 **15 Bxf6 Bxf6 16 0-0 Be6 17 Nc5 Qe7 18 Nxe6 Qxe6 19 Nd5 Rad8** 19...Rac8 20 Qe4 Bd8 21 exd4 Nxd4 22 Bg4! f5 23 Rxd4 **20 Bd3?** 20 e4 Ne7 21 Bf3 Nxd5 22 exd5 Δ c5± **Ne7 21 Nxf6+ Qxf6 22 exd4 exd4 23 Rfe1 Rd7?** 23...Ng6 **24 Re4 Nc6 25 Qe2 g6 26 Re1 Kg7 27 b4 b6 28 Qg4! Rfd8** 28...Qd6? 29 Re6! fxe6 30 Qxg6+ Kh8 31 Qxh6+ Kg8 32 Rxe6 +− **29 h4 h5 30 Qg3** 30 Qg5 **Qd6 31 f4** Δ Re6! **Re7 32 Rxe7 Nxe7 33 Re5 a5! 34 Rxh5** 34 bxa5 bxa5 35 Rxa5± **axb4 35 axb4 Qxb4**

Diagram

36 Rb5 Zeitnot 36 Re5! (Δ f5/h5) Nc6 37 Re2 Qc3 38 f5 Nb4 39 Qe5+ Kg8 40 fxg6 Qxd3 41 gxf7+ +− **Qd2 37 Kh2 Qe3 38 Rxb6 Ra8 39 Qxe3** 39 f5 **dxe3 40 Rb2 Ra3 41 Be4 Rc3 ½-½**

66 Korchnoi-Karpov (21) 78

1 c4 Nf6 2 Nc3 e6 3 Nf3 d5 4 d4 Be7 5 Bf4 0-0 6 e3 c5 7 dxc5 Bxc5 8 Qc2 Nc6 9 Rd1 Qa5 10 a3 Re8 11 Nd2 11 b4? Nxb4! 12 axb4 Bxb4 **e5 12 Bg5 Nd4 13 Qb1!** 13 exd4 exd4+ 14 Ne2 Ne4 15 Bh4 dxc4 16 Qxc4 Be6; 14...Ng4 (Δ Nxf2 16 Kxf2 d3+ −+) 15 Bh4 dxc4 16 b4 cxb3 17 Qxb3 Be6; 16 Qxc4 Ne5 Δ d3/Nd3+ **Bf5** 13...Bg4 14 Bxf6 gxf6 15 Nxd5! Bxd1 16 Kxd1 Δ b4/exd4/Nxf6+ **14 Bd3 e4 15 Bc2 Nxc2+ 16 Qxc2 Qa6** 16...dxc4 17 Bxf6 gxf6 18 b4 cxb3 19 Nxb3 Qxa3 20 Ra1 Qb4 21 Ra4 Qb6 22 Nd5; 16...d4 17 Bxf6 gxf6 18 Nd5 d3 19 Qb3 **17 Bxf6 Qxf6 18 Nb3 Bd6 19 Rxd5 Re5 20 Nd4 Rc8 21 Rxe5 Qxe5** 21...Bxe5? 22 Nd5 Qe6 23 Nxf5 +− **22 Nxf5 Qxf5 23 0-0** 23 Qxe4? Qxe4 24 Nxe4 Rxc4 25 Nc3 Bxa3!; 23 Nxe4 b5 **Rxc4 24 Rd1!** 23 Qb3 Qc8 **Qe5** 24...Be7! 25 f3 h6 26 fxe4; 25 Rd4 Rxd4 26 exd4 Bf6! **25 g3 a6 26 Qb3 b5 27 a4 Rb4 28 Qd5 Qxd5 29 Rxd5 Bf8 30 axb5 a5** 30... axb5 31 Rxb5; 30...Rxb2 31 bxa6 **31 Rd8 Rxb2 32 Ra8 f5** 32...Rb3 33

♘d5 Δ ♘e7+ **33 ♜xa5 ♝b4 34 ♜a8+ ♚f7 35 ♞a4 ♜b1+ 36 ♚g2 ♝d6 37 ♜a7+ ♚f6 38 b6 ♝b8** 38...♖b3 39 ♖d7 ♗e5 40 f4; 39 ♖c7? ♖b4! **39 ♜a8 ♝e5 40 ♞c5 ♝d6 41 b7 ♚e7 42 ♜g8 ♝e5** 42...♔f7? 43 ♖d8 ♗e5 44 ♖d5 +− **43 f4! exf3+ 44 ♚xf3 ♚f7 45 ♜c8** 45 ♖d8 ♔e7 46 ♖d7+ ♔e8 47 e4 ♖b5 48 exf5 ♖xc5 49 ♖xg7 h6! **♚e7 46 h3! h5?** 46...♖b5 **47 ♜g8 ♚f7 48 ♜d8 g5** 48...♔e7? 49 ♖d7+ ♔e8 50 ♖d5 ♗f6 51 ♖xf5 +− **49 g4!**

49...hxg4+ 49...fxg4+ 50 hxg4 h4 51 ♘d7 ♔e7 52 b8♕ ♖xb8 53 ♖xb8 ♔xd7 54 ♖g8 ♗f6 55 ♔e4 ♔e6 56 ♖g6+ ♔f7 57 ♔f5 +− **50 hxg4 ♚e7 51 ♜g8 fxg4+ 52 ♚xg4 ♚f7 53 ♜c8** 53 ♖xg5? ♗d6 54 ♘e4 ♗e7= **♝d6 54 e4** 54 ♔xg5 ♗xc5 55 b8♕ ♖xb8 56 ♖xb8 ♗xe3+ = **♜g1+ 55 ♚f5 g4 56 e5 ♜f1+ 57 ♚e4 ♜e1+ 58 ♚d5 ♜d1+** 58...♗xe5 59 ♘d3 **59 ♞d3! ♜xd3+ 60 ♚c4 1-0**

67 Korchnoi-Karpov (13) 78

1 c4 ♞f6 2 ♞c3 e6 3 ♞f3 d5 4 d4 ♝e7 5 ♝g5 h6 6 ♝h4 0-0 7 ♜c1 b6 8 ♝xf6 8 cxd5 **♝xf6 9 cxd5 exd5 10 g3** N **c6 11 ♝g2 ♝f5 12 0-0 ♛d6 13 e3 ♞d7 14 ♞e1 ♜fe8 15 ♞d3 g6** 15... h5 **16 ♞f4 ♝g7 17 g4 ♝e6 18 h3 ♞f8 19 ♞xe6 ♞xe6 20 ♛d3 ♜ad8** 20...♕e7 Δ ♕h4, f5 **21 ♜c2 ♞c7 22 ♞a4 ♛d7 23 b3** 23 b4!? c5 24 bxc5 ♕xa4 25 cxb6 ♘e6 26 b7 **♜e6** 23...♗f8; 23... ♘b5 **24 ♞c3** 24 b4!? **♜d6 25 b4 ♝f8 26 ♞e2 b5 27 ♛b3 ♞a8 28 a4 bxa4!?** 28...a6 29 a5 Δ ♘f4-d3 **29 ♛xa4 ♞b6 30 ♛b3 ♜b8 31 ♞f4 ♞c4 32 ♛a4 f5?!** 32...♖b5 Δ a5 **33 gxf5 ♛xf5 34 ♛xa7! ♜xb4 35 ♜a2 ♛c8 36 ♜c1 ♜b7 37 ♛a4?** 37 ♕a6!; 37 ♕a8! ♖b8 38 ♕a6 **♜f7!** Δ ♖xf4 **38 ♜xc4!? dxc4** 38...♖xf4 39 ♖xc6! **39 ♛xc4 ♛f5 40 ♞d3?** 40 ♖a8; 40 ♗xc6? ♖xc6 41 ♕xc6 ♕b1+ **♝g7?** 40...♕b5 **41 ♜a7** 41 ♘b4? c5 42 ♕xc5 ♕xc5 43 dxc5 ♖d1+ 44 ♔h2? ♗e5+ 45 f4 ♖xf4 −+; 44 ♗f1!? **♜df6** Δ ♕b5; 41...♕e6 42 ♕xe6 ♖xe6 43 ♖a6 ♖c7? 44 ♗d5! +− **42 ♜xf7** 42 ♘e5 ♕xf2+ 43 ♔h1 ♕e1+ 44 ♔h2 ♕xe3 45 ♘xf7 ♕f4+ =; 42 ♖b7!? ♔h7? 43 e4!; 42... ♗f8 **♜xf7 43 d5** 43 ♗xc6 ♔h7 **♝e5 44 dxc6** 44 ♕xc6 ♕xd3 45 ♕e8+ ♖f8 46 ♕xe5 ♕d1+ **♚g7 45 ♝e4 ♛g5+ 46 ♚f1 ♝d6 47 ♝d5 ♜e7 48 ♝f3?** 48 ♗e6 **h5 49 ♝d1 ♛f5 50 ♚e2 ♜e4** 50...♕xh3? 51 ♕d4+ Δ ♕xd6 **51 ♛c3+ ♛f6 52 ♛b3 ♛f5 53 ♛b7+ ♜e7 54 ♛b2+ ♚h7 55 ♛d4 ♝c7 56 ♛h4?** Zeitnot 56 h4 ♖e4 57 ♕d7+ ♕xd7 58 cxd7 ♖xh4 59 ♘f4 ♖xf4= **♜e4 57 f4 ♝b6 58 ♝c2 ♜xe3+ 59 ♚d2 ♛a5+ 60 ♚d1 ♛a1+ 61 ♚d2 ♜e4 0-1**

68 Korchnoi-Karpov (1) 78

1 c4 ♞f6 2 ♞c3 e6 3 ♞f3 d5 4 d4 ♝e7 5 ♝g5 h6 6 ♝h4 0-0 7 e3 b6 8 ♜c1 ♝b7 9 ♝d3 9 ♗xf6 ♗xf6 10 cxd5 exd5 11 b4; 11 ♗e2 **dxc4?** 9...c5 **10 ♝xc4 ♞bd7 11 0-0 c5** 11...♘e4 12 ♗xe7 ♕xe7 13 ♘xe4 ♗xe4 14 ♗b5! **12 dxc5?** 12 ♖e1; 12 ♕e2 ♘e4 13 ♘xe4 ♗xh4 14 ♘c3 ♗f6 15 ♖fd1 ♕e7 16 ♗a6 ♖ab8 17 ♗xb7 ♖xb7 18

♘e4± Alekhine-Bogolyubov, Mannheim 37; 12...a6 13 ♖fd1 b4 14 a4 += **♘xc5 13 ♕e2 a6 14 ♖fd1 ♕e8 15 a3 ♘fe4 16 ♘xe4 ♘xe4 17 ♗xe7 ♕xe7 18 ♘d4** 18 ♘e5 b5 19 ♖d7 ♕c5! 20 ♘g6 bxc4 21 ♘e7+ ♔h8 22 ♖xb7 ♘d6! 23 b4 ♕g5; 21 ♘xf8 ♗d5; 20 ♖xb7? ♕xe5; 20 ♘xf7? bxc4 **♖fc8 ½-½**

69 Kuligowski-Byrne
Buenos Aires 78
1 d4 ♘f6 2 c4 e6 3 ♘f3 d5 4 ♘c3 ♘bd7 4...c5 5 cxd5 ♘xd5 6 e4 ♘xc3 7 bxc3 cxd4 8 cxd4 ♗b4+ 9 ♗d2 ♗xd2 10 ♕xd2 0-0 11 ♗c4± Browne-Peters, USA 76; 5...exd5 6 g3 ♘c6 7 ♗g2 **5 ♗g5 ♗e7 6 e3 0-0 7 ♖c1 c6** 7...a6 8 cxd5 exd5 9 ♗d3 c6 10 ♕c2 ♖e8 11 0-0 ♘f8 12 ♘a4! ♘g6 13 ♘c5 ♘e4!∝ Browne-Tisdall, Orense 77; 8 a4!? **8 ♗d3 a6** 8...dxc4 9 ♗xc4 ♘d5 10 ♗xe7 ♕xe7 11 0-0 += **9 a4 dxc4 10 ♗xc4 ♘d5 11 ♗xe7 ♕xe7 12 0-0 ♘xc3 13 bxc3 b5 14 ♗d3 ♗b7 15 c4 b4** 15...bxc4 16 ♗xc4 c5 17 d5± **16 c5 a5 17 ♕c2 g6 18 e4 e5 19 d5 ♖fc8 20 d6 ♕f6 21 ♕b2 ♗a6 22 ♗xa6 ♖xa6 23 ♘d2! ♖e8 24 g3 ♖aa8 25 ♘b3 ♕f3 26 ♕c2 ♖e6 27 ♖ce1 g5 28 ♖e3 ♕g4 29 f3 ♕h3 30 ♖e2 ♖g6 31 ♘d2 ♕e6 32 ♘c4! b3 33 ♕c3!**

33...♘xc5?! 34 ♘b6 ♘xa4 35 ♘xa4 ♕xd6 36 ♕xb3 ♕d4+ 37 ♔g2 +− ♖d6 38 ♖c1 ♖ad8 39 ♘c5 h5 40 ♕c4 g4 41 fxg4 hxg4 42 ♘b7 ♕xc4 43 ♖xc4 ♖d2 44 ♖c2 ♖xc2 45 ♖xc2 ♖d4 46 ♘c5 1-0 Filipowicz

70 Guil.Garcia-De Corvahlo
Mexico 78
1 c4 ♘f6 2 ♘c3 e6 3 ♘f3 3 e4!? **d5** 3...b6!? 4 e4!? **4 d4 ♗e7 5 ♗g5 0-0 6 e3 ♘bd7 7 ♕c2 c6** 7...c5 **8 cxd5!?** 8 ♖c1 a6 9 cxd5 **exd5** 8...♘xd5 9 ♗xe7 ♕xe7 10 ♗e2 +=/=; 8...cxd5 **9 ♗d3 ♖e8 10 0-0** 10 0-0-0!?; 10 h3 **♘f8 11 ♖ab1** 11 ♗xf6 ♗xf6 12 b4; 11 ♖ae1; 11 ♘e5 **♘e4** 11...g6 Δ ♘e6-g7, ♗f5; 11...a5! 12 a3 ♘e4; 12... g6 **12 ♗xe7 ♕xe7 13 b4 += ♘g6?!** 13...a6 14 a4 ♘g6; 13...♗g4!? **14 b5 ♗g4** 14...f5 15 bxc6 bxc6 16 ♘e2 ♗d7 17 ♘f4± Glatman-Semenov, USSR 72 **15 ♗xe4** 15 ♘d2? ♘xd2 16 ♕xd2 ♘h4 **dxe4 16 ♘d2 f5?!** 16... ♗f5 17 bxc6 bxc6 18 ♘e2± **17 bxc6 bxc6 18 h3!?** 18 ♖fc1!? ♘h4 19 ♘f1 ♘xg2!? 20 ♔xg2 ♗f3+ 21 ♔g1 ♕g5+ 22 ♘g3 h5 23 ♘e2 h4 24 ♘f4; 21... ♕h4!? 22 ♘c2; 18 ♖fc1 ♕g5 19 ♘f1 **♗h5 19 ♖fc1 ♕g5** 19...♘h4 **20 ♘f1 ♘h4 21 ♘g3 ♖e6?!** 21...♗f7 22 ♖b7 h5 Δ ♘xg2!?; 22 ♘e2 ♗d5 23 ♘f4 **22 ♖b7 h6?** Δ ♖g6; 22...♖g6? 23 ♕b3+; 22...♗f7± **23 ♕b3! ♖ae8** 23...♗f7 24 ♖xf7 +− **24 ♘cxe4! +− fxe4 25 ♖c5 ♕f6** 25...♕g6 26 ♖xh5 ♕f6 27 ♘xe4 **26 ♘xh5 ♘f3+ 27 gxf3 ♕g6+ 28 ♔f1 ♔f8 29 ♖xg7 1-0 Speelman**

71 Formanek-Zilber Israel 78
1 d4 d5 2 c4 e6 3 ♘c3 ♗e7 4 ♘f3 ♘f6 5 ♗g5 0-0 6 e3 h6 7 ♗h4 b6 8 cxd5 ♘xd5 9 ♗xe7 ♘xe7 9...♕xe7 10 ♘xd5 exd5= Alekhine **10 ♗d3 ♗b7 11**

0-0 ♞d7 12 b4? c5 13 b5 13 bxc5 bxc5 14 dxc5 ♘xc5 **♝xf3! 14 gxf3** Δ f4, ♗e4; 14 ♕xf3 cxd4 15 exd4 e5! 16 dxe5 ♘xe5 −+ **♞d5 15 ♜c1 ♞xc3 16 ♜xc3 ♛f6 17 ♜c2 ♜fd8 18 f4 ♜ac8 19 dxc5 bxc5 20 ♝e4 ♞b6 21 ♛f3 c4 22 ♜fc1 ♜c5 23 ♝c6 c3 24 e4? ♞a4 25 e5 ♛g6+ 26 ♚h1 ♜d4 27 ♛e3 ♜cc4 28 f3 ♛d3!** 28... ♖xf4 29 ♗e4 ♖fxe4 30 fxe4 ♕xe4+ 31 ♕xe4 ♖xe4 **29 ♛xd3 ♜xd3 30 ♚g2 ♜xf4 31 ♝e4 ♜d4 32 ♜xc3 ♞xc3 33 ♜xc3 g5 34 ♜a3 ♜d2+ 35 ♚g3 h5 36 ♝c6** 36 ♖xa7 h4+ 37 ♔h3 g4+ 38 ♔xh4 gxf3+ −+ **♜h4 37 h3 ♜f4** Δ h4 mate **38 h4 ♜xh4 39 f4 ♜dh2 0-1** 40 ♗g2 gxf4+ 41 ♔f3 ♖h3+ −+

72 Mihaljcisin-Raicevic
Vrnjacka Banja 78
1 ♞f3 d5 2 c4 e6 3 d4 ♞f6 4 ♝g5 ♞bd7 5 e3 c6 6 ♞bd2 6 ♘c3 **♝e7 7 ♝d3 0-0 8 0-0 h6 9 ♝h4 b6 10 ♛e2 ♝b7 11 ♜ac1 c5= 12 ♜fd1 cxd4 13 ♞xd4 ♞e5?!** 13...♖c8= **14 ♝b1 += ♝a6?**

15 f4! ♞xc4 15...♘ed7 16 ♘c6 ♕e8 17 e4± **16 ♞xc4 ♜c8** 16...♗xc4 17 ♖xc4 dxc4 18 ♕c2 g6 19 ♘xe6 **17 ♝xf6 ♝xf6 18 ♛c2 g6 19 ♞xe6! +− ♛e7 20 ♞xf8 ♜xc4 21 ♛d2 ♚xf8 22 ♜xc4 dxc4 23 e4 ♛c5+ 24 ♚h1 ♝b7 25 e5 ♝e7 26 f5 ♛xe5 27 fxg6 ♝g5 28 ♛b4+ ♚g7 29 ♛xc4 fxg6 30 ♛d3 ♚h8 31 ♛d4 1-0 Gufeld**

Catalan

73 Gulko-Mikenas Vilnius 78
1 c4 e6 2 ♞f3 d5 3 g3 c5 4 ♝g2 ♞c6 5 0-0 5 cxd5 exd5 6 d4 **♞f6 6 d4 dxc4 7 ♛a4** 7 ♘e5!? ♗d7! 8 ♘xc6 ♗xc6 9 ♗xc6+ bxc6 10 ♕a4 cxd4 11 ♕xc6+ ♘d7 12 ♕xc4 ♗c5 13 b4 ♗b6 14 a4 a6! Panno-Browne, Manila 76 **♝d7 8 ♛xc4** 8...dxc5 **b5!?** 8... cxd4 9 ♘xd4 ♖c8 **9 ♛d3** 9 ♕xb5? ♘xd4 **♛b6** 9...c4!? **10 ♞c3 ♞b4** 10...cxd4? 11 ♘xd4; 10...c4!? 11 ♕b1 **11 ♛b1 cxd4 12 ♞xd4 ♜c8** 12...♖d8!?

13 a3 13 ♗e3? ♘g4! 14 ♘xe6?? ♕xe6; 13 ♘b3!? **♛xd4** 13...♘a6 **14 ♜d1** 14 ♗e3?! ♕c4 15 axb4 ♗xb4 16 ♖xa7 ♗c5; 16...♗xc3!? **♛b6** 14...♕c4 15 axb4 ♗xb4 16 ♖xa7 ♗c5 17 ♖b7∞ b4!? 18 ♘e4 ♘xe4 19 ♕xe4 (19 ♗xe4) ♕xe4 20 ♗xe4 ♗a4! **15 ♝e3 ♝c5 16 ♝xc5 ♛xc5 17 axb4 ♛xb4** 17...♕b6? 18 ♕a2± ♖c7 19 ♕a5 **18 ♜xa7 0-0 19 ♞e4!** 19 ♖xd7 ♘xd7 20 ♖xd7 ♖xc3! **♝c6** 19...♘xe4 20 ♗xe4! **20 ♞xf6+ gxf6 21 ♝xc6 ♜xc6 22 ♜b7 ♛c4** 22...♖fc8? 23 ♕d3

Qxb2?? 24 Qd7 **23 Qd3 Qxd3 24 Rxd3 Rc2 25 Rxb5 Rxe2 26 Kf1 Rc2 27 Ke1** 27 Rb7 Ra8? 28 Rdd7 Ra2?? 29 Rxf7 Raxb2 30 Rg7+! Kf8 31 Rbf7+! Ke8 32 Rxf6 +−; 27...f5 **Ra8 28 Rd2 Rc7 29 Ke2 f5 30 b4 Ra3 31 Rb2 Rcc3 32 Rb8+ Kg7 33 Rd8 Ra6 34 Kd2 Rf3 35 Ke2 Rc3 36 Rb8 Raa3 37 b5 Rab3 38 Rxb3 Rxb3 39 b6 Kf6 40 Kd2 Rf3 41 Kc2 ½-½ Speelman**

74 Kozlov-Sveshnikov USSR 78

1 d4 d5 2 c4 e6 3 Nf3 Nf6 4 g3 dxc4! 5 Bg2 5 Qa4+ Bd7 6 Qxc4 Nc6 7 0-0 Be7 8 e4 Rc8 9 Bd2! += Vaganian-Dvoretsky, USSR 75 **a6!?** 5...Nbd7 6 0-0 Be7 7 Nbd2 c5 8 Nxc4 += Polugaevsky-Csom, Montilla 75; 5... b5?! 6 Ne5 Nd5 7 a4 c6 8 0-0 Bb7 9 b3 cxb3 10 axb5! += Nesis-Zelinsky, corr 76 **6 0-0 b5 7 Ne5 Nd5 8 Nc3?!** 8 a4!? **Bb7 9 Nxd5 exd5 10 e4?!** 10 b3∝ **dxe4 11 Qh5** 11 Re1 **g6 12 Qe2 Qxd4! =+ 13 Bf4 Bg7 14 Rad1 Qb6 15 Bxe4 0-0 16 Rfe1 Ra7 17 h4∓** 17 Qf3!? **c5! 18 h5 Re8 19 Bxb7** 19 hxg6∓ **Rxb7 20 Nxc4!? Rxe2 21 Rxe2** 21 Nxb6 Rxe1+ 22 Rxe1 Rxb6 23 Re8+ Bf8 24 Bxb8 gxh5 −+ **bxc4 22 Re8+ Bf8 23 Bh6 Nd7 24 Rxd7 Rb8! −+ 25 Rde7 Qb5! 0-1 Gufeld**

75 Sosonko-Schneider
Buenos Aires 78

1 d4 Nf6 2 c4 e6 3 g3 d5 4 Bg2 dxc4 5 Nf3 a6 6 0-0!? 6 a4; 6 Ne5 **b5 7 Ne5 Nd5 8 Nc3 Bb7?!** 8...Bb4 9 Nxd5 exd5 10 e4 0-0 11 a3 Bd6 12 exd5 f6 13 Nc6 Nxc6 14 dxc6 Bf5∝ Gulko-Sveshnikov, Lvov 78; 8...c6 9 Nxd5 cxd5 10 e4∝; 8...f6!? **9 Nxd5! Bxd5?** 9...exd5 10 e4∝ **10 e4 +− Bb7 11 Qh5 g6** 11...Qe7 12 Bg5 +−; 11... Qf6 12 Bg5 +− **12 Nxg6 fxg6** 12... Rg8 13 Nxf8 Rxf8 14 d5 +− **13 Qe5 Nd7 14 Qxh8 Qe7 15 h4 0-0-0 16 Bg5 Qf7**

17 d5! 17 Bxd8 Bg7 18 Qxh7 Nf8 **Re8** 17...exd5 18 exd5 Be7 19 Qd4 Bc5 20 Qd2 Re8 21 Rae1 Nc5 22 Qf4 1-0 Sosonko-Steinbacker, Lugano 76 **18 dxe6 Rxe6 19 Rad1 Bc6** 19... Re8 **20 Bh6 Kb7 21 Rxd7 1-0 Sosonko**

76 Korchnoi-Karpov (15) 78

1 c4 Nf6 2 Nc3 e6 3 Nf3 d5 4 d4 Be7 5 g3 0-0 6 Bg2 dxc4 7 Ne5 Nc6 8 Bxc6 bxc6 9 Nxc6 Qe8 10 Nxe7+ Qxe7 11 Qa4 c5 12 Qxc4 cxd4 13 Qxd4 e5 14 Qh4 Rb8 15 Bg5 15 0-0 Rb4 16 e4 Qb7 17 f3 Qb6+ 18 Kh1 Ba6 Δ Qf2 **Rxb2 16 0-0** 16 Nd5 Qb7 17 Nxf6+ gxf6 18 0-0 fxg5 19 Qxg5+ **Qe6 17 Bxf6 Qxf6 18 Qxf6 gxf6 19 Rab1 Rxb1 20 Rxb1 Be6 21 f3** 21 Rb7? Rc8 **Rc8 22 Rc1 Rb8 23 Rc2 Rc8 24 Kf2 Bxa2 25 Rxa2 ½-½**

77 Korchnoi-Karpov (19) 78

1 c4 Nf6 2 g3 e6 3 Bg2 d5 4 Nf3 Be7 5 d4 0-0 6 Nbd2 b6 7 0-0 Bb7 8 cxd5 8 b3 **exd5 9 Ne5 Nbd7 10**

♘df3 c5 11 b3 a5 12 ♗b2 ♘e4 13 ♖c1 ♖e8 14 ♘xd7 ♕xd7 15 ♘e5 ♕e6 16 ♘d3 ♗d6 17 dxc5 bxc5 18 e3 18 ♗xe4 ♕xe4 19 ♘xc5 ♗xc5 20 ♖xc5 d4 21 f3 ♕e3+ Δ d3 **a4 19 bxa4 ♗a6 20 ♖e1 ♗xd3?** 20...♕f5 21 ♖c2 ♗c4 **21 ♕xd3 ♖xa4 22 ♕b3 ♖aa8 23 ♗xe4 dxe4** 23...♕xe4 24 ♖ed1 c4= **24 ♕xe6 ♖xe6 25 a3 ♖a4 26 ♖ed1 f6 27 ♔f1** 27 ♖c3 Δ ♖b3 **♔f7 28 ♖c2 ♗e7 29 ♖d7 ♖b6 30 g4** 30 ♖xc5 ♔e8 31 ♖cc7 ♗d6 32 ♖xd6 ♖xd6 33 ♖xg7 += **♔e6 31 ♖c7 ♖a8 32 ♖d2 g6** 32...♖d8 **33 ♔g2 f5 34 g5! ♖d6 35 ♖c2 ♖da6 36 h4 ♖8a7 37 ♖c8 ♖a8 38 ♖c7 ♖8a7 39 ♖c8 ½-½**

Dutch

78 Pytel-Hjartarsson Gausdal 78
1 c4 b6 2 d4 e6 3 ♘c3 ♗b7 4 e4 ♗b4 5 f3 ♘ge7 5...f5 6 exf5 exf5 7 ♘h3 ♕h4+ 8 g3 ♕h5 9 ♔f2!± Pytel-Helmers, Fredrikstadt 78 **6 ♗d3 0-0 7 ♘ge2 f5 8 0-0 ♗xc3 9 ♘xc3 d6? 10 exf5!± ♘xf5 11 d5 e5 12 f4 ♕e7? 13 fxe5 ♕xe5**

14 g4! ♕d4+ 15 ♔h1 15 ♖f2 ♘h4 **16 ♖xf8+** 16 ♗xh7+? ♔xh7 17 ♕xd4 ♖xf1+ −+ **♔xf8 17 ♗g5 ♘g6 18 ♕f3+ ♔g8 19 ♖f1 ♘a6 20 ♗xg6 hxg6 21 ♕f7+ ♔h8 22 ♖f4! 1-0** 22...♕d2 23 ♖f3 ♕xg5 24 ♖h3+ ♕h6 25 ♖xh6+ gxh6 26 ♘e4 **Pytel**

79 W.Schmidt-Spassky
Buenos Aires 78
1 ♘f3 e6 2 c4 f5 3 g3 ♘f6 4 ♗g2 ♗e7 5 0-0 0-0 6 d4 d5 7 b3 ♘c6!? 7...c6 8 ♗a3!? **8 ♗b2 ♗d7 9 ♘e5 ♗e8 10 ♘d3 ♗f7 11 ♘d2 a5!? 12 ♘f3 ♘e4 13 c5** 13 a3 **♗f6** 13...b6!? **14 a3 b6 15 ♖c1 ♗e8 16 ♕c2 bxc5!? 17 ♘xc5 ♘xc5 18 ♕xc5 ♕b8 19 ♘d2 ♖a6 20 e3 ♖b6= 21 ♖b1 ♗d7 22 ♖fc1 ♕b7 23 ♕c2 ♖b8 24 ♕d1 ♕c8 25 ♖c2 ♗e7 26 ♖c3 ♘a7 27 ♕c1 ♗d6 28 ♗f1 ♖8b7** 28...♗b5!? **29 ♖c5** 29 ♕c2!? Δ ♖c5 **♘c6?!** 29...♗xc5!? 30 dxc5 ♖xb3 **30 ♗c3 ♕a8 31 ♕c2 ♖b8 32 f4! ♗c8 33 ♘f3 ♕b7 34 ♘d2∞ ♖a8 35 ♗d3 ♗d7 36 g4!? ♗xc5?! 37 dxc5 ♖b5 38 ♗d4!? ♖e8!? 39 gxf5 ♘xd4 40 exd4 exf5 41 ♘f3 ♖e4 42 ♗xe4?!** 42 ♘e5 ♗e6 43 b4! axb4 44 ♕a4± Spassky **fxe4** 42...dxe4? 43 ♕c4+ **43 ♘e5 ♗f5 44 ♖b2 h6 45 ♕c3 ♕a6 46 ♕g3 ♕f6 ½-½ W.Schmidt**

Benoni

80 Guil.Garcia-Gild.Garcia
Mexico 78
1 c4 ♘f6 2 ♘c3 b6 3 d4 e6 4 a3 4 e4!? **c5!?** 4...♗b7 5 d5; 4...d5 **5 d5 exd5 6 cxd5 d6 7 e4 g6 8 f4 ♗g7 9 e5 ♘fd7** 9...dxe5!? 10 fxe5 ♘d7 11 e6 fxe6 12 dxe6 ♕h4+ 13 g3 ♗xc3+ 14 bxc3 ♕e4+ 15 ♕e2 ♗b7! 16 exd7+ ♘xd7 17 ♘f3 0-0 18 ♗g2 ♕xe2+ 19 ♔xe2 ♖ae8+ 20 ♗e3 ♘e5 21 ♘xe5 ♗xg2 22 ♘c4 ♗xh1!? 23 ♖xh1 +=; 22...♗f3+!?; 22...b5!?; 22 ♘d3? ♖f3!; 22 ♖g1? ♖xe5 23 ♖xg2 ♖fe8; 18 ♕xe4!? ♗xe4 19 ♗c4+ **10 e6! ♘f6 11 ♗b5+ ♔f8 12 f5 gxf5**

13 exf7 a6 14 ♗d3 ♔xf7 15 ♘ge2 ♖e8 16 0-0 ♔g8 17 ♗g5 ♖a7 18 ♘g3 ♖f7 19 ♗xf5 ♗xf5 20 ♘xf5 ±/+–

20...♗f8 21 ♕d3 b5 22 ♕g3 ♔h8 23 ♖ae1 ♘bd7 23...b4 24 ♖xe8 ♕xe8 25 ♘xd6 +– **24 ♖e6 b4 25 ♘e2 ♕a8 26 ♘xd6 ♗xd6 27 ♕xd6 ♖xe6 28 ♕xe6 +–** 28 dxe6 ♘e4 29 exd7! +– **♕f8 29 ♘g3 bxa3 30 bxa3 c4 31 d6 ♕g7 32 ♗d2 ♘b6 33 ♘h5 ♘xh5 34 ♖xf7 ♕a1+ 1-0 Speelman**

81 Miles-Botterill
Wales-England 78

1 d4 ♘f6 2 ♘f3 e6 3 c4 c5 4 d5 b5!? 5 ♗f4!? N 5 ♗g5 **exd5** 5...♗b7!? 6 ♘c3 a6!? 7 dxe6 fxe6 8 cxb5∝; 7 d6!?; 6...exd5 7 ♘xb5!? d6∝; 7 ♘xd5 +=; 6...b4? 7 ♘b5±; 6 dxe6 fxe6 7 cxb5∝; 5...♕b6?! 6 ♘c3 bxc4 7 e4 ♕xb2 8 ♖c1 ∝/± **6 cxd5 d6 7 e4 a6** 7...♘xe4? 8 ♗xb5+ Δ 0-0± **8 ♘bd2** 8 a4?! ♕e7!∝ **♗e7** 8...♘bd7!? 9 a4 ♖b8 10 axb5 axb5 11 ♗d3 += **9 a4 bxa4** 9...b4 10 a5± **10 ♕xa4+ ♘bd7** 10...♗d7? 11 ♕b3± **11 ♘c4!?** 11 ♗d3 Δ 0-0 += **0-0** 11...♘xe4? 12 ♗d3 f5 13 ♗xe4 fxe4 14 ♘xd6+ ♗xd6 15 ♗xd6 exf3? 16 ♕e4+ ♔f7 17 ♕e6 mate; 12...♘f6 13 ♘xd6+ ♗xd6 14 ♗xd6 ♕b6 15 ♕c6 +–; 12... g5± **12 ♘a5!?** 12 ♗d3 ♘b6 += **♖e8 13 ♗d3 ♘b6 14 ♕c2 ♗g4** 14...♘fxd5?! 15 exd5 ♗g5+ 16 ♗e3 ♗xe3 17 fxe3 ♘xd5 18 ♔f2± **15 0-0! +=** 15 ♘d2? ♘fxd5! 16 exd5 ♗g5+ 17 ♗e3 ♗xe3 18 fxe3 ♖xe3+ 19 ♔f2 ♕f6+ –+ **♗xf3 16 gxf3 ♘h5 17 ♘c6** 17 ♗g3? ♗g5 =+ **♕c7 18 ♘xe7+ ♕xe7 19 ♗g3 a5** 19...♘d7! =+ 20 f4 ♕f6 21 f5 g6!; 20 ♗xa6 ♘e5 Botterill; 19...♕f6 20 ♗xa6 ♕xf3? 21 ♗e2 +– **20 ♗b5 ♖f8 21 ♖a3** 21 ♖ae1 Δ f4, e5± **♔h8** 21...g6 (Δ f5) 22 ♖e3! ♕d8 23 e5± **22 ♗c6 ♖a7 23 ♖fa1 ♘d7?** 23...a4!? 24 b3 axb3 25 ♕xb3 ♖xa3 26 ♖xa3 +=/±; 26...♕c7 27 ♖a6 ♖b8 28 ♗xd6! +– Botterill; 25 ♖xa7?! ♕xa7; 24 ♗xa4 f5∝ **24 ♗xd7 +– ♕xd7 25 ♖xa5 ♖xa5 26 ♖xa5 f5 27 exf5** 27 ♕a4? ♕xa4 28 ♖xa4 f4 29 ♗h4 g5! **h6 28 ♖a6 ♖f6** 28...♘xg3 29 hxg3 ♕xf5 30 ♕xf5 ♖xf5 31 ♖xd6 ♖xf3 32 ♖c6 ♖b3 33 d6 ♖d3 34 ♔f1 +– **29 ♕e4 ♔h7 30 ♗h4** 30 ♖xd6! ♖xd6 31 ♗xd6 ♕xd6 32 f6+ g6 33 ♕e7+ ♕xe7 34 fxe7 ♘f6 35 d6 +– Botterill **♖xf5 31 ♖xd6 ♕f7 32 ♗g3 g5 33 ♖e6 ♘g7 34 ♖e7 ♕xd5 35 ♗e5 1-0 Miles**

82 Tatai-Povah England 78

1 d4 ♘f6 2 c4 c5 3 d5 e6 4 ♘c3 exd5 5 cxd5 d6 6 ♘f3 g6 7 ♘d2 ♗g7 8 e4 0-0 9 ♗e2 ♖e8 10 0-0 ♘bd7 11 a4 g5 12 ♕c2 12 f3 ♘e5 13 ♘c4 ♘xc4 14 ♗xc4 h6 15 ♘e2 a6 16 ♘g3 ♘h7= Popov-Spassov, Varna 71; 12 ♘c4 ♘xe4 13 ♘xe4 ♖xe4 14 ♘xd6 ♖d4 15 ♕b3 ♘b6 16 a5 ♘xd5 17 ♘xc8 ♖xc8 18 ♕xb7 ♖c7 19 ♕b3? c4 20 ♕g3 h6 =+; 19 ♕b5!? **♘e5 13 ♖a3** 13 ♘c4 ♘xc4 14 ♗xc4 ♘g4 15 ♘e2 Najdorf-Ree, Beverwijk 71 15...♘e5! Δ g4; 13 ♘f3 ♘xf3+ 14 ♗xf3 Gligoric-Fischer, Palma 70; 14...♘d7 15 ♗g4

♘e5 16 ♗xc8 ♖xc8=; 13 ♘d1 g4 14 ♘e3 ♘h5 15 g3?! ♕f6! 16 f4? gxf3 17 ♘xf3 ♗h3 18 ♖f2 ♘xf3+ 19 ♗xf3 ♕g6 20 ♘g2 ♗d4 21 ♘h4 ♕f6 22 ♗xh5 ♖xe4! 23 ♘g2 ♖ae8 24 ♗f4 ♕f5 25 g4 ♕xf4!! 0-1 Farago-Szilagyi 74; 13 b3 g4 14 ♗b2 ♘h5 15 ♘c4 ♘xc4 16 ♗xc4 ♘f4 17 ♘d1 ♗e5= Gligoric-Tatai, Venice 71 **g4 14 b3!** 14 ♗b5 ♖f8 =+ 15 ♖e1 ♘h5 16 ♘f1 f5 17 ♘g3 ♘xg3 18 hxg3 ♕f6 19 ♗e3 ♕g6 20 ♗f4 a6 21 ♗f1 fxe4!∓ Dzieciolowski-Holm, Zabrze 77 **♘h5 15 ♘c4 ♕f6 16 ♘b5 ♘xc4 17 bxc4 ♖e7** 17...♕e7!? **18 h3?!** 18 g3! += Δ ♗d3, ♖b3, ♘c3-e2-f4; 18 f4!? a6 19 e5 dxe5 20 fxe5 ♕xe5 21 ♖e3 ♕xe3+ 22 ♗xe3 ♖xe3 23 ♘d6∞ **a6 19 ♗xg4** 19 hxg4 ♘f4! 20 ♘c3 ♕g5 21 ♕d2 ♘xe2+ 22 ♕xe2 ♕h4! 23 f3? ♗e5!∓; 22...♕xg4? 23 ♕xg4 ♗xg4 24 f3± **axb5! 20 ♗xh5 ♖xa4 21 ♖xa4** 21 ♖g3!? ♖xc4 22 ♕b2 ♔h8! 23 ♕xb5 ♖xc1! 24 ♖xc1 ♕h6∞; 22...♔f8? 23 ♖xg7! Δ ♗h6 +− **bxa4 22 ♕xa4 ♖xe4= 23 ♕a8 ♕d8 24 ♗g4 ♖e8 25 ♗f4** 25 ♗xc8 ♕xc8 26 ♕xc8 ♖xc8 27 ♗f4 ♗f8 28 ♖b1 ♖a8! 29 ♖xb7 ♖a4= **♗xg4 26 ♕xd8 ♖xd8 27 hxg4 ♗f8! 28 ♖b1 ♖a8! 29 ♖xb7 ♖a4 30 ♖d7 ½-½** 30...♖xc4 31 ♗xd6 ♗xd6 32 ♖xd6 ♖xg4 33 ♖c6 c4 34 d6 ♖d4= **Povah**

83 Danielsen-Filipowicz
Roskilde 78

1 d4 ♘f6 2 c4 c5 3 d5 e6 4 ♘c3 exd5 5 cxd5 d6 6 e4 g6 7 ♘f3 ♗g7 8 ♗e2 0-0 9 0-0 ♖e8 10 ♘d2 ♘a6 10...♘bd7 11 a4 a6 12 ♕c2 ♘e5 13 ♖a3! ♕e7 14 a5 ♗d7 15 ♖b3 ♖ab8 16 ♖b6 ♗g4 17 f3 ♗c8 18 ♔h1∞ Portisch-Velimirovic, Ljubljana 75 **11 f3** 11 ♔h1! **♘c7 12 a4 b6 13 ♘c4 ♗a6 14 ♗d2?** 14 ♗g5! h6 15 ♗e3 ♗xc4 16 ♗xc4 a6 17 ♕d2 ♔h7 18 ♖ab1± **♕d7!** 14...♗xc4 15 ♗xc4 a6= **15 ♘e3 ♗xe2 16 ♕xe2 a6 17 ♖ab1 b5 18 b3** 18 b4? cxb4 19 ♖xb4 a5∓ **♘h5! 19 g3 f5!**

20 exf5? 20 ♘ed1; 20 ♕d3? f4!∓ **♖xe3! −+ 21 ♗xe3 ♗xc3 22 ♕d3** 22 fxg6 ♖e8! 23 gxh7+ ♔h8 −+ **b4 23 fxg6 ♖e8! 24 ♗f2 ♘f6 25 gxh7+ ♕xh7 26 ♕c4 ♘d7! 27 ♕f4 ♘e5 28 ♔g2 ♕g6 29 ♗g1 ♘xd5** 29...♘d3 30 ♕c4 ♘e1+ 31 ♖bxe1 ♗xe1 32 ♗xc5!∞ **30 ♕e4 ♕xe4 31 fxe4 ♘c7 32 ♖bd1 ♘f7 33 ♖f4 ♘e6 34 ♖f5 ♗d4! 35 h4 ♗xg1 36 ♖xg1 ♘d4 37 ♖f6 ♖xe4 38 ♖gf1 ♖e7 39 g4 ♘xb3 40 g5 ♘d2 41 ♖1f4 b3 0-1** 42 g6 b2 43 gxf7+ ♔f8 44 ♖g6 ♖xf7 −+ **Filipowicz**

84 Malich-Nunn Budapest 78

1 ♘f3 ♘f6 2 c4 e6 3 d4 c5 4 d5 exd5 5 cxd5 d6 6 ♘c3 g6 7 e4 ♗g7 8 ♗f4!? 0-0 8...a6? 9 ♕a4+ ♗d7 10 ♕b3 ♕c7 11 e5± **9 ♗e2** 9 ♘d2 ♘h5 10 ♗e3 ♘d7 11 ♗e2 ♘e5 12 0-0 ♕h4∞; 11 g4 ♗d4!?∞ **a6 10 a4 ♗g4** 10...♖e8 11 ♘d2± **11 h3** 11 ♘d2 ♗xe2 12 ♕xe2 ♘h5 13 ♗e3 ♘d7 14 g4 ♘hf6 15 ♘c4? b5! 16 ♘xd6 ♕e7 17 g5 ♘h5 18 ♘f5 gxf5 19 ♕xh5 f4! 20 ♗d2 ♗xc3 21 ♗xc3 ♕xe4+ 22 ♔d2 b4

23 ♗f6 ♕xd5+ 0-1 Benjamin-Nunn, England 77; 15 0-0= **♗xf3 12 ♗xf3= ♕c7 13 0-0 ♘bd7 14 ♕c2 c4!** 14... ♖fe8? 15 b3! += c4 16 b4 Dieks-Nunn, Groningen 74/5 **15 ♖ac1 ♘c5 16 ♘e2 b5** 16...♘d3? 17 ♕xd3 **17 axb5 axb5 18 b4 cxb3 19 ♕xb3 ♕b6 20 ♕c2 ♘fd7 21 ♗e3 b4 22 ♖b1 b3 23 ♕d1 b2 24 ♘d4 ♖fb8 25 ♕c2** 25 ♘c6 ♖b7 **♖a3 26 ♖fd1 ♘e5∓ 27 ♗e2** 27 ♔h2 ♕b4 28 ♖d2 ♘c4 29 ♘c6 ♘xd2 30 ♘xb4 ♘xb1 31 ♘c6 ♘c3 −+ **♕b4 28 ♖d2** 28 ♘c6 ♘xc6 29 ♗xc5 ♕xc5 30 ♕xc5 dxc5 31 dxc6 ♖c8 32 c7 ♖a1! 33 ♖d8+ ♗f8 34 ♖xc8 ♖xb1+ 35 ♔h2 ♖h1+ 36 ♔g3 b1♕ 37 ♖xf8+ ♔xf8 38 c8♕+ ♔g7 −+; 32...♖xc7? 33 ♖d8+ ♗f8 34 ♖xb2 **♖a1 29 ♖dd1 ♖xb1 30 ♖xb1 ♘g4! 31 ♘c6** 31 ♗xg4 ♗xd4 32 ♗xd4 ♕xd4 −+ **♘xe3 32 fxe3 ♕b3 33 ♕xb3 ♖xb3 34 e5 dxe5 35 d6 e4 36 ♔f2 ♖b6 37 ♘d4 ♗xd4!** −+ 37...♖xd6? 38 ♖xb2 ♗xd4 39 exd4 ♖xd4 40 ♔e3∓; 38...♖xd4? 39 ♖b8+ **38 exd4 ♘a4 39 d7 ♖d6 40 ♔e3** 40 ♗b5 ♘c3 41 ♖xb2 ♘d1+; 40 ♔e1 ♖xd7 41 ♗b5 ♖xd4 −+ **♖xd7 41 ♗b5 ♘c3 42 ♖xb2 ♖b7 43 ♖b3 ♘xb5 0-1 Nunn**

85 Alburt-Gofstein USSR 78

1 d4 ♘f6 2 c4 c5 3 d5 e6 4 ♘c3 exd5 5 cxd5 g6 6 ♘f3 ♗g7 7 e4 d6 8 ♗g5!? h6 8...0-0?! 9 ♘d2 ♖e8 10 ♗e2 a6 11 a4 ♘bd7 12 0-0 ♖b8 13 ♗h4 += Kavalek-Ljubojevic, Manila 76 **9 ♗h4 a6!** 9...g5 10 ♗g3 ♘h5 11 ♗b5+ ♔f8 12 e5!? ♘xg3 13 fxg3! += Stean-Nunn, Birmingham 76 **10 ♘d2** 10 a4?! g5! **b5 11 ♗e2 0-0 12 0-0 ♖e8 13 ♕c2** 13 f4? ♘bd7 14 ♕c2 ♕c7 15 ♖ae1 ♘b6! =+ Spassov-Hulak, Athens 76 **♘bd7 14 a4!?** 14 ♗g3∞ **b4 15 ♘d1 g5 16 ♗g3 ♘xd5 17 ♘c4** 17 exd5 ♖xe2 18 ♘e3∞ **♘f4 18 ♘xd6?** 18 ♗xf4 Δ ♘xd6 **b3! 19 ♕d2 ♘e5∓ 20 ♘c3 ♖a7! 21 ♗xf4 gxf4 22 ♖fd1 ♖d7 23 ♕d5 ♖e6 24 ♘xf7 ♘xf7 25 ♕xb3** 25 ♕xe6? ♖xd1+ Δ ♗xe6 −+ **♕g5?** 25...♖d4 −+; 25... ♖b6 −+ **26 ♕b8! ♖e8 27 ♗xa6 ♖xd1+ 28 ♖xd1 ♗d7 29 ♕c7 ♗h3 30 g3 ♘e5 31 ♗e2! ♗g4 32 h4 ♕h5 33 ♖d8 fxg3 34 ♖xe8+ ♕xe8 35 fxg3 ♗xe2 36 ♘xe2 ♕xa4?** 36...c4! −+ **37 ♕c8+ ♗f8 38 ♕e6+ ♘f7 39 ♕g4+ ♔h8 40 ♕e6 ♕d1+ 41 ♔f2= ♘d6 42 ♘f4 ♕d4+ ½-½ Gufeld**

86 Legky-Shvedchikov USSR 78

1 d4 ♘f6 2 c4 c5 3 d5 e6 4 ♘c3 exd5 5 cxd5 d6 6 e4 g6 7 f4 ♗g7 8 e5 ♘fd7 9 ♘b5 dxe5 10 ♘d6+ ♔e7 11 ♘xc8+ ♕xc8 12 ♘f3 ♖e8 13 fxe5 ♘xe5 14 ♗b5 ♘bd7 15 ♘xe5! 15 0-0 a6?! 16 ♘xe5 ♗xe5 17 d6+!± **♔f8!** 15...♗xe5 16 0-0 ♕c7 17 ♕g4± **16 0-0 ♖xe5!** 16...♗xe5?± **17 ♗f4 c4!** 17...a6?! 18 ♗xd7 ♕xd7 19 ♗xe5 ♗xe5 Shereshevsky-Savon, USSR 74 20 ♕f3! **18 ♕d4!** 18 ♗xe5 ♘xe5 19 ♔h1 ♕c5 20 ♗a4 ♖d8∓; 18 ♗xd7 ♕c5+! 19 ♔h1 ♖xd5 =+ Juferov-Kapengut, USSR 76 **♖f5! 19 ♗h6??** 19 ♕xc4!= **♗xh6 20 ♗xd7 ♗g7! −+**

21 ♕xg7+ ♔xg7 22 ♗xc8 ♖xf1+ 23

Kxf1 Rxc8 24 Re1 Kf6 25 d6 Rd8 26 Re7 Rxd6 27 Rxb7 Rb6! 28 Rxa7 Rxb2 29 Rc7 Rb4! 30 Ra7 Ke5! 31 Rxf7 Rb2! 32 Ke1 c3?? 32...h5! −+ **33 Kd1!= h5 34 Re7+ Kd4 35 Rd7+ Ke4 36 Re7+ Kd3 37 Rd7+ Kc4 38 Rc7+ Kd4 39 Rd7+ Ke4 40 Re7+ Kd3 41 Rd7+ Ke3 42 Rc7 Rd2+ 43 Kc1 Kd3 44 Rd7+ Ke2 45 Rc7 Rxa2 46 Rc6 Kf1 47 g3 g5 48 Rc5 h4 49 gxh4! gxh4 50 h3 Rh2 51 Rxc3 Kg2 52 Kd2 Rxh3 53 Rc4 Kg3 54 Rc3+ Kg4 55 Rc4+ Kg3 56 Rc3+ Kg2 57 Rc4 Kf2 58 Rf4+ Kg3 59 Ke3 Rh1 60 Rf3+ Kg2 61 Rf2+ Kg1 62 Ra2 Rh3+ 61 Kf4 ½-½ Sher**

87 L.Bronstein-Tringov
Buenos Aires 78
1 d4 Nf6 2 c4 c5 3 d5 3 dxc5!? **e6 4 Nc3 exd5 5 cxd5 d6 6 Nf3 g6 7 Bf4** Δ Nb5 **a6 8 a4 Bg7 9 e4 0-0 10 Be2 Bg4 11 Nd2** 11 0-0 Bxf3 12 Bxf3= Polugaevsky **Bxe2 12 Qxe2 Nh5 13 Be3 Nd7 14 g4!?** 14 0-0 += **Nhf6 15 0-0 Re8 16 a5 Qc7 17 f3** 17 h3! Δ f4 **b5 18 axb6 Nxb6 19 Kh1 Qb7 20 Ra2 Nfd7 21 Rfa1 Bd4 22 Bh6?** 22 Nd1! f5 23 gxf5 gxf5 24 Bxd4 cxd4 25 Qg2+ Kh8 26 Qf2 +−; 22...Nb8± **Nxd5 23 Nxd5 Qxd5 24 Rxa6 Rxa6 25 Qxa6 Qe6 26 Nc4 Qf6 27 Kg2 Qh4 28 Be3 d5! 29 Bxd4 cxd4 30 Nd6 Rb8 31 Ra2 Qf6 32 exd5 Ne5 33 Ra3 d3! 0-1 Neikirch**

88 Zaichik-Gedevanishvili USSR 78
1 d4 Nf6 2 c4 e6 3 g3 c5 4 d5 exd5 5 cxd5 g6 5...b5!? 6 e4?! Nxe4 7 Qe2 Qe7 8 Bg2 Nd6 9 Be3 b4≈ Sosonko-Olafsson, Wijk aan Zee 77; 6 Bg2 d6 7 a4 Qa5+!? 8 Nd2 Bb7 9 e4∞; 6 a3!? **6 Nc3 Bg7 7 Bg2 0-0 8 Nf3 b5?** 8...d6 **9 Nxb5 Qa5+ 10 Nc3 Ne4 11 0-0** 11 Qc2? Nxc3 12 Bd2 Qa4! −+ **Nxc3 12 bxc3 Qxc3 13 Rb1 Qc4!?** 13...Ba6 14 Bf4 +=; 13... d6 14 Bf4± **14 Bf4 Ba6 15 Re1 Re8 16 e4 Qxa2** 16...h6 17 e5 g5 18 Bxg5! hxg5 19 Nxg5 Qd3 20 e6! +− **17 e5± h6** 17...Bc4 18 Ng5 h6 19 Ne4 +− **18 e6! dxe6**

19 Ne5! +− 19 dxe6? Nc6 **Bxe5 20 Bxe5 Nd7 21 Ra1 Qc4 22 dxe6** 22 Bf1? Qxd5 **Nxe5** 22...Qxe6 23 Bd5! Qb6 24 Bxa8 +− **23 Rxe5 f6 24 Bxa8 fxe5 25 Qf3 Bb5** 25...Rf8 26 e7! +− **26 Bd5 Qd3 e7+ 1-0 Gufeld**

89 Bohlig-Filipowicz Warsaw 78
1 d4 Nf6 2 g3 c5 3 d5 e6 4 c4 exd5 5 cxd5 d6 6 Nc3 g6 7 Bg2 Bg7 8 Nf3 0-0 9 0-0 Na6 9...Nbd7 10 Nd2 a6 11 a4 Rb8 12 Nc4 Ne5; 9...a6; 9...Re8 **10 Nd2** 10 h3 Nc7 11 e4 Nd7 12 Bf4 Ne5 13 Nxe5 dxe5 14 Be3 += b6 Δ Ne8-d6 Sosonko-Taimanov, Hastings 75/76; 10...Re8? 11 Nd2 Nc7 12 Nc4! a6 13 Bf4 Bf8 13 a4 Rb8 14 e4 b5 16 Na5!± Sosonko-Ornstein, Haifa 76; 10...Bd7 11 e4 Qc8 12 Kh2 Re8 13 Re1 c4≈ Marovic-Planinc, IBM 73 **Nc7 11 a4 b6 12 Nc4 Ba6 13 Na3?!** 13 Qb3 Bxc4 14 Qxc4 a6 15 Rb1 +=; 15 e4 += **Re8 14 Re1 Ng4!** Δ Bd4 **15 h3**

♞e5 16 ♝d2? ♜b8 17 ♛b3 b5! 18 axb5 ♝xb5!∓ 19 ♞cxb5 a6 19...♘xb5 20 ♘xb5 ♕b6 21 ♗c3 a6! =+; 21 f4? c4+ 22 ♕e3 ♘f3+ −+ **20 f4 ♞d7 21 ♞c4 ♜xb5 22 ♛d3 ♞b6 23 ♞xb6 ♜xb6 24 ♝c3 ♛b8 25 ♜a2 ♜b3 −+ 26 e3 ♛b4 27 ♜c1 ♞b5 28 ♝xb4 ♜xd3 29 ♝e1 ♜dxe3 30 ♝f2 ♝d4! 31 ♜xa6 ♜xg3 32 ♜b6 ♜e2 33 ♜f1 ♜xb2 34 ♚h2 ♜gb3 0-1 Filipowicz**

90 Andrianov-Azmajparashvili
USSR 78

1 d4 ♞f6 2 c4 e6 3 g3 c5 4 d5 exd5 5 cxd5 d6 6 ♞c3 g6 7 ♞f3 ♝g7 8 ♝g2 0-0 9 0-0 ♜e8! 9...a6 10 a4 ♘bd7 11 ♘d2 **10 ♞d2** 10 ♗f4?! ♘h5!∝ **♞bd7 11 a4 a6 12 a5** 12 ♘c4 ♘e5 13 ♘a3 ♖b8 14 h3 ♘h5 15 e4! += **b5 13 axb6 ♞xb6 14 ♞b3 ♝f5!?** N 14...♘c4!? 15 ♖a4 ♘b6 16 ♖a2 ♘c4= **15 ♞a5 ♞e4! 16 ♜a3** 16 ♘xe4 ♗xe4 17 ♘c6 ♕c7 =+ **♛c7 17 ♜e1 ♝d4! 18 e3 ♝g7 19 ♝d2 c4!=**

20 g4? ♝xg4 21 ♛xg4 ♞xd2 22 ♛e2 ♝xc3? 22...♘b3! 23 ♘xb3 cxb3 24 ♖xb3 ♘c4∓ **23 ♜xc3 ♞a4 24 ♜a3 ♛xa5 25 ♜ea1 ♞e4?!** 25...♘b3! 26 ♖xa4 ♕b5 27 ♖1a3 ♖ec8∓ **26 ♜xa4 ♛xd5 27 ♛xc4 ♛xc4 28 ♜xc4 d5 29 ♜d4 ♜ab8 30 ♜xd5 ♜xb2 31 ♝xe4 ♜xe4= 32 ♜xa6 ♜g4+ 33 ♚f1 ♜b1+ 34 ♚e2 ♜g2 35 ♚f3?** Zeitnot 35 ♖f6= **♜xh2 36 ♚g3 ♜hh1 37 ♜a8+ ♚g7 38 ♜a7 ♜b6 39 ♜d4! ♜f6 40 ♜f4 ♜xf4** 40...♖g1+ 41 ♔h2 ♖xf4 42 ♔xg1 =+ **41 exf4! =+** 41 ♔xf4 ♖g1∓ **♜g1+ 42 ♚h3! ♚f6 43 f3 h6 44 ♚h2 ♜d1 45 ♚g3 ♚e6 46 ♜a6+ ♜d6 47 ♜a5 ♜d5 48 ♜a7 f6 49 ♜a6+ ♚f5 50 ♜c6 h5 51 ♜a6 ♜c5! 52 ♜b6 ♜a5 53 ♜c6 g5 54 fxg5 fxg5 55 ♜c3? h4+ 56 ♚g2 ♜a4! 57 ♜c5+?** 57 ♖c8! ♖a2+ 58 ♔h3 ♖f2 59 ♖f8+ ♔e5 60 ♔g4! ♖g2+ 61 ♔h3 ♖g3+ 62 ♔h2 =+ **♚f4∓ 58 ♜c2 ♜d4! 59 ♜a2 ♚e3 60 ♜a5 ♜d2+ 61 ♚g1 ♚f4 −+ 62 ♜a3 ♚g3 63 f4+ ♚xf4 64 ♜b3 ♜e2 65 ♜b4+ ♚f3 66 ♜b3+ ♜e3 67 ♜b8 g4 68 ♜f8+ ♚g3 69 ♜f1 h3 70 ♜a1 ♜c3 71 ♜b1 ♚h4 72 ♜b4 ♚g5 73 ♜b5+ ♚f4 74 ♜b4+ ♚f3 75 ♜b8 ♜c1+ 76 ♚h2 g3+ 0-1 Gufeld**

91 Reicher-Pytel
Val Thorens 78

1 d4 ♞f6 2 c4 c5 3 d5 g6 4 ♞c3 ♝g7 5 e4 d6 6 ♝d3 0-0 7 ♞ge2 e5 8 h3 a6 9 g4 b5! 10 cxb5 axb5 11 ♝xb5 ♛a5 12 ♞g3 ♝a6 13 ♛e2 ♜c8 14 ♝d2 c4 15 ♝xa6 15 a4? ♗xb5 16 ♘xb5 ♕xb5! 17 axb5 ♖xa1+ 18 ♗c1 ♖xc1+ 19 ♔d2 ♗h6+! **♞xa6 16 0-0 ♛b6 17 ♝e3 ♛b4 18 ♜ab1 ♞d7 19 ♜fc1 ♞ac5 20 ♜c2 ♞d3 21 ♞f1 ♞f4 22 ♛f3 ♞c5!? 23 ♞d2** 23 ♗xf4!? **♞cd3 24 ♞f1 ♛b7! 25 ♝d2 ♞b4 26 ♜cc1 ♞fd3 27 ♜d1 ♞c2 28 ♞e3 ♞d4 29 ♛g2 ♞f4 30 ♛h1 ♛e7 31 ♚f1 ♛f6 32 ♝e1 h5 33 ♜d2 ♞d3 34 ♜bd1 ♜ab8 35 gxh5 gxh5 36 ♞f5 ♞xb2** 36...♘xf5! **37 ♜xd4!? exd4 38 ♜xd4 ♞d3 39 ♝d2 ♚h7?! 40 ♚f3 ♛g6 41 ♝e3** 41 ♘g3 ♗xd4!∓ **♝xd4 42 ♝xd4 ♜g8 43 ♞g3 h4 44 ♞ge2 ♞e5 0-1 Pytel**

92 Peev-Timoshenko Decin 78
1 d4 Nf6 2 c4 c5 3 d5 d6 4 Nc3 g6 5 e4 Bg7 6 f4 0-0 7 Bd3 e6 8 dxe6 fxe6 9 Nge2 Nc6 10 0-0 Bd7 10... Nd4 **11 Ng3!?** 11 f5!? Qe7!? 12 Bg5!±; 11...Nd4∞ **Qe7 12 Be3!?** 12 f5!? **Rad8 13 h3** 13 Qe2!? Nd4; 13 Qd2!? Ng4 =+ **d5! =/=+ 14 Bd2?** 14 e5 d4 15 exf6 Bxf6 16 Bd2 dxc3 17 bxc3! e5 18 Qc2∞ **Nb4!∓ 15 Bb1?** 15 Qe2 Nxd3 16 Qxd3 dxc4 17 Qxc4 b5 18 Qe2 b4!∓ **dxc4 −+ 16 Qe2 Bc6 17 e5 Nfd5 18 Qxc4 Nxf4 19 Bxf4 Rd4 20 Qe2 Rdxf4 21 Rxf4 Rxf4 22 Qe3 Qg5** Δ Rf1+! **23 Be4 Nc2! 0-1** 24 Bxc2 Rf1+ −+ **Pritchett**

93 Padevsky-Ghitescu
Balkaniad 78
1 d4 Nf6 2 c4 c5 3 d5 d6 4 Nc3 g6 5 e4 Bg7 6 f4 0-0 7 Nf3 e6 8 Be2 exd5 9 cxd5 Bg4 9...Re8 10 e5 dxe5 11 fxe5 Ng4 12 Bg5 f6 13 exf6 Bxf6 14 Qd2 Bf5∞ **10 0-0 Bxf3 11 Bxf3 Nbd7 12 Be3** 12 Kh1 a6 13 Be3 Re8 14 g4 h6 15 g5 hxg5 16 e5 gxf4!∓ **Re8 13 Bf2!? a6 14 Qc2! += Rc8** 14...b5?! 15 a4!± **15 a4 c4 16 Kh1 Qa5 17 Rfe1 h6 18 Bg3 Nh7 19 Bg4 Nhf6 20 Bh3 Rcd8!**

21 e5?! 21 Rad1 Nh5= **Nxd5 22 Nxd5 Qxd5 23 Red1 Qc5 24 Rxd6 Nf8!= 25 Bf2 Qb4 26 Rad1?! Rxd6 27 Rxd6 c3!∓ 28 Bd4? Qxd6! 0-1 Ghitescu**

Nimzo-Indian

94 Niklasson-Iskov Bergen 78
1 d4 Nf6 2 c4 e6 3 Nc3 Bb4 4 a3 Bxc3+ 5 bxc3 b6 6 f3 Ba6 7 e4 Nc6 8 e5! Ng8 9 Nh3 Na5 10 Qa4 Ne7 11 Bg5 h6 12 Bh4 0-0 13 Bd3 d5?? 13...Qe8! 14 Bb1 Bxc4 15 Qc2 Ng6 16 Nf4 Bb3 17 Qe4 d5 18 exd6 Bd5 =+ **14 Bb1! Bxc4** 14...g5 15 Qc2 Ng6 16 Nf4! gxh4 17 Nxg6 Re8 18 Nh8! +− Kotov-Keres, Budapest 50 **15 Qc2 g6 16 Nf2 c5 17 Ng4 Nb3 18 Nxh6+ Kh7 19 Bf6! b5** 19...Nxa1 20 Qf2 +−; 19...Kxh6 20 Qf2 +− **20 Ng4** 20 Qf2 Qa5!∞ **Rh8 21 Ra2 cxd4 22 Qf2 Kg8 23 Bxh8 Qa5 24 Qh4 Qxc3+ 25 Kf2 1-0 Iskov**

95 Korchnoi-Panno
Wijk aan Zee 78
1 c4 Nf6 2 Nc3 e6 3 Nf3 Bb4 4 Qc2 c5 5 a3 Ba5 6 e3 0-0 7 d4 b6? 8 Bd3 Bb7 9 0-0 Bxc3 10 Qxc3 Be4 11 Be2! Nc6 12 dxc5 bxc5 13 b4!± Rc8 14 b5 Na5 15 Bd2 Nb7 16 Qb2! Qe7 17 a4 d5?! 18 Ne5 Nd6 19 f3 Bg6 20 Nc6 +− Qb7 21 cxd5 exd5 22 Qa3! Rxc6 22...Nd7 23 Ne7+ **23 bxc6 Qxc6 24 Rac1 Rc8 25 Rfd1 Nd7 26 Be1 Nb6 27 Qa2 c4 28 a5 Na8 29 Qd2 1-0** 29...Nc7 30 e4 **Pytel**

96 Soos-Kokkinosz Athens 78
1 d4 Nf6 2 c4 e6 3 Nc3 Bb4 4 Qc2 c5 5 dxc5 Na6?! 6 a3 Bxc3+ 6...Qa5 **7 Qxc3 Nxc5 8 b4!?** 8 f3 (Δ e4) d5 9 cxd5 **Nce4 9 Qd4 d5 10 c5 h6?** 10...b6 **11 f3 Ng5 12 h4 Ngh7 13 g4**

0-0 14 ♝f4 ♞e8 15 e4 f6 16 e5 ♜f7 17 ♝d3 f5 18 ♞e2 ♞c7 19 g5! hxg5 20 hxg5 ♞xg5 21 ♝xg5 ♛xg5 22 ♚f2 ♛d8 23 ♜ag1 ♞e8 24 ♞f4 g5 25 ♞h3 g4 26 fxg4 f4 27 g5 ♞g7 28 g6 ♜f5 29 ♝xf5 ♛h4+ 30 ♚f1 ♞xf5 31 ♛xf4 ♛h5 32 ♞f2 1-0

97 Korchnoi-Karpov (17) 78

1 c4 ♞f6 2 ♞c3 e6 3 d4 ♝b4 4 e3 0-0 5 ♝d3 c5 6 d5 b5 6...h6 7 e4 exd5 8 exd5 ♗xc3+ 9 bxc3 ♖e8+ 10 ♘e2 d6 **7 dxe6 fxe6 8 cxb5 a6 9 ♞e2 d5 10 0-0 e5 11 a3 axb5** 11...♗a5; 11...♗xc3 **12 ♝xb5 ♝xc3** 12...♗a5 13 b4!; 12...c4 13 e5! **13 bxc3** 13 ♘xc3 **♝a6 14 ♜b1 ♛d6 15 c4 d4 16 ♞g3 ♞c6 17 a4 ♞a5 18 ♛d3 ♛e6 19 exd4 cxd4** 19...exd5 20 ♗a3± **20 c5 ♜fc8 21 f4!** 21 ♗g5; 21 ♗a3 ♘d5! 22 ♘e4 ♘f4; 21...♘c4? 22 ♗b4 **♜xc5 22 ♝xa6 ♛xa6 23 ♛xa6** 23 ♖b8+ ♔f7 24 ♖b5 **♜xa6 24 ♝a3 ♜d5 25 ♞f5 ♚f7 26 fxe5 ♜xe5 27 ♜b5?!** Zeitnot 27 ♘xd4 ♘c4 28 ♖b7+ ♔g8 29 ♗e7; 28...♔g6 ♗f8; 28...♔e8 29 ♗c1; 27...♔g6 28 ♖a1 **♞c4! 28 ♜b7+** 28 ♘d6+ ♖xd6 29 ♖xe5 ♖d7 −+ **♚e6 29 ♞xd4+** 29 ♘xg7+ ♔d4 **♚d4 30 ♞f3?** 30 ♘c2 ♘xa3 31 ♘b4+; 30...♖xa4 31 ♗f8; 30 ♗f8 ♔xd4 31 ♗xg7 ♖ee6 32 ♖f7 ♔e5 33 g4 h6 34 ♖f5+; 33...♘e3 34 ♖1xf6 ♖xf6 35 g5 +−; 31...♘e4 **♞xa3 31 ♞xe5** 31 ♖d1+ ♔e6 32 ♘d4+! ♔d5 33 ♘b5+ ♔c6 34 ♖c7+ ♔b6 35 ♖d6+ ♔a5 36 ♖xa6+ ♔xa6 37 ♘xa3; 31...♔c6! 32 ♖b3 ♖e4 33 ♖xa3 ♖exa4 34 ♖c3+ ♔b3= **♚xe5 32 ♜e7+ ♚d4 33 ♜xg7?** 33 ♖d1+! Δ ♖c7+, ♖xg7 **♞c4 34 ♜f4+** 34 ♖f7 ♔e5 35 ♖e7+ = **♞e4 35 ♜d7+** 35 ♖xh7 **♚e3 36 ♜f3+ ♚e2 37 ♜xh7 ♞cd2 38 ♜a3? ♜c6**

39 ♜a1?? 39 h4? ♖c1+ 40 ♔h2 ♘f1+ 41 ♔h3 ♘f2 mate; 39 g4 ♘f3+ 40 ♖xf3 ♔xf3 41 h4= **♞f3+! 0-1** 40 ♔h1 ♘f2 mate; 40 gxf3 ♖g6+ 41 ♔h1 ♘f2 mate

98 Korchnoi-Karpov (7) 78

1 d4 ♞f6 2 c4 e6 3 ♞c3 ♝b4 4 e3 0-0 5 ♝d3 c5 6 d5 N **b5** 6...exd5 7 cxd5 ♘xd5 8 ♗xh7+ ♔xh7 9 ♕xd5 +=; 7...d6 **7 dxe6 fxe6 8 cxb5 ♝b7 9 ♞f3 d5 10 0-0 ♞bd7 11 ♞e2 ♛e8 12 ♞g3 e5 13 ♝f5 g6 14 ♝h3 a6 15 ♞g5!** 15 bxa6?! ♗xa6 16 ♗xd7 ♕xd7 17 ♘xe5; 15 e4! axb5 16 ♗h6 ♖f7 17 ♘g5 ♖e7 18 exd5 ♗xd5 19 ♘3e4!; 15...d4 16 ♕b3+ ♔h8 17 ♗h6 axb5 18 a3 ♗a5 19 ♕xb5 ♗a6 20 ♕xa5 ♗xf1 21 ♕c7 **axb5 16 ♞e6 c4 17 ♝d2 ♝c5!** 17...♗d6 18 ♘xf8 ♘xf8 19 f4 exf4 20 exf4 ♗c5+ 21 ♔h1 d4 22 f5 **18 ♞c7 ♛e7 19 ♞xa8 ♜xa8 20 a3 ♞b6 21 ♛c2 ♝c8 22 ♝xc8 ♜xc8 23 ♝a5** 23 ♗b4 ♗xb4 24 axb4 ♕xb4 25 ♖a7 **♞bd7 24 ♛d2 ♝d6 25 ♝b4 ♞c5 26 ♝xc5 ♝xc5 27 ♚h1 ♛d6 28 ♜ad1** 28 f4 **♚h8 29 ♛c2?** 29 e4 d4 30 ♕g5 ♘d7 31 f4 exf4 32 ♘e2 Δ ♘xf4, ♘d5± **♛e6 30 ♞e2 ♛c6 31 h3 ♜e8 32 b4?? ♝b6 33 ♛b2 ♚g8 34 ♜fe1 ♚f7** 34...♘e4 35 ♘c3 ♘xc3 36 ♕xc3 d4 37 exd4 exd4 38 ♖xe8+ ♕xe8 39 ♖xd4 ♗xd4 40 ♕xd4 ♕c6

35 Qc2? d4 36 Ng3 Rd8 37 exd4 exd4 38 Qd2 d3 38...Rd7 **39 Qh6 c3** 39...Bd4 20 Qf4 Qd6 41 Qf3 Qd5 **40 Ne4** 40 Re7+ Kxe7 41 Qg7+ Ke6 42 Re1+ Kd5 43 Qf7+ Kd4 44 Re6 **Nxe4?** 40...Kg8 **41 Qxh7+ Kf8**

42 Qh8+ ½-½ 42...Kf7 43 Qh7+ Kf6 44 Qh4+ Kg7 (44...Ng5 45 f4) 45 Rxe4 Re8 46 Rxe8 Qxe8 47 Rxd3 Qe1+ 48 Kh2 Bc7+ 49 g3 Qxf2+ =; 47...c2 48 Qf4 Qe1+ 49 Kh2 c1Q 50 Rd7+ +−; 43...Ke8 44 Qg8+ Kd7 45 Rxd3+ Kc8 46 Rxd8+ Bxd8 47 Qg1!; (1) 47...Kd7 48 a4 bxa4 49 b5 Qxb5 50 Qxc3 Nd6 51 Qg7+ Δ Qxg6; 50 Rxe4? Qb1+; (2) 47...g5 48 a4 Nf6 49 axb5 Nxg8 50 bxc6 Ne7 51 Re5 Ng6 52 Re2 Δ Rc2=; 48...bxa4? 49 b5; (3) 47...Nd2 48 Rc1 Qc4 49 Qxg6 Ne4 50 Rc2 Qd3 51 Rxc3+ Qxc3 52 Qxe4=; 50...Qd4; 49...Nb3 50 Qf5+; 48...g5 49 h4 gxh4 50 Qg4+ Kb8 57 Qg8; (4) 47...c2 48 Rc1 Δ Qb3/Qa2

99 Vaiser-Zilberstein USSR 78

1 d4 Nf6 2 c4 e6 3 Nc3 Bb4 4 e3 0-0 5 Bd3 c5 6 Nf3 d5 7 0-0 Nc6 8 a3 Bxc3 8...cxd4 9 exd4 dxc4 10 Bxc4 Be7 11 Re1 b6 12 Bd3 += **9 bxc3 Qc7!?** 9...dxc4 10 Bxc4 Qc7 11 Bd3 e5 12 Qc2 Re8 13 dxe5 Nxe5 14 Nxe5 Qxe5 15 f3 Be6 16 Re1 Rad8∞ Hort-Spassky (2) 77 **10 cxd5!** 10 Qe2? dxc4 11 Bxc4 e5 =+ Fraguela-Byrne, Torremolinos 76; 10 Bb2!? dxc4 11 Bxc4 e5 12 Be2 Rd8 13 Qc2 Bg4 14 dxe5 Δ c4 += Lim-Tisdall, Hastings 2 76/77 **exd5 11 Nh4!?** 11 a4?! Re8 12 Ba3 c4 13 Bc2 Ne4 14 Qe1 f5!=; 11 Bb2!? **c4!?** N 11...Ne7 12 a4 c4 13 Bc2 Re8 14 Qe1! Kh8!∞ Unzicker-Byrne, Haifa 76 **13 Bb1** 13 Bc2!? **Ne4 14 Qc2?!** 14 Qe1= **Qe7 14 f3 Qxh4 15 fxe4 Qxe4 16 Qxe4 dxe4 17 Bxe4 Bd7 =+ 18 Bf3 Rac8 19 e4** 19 Bxc6!? =+ **Na5 20 Bf4 Rc6! 21 Ra2 Ra6 22 h3 Re8 23 g4 Nb3 24 Kg2 Bc6 25 Re1 b5∓ 26 Ree2 Bb7 27 e5** 27 d5!? **Bxf3+ 28 Kxf3 Kf8! 29 Ke4 f6! 30 Rf2 Ke7 31 Rf1 Kd7 32 g5?! Re7 33 gxf6 gxf6 34 Rg1 fxe5 35 Bxe5 Rh6 36 Rag2** 36 Rg3 **Ke6! 37 Rg7 Rh4+ 38 Bf4 Nd2+ 39 Ke3 Rxg7 40 Rxg7 Nb1 −+ 41 Kf3 Rxh3+ 42 Kg4 Rh1 43 Rxa7 h5+ 44 Kg3 Nxc3 45 Bd2?! Ne4+ 46 Kg2 Nxd2! 47 Kxh1 c3 48 Rc7** 48 Rg7 c2 49 Rg1 Nb3 −+ **Nc4 49 Rg7 c2 50 Rg1 Kd5 51 Rc1 Nxa3 0-1 Gufeld**

100 Sherbakov-Grigorian USSR 78

1 d4 Nf6 2 c4 e6 3 Nc3 Bb4 4 e3 c5 5 Ne2 5 Bd3 **cxd4** 5...Ne4 6 Qc2 cxd4 7 exd4 d5 8 a3 +=; 5...d5; 5...b6!? 6 a3 Ba5 7 Qa4! Nc6 8 g3 += **6 exd4 d5** 6...0-0 7 a3 Be7 8 d5!? **7 a3** 7 c5 Ne4 8 Bd2 Nxd2 Δ b6∞ **Be7 8 c5** 8 g3!? **0-0** 8...b6!? **9 b4** 9 Bf4! += **Nc6!?** 9...b6 **10 f4 a6 11 g3 Ne4 12 Bg2 f5= 13 0-0 Bf6 14 Be3 Bd7 15 Bxe4 fxe4 16 g4 Qe8! 17 Ng3 Kh8 18 Ra2** Δ Raf2 **b6 19 f5** 19 g5!? **bxc5 20 bxc5 Bh4! 21**

♜af2 ♞e7 22 ♞ce2 22 ♕d2 **exf5 23 gxf5 ♝b5!∓ 24 a4!? ♝c4!** 24...♗xa4∓ **25 ♛d2 ♞g8 26 ♝g5 ♝xg5 27 ♛xg5 ♞f6 28 ♚h1 ♜a7 29 ♜c1 ♝xe2 30 ♜xe2 ♛xa4 31 ♜e3 ♛xd4 32 ♞e2 ♛e5 −+ 33 ♞f4 d4 34 ♜h3 ♚g8 35 ♞e6 ♜8f7 36 ♛d2** Zeitnot **♛xf5 37 ♞g5 h6 0-1 Gufeld**

101 Korchnoi-Karpov (3) 78

1 c4 ♞f6 2 d4 e6 3 ♞c3 ♝b4 4 e3 c5 5 ♞e2 cxd4 6 exd4 d5 7 c5 ♞e4 8 ♝d2 ♞xd2 9 ♛xd2 a5 9...b6 10 a3 ♗xc3 11 ♘xc3 bxc5 12 dxc5 a5 13 ♗b5+ ♗d7 14 ♖c1 a4= Averbakh-Panno, Portoroz 58; 9...♘c6 10 a3 ♗a5 11 b4 ♗c7 12 g3 b6 13 ♗g2 bxc5 14 dxc5 ♖b8 15 ♖b1 0-0 16 0-0 ♗e5 17 ♖fd1 += Korchnoi-Spassky, USSR Final 73; 16 f4!? **10 a3 ♝xc3 11 ♞xc3 ♝d7 12 ♝d3 a4 13 0-0 0-0 14 f4** 14 ♖ac1 b6 15 ♘b5 += Korchnoi **g6** 14...f5 **15 ♚h1** 15 g4 **♞c6 16 ♝c2 ♞e7** 16...♘a5 17 ♕e2 ♘c4 18 ♗d3 **17 ♜ae1 b6 18 ♜f3!** 18 f5 ♘xf5 19 ♗xf5 exf5; 18...gxf5!? **♜e8!** 18...bxc5 19 dxc5 f6! **19 ♜fe3! ♝c6 20 cxb6 ♛xb6**

21 g4 21 f5 gxf5 (21...♘xf5 22 ♗xf5 exf5 23 ♘xd5! ♕d8 24 ♖xe8+ ♗xe8 25 ♖xe8+ ♕xe8 26 ♘f6+ +−) 22 ♖g3+ ♘g6 23 h4 ♕c7 (23...♕d8 24 h5 ♕h4+ 25 ♖h3 ♕f4 26 ♖ee3 +−) 24 ♘e2! ♗b5 25 ♘f4 ♔h8 (25...♕d8 26 ♘h5 ♕xh4+ 27 ♖h3 ♕e7 28 ♕h6 f6 29 ♖xe6! +−) 26 ♘h5; (1) 26... ♕d8 27 ♕h6 ♕xh4+ 28 ♖h3 ♕xe1+ 29 ♔h2 ♖g8 30 ♘f6 ♖g7 31 ♕xh7+ ♖xh7 32 ♖xh7 mate; (2) 26...♕a5 27 ♕g5! ♕xe1+ 28 ♔h2 +−; (3) 26... ♖g8 27 ♕g5 ♕d8 28 ♘f6 Δ h5 +−; (4) 26...f6! 27 ♖xg6 hxg6 28 ♕h6+ ♕h7 29 ♕xh7+ ♔xh7 30 ♘xf6+ ♔g7 31 ♘xe8+ ♖xe8 32 ♖e3 += **♛c7! 22 f5** 22 ♖h3 ♔g7 23 f5 ♘g8 24 f6+ ♘xf6 25 ♕h6+ ♔g8 26 ♖f1 ♕e7 27 g5 ♘h5 28 ♖xh5 gxh5 29 ♕xh7+ ♔f8 30 ♕h8 mate; 22...♕d6! 23 f5 exf5 24 ♕h6 ♕f6! **exf5 23 gxf5 ♛d6** 23...♕f4 24 ♗d3 (Δ ♗b5) ♕xd4 25 ♖xe7 ♖xe7 26 ♖xe7 ♕f6 27 ♖e2! d4+ 28 ♘e4 ♕xf5 29 ♔g1; 28...gxf5 29 ♖g2+ **24 ♜h3?** 24 ♖e5! ♕f6 25 ♕h6; 24 ♖g3 **♞xf5 25 ♝xf5 gxf5 26 ♜g1+ ♚h8 27 ♜h6 ♜e6 28 ♜xe6 ♛xe6!** 28...fxe6 29 ♕g5 ♕f8 30 ♘e2 (Δ ♘f4) e5 31 ♘g3 exd4 32 ♘xf5 d3 33 ♘d4! **29 ♛g5 ♛g6 30 ♛h4 ♛e6 ½-½**

102 Ghitescu-Schneider Roskilde 78

1 d4 ♞f6 2 c4 e6 3 ♞c3 ♝b4 4 e3 c5 5 ♞e2 d5 5...cxd4; 5...b6; 5...♘e4?! **6 a3 ♝a5 7 dxc5** 7 g3?! ♘e4! 8 ♕c2 ♘xc3 9 ♘xc3 cxd4 10 exd4 ♘c6 11 ♗e3 e5 =+ Gligoric-Ivkov, IBM 71 **dxc4 8 ♛xd8+** 8 ♕a4+ ♘c6 9 ♕xc4 ♘e5∓ **♚xd8 9 ♝d2 e5 10 ♞g3 ♝e6 11 ♞ce4 ♝xd2+ 12 ♚xd2?!** 12 ♘xd2 **♞xe4+ 13 ♞xe4 ♚e7 14 ♜c1?** 14 ♘g5 **♜d8+ 15 ♚c3 ♝d5! 16 ♞d6 ♞a6 17 e4?** 17 ♖d1!; 17 ♗xc4? ♘xc5 18 ♗xd5 ♖xd6 19 ♖hd1 ♖ac8 20 ♔b4 ♘d3+∓ **♞xc5? 18 ♞f5+ ♚f6 19 exd5 ♞e4+ 20 ♚b4** 20 ♔c2 ♔xf5 −+ **a5+ 21 ♚a4 b5+ 22 ♚xb5 ♜ab8+ 0-1** 23 ♔c6

♖dc8+ 24 ♔d7 ♘c5+ 25 ♔d6 ♖b6 mate: 23 ♔xa5 ♖xb2 24 ♗xc4 ♘c5 −+ **Filipowicz**

103 Korchnoi-Karpov (5) 78

1 c4 ♞f6 2 d4 e6 3 ♞c3 ♝b4 4 e3 c5 5 ♞e2 d5 6 a3 ♝xc3+ 7 ♞xc3 cxd4 8 exd4 dxc4 9 ♝xc4 ♞c6 10 ♝e3 0-0 11 0-0 b6 12 ♛d3 12 ♕f3 ♗b7 13 ♗d3 **♝b7 13 ♜ad1 h6** 13... ♘e7 14 ♗g5 Botvinnik-Tolush 65 **14 f3!** N 14 ♖fe1 **♞e7 15 ♝f2 ♞fd5 16 ♝a2 ♞f4?! 17 ♛d2! ♞fg6** 17... ♘ed5?! 18 ♘e4 f5?!; 18...♖c8 **18 ♝b1 ♛d7 19 h4 ♜fd8 20 h5 ♞f8 21 ♝h4 f6 22 ♞e4 ♞d5**

23 g4!? ♜ac8 24 ♝g3 ♝a6 25 ♜fe1 ♜c6 26 ♜c1 ♞e7 27 ♜xc6 ♛xc6 27... ♘xc6 28 ♘d6 **28 ♝a2 ♛d7 29 ♞d6 ♝b7** 29...♘c8? 30 ♖xe6! ♘xe6 31 ♕e3 ♔f8 32 ♗xe6 ♕e7 33 ♘f5; 29... ♘d5 30 ♗xd5 exd5 31 ♕e3 **30 ♞xb7 ♛xb7 31 ♛e3 ♚h8 32 ♜c1 ♞d5 33 ♛e4 ♛d7 34 ♝b1 ♛b5 35 b4 ♛d7** 35...a5 36 ♗d6! ♖xd6 37 ♖c8 ♔g8 38 ♕h7+ +− **36 ♛d3 ♛e7 37 ♚f2 f5?! 38 gxf5 exf5 39 ♜e1 ♛f6** 39...♕g5! 40 ♖e5 ♘e7? 41 ♕e2 ♖xd4 **40 ♝e5** 40 ♖e5 f4 41 ♖f5 fxg3+ 42 ♔g1 ♘f4! 43 ♕e4 ♖xd4 44 ♖xf6 ♖d1+ −+ **♛h4+ 41 ♝g3 ♛f6** 41...♕g5! **42 ♜h1 ♞h7!** 42...♘e6; 42...♕g5 **43 ♝e5 ♛g5 44 ♛xf5 ♛d2+** 44...♕e3+ 45 ♔g3 ♘g5 46 ♖f1 ♘e7 47 ♕d3! **45 ♚g3 ♞hf6 46 ♜g1 ♜e8 47 ♝e4!** 47 ♔h3? ♖xe5 Δ ♘f5+ +− **♞e7 48 ♛h3 ♜c8 49 ♚h4 ♜c1 50 ♛g3** 50 ♕g2 **♜xg1** 50...♕g5+ 51 ♕xg5 hxg5+ 52 ♖xg5 ♖h1+ 53 ♔g3 ♖g1+ 54 ♔f4 ♘fd5+ 55 ♗xd5 ♘xd5+ 56 ♔f5 ♘e7+ 57 ♔e6 ♖xg5 58 ♔xe7 ♖xh5 59 f4 Δ d5-d6 +− **51 ♛xg1 ♚g8 52 ♛g3** 52 ♗xf6? ♕f4+ **♚f7? 53 ♝g6+ ♚e6? 54 ♛h3+ ♚d5 55 ♝e4+??** Zeitnot 55 ♗f7+ ♔c6 56 ♕e6+ ♔b5 57 ♕c4+ ♔a4 58 ♕a6 mate **♞xe4 56 fxe4+ ♚xe4 57 ♛g4+ ♚d3 58 ♛f3+ ♚e3 59 ♚g4 ♛xf3+ 60 ♚xf3 g6? 61 ♝d6 ♞f5 62 ♚f4 ♞h4** 62...♘xd6 63 hxg6 ♘e8 64 d5 +− **63 ♚g4 gxh5+ 64 ♚xh4 ♚xd4 65 ♝b8 a5 66 ♝d6 ♚c4 67 ♚xh5 a4 68 ♚xh6 ♚b3 69 b5 ♚c4 70 ♚g5 ♚xb5 71 ♚f5 ♚a6 72 ♚e6 ♚a7 73 ♚d7 ♚b7 74 ♝e7 ♚a7 75 ♚c7 ♚a8 76 ♝d6 ♚a7 77 ♚c8 ♚a6 78 ♚b8 b5 79 ♝b4 ♚b6 80 ♚c8 ♚c6 81 ♚d8 ♚d5 82 ♚e7 ♚e5 83 ♚f7 ♚d5 84 ♚f6 ♚d4 85 ♚e6 ♚e4 86 ♝f8 ♚d4 87 ♚d6 ♚e4 88 ♝g7 ♚f4 89 ♚e6 ♚f3 90 ♚e5 ♚g4 91 ♝f6 ♚h5 92 ♚f5 ♚h6 93 ♝d4 ♚h7 94 ♚f6 ♚h6 95 ♝e3+ ♚h5 96 ♚f5 ♚h4 97 ♝d2 ♚g3 98 ♝g5 ♚f3 99 ♝f4 ♚g2!** 99...♔f2 100 ♔e4 ♔e2 101 ♗b8 ♔f2 102 ♔d5 ♔f3 103 ♔c5 ♔e4 104 ♔xb5 ♔d5 105 ♗h2 ♔e6 106 ♔xa4 ♔d7 107 ♔b5 ♔c8 108 ♔c6 +− **100 ♝d6 ♚f3 101 ♝h2 ♚g2 102 ♝c7 ♚f3 103 ♝d6 ♚e3 104 ♚e5 ♚f3 105 ♚d5 ♚g4 106 ♚c5 ♚f5 107 ♚xb5 ♚e6 108 ♚c6 ♚f6 109 ♚d7 ♚f7 110 ♝e7 ♚g8 111 ♚e6 ♚g7 112 ♝c5 ♚g8 113 ♚f6 ♚h7 114 ♚f7 ♚h8 115 ♝d4+ ♚h7 116 ♝b2 ♚h6 117 ♚g8 ♚g6 118 ♝g7 ♚f5 119 ♚f7 ♚g5 120 ♝b2 ♚h6 121 ♝c1+ ♚h7 122 ♝d2 ♚h8 123**

♗c3+ ♔h7 124 ♗g7= ½-½

104 Gipporel-Pytel
Bagneux 78
1 d4 ♘f6 2 c4 e6 3 ♘c3 ♗b4 4 e3 d5 5 ♕a4+ ♘c6 6 ♘f3 ♗d7 7 ♕c2 a6 7...0-0! 8 a3 ♗xc3+ 9 ♕xc3 a5 **8 a3 ♗d6?!** 8...♗xc3+ **9 c5 ♗f8 10 ♗d3 g6 11 e4** 11 b4! Δ ♗b2± **dxe4 12 ♘xe4 ♘xe4 13 ♗xe4 ♗g7** 13...f5! **14 ♗e3 0-0** 14...f5 **15 0-0-0± f5 16 d5! fxe4 17 dxc6 exf3 18 ♖xd7** 18 cxd7! fxg2 19 ♖g1 Δ ♕e4 +− **fxg2∝ 19 ♖g1 ♕e8 20 ♖xg2 bxc6 21 ♖xc7 ♕b8** 21...♖f7!∓ **22 ♖d7 ♕e5 =+ 23 ♕d2 ♖f7 24 ♖xf7 ♔xf7 25 ♖g4! ♔g8 26 ♖b4= ♕xh2 27 ♕d7 ♕h1+ 28 ♔c2 ♕d5 29 ♖b7 ♕c4+ 30 ♔b1 ♕e4+ 31 ♔c1 ♕c4+ 32 ♔b1 ½-½ Pytel**

105 Kagan-A.Saharov
corr 77
1 d4 ♘f6 2 c4 e6 3 ♘c3 ♗b4 4 e3 0-0 5 ♗d3 d5 6 a3 ♗xc3+ 7 bxc3 dxc4 8 ♗xc4 c5 9 ♘f3 ♕c7 10 ♗a2 ♘c6 11 0-0 e5 12 h3 e4 13 ♘h2 ♗f5 14 ♘g4 ♘xg4 15 hxg4 ♗g6 16 a4 ♖ad8! 16...♖fd8 17 f4! exf3 ♕xf3 **17 ♕e2** 17 f4 exf3 18 ♕xf3 ♖fe8 19 ♗a3 cxd4 20 cxd4 ♖xd4! 21 exd4 ♘xd4= **♖fe8! 18 ♗a3 b6 19 ♖ad1** 19 dxc5 ♘e5 20 cxb6 axb6∝ **♔h8! 20 ♖d2** 20 f4 exf3 21 ♕xf3 f6 **f5** 20...♘e7? 21 dxc5 bxc5 22 ♕b5!±; 20...cxd4? 21 cxd4± **21 gxf5 ♗xf5 22 f4** 22 ♖fd1 ♖d6? 23 dxc5 ♖h6 24 ♖d6±; 22...♕e7! 23 dxc5 ♖xd2 24 ♕xd2 ♘e5 25 ♕d6 ♕g5; 23 ♕b5 ♖d6 24 dxc5 ♖g6 **exf3** 22...♕d7 23 ♖f2 cxd4 24 cxd4± **23 ♕xf3 ♗e4 24 ♕f4** 24 ♕f7 ♕c8 25 ♖df2 ♗d3 **♕e7 25 ♕f7 ♕g5 26 ♕f4 ♕e7 ½-½ Kasparov**

106 Botterill-Ligterink
Middlesborough 78
1 d4 ♘f6 2 c4 e6 3 ♘c3 ♗b4 4 e3 0-0 5 ♘f3 d5 6 ♗d3 c5 7 0-0 ♘c6 8 a3 cxd4 9 exd4 ♗xc3 10 bxc3 dxc4 11 ♗xc4 ♕a5!? Δ e5 **12 ♗d2** 12 ♕e2!? ♕xc3 13 ♗d2 ♕c2 14 ♗d3 ♕a4 15 ♗b5 ♘xd4 16 ♘xd4 ♕xd4 17 ♗b4 ∝/∓ **e5 13 ♕b3!?** 13 ♘xe5 ♘xe5 14 dxe5 ♕xe5 15 ♕f3= **e4 14 ♘g5 ♕c7 15 ♕c2 b5! 16 ♗b3** 16 ♗xb5 ♘xd4∓ **♘a5 =+ 17 ♗a2** 17 f3!? **♗b7 18 f3 exf3 19 ♖ae1! ♘c4! 20 ♘xf3 ♖ae8 21 ♗xc4?!** 21 ♕c1!? **♕xc4 22 ♖xe8 ♖xe8 23 ♘e5 ♕d5 24 ♖f3?** 24 ♗e1 Δ ♗h4 **♘e4! 25 ♘xf7 ♖e7 26 ♘e5 ♘xd2 27 ♕xd2 ♖xe5 −+ 28 ♕f2 ♖e8 29 ♖f5 ♖e1+! 0-1 Botterill**

107 Cooper-Petrosian
Buenos Aires
1 d4 ♘f6 2 c4 e6 3 ♘c3 ♗b4 4 ♗g5 c5 5 d5 5 e3? ♕a5 6 ♕c2 ♘e4! 7 ♕xe4 ♗xc3+ 8 ♔d1 ♗xb2 −+ **d6 6 e3 ♗xc3+ 7 bxc3 e5 8 ♗d3 ♘bd7 9 f4!** 9 f3 ♘f8 10 ♘e2 ♘g6∝ **h6 10 ♗h4 ♖g8!?** Δ g5 **11 ♘h3 ♕a5 12 ♕d2 e4 13 ♗e2 ♕a4 += 14 ♘f2 g5 15 fxg5 hxg5 16 ♗g3 ♘b6 17 ♕d1!** 17 ♗xd6? ♘xc4 18 ♗xc4 ♕xc4 19 ♖d1 ♗f5∓ **♕xd1+ 18 ♖xd1 ♔e7 19 h4 ♗f5 20 0-0 ♘bd7 21 ♖b1 b6 22 h5** 22 hxg5?! ♖xg5 23 ♗h4 ♖g6 24 ♘h1 ♖ag8 25 ♘g3 ♖xg3 26 ♗xg3 ♖xg3 27 ♖xf5 ♖xe3∝; 24...♗g4 25 ♗xg4 ♖xg4 26 ♘g3!± **♖g7 23 ♗h2!** Δ ♘h1-g3 **g4 24 ♘h1 ♗h7 25 h6 ♖g6 26 ♗f4 ♘h5 27 ♘g3 ♘xg3?** 27...♘xf4! 28 ♖xf4 ♖xh6 29 ♗xg4 ♘e5 30 ♗f5 ♖g8 += **28 ♗xg3 ♖ag8 29 ♗f4± ♘e5 30 g3 ♘f3+ 31 ♗xf3 exf3 32 e4 ♔d7 33 a4! ♖e8?!** 33...f6 34 a5 ♖b8± **34 a5 ♖xe4 35 axb6 axb6 36 ♖xb6 ♖xf4?** 36...♔e7!

37 gxf4?? 37 ♖b7+! ♔d8 38 ♖a1 ♔c8 39 ♖ab1 (Δ ♖b8+, ♖1b7 mate) ♔d8 40 ♖a7 ♔c8 41 ♖a8+ ♔c7 42 ♖ab8 f2+ 43 ♔f1 Δ ♖1b7 mate; 37...♔e8 38 ♖e1+ **♜xh6 38 ♜b7+ ♚e8 39 ♜a1 ♚f8 40 ♜aa7 ♜f6 41 ♚f2 ♜xf4 −+ 42 ♜a1 ♜xc4 43 ♚g3 ♝e4 44 ♜b8+ ♚e7 45 ♚xg4 ♝xd5+ 46 ♚g3 ♜xc3 47 ♜a7+ ♚f6 48 ♜d8 ♜c2 49 ♜xd6+ ♚e5 0-1 Gipslis**

Bogoljubow Indian

108 Bagirov-Rashkovsky USSR 78

1 d4 ♞f6 2 c4 e6 3 ♞f3 ♝b4+ 4 ♞bd2 4 ♗d2 ♕e7 5 g3 ♘c6 6 ♗g2 ♗xd2+ 7 ♘bxd2 d6 8 0-0 e5 9 d5 ♘b8 10 e4 a5=; 5 ♘c3 b6 6 e3 ♗b7 7 ♗d3 0-0 8 0-0 c5= **d5** 4...c5 5 a3 ♗xd2 6 ♕xd2 cxd4 7 ♘xd4 0-0 8 b4!?; 4...0-0 5 e3 b6 6 ♗d3 ♗b7 7 0-0 d5 8 a3 ♗d6 9 b4 += **5 e3 0-0 6 ♝d3** 6 a3 ♗e7 7 b4 a5!=; 7 ♗d3 b6 8 0-0 ♘bd7 9 b4 c5= **c5 7 0-0 ♞c6 8 dxc5!** 8 a3 ♗xd2 9 ♕xd2 cxd4 10 exd4 dxc4 =+ **♝xc5 9 a3 a5 10 ♛c2 ♝d6** 10...♗b6! Δ d4 **11 b3 ♛e7 12 ♝b2 h6 13 cxd5 exd5 14 ♝f5 ♝e6 ½-½** 15 ♘d4 ♘xd4 16 ♗xd4 ♕d7! **Gufeld**

109 Miles-Gonzalez
Buenos Aires 78

1 d4 e6 2 c4 ♝b4+ 3 ♞d2 ♞f6 4 ♞f3 0-0 5 a3 ♝xd2+ 6 ♛xd2 6 ♗xd2 **b6 7 g3 ♝b7 8 ♝g2 d6 9 0-0 ♞bd7 10 b4 a5 11 ♝b2 ♛e7 12 ♜fd1 axb4 13 axb4 b5! 14 c5** 14 cxb5 ♘b6 ∝/=+ **♝xf3?** 14...♗e4! ∝/=+ **15 ♝xf3 d5 16 ♛f4! += ♜xa1** 16...c6 17 ♖xa8 ♖xa8 18 ♕c7 +− **17 ♜xa1 ♞b8 18 ♜a7 ♜c8 19 ♝c3 ♞c6 20 ♜a6 ♛d7 21 g4!?** 21 ♕d2!? **♞e7 22 g5 ♞e8 23 ♝g4** 23 ♕c1 **c6 24 ♛c1 ♞c7 25 ♜a7 ♜a8 26 ♛a1 ♛c8 27 ♝d2! ♛b8?** 27...♘g6!?; 27...♖xa7 **28 ♜xa8 ♛xa8** 28...♘xa8 29 ♗f4! **29 ♛xa8+ ♞xa8 30 ♝f4 ♚f8 31 ♚g2 ♚e8 32 ♝e5 g6?** 32...♘f5? 33 ♗xf5 exf5 34 ♔f3 +−; 32...♔d7! 33 ♗xg7!? ♘c7 Δ ♘a6-xb4∝ **33 ♚f3± ♚d7 34 ♚f4 ♞c7?** 34...♘g8 35 h4 ♘c7 36 ♗xc7 ♔xc7 37 ♔e5 ♔d7 38 h5 ±/+− **35 ♝xc7 ♚xc7 36 ♚e5 ♞g8 37 ♝xe6!** 37 h4 ♔d7 38 f3 ±/+− **fxe6 38 ♚xe6 ♚d8 39 ♚d6 ♞e7 40 e3 ♚e8 41 ♚c7 ♚f7 42 ♚d7 ♚f8 43 f3 ♞f5** 43...♔f7 44 e4 dxe4 45 fxe4 ♔f8 46 h3 ♔f7 47 e5 ♔f8 48 e6 ♘d5 49 ♔xc6 ♘xb4+ 50 ♔xb5 +− **44 ♚xc6 ♞xe3 45 ♚d7 ♞c4 46 c6 ♞b6+ 47 ♚d8 1-0** 47...♔f7 48 c7 ♔e6 49 c8♕ ♘xc8 50 ♔xc8 ♔f5 51 ♔d7 +− **Miles**

Queen's Indian

110 Botterill-Short
British Final 78

1 d4 e6 2 c4 b6 3 a3 ♝a6 4 ♛a4 ♞f6 5 ♞c3 ♝e7 6 ♞f3 0-0 7 d5!? ♛c8 7...c6 8 ♗f4 d6 9 dxc6 ♕c7≈; 7...c6 8 dxc6 dxc6 9 ♗f4∝ **8 e4 exd5 9 e5!?** 9 cxd5 ♗xf1 10 ♔xf1 += **♞e8 10 ♞xd5 ♝d8 11 ♝d3 c6 12 ♞b4** 12 ♕c2? cxd5 13 ♗xh7+ ♔h8 14 ♕f5 (Δ ♕h5/♕h3) 14...♕xc4 15 ♘d4 ♕xd4 16 ♕h5 ♘f6! −+ **♝b7 13 ♛c2 h6 14 0-0 a5 15 ♞a2 ♞a6 16 ♝e3**

♞c5 17 ♝xc5 bxc5 18 ♞c3± ♞c7 19 ♜ad1 ♞e6 20 ♛e2! Δ ♕e4 **♞f4 21 ♛e3 ♞xd3 22 ♜xd3 ♝b6 23 ♞e4** Δ ♘f6+! **d5 24 exd6 ♛e6 25 ♛f4 ♝a6 26 ♞ed2 ♜fe8 27 ♜e1 ♛g6 28 ♜xe8+ ♜xe8 29 d7 ♜d8 30 ♜b3!**

30...♛c2 31 ♜xb6 ♛c1+ 32 ♞e1! ♛xe1+ 33 ♞f1 ♝xc4 34 ♛xc4 ♜xd7 35 ♜b8+ ♚h7 36 ♛c2+ g6 37 ♛c3 +− ♛xc3 38 bxc3 ♜d3 39 c4?! ♜xa3 40 ♜c8 ♜c3 41 ♜xc6 ♜xc4 42 g3 a4 43 ♞e3 ♜c1+ 44 ♚g2 a3 45 ♜a6 ♜c3 46 ♜a4 h5 47 ♞c4 a2 48 ♞e3 g5 49 ♜xa2 ♜c1 50 ♜a6 c4 51 ♜c6 1-0 Botterill

111 Djuric-Hartmann
Il Ciocco 78

1 d4 ♞f6 2 c4 e6 3 ♞f3 b6 4 a3 ♝b7 5 ♞c3 ♞e4 5...d5! **6 ♞xe4 ♝xe4 7 ♞d2!?** 7 ♗f4; 7 e3 Petrosian-Magrin, Venice 67 **♝b7 8 e4 ♛f6 9 d5 ♝c5 10 ♞f3 ♛g6 11 b4 ♛xe4+** 11...♗e7 12 ♗d3 ♕xg2 13 ♖g1 ♕h3 14 ♖xg7 ♗f6 15 ♖g3 ♕xg3 16 hxg3 ♗xa1 17 ♗h6!± **12 ♝e2 ♝d6!?** 12...♗e7 13 0-0 0-0 14 ♖e1 ♕g6 Tseitlin-Zilberstein, USSR 77; 14 h3 ♕g6 15 ♗d3 f5 16 ♘e5 ♕e8∝; 14 ♗d3 ♕g4 15 ♗xh7+! ♔h8 16 ♖e1 ♕xc4∝; 15... ♔xh7 16 ♘g5+ ♕xg5 17 ♗xg5 ♗xg5 18 ♕h5+ ♗h6 19 g4 g5 20 f4± Tseitlin **13 0-0 ♛g6 14 ♜e1 0-0 15 ♝d3 ♛h5 16 ♜b1 ♞a6 17 ♜e4 f5 18 ♜h4 ♛e8** 18...♕g6 **19 ♛c2 ♛g6 20 ♝b2** 20 c5 bxc5 21 ♗xa6 ♗xa6 22 bxc5 ♗e7 23 ♖a4 ♗c8 24 ♘e5 ♕e8! 25 dxe6 d6! =+ **c5 21 ♞e5 ♛f6 22 ♞f3 ♛e7 23 b5 ♞c7 24 ♜e1** 24 g4? ♘xd5! 25 cxd5 ♗xd5 26 ♖h3 ♗xf3 27 ♖xf3 ♕g5!∓ **♞xd5! 25 cxd5 ♝xd5 26 ♛c3 ♝xf3! 27 gxf3 ♜f7 28 ♜h5 ♛f6 29 ♛c1 ♝f4! 30 ♛xf4 ♛xb2 31 ♝f1 g6 32 ♜h3** 32 ♖h4?? g5 **♜c8 33 ♛c4 d5** 33...♕xa3 Zeitnot **34 ♛f4 ♜e8 35 ♛d6 ♛f6 36 f4 ♛e7 37 ♛e5 ♛f6 38 ♛e2 c4 39 ♜e3 ♜fe7 40 ♜e5 ♛f7 41 ♝g2 ♜d8 42 ♛d2 ♜d6 43 ♛c3 ♜ed7 44 ♛d4 ♛d8 45 ♜1e3 ♛c7 46 ♜h3 h5 47 ♜5e3 ♜d8 48 ♜eg3 ♛c5 49 ♛d1 d4??** 49...♖h8 **50 ♜xg6! ♜h8 51 ♜xh5 ♜dd8 52 ♜hh6 ♜xh6 53 ♜xh6 ♛xb5 54 ♛h5+ ♚e7 55 ♛g5+ ♚d7 56 ♜h7+ 1-0 Paoli**

112 Hoi-Botterill
Middlesborough 78

1 d4 ♞f6 2 c4 e6 3 ♞c3 ♝b4 4 e3 b6 5 ♞e2 ♝a6 6 a3 ♝xc3+ 6...♗e7 7 ♘f4 d5 8 cxd5 ♗xf1 9 ♔xf1 exd5 10 g4 0-0!? 11 g5 ♘e4∝ Pritchett **7 ♞xc3 d5 8 b3 0-0 9 ♝e2 ♞c6 10 a4 ♛d7 11 0-0 dxc4** 11...♘a5 12 ♖b1!? Δ dxc4? 13 b4 +− **12 bxc4** 12 ♗a3! ♖e8 13 b4 Δ b5, ♗xc4 += **♞a5 13 ♞b5 c6 14 ♞a3 c5!** 14... ♖ac8 15 ♗d2 += Botterill-P. Littlewood, London 78 **15 ♞b5?** 15 ♗b2 cxd4 16 exd4 ♖ac8? 17 d5! exd5 18 ♗xf6 gxf6 19 ♗d3!±; 16...♘e4! = Δ ♘d6, ♖ac8 **cxd4 16 exd4 ♜fc8 =+ 17 ♝f3 ♝b7 18 ♝xb7 ♞xb7 19 ♛d3 a6 20 ♞a3 ♞c5 21 ♛e3 ♞xa4∓ 22 ♝d2 ♜d8 23 ♞c2 ♜ac8 24 ♛b3 b5 25 ♝a5 ♜e8** 25...♖xc4!? 26 ♗xd8 ♕xd8∓ **26 ♞e3! ♜b8** Δ ♘b6 **27 ♜fd1 ♞b6 28 c5**

28 ♗xb6 ♖xb6 29 c5 ♖c6∓ **♘bd5 29 ♗d2 ♕c6 30 ♖a5 ♖a8 31 f3? e5!** Zeitnot **32 ♘xd5 ♘xd5 33 ♕d3 ♘c7 34 ♗e3 ♖ad8 35 ♕a3 exd4 36 ♖xd4 ♖xd4 37 ♗xd4 ♕d5 38 ♕c3 ♖d8! 39 ♗e3** 39 ♗xg7 ♕d1+ 40 ♔f2 ♖d2+ 41 ♔g3 ♕e1+ 42 ♔h3 ♕f2 −+ **♕d1+ 40 ♔f2 ♘d5 41 ♕d2 ♘xe3 42 ♕xe3**

42...♖d2+ 43 ♔g3 ♖e2! 44 ♕f4 44 ♖a1 ♕c2 −+ **♕e1+ 45 ♔h3 ♖e5!** Δ ♖h5+, ♕h4+ **46 ♔g4** 46 ♕g3 ♕e3 47 f4 ♖h5+ 48 ♔g4 ♕xc5 49 ♖xa6 ♕c8+ 50 ♔xh5 ♕xa6 −+; 46 g4 h5! 47 ♖xa6 ♕f1+ 48 ♔g3 h4+ −+; 47 g5 f6! 48 gxf6 ♕f1+ 49 ♔g3 h4+ 50 ♔g4 ♕g2+ −+ **f6** Δ ♖g5+/♕xa5; 46...h5+ 47 ♔h3 g5 48 ♕d4 ♖d5!!; 48 ♕g3 ♕e3 49 f4 ♕e4! −+ **0-1 Botterill**

113 Petrosian-Browne
Buenos Aires 78

1 d4 ♘f6 2 ♘f3 b6 3 e3 ♗b7 4 ♗d3 e6 5 0-0 ♗e7 6 b3 0-0 7 ♗b2 c5 8 c4 cxd4 9 exd4 d5 10 ♘bd2 ♘bd7 11 ♖c1 ♖c8 12 ♕e2 ♖c7 13 ♘g5?! h6 14 ♘h3 ♖e8 =+ **15 f4 ♕a8 16 ♘f3 dxc4 17 bxc4 ♗e4! 18 ♘d2 ♗xd3 19 ♕xd3 ♗b4 20 ♘f3 ♕e4 21 ♕b3 ♗a5! 22 ♗c3** 22 ♘e5!? **♗xc3 23 ♖xc3 ♖ec8∓ 24 g3 ♘d5?!** 24...♘e8! Δ ♘d6∓ **25 ♖cc1 ♕g6?** 25...♘5f6!= **26 ♖fe1 ♘e7 27 ♘f2 ♘f5 28 ♕d3!± ♘e7 29 ♘e4 ♘d5 30 ♕f1 ♘b4** 30...♘xf4 31 ♘h4 +− **31 a3 ♘c6 32 d5! exd5 33 cxd5 ♘a5 34 f5! +− ♕h5 35 ♖xc7 ♖xc7 36 ♘d6! ♘f6 37 h3! ♖c3 38 ♔g2 ♘xd5** 38...♖c2+ 39 ♖e2 ♘xd5 40 ♕f2 +− **39 g4 ♘f4+ 40 ♔g3 ♕xh3+ 41 ♕xh3 1-0** 41...♘xh3 42 ♖e8+ ♔h7 43 ♘xf7 Δ ♖h8 mate **Gipslis**

114 Malich-J.Fernandez
Budapest 78

1 ♘f3 ♘f6 2 d4 e6 3 c4 b6 4 ♘c3 4 a3 c5! 5 d5 ♗a6 6 dxe6?! dxe6 =+ Malich-Csom, Budapest 78 **♗b7** 4... ♗b4 5 e3 ♗b7 6 ♗d2 += Malich-Fernandez, Budapest 78 **5 a3 d5 6 ♗g5** 6 cxd5 exd5 7 g3 ♗e7 8 ♗g2 0-0 9 0-0 ♘e4!= N Malich-Kuzmin, Budapest 78; 6...♘xd5 7 e3 ♗e7 8 ♗b5+ c6 9 ♗d3 +=; 7...♘d7!= **♗e7 7 ♗xf6 ♗xf6 8 cxd5 exd5 9 g3!?** N 9 e3!? **0-0 10 ♗g2 ♖e8 11 0-0 ♘c6!?** 11...♕d6!? 12 ♖c1 a6 += **12 e3 ♘a5?! 13 b4 ♘c4 14 ♘d2! ♘xd2** 14...♖xe3 15 fxe3 ♘xe3 16 ♕f3 ♘xf1 17 ♖xf1 ♗xd4+ 18 ♔h1± **15 ♕xd2 c6 16 a4?!** 16 ♖fc1!? **♖c8 17 ♖ab1 ♖c7 18 ♖fc1 ♖ee7 19 ♕a2** Δ b5 +− **♖ed7 20 ♖c2 g6 21 ♖bc1 ♔g7 22 ♘e2 ♗a6?! 23 ♖xc6! ♗c4 24 ♖1xc4 dxc4 25 ♕xc4 ♖xc6 26 ♗xc6 ♖d6 27 b5?!** 27 ♗f3 h5 28 ♔g2± **h5 28 ♘c3 ♕e7** 28...♗xd4 29 exd4 ♖xd4 30 ♕e2 +− **29 h3?!** 29 ♘e4 ♖d8 30 ♘xf6 ♕xf6±; 30 d5 ♗e5 31 f4 ♗d6 32 ♕d4+ f6 33 ♘xd6 ♖xd6 34 e4± **♕e6 30 ♕xe6 fxe6 31 ♔g2?** 31 ♔f1 ♗xd4 32 exd4 ♖xd4 33 ♔e2 ♖c4 34 ♔d3 +− **♗xd4!= 32 exd4 ♖xd4 33 h4?! ♖c4 34 ♘e4 a5 35 ♔f3?** 35 ♘d6! ♖xa4 36 ♘c8 ♖b4 37 ♘xb6 a4 38 ♘xa4 ♖xa4 39 b6 ♖b4 40 b7= **♖xa4**

36 ♝d7 ♜b4? 36...e5! −+ **37 ♝xe6 ♜xb5 38 ♞c3 ♜c5 39 ♞e4 ♜e5 40 ♝d7 b5 41 ♚f4 ♜d5 42 ♝e6 ♜d8 43 ♚e5! a4 44 ♞c3 ♜b8 45 ♚d4 ½-½** 45...a3 46 ♗b3! b4 47 ♘a2= **Malich**

115 Miles-Spassky
Buenos Aires 78

1 d4 ♞f6 2 ♞f3 b6 3 c4 e6 4 ♝f4 ♝b7 5 e3 ♝e7 6 h3 0-0 7 ♞c3 d5 8 cxd5 exd5 9 ♝d3 c5 10 0-0 ♞c6 11 ♞e5 a6 12 ♛f3 ♜e8 12...c4?? 13 ♘xc6 ♗xc6 14 ♗xc4 +− **13 ♜ad1 cxd4 14 ♞xc6** 14 exd4!? ♘xd4 15 ♗xh7+ ♘xh7 16 ♖xd4 ♘f6∞ **♝xc6 15 exd4 += b5** Δ b4, ♘e4 **16 a3 ♞e4! 17 ♝b1! ♛b6 18 ♜fe1 ♞xc3 19 ♛xc3 b4 20 ♛g3 bxa3 21 bxa3 ♝a4?!** 21...g6 += **22 ♜c1 ♛b2?** 22...♕xd4?? 23 ♗e5 +−; 22...g6 += **23 ♝xh7+! ♚xh7 24 ♜xe7 ♜xe7 25 ♛h4+ ♚g8 26 ♛xe7 ♛xd4 27 ♝e5!± ♛b6** 27...♕d2 28 ♖c7 ♕e1+ 29 ♔h2 ♕xf2 30 ♕g5 +−; 28...♖f8 29 ♗d6 +−; 28...♗e8 29 ♖c3 Δ ♖g3 ±/+−; 27...♕d3 28 ♕g5 ♕h7 29 ♖c3 ±/+− **28 ♛g5! ♛h6** 28...f6 29 ♗xf6 ♕xf6 30 ♕xd5+ +−; 28...♕g6 29 ♕xg6 fxg6 30 ♖c7 +− **29 ♛xh6 gxh6 30 ♜c3 ±/+− ♚f8 31 ♜c5! ♜d8** 31...♗b3 32 ♖c6 +− **32 ♝f6 ♜d6 33 ♜c8+ ♝e8 34 ♝d4 ♜e6 35 ♜d8 +− ♚g8 36 ♜xd5 ♜e1+** 36...♗c6 37 ♖c5 +− **37 ♚h2 ♜d1 38 ♜d8 ♚h7 39 g4 ♜d3 40 f4 h5 41 f5 1-0 Miles**

116 Miles-Spassky Montilla 78

1 d4 ♞f6 2 ♞f3 b6 3 c4 e6 4 ♝f4 ♝b7 5 e3 ♝e7 6 h3 0-0 7 ♞c3 d5 8 cxd5 exd5 N 8...♘xd5 9 ♘xd5 ♕xd5 10 ♗d3 += Miles-Browne, IBM 78 **9 ♝d3 c5 10 0-0 ♞c6 11 ♞e5 c4!?** 11...cxd4 12 ♘xc6 ♗xc6 13 exd4 += **12 ♝c2 a6 13 g4 b5 14 g5 ♞e8 15 ♛g4 += g6 16 ♜ad1 ♞g7 17 h4 ♝b4?** 17...b4 18 ♘e2 f6 += **18 ♞d7! ♝c8** 18...♗xc3 19 ♘f6+ ♔h8 20 bxc3 ±/+−; 18...f5 19 gxf6± **19 ♞xd5** 19 ♘f6+? ♕xf6 20 ♕xc8 ♕e6! =+ **♚h8 20 ♞5f6 ♜a7** 20...♗e7 21 ♗e4±; 20...♘e8 21 ♗e5± **21 d5! ♞e7** 21...♘a5 22 h5! (Δ ♕h4 +−) ♖xd7 23 ♕h4 gxh5 24 ♗e5 ♖e7 (24...♕e7 25 ♕e4) 25 ♗d4! +− **22 ♝e5!** 22 h5? ♗xd7 23 ♕h4 gxh5∞ 24 ♗e5 ♘g6 **♜xd7** 22...♗xd7? 23 ♕d4 +− **23 h5!** 23 ♘xd7? ♕xd7 Δ ♕g4+; 23 ♕d4? ♘c6! **♜xd5** 23...♖b7 24 ♕f4 +− **24 ♛f4 ♜xd1 25 ♜xd1 +− ♛a5** 25...♕b6 26 h6 +− **26 ♞e8! f6** 26...♖xe8 27 ♕f6 ♖g8 28 h6 ♘f5 29 ♗xf5 ♗f8 30 ♗xc8 +−; 27...♘f5 28 ♗xf5 ♖xe5 29 h6 ♗f8 30 hxg7+ ♗xg7 31 ♖d8+ +− **27 gxf6 ♚g8** 27...♖xe8 28 f7! ♖f8 29 h6 ♘f5 30 ♕xf5 ♗xf5 31 hxg7 mate **28 ♞xg7 1-0** 28...♘c6 29 hxg6 +− **Miles**

117 Kuligowski-Keene
Buenos Aires 78

1 d4 ♞f6 2 c4 e6 3 ♞f3 b6 4 g3 ♝a6 4...♗b7 5 ♗g2 d5 6 cxd5 exd5 7 0-0 ♗d6 8 ♘c3 a6 9 ♘h4 0-0 10 ♘f5 ♖e8 11 ♘xd6?! Heilemann-Ornstein, Hanover 76; 11 ♗g5!± **5 b3** 5 ♕a4 ♗b7 6 ♗g2 c5 7 0-0 ♕c8 **♝b4+ 6 ♝d2 ♝e7 7 ♞c3 0-0** 7...♗b7 8 ♗g2 c5 9 0-0 0-0 10 ♖c1 ♘a6! 11 ♗g5! += Browne-Larsen, Las Palmas 77; 9 ♗f4? d6!; 7...c6! **8 e4 d5!? 9 cxd5 ♝xf1 10 ♚xf1 exd5 11 e5 ♞e4 12 ♛e2 ♞xc3 13 ♝xc3 ♛d7 14 ♚g2 c5 15 e6! ♛xe6 16 ♛xe6 fxe6 17 ♜he1 ♝f6 18 ♜xe6 += ♞a6 19 ♜c1 ♞c7 20 ♜e2!** 20 ♖c6 ♘b5 21 ♗a1 cxd4 22 ♖d1 ♖ac8 =+ **♞b5 21 ♝a1 cxd4 22 ♜d2 ♜ac8 23 ♜xc8 ♜xc8 24 ♝xd4 ♞xd4 25 ♞xd4 ♝xd4 26 ♜xd4**

Rd8 27 Rd2 += Kf7 28 Rc2! Rd7 29 Rc6± d4 30 Kf3 d3 31 Rc1 Re7 32 Rd1 Re2 33 a4 Rb2 34 Rxd3 Ke6 35 h4 a6 36 Ke3 Ke5 36...h5± 37 g4 Ke6 38 f3 Ke5 39 f4+ Ke6 40 Ke4 g6 41 f5+ gxf5 42 gxf5+ Ke7 43 Ke5 1-0 Filipowicz

118 Tukmakov-Kuzmin USSR 78

1 Nf3 Nf6 2 c4 e6 3 d4 b6 4 g3 Bb7 5 Bg2 Be7 6 Nc3 Ne4 7 Qc2 Nxc3 8 Qxc3 0-0 9 0-0 c5 10 Rd1 Bf6 10...d6 11 b3 Nd7 12 Bb2 Nf6 13 d5 e5 14 Nxe5 dxe5 15 d6 += Petrosian-Karpov, USSR 76; 11 Bf4!? 11 Qd3!? 11 Be3 Nc6 11...d6!? 12 dxc5 bxc5 13 Qxd7 Qb6 14 Bf4 Rac8 15 Qd3 Rfd8∝ 16 Qc2 h6 16...Qxb2 17 Rxd8+ Δ Rb1 17 Bd2 e5! 18 e4 Rb8 19 Rab1 a5 20 a3 Ba6 Δ Qb3 21 Bf1! Re8 22 Qa4 Bb7 Δ Nd4 23 Bg2 Ra8 24 Re1 Qc7 25 h3 Nd4 26 Nxd4 exd4 27 Bf4 Be5 28 Bxe5 Rxe5 29 f4 Re6! Δ Rb6 30 Qc2 Rae8= 31 Re2 Rb6 32 Qa4 Rbe6 33 Rbe1 Qd8 34 Qd1 d3 35 Re3 Bxe4! 36 Bxe4 Qd4 37 Qxd3 Qxd3 38 Rxd3 Rxe4 39 Rxe4 Rxe4 40 Kf2 40 Rc3 Re2 41 b3 Ra2= Rxc4 41 Rc3 Rxc3 42 bxc3 Kf8 43 Ke3 Ke7 44 Kd3 Kd6 45 Kc4 Kc6 46 a4 f5 ½-½ Gufeld

119 Beljavsky-Petrosian
Vilnius 78

1 d4 Nf6 2 c4 e6 3 Nf3 b6 4 g3 Bb7 5 Bg2 Be7 6 Nc3 Ne4 7 Qc2 Nxc3 8 Qxc3 0-0 9 0-0 Be4 9...c5; 9...d6; 9...Qc8 10 Bf4 10 Ne1 Bf6 10...c6!? 11 Rac1 d5 12 cxd5 Qxd5 =/+= 11 Rfd1 Nc6 12 Ne5 Bxg2 13 Kxg2 Rc8 13...Bxe5!? 14 dxe5 +=/±? 14 h4 Qe8?! 15 Ng4! Be7 16 d5 Nd8 17 h5 f6 18 h6 g6

19 Bxc7! Rxc7 20 d6 Bxd6 21 Rxd6 Qe7 22 Rad1 Nb7 23 R6d4 d5 24 Qd3 Nd6 24...Nc5 25 cxd5 e5! 26 Rb4 26 Ra4? Qd7! f5 27 Ne3 Rfc8 27...e4!?; 27...f4 28 Ra4 Qg5? 29 Qa3? Qe7 30 b3 Kf8 31 Qb2 Rc5 32 Nc4! Nf7 33 Qa3! +- b5 34 Rxa7 Qf6 35 Ra6 Zeitnot Qe7 35...Qd8 36 Rc6! 36 Ra7 Qd8 36...Qf6 37 Na5 Qb6 38 Nb7 b4 39 Nxc5! 1-0 Speelman

120 Buturin-Chechelian
USSR 78

1 d4 Nf6 2 Nf3 e6 3 c4 b6 4 g3 Bb7 5 Bg2 Be7 6 Nc3 0-0?! 6...Ne4 7 d5!± Bb4 7...exd5 8 cxd5 Bb4 9 Nh4±; 8 Nxd5! Nxd5 9 cxd5 c5 10 d6 11 Rb1!± Dorfman-Mordasov, USSR 78 8 Bd2 d6 9 0-0 e5 10 Qc2 a5 11 e4 Na6 12 Nh4 Nc5 13 f4?! exf4 14 Nf5 Bc8! 15 Rxf4 Bxf5 16 Rxf5 Ng4 17 a3 Bxc3 18 Qxc3 a4 19 Raf1 Qe7 20 Qf3 Ne5 21 Qe2 Rae8 22 Bc3 Ng6! 23 Re1 Qd7 24 h4! Re7 24...Qxf5!? 25 exf5 Rxe2 26 Rxe2 Ne5 27 Bxe5 Re8 28 Bxd6 Rxe2 29 Bxc7 Rxb2 30 d6 Rb3 31 Bc6 Rd3 32 Bb5! +- 25 h5 Rfe8 26 Ref1 Ne5 27 h6! g6 28 Bh3! Qd8 28...gxf5 29 Bxf5 Qd8 30 Bxe5 Rxe5 31 Qg4+ Kf8 32 Qg7+ Ke7 33 Bg6! +- 29 Rf6 Ned7? 29...Rf8!

30 Qf3! Nxe4 31 Rxf7!! Ng5

32 Be6!! +– Nxf3+ 33 Rxf3 Rxe6 34 Rg7+ Kh8 35 Rxd7+ Re5 36 Bxe5+ dxe5 37 Rxd8 Rxd8 38 Rf7 e4 39 Kf2 Kg8 40 Rg7+ Kf8 41 Rxh7 Rd6 42 Rxc7 1-0 Sher

121 Hort-Romanishin IBM 78
1 c4 Nf6 2 d4 e6 3 Nf3 b6 4 g3 Bb7 5 Bg2 Be7 6 0-0 d6!? Romanishin **7 Nc3 Ne4 8 Qa4+! Nd7 9 Nxe4 Bxe4 10 Rd1 0-0 11 Ne5 Nf6!** 11...dxe5 12 Bxe4 +–; 11...Nxe5 12 Bxe4 +– **12 Nc6 Qe8 13 b4 Bxg2 14 Kxg2 Ne4 15 Rd3 f5 16 f3 Nf6 17 b5 Nd7 18 Qd1?! Bf6 19 Bb2 a5 20 e3 Qf7 21 f4?** 21 a4 Rae8 =+/∓; 21 e4 fxe4 22 fxe4 Nc5∓ **Be7 22 Qf3 Nf6 23 Nxe7+ Qxe7 24 Qc6 Ne4 –+ 25 d5 Nc5 26 Rd2 Rae8 27 Re1 Qf7 28 dxe6 Rxe6 29 Qd5 Rfe8 30 Bd4 Ne4 31 Rc2 Qh5 32 Qc6 Qf7 33 Qd5 h5 34 Kh1 Qg6 35 Rg2 Qg4 36 Bb2 Kh7 37 Qd1 Qh3 38 Qf3 Rh6 39 Bd4 Ree6 40 Rf1 Reg6 41 Kg1 Rg4 42 Rc2 h4 0-1 Taulbut**

122 Rashkovsky-Pripis USSR 78
1 Nf3 Nf6 2 c4 e6 3 g3 b6 4 Bg2 Bb7 5 0-0 Be7 6 d4 0-0 7 Nc3 Ne4 8 Bd2 8 Qc2! += **d6** 8...Bf6 9 Qc2 Nxd2 10 Qxd2 d6 11 e4 Nd7 12 d5 Ne5!= Mecking-Polugaevsky, (10) 77; 9 Rc1 c5 10 dxc5 bxc5 11 Qc2 Nxd2 12 Nxd2! Bxg2 13 Kxg2 += Rashkovsky-Pokojowczyk, Sochi 76; 8...Nxc3 9 Bxc3 Bf6!? **9 d5! Nxd2** 9...Nxc3?! 10 Bxc3 e5 11 b4 Nd7 12 e4 += **10 Nxd2 e5** 10...Kh8! **11 f4! += exf4 12 gxf4 Bf6** 12...a5 Δ Nd7-c5 **13 Nde4 Nd7 14 Nxf6+ Qxf6 15 Qd2 a6 16 Rae1 Rae8 17 e4 Qh4 18 Ne2 Re7 19 Nd4 g6 20 Re3 Rfe8 21 Rg3! Rxe4** 21...Kh8 22 Nf3 Qf6 23 Ng5 Δ e5± **22 Bxe4 Rxe4 23 Re3! Qg4+ 24 Kh1 Rxe3 25 Qxe3 Nf6 26 Qg3! Qd7 27 f5! Nh5 28 Qe3 c6 29 Re1! Kf8 30 dxc6 Bxc6+ 31 Nxc6 Qxc6+ 32 Qe4 Qc5 33 Rf1 +– Kg8 34 Qd5 Qc7 35 Qd4 Kf8 36 Qh8+ 1-0 Gufeld**

Grunfeld

123 Smejkal-Boll
Val Thorens 78
1 Nf3 Nf6 2 c4 g6 3 Nc3 d5 4 Qa4+!? N **Nc6** 4...c6; 4...Bd7! 5 Qb3 dxc4 **5 cxd5 Nxd5 6 Ne5 Bd7?** 6...Nb6 7 Nxc6 Nxa4 8 Nxd8 Nxc3 9 Nxf7±

7 Nxf7! Ncb4 8 Qb3 Kxf7 9 Nxd5 Nxd5 10 Qxd5+ e6 11 Qxb7 Bc5 12 Qf3+ Ke7 13 Qc3 Bb6 14 d3 Qf8 15 Bg5+ +– 1-0 Pytel

124 Larsen-O.Rodriguez Spain 78
1 c4 ♞f6 2 ♞c3 c5 3 ♞f3 d5 4 cxd5 ♞xd5 5 e3 ♞xc3 6 bxc3 g6 7 d4 ♝g7 8 ♝e2 0-0 9 0-0 ♛c7 10 ♛b3 b6 11 ♜d1!? 11 a4? ♘c6! **♝b7?** 11...e6! **12 d5! += ♞d7 13 ♝b2 ♞e5 14 c4 ♜ad8** 14...♖fd8!? **15 a4!? e6 16 a5 exd5 17 ♝xe5 ♝xe5 18 axb6 axb6 19 ♞xe5 ♛xe5 20 ♛xb6 ♝a8 21 ♜a5?!** 21 ♕xc5 ♖c8 22 ♕d4 += **♜b8 22 ♛xc5 ♛b2 23 ♝f1 ♜fc8 24 ♛e7 dxc4 25 ♜a7 ♛g7 26 ♜c7 c3?** 26...♕f8 27 ♕xf8+ ♔xf8 28 ♖xc4 ♖xc4 28 ♗xc4 ♗e4 += **27 ♛c5! ♜xc7 28 ♛xc7 ♜e8 29 ♜d4 ♝e4 30 ♛xc3** 30 ♗b5 ♕e5! **♝d5 31 h4 h5? 32 ♛a5 ♝e6 33 ♛g5± ♛f8?!** Δ ♕e7 **34 ♝b5! ♜c8 35 ♝d3 ♜c5? 36 ♛f6 ♛g7 37 ♜d8+ ♚h7 38 ♝xg6+! 1-0 Larsen**

125 Volchikhin-Timoshenko USSR 78
1 d4 ♞f6 2 c4 g6 3 ♞c3 d5 4 cxd5 ♞xd5 5 e4 ♞xc3 6 bxc3 ♝g7! 6...c5 7 ♗b5+!? **7 ♝c4 c5 8 ♞e2 0-0 9 0-0 ♞c6 10 ♝e3 ♛c7** 10...cxd4 11 cxd4 ♗g4= **11 ♜c1 ♜d8 12 ♛e1** 12 ♕d2! ♕a5 13 ♖fd1 += **b6** 12...♕a5 13 ♖d1 cxd4 14 cxd4 ♕xe1 15 ♖fxe1 b6=; 12...e6 13 f4 ♘a5 14 ♗d3 f5 15 ♖d1 b6 16 ♕f2 fxe4 17 ♗xe4 ♗b7 **13 ♚h1** 13 f4 **♝b7 14 f3 ♛d7= 15 ♝b5 e6 16 dxc5** 16 ♕f2∝ **bxc5 17 ♝xc5 ♛c7 18 ♝e3 ♛a5 19 ♝xc6 ♝xc6 20 ♞d4 ♝e8≈ 21 ♜f2 ♜ac8 22 ♞b3 ♛a3 23 ♜d2 ♜xd2 24 ♛xd2 ♝a4! 25 c4** 25 ♗d4 e5 **♝xb3 26 axb3 ♛xb3 27 ♝xa7** 27 c5 a5!= **♜xc4 28 ♜xc4 ♛xc4 29 ♛d8+ ♝f8 30 ♝g1 ♛c1 31 ♛d4 h5 32 ♛e3 ♛c8 33 g3 ½-½ Gufeld**

126 Nikolac-Hort IBM 78
1 d4 ♞f6 2 c4 g6 3 ♞c3 d5 4 cxd5 ♞xd5 5 e4 ♞xc3 6 bxc3 ♝g7 7 ♝c4 c5 8 ♞e2 0-0 9 0-0 ♞c6 10 ♝e3 ♝g4 11 f3 ♞a5 12 ♝d3 cxd4 13 cxd4 ♝e6 14 d5 ♝xa1 15 ♛xa1 f6 16 ♜b1 ♝d7 17 ♞f4 ♛b8 18 ♛c3 b6 19 ♝a6 ♛d6 20 ♞d3

20...♝c8! 20...e6 21 ♗h6 ♖f7 22 e5; 20...e5 21 f4 **21 ♝b5 ♝b7 22 ♞f4 ♜fc8 23 ♛d3 a6 24 ♝a4 b5 25 ♝d1 ♞c4 26 ♞e6** 26 ♗c1 ♕c5+ Δ ♘e5, ♕f2 **♞xe3 27 ♛xe3 ♚h8 28 f4 ♛b8 29 ♛a3 ♜e8 30 ♛a5 ♛a7+ 31 ♚h1 ♛e3 32 ♝f3 ♜ac8 33 h3 ♜c1+ 34 ♜xc1 ♛xc1+ 35 ♚h2 ♝c8 36 ♛c7 ♛xc7 37 ♞xc7 ♜d8 38 e5 fxe5 39 fxe5 ♚g7 40 ♚g3 ♚f7 41 ♚f4 ♝b7 42 ♚g5 ♝c8** 42...♖c8! 43 ♘e6 a5 44 ♘d4 ♖c5 45 ♘b3 ♖xd5 −+ **43 ♚h6 ♚g8 44 d6 exd6 45 e6 ♚f8 46 ♚xh7 ♚e7 47 ♝d5 g5 48 ♚g6 ♜g8+ 49 ♚f5 ♜f8+ 50 ♚xg5 ♜f2 51 ♝f3 ♝xe6 52 h4 ♝xa2 53 ♞xa6 ♝b1 54 ♞b4 ♜b2 55 ♞d5+ ♚f7 56 ♚f4 b4 57 ♚e3 ♚e6 58 ♞b6 ♜c2 59 ♚d4 ♝a2 59 h5 ♜c1 50 ♝e4 d5 61 ♝f3 ♜c6 62 ♞a4 ♜c4+ 63 ♚d3 ♚e5 64 ♞b6 ♜c3+ 65 ♚d2 ♜c6 66 ♞d7+ ♚d4 0-1 Taulbut**

127 Kozlov-Mishuchkov USSR 78
1 d4 ♞f6 2 c4 g6 3 ♞c3 d5 4 ♞f3 ♝g7 5 ♛a4+!? ♝d7 6 ♛b3 dxc4 7

♛xc4 7 ♕xb7? ♘c6∓ **0-0** 7...♗c6 8 ♘e5 0-0 9 ♗g5 ♗d5 10 ♘xd5 ♘xd5 11 ♘f3! += **8 e4 ♞a6!?** 8...♘c6 9 ♗e2!? a6 10 d5 b5 11 ♕c5 ♘a5 12 0-0∝; 8...♗g4! **9 e5** 9 ♕b3 c5 10 d5 b5! 11 ♗xb5 ♖b8≈; 9 ♗e2 c5 10 d5 e6 11 0-0 exd5 Δ ♖b8= **♝e6!** 9...♘e8 10 ♕b3! c5 +=; 9...♘g4!? 10 ♗f4 c5 11 d5 ♕b6∝ **10 exf6!? ♝xc4 11 fxg7 ♚xg7 12 ♝xc4 += ♞b4 13 ♝b3** 13 0-0!? ♘c2 14 ♖b1 ♘xd4 15 ♘xd4 ♕xd4 16 ♗e3 += **♞d3+!?** N 13...c5 Δ ♘d3+ **14 ♚e2 ♞xc1+ 15 ♜axc1 c6 16 ♜he1 e6 17 ♚f1 ♜c8 18 ♞e4 ♜c7 19 g3 ♜e7 20 ♜c3 ♛b6 21 ♚g2 ♜d8 22 ♞c5 ♜d6 23 ♜e4 ♛d8 24 h4?!** 24 ♗c2 += **b6! 25 ♞a6** 25 ♘d3 c5 **♛a8 26 ♜e2 ♜ed7 27 ♝c2** ♘b4!? **♜xd4! 28 ♞c7!** 28 ♘xd4 ♖xd4 Δ c5 =+ **♛b8!** 28...♕b7? 29 ♘e8+ ♔f8 30 ♘f6 **29 ♜xc6 ♜4d6 30 ♜xd6 ♜xd6 31 ♞b5 ♜d5** 31...♖d8 32 ♘e5!± **32 ♞c3 ♜c5! 33 ♜d2 ♛c7 34 a4 += a6 35 ♝d3 ♛b7 36 ♝e4 ♛e7 37 ♜d4 h6 38 ♝d3 ♛b7 39 ♜b4 a5 40 ♜d4 g5 41 hxg5 hxg5 42 g4?!** 42 ♗e4 += **f5!= 43 ♞b5 ♜d5! 44 ♚g3 ♛b8+ 45 ♚g2 ♛b7 ½-½ Gufeld**

128 Diez del Corral-W.Schmidt
Buenos Aires 78

1 d4 ♞f6 2 c4 g6 3 ♞c3 d5 4 ♞f3 ♝g7 5 ♛b3 dxc4 6 ♛xc4 0-0 7 e4 ♝g4 8 ♝e3 ♞fd7 9 ♜d1 ♞b6 9...♘c6!?∝ **10 ♛b3 ♞c6** 10...e6 11 ♗e2 ♘c6 12 e5 ♘e7 13 ♘e4± **11 d5 ♞e5 12 ♝e2 ♞xf3+ 13 gxf3 ♝h5 14 f4** 14 ♖g1!? **♝xe2 15 ♚xe2!?** 15 ♘xe2 c6! **♛d7 16 ♜hg1 c6 17 f5 cxd5 18 ♝xb6 axb6 19 ♞xd5 ♛a4 20 ♞xe7+ ♚h8 21 ♚f3! ♛xa2 22 ♛xa2 ♜xa2 23 b3 ♜b2 24 ♜d3 ♜e8 25 ♞d5 ♜d8 26 h3 ♝e5 27 ♜gd1 gxf5 28 exf5 f6 29 ♞e3** 29 ♘xb6?! ♖xb3! **♜xd3 30 ♜xd3 b5 31 ♞g4** 31 ♘d1 **h5!? 32 ♞xe5 fxe5 33 ♚e4 ♚g7 34 ♚xe5 ♜e2+ 35 ♜e3 ♜xf2 36 ♚e6 h4 37 ♜e5 ♜f3 38 b4 ♜xh3 39 f6+ ♚f8 40 ♜xb5 ♜e3+ 41 ♚f5 h3 42 ♜xb7 h2 ½-½ W.Schmidt**

129 Botterill-Miles
Wales-England 78

1 d4 ♞f6 2 c4 g6 3 ♞c3 d5 4 ♞f3 ♝g7 5 e3 0-0 6 cxd5 ♞xd5 7 ♝c4 ♞b6 8 ♝b3 ♞c6 8...c5!? **9 0-0 e5!?** 9...♘a5!? Botterill; 9...a5 10 ♘a4! += Gligoric-Honfi, Hague 66 **10 ♞xe5** 10 d5?! ♘a5 11 ♗c2 c6 ≈/=+ Botterill **♞xe5 11 dxe5 ♝xe5 12 e4 ♛e7!** 12...♕h4? 13 f4 ♗g4 14 ♕e1± Botterill-Corden, Birmingham 77 **13 ♝e3** 13 f4? ♗xc3 14 bxc3 ♕xe4 15 ♖e1 ♕c6 16 ♗a3 ♖e8∓ Botterill **♝e6 =+ 14 ♛c2! ♜fe8 15 ♜ae1** 15 ♗xe6 ♕xe6 16 ♖ae1 =+ **♝xb3! 16 axb3** 16 ♕xb3?! ♕e6 17 ♕c2!∝; 16...♕h4 =+ Botterill 17 g3 ♕g4!? 18 f3 ♕h3∓ **♛b4!** 16...♖ad8? 17 f4 += **17 ♞e2** 17 f4? ♗xc3∓; 17 ♘a2!? **♝d6 18 ♞c3 ♝e5 19 ♞e2 ♝g7 20 f3** 20 ♕xc7 ♖e7 21 ♕c2 ♖c8∓; 21 ♗c5? ♕xe1! −+ **♜e6!∓ 21 ♝d2** 21 ♕xc7 ♕xb3∓; 21 ♖d1 ♖c6∓; 21 ♗c5 ♖c6∓ **♛e7 22 ♝c3 ♜d8 23 ♜d1 ♛c5+ 24 ♚h1 ♜ed6 25 ♜xd6 ♛xd6 26 ♝xg7 ♚xg7 27 ♛c3+** 27 ♘c3 ♕d2 ∓/−+ **♚g8 28 ♜c1 ♛d2 29 ♞g1 c6** 29...♕xc3 30 bxc3 ♖d2∓ Botterill **30 ♜a1 a6?** 30...♕xc3 31 bxc3 a6 Δ ♖d2 −+ **31 ♛f6! ♛d4 32 ♛g5 ♚g7 33 e5 ♜e8 34 ♜e1** 34 f4 ♘d5∓ **h6** 34...♘d5? 35 ♖e4 Δ ♖h4 **35 ♛f6+ ♚g8 36 ♜e4 ♛xb2**

Diagram

37 ♛f4 Zeitnot 37 ♕h4!? ♖xe5?

38 ♕f6! ♘d7 39 ♕d8+ ♘f8 40 ♕f6= **♘d5 38 ♕xh6 ♖xe5 39 ♖h4 ♖e1!** −+ 39...♖h5!? 40 ♖xh5 gxh5 41 ♕xh5 ♕xg2+ −+ **40 ♕h7+ ♔f8 41 ♕h6+ ♔e7 42 ♖e4+ ♖xe4 43 fxe4 ♘f6 44 ♕e3 ♕e5 45 ♕b6 ♕b5 46 ♕c7+ ♘d7 47 ♕g3 ♕b4 0-1 Miles**

130 Farago-Swic Polanica 78

1 d4 ♘f6 2 c4 g6 3 ♘c3 d5 4 ♘f3 ♗g7 5 ♗f4 5 ♗g5; 5 e3; 5 ♕b3 **0-0 6 e3 c5** 6...c6 7 ♗d3 ♗e6 8 ♕e2 ♘h5 9 ♗g5 ♘d7 10 cxd5 += **7 dxc5 ♕a5** 7...♘e4 8 ♗e5 ♘xc3 9 bxc3 ♗xe5 10 ♘xe5 ♕c7 11 ♕d4 f6∞ Ribli-Ghizdavu, Nice 74 **8 ♖c1!** 8 ♕a4 ♕xc5 9 ♕b5 ♕xb5 10 ♘xb5 ♘a6 11 ♖d1 ♗e6 12 ♘fd4 ♗d7 13 ♗e5 ♖fc8 += Levenfish-Botvinnik, Moscow 37 **dxc4 9 ♗xc4 ♘c6** 9...♕xc5 10 ♗b3 ♘c6 11 0-0 ♕a5 12 h3 ♗f5 13 ♘d4 ♗d7 14 ♕e2 ♖fd8 15 ♖fd1 ♖ac8= Farago-Schmidt, Polanica 78 **10 0-0 ♕xc5** 10...♗g4 11 h3 ♖ad8 12 ♕e2 ♗xf3 13 ♕xf3 ♕xc5 14 ♘a4 ♕b4 15 ♘c5 += **11 ♘b5 ♕h5?! 12 h3 ♗e6 13 ♗e2 ♖ad8 14 ♕a4 a6 15 ♘c3± ♘d5?** 15...♕a5? 16 ♕xa5 ♘xa5 17 ♗c7 +−; 15...♕c5 **16 ♘d4 +− ♘xc3 17 bxc3 ♖xd4 18 ♕c2 ♕d5 19 cxd4 ♘b4 20 ♕c5 ♕xc5 21 ♖xc5 1-0 Filipowicz**

131 Ribli-Timman IBM 78

1 ♘f3 ♘f6 2 c4 g6 3 ♘c3 d5 4 d4 ♗g7 5 ♗f4 0-0 5...c5 6 dxc5 ♕a5 7 cxd5 ♘xd5 8 ♕xd5 ♗xc3+ 9 ♗d2 ♗e6! Grigorian-Tseshkovsky, USSR Final 77 **6 e3 c5 7 dxc5 ♘e4!** 7...♕a5 8 ♖c1 dxc4 9 ♗xc4 += Farago-Portisch 74 **8 ♖c1 ♘xc3 9 bxc3 dxc4 10 ♕xd8** 10 ♕a4 ♘d7 11 ♕xc4 ♕a5 =+ **♖xd8 11 ♗xc4** 11 ♗xb8 ♖xb8 12 ♗xc4 ♗d7= **♘d7 12 ♗g5?!** 12 ♘g5! Δ ♘e4 **♖e8 13 ♗b5** 13 ♘d4 ♘xc5 14 ♘b5 ♗e6; 13 0-0 ♘xc5 =+ **a6 14 ♗a4** 14 ♗xd7 ♗xd7 =+ **h6 15 ♗h4 g5**

16 c6?! 16 ♗g3 ♖f8! Δ ♘xc5 **♘c5 17 cxb7 ♗xb7 18 ♗xe8 gxh4 19 ♗d7 ♘xd7 20 ♘xh4 ♘e5 21 0-0 e6 22 ♖fd1 ♗f6 23 ♖d4 a5** Δ ♘g6 **24 h3 ♗a6 25 ♖e4 ♗c4 26 a4 h5 27 ♖d1 ♗b3 28 ♖d6 ♘c4 29 ♖d7 ♗xa4 30 ♖c7 ♗b3 31 ♖exc4 ♗xc4 32 ♖xc4 a4 33 ♘f3 a3 34 ♘d2 a2 35 ♘b3 ♖a3 0-1 Taulbut**

132 Haik-Emerson
England 78

1 d4 ♘f6 2 c4 g6 3 ♘c3 d5 4 ♘f3 ♗g7 5 ♗g5 5 ♗f4; 5 e3; 5 ♕b3 **dxc4** 5...♘e4 **6 e3** 6 e4 c5 7 d5 b5 8 e5 b4 9 exf6 exf6! 10 ♕e2+ ♔f8 11 ♗e3 bxc3 12 ♗xc5+ ♔g8∞ Hort-

Kouatly, England 78; 9 Nb5 a6 10 Bxc4 0-0!? **Be6 7 Ne5** 7 Nd2 c5 8 dxc5 Nd5 9 Bxc4 Nxc3 10 bxc3 Bxc4 11 Qa4+ Nc6 12 Qxc4 0-0 13 Nb3 Ne5 14 Qe2 += Petrosian-Savon 69; 13...Qd7!? Δ Rfd8 **Nd5 8 Nxc4** 8 Bxc4? Nxc3 9 bxc3 Bxc4 10 Nxc4 Qd5 −+ **c5 9 Qa4+ Nc6 10 Nxd5 Qxd5 11 Nb6 Qxg5 12 Nxa8 Kd7!?** 12...0-0! 13 Nc7 cxd4∓ 14 f4 Qf6 15 Bb5 dxe3 16 Bxc6 Qxb2 17 0-0 e2 18 Rfc1 Qb6+ 19 Kh1 Bxa1 20 Nxe6 Qf2 0-1 Bennett-Stean, England 75; 14 Qb5 Qh4!∓ **13 Qb5** 13 d5 Bxd5 14 0-0-0 Kc8! 15 f4 Qf6∓ **Kc8 14 Rc1** 14 0-0-0 Nxd4 **Bxd4! 15 f4 Qd5 16 exd4 Qe4+ 17 Be2** 17 Qe2 Qxd4 **c4! 18 0-0 Nxd4** 18...Qxe2 19 d5 **Qc5+ Kb8 20 Bf3 Nxf3+** 20...Qe3+! 21 Kh1 Rc8 22 Qxe7 Nxf3 23 Qd6+ Kxa8 24 gxf3 Qe2∓ **21 Rxf3 Kxa8 22 Qxe7 Qd4+ 23 Rf2 h5 24 Re1 a6 25 Qc7 Rd8 26 h3 Rd5 27 Re5 Rd7 28 Qc5 Qxc5 29 Rxc5 Rd1+ 30 Kh2?!** 30 Rf1! Rd2 31 Rf2= **Ra1 31 a3 Ra2! 32 Kg3 Ka7 33 f5!?** 33 Kf3 Kb6 34 Re5 Δ g4, f5 **gxf5 34 Kh4 b6 35 Re5 c3 36 Ree2 cxb2 37 Rxb2 Rxa3 38 Kxh5?** 38 Rf3! Ra1 39 Kxh5 a5 40 Kg5 a4 41 h4 a3 42 Rd2 a2 43 h5 b5 44 h6 Rh1 45 Rxa2+ Bxa2 46 Rh3 +−; 38...Rxf3! 39 gxf3 f4! 40 Rh2 a5 41 Kxh5 a4 42 Kg5 a3 43 h4 a2 44 Rh1 b5 45 h5 b4 46 h6 b3 47 h7 b2 48 h8Q b1Q 49 Kxf4!= **Rg3 −+ 39 Rf3 Rg6 40 Rc3 b5 41 Rc6 Kb7 42 Rd6 Rg8 43 h4 Bc4 44 Kh6 Rh8+ 45 Kg5 a5 46 h5 a4 47 g3 a3 48 Rh2 a2 49 Rd1 b4 50 h6 b3 51 Re1 Kb6 52 h7 Rxh7! 53 Rxh7 b2 54 Rh6+ Kc5 55 Rhh1 Bd3 56 g4 b1Q 57 gxf5 a1=Q 58 Rxb1 Bxb1 59 Re1 Qg7+ 60 Kh4 Qh6+ 61 Kg4 Bxf5+! 62 Kf3** 62 Kxf5 Qh5+ Δ Qh4+ **Qh3+ 63 Ke2 Qg2+ 64 Kd1 Qc2 mate 0-1 Povah**

133 Haik-Roos Bagneux 78

1 d4 Nf6 2 c4 g6 3 Nc3 d5 4 **Nf3 Bg7 5 Bg5 Ne4** 5...dxc4!? **6 cxd5 Nxc3 7 bxc3 Qxd5 8 e3 c5 9 Bb5+ Bd7 10 c4! Qf5** 10...Qe4!? **11 Rb1 cxd4 12 exd4 Bxb5 13 Rxb5 Qe6+ 14 Qe2 Qxe2+ 15 Kxe2 b6 16 Kd3 e6 17 c5!± bxc5 18 dxc5 Nc6 19 Kc4 0-0 20 Rd1 Rfc8 21 Rd7 h6 22 Bd2!** Δ Rbb7 **Bf8 23 Rbb7 Nb8 24 Rxf7 Rxc5+ 25 Kd3 Nc6 26 Rf6 Rd8+ 27 Ke2 g5 28 Rxe6 Rc2** 28...g4? 29 Rg6+ **29 Kd1 Rc4 30 Rc7! Rd6 31 Rxd6 Bxd6 32 Rc8+ Kh7 33 Be3 a6 34 Nd2 Rc3 35 Ne4 Rd3+ 36 Ke2 Ne5 37 Rd8 1-0** 37...Nf7 38 Rd7 **Pytel**

134 Kochiev-Kuzmin USSR 78

1 Nf3 Nf6 2 g3 g6 3 Bg2 Bg7 4 c4 0-0 5 0-0 c6 6 d4 d5 7 cxd5 cxd5 8 Ne5 Ng4!? 8...Bf5; 8...Nbd7 **9 Nxg4 Bxg4 10 h3** 10 Nc3 Nc6 11 h3 Be6 12 e3 Rc8 13 Bd2 Qd7 14 Kh2 f6 15 Qa4 Bf7 16 b4 += Smyslov-Korchnoi, USSR 75 **Bd7 11 e3** 11 Bf4 Nc6 12 e3 Qb6 **Nc6 12 Nc3 e6 13 Na4!?** 13 Bd2= **b6 14 Bd2 Qe7 15 Nc3 Rac8 16 Ne2!?** Δ Nf4 **Rfd8 17 Nf4 Be8= 18 Qb3 f6!? 19 Rfc1 Bf7**

Diagram

20 Qb5 Qd6 21 Nd3 Δ Nb4 += **Bf8 22 a3 Be8! 23 Qa6 Qd7 24 Qa4 Qf7 25 Qb3 Rc7 26 Rc2 Rdc8 27 Rac1 g5∞ 28 Bf1 Qd7** Δ Bg6 **29 Qa2 Bg6 30 b4 Bd6 31 b5 Ne7 32 Rxc7 Rxc7 33 Rxc7 Qxc7 34 Bb4 Nf5**

35 Bxd6 Nxd6 36 Qb2 36 Qb3 Qc4 **Be8 37 a4 Ne4 38 Kg2 Bh5 39 Be2 Bxe2 40 Qxe2 Kg7 41 Qg4= ½-½ Gufeld**

King's Indian

135 Flecker-Pytel Graz 78
1 c4 Nf6 2 Nc3 c5 3 Nf3 g6 4 d4 Bg7 5 g3 0-0 6 Bg2 d6 7 0-0 Nc6 8 dxc5 dxc5 9 Be3 9 Bf4 Petrosian-Smejkal, Biel 76 **Qa5!** 9...Be6 10 Bxc5 Qa5!= **10 Qa4 Qxa4 11 Nxa4 b6! 12 Nc3** 12 Ne5? Nxe5 13 Bxa8 Bd7∓ **Bd7 13 Rad1 Rac8 14 Rd2?** 14 Bf4 **Be6 15 b3** 15 Nd5 Ne4 **Ng4 16 Nd5 Nxe3 17 fxe3** 17 Nxe3 Bh6 **Bh6 18 Kf2 g5! 19 Rfd1 Kh8 20 h4 gxh4 21 Nxh4 Rfd8 22 Be4 Rd6∓ 23 Ng2? f5!+ 24 Bf3 Rcd8 25 Ke1 Bg7 26 a3 Bf7 27 Rd3 Ne5 28 Nxe7 Nxd3+ 29 exd3 Rxd3 30 Nxf5 Bc3+ 0-1 Pytel**

136 Doroshkevich-Gufeld
USSR 78
1 d4 Nf6 2 c4 g6 3 Nc3 Bg7 4 e4 d6 5 Nf3 0-0 6 Be2 e5 7 d5 a5 8 0-0 Na6 9 Be3!? Ng4 10 Bg5 f6 11 Bh4 Nh6?! 11...h5 **12 Nd2 Nc5 13 Nb3** 13 b3 Δ a3, b4 += **b6 14 Nxc5 bxc5** 14...dxc5 Δ Nf7-d6= **15 a3 g5 16 Bg3 f5 17 f3** 17 exf5 Bxf5! Δ g4∞ **f4 18 Bf2 Rf6 19 b4 Rg6** 19...axb4? 20 axb4 cxb4 21 Nb5± **20 h3** 20 bxc5 g4∓ **Nf7 21 bxc5 h5 22 cxd6 cxd6 23 Na4 g4 27 fxg4 hxg4 25 hxg4 Rb8** 25...Nh6 26 Nb6 Bxg4 27 Bxg4 Nxg4 28 Nxa8 Ne3! 29 Bxe3 Rxg2+! 30 Kg2 Qg5+ =; 27 Nxa8 Bh3 ∞/=+

26 c5! 26 Rb1 Rxb1 27 Qxb1 Bxg4 28 Bxg4 Rxg4 29 Qd3 Ng5!∓; 28 Qd1 Qg5 29 Qf3 Qh5 Δ Ng5∓ **Nh6 27 c6 Nxg4** 27...Bxg4? 28 Bxg4 Nxg4 29 Qf3± **28 Rb1!** 28 Bf3? Qg5∓ **Rxb1 29 Qxb1 Ne3! 30 Bxe3 Rxg2+ 31 Kxg2 Qg5+ 32 Kh1 Qh4+ 33 Kg1 Qg3+ ½-½ Gufeld**

137 W.Schmidt-Torre
Buenos Aires 78
1 Nf3 Nf6 2 c4 g6 3 Nc3 Bg7 4 e4 d6 5 d4 0-0 6 Be2 e5 7 0-0 Nc6 8 d5 Ne7 9 Nd2!? c5 9...a5 **10 dxc6 bxc6 11 b4 d5 12 Ba3 d4?!** 12...a6 13 Re1 Be6 14 Bf1 += **13 Na4 Bh6 14 Nc5 Re8** 14...Qc7 15 Ndb3 Ne8 16 Bc1! Bg7 17 Bd2 f5 18 Rc1 Nd6 19 f3 Kh8 20 b5± Smejkal-Ciocaltea, Sandomierz 76 **15 Ndb3 Nd7 16 Re1** 16 Rc1! **Kh8** Δ Ng8-f6 **17 Rb1 a6 18 Bc1 Bg7 19 Bd2 Qc7 20 Qc2 Ng8 21 b5!? Nxc5 22 Nxc5 cxb5 23 cxb5 axb5 24 Bxb5 Rd8 25 Rec1±**

♞f6 26 ♛b3 ♛e7 26...♕a7? 27 ♗c6 27 ♝b4?! 27 ♗c6!?; 27 a4 ♛a7 28 a4 ♜b8 29 ♛c4 ♞e8!∝ 30 ♝c6?! ♞d6 32 ♛c2 ♝h6 33 ♜e1 ♛c7! =+ 33 ♝d5 ♝b7 34 ♝b3 ♝a8 35 ♝a3 ♛a5 36 ♛a2 ♜bc8 37 ♞d3 ♝xe4 38 ♝xd6 ♝xd3 39 ♝xe5+ ♝g7 40 ♝xg7+ ♚xg7 41 ♜bd1 =+ ½-½ W.Schmidt

138 Kozlov-Gufeld USSR 78

1 d4 ♞f6 2 c4 g6 3 ♞c3 ♝g7 4 e4 d6 5 ♝e2 0-0 6 ♞f3 e5 7 0-0 ♞c6 8 d5 ♞e7 9 ♞e1 ♞d7 10 f3 f5 11 g4 ♞f6 12 ♞d3 h6 12...c6 13 h4 c6 14 ♞f2 a6 15 ♚g2 15 a4 a5= b5! 16 b3 16 dxc6 ♘xc6?! 17 exf5! gxf5 18 g5 +−; 17 g5 ♘h5 18 ♕d5+ ♖f7 19 ♕xc6?? ♗b7 −+; 16...♗e6!? 17 cxb5 d5!∝ ♝d7 17 ♝e3 ♜c8 18 ♜c1 ♛a5?! 18...cxd5= 19 dxc6 += ♞xc6?! 19...♖xc6 += 20 cxb5 ♞d4 21 ♝c4+ ♚h8?! 21...♗e6! +=; 21...♔h7 22 bxa6± fxg4 23 fxg4 h5 24 g5! ♞g4 25 ♞xg4 ♝xg4 26 ♛d2 ♝f3+?! 27 ♚h2 ♛d8 27...♕c7 28 ♘b5! ♕d7 29 ♘xd4 exd4 30 ♗xd4 +− 28 ♜f2 ♛d7 29 ♜g1 ♝g4 30 ♜g3! 30 ♖gf1 ♗f3! ♜xf2+ 31 ♝xf2 ♜f8 32 ♞d5 +− ♞f3+ 33 ♜xf3 ♝xf3 34 ♞f6! ♝xf6 35 gxf6 ♚h7 36 ♝d5 ♛g4 37 ♛g5 ♛c8 38 ♝e3 ♛c2+ 39 ♝d2 1-0 Gufeld

139 Rashkovsky-Gufeld
USSR 78

1 d4 ♞f6 2 c4 g6 3 ♞c3 ♝g7 4 e4 d6 5 ♞f3 0-0 6 ♝e2 e5 7 0-0 ♞c6 8 d5 ♞e7 9 ♞e1 ♞d7 10 ♞d3 f5 11 ♝d2 ♞f6 12 f3 f4 13 c5 g5 14 cxd6 cxd6 15 ♞b5 ♞g6 16 ♜c1 ♜f7 17 ♛c2 ♞e8 18 ♞f2 ♝f8 19 a4 h5 20 b4?! N 20 ♘xa7 ♖c7 21 ♗a5 ♖xc2 22 ♗xd8 ♖xd2 23 ♘xc8 ♖xa4= ♜g7? 20...a6; 20...♗d7

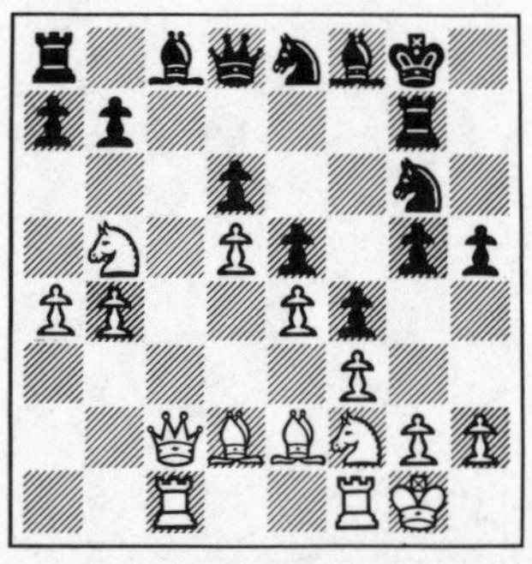

21 ♞xa7! ♜c7 22 ♞c6 bxc6 23 dxc6± g4?! 23...♘f6 24 b5± 24 fxg4 ♞f6 25 gxh5 ♞h4 26 g3 ♜h7 27 b5! 27 gxh4? ♘xh5∓ Δ ♕xh4 ♞xh5 28 ♛b3+ ♚h8 29 ♝xh5! ♜xh5 30 b6 ♜h7 30...♗e6 31 ♕xe6 ♘f3+ 32 ♔g2 +− 31 b7 ♜b8 32 c7! 32 bxc8♕?? ♖xb3 33 ♕xd8 ♘f3+ −+ ♜xc7 33 ♜xc7 ♛xc7 34 bxc8♛ ♛xc8 35 ♛c3? 35 ♕d1! +− ♛xc3 36 ♝xc3 ♜b3? 36...fxg3 37 hxg3 ♘f3+ 38 ♔g2 ♘g5± 37 ♞d1 ♞g6 38 gxf4 +− ♝h6 39 fxe5 dxe5 40 a5 ♝f4 41 ♚f2 41 ♖xf4 ♘xf4 42 ♗xe5+ ♔g8 43 ♗xf4 ♖b1= ♝c1 42 ♚g3 ♚g7 42...♗d2 43 ♖f3 +− 43 ♚g4 1-0 Gufeld

140 Kozlov-Zelnin
USSR 78

1 d4 ♞f6 2 c4 g6 3 ♞c3 ♝g7 4 e4 d6 5 ♝e2 0-0 6 ♞f3 e5 7 0-0 ♞c6 8 d5 ♞e7 9 ♞e1 ♞e8 9...♘d7 10 f3 10 ♘d3 f5 11 f3 ♘f6 12 ♗d2 f4 13 c5 g5 14 cxd6 Δ ♖c1 +=; 10 ♗e3! f5 11 f3 f4 12 ♗f2 g5 13 c5 ♘g6 14 a4! += ♚h8!? 10...f5 11 ♞d3 ♞g8 12 f4 12 ♗e3; 12 b4 f5 13 exf5 gxf5 14 ♝e3 ♛e7 15 ♛d2 e4 16 ♞b4 16 ♘f2 Δ g4 ♞gf6 17 ♞c2 ♜g8 18 b4 ♛f7 19 ♝d4 19 c5 ♛g6 20 ♞e3∝ h5 21 c5 ♚h7 22 cxd6 cxd6 23 ♜ac1 ♝d7 24 ♚h1 a6! 25 g3 ♜c8 26 ♜g1 ♝h6 27 a4 ♛f7 28 h4 ½-½ Gufeld

141 Christiansen-Kochiev
Mexico 78

1 c4 g6 2 d4 Bg7 3 Nc3 d6 4 e4 e5 5 Nf3 5 dxe5!? **Nd7 6 Be2 Nf6 7 0-0 0-0 8 Qc2** 8 Re1 Δ Bf1; 8 Be3!? **c6** 8...exd4 9 Nxd4 Nc5 10 Nb3 Nxb3 11 axb3 += Korchnoi-Timman (8) 76; 10...Nfd7; 9...Re8 Δ Nc5 **9 d5!? a5** 9...c5!? **10 Be3 Ng4 11 Bg5 f6 12 Bd2 Nc5** 12...Nh6 13 dxc6!? bxc6 14 Na4 Δ c5 **13 Ne1 h5** 13...Nh6 **14 h3 Nh6 15 Nd3 Nxd3 16 Qxd3 c5** 16...Nf7 **17 Qg3 Kh7 18 f4**

18...exf4 19 Bxf4 Nf7 20 Nb5 Ne5 21 Rf2 21 Bxe5!? **Qe7 22 Bxe5 fxe5 23 Rxf8 Bxf8 24 Rf1 Bg7** 24...Bh6!? 25 Qf2 Bf4!? 26 g3 Bxh3 27 gxf4 Bxf1 28 Bxf1 Rf8 29 f5∞; 27...Rf8; 26 h4!?; 25 Qf3 **25 Qf2 Kg8 26 Qg3 Kh7 27 Qf2 ½-½ Speelman**

142 Speelman-Cooper
British Final 78

1 c4 Nf6 2 Nf3 g6 3 Nc3 Bg7 4 e4 d6 5 d4 0-0 6 Be2 e5 7 0-0 Nbd7 8 Re1 c6 9 Bf1 a5 10 Rb1 Ng4 11 d5 11 h3 exd4 12 Nxd4 Qb6 13 hxg4 Bxd4 14 Be3 +=; 11...Nh6 **c5 12 a3** 12 h3 **Kh8** 12...Bh6!? 13 Nb5 Ra6 14 h3 Bxc1 15 Qxc1 Nf6 16 Qh6!? **13 h3 Nh6 14 Nb5 Ra6 15 b4 axb4 16 axb4 f6** 16...cxb4!? 17 Bd2!? Nc5 18 Bxb4 b6 **17 Be3 Nf7** 17...cxb4 18 Nxd6! **18 Qc2** 18 bxc5 Nxc5 19 Bxc5 dxc5 =+ **Bh6!? 19 Bxh6 Nxh6 20 Nd2 Nf7 21 Be2 cxb4 22 Nxd6 Nxd6 23 c5 Nxc5! 24 Qxc5 Ra2 25 Qxb4 f5?** 25...b5! 26 Bd1 Qb6 27 Bb3 (Δ Nc4) Ra6! 28 Rec1 Bd7 29 Rc6!? Bxc6 30 Qxd6 Qd8! 31 Qxd8 Rxd8 32 dxc6 Rxc6! += **26 Qc3 fxe4 27 Qxe5+ Qf6 28 Qxf6+ Rxf6 29 Nxe4! Nxe4 30 Bc4 Raxf2** 30...Ra8 31 Rxe4 Bf5 32 Rf4! **31 Rxe4± Kg7 32 Re7+** 32 Re8 Rf8 **Kh6 33 Rc7 Rc2!?** Zeitnot 33...Bf5 34 Kxf2 Bxb1+ 35 Ke3 Rb6 ±/+−; 34 Rxb7?? Be4! **34 Rxc8 Rf4** 34...Rff2 35 Kh1 Rxg2 36 Bf1! **35 Rb4 b5** 35...Rff2 36 Kh1 Rc1+ 37 Kh2 Rcc2 38 Kg3 **36 d6** 36 Be2! **Rd4 37 Be6 1-0** 37...Rd1+ 38 Kh2 Rxc8 39 Bxc8 Rxd6 40 Rxb5 +− **Speelman**

143 Hort-Vogt Halle 78

1 d4 Nf6 2 c4 d6 3 Nc3 Nbd7 4 e4 e5 5 Nf3 g6 6 Be2 Bg7 7 0-0 0-0 8 Be3 8 Re1; 8 d5 **a5 9 Re1** 9 Qc2; 9 d5 **Ng4 10 Bg5 f6 11 Bc1 c6 12 h3** 12 b3 Qb6 **Nh6 13 b3?! exd4 14 Nxd4 Nc5 15 Bf4?** 15 Be3 **f5 16 Qd2 Qf6 17 Rad1** 17 Bxh6? Bxh6 18 Qxh6 Qxd4∓ **fxe4!∓**

18 Bxh6 Qxf2+ 19 Kh1 19 Kh2?

♗e5+ Δ ♕g3 −+ **♗xh3! 20 gxh3** 20 ♗f1 ♗xg2+ 21 ♗xg2 ♕h4+ 22 ♔g1 ♗xh6 −+ **♕h4 21 ♗g4** 21 ♗e3 ♕xh3+ 22 ♔g1 ♗h6 23 ♗xh6 ♕g3+ 24 ♔h1 ♖f2 −+; 23 ♘c2 ♕g3+ 24 ♔h1 ♗f4 25 ♗f1 ♖f5 26 ♕g2 ♕h4+ 27 ♔g1 ♖g5 −+; 23 ♗f1 ♖xf1+ −+ **♗xh6 22 ♕g2 ♖f2 23 ♕g1** 23 ♖xe4 ♘xe4 24 ♕xe4 ♕g3 −+ **e3 24 ♘e6 ♖e8** 24... ♘xe6 25 ♗xe6+ ♔h8 26 ♕g4∝ **25 ♘xc5** 25 ♖xd6 ♖f6! 26 ♖xe3 ♗xe3 27 ♕xe3 h5 −+ **dxc5 26 ♖d3** Zeitnot 26 ♘e2 **♗f4 27 ♖e2 h5 28 ♗f5 g5 29 ♕xf2?** 29 ♖d7 g4 30 ♗xg4 hxg4 31 ♕xg4+ ♕xg4 32 hxg4 ♖f3!∓ **exf2 −+ 30 ♖xe8+ ♔f7 31 ♔g2 ♔xe8 32 ♘e4 ♗e5 33 ♘xf2 ♗d4 34 ♘e4 ♕e1 35 ♖d2 g4 36 hxg4 hxg4 37 ♖f2 0-1 Vogt**

144 Azmajparashvili-Taborov
USSR 78

1 c4 e5 2 ♘c3 d6 3 ♘f3 ♘d7 4 d4 g6 5 e4 ♗g7 6 ♗e2 ♘gf6 7 0-0 0-0 8 ♗e3 exd4 8...♘g4!? **9 ♘xd4 c6 10 ♕c2 ♕e7 11 ♖fe1 ♘c5 12 f3 ♘h5?!** 12...d5 13 cxd5 cxd5 14 ♘cb5! dxe4 15 ♘xc6 bxc6 16 ♗xc5 +−; 12... ♗d7 += **13 ♗f1 ♗e5 14 g3 ♕f6 15 ♖ad1 g5 16 ♗g2 ♔h8 17 ♖f1 ♖g8 18 ♘ce2 ♘e6** 18...♘f4 19 gxf4 gxf4 20 ♗c1 ♗h3 21 ♖f2 ♖g7 22 ♔h1 +− **19 ♘f5 ♘eg7** 19...♗xb2 20 ♖xd6 +− **20 ♗xg5! ♕xg5 21 f4 ♘xf5** 21...♕f6 22 fxe5 dxe5 23 ♘d6 +−; 21...♕d8 22 ♘h6 +− **22 fxg5 +− ♘e3 23 ♕c1 ♘xd1 24 ♕xd1 ♖xg5 25 ♖xf7 ♗g4 26 ♕d2 ♖g6 27 ♗f3 ♗e6 28 ♖xb7 ♖f8 29 ♗xh5 ♗h3 30 ♖b8! ♖xb8 31 ♗xg6 1-0 Gufeld**

145 Alburt-Kasparov
Daugavpils 78

1 d4 ♘f6 2 c4 g6 3 ♘c3 ♗g7 4 e4 d6 5 ♗e2 0-0 6 ♗g5 c5 7 d5 h6 8 ♗f4 e6 9 dxe6 ♗xe6 10 ♗xd6 ♖e8 11 ♘f3 ♘c6 12 0-0 ♕a5 13 ♘d2 N 13 a3 ♖ed8 14 b4 cxb4 15 axb4 ♕xa1 16 ♕xa1 ♘xe4∝ **♖ed8!** 13...♖ad8 14 e5 ♘d7 15 f4± **14 ♘b3** 14 e5 ♘e8 **♕b6 15 ♘a4 ♕b4 16 ♘bxc5** 16 ♘axc5 ♘e8 17 a3 ♕b6 18 ♘a4 ♖xd6 19 ♘xb6 ♖xd1 20 ♘xa8 ♖d8 =+ **♗xc4 17 ♗xc4 ♕xc4 18 ♘xb7 ♘xe4 19 ♖c1 ♕b5 20 ♘xd8 ♖xd8 21 ♕c2 ♘d4! 22 ♕xe4 ♘e2+ 23 ♔h1 ♘xc1 24 ♖xc1 ♖xd6∝ 25 ♕c2?!** 25 b3 **♕g5 26 ♖d1? ♕f5 27 ♕c1 ♖xd1+ 28 ♕xd1 ♕xf2∓ 29 ♕g1?** 29 ♕b1 **♕c2! 30 b3 ♕xa2 31 ♘c5 ♕d2 32 ♕b1 ♗d4 33 ♘d3 ♕e3 34 ♘b4 h5 35 ♕d1 h4 36 ♘c2** 36 h3 ♗e5 Δ ♕g3 −+ **♕xb3 37 ♕xd4 ♕xc2 39 ♕xa7 ♕d1+ 40 ♕g1 ♕xg1+ 41 ♔xg1 ♔g7 42 ♔f2 ♔f6 43 ♔e3 ♔e5 44 ♔f3 f5 45 ♔e3 g5 46 h3 ♔d5 47 ♔d3 ♔c5 48 ♔c3 g4 49 ♔d3 gxh3 50 gxh3 ♔d5 51 ♔e3 ♔e5 52 ♔f3 f4 53 ♔f2 ♔e4 54 ♔e2 f3+ 55 ♔f1 ♔f5! 56 ♔g1 ♔e5 57 ♔f1 ♔e4 0-1 Kasparov**

146 Forintos-Kristiansen
Esbjerg 78

1 d4 ♘f6 2 c4 g6 3 ♘c3 ♗g7 4 e4 d6 5 ♗e2 0-0 6 ♗g5 c5 7 d5 h6 8 ♗f4 ♖e8!? 8...e5 9 dxe6 ♗xe6 10 ♗xd6 ♖e8; 8...a6 9 a4 ♖e8!? **9 ♘f3** 9 ♕d2 g5!?∝ **e6 10 ♘d2!?** 10 dxe6 ♖xe6 11 e5 ♘h5 12 ♗e3 ♗xe5 **a6 11 a4 ♕e7 12 h3 ♘bd7 13 0-0 e5!?** 13... exd5 **14 ♗e3 a5 15 ♕c2 ♖f8** 15...g5 Δ ♘f8-g6 **16 ♖ae1 ♔h8 17 ♔h2 ♘g8 18 ♗d3 h5 19 ♘f3 ♗h6 20 ♕d2 ♗xe3 21 ♕xe3 22 g3** 22 ♕g5! f6 23 ♕g3 **♘df6 23 ♔g2 ♘h7 24 ♘h4 ♗d7 25 ♗c2 ♖ae8 26 ♘d1 ♘g5 27 ♖h1 ♘h6?** 27...b6 **28 ♕c3! b6 29 f4 ♘h7 30 ♘e3?** 30 ♘f2 Δ ♘d3, ♘f3 **♔g8 31 ♘f3**

♕f6 32 fxe5 dxe5 33 ♖ef1 ♕e7 34 ♕d2 ♔g7 35 ♘h4 f6 36 ♖f2 ♘g5 37 ♕e2 ♘hf7 38 ♘f1 ♖h8 39 ♘d2 ♕d8 40 ♕f1 ♕c8! 41 g4!? hxg4 42 ♔g3 gxh3 43 ♖xf6 ♖xh4! 44 ♔xh4 ♕d8 0-1

147 Botterill-Whiteley
England 78

1 c4 ♘f6 2 d4 g6 3 ♘c3 ♗g7 4 e4 d6 5 f3 0-0 6 ♗e3 ♘c6 7 ♕d2 ♖e8 8 ♘ge2 ♖b8 9 0-0-0 a6 10 h4 10 g4 b5 11 h4 e5 12 d5 ♘a5 13 ♘g3 b4 14 ♘b1 c6∞ Haygarth-Botterill, England 78 **h5 11 ♗h6 ♗h8 12 ♕e3** Δ e5 **e5 13 d5 ♘a5 14 ♘g3 c5** 14... b5?! Tarjan 15 c5!± **15 ♗d3 b5 16 ♘f1 ♔h7?** 16...♘d7!? 17 g4 ♘b6!∞ **17 ♗g5 ♘xc4 18 ♗xc4 bxc4 19 g4!± ♕b6 20 ♖d2 hxg4 21 h5! ♘xh5 22 ♘g3 f6 23 ♘xh5 gxh5 24 ♖xh5+ ♔g6**

25 ♖h6+ ♔f7 26 ♖h7+ ♔g6 27 ♗xf6!! Δ ♕h6 mate **♔xh7 28 ♖h2+ ♔g8 29 ♕g5+ 1-0 Botterill**

148 Martin-Botterill
England 78

1 e4 d6 2 d4 g6 3 c4 ♗g7 4 ♘c3 ♘f6 5 f4 0-0 6 ♗e2 c5 7 d5 e6 8 ♘f3 exd5 9 cxd5 b5!? 10 e5 10 ♗xb5 ♘xe4 11 ♘xe4 ♕a5+ 12 ♔f2 ♕xb5 13 ♘xd6 ♕b6! 14 ♘xc8 ♖xc8≈ **dxe5 11 fxe5 ♘g4 12 ♗f4** 12 ♗xb5 ♘xe5 13 0-0 ♗g4 14 ♗e2 ♗xf3 15 ♗xf3 ♘bd7= Geller **b4 13 ♘e4 ♘d7 14 e6 fxe6 15 dxe6 ♖xf4 16 ♕d5 ♔h8 17 ♕xa8** 17 0-0-0!? **♘b6 18 ♕c6 ♘e3 19 g3 ♘c2+!** N 19...♖xf3 20 ♗xf3 ♘c2+ 21 ♔f2 ♕f8∞ Thanhauser-Gerer, Corr. 68 **20 ♔f2?** 20 ♔f1 ♖xf3+ 21 ♗xf3 ♕f8∞; 20...♖f5!∓ **♕d4+ 21 ♔g2 ♕xe4 −+ 22 ♕xe4 ♖xe4 23 ♗d3 ♖xe6 24 ♖ac1 ♘e3+ 25 ♔f2 c4 0-1 Botterill**

149 Peev-Trapl Decin 78

1 d4 ♘f6 2 c4 g6 3 ♘c3 ♗g7 4 e4 d6 5 f4 0-0 6 ♘f3 c5 7 d5 e6 8 ♗e2 exd5 9 cxd5 ♖e8 10 e5 dxe5 11 fxe5 ♘g4 12 ♗g5 ♕b6 13 0-0 ♘d7 13...c4+? 14 ♔h1 ♘f2+ 15 ♖xf2 ♕xf2 16 ♘e4 ♕b6 17 ♘d6± Kakageldyev-Lerner, Riga 72 **14 d6 c4+ 15 ♔h1 ♘f2+ 16 ♖xf2 ♕xf2 17 ♘d5 ♘xe5 18 ♗h4?** 18 ♘e7+ **♘g4! −+ 19 ♘e7+ ♔f8 20 ♗xc4 ♕xh4! 21 ♕c1 ♕h6 22 ♕e1 ♗d4 23 ♕f1 ♘f2+ 24 ♔g1 ♗e3 25 ♕e2 ♘e4+ 0-1** 26 ♔f1 ♘g3+ −+ **Pritchett**

150 Hausner-Vogt
CSSR-DDR 78

1 c4 g6 2 ♘c3 ♗g7 3 d4 d6 4 e4 ♘f6 5 f4 0-0 6 ♘f3 c5 7 d5 e6 8 ♗e2 exd5 9 cxd5 ♗g4 9...♖e8 10 e5 dxe5 11 fxe5 ♘g4 12 ♗g5 f6∞ **10 0-0** 10 e5 ♗xf3 11 ♗xf3 dxe5 12 fxe5 ♘fd7 13 e6 ♘e5 14 exf7+ ♖xf7 15 0-0 ♘bd7 16 ♗e3 ♘xf3+ 17 ♖xf3 ♖xf3 18 ♕xf3 ♘e5 19 ♕d1 c4∓ **♘bd7 11 a4 ♖e8 12 h3 ♗xf3 13 ♗xf3 c4** 13...a6 14 g4± **14 ♗e3 ♕a5 15 ♗d4 ♘c5?!** 15...♖e7! 16 ♔h1 a6 17 g4 ♖ae8 18 g5 ♘xe4 19 ♘xe4 ♖xe4 20 ♗xe4 ♖xe4 21 ♗xg7 ♔xg7 22 ♕f3 f5=

Peev-Velimoric, Balkaniad 72 **16 e5 Nfd7 17 e6 fxe6 18 dxe6** 18 Bxg7 Kxg7 19 Qd4+ e5 **Nxe6 19 Bxg7 Kxg7 20 Kh1!** 20 Qxd6 Nf6 **Qb6** 20...Nf6 21 Nd5 Qd8 22 Qd2 += **21 Bd5** 21 Nd5 Qc5∞ **Nf6 22 f5± Qxb2 23 Nb5?** 23 Rb1 Qxc3 24 Rxb7+ Kh8 25 fxe6± **Nf4! 24 Rxf4 Nxd5 25 Rb1 Qe5 =+** 25...Qxb1? 26 Qxb1 Nxf4 27 Nxd6 **26 Rxc4 Re7! 27 Qd4!** 27 fxg6 Ne3 −+ **Ne3 28 Rc7 Nxf5** 28...Rae8 29 Qxe5+ dxe5 30 Nd6 +− **29 Rxe7+ Nxe7 30 Qxd6 Qxd6 31 Nxd6 b6 32 Rc1= Nd5 33 Nb5 Kf6 34 Nc7 Nxc7** 34...Rd8 35 Rd1 Ke5 36 Re1+ += **35 Rxc7 h5 36 Kg1 Ke6 37 Rg7 Kf5 38 Kf2 g5 ½-½ Vogt**

151 Rogoff-Villareal Mexico 78
1 Nf3 Nf6 2 c4 g6 3 g3 Bg7 4 Bg2 0-0 5 d4 d6 6 0-0 Nc6 7 Nc3 a6 8 Qd3!? 8 d5; 8 h3; 8 Nd5!? **Bf5! 9 e4 Bg4 10 Be3** 10 d5 Bxf3 11 Qxf3 Nd4 12 Qd1 c5 13 dxc6 Nxc6 14 Be3 Nd7= Furman-Boleslavsky, Moscow 57 **Nd7 11 Ne1!** 11 Ne2!? **e5 12 d5 Nd4 13 f3 Nc5 14 Qd1 Bc8 15 Nc2** 15 b4!? Nd7 16 Nc2 **Nxc2 16 Qxc2 a5 17 a3 f5 18 Bf2** 18 b4 f4!? **fxe4 19 fxe4 Bh6 20 b4 axb4 21 axb4 Rxa1 22 Rxa1 Na6 23 Rb1**

23...Qg5!? 23...b6 24 Nb5 Δ Na7-c6; 23...Nb8!? 24 c5 Nd7 25 Nb5?! Nf6 26 cxd6 cxd6 27 h3!? Ne8; 27 Qc7?! Qxc7 28 Nxc7 Bd7 =+; 27...Nh5!?; 25 c6!? Nf6 26 cxb7 Bxb7∞; 25...bxc6!? 26 dxc6 Nf6 **24 c5 Qd2!? 25 Qxd2 Bxd2 26 Na2! Bg4?! 27 h3 Bc8** 27...Be2? 28 Rb2; 27...Bf3 28 Rb3? **28 Rb2 Bg5 29 Rc2 +=/± Be7 30 Rc3 Bd7 31 Bf1 Nb8 32 Nc1** Δ Nb3-a5 **c6!? 33 Nb3 Rc8 34 g4 cxd5 35 exd5 Ba4 36 Nd2 Nd7 37 Ra3 Bd1 38 Ra1 Bc2 39 Ra2 Bd1 40 Ra1 Bc2 41 Ra2 Bd1 42 c6! +− bxc6 43 dxc6 Rxc6 44 Ra7 Bg5 45 Ne4 1-0 Speelman**

152 Romanishin-Adorjan IBM 78
1 d4 Nf6 2 Nf3 g6 3 c4 Bg7 4 g3 0-0 5 Bg2 d6 6 0-0 Nc6 7 Nc3 a6 8 Nd5!? Nd7?! 8...Ne4!? 9 Ne3 f5 10 d5 Na5 11 Nd2 Ng5∞ Bilek-Liberzon, Venice 74; 8...Bd7 9 Nxf6+ Bxf6 10 Bh6 Re8 11 Qd2 Qc8 12 d5 Ne5 13 Nxe5 Bxe5 14 f4 Bg7= Bilek-Ciocaltea, Szombathely 66 **9 Be3 b5 10 cxb5 axb5 11 Rc1 Bb7 12 Nxc7! Qxc7 13 d5 Ndb8 14 dxc6 Nxc6 15 Nd4 Bxd4 16 Qxd4!** Δ Bxc6/Bh6 **Nxd4 17 Rxc7 Bxg2** 17...Nxe2+? 18 Kh1 Δ Re1 **18 Kxg2 Nf5 19 Ba7 d5 20 a3 Rfc8 21 Rfc1 Nd6 22 R1c6 b4 23 Rxc8+ Nxc8** 23...Rxc8 24 Rxc8+ Nxc8 25 Bc5 Δ a4 +− **24 Bc5 bxa3 25 Bxa3 Rb8 26 Rc5 Nb6 27 Rc7 Nc4 28 Bxe7 Nxb2 29 Bf6 Na4 30 Rd7 Nb6 31 Rd6 Kf8 32 Bd4 Nc4 33 Rxd5 Ke7**

Diagram

34 Bc5+ Ke6 35 Rd4 Na5 36 Rd6+ Ke5 37 f4+ Ke4 38 Rd4+ Kf5 39 Rd5+ Ke6 40 Re5+ Kd7 41 Ba7

1-0 Taulbut

153 Birnboim-Westerinen
Gausdal 78

1 d4 ♘f6 2 c4 g6 3 ♘f3 ♗g7 4 ♘c3 0-0 5 g3 d6 6 ♗g2 ♘c6 7 0-0 e5 8 d5 ♘e7 9 c5 9 e4 ♘e8 10 ♘g5 h6 11 ♘h3∞ **♘e8 10 cxd6 cxd6 11 ♘d2?!** 11 a4 h6 12 e4 f5 13 exf5 gxf5 14 a5 ♘c7 15 ♘e1 ♗d7= Korchnoi-Bogdanovic, Sarajevo 69; 14 ♘d2!? **f5 12 ♘c4 ♗d7 13 a4 ♖c8 14 ♕b3?!** 14 b3∞ **f4 15 ♘b5 ♘f5 16 e3 a6 17 ♘ba3** 17 ♘a7!? ♖c7 18 ♘b6 ♘h4!? 19 ♘c6 ♕f6 20 ♘xd7 ♖xd7 21 gxh4 f3 22 ♗h3 ♕xh4 23 ♗e6+ ♔h8 24 ♔h1 e4∞ **♘h4! 18 exf4** 18 gxh4 f3 19 ♗h1 ♕xh4 20 ♖d1 ♕h3 −+ **♘xg2 19 ♔xg2 b5 20 axb5 axb5 21 ♘xb5** 21 ♘d2 exf4 ∓/−+ **♖b8 22 ♖a5 ♘c7 23 fxe5 ♗xb5 24 exd6 ♗c6! 25 ♕d3 ♘xd5 26 ♔g1** 26 ♖xd5 ♖f5 27 ♘e3 ♖xd5 28 ♘xd5 ♕xd6 −+ **♘b4 27 ♕e2 ♕d7 28 ♗f4 ♖be8 29 ♕d2 ♕h3 30 f3 ♗d4+ 31 ♗e3** 31 ♕xd4 ♖e2 32 ♖f2 ♖e1+ −+ **♖xf3 32 ♖xf3 ♗xf3 33 d7 ♖xe3 34 d8♕+ ♖e8+ 35 ♕2xd4** 35 ♕8xd4 ♖e1+ 36 ♔f2 ♕f1 mate **♕g2 mate 0-1 Westerinen**

154 Rogoff-Guil.Garcia
Mexico 78

1 d4 ♘f6 2 c4 d6 3 ♘c3 ♘bd7 4 e4 e5 5 ♘f3 g6 6 g3 ♗g7 7 ♗g2 0-0 8 0-0 c6 9 ♖b1 a5 10 h3 ♖e8 11 ♖e1 exd4 12 ♘xd4 ♘c5 13 ♗f4 ♗f8 13...♘h5 14 ♗e3 a4; 14...♘f6!? **14 b3 ♘fd7 15 ♖e2 ♘e5 16 ♖d2 ♕c7 17 ♗e3** △ f4, ♗f2 **f5!?** △ ♘xe4 **18 exf5 gxf5 19 ♕c2 ♕f7 20 ♖e1 ♘e4 21 ♘xe4 fxe4 22 ♗xe4 ♗xh3** △ ♘g4 **23 f3**

23...♗d7!? 23...d5!? 24 cxd5 cxd5 25 ♗xh7+ (1) 25...♔g7 26 ♖h2 ♖ac8 27 ♕b1 ♕h5 28 ♗f5 ♘xf3+ 29 ♘xf3 ♖xe3 30 ♖xe3 ♕xf5 31 ♕xf5 ♗xf5 32 ♘d4±; 31 ♕a1+!? ♔g8 32 ♘d4 ♕g5; 30...♗c5? 31 ♖xh3 ♕xf3 32 ♕b2+! +−; 27...♘xf3+? (27...♕d7? 28 f4 +−) 28 ♘xf3 ♖xe3 29 ♖xe3 ♗c5 30 ♖xh3 ♗xe3+ 31 ♔g2 +− (2) 25...♕xh7! 26 ♕xh7+ ♔xh7 27 ♖h2 ♘xf3+!? 28 ♘xf3 ♖xe3!? 29 ♖xh3+ ♔g7 30 ♖xe3 ♗c5 31 ♔f1 ♗xe3 32 ♖h5 ♖c8 ∞/+=; 32 ♔e2!? ♖e8; 31 ♔g2!?; 27...♗c5!?; 27...♘d3!? **24 ♖h2 h5 25 ♕f2 d5 26 cxd5 cxd5 27 ♗b1 ♗c5 28 ♔g2 ♖f8 29 ♗f4! ♘g6** 29...♘c6 30 ♘xc6! ♗xf2 31 ♘e7+ ♔g7 32 ♔xf2 **30 ♗xg6 ♕xg6 31 ♕c2 ♕xc2 32 ♘xc2 ♖f5 33 ♗e3 ♗b4 34 ♖d1 ♖e8 35 ♔f2? ♖fe5?** 35...♖xf3+! **36 ♘xb4 axb4 37 ♗c5 ♖e2+ 38 ♔g1 ♖xh2 39 ♔xh2 ♖e2+ 40 ♔g1 ♗c6 41 ♗xb4 ♖xa2 42 ♖d2 ½-½ Speelman**

155 Petrosian-Ciocaltea
Buenos Aires 78
1 d4 g6 2 c4 ♗g7 3 ♘c3 d6 4 ♘f3 ♘f6 5 g3 0-0 6 ♗g2 ♘bd7 7 0-0 e5 8 e4 c6 9 h3 9 ♖b1!? **♖e8** 9...♕a5; 9...♕b6 **10 ♗e3 a5 11 ♕c2 a4 12 ♖ab1! exd4 13 ♘xd4 ♘c5 14 ♖fe1 ♕e7** 14...♕a5!? 15 b4 axb3 16 axb3 ♕b4 **15 ♖bd1**

15...♘fd7 15...♘fxe4?! 16 ♘xe4 ♘xe4 17 ♗xe4 ♕xe4 18 ♗d2 ♕xe1+ 19 ♗xe1 ♗xd4∞; 17 ♗f4! f5 18 f3 ♗xd4 (18...g5 19 ♗c1 ♗xd4+ 20 ♖xd4 ♕e5 21 ♖dd1 ♕xg3 22 fxe4 fxe4 23 ♕f2 +−) 19 ♖xd4 ♕g7 20 ♕d1 ♘f6 21 ♖xd6 ♖xe1+ 22 ♕xe1 ♗d7 23 ♗e5 ♖e8 24 ♕c3 +−; 16 ♘xc6 bxc6 17 ♗xc5 dxc5= **16 ♖e2 ♘e5 17 b3 axb3 18 axb3 += f6?** 18...♖a3!? 19 f4 ♘xb3!? 20 fxe5 ♗xe5∞ **19 f4 ♘f7 20 ♗f2± ♗d7 21 b4 ♘a6 22 ♖b1 ♘c7 23 ♕c1 ♕f8 24 ♖d2 ♕e7 25 ♕d1 ♘e6 26 ♘de2** 26 c5! dxc5 27 ♘f5! gxf5 28 ♖xd7 **♗c8 27 ♘a4 ♘f8 28 ♘b6 ♖b8 29 c5 dxc5 30 bxc5 ♗e6 31 ♘d4 ♖bd8 32 ♕c2 ♗h6 33 ♖bd1 ♗g7 34 ♗f1 h5?! 35 f5! gxf5 36 ♘xe6 +− ♖xd2 37 ♖xd2 ♕xe6 38 exf5 ♕e7 39 ♗c4 +− ♔h7 40 ♕d1 ♗h6 41 ♕xh5 ♘e5 42 ♖d4! 1-0 Gipslis**

156 F.Portisch-Ujtelky
Zamardi 78
1 d4 g6 2 c4 ♗g7 3 ♘c3 d6 4 e4 ♘c6 5 d5 5 ♘ge2; 5 ♗e3 **♘d4 6 ♗e3 c5 7 ♘ge2 ♘xe2?** 7...♕b6 **8 ♗xe2 ♕a5 9 ♗d2! a6 10 0-0 ♘f6 11 a3!? 0-0?** 11...♕c7 12 b4 ♘d7 **12 b4! cxb4 13 axb4 ♕c7** 13...♕xb4?? 14 ♘a4 +− **14 ♕b3 b6 15 ♖a3 ♖b8 16 ♗e3 ♘d7 17 ♖c1 ♗b7 18 ♖a2 ♗c8 19 ♕a3 ♗e5 20 ♖ac2** Δ ♘a4, c5 **f5 21 exf5! gxf5 22 f4 ♗f6 23 ♘a4 ♔h8 24 ♕d3 ♗g7 25 ♗d4 ♘f6 26 ♕e3! ♘g4 27 ♗xg4 fxg4 28 ♘xb6 ♗f5 29 ♖c3 ♗g6 30 c5 dxc5 31 bxc5 ♕xf4 32 ♗xg7+ ♔xg7 33 ♘d7 ♖b2 34 ♘xf8 1-0**

157 Speelman-Biyiasas
Lone Pine 78
1 c4 g6 2 e4 d6 2...e5!? 3 d4 ♘f6 4 ♘f3 ♗b4+ 5 ♗d2 ♗xd2+ 6 ♕xd2!= Speelman-Sax, Hastings 77/78 **3 d4 e5 4 ♘f3 ♗g7 5 ♘c3** 5 dxe5?! **♗g4?!** 5...♘d7 Δ c6, ♘h6?!; 5...exd4!? 6 ♘xd4 ♘e7 Δ ♘bc6, f5!?; 5...c6!?; 5...♗g4 **6 d5 ♘f6** 6...f5? 7 h3 ♗xf3 8 ♕xf3 += Polugaevsky-Seirawan, Lone Pine 78; 6...♔f8 Δ 7...♗h6 8 ♗xh6+ ♘xh6 9 ♕d2 ♔g7 Biyiasas; 6...a5 7 ♗e2 ♘a6 8 0-0; 8 ♕a4+!? Korchnoi-Hubner, Wijk aan Zee 71 **7 h3 ♗c8** 7...♗xf3? 8 ♕xf3+= **8 ♗e3 0-0 9 ♗e2** 9 g4!? h5!? 10 ♗g5 **♘bd7 10 g4 ♘c5 11 ♘d2 a5 12 h4 c6** 12...♗xg4? 13 ♗xg4 ♘d3+ 14 ♔f1 ♘xb2 15 ♕e2 ♘xg4 16 ♕xg4 f5 17 ♕e2 f4 18 ♖b1 fxe3 19 ♕xe3 +− **13 h5 ♘e8 14 ♘f1** 14 ♘b3!? **cxd5 15 cxd5 gxh5!? 16 gxh5?!** 16 ♗xc5 dxc5 17 ♖xh5; 16 ♖xh5 ♘f6 17 ♖h2!? (17 ♗g5) ♘cxe4 18 ♘xe4 ♘xe4 19 ♗d3 f5! 20 gxf5 ♘f6∞ 21 ♘g3 e4! **♔h8** 16...f5? **17 ♖g1 ♗f6 18 ♕d2 ♗d7 19**

♝h6 ♞g7 20 ♛e3 ♜g8 21 ♛f3 ♛e7 22 ♝b5? 22 ♘e3 b5? 23 ♗xb5! ♗xb5 24 ♘xb5 Δ ♗xg7+, ♘f5!; 22...♖af8 23 ♗b5 ♗e8! Δ ♗h4, f5 ∝/=+

22...♞f5!! 22...♗xb5?! 23 ♘xb5 ♘xh5?! ±/+− **23 ♜xg8+ ♜xg8 24 exf5** 24 ♗xd7 ♘d4 −+/∓ **♝xb5 25 ♞xb5 e4 26 ♛e2 ♞d3+ 27 ♚d2 ♛e5! −+ 28 ♚e3?** 28 ♘c3 ♘xb2 29 ♖c1 ♕d4+!; 28 ♘a3 ♕xb2+ 29 ♘c2 ♖c8 30 ♘e3 ♕c3+ 31 ♔d1 ♕xa1+! 32 ♘xa1 ♖c1+ 33 ♔d2 ♗c3 mate **♜g5! 0-1 Speelman**

158 Rashkovsky-Shtukaturkin
USSR 78

1 ♞f3 g6 2 c4 ♝g7 3 e4 d6 4 d4 ♝g4 4...♘d7; 4...e5 5 ♘c3 ♘c6 6 d5 ♘ce7 7 ♗e2 f5 8 exf5 gxf5 9 ♘g5! +=; 5...♗g4!? **5 ♝e2** 5 ♘c3 **e5 6 d5** 6 dxe5 ♗xf3 7 ♗xf3 dxe5 8 ♕xd8+ ♔xd8 =+ **a5 7 0-0 ♞a6 8 ♞e1! ♝xe2 9 ♛xe2 ♝h6!? 10 ♝xh6 ♞xh6 11 ♛d2! += ♛h4 12 ♞f3 ♛h5** 12...♕f4 13 ♕xa5 ♕xe4 14 ♕b5+ ♔e7 15 ♘c3 ♕f4 16 ♖fe1 +=; 13 ♕xf4! exf4 14 e5 += **13 ♛xa5 0-0 14 ♛d2 f5 15 ♛g5 fxe4 16 ♛xh5 gxh5 17 ♞fd2** 17 ♘g5 ♘b4 18 ♘c3 e3 19 fxe3 ♘c2 **♞b4 18 ♞c3 e3 19 fxe3 ♞g4** 19...♘c2 20 ♖xf8+ ♖xf8 21 ♖f1! ♘xe3 22 ♖xf8+ Δ ♘b5± **20 e4!± ♞d3 21 b3 ♞e3 22 ♜xf8+ ♜xf8 23 ♞f1 +− ♞c2 24 ♜d1 ♞c5 25 ♜d2 ♞b4 26 a3! ♞ba6 27 b4 ♞b3 28 ♜f2 ♞d4 29 ♜xf8+ ♚xf8 30 ♚f2 ♚f7 31 ♚e3 ♚g6 32 h4 ♞b8 33 ♞b5! ♞xb5 34 cxb5 ♞d7 35 a4 ♞b8 36 a5 ♚f7 37 ♞g3 ♚e7 38 ♞xh5 c6 39 dxc6 bxc6 40 a6 1-0 Gufeld**

Sicilian 2 c3

159 P.Littlewood-Speelman
London 78

1 e4 c5 2 c3 b6!? 3 d4 ♝b7 4 ♝d3 4 d5 ♘f6 5 ♗d3 c4!?; 5...g6; 4...g6 **cxd4?! 5 cxd4 ♞c6 6 ♞f3 ♞b4 7 ♝c4!?** 7 ♘c3 ♘xd3+ 8 ♕xd3+ =/± **♜c8 8 ♞e5 e6 9 ♞c3 f6** 9...♗d6 10 ♘b5 ♗b8! **10 ♛h5+ g6 11 ♞xg6 hxg6 12 ♛xh8 ♚f7 13 ♛h7+** 13 ♗b3; 13 ♘b5!? **♝g7 14 ♝b3** 14 ♘b5!? d5! 15 ♗f4 ♖c6! **♞d3+ 15 ♚e2 ♝a6 16 ♚f3 ♞xc1!? 17 ♜axc1 ♞h6**

18 ♞d5 18 h4! f5!? 19 h5 ♖xc3+ 20 ♖xc3 fxe4+ 21 ♔xe4 d5+ 22 ♔f3 ♕f6+ 23 ♔g3 ♕g5+ 24 ♔h2 +−; 23...♘f5+ 24 ♔h2 **f5 19 ♜xc8??** 19 ♘f4! ♕g5 20 ♕xg6+!∝ **fxe4+!** 19...♕h4 20 ♖f8+! ♔xf8 21 ♕xg6 **20 ♚xe4 ♛h4+ −+ 21 f4** 21 ♘f4 d5+! −+ **♝xc8 22 ♞e3 ♛f2 23 ♜c1 d5+ 24 ♞xd5** 24 ♗xd5 exd5+ 25

♔xd5 ♗b7+ 26 ♔d6 ♕xf4+ −+ **♕e2+ 25 ♘e3 ♗b7+ 26 d5 exd5+ 27 ♗xd5+ ♗xd5+ 28 ♔xd5 ♕d2+ 29 ♔e4 ♕xc1 30 g4 ♕c6+ 31 ♔d3 ♘xg4 32 ♘xg4 ♕d7+ 0-1 Speelman**

160 Corden-Speelman
British Final 78

1 e4 c5 2 c3 ♘f6 3 e5 ♘d5 4 d4 cxd4 5 cxd4 b6!? 6 ♕f3 ♗b7 7 ♘c3 7 ♗c4 ♕c8! **e6 8 ♕g3** 8 ♗c4!? **♘xc3 9 bxc3 ♕c8 10 ♘h3 ♘c6 11 ♗e2?!** 11 ♘f4 ♘e7 **♗a6! 12 ♘f4 ♗xe2 13 ♔xe2!?** 13 ♘xe2 ♕a6 **♕a6+ 14 ♕d3 ♕xd3+ 15 ♔xd3** 15 ♘xd3 **d6! =+ 16 exd6 ♗xd6 17 ♘h5!? 0-0 18 ♗e3 ♖fd8 19 ♖hd1 ♖ac8∓ 20 c4?**

20...♗a3? 20...e5! 21 d5 ♘b4+ 22 ♔c3 b5 23 c5 ♗xc5 24 ♗xc5 ♘a6!; 21 ♔e2 ♘a5! **21 ♔e2 ♘a5 22 c5 bxc5 23 dxc5 ♖e8 24 ♔d3! ♘b7!?** 24... ♗xc5 **25 ♔e2** 25 c6!? **♘xc5 26 ♗c1 ♗b4 27 ♗b2** 27 ♗d2 **e5 28 ♖ac1 ♘a4 29 ♗a1 ♘c3+ 30 ♗xc3 ♗xc3 31 ♖d7 a5 32 ♔d3** 32 ♘g3 **♗b4! 33 ♖xc8** 33 ♖cc7 **♖xc8 34 g4** Zeitnot **h6 35 h4?! ♖c3+ 36 ♔e4 ♖c2 37 ♔xe5 ♖xf2 38 a4 ♖e2+ 39 ♔f4 ♖d2 40 ♖xd2? ♗xd2+ −+ 41 ♔f3** 41 ♔g3 ♗b4! 42 ♘f4 ♗d6 −+ **♗e1 42 ♘g3 ♗xg3 43 ♔xg3 ♔f8 44 ♔f4 ♔e7 45 ♔e5 g6 46 ♔d5 f6 47 h5 gxh5 48 gxh5 ♔d7 49 ♔e4** 49 ♔c5 f5?? 50 ♔d5; 49...♔e6! 30 ♔b5 f5 **♔e6 50 ♔f4 f5 51 ♔e3 ♔e5 52 ♔f3 f4 53 ♔e2 ♔f5 0-1 Speelman**

161 Hazai-Honfi
Budapest 78

1 e4 c5 2 ♘f3 e6 3 c3 ♘f6 4 e5 ♘d5 5 d4 cxd4 6 cxd4 d6 7 a3!? N **♗d7 8 ♗d3 ♗c6 9 0-0 ♗e7 10 ♗c2 ♘d7 11 ♘bd2 ♕c7 12 ♖e1 0-0 13 ♘e4 dxe5 14 dxe5 ♖fd8 15 ♘fg5?** 15 ♘g3; 15 ♗g5 **♘xe5 16 ♕h5 h6 17 f4 ♗e8 18 ♘c3 ♘xc3 19 fxe5 ♘d5 0-1** 20 ♖e2 f5 **Honfi**

162 Regan-Adorjan
Budapest 78

1 e4 c5 2 ♘f3 ♘c6 3 c3 ♘f6 4 e5 ♘d5 5 d4 cxd4 6 cxd4 d6 7 ♗c4 ♘b6 7...dxe5 8 dxe5 e6 9 0-0 ♘b6 10 ♕xd8+ ♘xd8 11 ♗b3 ♗d7 12 ♘c3 ♗c6 13 ♘d4 ♗e7 14 ♗e3 0-0 15 ♖fd1 ♖e8 16 ♘db5 ♖f8 17 ♘xa7 ♖xa7 18 ♗xb6 ♖a6 19 ♗e3?! (19 ♗d4!? Ochoa) ♖a5 20 ♗d4 b5! 21 a3 ♘b7 22 ♖ac1 ♖a6! 23 ♘xb5 ♗xb5 24 ♖c7 ♘a5! 25 ♗c2 ♖c6 26 ♗xh7+? ♔xh7 27 ♖xe7 ♖d8 0-1 O.Castro-Ochoa, Manresa 78 **8 ♗b5 dxe5 9 ♘xe5 ♗d7 10 ♗xc6 ♗xc6 11 ♘xc6 bxc6 12 0-0 g6 13 ♖e1 ♗g7 14 ♗g5 0-0!** N 14...♘c8± **15 ♗xe7 ♕xd4 16 ♘c3 ♕xd1 17 ♖axd1 ♖fe8 18 ♔f1 ♘c4 19 ♖d7 f5 20 ♘a4 ♘xb2** 20...♘b6 **21 ♘xb2 ♗xb2 22 ♖b1 ♖ab8 23 ♖xa7 ♗d4 24 ♖ab7 ♖a8 25 a3 c5 26 ♖c7 ♖xa3 27 ♗xc5 ♖c3 28 ♗b6 ♖b8 29 ♖xc3 ♗xc3 30 ♖c1 ♖xb6 31 ♖xc3 ½-½ Haag**

163 Regan-Malich
Budapest 78

1 e4 c5 2 c3 ♘f6 3 e5 ♘d5 4 d4 cxd4

5 cxd4 d6 6 ♞f3 e6 7 ♝d3 7 a3 ♗e7 8 ♗d3 ♗d7 9 0-0 ♗c6 10 ♕e2 ♘d7 11 ♗d2 0-0 12 ♘c3 dxe5 13 dxe5 ♘c5 14 ♗c2 ♘xc3 12 ♗xc3 ♘a4= Groszpeter-Malich, Budapest 78 **dxe5 8 ♞xe5 ♝b4+ 9 ♝d2 ♞d7! 10 0-0 0-0?!** 10...♗xd2! 11 ♘bxd2 0-0= **11 ♛c2! ♞7f6 12 ♞c3** Δ ♘xd5 +– **♝e7 13 a3 ♞b6!?** 13...♗d7 14 ♘xd5 exd5 15 ♕b3±; 13...♘xc3 14 bxc3 ♗d7 15 ♖ab1± **14 ♜fe1!** 14 ♗e3 ♗d7 15 ♖ad1 ♗c6 += **♛xd4** 14...♗d7

15 ♜ad1 15 ♕d1! ♕d8 16 ♕f3 ♘bd5 17 ♕h3± **♛c5 16 b4?!** 16 ♕b1!? ♘bd5? 17 ♘xd5 exd5 18 ♗b4 ♕c7 19 ♗xe7 ♕xe7 20 ♘g6+ –; 16...♗d7 **♛c7 17 ♝f4 ♝d6 18 ♜e3?!** 18 ♘b5? ♕xc2 19 ♗xc2 ♘bd5∓ **♞bd5 19 ♞xd5 exd5 20 ♛e2 d4! –+ 21 ♜g3 ♜e8 22 ♜e1 g6 23 ♝c4 ♝e6 24 ♝b5 ♝d7 25 ♝c4 ♜e7 26 ♛c2 ♚g7 27 ♜g5 b5 28 ♝d3 ♛xc2 29 ♝xc2 ♜ae8 0-1 Malich**

164 Maric-Hoffmann
Il Ciocco 78

1 e4 c5 2 c3 ♞f6 3 e5 ♞d5 4 d4 cxd4 5 ♛xd4 e6 6 ♞f3 ♞c6 7 ♛e4 d6 8 ♞bd2 dxe5 9 ♞xe5 ♞xe5 9...♘f6 10 ♕a4 Hort-Polugaevsky, Belgrade 70 **10 ♛xe5 ♝d7?! 11 ♞e4!?** Δ ♘d6+ += **♛c7** 11...♗c6 12 ♗h6! ♖g8 13 ♗g5 += **12 ♛xc7 ♞xc7 13 ♝f4 ♝c6** 13...♘d5 14 ♘d6+ ♗xd6 15 ♗xd6± **14 ♝xc7! ♝xe4 15 ♝b5+ ♝c6 16 ♝xc6+ bxc6 17 0-0-0± ♝c5 18 ♝g3 ♚e7** 18...♖d8 19 b4! ♗b6 20 ♖xd8+ ♗xd8 21 ♖d1± **19 b4 ♝b6 20 c4 ♜ac8 21 ♝d6+ ♚f6 22 ♜d3 ♝c7 23 ♜hd1 ♝xd6 24 ♜xd6 ♜c7** Δ ♔e7 **25 ♜d7! ♜hc8 25 ♚c2 a5 26 a3 a4 27 ♚c3 e5 28 ♜1d6+ +– ♚f5 29 c5 ♚f4 30 ♜xc7 ♜xc7 31 b5! cxb5 32 ♚b4 ♜b7 33 c6 1-0** 33...♖b8 34 c7 ♖c8 35 ♖d7 ♔f5 36 ♔xb5 ♔e6 37 ♔c6 +– **Maric**

2 ♞c3/2 d3

165 Ekstrom-Hjartarson
Gausdal 78

1 e4 c5 2 ♞c3 ♞c6 3 f4 d6?! 3...e6! **4 ♞f3 g6 5 ♝c4 ♝g7 6 0-0 e6 7 f5 exf5** 7...♘ge7 8 fxe6 fxe6 9 ♗g5 **8 d3 ♞ge7 9 a3** 9 ♕e1!? **0-0?** 9...h6! Δ ♗e6 =+ **10 ♝g5! h6 11 ♝h4 ♝e6 12 exf5 ♝xf5 13 ♞d5 g5? 14 ♞xg5! ♞xd5 15 ♝xd5 hxg5 16 ♜xf5 gxh4 17 ♛h5** Δ ♗xf7+ **♛e7 18 ♜af1 ♞d8 19 ♝e4 ♞e6 20 ♜f6 ♞g5 21 ♛xg5 d5 22 ♝h7+ 1-0 Pytel**

166 Kaizauri-Peshina Vilnius 78

1 e4 c5 2 ♞f3 e6 3 d3 ♞c6 4 g3 ♞ge7 5 ♝g2 g6 6 0-0 6 d4!? ♗g7 **7 ♜e1 d6** 7...0-0 8 e5 b6 **8 c3 e5** 8...0-0 **9 ♝e3 0-0 10 d4!? exd4 11 cxd4 ♝g4 12 dxc5 ♝xf3 13 ♝xf3 ♝xb2 14 ♞d2 ♝xa1 15 ♛xa1 dxc5 16 ♞b3**

Diagram

16...♞d4 16...b6!? 17 ♗h6 f6 18 ♖d1 ♕c7 (18...♕e8!?; 18...♕c8!?) 19 ♗g4 (19 ♗e2!?) ♕e5 **17 ♞xd4**

cxd4 18 ♝xd4 ♞c6 19 ♝f6 ♛d2 20 ♜d1 ♛c2 20...♕h6!? **21 ♝h8! f6 22 ♝xf6 ♜xf6** 22...♖ad8 23 e5!; 23 ♗xd8!?/?! ♖xf3; 23 ♖xd8!? ♘xd8 24 e5 **23 ♛xf6 ♜f8 24 ♛e6+ ♚h8 25 ♜d7 ♛c3 26 ♜f7 ♜xf7 27 ♛xf7 ♛g7 28 ♛e8+ ♛g8 29 ♛d7** 29 ♕xg8+ **♛xa2 30 ♛c8+ ♛g8 31 ♛xb7 ♛e6 32 h3 ♛c4??** 32...a5 **33 ♛c8+ ♚g7 34 ♛c7+ ♚h6 35 e5 1-0 Speelman**

167 Korchnoi-Karpov (11) 78

1 g3 c5 2 ♝g2 ♞c6 3 e4 g6 4 d3 ♝g7 5 f4 d6 6 ♞f3 ♞f6 7 0-0 0-0 8 c3 ♜b8 9 ♛e2 ♞e8 9...b5 10 e5 ♘d5 **10 ♝e3 ♞c7** 10...♗g4 11 h3 ♗xf3 12 ♗xf3 Δ ♖d1 **11 d4 cxd4 12 cxd4 ♝g4 13 ♜d1 d5** 13...♘e6 14 ♕f2 ♕b6 15 d5 ♕xb2 16 ♘bd2 +− **14 e5 ♛d7 15 ♞c3 ♜fc8** 15...♗h3 16 ♗h1 Δ ♖dc1, ♘d1-f2 **16 ♛f1 b5 17 h3 ♝xf3 18 ♝xf3** 18 ♕xf3 e6 19 g4 Δ ♘e2-g3 **b4?** 18...e6= **19 ♝g4 e6 20 ♞a4 ♞a5?** 20...♘xe5!? 21 ♘c5 ♘xg4 22 ♘xd7 ♘xe3; 20...♗f8 **21 ♞c5 ♛e8 22 ♝e2 ♞b7?** 22...♘c4!? 23 ♗xc4 dxc4 24 ♕xc4 ♘d5 **23 ♞xb7 ♜xb7 24 ♜dc1 ♛d7 25 ♜c2 b3?** 25...♖cb8 **26 axb3 ♜xb3? 27 ♛c1!** Δ ♗a6 **♜b7 28 ♝a6 ♜cb8 29 ♝xb7 ♜xb7 30 ♜a3 h6 31 ♜ac3 ♞b5 32 ♜c8+ ♚h7 33 ♜2c6 f6 34 ♚g2 ♛f7 35 ♛c2 a5 36 g4 fxe5 37 fxe5 a4 38 ♜a8 ♞a7 39 ♜a6 ♛e7 40 ♜xa4 ♜c7 41 ♛b3** Δ ♕b8 **♞c6 42 ♜a1 ♞b4 43 ♜c1 ♜c4 44 ♜b8** 44 ♖xc4? dxc4 45 ♕xc4 ♕b7+ **♜xc1 45 ♝xc1 ♛c7 46 ♜xb4 ♛xc1 47 ♛d3 h5 48 ♜b6 ♝h6 49 gxh5 ♛g5+ 50 ♛g3 ♛d2+ 1-0**

3 ♗b5

168 Nicevski-Schinzel
Budapest 78

1 e4 c5 2 ♞f3 ♞c6 3 ♝b5 e6 4 0-0 4 ♗xc6!? bxc6 5 0-0 ♘e7 6 b3 ♘g6 7 ♗b2 f6 8 d4 cxd4 9 ♘xd4 ♗e7= **♞ge7 5 ♜e1 a6 6 ♝f1 d5 7 exd5 ♞xd5 8 d4 cxd4 9 ♞xd4 ♝e7!?** 9...♕b6 10 ♘b3 (10 ♘f5!? ♘ce7) ♗e7 11 c4 ♘f6 12 ♗e3 ♕c7 13 ♘c3 0-0 14 ♕f3 b6 15 ♖ad1 ♗b7 +=; 9...♘db4 10 c3 ♘xd4 11 cxd4 ♗e7 12 ♘c3 0-0 13 a3 ♘d5= **10 ♞xc6! bxc6 11 c4 ♞b6** 11...♘f6 **12 ♛f3 ♝d7 13 ♞c3 0-0 14 ♝f4 f6 15 ♜ad1 += e5 16 ♝e3 ♞c8!?** 16...♖c8 17 c5±; 16...c5 17 ♘d5 ♖c8 += **17 c5 ♚h8 18 ♝c4 ♛c7 19 ♞a4 f5 20 ♞b6! +− ♞xb6 21 cxb6 ♛b7 22 ♝d4 exd4 23 ♜xe7 ♜ae8 24 ♜de1 ♛b8 25 ♛g3! ♛xg3 26 hxg3 c5 27 ♜xe8 ♝xe8 28 ♝xa6 ♝f7 29 ♜c1 ♜d8 30 ♜xc5 d3 31 ♝xd3 1-0 B.Balogh**

169 Filguth-Panchenko
Mexico 78

1 e4 c5 2 ♞f3 ♞c6 3 ♝b5 e6 3...g6; 3...♘f6; 3...♕b6!? **4 0-0 ♞ge7 5 ♜e1** 5 b3!? a6 6 ♗xc6 ♘xc6 7 ♗b2; 5 ♘c3 **a6 6 ♝f1** 6 ♗xc6 ♘xc6 7 d4 cxd4 8 ♘xd4 d6 9 c4; 8...♗e7?! 9 ♘xc6 bxc6 10 ♕g4 ♔f8; 9 ♘c3 += **d5** 6...♘g6!? **7 exd5 ♛xd5** 7...♘xd5 8 d4! **8 b3 ♞f5 9 ♝b2 ♝e7 10 ♞a3 0-0 11 ♞c4 += ♛d8 12 c3 b6** 12...b5 **13 ♞e3 ♞h4!?** 13...♘xe3 14 fxe3!? e5

15 d4 exd4 16 exd4 ♗e6; 13...♘xe3 14 ♖xe3!?; 14 dxe3= **14 d4! cxd4 15 cxd4 ♝b4!?** 15...♗b7 16 d5 **16 ♞xh4! ♝xe1 17 g3 ♝a5 18 ♝g2 ♝d7 19 d5! exd5 20 ♝xd5 ♛g5 21 ♜c1 ♜ad8**

22 f4! ♛h6 22...♕e7 23 ♘hf5 ♗xf5 24 ♘xf5 ♕e1+ 25 ♕xe1 ♗xe1 26 ♗xc6 +−; 24...♕d7 25 ♕g4 g6 26 ♘h6 mate **23 ♜xc6! ♛xc6** 23...♗xc6 24 ♘hf5 ♕h3 25 ♕d4; 24...♕g6 25 ♘e7+ **24 ♝xc6 ♝xc6 25 ♛g4 g6 26 ♞hf5 ♜fe8 27 ♛g5 ♝d2 28 ♞h6+ ♚f8 29 ♝a3+ 1-0 Speelman**

170 Ciocaltea-Petursson
Buenos Aires 78

1 e4 c5 2 ♞f3 ♞c6 3 ♝b5 g6 4 0-0 ♝g7 5 c3 ♞f6 6 ♜e1 6 d4!? cxd4 7 cxd4 ♘xe4 8 d5 ♘d6! 9 ♘a3 ♘b4! 10 ♗f4 0-0= Lutikov-Mihalchishin, USSR 77; 6...♘xe4 7 d5 ♘d6 8 ♘a3 ♘xe5 9 ♘xe5 ♗xe5 10 ♖e1 ♗f6! 11 ♗f4≈ Florian-Balogh, Hungary 77 **0-0 7 h3 a6?!** 7...e5!? **8 ♝xc6 bxc6 9 d4 cxd4 10 cxd4 d5 11 e5 ♞e4 12 ♞bd2** 12 ♘c3!? **c5?!** 12...♘xd2!? += **13 dxc5 ♞xc5 14 ♞b3 ♞xb3 15 ♛xb3 ♝e6 16 ♞d4 += ♛a5?!** 16...♖b8!? 17 ♕c3 ♕b6; 17 ♕a3!? **17 ♛e3! ♜ac8** 17...♗h6 18 ♕e2 ♗xc1 19 ♖exc1± **18 ♝d2 ♛a4 19 ♝c3 ♛d7 20 g4! ♜ce8** 20...h5 21 f3! **21 ♜ad1 ♛c8 22 ♚h2 ♝d7 23 f4± ♚h8 24 ♜d2! ♜g8 25 ♞b3! ♛c4 26 ♞c5 ♝c6** 26...♗c8 27 a4! Δ b3 **27 b3 ♛b5 28 a4 ♛b8** Zeitnot **29 b4! ♛b6 30 ♜b2 ♜c8 31 ♝d4 ♛d8 32 b5! +− axb5 33 axb5 ♝e8 34 b6 ♝c6 35 b7 ♜b8 36 ♜eb1 ♛a5 37 ♜b6 1-0** 37...♗e8 38 ♖a6 ♕c7 39 ♖a8 Δ ♘a6; 38...♕d8 39 ♖a7 Δ ♘a6 **Ciocaltea**

171 Hardicsay-Mednis
Budapest 78

1 e4 c5 2 ♞f3 ♞c6 3 ♝b5 g6 4 0-0 ♝g7 5 c3 ♞f6 6 ♜e1 0-0 7 h3 7 d4! **♛c7! 8 ♞a3** 8 ♗f1 e5 9 a3 d5 10 d3 a5! 11 a4 h6 12 ♘a3 ♗e6 13 ♕c2 ♖ad8= Ciocaltea-Mednis, Nis 77 **e5!= 9 ♞c2 a6 10 ♝f1?!** 10 ♗xc6! dxc6= **d5 =+ 11 d3 h6 12 ♛e2 ♝e6 13 ♞d2** 13 ♗d2!? **♞h5! 14 g3 f5 15 exf5 ♜xf5 16 ♞e3 ♜f7 17 ♝g2 ♛d7 18 ♚h2 ♜af8 19 ♜f1** 19 ♘g4!? **♚h7 20 a3 ♛d6** Δ ♘f4 **21 ♚g1 ♛d7 22 ♚h2 b5! 23 ♞g4 c4! 24 dxc4 bxc4 25 b3 cxb3 26 ♞xb3**

26...♝xg4!∓ 27 hxg4 27 ♕xg4 ♕xg4 28 hxg4 ♘f6 29 ♔g1 e4∓ **♞f6 28 f3** 28 ♘c5 ♕xg4 29 ♗f3 ♕c8 30 ♘xa6 e4∓ **e4! 29 ♝f4 exf3 30 ♝xf3 ♜e8 31 ♛d1 ♞e5 32 ♝xe5 ♜xe5 33 ♞d4 ♜fe7 34 ♞c2 ♛c7 35 ♛d3 ♞e4 36**

♜ae1? 36 ♗xe4 ♖xe4 ∓/−+ **♞xg3! −+ 37 ♜xe5 ♞xf1+ 38 ♛xf1 ♛xe5+ 39 ♚h3 ♛xc3 40 ♛d1 d4 41 g5 a5 42 gxh6 0-1 Mednis**

172 Adorjan-Mednis Budapest 78

1 e4 c5 2 ♞f3 ♞c6 3 ♝b5 g6 4 0-0 ♝g7 5 ♜e1 e5 6 ♝xc6 dxc6 6...bxc6 += Haag **7 d3 ♛e7** 7...♗g4 += Haag **8 ♞bd2** 8 a4 ♘h6 9 ♘a3 0-0 10 ♗d2 f6 11 ♖b1 ♖d8! 12 b4 cxb4 13 ♗xb4 ♕c7 = Torre-Mednis, Cleveland 75 **♞h6** 8...♗g4; 8...♘f6 += Haag **9 ♞c4 f6 10 b4!?** N **♝e6?!** 10...cxb4 11 a3 0-0! 12 axb4 ♗e6 13 ♗a3 ♖d8= **11 bxc5 ♝xc4 12 dxc4 ♛xc5?** 12...♘f7! += **13 ♛d3! ♛e7** 13...♘g4 14 ♖f1 ♖d8 15 ♕b3 ♘xf2? 16 ♗e3 +− **14 a4!** 14 ♗a3 c5! += **♛d7** 14...0-0 15 ♗a3 c5 16 ♕d5+ ♕f7 17 ♖ab1! b6 18 a5± Haag **15 ♛b3 0-0 16 ♝a3± ♜fd8 17 ♜ab1 b6** 17...♖ab8? 18 ♗d6 Haag **18 c5+ ♚h8** 18...♕f7 19 ♕c3± **19 h3 ♜ab8** 19...g5 20 ♖e3! **20 cxb6! ♜xb6** 20...axb6 21 a5 **21 ♛c4 ♛f7 22 ♛xf7 ♞xf7 23 ♜xb6 axb6 24 ♜b1 ♜b8?** 24...b5! 25 axb5 cxb5 26 ♖xb5± **25 ♝c5 b5 26 c4! +− ♝f8 27 ♝xf8 ♜xf8 28 cxb5 cxb5 29 axb5 ♞d6 30 ♞d2 ♜d8?!** 30...♖b8! **31 b6 ♞b7 32 ♞f1! f5 33 exf5 gxf5 34 ♞g3 f4 35 ♞e4 ♚g7 36 ♜c1 ♞a5 37 ♜c5 ♞b3 38 ♜xe5 ♚f7 39 b7 ♜b8 40 ♞d6+ ♚f6 41 ♜e8 1-0 Mednis**

173 Kapengut-Kim
Daugavpils 78

1 e4 c5 2 ♞f3 ♞c6 3 ♝b5 g6 4 0-0 ♝g7 5 ♜e1 ♞f6 6 c3 0-0 7 h3 e5! 8 ♞a3!? 8 d3 d6 9 a3 ♗d7 10 ♗a4 a6 11 b4 cxb4 12 axb4 Razuvaev-Vasyukov, Baku 72; 8 ♗xc6?! dxc6 9 ♘xe5 ♖e8 10 f4 ♘xe4! 11 ♖xe4 f6 12 ♕b3+ ♗e6 13 ♘c4 ♗d5∓ Veingold-Kapengut, Minsk 75; 8 d4 cxd4 9 cxd4 ♘xd4 10 ♘xd4 exd4 11 e5 ♘e8 12 ♕xd4 d6 13 ♘c3 ♗f5 14 ♗f4 dxe5 15 ♕xd8 ♖xd8 16 ♗xe5= Kim-Makarichev, Daugavpils 78 **♞h5!?** N 8...♕c7 9 d4! cxd4 10 cxd4 exd4 11 e5 ♘d5?! 12 ♗c4 ♘b6 13 ♗f4 ♘xc4 14 ♘xc4 ♘d8 15 ♖c1 ♘e6 16 ♗g3 b5 17 ♘e3 ♕a5 18 ♘xd4 ♗b7 19 ♕d3 a6± Kapengut-Shustin, Yalta 76; 11...♘e8!? **9 ♞c2 ♛b6 10 ♝f1 d6 11 b4 cxb4 12 cxb4 ♝d7?!** 12...♗e6 **13 ♜b1 ♝e6 14 a4 ♜ad8 15 ♝a3 ♞e7 16 b5 ♜fe8 17 d4± d5?! 18 ♝c5! ♛a5** 18...♕c7 19 b6 **19 ♞xe5 dxe4** 19...♗xe5 20 dxe5 dxe4 21 ♘d4± **20 ♞c4 ♝xc4 21 ♝xc4 ♛c3 22 ♞e3! +− ♞f4** 22...♗xd4 23 ♗b4 **23 ♜c1 ♛a5 24 ♛b3 ♞d3 25 ♝xf7+ ♚h8 26 ♝xe8 ♜xe8 27 ♝xe7 1-0 Kapengut**

2...♞c6, 5...e5

174 Kovacs-Adorjan
Hungary 78

1 e4 c5 2 ♞f3 ♞c6 3 ♞c3 ♞f6 4 d4 cxd4 5 ♞xd4 e5 6 ♞db5 d6 7 a4 a6 8 ♞a3 ♝e6 9 ♞c4 9 ♗c4 **♝e7 10 ♝e3?! 0-0 11 f3 b5!? 12 ♞b6?!** 12 axb5 axb5 13 ♖xa8 ♕xa8 14 ♘xb5 ♕b8 15 ♘b6!?; 14...♖b8 15 ♘d2 d5! 16 ♘c7 ♕a5 17 ♘xd5 ♘xd5 18 exd5 ♗xd5; 16 c3 **♜b8 13 ♞bd5 ♝xd5 14 exd5**

Diagram

14...♞d4! 15 axb5 axb5 16 ♝xd4 exd4 17 ♛xd4 17 ♘xb5 ♘xd5 18 ♕xd4 ♘c7∓ **b4 18 ♞d1** 18 ♘b5 **♞d7 19 ♝d3** 19 ♗e2 **♝f6 20 ♛a7 ♜e8+ 21 ♚f2 ♞c5! 22 ♚f1** 22 ♖e1 ♗d4+ 23 ♘e3 ♘xd3+; 23 ♔f1 ♖xe1+

24 ♔xe1 ♘xd3+ **♜b7 23 ♛a5 ♛e7 24 ♚f2 ♝h4+! 25 g3 ♞xd3+ 26 cxd3 ♛e2+ 27 ♚g1 ♝d8 0-1**

175 Torre-Suradiradja
Jakarta 78

1 e4 c5 2 ♞f3 ♞c6 3 d4 cxd4 4 ♞xd4 ♞f6 5 ♞c3 e5 6 ♞db5 d6 7 ♞d5 ♞xd5 8 exd5 ♞e7 9 c4 ♞f5 9...♘g6 Δ ♗e7 **10 ♝d3 ♝e7** 10...g6 11 ♕a4! ♗d7 12 ♗xf5 gxf5 13 ♕b4 ♗xb5 14 ♕xb5+ ♕d7 15 a4 Quinteros-Chandler, Jakarta 78; 10...a6 11 ♕a4 ♔e7 12 ♘c3 f6 13 0-0 g6 14 ♘e4 Mestel-Fedorowicz, Hastings 77/78 **11 0-0 a6** 11...0-0 12 f4! ♕b6+ 13 ♔h1 ♘e3 14 ♗xe3 ♕xe3 15 ♕c2 g6 16 ♖ae1 Sampouw-Chandler, Jakarta 78 **12 ♞c3 0-0 13 ♚h1 ♞d4 14 ♝e3 f5** 14...♘f5 15 ♗c1 ♘d4 16 f4 **15 ♝xd4 exd4 16 ♞e2 ♝f6 17 ♛d2 ♝d7 18 ♜ad1 b5 19 cxb5** 19 b3 **axb5 20 ♝b1 d3 21 ♞c1** 21 ♘f4 ♗g5 **♜a4 22 ♝xd3** 22 ♘xd3 ♖d4 **♛a8** 22...♖d4 23 ♘e2 **23 b3! ♜h4 24 f4! ♚h8 25 ♝e2 ♛a3 26 ♞d3 ♜a8 27 ♞b4! ♝d8 28 ♞c6 ♝f6 29 ♝xb5 ♛xa2 30 ♛xa2 ♜xa2 31 ♞b4! ♝xb5 32 ♞xa2 ♝xf1 33 ♜xf1 g5 34 g3 ♜g4 35 ♞b4 gxf4 36 ♜xf4 ♜g5 37 ♞c6 ♝e5 38 ♜f3 ♚g7 39 b4 ♚f6 40 b5 ♜g7 41 b6 h5 42 ♜b3 h4** 42...♖b7 43 ♘a5 **43 b7 1-0**

176 Ristic-Dolmatov
Graz 78

1 e4 c5 2 ♞f3 e6 3 d4 cxd4 4 ♞xd4 ♞f6 5 ♞c3 ♞c6 6 ♝f4?! d6 7 ♝g3 ♝e7!? 7...♘xd4 8 ♕xd4 ♘h5!? **8 ♞db5** 8 ♗b5 **e5 9 ♞d5 ♞xd5 10 exd5 ♞b8! 11 f4?!** 11 c4 a6 12 ♘c3 f5 13 f3 Δ ♗d3, 0-0 **a6 12 ♞a3 ♞d7 13 fxe5 ♞xe5! 14 ♝xe5?** 14 ♘c4 =+ **dxe5 15 ♞c4 0-0!∓ 16 ♛d3?** 16 ♘xe5? ♗h4+ 17 g3 ♖e8; 16 a4!?∓ **e4! 17 ♛d2** 17 ♕xe4? ♗b4+ 18 ♔f2 ♗c5+ −+ **b5 18 ♞e5 ♝b7 19 ♞c6** 19 0-0-0?? ♗g5 −+ **♝xc6 20 dxc6 ♛b6 21 ♛d7 ♜ad8! 22 ♛h3** 22 ♕xe7? ♕e3+ 23 ♗e2 ♖d2 −+ **♛xc6 −+ 23 c3 ♛d5 24 ♛e3 ♝g5 25 ♛e2 ♝d2+ 26 ♚f2 ♛c5+ 27 ♚g3 ♜d3+ 0-1 Maric**

177 Chiburdanidze-Dvoretsky
Vilnius 78

1 e4 c5 2 ♞f3 e6 3 d4 cxd4 4 ♞xd4 ♞f6 5 ♞c3 ♞c6 6 ♞db5 d6 7 ♝f4 e5 8 ♝g5 a6 9 ♞a3 b5 10 ♞ab1 10 ♗xf6 **♝e7 11 ♝xf6 ♝xf6 12 a4 b4 13 ♞d5 0-0 14 ♝c4** 14 ♘d2 ♗g5 15 ♘c4!? **♝g5 15 ♞d2 ♝b7** 15...♗e6?! 16 0-0 ♘a5!? 16 ♗a2 ♕b8 17 ♘c4 ♘xc4 18 ♗xc4 a5 19 ♕d3 +=/± Savon-Ostojic, Erevan 76; 15...♔h8 16 0-0 f5!? (16...♗b7) 17 f3 f4 (17... g6!?) 18 c3 bxc3 19 bxc3 =/+= Savon-Timoshenko, Odessa 76 **16 0-0 ♜c8** 16...♔h8!? 17 ♘b3?! a5 =/=+ Mnatsakanian-Vasyukov, Erevan 76 **17 ♞f3**

Diagram

17...♞d4 18 b3 ♝xd5 19 ♝xd5 ♜xc2 20 ♞xd4 ♜d2 21 ♞c6 ♜xd1 22 ♞xd8 ♜xa1 23 ♜xa1 ♜xd8= ½-½ Speelman

178 Bugor-Hardicsay
Prievidza 78
1 e4 c5 2 ♞f3 ♞c6 3 d4 cxd4 4 ♞xd4 ♞f6 5 ♞c3 e5 6 ♞bd5 d6 7 ♝g5 a6 8 ♞a3 b5 9 ♞d5 ♝e7 10 ♝xf6 10 ♘xe7 ♘xe7 11 ♗xf6 gxf6≈ **♝xf6 11 c3 0-0 12 ♛f3?!** 12 ♘c2 ♗g5! 13 a4 bxa4 14 ♖xa4 a5 15 ♗c4 ♔h8! Δ f5 =+; 12 h4!? **♝g5 13 h4** 13 ♘c2 f5∓ **♝h6 14 ♝d3** 14 g4 f6!; 14...♗f4!? ∓ **♞e7! 15 ♞xe7+ ♛xe7 16 ♞c2 f5 17 ♞e3 ♝xe3 18 ♛xe3** 18 fxe3 f4 −+ **♜b8 19 exf5 ♝xf5 20 ♝xf5 ♜xf5 21 g3 ♛e6! 22 0-0 d5 23 ♜ad1 h6 24 ♛c5 e4 25 ♜d2 ♜d8 26 ♜fd1?** 26 ♕d4 ♖f3 Δ e3 −+ **d4! 27 ♛b4** 27 ♕c7 ♖c8 28 ♕a7 e3 −+; 28 ♕b7?? ♖f7 −+ **e3 28 fxe3** 28 ♖e2 exf2+ 29 ♔f1 ♕c6 −+ **♛xe3+ 29 ♚h2 ♜f2+ 30 ♜xf2 ♛xf2+ 0-1** 31 ♔h3 ♕f5+ 32 ♔g2 ♕c2+ −+ **Hardicsay**

179 Honfi-Diesen Bajmok 78
1 e4 c5 2 ♞f3 ♞c6 3 d4 cxd4 4 ♞xd4 e6 5 ♞b5 ♞f6 6 ♞1c3 d6 7 ♝f4 e5 8 ♝g5 a6 9 ♞a3 b5 10 ♝xf6 gxf6 11 ♞d5 f5 12 ♝xb5 axb5 13 ♞xb5 ♜a4 13...♖a7!? **14 ♞bc7+ ♚d7 15 0-0 ♞e7** 15...♖xe4 Honfi-Piasetski, Subotica 78 **16 c4 ♜a7** 16...♖xc4 17 ♕b3 ♖xc7?? 18 ♘f6+ ♔c6 19 ♖ac1+ **17 ♞b5 ♜a5 18 exf5 ♞xd5 19 ♛xd5 ♚e7 20 ♜fe1?!** 20 c5! ♖xb5 21 cxd6+ ♕xd6 22 ♕xb5 +− **♝g7 21 c5?!** 21 a4!? Δ c5 **♜xb5 22 cxd6+ ♛xd6 23 ♛xb5 ♝xf5 24 ♜ad1 ♜b8 25 ♛a5 ♛b6 26 ♜xe5+ ♝xe5 27 ♛xe5+ ♝e6 28 ♛g5+ ♚f8 29 b3 ♛b5 30 ♛f6 ♛e2 31 ♛h8+ ♚e7 32 ♛d4 ♜a8 33 a4 ♛c2** 33...♗xb3 34 ♕d6+ ♔e8 35 ♕c6+ +− **34 ♛d6+ ♚f6 35 ♛d4+ ♚e7 36 f4!? h6?!** 36...♖c8!≈ **37 h3 ♛xb3?** 37...♖c8! **38 f5 ♝d5** 38...♗xf5 39 ♕d6+ ♔e8 40 ♖e1+ ♗e6 41 ♕c6+ +− **38 ♛e5+ ♝e6 39 ♛d6+ ♚f6 40 fxe6 ♛e3+?!** 41...♕xe6!? 42 ♕g3 ♕b6+ 43 ♔h1 ♖a6 44 ♖f1+ ♔e7 45 ♕f3! ♕e6 46 ♕b7+ ♔f8 47 ♖xf7+ ♕xf7 48 ♕xa6 +−; 43...♖d8? 44 ♖xd8 ♕xd8 45 ♕h4+ +− **41 ♚h1 ♛xe6 42 ♛g3 ♛f5 43 ♜d6+ ♚e7 44 ♜xh6 ♜d8 45 ♛e3+ ♚d7 46 ♛a7+ 1-0 Honfi**

180 Nunn-F.Portisch Budapest 78
1 e4 c5 2 ♞f3 ♞c6 3 d4 cxd4 4 ♞xd4 ♞f6 5 ♞c3 e5 6 ♞db5 d6 7 ♝g5 a6 8 ♞a3 b5 9 ♝xf6 gxf6 10 ♞d5 f5 11 ♝xb5!? axb5 12 ♞xb5 ♜a4 12...♖a7 13 ♘xa7 ♘xa7 14 exf5 +=; 12...♕a5+ 13 c3 ♕a4 14 ♘bc7+ ♔d8 15 ♘xa8 ♕xa8 16 exf5 +=; 12...♖b8!? ∝ **13 ♞bc7+ ♚d7 14 0-0!** 14 c4 ♖a7! 15 ♘b5 ♕a5+∓; 15 ♕h5! ♖xc7?! 16 ♕xf5+ ♔e8 17 ♘f6+ = **♛g5** 14...♖xe4 15 ♕h5 ♘e7 16 ♕xf7 ♔c6 17 c4! ♖g8 18 ♖fc1 ♖g7 19 ♘e6!± Honfi-Piasetski, Subotica 78; 18...♖eg4 19 g3 ♖4g6 20 c5! dxc5 21 ♖xc5+ ♔xc5 22 ♖c1+ ♔d6 23 ♘xe7 ♗e6 24 ♖c6+ ♔d7 25 ♘xe6 ♕xe7 26 ♘xf8+ ♖xf8 27 ♖c7+ +−; 14...♘e7 15 c4! ♖xc4 16 ♕b3 ♖c5 17 ♕a4+ ♘c6 18 b4 ♖c4 19 ♕b5 +− **15 c4 ♜xc4** 15...♖a7!? Haag **16**

b4! 16 Nb6+ Kxc7 17 Nxc4 Nd4∓ 18 Rc1? Qxc1; 16 Qd3 Rc5 17 b4 Nxb4 18 Nxb4 Rxc7 19 Qb5+∞; 18...Kxc7 19 Na6+∞ **Bh6 17 Nb5** Δ Nb6+ **Rd4** 17...Nd4 18 Nb6+ Ke7 19 Nxc4 Nxb5 20 Qd5 Bd7 21 a4 +− **18 Qa4** 18 Qc2 Qd8! **fxe4** 18... Bb7 19 Nxd4 exd4 20 f4!± **19 Nxd4 exd4 20 Nb6+ Kc7 21 Rfc1 Qxc1+** 21...Bb7 22 b5 Kxb6 23 bxc6 +− **22 Rxc1 Bxc1 23 Nd5+ Kd7 24 Qd1!**± 24 Nb6+?=

24...Ke6! 24...Bb2 25 Qg4+ Kd8 26 Qg5+ Ke8 27 Qf6 Rg8 28 Qxd6 +−; 24...e3 25 Qxc1 e2 26 b5! +− **25 Nb6!** 25 Nc7+? Kd7 26 Qxc1 Kxc7 27 b5 Bb7 28 bxc6 Bxc6= **Ne5** 25... Bb2 26 Qb3+; 25...Bg5 26 Qg4+ Kf6 27 Nxc8; 25...Bh6 26 Qh5 Δ Qd5+ **26 Qxc1 Ba6?** +− 26...Bb7!± **27 Qh6+ Ng6 28 Qh3+ f5 29 Qb3+ Kf6 30 Nd5+ Kg5** 30...Kg7 31 Qb2; 30...Ke5 31 Nc7 +− **31 Qg3+ Kh6 32 Qh3+ Kg5** 32...Kg7 33 Qxf5 **33 f4+ exf3 34 gxf3** Δ f4+ **f4 35 Qg4+ Kh6 36 Nxf4 Rg8 37 Kf2 d3 38 Ne6 Ne7 39 Qh4+ Kg6 40 Qxe7 d2 41 Nf4+ 1-0 Nunn**

181 Nunn-Bhend
Buenos Aires 78

1 e4 c5 2 Nf3 Nc6 3 d4 cxd4 4 Nxd4 Nf6 5 Nc3 e5 6 Ndb5 d6 7 Bg5 a6 8 Na3 b5 9 Bxf6 gxf6 10 Nd5 f5 11 Bxb5!? axb5 12 Nxb5 Rb8!? 12...Ra7 13 Nxa7 Nxa7 14 exf5 +=; 12...Qg5 13 Ndc7+ Kd8 14 Nxa8 Qxg2 15 Rf1 Qxe4+ 16 Qe2 Qa4 =+ Honfi-Horvath, Subotica 78; 14 Qd5∞; 12...Qa5+ 13 c3 Qa4 14 Nbc7+ Kd8 15 Nxa8 Qxa8 16 exf5∞ **13 Nbc7+ Kd7 14 Qh5 Nd4** 14...Ne7 15 Qxf7 Kc6 16 a4 Rb7! 17 Nxe7+ Bxe7 18 Qc4+ Kd7 19 Nd5∞; 16 b4! Nxd5 17 b5+ Kb7 18 Qxd5+! Ka7 19 Qc6 Δ b6+ +−; 17...Kb6 18 Nxd5+ +− **15 0-0 Kc6 16 b4! fxe4** 16... Ne6 17 b5+ Kb7 18 b6; 16...Rxb4 17 c3; 16...Rb7 17 c3 Rxc7 18 cxd4± **17 c3** 17 a4 Rg8 Δ Bg4, Qg5 **Ne6** 17...Nb5 18 Nxb5 Rxb5 19 c4 Rb8 20 b5+ Kb7 21 a4∞ **18 b5+ Kb7** 18...Rxb5 19 Nxb5 Kxd5 20 Na7!± **19 b6 Kc6?** 19...Qg5! 20 Qxf7? Nd8! 21 Qe8 Bh3 22 Ne3 Nc6 −+; 20 Nxe6? Qxh5 21 Nd8+ Ka6 22 Rfb1 Δ 23 Nc7+ Ka5 24 Nc6+ Ka4 25 Rb4+ Ka3 26 Nb5 mate; 22... Rb7? 23 Rb3∞; 22...Bd7! −+; 20 Qe2 Nc5∓; 20 Qxg5! Nxg5 21 a4∞ Be6 22 a5 Bxd5 23 Nxd5 Kc6 24 c4; 19...Nc5 20 a4 Be6 21 a5 Ra8 22 Nxa8 Bxd5 23 Nc7 Bc4 24 a6+ Nxa6 25 Nxa6 Kxb6 26 Rfb1+ Kc6 27 Nb8+ Kc7 28 Ra7+ Kc8 29 Nc6 1-0 Juhnke-Kindermann, BRD 77 **20 Rab1 +− Qg5** 20...Kb7 21 a4 Qg5 22 Nxe6! **21 Qe2 Nc5 22 b7! Nd3 23 Qxe4 Nc5 24 Qc4 Rxb7 25 Rxb7 1-0 Nunn**

182 Botterill-Povah
England 78

1 e4 c5 2 Nf3 e6 3 d4 cxd4 4 Nxd4 Nf6 5 Nc3 Nc6 6 Ndb5 d6 7 Bf4 e5 8 Bg5 a6 9 Na3 b5 10 Bxf6 gxf6

11 ♘d5 f5 12 c3 ♗g7 13 ♗d3 ♗e6 14 ♕h5 0-0 15 exf5 ♗xd5 16 f6 e4 17 fxg7 ♖e8 18 ♗e2 ♖e5 19 ♕h6 ♖g5 19...b4!? **20 ♘c2 ♘e5 21 ♘e3 ♗c4 22 ♗xc4 bxc4 23 0-0 ♖c8** 23...♖b8 24 b3 ♖b5!; 23...♖b8 24 ♖ad1! **24 b3?!** 24 ♖ad1! ♘d3 25 f3 += **♖c5! 25 ♔h1 ♘g6 26 ♘xc4 ♕f6?** 26...♖h5∞ Nunn-Piasetski, Islington 77; 26...e3!? 27 ♖ae1∞; 26...♖cf5!!∓ Wade **27 ♖ad1 d5 28 f4!± ♖f5** 28...exf3?? 29 ♖xf3 Δ ♖h3 **29 ♘e3 ♖xf4**

30 c4! ♖f2 31 ♔g1 ♖xf1+ 32 ♖xf1 ♕d4 33 ♖d1 ♕xg7 34 ♕xg7+ ♔xg7 35 ♖xd5 +− ♖xd5 36 ♘xd5 ♘e5 37 ♔f2 f5 38 ♔e3 ♘d3 39 b4 ♔f7 40 a3 ♔e6 41 ♘f4+ ♘xf4 42 ♔xf4 h5 43 g3 1-0 Botterill

183 Chiburdanidze-Gaprindashvili (3) 78

1 e4 c5 2 ♘f3 e6 3 d4 cxd4 4 ♘xd4 ♘f6 5 ♘c3 ♘c6 6 ♘db5 d6 7 ♗f4 e5 8 ♗g5 a6 9 ♘a3 b5 10 ♗xf6 gxf6 11 ♘d5 f5 12 ♗d3 ♗e6 13 ♕h5 ♗g7 14 0-0 14 c3 0-0 15 exf5 ♗xd5 16 f6 e4 17 fxg7 ♖e8 18 ♗e2 ♖e5 19 ♕h6 ♕g5 **f4 15 c4 b4** 15...bxc4 16 ♗xc4 0-0 17 ♖ac1 ♖b8 18 b3 ♗xd5 19 ♗xd5 Stean-Sax, Las Palmas 78; 15...0-0 16 cxb5 ♘d4 17 ♘c2 ♘xc2 18 ♗xc2 axb5 19 ♗b3 **16 ♘c2 ♖b8 17 b3 h6 18 g3 a5** 18...0-0; 18...♕g5 **19 ♖ad1 ♕g5 20 ♗e2 0-0 21 ♔h1 ♕xh5** 21...♘d4 22 ♘xd4 ♗xd5 23 exd5 exd4; 22 ♕xg5 hxg5 23 ♘e7+ ♔h7 24 ♘xd4 exd4 25 ♘c6; 21...♔h7 **22 ♘xh5 f5 23 ♘c7 ♗f7 24 ♗xf7+ ♖xf7 25 ♘b5!± fxe4 26 ♘xd6** 26 ♖xd6 **♖d7 27 ♘xe4 ♖bd8 28 ♖xd7 ♖xd7 29 ♔g2 ♖d3 30 f3 ♔f7 31 ♔f2 ♖d8 32 ♔e2 a4! 33 ♖d1** 33 bxa4 ♖a8 **axb4 34 axb4** 34 ♖xd8?? bxc2 −+ **♖xd1 35 ♔xd1 ♗f8 36 ♔e2 ♘a5 37 ♘d2 ♔e6 38 ♔d3** 38 g4; 38 gxf4 **fxg3 39 hxg3 ♘b7 40 ♘e3 ♘a5 41 ♘g4** 41 ♘d5 **h5 42 ♘f2 ♗c5 43 ♘fe4 ♗e7 44 ♔e3 ♔f5 45 ♔e2 ♘c6 46 ♔d3 ♘a5 47 ♔c2 h4! 48 gxh4 ♗xh4 49 c5 ♔e6 50 ♘c4 ♘c6 51 ♔d3 ♗e7 52 ♘e3 ♘a5 53 ♘c2 ♘xb3 54 ♔c4 ♘xc5 55 ♘xc5+ ½-½**

184 Gaprindashvili-Chiburdanidze (12) 78

1 e4 c5 2 ♘f3 e6 3 d4 cxd4 4 ♘xd4 ♘f6 5 ♘c3 ♘c6 6 ♘db5 d6 7 ♗f4 e5 8 ♗g5 a6 9 ♘a3 b5 10 ♗xf6 gxf6 11 ♘d5 f5 12 ♗d3 ♗e6 13 ♕h5 ♗g7 14 0-0 f4 15 c4 b4 16 ♘c2 ♖b8 17 ♖fd1 h6 17...0-0; 17...a5 **18 ♗e2 0-0 19 c5 dxc5 20 ♘xf4**

20...♗d7 20...♕e7 21 ♘xe6 ♕xe6 22 ♘e3! ♘d4 23 ♗c4; 20...exf4?!

21 Rxd8 Rfxd8 22 Qxc5 Nd4 23 Nxd4 Rxd4 24 Qc7 Rbd8 25 Qxf4 Rd2 26 Bg4 Bxa2 27 e5 Rxb2; 24 Rd1 Rxd1+ 25 Bxd1 Bxb2 26 Qc7 Rc8 27 Qxf4 Rc1 28 Qd2 b3 **21 Nd5 a5 22 Nce3 Nd4 23 Rac1 Rc8 24 Bc4 Rc6 25 Nf5 Bxf5 26 exf5 Rd6 27 Qg4 h5 28 Qe4 Re8 29 Re1 Qg5 30 Ne3 Rf6 31 h4 Qh6** 31...Qf4? 32 Nd5 Qxe4 33 Nxf6+! +− **32 Bd3 Rc6 33 g3 a4 34 Kg2 Rcc8 35 Nd5 Kf8 36 Bc4 Bh8 37 Ne3 Qf6 38 Bd5 Bg7 39 Bb7 Rb8 40 Bd5** 40 Rxc5? Qb6! **Rbc8 41 Qd3 Red8 42 Qc4 Nxf5 43 Nxf5 Qxf5 44 Rcd1 Qg4 45 Qc2 Bf6** 45...c4! 46 Bf3 b3 **46 Bf3 Qe6 47 Rxd8+ Bxd8 48 Qxa4 Be7 49 Qc2 Rd8** 49...c4! **50 Qh7 Bf6 51 Qh6+ Ke7 52 Qe3 Rd4 53 b3 Qf5 54 Rc1 Kd6 55 Rc4 Bg7 56 Qe2 Qd3 57 Rxd4+ Qxd4 58 Qa6+ Ke7 59 Qa7+ Ke6 60 Qa6+ Qd6 61 Qc4+ Kf6 62 Bxh5 Qe7 63 Qc1 Ke6 64 Qc4+ Kf6 65 Qe4 Bh6 66 Qh7 Bd2 67 Qh8+ Ke6 68 Bg4+ Kd6 69 Qa8 Bc3 70 Bf3 Qc7 71 Be4 Ke7 72 h5** 72 g4 (Δ g5) Qd7! 73 Bf5 Qd4! **Bd2 73 Bd5 Qd7 74 Bc4 f5** 74...Qc7 75 Qd5; 74...Bc1 75 Qa6 **75 Qa6 Qd6 76 Qa7+ Kd8 77 Qf7 f4** 77...Qd7 78 Qf6+! **78 g4 e4 79 Qg8+ Kd7 80 Qf7+ Kd8 81 Qg8+ Kd7 82 Qh7+ Qe7 83 Qf5+ Kc7 84 Kh3 f3 85 Bd5 e3 86 fxe3 Qxe3 87 Bxf3 Kd6 88 Qf6+ Kd7 89 Kg2 Qg5 90 Bc6+ Kc7 91 Qe6 Qd8 92 Bf3 Qd6 93 Qf7+ Qd7 94 Qf6 Qd6 95 Qg7+ Kd8 96 g5 Qf4 97 g6 Be1 98 Kf1 Qxf3+ 99 Kxe1 Qe3+ 100 Kd1 Qd3+ 101 Kc1 Qe3+ ½-½**

185 Vogt-Meduna Halle 78

1 e4 c5 2 Nf3 e6 3 d4 cxd4 4 Nxd4 Nf6 5 Nc3 Nc6 6 Ndb5 d6 7 Bf4 e5 8 Bg5 a6 9 Na3 b5 10 Bxf6 gxf6 11 Nd5 f5 12 Bd3 Be6 13 Qh5 Bg7 14 0-0 f4 15 c4 bxc4 15...0-0 16 cxb5 Nd4 17 Nc2 Nxc2 18 Bxc2 axb5 19 Bb3 +=; 17...Nxb5 18 a4 Nc7 19 Ncb4± **16 Bxc4 Nd4** 16...0-0 Stean-Sax, Las Palmas 78 **17 Rac1 0-0 18 Nc2 Nxc2 19 Rxc2 Kh8 20 Rfc1 Ra7 21 b4± Rg8 22 a4 Bf8 23 h3 Rg5 24 Qf3 f5 25 exf5 Bxf5 26 Bd3 Be6 27 Nc7 Bg8 28 Be4** 28 Bxa6? Rg7 **Rg7 29 Nd5 Be6 30 b5 axb5 31 axb5 Qh4 32 b6 Raf7 33 Rc7 Qd8 34 Rxf7 Rxf7 35 Nc7 +− Bc8 36 Qh5 Re7** 36...Rg7 37 Qe8 +− **37 Qh4 d5 38 Nxd5 1-0 Vogt**

186 Vogt-Georgadze Halle 78

1 e4 c5 2 Nf3 e6 3 d4 cxd4 4 Nxd4 Nf6 5 Nc3 Nc6 6 Ndb5 d6 7 Bf4 e5 8 Bg5 a6 9 Na3 b5 10 Bxf6 gxf6 11 Nd5 f5 12 Bd3 Be6 13 Qh5 Bg7 13...f4 14 g3 f3 15 c3 Bg7 16 Nc2 0-0± **14 0-0 f4 15 c4 Bxd5?! 16 exd5 Ne7 17 Rad1± b4 18 Nb1 Ng6** 18...Kf8 **19 g3 e4?!** 19...0-0 20 Nd2 Δ Bf5, Ne4 **20 Bxe4 Bxb2 21 c5** 21 Bxg6? fxg6 22 Qe2+ Be5 23 gxf4? Qh4 **0-0** 21...dxc5? 22 Bxg6 fxg6 23 Qe2+ +− **22 c6 a5 23 Nd2 a4 24 Nc4 Bf6 25 Qf5 Re8 26 h4 h5 27 Bb1 Kg7 28 Qxh5 Rh8 29 Qg4 Bxh4 30 Bxg6 fxg6 31 Qxf4 +−** 31 gxh4?? Rxh4 32 Qd7+ Qxd7 33 cxd7 f3! 38 Rfe1 Rah8 35 Re7+ Kf6 36 Re6+ Kg5 −+ **b3 32 axb3 Bg5 33 Qxd6 Qc8 34 Ne5 Bf6 35 Nd7 1-0 Vogt**

187 Wedberg-Bouaziz Gausdal 78

1 e4 c5 2 Nf3 Nc6 3 d4 cxd4 4 Nxd4 Nf6 5 Nc3 e5 6 Ndb5 d6 7 Bg5 a6 8 Na3 b5 9 Bxf6 gxf6 10 Nd5 f5 11 Bd3 Be6 12 Qh5 Bg7 13 0-0

f4 14 ♚h1!? N **♜b8 15 ♞b1 h6** 15... 0-0!? **16 ♞d2 0-0 17 g4! fxg3 18 ♜g1! ♛g5?** 18...♘e7 19 ♘xe7+ ♕xe7 20 ♖xg3±

19 ♜xg3! ♛xh5 20 ♞f6+ ♚h8 21 ♞xh5 f5 21...♖g8 22 ♖ag1 +− **22 ♞xg7 1-0 Iskov**

188 Iskov-Delaney
Middlesborough 78

1 e4 c5 2 ♞f3 ♞c6 3 d4 cxd4 4 ♞xd4 ♞f6 5 ♞c3 e5 6 ♞db5 d6 7 ♝g5 a6 8 ♞a3 b5 9 ♝xf6 gxf6 10 ♞d5 f5 11 ♝d3 ♝e6 12 ♛h5 ♝g7 13 0-0 f4 14 ♚h1!? 0-0?! 15 g4! fxg3 16 ♜g1 f5 17 ♜xg3 f4 18 ♜g5 18 ♖xg7+?! ♔xg7 19 ♖g1+ ♔h8 20 ♕h6 ♕d7 **♚h8 19 ♜ag1 ♜a7 20 ♞b1 ♝f6?** 20...♕e8 21 ♕xe8 ♖xe8 22 ♘d2 += **21 ♜g6! +− ♝xd5?** 21...♗f7 22 ♕xh7+! ♔xh7 23 ♘xf6+ ♕xf6 24 ♖xf6 **22 exd5 e4 23 ♝xe4 ♞e5 24 ♜g7! ♜xg7 25 ♜xg7 1-0 Iskov**

189 Edocs-Hardicsay Hungary 78

1 e4 c5 2 ♞f3 ♞c6 3 d4 cxd4 4 ♞xd4 ♞f6 5 ♞c3 e6 6 ♞db5 d6 7 ♝f4 e5 8 ♝g5 a6 9 ♝xf6 gxf6 10 ♞a3 b5 11 ♞d5 f5 12 ♛d3!? f4 N 12...♗g7; 12...fxe4! **13 ♝e2 ♝g7 14 g3! 0-0 15 gxf4 exf4 16 ♜g1 ♚h8 17 0-0-0** 17 c3!? **♞e5** 17...♗e6? 18 ♖xg7 ♔xg7 19 ♖g1+ ♔h8 20 ♘xf4±; 17... ♗e5!?≈ **18 ♛d4** 18 ♕d2 ♗h6 −+ **♝h6 19 ♚b1 ♝e6 20 c4!?** 20 c3 △ ♘c2≈ **♜b8 21 c5?** 21 cxb5 axb5 22 ♘xb5 f3! 23 ♗f1 ♗xd5 24 ♕xd5 ♕a5 25 ♕xd6 f6 +=/≈ **f6 22 f3 ♜f7! 23 ♞b6 ♝f8 24 ♜g2 ♛c7 25 ♛g1 ♜g7 26 ♜xg7 ♛xg7 27 ♞d5 ♛xg1 28 ♜xg1 ♝xd5 29 exd5 dxc5 0-1 Hardicsay**

190 Kolker-Bigeldin USSR 78

1 e4 c5 2 ♞f3 ♞c6 3 d4 cxd4 4 ♞xd4 ♞f6 5 ♞c3 e5 6 ♞db5 d6 7 ♝g5 a6 8 ♝xf6 gxf6 9 ♞a3 b5 10 ♞d5 f5 11 ♛d3!? f4 11...♗g7!? 12 exf5 0-0 13 ♕e4 ♘d4 14 f6?! ♗xf6 15 ♘xf6+ ♕xf6 16 ♕xa8 b4 17 ♗d3 ♗f5∓ Chekov-Sveshnikov, USSR 76; 11... fxe4 12 ♕xe4 ♗d7 13 f4 f5 14 ♕f3 ♗g7 15 ♕h5+ ♔f8 16 0-0-0 ♗e6 17 fxe5 dxe5 18 ♘f4 ♕f6 19 ♘xe6 ♕xe6 20 g4 ♘d4 21 ♗g2 ♖c8 22 ♖hf1 b4 Isserman-Shestoperov, USSR 76; 22 gxf5! ♕xa2 23 ♖xd4! exd4 24 f6! +− **12 g3 ♝g7 13 ♛c3 ♝d7** 13...♗b7 14 gxf4 ♔f8 15 ♖g1 ♘e7 16 0-0-0 ♗xd5 17 exd5 ♗h6= Boidman-Tilenko, USSR 77 **14 gxf4 b4! 15 ♛g3!** 15 ♘xb4? ♕a5! 16 ♘d5 ♕xc3+ 17 bxc3 exf4= **♚f8 16 ♜g1 ♜g8 17 ♞c4 ♞d4?!** 17...exf4!? 18 ♕xf4 ♗e6! △ ♗c3+ −+ **18 0-0-0 ♝b5 19 ♞ce3! ♝xf1**

20 ♖xd4! exd4 21 ♘f5 21 ♘xf1? d3! Δ ♗xb2+ −+ **♗c4 22 ♘h6!!± ♗xd5 23 ♘xg8 ♗h8 24 exd5 d3!? 25 ♕h3!! d2+?** 25...♖c8! 26 ♕h6+ ♔e8 27 ♘f6+ ♕xf6 28 ♖g8+ ♔d7 29 ♕h3+ ♔e7 30 ♕xc8! ♕xf4+ 31 ♔b1 dxc2+ 33 ♕xc2± **26 ♔xd2 ♗xb2 27 ♕h6+ ♔e8 28 ♘f6+ 1-0 Maric**

191 Artishevsky-Fridman
Minsk 78

1 e4 c5 2 ♘f3 ♘c6 3 d4 cxd4 4 ♘xd4 ♘f6 5 ♘c3 e5 6 ♘db5 d6 7 ♗g5 a6 8 ♘a3 b5 9 ♗xf6 gxf6 10 ♘d5 f5 11 ♕d3 ♗g7 11...fxe4 12 ♕xe4 ♗d7 13 f4 f5 14 ♕f3 ♗g7 15 ♕h5+ ♔f8 16 0-0-0 ♗e6 17 fxe5 dxe5 18 ♘f4∞ Isserman-Shestoperov, USSR 76; 13 ♗g4 ♖c8 14 h4 ♗g7 15 0-0-0 ♘e7 16 ♘xe7 ♕xe7 17 ♖h3 ♗c6 18 ♕f5 0-0 19 ♔b1 ♗d7 =+ Muratov-Peev, Moscow 78; 12...♗g7 13 ♘f6+?! ♗xf6 14 ♕xc6+ ♗d7 15 ♕xd6 ♕e7 16 0-0-0 ♕xd6 17 ♖xd6 ♗e7 18 ♖d5 f6 19 ♖d2 ♗e6 20 ♔b1 ♖c8 21 ♔a1 ♗b4 22 ♖e2 ♔f7 23 ♘b1 ♖hd8 24 c3 ♗c5 =+ Muratov-Timoshenko, Beltsi 77; 16 ♕xe7+ ♗xe7 17 ♗d3 f5 18 f3 0-0 19 0-0-0 ♗c6 20 ♖hf1 ♖ac8 21 ♖de1 e4 22 fxe4 ♗g5+ 23 ♔d1 fxe4 =+ Saharov-Vaiser, USSR 78; 13 ♘e3!? d5! 14 ♕xd5 ♕xd5 15 ♘xd5 0-0 16 c3 ♗b7 17 ♘c2 ♖fd8 18 ♘ce3 ♘d4 19 ♘e7+ ♔f8 20 ♘7f5 ♘xf5 21 ♘xf5 ♗f6 22 h4 b4∞ Kapengut-Kalinechev, USSR 78 **12 exf5 0-0 13 ♕e4** 13 0-0-0!? e4 14 ♕xe4 ♖e8 15 ♕g4 ♘e5 16 ♕h3 +=; 13...♘d4 14 g4 ♗b7 15 ♗g2 ♖c8 Δ ♖c5=; 13...♕g5+ 14 ♘e3 d5!∞ **♘d4 14 g4** 14 f6? ♗xf6 15 ♘xf6+ ♕xf6 16 ♕xa8 b4 17 ♗d3 ♗f5 18 ♕d5 ♗xd3 19 cxd3 bxa3 −+ **♗b7 15 0-0-0** 15 ♗d3 ♗xd5 16 ♕xd5 ♕g5 17 0-0 e4 18 ♗xe4 ♘e2+ 19 ♔h1 ♗xb2 20 ♖ae1 ♘f4 21 ♕b3 ♗e5 22 ♗xa8 ♖xa8∞ Katalimov-Sveshnikov, Rostov 76; 16...♖c8 17 c3 e4! 18 cxd4 exd3 19 0-0 ♕g5 20 h3 ♕f4 21 ♖ad1 d2 22 ♔g2 ♗xd4 23 ♕f3 ♕xf3+ 24 ♔xf3 ♗xb2 =+ Razuvaev-Boumeester, USSR-Netherlands 78; 15 c3?! (Suetin) b4! 16 cxb4 ♗xd5 17 ♕xd5 e4∞ **♗xd5!** N 15...♖c8 16 h4 ♖c5 17 ♖xd4 exd4 18 ♘e7+ ♔h8 19 ♕xb7 ♖c7 20 ♕xa6 ♕xe7 21 ♗d3 b4 22 ♘b5 ♖cc8 23 ♕xd6 += Rogulj-Semkov, Varna 77; **16 ♕xd5 ♖c8 17 ♗d3∓** 17 f6!? **♖c5 18 ♕b7 e4 19 ♕xe4** 19 ♗xe4 ♘e2+ 20 ♔b1 ♕f6 21 c3 ♘xc3+ 22 bxc3 ♕xc3 −+; 20 ♔d2 ♗xb2 21 ♔e2 ♗xa3 **d5! 20 ♕g2 b4 21 g5** 21 ♘b1 b3! 22 ♘c3 ♖xc3 −+ **bxa3 22 f6 ♕c7 23 ♖d2** 23 c3? ♖xc3+; 23 c4 ♖xc4+ 24 ♔b1 ♖c2 −+ **♘b3+! 24 ♔d1 axb2 25 cxb3 ♖e8 −+ 26 ♗xh7+ ♔xh7** 26...♔f8 27 fxg7+ ♔xg7 **27 ♕h3+ ♔g8 28 ♖xb2 ♖c1+ 29 ♔d2 ♕f4+ 30 ♕e3 ♕xe3+ 31 fxe3 ♖xh1 0-1 Kapengut**

2...♘c6, 4...g6

192 Speelman-de Silva
London 78

1 e4 c5 2 ♘f3 ♘c6 3 d4 cxd4 4 ♘xd4 g6 5 c4 ♗g7 6 ♘c2 6 ♗e3 **♘f6 7 ♘c3 d6 8 ♗e2 ♘d7 9 ♗d2 0-0 10 0-0 ♘c5 11 b4!?** 11 b3!? ♗xc3 12 ♗xc3 ♘xe4 13 ♗b2 a5 ∞/=+ Goldstein-Buslajev, Suhumi 73; 11...a5 12 ♖b1 f5 13 exf5 ♗xf5 Korchnoi-Matulovic, Sarajevo 79; 11 f3 **♘e6** 11...♗xc3 12 ♗xc3 ♘xe4 13 ♗b2 a5∞ **12 ♖c1 a5 13 a3 axb4 14 axb4 ♘ed4 15 ♘xd4 ♘xd4 16 ♗e3 ♘xe2+ 17 ♕xe2 ♗e6**

Diagram

18 Rfd1 18 Nd5 Bxd5 19 exd5 Ra4!? 20 Bg5!?; 19 cxd5=; 18 f4!? **Ra3 19 Nb5** 19 Nd5 Bxd5 20 cxd5=; 20 exd5!?; 20 Rxd5 **Rb3! 20 Qd2 Rb2! 21 Rc2** 21 Qe1?! =+/∓ ½-½ 21...Rxc2 22 Qxc2 =/=+ **Speelman**

Najdorf

193 Silva-Ochoa
Portugal Final 78
1 e4 c5 2 Nf3 d6 3 d4 cxd4 4 Nxd4 Nf6 5 Nc3 a6 6 Bc4 e6 7 Bb3 b5 8 0-0 Be7 9 Qf3 Qb6!? 9...Qc7! **10 Be3 Qb7 11 Qg3 0-0!** N 11...g6?! **12 Bh6 Nh5! 13 Qg4 Bf6 14 Rad1 b4 15 Na4 Nd7! 16 Qxh5 gxh6 17 Rfe1 Bg7 18 Rd3 Kh8 19 Nf3 Qb5 20 Qh4 Nc5 21 Nd4 Qa5 ½-½ Ochoa**

194 Sampouw-Ghitescu
Buenos Aires 78
1 e4 c5 2 Nf3 d6 3 d4 cxd4 4 Nxd4 Nf6 5 Nc3 a6 6 Be2 e5 7 Nb3 Be7 8 Be3 0-0 9 g4 Be6 10 g5 Nfd7 11 Qd2 Nc6 12 Nd5 a5! 13 a3 a4 14 Nc1 Nc5 15 f3 Nd4! 16 Bxd4 exd4 17 Nxe7+?! 17 h4 Bxd5 18 exd5 Re8 19 Qd4 Bf8 Δ g6, Bg7∓ **Qxe7 18 Qxd4 Qxg5∓ 19 Nd3 Nxd3+ 20 Bxd3 Qf4 21 Ke2 Ra5! 22 Rag1 g6 23 Qe3 Qf6 24 Qb6 Rc5 25 h4 Rfc8** Δ Rxc2+! **26 c3 d5!** Δ 27...dxe4 28 Bxe4 Bc4+ −+ **27 Ke3! dxe4 28 Bxe4 Qe7 29 Kf2! Rd8?!** 29...Bf5!∓ **30 h5 Bf5 31 hxg6 hxg6 32 Rd1! Re8** 32...Rxd1 33 Rxd1 Bxe4 34 Qd8+! Qxd8 35 Rxd8+ Kg7 36 fxe4 Rb5 37 Rd2 += **33 Rde1 Re5 34 Qd4 Rd8?**

35 Bd5!! +− **Rdxd5** 35...Re8 36 Bxf7+! **36 Qxd5 Rxe1 37 Rxe1 Qh4+ 38 Ke2 Qh2+ 39 Ke3 Qxb2 40 Qd8+ Kg7 41 Qd4+ f6 42 Qb4 Qb3 43 Qe7+ Qf7 44 Qd4 g5 45 Qd8! 1-0 Ghitescu**

195 Chiburdanidze-Tukmakov
Vilnius 78
1 e4 c5 2 Nf3 d6 3 d4 cxd4 4 Nxd4 Nf6 5 Nc3 a6 6 Be2 e5 7 Nb3 Be7 8 0-0 0-0 8...Be6 **9 a4 Nc6 10 f4** 10 Kh1 Be6 11 f4 Nb4 12 f5 Bd7 13 Bg5 Bc6 14 Bf3 Rc8 (14...b5) 15 Qe2 h6?! 16 Bh4 b6 17 Rfd1 Qc7 18 Bg3 +=/± Karpov-Bukic, Bugojno 78 **Nb4 11 Kh1 b6 12 Bf3 Bb7 13 Be3 Qc7** 13...d5?! 14 exd5 Nfxd5 (14...e4!?) 15 Nxd5 (15 Bxd5) Nxd5 (15...Bxd5!?) 16 Bxd5 Bxd5 17 fxe5± (17 Bxb6!? Bxg2+!) **14 Qd2**

Diagram

14...d5! 15 exd5 e4! 16 Nxe4 Nfxd5

Δ Nxe3, Nxc2 **17 Nd4 Rad8 18 c3 Nxe3 19 Qxe3 Nd5 20 Qf2 Qxf4 21 Rae1** 21 g3! Qe3?! 22 Nf5 Qxf2 23 Nxf2; 21...Qe5?! 22 Rae1; 21...Qc7/21...Qb8 22 Nf5 **g6** =+ **22 Qg3?! Qxg3 23 Nxg3 Rd7 24 Nc2 Kg7 25 c4!? Nf6** 25...Nb4?? 26 Rxe7! **26 Bxb7 Rxb7 27 Ne4** 27 b3 **Rd8 28 b3 Rd3∓ 29 Nxf6 Bxf6 30 Re3 Rbd7 31 h3 a5 32 Ref3?** 32 Rff3 **Rxf3 33 gxf3** 33 Rxf3 Rd1+ 34 Kh2 Be5+ 35 g3 Rd2+ −+ **Rd3 34 Rb1 Rxf3 −+ 35 Kg2 Rc3 36 Ne1 Be7 37 Nf3 Rc2+ 38 Kf1 Bc5 39 Ke1 Rc3 0-1 Speelman**

196 Sznapik-Adamski Lodz 78

1 e4 c5 2 Nf3 d6 3 d4 cxd4 4 Nxd4 Nf6 5 Nc3 a6 6 Be2 e6 7 0-0 Be7 8 f4 0-0 9 Kh1 Nc6 10 Be3 Bd7 11 Qe1 11 a4!? Qc7 12 Nb3 b6≈ **b5 12 a3 Qb8!? 13 Rd1** 13 Qg3 b4 14 axb4 Qxb4 =+ **Nxd4** 13...b4?! 14 axb4 Qxb4 15 Nd5! Nxd5 16 exd5 Qxe1 17 Rfxe1 += **14 Bxd4 Bc6 15 Qg3 Qb7** 15...b4!? **16 Bf3 Rad8 17 Rfe1 a5?** 17...Kh8≈ **18 Nd5! Kh8** 18...exd5 19 exd5 Be8 20 Rxe7 Qxe7 21 Re1 +− **19 Nxe7 Qxe7 20 Bc3± Qc7 21 Qg5** 21 Bxf6! gxf6 22 Qh4 Qe7 23 e5 Bxf3 24 gxf3 +− **h6 22 Qg3 Ne8 23 Re3 Rb8** 23...Ra8 **24 Qe1 Ra8 25 Red3 Ra6 26 Qh4 Kh7 27 Re1 Qb7 28 f5 b4?** 28...e5± **29 axb4 axb4 30 Bd2 e5 31 f6! Nxf6 32 Bxh6 1-0 Webb**

197 Sax-Tukmakov
Las Palmas 78

1 e4 c5 2 Nf3 d6 3 d4 cxd4 4 Nxd4 Nf6 5 Nc3 a6 6 Be3 e6 7 g4 h6 7...e5!? **8 Qf3 Nbd7?!** 8...Nc6 **9 Qh3! Nc5 10 f3 e5 11 Nb3 Be6** 11...Nxb3 12 axb3 Be6 13 Bc4 **12 Nxc5 dxc5 13 Qg3 Be7 14 h4** 14 Qxe5? Bd6 **Qa5!?** 14...Nd7 15 Nd5 **15 Qxe5 0-0-0 16 Bc4!** 16 Qg3 Bxg4! 17 fxg4 Nxe4 **Bd6** 16...Bxc4 17 Qxe7 **17 Bxe6+ Kb8! 18 Qf5 fxe6 19 Qxe6 Rhe8 20 Qf7!** 20 Qf5 Nd5 **Nd5? 21 0-0-0! Nxe3 22 Rxd6 Rf8 23 Qxg7 Rxf3 24 Qe5 Rxd6 25 Qxd6+ Ka7 26 Qd3 Rg3 27 Ne2? Nf5??** 27...Rh3! **28 Nxg3 1-0**

198 Ermenkov-Polugaevsky
Buenos Aires 78

1 e4 c5 2 Nf3 d6 3 d4 cxd4 4 Nxd4 Nf6 5 Nc3 a6 6 Be3 e6 7 g4 7 f4!? **h6! 8 Qf3** 8 h4 e5 Nf5 g6 **Nbd7 9 Qh3** 9 Qg3!? **e5! 10 Nf5?** 10 Nb3! b5 11 a3 Bb7 =+ **g6∓ 11 Ng3** 11 Nxh6 Bxh6 12 Bxh6 g5 −+ **Nb6 12 Be2** 12 f3 Be6 13 0-0-0 Rc8 Δ Rxc3∓; 12...h5!?∓ **h5 13 Qh4 Be7 14 g5 Nh7 15 0-0-0 Nxg5 16 Bxb6 Qxb6 17 Nd5 Qd8 18 Nf1**

Diagram

18...Nh3 19 Qg3 Bh4 −+ **20 Qc3 0-0 21 Nfe3** 21 Rd2 Nxf2 22 Rg1 Nxe4 −+ **Nxf2 22 Nc4 Be6 23 Ncb6 Qg5+ 24 Kb1 Nxh1 25 Rxh1 Rab8** 25...Rac8! **26 Qf3 Qg4! 27 Qd3 Qh3 28 Qd1 Bd8! 29 Nc4 Bxd5 30 Qxd5 Qg2 31 Re1** 31 Qd1 Qxe4

—+ **b5! 32 ♞xd6 ♛f2 33 ♛d1 ♛d4 34 ♜g1 ♛xd1+ 35 ♝xd1 ♝b6 36 ♜f1 ♜bd8 0-1 Polugaevsky**

199 Kapengut-Juferov Minsk 78

1 e4 c5 2 ♞f3 d6 3 d4 cxd4 4 ♞xd4 ♞f6 5 ♞c3 a6 6 f4 ♛c7 7 ♝d3 g6 8 0-0 ♝g7 9 ♚h1 ♞bd7 10 a4 e5 11 fxe5 dxe5 12 ♞b3!? N 12 ♘f3 0-0 13 ♕e2 ♘c5 14 ♗g5 ♗e6 15 ♘h4 ♘h5 16 ♘f5 ♘f4 17 ♗xf4 exf4 18 ♘xg7 ♔xg7 Tseshkovsky-Bukic, Ljubljana 77; 15 ♘d2!; 14 ♗c4!? ♗e6! 15 ♘g5 ♗xc4 16 ♕xc4 ♖ac8 17 ♗e3 h6 =+ Kapengut-Juferov, Minsk 78 **b6 13 ♝g5 h6 14 ♝e3 0-0** 14...♗b7 15 ♕d2 0-0-0? 16 ♕e2 +−; 15...♘h5?! 16 a5 b5? 17 ♗xb5 +− **15 ♛d2 ♚h7 16 ♜f3 ♝b7 17 ♜af1 ♜ae8** 17...♗c6 18 ♕e1! b5 19 axb5 axb5 20 ♕h4 b4 21 ♘d5! ♘xd5 22 exd5 ♗xd5 23 ♖h3 ♖h8 24 ♕xb4± **18 ♛e2 ♜e7 19 ♞d2± ♜a8 20 ♜h3 ♞g8** 20...♘h5? 21 ♖xh5 gxh5 22 ♘d5 +− **21 ♝c4 ♞df6 22 ♜h4! ♜d7 23 ♝b3 ♝c6 24 ♞f3 ♝f8** 24...♘h5 25 ♖xh5! gxh5 26 ♘h4 ♘f6 27 ♖xf6! ♗xf6 28 ♕xh5 ♗xh4 29 ♕xh6+ ♔g8 30 ♕g6+ ♔h8 31 ♕h5+ ♔g8 32 ♕g4+ ♔f8 33 ♗h6+ ♔e7 34 ♕xh4+ +− **25 ♛c4 ♜e7** 25...b5!? 26 axb5 axb5 27 ♘xb5 ♕b7 28 ♘c3± **26 ♞d5! +− b5 27 axb5 axb5 28 ♛c5 ♞xd5?** 28...♗xd5 20 exd5 ♕xc5 21 ♗xc5 ♖ee8 22 ♗xf8 ♖xf8 22 ♘xe5 +− **29 exd5 ♝e8 30 d6 ♛d8 31 ♝g5 1-0 Kapengut**

200 Tseshkovsky-Tukmakov
Lvov 78

1 e4 c5 2 ♞f3 d6 3 d4 cxd4 4 ♞xd4 ♞f6 5 ♞c3 a6 6 f4 ♛c7 7 ♝e2 7 a4; 7 ♗d3 **e5 8 ♞b3 b5 9 ♝f3 ♝b7 10 0-0 ♞bd7 11 a3 exf4** 11...♗e7 **12 ♝xf4 ♞e5 13 ♞d4 g6** 13...♘c4 14 b3! ♘xa3 15 ♘d5; 15 e5; 14...♘e3 15 ♗xe3 ♕xc3 16 ♘f5! **14 ♚h1 ♜d8** 14...♗g7 15 ♘dxb5! axb5 16 ♘xb5 Δ ♘xd6+ **15 ♝g5 ♝e7** 15...♗g7 16 ♗e2! ♘ed7 17 ♗xb5 axb5 18 ♘dxb5; 16...♕e7 17 a4 b4 18 ♘d5 ♗xd5 19 exd5 ♖a8 20 ♕d2 **16 ♝h6 ♛c5** 16... ♗f8 17 ♕c1 ♘xf3 **17 ♞b3 ♛c8 18 ♞a5 ♝a8 19 ♝g7 ♜g8 20 ♝xf6 ♝xf6 21 a4 b4 22 ♞d5 ♝xd5 23 ♛xd5 ♚e7** 23...♕xc2? 24 ♗d1! ♕xb2 25 ♖a2 ♕c3 26 ♖af2! ♗e7 27 ♖xf7 ♘xf7 28 ♕xf7+ ♔d7 29 ♗g4+ ♔c7 30 ♕xe7+ ♔b6 31 ♘b3! ♕xb3 32 a5+ **24 ♝e2 ♛c5** 24...♕xc2 25 ♗xa6 ♕xb2? 26 ♖a2! ♕c3 27 ♖af2; 25...♕c5 26 ♘b3 ♕xd5 27 exd5 **25 ♜ae1!** 25 ♕xc5 dxc5 26 ♗xa6? ♖a8!; 25 ♕b7+ ♖d7 26 ♕xa6 ♕xc2!; 23 ♗xa6? ♕xd5! 26 exd5 ♖a8 **♜d7** 25...♕xd5 26 exd5 ♖a8 27 ♗g4! **26 ♜f4 ♜c7** 26...♗g5 27 ♘c6+! ♕xc6 28 ♖xf7+ ♔e8 29 ♕e6+ ♗e7 30 ♖xe7+ ♖xe7 31 ♕xg8+ ♔d7 32 ♕b3; 27...♔e8 28 ♕xc5 dxc5 29 ♘xe5 ♗xf4 30 ♘xd7 ♔xd7 31 ♖f1!; 26...♗g7 27 ♗xa6 ♕xd5 28 exd5 ♖a7 **27 ♜ef1 ♛xd5 28 exd5 ♜xc2** 28... ♖c5 29 ♘b3 ♖xc2 30 ♗d1 **29 ♝xa6 ♝g5** 29...♖a8 30 ♘c6 ♘xc6 31 ♗b7! ♘d8 32 ♗xa8 ♗xb2 33 ♖xb4 **30 ♞c6+ ♜xc6** 30...♘xc6 31 ♖xf7+ ♔d8 32 dxc6 ♖xc6 33 ♖a7; 30...♔f8! **31 dxc6**

♝xf4 32 c7 ♝e3 33 c8♛? 33 ♖e1 ♗d4 34 ♖e4! **♜xc8 24 ♝xc8 ♞d3 35 g3**

35...d5 35...♘xb2! 36 ♖e1 ♘c4? 37 ♗a6 d5 38 ♗xc4 dxc4 39 ♖xe3+ ♔d6 40 ♖e8! c3 41 ♖c8; 36...♔d8!; 36 ♗a6! ♗b6? 37 ♗b5! f5 38 a5! ♗d4 39 a6 ♔d8 40 ♖a1? ♔c7! 41 a7 ♗xa7 42 ♖xa7+ ♔b6 43 ♖a2 ♔xb5 44 ♖xb2 ♔c4; 40 ♖f4! ♗c5 41 ♖xb4 +−; 36...♗d4! 37 ♗b5 f5 38 a5 ♔d8! 39 g4! fxg4 40 ♖f8+ ♔c7 41 ♖f7+ ♔b8 42 a6; 40...♔e7 41 ♖f4; 39... ♔c7 40 gxf5 gxf5 41 ♖xf5 ♘d1 42 ♖f7+; 37...d5 38 a5 ♘c4 39 ♖d1! ♗f2! 40 a6! ♘b6 41 a7 ♔d6 42 ♖f1 ♗e3 43 ♖xf7; 40...b3 41 ♖b1! ♘a5 42 ♗a4! **36 a5 ♚d8** 36...♘xb2 37 ♖e1! ♔d8 38 ♖xe3 ♔xc8 39 ♖b3 ♘c4 40 a6 ♔b8 41 ♖xb4+ ♔a7 42 ♖b7+ ♔xa6 43 ♖xf7 **37 ♝b7 f5 38 ♝xd5 ♞xb2 39 ♜b1 ♝d4 40 a6 ♞d3 41 ♜b3 1-0**

201 Rantanen-Morris Gausdal 78

1 e4 c5 2 ♞f3 d6 3 d4 cxd4 4 ♞xd4 ♞f6 5 ♞c3 a6 6 f4 ♞bd7 6...♕b6!? **7 ♝d3 g6 8 ♞f3 ♛c7 9 0-0 e5 10 a4 ♝g7 11 ♛e1 0-0 12 fxe5 dxe5 13 ♛h4 b6 14 ♝h6 ♝b7 15 ♞g5 ♜fe8?** 15...♘h5? 16 ♗xg7 ♔xg7 17 ♖xf7+ ♖xf7 18 ♘e6+ +−; 15...♖ae8! 16 ♖f3 ♘h5= **16 ♝xg7 ♚xg7 17 ♞xf7! +− ♚xf7 18 ♛xh7+ ♚e6 19 ♜xf6+!! ♚xf6 20 ♜f1+ ♚e6 21 ♝c4+ ♚d6** 21...♕xc4 22 ♕f7+ **22 ♜d1+ ♚c6 23 ♝d5+ ♚c5 24 ♝xb7 1-0 Pytel**

202 Nordby-Pytel Skien 78

1 e4 c5 2 ♞f3 d6 3 d4 cxd4 3...♘f6 4 dxc5 ♕a5! 5 ♗d2 ♕xc5 6 ♗d3 g6 =+ Bohmfeldt-Pytel, Dortmund 77 **4 ♞xd4 ♞f6 5 ♞c3 a6 6 f4 e5 7 ♞f3 ♛c7 8 a4 ♝e7 9 ♝d3 0-0 10 0-0 ♞bd7 11 ♛e1 ♜e8 12 ♞h4 exf4 13 ♝xf4 ♞c5 14 ♚h1 ♝e6 15 ♞f5** 15 ♗g5 d5 16 e5 ♘g4 17 ♗xe7 ♕xe7 18 ♘f3 ♖ad8 19 h3 d4! 20 ♘e4 ♘e3 21 ♘xc5 ♕xc5 22 ♕h4 h6 23 ♖f2 ♗d5 24 ♕f4 ♖e7 25 ♕xd4 ♕xd4 26 ♘xd4 ♘xg2! 27 ♔h2 ♖xe5 28 ♘f5 ♘e3! −+ Goichberg-Pytel, Skien 78 **♝xf5 16 exf5 ♞xd3 17 cxd3 ♛b6 18 ♛f2 ♛b3 19 a5 d5 =+ 20 h3 ♜ac8 21 ♝e3 h6 22 ♝d4 ♞d7! 23 ♜fe1 ♝f6 24 ♝xf6 ♞xf6 25 ♜xe8+ ♜xe8 26 ♜a3 ♛b4 27 ♜a4 ♛e7 28 ♜a1 ♛e5 29 d4 ♛c7∓ 30 ♛f3 ♛c4 31 ♜d1 ♛b3 32 ♚h2 ♛c2 33 ♜f1?! ♛xb2 34 ♞xd5 ♛xd4 35 ♞xf6+ ♛xf6 36 ♛xb7 ♛e5+ 37 ♚h1 ♛xa5 38 ♛b1** 38 f6? ♖e1! **♛e5 39 ♛c1 a5 40 f6 g5 41 ♛b1 ♛e4 42 ♛xe4 ♜xe4 43 ♜f5 a4 44 ♜a5 ♚h7 45 ♜a6 h5 46 ♚g1 ♜f4 47 g3? ♜b4 48 ♚f2 ♚g6 49 ♚f3 ♚f5 50 g4+ hxg4+ 51 hxg4+ ♚e5 52 ♚g3 ♜b3+ 53 ♚g2 a3 0-1 Pytel**

203 Ljubojevic-Ribli IBM 78

1 e4 c5 2 ♞f3 d6 3 d4 cxd4 4 ♞xd4 ♞f6 5 ♞c3 a6 6 f4 e5 7 ♞f3 ♞bd7 7...♕c7 8 ♗d3 ♗e7 9 0-0 0-0 10 ♕e1 b5 11 a3 ♘bd7 12 g4?! =+ Beljavsky-Juferov, USSR 77 **8 ♝c4 ♝e7 9 a4 0-0 10 ♛e2** 10 0-0 exf4 11 ♗xf4 ♕b6+ Δ ♕xb2 **♛a5!** Δ b5

11 ♗d2 exf4 12 ♘d5 ♕d8 13 ♗xf4 ♘xd5 14 ♗xd5 14 exd5? ♗f6 Δ ♖e8 **♗f6 15 ♗xd6** 15 c3 ♘e5= **♗xb2 16 ♖b1** 16 ♗xf8 ♗xa1 17 ♗b4 ♕b6 **♗c3+ 17 ♔f2 ♖e8**

18 ♗xb7 18 ♕c4 ♕f6 19 ♗xf7+ ♕xf7 20 ♕xc3 ♘f6∓; 18 ♕c4 ♕f6 19 ♖hf1 ♗e5 =+ **♗xb7 19 ♖xb7 ♘f6 20 e5 ♘g4+ 21 ♔g3** 21 ♔f1 ♘xe5 22 ♗xe5 ♗xe5 23 ♘xe5 ♕f6+ 24 ♕f3 ♕xe5 25 ♕f7+ ♔h8; 25 ♔g1?? ♕xd6 **♘xe5 22 ♖d1** 22 ♗xe5 ♗xe5+ 23 ♘xe5 ♕g5+ −+ **♕f6 23 ♕e4 ♘xf3 24 ♕xf3 ♕g6+ 25 ♔f2** 25 ♕g4?? ♖e3+ **♕xc2+ 26 ♔g1 ♗f6 27 ♕b3** 27 ♕d5 ♕g6 **♕xb3 28 ♖xb3 ♖ac8 29 ♔f1 h6 30 ♖b6 a5** 30...♖e6!? 31 ♖db1 ♗d4 Δ ♖c2; 31 ♖xa6 ♖d8 Δ ♗e5; 31 a5 ♖d8 **31 ♖b5 ♗c3 32 ♖c1 ♔h7 33 ♖c5 ♖xc5 34 ♗xc5 ♗d2 35 ♖c2 ♖c8 36 ♖xd2 ♖xc5 37 ♖d4 g5! 38 h4 ♔g6 39 hxg5 hxg5 40 ♔f2 ♔h5 41 g3 ♖c2+ 42 ♔f3 ♖a2 43 ♖c4 f5 44 ♖d4 g4+ 45 ♔f4 ♖f2+ 46 ♔e5 ♔g5 47 ♖d5 ♖e2+ 48 ♔d6 ♖e3 49 ♖xa5 ♖xg3 50 ♖a8 f4 51 ♖g8+ ♔f5 52 ♖f8+ ♔e4 53 ♖e8+ ♔d4 54 ♖f8 f3 55 a5 ♖g1 56 ♔c6 ♔e3 57 ♖e8+ ♔f2 58 ♖e4 g3 59 ♖a4 g2 0-1** 60 a6 ♖h1 61 a7 ♖h8 **Taulbut**

204 Honfi-Nemet Stip 78

1 e4 c5 2 ♘f3 d6 3 ♘c3 a6 4 d4 cxd4 5 ♘xd4 ♘f6 6 f4 e5 7 ♘f3 ♘bd7 8 ♗c4 ♗e7 8...b5!? **9 0-0 0-0 10 a4 ♕c7** 10...b6 **11 ♕e2 exf4 12 ♗xf4 ♘e5 13 ♗b3 ♗e6 14 ♔h1 ♘g6 15 ♗e3 ♖fe8 16 a5 ♖ac8** 16...♗xb3 17 cxb3 ♖ac8 18 ♗b6 ♕b8 19 ♘d4 += **17 ♗b6 ♗c4** 17...♕b8 18 ♗xe6 fxe6 19 ♘d4 ♗f8 20 ♕f3 Δ ♕h3± **18 ♕f2 ♕b8 19 ♗xc4 ♖xc4 20 ♘d2 ♖cc8 21 ♗d4 ♘e5 22 ♕g3 g6 23 ♖f5 ♘fg4** 23...♔h8 24 ♖xe5 +− **24 ♖f4 ♘f6** 24...♗g5 25 ♖xg4 ♗xd2 26 ♘d5 ♘xg4 27 ♕xg4 ♖xc2 28 ♕xe6!; 27...♖ce8 28 ♕f3 +−; 27...h5 28 ♕f3 ♖c7 29 ♗b6 +− **25 ♕h3 ♘h5 26 ♖f2 ♗f6 27 ♘d5 ♖xc2?** 27...♗g7 28 c3!± **28 ♕b3! ♖xd2** 28...♘g4 29 ♘xf6+ ♘hxf6 30 ♖xf6 +− **29 ♖xd2 ♗g7 30 ♖f1 ♕d8 31 ♕xb7 ♖f8 32 ♕e7 ♕c8 33 ♕xd6 ♕c4 34 ♖dd1 ♖e8 35 ♘e7+ ♔h8 36 ♗xe5 f6 37 ♗c3 ♕xe4 38 ♘d5 1-0 Honfi**

205 Kapengut-Tseshkovsky
Daugavpils 78

1 e4 c5 2 ♘f3 d6 3 d4 cxd4 4 ♘xd4 ♘f6 5 ♘c3 a6 6 f4 g6 7 ♗d3 (1) 7 e5?! dxe5 8 fxe5 ♘g4 9 e6 f5 10 ♗c4 ♗g7 11 ♘ce2 ♘c6 12 ♘xc6 ♕xd1+ 13 ♔xd1 bxc6 Honfi-Barczay, 70; 10 h3 ♘e5 11 ♗e3 ♘bc6 12 ♘xf5!? ♗xe6 13 ♘d4 ♗f7∞ Bronstein-Tukmakov, Leningrad 71; 8...♘d5 9 ♗c4 ♘xc3 10 bxc3 ♗g7 11 0-0 0-0 12 e6 f5 13 ♗g5 ♕c7 Kozlov-Zhelmin 72; (2) 7 ♘f3 ♗g7 8 e5 ♘g4 9 h3 ♘h6 10 ♗c4 0-0 11 g4 ♘c6 12 ♗e3 dxe5 13 ♘xe5 ♗e6! 14 ♗xe6 fxe6∞ Ghizdavu-Ghitescu 72; 10...♘c6 11 0-0 0-0 12 exd6 ♘f5! 13 dxe7 ♕xe7 14 ♔h2 ♗e6 15 ♗xe6 ♕xe6 16 ♖e1 ♕c4 17 ♕e2 ♕xe2 18 ♖xe2 ♘fd4

19 ♘xd4 ♘xd4 20 ♖f2 ½-½ Platonov-Savon, Rostov 76; 7...♘c6 8 e5 ♘g4 9 h3 ♘h6 10 exd6 ♗g7!? 11 dxe7 ♕xe7+ 12 ♗e2 ♗e6 13 0-0 ♖d8 14 ♗d3 0-0 Kirpichnikov-Vitolins, Riga 73; 8...dxe5 9 ♕xd8+ ♔xd8 10 fxe5 ♘g4 11 ♗f4 ♗e6 12 h3 ♗h6! 13 ♗xh6 ♘xh6 14 g4 ♔c7 Tseshkovsky-Hort, Ljubljana 77; (3) 7 ♗e2 **♗g7 8 ♘b3!?** N 8 ♘f3 ♘c6 9 0-0 ♗g4 10 ♕e1 0-0 11 ♕h4 ♗xf3 12 ♖xf3 e6 13 ♖h3 h5 Tringov-Barczay, Havana 71; 11 a4 ♗xf3 12 ♖xf3 e6 13 ♔h1 ♖c8 14 ♗d2 ♘d7 15 ♖h3 ♘b4 16 ♕g3 ♘xd3 17 ♕xd3 ♘c5 18 ♕e2 d5 19 e5 f6! 20 exf6 ♕xf6 Sigurjonsson-Tseshkovsky, Ljubljana 77; 10...♗xf3 11 ♖xf3 ♖c8 12 ♔h1 ♘d7 13 ♗e3 ♘a5 14 ♖d1 ♘c4 15 ♗c1 ♕a5 16 ♗f1 ♘db6 17 ♕g3 0-0 18 b3 ♘e5 19 fxe5 ♗xe5 20 ♕h4 ♗xc3 21 ♕xe7± Kapengut-Zhidkov, Minsk 75 **0-0 9 0-0 ♘c6 10 ♕e1 ♘b4?!** 10...e6 **11 ♔h1 e5 12 fxe5 ♘xd3 13 cxd3 dxe5 14 ♗g5 h6 15 ♗h4!?** 15 ♗xf6! ♗xf6 16 ♘d5 ♗g5 17 ♕c3 ♕d6 18 ♘a5 +=; 16...♗g7 17 ♕b4 += **g5 16 ♗g3 ♘h5 17 ♖d1 ♗e6 18 ♘c5 ♕b6?!** 18...♗g4 19 ♖d2 b6 20 ♘5a4 ♘f4 21 d4∝ **19 ♗f2 ♕xb2 20 ♘5a4 ♕b4 21 ♗c5 ♕a5 22 ♗b6** 22 ♗xf8 ♗xf8 ∝/=+ **♕b4 23 ♗c5** 23 ♖b1 ♕e7 24 ♗c5 ♕c7 25 ♗xf8 ♖xf8 26 ♕e3 += **½-½ Kapengut**

206 Kagan-Polugaevsky
Buenos Aires 78

1 e4 c5 2 ♘f3 d6 3 d4 cxd4 4 ♘xd4 ♘f6 5 ♘c3 a6 6 g3 e5 6...e6 7 ♗g2 ♗e7 8 0-0 0-0 9 b3 ♘c6 10 ♘xc6?! bxc6 11 e5 dxe5 12 ♕xd8 ♖xd8 13 ♗xc6 ♖a7 14 ♗b2 ♖c7? 15 ♗g2 ♖d2 16 ♘e4 += Estrin-Tal, Dubna 73; 6...g6!? **7 ♘de2 ♘bd7 8 a4 b6 9 ♗g2 ♗b7 10 h3 ♗e7 11 g4 ♘c5 12 ♘g3 0-0** 12...♘e6 13 ♗e3 g6 14 ♕d2 0-0 15 0-0 ♖c8 16 ♖ac1 ♘d7 17 ♘ge2 ♘dc5 18 b4 ♘d7 19 ♘d5 ♗g5 20 ♗xg5 ♘xg5 21 h4 ♘e6 22 g5± Ciric-Polugaevsky, Vrnjacka Banja 65 **13 ♗e3 g6 14 ♕d2 b5 15 g5 ♘fd7 16 a5!?** 16 axb5 axb5 17 0-0= **b4 17 ♘d5 ♗xd5 18 exd5 ♖b8 19 ♗f1?!** 19 0-0 **f5! 20 gxf6 ♗xf6 21 ♗e2 e4∓ 22 ♖a2 b3 23 cxb3 ♖xb3 24 0-0 ♕e7 25 ♖c1 ♗e5 26 ♔g2 ♕h4 27 ♖a3 ♖xa3 28 bxa3 ♘b3 29 ♕d1 ♘xc1 −+ 30 ♕xc1 ♗xg3 31 fxg3 ♕f6 32 ♕d2 ♘c5 33 ♕b4 ♕e5 34 ♗d4 ♕e7 35 ♗xc5 dxc5 36 ♕c4 ♕e5 37 d6+ ♔g7 38 ♕xa6 e3 39 ♕b7+ ♔h6 40 h4 ♖f2+ 41 ♔h3 ♖xe2 0-1 Filipowicz**

207 Wibe-Sigurjonsson Gausdal 78

1 e4 c5 2 ♘f3 d6 3 d4 cxd4 4 ♘xd4 ♘f6 5 ♘c3 e6 6 ♗g5 ♗e7 7 ♕d2 a6 8 0-0-0 b5 9 ♗d3 ♗b7 10 ♖he1 ♘bd7 11 f4 ♕b6

12 ♘xe6?! fxe6 13 e5 b4? 13...♘d5! 14 ♘xd5 ♗xd5 15 ♗xe7 ♔xe7 16 f5 ♘xe5∓; 14 ♗xe7 ♔xe7 15 ♘e4∝; 14...♘xe7 15 exd6 ♕xd6?? 16 ♗g6+ +− **14 ♘a4± ♕a5 15 exf6 gxf6 16 ♖xe6! ♕xa4** 16...fxg5 17 ♖de1 ♕xa2 18 ♖xe7+ ♔d8 19 ♗f5 +− **17 ♗h4**

♔d8 17...♕xa2 18 ♕e2 **18 ♗c4 ♕c6 19 ♕e2 ♗f8 20 ♖e8+ ♔c7 21 ♖xa8 ♗xa8 22 ♗d5 ♕xd5 23 ♖xd5 ♗xd5 24 ♕xa6 ♗h6 25 ♕a5+ ♘b6 26 g3 +– ♗g7 27 g4 h5 28 ♗f2 ♖b8 29 ♗xb6+ ♖xb6 30 ♕xd5 hxg4 31 ♕f7+ 1-0 Pytel**

208 Westerinen-Vitolins Jurmala 78
1 e4 c5 2 ♘f3 d6 3 d4 cxd4 4 ♘xd4 ♘f6 5 ♘c3 a6 6 ♗g5 e6 7 f4 ♘bd7 8 ♗e2 8 ♘f3! **♕b6 9 ♕d2 ♗e7 10 0-0-0 h6 11 h4!?** 11 ♗h4? ♘xe4 **hxg5? 12 hxg5 ♖xh1 13 ♖xh1 ♘g8 14 ♖h8 ♔f8 15 g6!± ♘c5 16 gxf7 ♔xf7 17 ♗h5+ ♔f8 18 ♗g6 ♗d7 19 ♗h7 ♔f7 20 ♕d1 ♗f6 21 ♕h5+?!** 21 ♘f5! exf5 22 ♕h5+ ♔e7 23 ♘d5+ +– **♔e7 22 ♘f5+ ♔d8 23 ♖xg8+ ♔c7 24 ♖xa8 ♘xe4?** 24...♗xc3 25 bxc3 ♘xe4∞ **25 ♘d4! +– ♘f2** 25...♗xd4!? **26 ♘ce2 e5 27 ♕f3 exd4 28 ♕xf2 ♕a5 29 a3 ♕d5 30 ♗g8 ♕h5 31 ♔b1 d3 32 cxd3 ♕b5 33 ♘c1 d5 34 ♕c2+ ♗c6 35 ♕b3 ♕c5 36 ♕b4 1-0 Pytel**

Sozin

209 Nunn-Spassov
Buenos Aires 78
1 e4 c5 2 ♘f3 d6 3 d4 cxd4 4 ♘xd4 ♘f6 5 ♘c3 ♘c6 6 ♗c4 e6 7 ♗e3 ♗e7 8 ♕e2 0-0 9 0-0-0 a6 10 ♗b3 10 ♖hg1? ♘xd4 11 ♗xd4 b5 12 ♗b3 b4 13 ♘a4 ♗d7! =+ Diaz-Spassov, Vrnjacka Banja 76 **♕c7 11 g4 ♘d7 12 ♘f5!? ♘c5!?** 12...exf5 13 ♘d5 ♕d8 14 gxf5 ♘a5 15 ♖hg1! ♘xb3+ 16 axb3 ♔h8 17 ♗d4 f6 18 ♖g3 b5 19 ♖dg1 +– ♖f7 20 ♘f4 ♕a5 21 ♕h5 ♔g8 22 ♘g6 ♗b7 23 ♕xh7+ 1-0 Nunn-Simm, England 77; 22... ♘f8 23 ♘h8! **13 ♘xe7+ ♘xe7** 13... ♕xe7 += **14 ♕d2! ♘xb3+ 15 axb3 e5** 15...♖d8 16 e5 d5 17 f4 +=/± **16 ♖hg1 ♖d8 17 f4 exf4** 17...♗e6 18 f5 **18 ♗xf4 ♗e6 19 ♗xd6 ♕c6 20 e5± b5 21 ♔b1 ♕b7 22 ♘e2 a5 23 ♘d4 ♘g6** 23...a4 24 ♗xe7 ♕xe7 25 ♘c6 +–; 23...♘d5 24 ♘f5 h6 25 ♘xh6+ gxh6 26 ♕xh6 a4 27 ♖d3 axb3 28 ♕g5+ **24 ♘xe6 fxe6 25 ♕e3 a4 26 b4 ♘e7**

27 ♗xe7! ♕xe7 28 ♕b6! +– ♖d5 28...♖ab8 29 ♖xd8+; 28...♖db8 29 ♕d6 **29 ♖xd5 exd5 30 ♕xb5 ♕xe5 31 ♖d1 ♖d8 32 h3 h5 33 ♕a5 ♖d6 34 b5 ♕e2 35 ♖e1 ♕c4 36 gxh5 d4 37 ♕a8+ ♔h7 38 ♕e4+ ♔g8 39 ♕f5 ♖d8 40 h6 d3 41 cxd3 ♕xd3+ 42 ♕xd3 ♖xd3 43 ♖g1 ♖b3 44 ♖xg7+ ♔h8 45 ♖a7 ♖xb5 46 ♖xa4 ♖b6 47 ♖h4 ♔h7 1-0 Nunn**

Boleslavsky

210 J.Fernandez-Csom Budapest 78
1 e4 c5 2 ♘f3 d6 3 d4 cxd4 4 ♘xd4 ♘f6 5 ♘c3 ♘c6 6 ♗e2 e5 7 ♘f3 7 ♘b3! **h6** 7...♗e7 8 ♗g5 += **8 0-0 ♗e7 9 b3 0-0 10 ♗b2 a6 11 ♘d2** 11 ♖e1 **♗e6!?** N 11...♘d4 12 ♗d3 b5 13 ♖e1 ♗b7 14 ♘e2 ♘e6 15 ♘g3 g6 16 c4 += Smyslov-Timman, Tillburg 77 **12 ♖e1 ♖c8 13 ♘c4** 13 ♗f1 b5 14 a3 ♕b6∓ **♘xe4! 14 ♘xe4 d5 15 ♘ed2?!** 15

♘xe5= **dxc4 16 ♝xc4 ♛d7 17 ♝xe6 ♛xe6 18 ♞c4?** 18 ♘f3 Δ c4 =+ **f6 19 ♞e3 ♝c5!?** 19...♖fd8∓ **20 ♛d5 ♛xd5 21 ♞xd5 ♞b4! 22 ♞xb4 ♝xb4 23 ♜e2 ♜fd8 24 c4 ♜d3 25 g3 ♚f7 26 ♚g2 a5! 27 ♜c1 b6 28 ♜cc2** 28...f4!? **♜cd8 29 ♜e4 h5 30 ♜ce2 ♝c5 31 ♝c1 a4! 32 bxa4 ♜a8 33 ♝e3 ♜xa4 34 ♝xc5 bxc5 35 f4 exf4 36 gxf4 ♚g6 37 ♜b2 ♜da3 38 ♜ee2 ♜xc4 39 ♜bc2 ♜xf4 40 ♜xc5 ♜fa4 41 ♜cc2 ♚g5 0-1**

Richter-Rauzer

211 Tabanne-Ghitescu
Buenos Aires 78

1 e4 c5 2 ♞f3 d6 3 d4 cxd4 4 ♞xd4 ♞f6 5 ♞c3 a6 6 ♝g5 ♞c6 7 ♛d2 ♝d7 8 ♝c4 e6 9 0-0 ♜c8 9...h6 10 ♗h4 ♘xe4! =+ **10 ♝b3 ♝e7 11 ♜ad1 0-0** 11...♘xd4 12 ♕xd4 ♗c6 13 ♗xf6?! ♗xf6 14 ♕xd6 ♕xd6 15 ♖xd6 ♗xc3 16 bxc3 ♗xe4∓ **12 ♜fe1 b5 13 ♞xc6 ♝xc6** 13...♖xc6? 14 e5! +− **14 ♝xf6 gxf6!? 15 ♛h6 ♚h8 16 ♛h5!** 16 ♖e3 ♖g8 17 ♖h3 ♖g7 18 ♖dd3 f5! 18 ♖dg3 ♗g5∓ **b4 17 ♜e3 ♜g8 19 ♞e2 ♝e8! 20 ♜h3 ♜g7 21 ♞g3 a5 22 ♛e2 ♛c7 22 ♞h5 ♜g5 23 c3 ♝b5 24 ♛f3 f5!∓ 25 exf5!? ♝c6 26 ♛e3 ♜xg2+ 27 ♚f1 ♜g4 28 f3 ♝b5+ 29 ♚f2 ♝g5 30 f4 ♝h4+ 31 ♚f3 ♜cg8 32 fxe6 ♝c6+! 33 ♝d5 ♝xd5 34 ♜xd5 fxe6 35 ♛xe6 ♛c4! −+**

Diagram

36 ♜xh4 ♛f1+ 37 ♚e4 ♛e2+ 38 ♚f5 ♜8g5+! 0-1 Ghitescu

212 Nogueiras-Lain Mexico 78

1 e4 c5 2 ♞f3 d6 3 d4 cxd4 4 ♞xd4 ♞f6 5 ♞c3 ♞c6 6 ♝g5 e6 7 ♛d2 a6 8 0-0-0 ♝d7 9 f4 b5 10 ♞xc6 ♝xc6 11 ♝d3 ♝e7 12 ♜he1 12 e5 dxe5 13 fxe5 ♘d7 14 ♗xe7 ♕xe7 15 ♕f4 ♘c5 16 ♘e4 ♗xe4 17 ♗xe4 ♖c8!= Mecking-Polugaevsky (8) 77 **0-0 13 e5 dxe5 14 ♛f2 h6!? 15 ♝xb5** 15 ♗h7+ ♔xh7 16 ♖xd8 ♖fxd8 =+; 15 ♗xf6?! ♗xf6 16 fxe5 ♗h4 17 g3 ♗g5+ 18 ♔b1 ♕c7 19 h4 ♗e7 =+ Karpov-Tal, USSR Final 76 **axb5** 15...♕c7 16 ♗xc6 ♕xc6 17 ♗xf6 ♗xf6 18 fxe5 += **16 ♜xd8 ♜fxd8 17 ♝xf6 ♝xf6 18 fxe5 ♝g5+** 18...♗e7!? b4 19 ♖f1!? **19 ♚b1 b4 20 ♛c5**

20...bxc3?! (1) 20...♗d2!? 21 ♖d1 bxc3 22 ♕xc6 ♖db8 23 b3 ♖a3 24 ♖xd2 cxd2 25 ♕d6 ♖ba8 26 ♕xd2 ♖xa2±; 22...♖a5!? 23 a4; 21 ♖f1? ♗xg2!; (2) 20...♖dc8 21 ♕xb4 ♗d2

22 ♖e2!± ♗xc3 23 ♕xc3 +−; 22 ♖d1? ♗xc3 23 ♕xc3 ♗e4! **21 ♛xc6 cxb2** 21...♗d2 22 ♖f1 ♖db8!? 23 b3 (Δ a4) ♖a3? 24 ♕c7 ♖ba8 25 ♖xf7!; 22 ♖d1!? **22 ♜f1 ♜dc8?** 22...♖a7 **23 ♛b7 +− ♜cb8 24 ♛xf7+ ♚h7 25 ♛xe6 ♜b5 26 ♜f7 1-0** 26...♖d8! +− **Speelman**

213 Inkiov-Spassov Pernik 78
1 e4 c5 2 ♞f3 d6 3 d4 cxd4 4 ♞xd4 ♞f6 5 ♞c3 ♞c6 6 ♝g5 e6 7 ♛d2 a6 8 0-0-0 ♝d7 9 f4 ♝e7 10 ♞f3 b5 11 ♝xf6 ♝xf6!? 11...gxf6 12 ♔b1 ♕b6 13 f5 += **12 ♛xd6 ♜a7** 12...♗e7 13 ♕d2 b4 Vogt-Suetin, Budapest 76 14 ♘a4 += **13 e5 ♝e7 14 ♛d2?!** 14 ♕d3 ♕a5 15 ♘d4 ♘b4 16 ♕e3 ♖c7 ≈ Hardicsay-Mista, Olomouc 77 **♛a5 15 ♚b1 ♝b4 16 ♞g5 ♝xc3 17 ♛xc3 ♛xc3 18 bxc3 ♞a5 =+ 19 ♜d6 ♝c6 20 ♝d3 h6** 20...♗xg2?! 21 ♖g1 ♗c6 22 ♘xh7 g6 23 ♘f6+≈ **21 ♝e4** 21 ♘e4 ♔e7 Δ ♖c8 **hxg5! 22 ♝xc6+ ♚e7 23 fxg5** 23 g3 gxf4 24 gxf4 ♖h3∓ **♞c4 24 ♜d4 ♞xe5 25 ♝e4 ♜c7 26 h4** 26 ♔b2 ♖c5 Δ ♘c4+∓ **♜xc3 27 h5 ♜g3 28 ♝b7 a5 29 g6 ♜xg6! −+ 30 hxg6 ♜xh1+ 31 ♚b2 ♞xg6 32 ♝c6 b4 33 ♜d7+ ♚f6 34 ♜a7 ♞e5 35 ♝b5** 35 ♗b7 ♖d1 Δ ♖d7; 35 ♗a8 ♘c4+ 36 ♔b3 ♘b6 **♜g1 36 ♜xa5 ♜xg2 37 ♜a4 ♚e7! 38 ♜xb4 ♚d6 39 a4 ♚c5 40 ♜b3 ♜g4 41 a5 ♜b4 42 ♝f1 ♜xb3+ 43 cxb3 ♞c6 44 ♚c3 ♞b4 45 a6 ♞d5+ 46 ♚d3 ♚b6 47 ♚e4 ♞c7 48 ♚e5 ♞xa6 49 ♚d6 ♞c7 50 ♚e7 f5 51 ♚f7 g5 52 ♚f6 g4 53 b4 g3 54 ♚e5 ♞d5 55 ♚xe6 ♞e3 56 ♝h3 f4 0-1 Webb**

214 Chiburdanidze-Gaprindashvili (11) 78
1 e4 c5 2 ♞f3 ♞c6 3 d4 cxd4 4 ♞xd4 ♞f6 5 ♞c3 d6 6 ♝g5 e6 7 ♛d2 a6 8 0-0-0 h6 9 ♝e3 9 ♗f4 e5 10 ♘xc6 dxc6 11 ♗xe5 **♛c7** 9...♘g4 10 ♘xc6 bxc6 11 ♗c5! ♗b7 12 h3 dxc5 ♕xd8+ **10 f3 ♜b8 11 g4 ♞xd4** 11...b5 12 ♗xb5!? axb5 13 ♘cxb5! **12 ♝xd4 b5 13 e5** 13 ♗xf6 gxf6 14 ♔b1 **♞d7** 14...dxe5 15 ♗xe5 ♕xe5 16 ♕d8 mate **14 exd6 ♝xd6 15 ♞e4 ♝f4 16 ♝e3 ♝xe3 17 ♛xe3 0-0 18 ♞d6?** 17 g5! h5? 19 ♘f6+! **♞b6 19 ♞xc8 ♜fxc8 20 ♝d3 ♞d5 21 ♛e4 ♞f6 22 ♛e2 ♛a5 23 ♚b1 ♞d5 24 ♝e4** 24 ♕e4 ♘b4; 24...b4 **♞b6!** 24...♘b4? 25 a3 ♘c6 26 ♗xc6 ♖xc6 27 ♕d2! b4 28 axb4 ♖xb4 29 ♕d8+ **25 ♜hg1** 25 ♖d3 ♘a4! 26 ♖hd1 b4 **♞a4! 26 ♛e1** 26 g5 ♕b4! **b4! 27 ♚a1** 27 ♖d3 ♘c3+! **♜c5 28 ♜b1 ♞b6 29 ♛g3 ♜bc8 30 ♜hd1 ♞c4 31 f4**

31...♞d2! 32 ♜xd2 32 ♗d3 ♕xa2+! 33 ♔xa2 ♖a5 mate **b3! 33 ♛xb3 ♛xd2 34 f5** 34 ♕g3 ♖c4! **♛d4 35 ♜e1 ♜e5 36 ♛f3 ♜xc2 37 ♝xc2 ♜xe1+ 38 ♝b1 ♛d1 39 ♛xd1 ♜xd1 40 fxe6 fxe6 0-1**

Scheveningen

215 Krug-Vogt DDR 78
1 e4 c5 2 ♞f3 e6 3 d4 cxd4 4 ♞xd4 ♞f6 5 ♞c3 d6 6 ♝c4 ♝e7 7 ♝b3 0-0

8 ♝e3 ♞a6 9 f3 9 f4 **♞c5 10 ♛d2 a6 11 g4 ♛c7 12 g5** 12 h4 b5 13 a3 ♘fd7 14 g5 ♘b6∞ **♞fd7 13 h4 b5 14 h5** 14 g6 ♘e5 15 gxh7+ ♔h8 16 a3 ♖b8∞ Reshevsky-Malich, Seigen 70 **♞e5 15 0-0-0 b4 16 ♞a4** 16 ♘ce2 a5 **♝d7 17 h6!? g6** 17...♗xa4 18 hxg7 ♔xg7 19 ♕h2 ♖h8 20 ♖dg1 Δ f4±; 19...h5 20 f4± **18 ♞xc5 dxc5 19 f4 ♞g4?** 19...cxd4 20 ♕xd4 a5 21 ♕xe5 ♕xe5 22 fxe5 ♗b5∓ **20 ♞f5! exf5 21 ♛xd7 ♜a7 22 ♛xc7 ♜xc7 23 ♜he1 c4 24 ♝a4 fxe4 25 ♝b6 += ♜b7 26 ♜xe4 ♜xb6 27 ♜xe7 ♜e6! 28 ♜ed7** 28 ♖xe6 fxe6 29 ♖d4 e5 **♞f2 29 ♜f1 ♞e4 30 ♜c7 ♜d8** Δ ♘g3 –+ **31 ♜d7 ♜xd7 32 ♝xd7 ♜e7** 32...♖d6 33 ♖e1 f5 34 gxf6 ♘xf6 35 ♗e6+ ♔f8 36 ♗xc4 ♘g4= **33 ♝c6 ♞c5 34 ♜d1 ♞e6 35 ♝d5 ♞xf4 36 ♝xc4 ♚f8 37 ♝xa6 ♜e4! 38 ♝c8 ♜e5 39 ♜f1 ♞d5 40 ♜g1 ♚e7= 41 ♚d2 ♞b6 42 ♝b7 ♞c4+ 43 ♚d3** 43 ♔c1 **♞xb2+ 44 ♚d4 ♜e2 45 ♝e4 ♚d6! 46 ♜b1 ♜d2+ 47 ♝d3** 47 ♔e3 ♘c4+ **♞xd3 48 cxd3 ♜xa2 49 ♜xb4 ♜a5 50 ♜b6+ ♚e7 51 ♚e4! ½-½ Vogt**

216 Sznapik-Mascarinas
Buenos Aires 78

1 e4 c5 2 ♞f3 d6 3 d4 cxd4 4 ♞xd4 ♞f6 5 ♞c3 e6 6 ♝e2 a6 7 f4 7 ♗e3 ♗e7 8 f4 0-0 9 g4!? ♕c7 10 g5 ♘fd7 11 ♗f3 ♘c6 12 a4 ♘a5 13 0-0! ♘c4 14 ♗c1 ♕b6 15 b3± Minic-Stean, Bar 77 **♞c6 8 ♝e3 ♛c7?!** 8...♗e7 9 0-0 0-0 10 ♕e1 ♗d7 **9 0-0 ♝e7 10 ♛e1 0-0 11 ♛g3 ♞xd4 12 ♝xd4 b5 13 a3 ♝b7 14 ♜ae1± d5 15 e5 ♝c5 16 ♜d1 ♞d7 17 ♛e3! ♜ac8 18 ♝d3 ♝xd4 19 ♛xd4 ♛c5 20 ♞e2 ♞b6 21 ♛xc5 ♜xc5 22 b3 ♞c4?! 23 ♝xc4** 23 bxc4 dxc4 =+ **dxc4 24 b4 ♜c7 25 ♜d6 ♜fc8 26 ♜fd1 ♚f8 27 c3 ♚e8 28 ♞d4 ♝c6 29 ♚f2 ♝b7 30 g4 g6 31 ♚e3 ♜a8 32 f5 +– exf5 33 gxf5 ♜e7 34 ♚f4 g5+ 35 ♚xg5 ♜xe5 36 ♚f6 ♜d5 37 ♜b6 ♜d7 38 ♜g1 ♚f8 39 ♜g7 ♜ad8 40 ♜xh7 ♜d6+ 41 ♞e6+! 1-0 Filipowicz**

217 Hund-Alexandria
Buenos Aires 78

1 e4 c5 2 ♞f3 e6 3 d4 cxd4 4 ♞xd4 ♞c6 5 ♞c3 ♛c7 6 ♝e2 a6 7 ♝e3 ♞f6 8 0-0 ♝e7 9 f4 d6 10 ♚h1 0-0 11 ♛e1 ♞xd4 12 ♝xd4 b5 13 a3!? 13 e5 dxe5 14 ♗xe5 ♕b6 15 ♗d3 ♗b7 16 ♕h4! += Gufeld-Platonov, USSR 74; 14 fxe5!? **♝b7 14 ♛g3 ♝c6** 14... ♖fd8 15 ♗d3 ♘e8 16 ♖ae1 ♗f8 17 ♕h3 += Smyslov-Kotov, Budapest 50 **15 ♜ad1!?** 15 ♖ae1; 15 ♗d3 **♜ad8 16 ♝f3!?** 16 ♗d3 ♕b7 17 ♖de1 a5 18 ♕h3!? b4 19 axb4 axb4 20 e5≈ Larsen **♛b7 17 ♝xf6 ♝xf6 18 e5 dxe5 19 fxe5 ♝e7 20 ♜d3! ♝xf3** 20...♖xd3 21 cxd3 Δ ♘e4 **21 ♜dxf3 b4 22 axb4 ♛xb4 23 b3 ♝h4?! 24 ♛h3 ♜d4 25 ♞e2 ♜e4 26 ♞f4 ♝e7 27 c4!** 27 ♘xe6? ♖h4 28 ♕f5 g6! **♛b8?** 27... ♕b6 28 ♕h5

28 ♞xe6! ♜h4 28...fxe6 29 ♕xe6+ ♔h8 30 ♖xf8+ ♗xf8 31 ♕f5 +– **29 ♛g3 fxe6 30 ♜xf8+ ♛xf8** 30... ♗xf8 31 ♕xh4 **31 ♜xf8+ ♚xf8 32**

Qf3+ Kg8 33 g3 +− Rd4 34 Qa8+ Kf7 35 Qxa6 Re4 36 Qb5 h5 37 h4 Re3 38 Kg2 g5 39 hxg5 Bxg5 40 b4 Kg6 41 Qe8+ Kf5 42 Qxh5 Re4 1-0 Samarian

218 Iskov-Goichberg Bergen 78

1 e4 c5 2 Nf3 d6 3 Nc3 Nf6 4 d4 cxd4 5 Nxd4 e6 6 f4 Nc6 7 Be3 Be7 8 Qf3 a6 9 0-0-0 Qc7 10 g4?! 10 Rg1 0-0 11 g4 Nxd4 12 Bxd4 b5 13 g5 Nd7 14 f5! += **Nxd4 11 Bxd4 e5 12 g5 exd4?** 12...Bg4 13 Qg3 Bxd1 14 gxf6 exd4 15 fxg7 Rg8 16 Nxd1 Bf6 17 Qb3 ∞/∓ **13 gxf6 dxc3 14 fxe7 cxb2+ 15 Kb1 Qxe7 16 Rg1! Bd7!?** 16...0-0 17 f5! Kh8 18 Qg3 Qe5 19 Rxd6±; 17...Qf6 18 Qg3 Rd8? 19 e5! **17 Rxg7 0-0-0 18 Bc4 Bc6 19 Qc3! Kb8** 19...Qxe4 20 Bd5! Qe2 21 Rd3! +−; 20...Qa4 21 Rd4 Qb5 22 Bxc6 bxc6 23 Rb4± **20 Rxf7 Qxe4 21 Re1 Qg6** 21...Qf3 22 Re3± **22 f5 Qh5** 22...Qg5 23 Kxb2± **23 Ree7!** Δ Rxb7+!, Rxb7+, Bd5+ +− **Rc8? 24 Be6 Qg5 25 Kxb2 Rce8 26 Rxb7+! 1-0** 26...Bxb7 27 Qc7+ Ka8 28 Qxb7 mate **Iskov**

Dragon

219 Kasparov-Gufeld USSR 78

1 e4 c5 2 Nf3 d6 3 d4 cxd4 4 Nxd4 Nf6 5 Nc3 g6 6 Be2 Bg7 7 0-0 0-0 8 Be3 Nc6 9 Nb3 Be6 10 f4 Qc8 11 Kh1 Bg4!? N 11...Rd8 **12 Bg1 Bxe2 13 Qxe2 Qg4 14 Qd2 Nh5 15 Rf3 f5** 15...Bxc3 16 bxc3 Δ Nd4 += **16 h3 Qh4 17 exf5 gxf5?!** 17...Ng3+? 18 Rxg3 Qxg3 19 Bf2 +−; 17...Rxf5 18 Bf2 Qf6 19 g4 Rxf4 20 Nd5±; 18...Bxc3! 19 bxc3! Qf6 20 Be3 += **18 Nd4 Ng3+?!** 18...Nxd4 19 Bxd4 e5? 20 fxe5 dxe5 21 Bxe5! Rad8 22 Qe1 +−; 18...e5 19 Bf2! Qe7 20 fxe5 Nxd4 21 Qxd4 dxe5 22 Qd5+ Qf7 23 Rxf5! Qxd5 24 Nxd5 +−; 18...Qf6!? **19 Kh2 Ne4 20 Nxe4 fxe4 21 Rg3 Qh6** 21...Qxf4? 22 Qxf4 Rxf4 23 Rxg7+ +−; 21...Kh8 22 Ne6 Rg8 23 Nxg7 Rxg7 24 Rxg7 Kxg7 25 Re1± **22 Be3 Rf7 23 f5 Qf6 24 c3 Kh8 25 Rf1± Qe5 26 Nxc6 bxc6 27 Bd4**

27...Qd5 27...Rg8 28 f6!! Qxg3+ 29 Kxg3 Bh6+ 30 Kh2 Bxd2 31 fxe7+ Rfg7 32 Rf8 +− **28 Rxg7 Rxg7 29 c4!** 29 Qh6 Rg8 30 Rf4? Qf7? 31 Qxh7+! +−; 30...Qxd4! −+ **Qxc4 30 Rf4 c5 31 Bxg7+ Kxg7 32 f6+! exf6 33 Qxd6 Qf7 34 Rxe4 Kh8 35 Rf4 Rg8 36 Rxf6 Qg7 37 Rf2 c4 38 Rc2 a5 39 a4 h6 40 Re2 Qg5 41 Qd4+ Qg7 42 Qxc4 Qg3+ 43 Kg1 Rd8 44 Qc3+ Qxc3 45 bxc3 Rc8 46 Re5 Rxc3 47 Rxa5 Kg7 48 Rh5 1-0 Kasparov**

220 Ljubojevic-Sosonko
Buenos Aires 78

1 e4 c5 2 Nf3 d6 3 d4 cxd4 4 Nxd4 Nf6 5 Nc3 g6 6 Be3 Bg7 6...Ng4? 7 Bb5+ +− **7 Bc4 Ng4!? 8 Bb5+ Kf8 9 Bg5** 9 0-0 Be5!∓ **h6** 9...Qb6?? 10 Bxe7+ +− **10 Bh4 g5 11 Bg3 Qb6 12 Nde2** 12 Nf5 Bxf5 13 exf5 Bxc3+

14 bxc3 ♕xb5 15 ♕xg4 ♕d7∓ **h5** 12...♘c6 13 h3±; 12...a6 13 ♗c4 ♕xb2 14 0-0 ♗xc3 15 ♖b1 ♕a3 16 ♖b3± **13 h4!** 13 h3 h4 14 hxg4 hxg3 15 ♖xh8+ ♗xh8 16 fxg3 ♗xg4∓ **gxh4 14 ♖xh4** 14 ♗xh4? ♗f6 −+ **♘c6** 14...♗f6 15 ♕d2 ♗xh4 16 ♗xh4 **15 ♕d2 ♘d4** 15...♗e6? 16 ♘f4 ♘d4 17 ♖xh5 ♖xh5 18 ♘xh5 ♘xb5 19 ♘xg7 +−; 15...♘e5? 16 ♘f4 **16 ♘xd4 ♕xd4 17 0-0-0 ♕xd2+ 18 ♖xd2 ♗f6! 19 ♖h1 h4 20 ♗f4 ♗e6= 21 ♘d5** 21 f3 ♗xc3 22 bxc3 ♘e5= **♗xd5 22 exd5 ♖c8 23 ♖h3** 23 ♗d7?! ♖c4 **♘e5 24 ♖b3 a6 25 ♗f1 ♘c4 26 ♖d1 b5 27 a4 ½-½** 27...♘a5 28 ♖b4!; 27...♖c5= **Sosonko**

221 Pokojowczyk-Marszalek
Pazardjik 78
1 e4 c5 2 ♘f3 d6 3 d4 cxd4 4 ♘xd4 ♘f6 5 ♘c3 g6 6 ♗e3 ♗g7 7 f3 ♘c6 8 ♕d2 0-0 9 ♗c4 9 0-0-0 ♘xd4! 10 ♗xd4 ♗e6 11 ♘d5 ♗xd5! 12 exd5 ♕c7 13 g4 ♖ac8 14 c3 ♕a5 15 g5 ♘h5 16 ♗xg7 ♘xg7 17 ♔b1 e5! 18 dxe6 fxe6 19 ♗h3 ♖xf3= Timman-Sosonko, Wijk aan Zee 78 **♗d7 10 h4 ♖c8 11 ♗b3 ♘e5 12 h5 ♘xh5 13 g4** 13 0-0-0 ♘c4 14 ♗xc4 ♖xc4 15 g4 ♘f6 16 ♘de2 ♕a5 17 ♗h6 ♗h8!? 18 ♗xf8 ♔xf8 19 ♔b1 ♗e6 20 ♘f4 g5! 21 ♘xe6 fxe6 22 ♘xe2 ♕e5! Chudinovsky-Jakmimainen, USSR 77 **♘f6 14 ♗h6 ♗xh6 15 ♕xh6**

Diagram

15...♖xc3!= 16 bxc3 ♕a5 17 0-0-0 ♕xc3 18 ♔b1 ♘c4! 19 ♗xc4 ♕xc4 20 ♕e3 ♖c8 21 ♖d2 a5 22 g5 ♘h5 23 f4 ♕b4+ 24 ♔c1 ♖c3! 25 ♖d3 ♖xd3 26 cxd3 ♕a4 27 ♘c2 ♕xa2 28 f5 ♗a4 29 ♖h2 ♕b3 30 e5! dxe5 31 ♕xe5 gxf5 32 ♕xe7 ♕xd3 33 ♕xb7 ♘g3 34 ♕b8+ ♔g7 35 ♕e5+ ♔g8 ½-½ Mechkarov

222 Trapl-Barczay Decin 78
1 e4 c5 2 ♘f3 d6 3 d4 cxd4 4 ♘xd4 ♘f6 5 ♘c3 g6 6 ♗e3 ♗g7 7 f3 0-0 8 ♕d2 ♘c6 9 g4!? ♗e6 10 g5 ♘h5 11 ♗e2? 11 0-0-0∝ **♘xd4 12 ♗xd4 ♗xd4 13 ♕xd4 ♕a5 14 ♕d2 ♕e5∓ 15 0-0-0 ♖ac8 16 ♔b1 ♖c5 17 h4?** 17 ♗d3 Δ ♘e2 **♘f4 18 ♗d3 ♖fc8 19 h5 ♖xc3! −+ 20 bxc3 ♖xc3 21 hxg6 fxg6 22 ♕h2 h5! 23 gxh6 ♔h7! 24 ♕h4 g5 25 ♕e1 ♘xd3 26 ♖xd3 ♕b5+ 27 ♔c1 ♕xd3 0-1 Pritchett**

4 ♕xd4

223 Gulko-Kuligowski
Buenos Aires 78
1 e4 c5 2 ♘c3 d6 3 f4 g6 4 d4?! 4 ♘f3 ♗g7 5 ♗c4 e6 6 f5 **cxd4 5 ♕xd4 ♘f6 6 e5?! ♘c6 7 ♗b5 dxe5 8 ♕xd8+ ♔xd8 9 fxe5 ♘xe5 10 ♗f4 ♘ed7! 11 0-0-0 a6 12 ♗c4 e6 13 a4** 13 ♘f3 b5 14 ♗b3 ♗b7 15 ♘e5 ♔e8 =+ **h6 14 ♘f3 ♗b4!** 14...♗g7 15 ♖he1± **15 ♘e5 ♔e7 16 ♖hf1 ♖h7 17 ♘xd7 ♗xd7 18 ♘a2 ♗c5 19 b4**

Diagram

19...g5! 19...♗a7 ♗d6+ +− **20 bxc5 gxf4 21 ♜xf4 ♝c6** 21...♗xa4?? 22 ♗d3 +− **22 g3 ♞d7 23 ♝d3 ♜g7 24 ♞b4 ♝xa4 25 ♞xa6 ♝c6 26 ♞b4 ♜a1+ 27 ♚d2 ♜xd1+ 28 ♚xd1 ♞xc5∓ 29 ♞xc6+ bxc6 30 ♜h4 ♞xd3 31 cxd3 ♜g6 36 ♚d2 =+ c5 37 ♚e3 ♚d6 38 ♜f4 f5 35 ♜a4 h5 36 ♜h4 ♜h6 37 ♚f4 ♚d5 38 ♚f3 ♜h8 39 ♚e3 ♜h7 40 ♚e2 e5 43 ♚e3 ½-½** 43...♖h6 44 ♔e2 ♖a6 45 ♖xh5 ♔d4 46 ♖xf5 ♖a2+ 47 ♔e1 ♖xh2 48 g4= **Filipowicz**

224 Braga-Ghitescu
Buenos Aires 78

1 e4 c5 2 ♞f3 d6 3 d4 cxd4 4 ♛xd4 ♞c6 5 ♝b5 ♝d7 6 ♝xc6 ♝xc6 7 ♞c3 7 c4 ♘f6 8 ♘c3 g6 **♞f6 8 ♝g5 e6 9 0-0-0 ♝e7 10 ♜d2** 10 ♖he1 **0-0 11 ♛e3 ♛a5 12 h4 ♜fc8! 13 ♞d4 ♝e8 14 ♜hd1 ♜c4 15 ♞b3 ♛c7 16 ♚b1** 16 ♖d4 b5 17 ♖xc4 bxc4 18 ♘d4 ♖b8∓; 16 ♗f4 ♘g4 17 ♕g3 ♘e5 **b5** Δ a5-a4 **17 ♝xf6 ♝xf6 18 ♜xd6 ♝xc3 19 bxc3 ♜xc3 20 ♛d2 ♚f8!** 20...♖c8? 21 ♖d8 ♖xc2? 22 ♖xc8 +− **21 ♜d3 ♜c4 22 ♜e3 ♜ac8 23 ♜e2 e5?!** 23...♔g8!∓ **24 ♛d6+ ♛xd6 25 ♜xd6 ♚e7 26 ♜a6 ♜8c7 27 f3 ♝d7 28 ♞c1 ♜b4+ 29 ♚a1 ♜d4 30 ♞d3 f6 31 ♚b2 ♝e6∓ 32 ♜d2 ♝c4 33 ♜d1 ♜cd7 34 ♚c1 ♜4d6 35 ♜a5 h5! 36 ♞f2 ♜c7 37 ♜xd6 ♚xd6 38 ♚b2 ♚c5 39 ♜a3 ♜d7 40 ♞d3+ ♚b6 41 ♜c3 a5 42 a3 ♜d6! −+ 43 ♞e1 ♜d1 44 ♜e3 ♚c5 45 c3 ♜d2+ 46 ♚b1 ♝e2 47 ♚c1 ♜d1+ 48 ♚c2 ♜xe1 49 ♚d2 ♜a1 50 ♚xe2 ♚c4! 51 g4** 51 ♖d3? ♖e1+ **♜xa3 52 ♜d3 ♜a2+ 53 ♚e3 hxg4 54 ♜d7 gxf3 0-1 Ghitescu**

225 Silva-Ferreira
Portugal Final 78

1 e4 c5 2 ♞f3 d6 3 d4 cxd4 4 ♛xd4 ♞c6 5 ♝b5 ♛d7 6 ♝xc6 bxc6 7 c4 e5 8 ♛d3 8 ♕d2!? **♞f6 9 ♞c3 ♝e7 10 0-0 ♛c7!** 10...0-0?! **11 b3?! 0-0 12 ♜d1 ♝e6 13 ♝b2** 13 ♗a3!? **♜ad8 14 ♜ac1 ♞h5!** N **15 ♞d5?! ♛d7 16 ♞e3** 16 ♘xe7+?! ♕xe7 17 c5 dxc5 18 ♕c3 ♘f4 19 ♔f1 ♖xd1+ 20 ♖xd1 ♖d8 21 ♖c1 =+ **♝g4 17 ♞f1 ♞f4 18 ♛e3 ♛e6 19 ♞g3 f5 20 exf5 ♝xf5 21 ♞xf5 ♛xf5 22 ♞e1 ♝g5! 23 ♜c2 ♞xg2 24 ♛d3 e4 25 ♛g3 ♞xe1 26 ♜xe1 e3! 27 ♜ee2 ♜de8 28 ♚h1 exf2 29 ♛xf2 ♜xe2 30 ♛xe2 ♛h3! 31 ♝d4 ♜f1+ 32 ♝g1 ♝e3 33 ♜c1 ♜xc1 0-1 Ochoa**

2...e6, 4...a6

226 Panchenko-Agramov USSR 78

1 e4 c5 2 ♞f3 e6 3 d4 cxd4 4 ♞xd4 a6 5 ♞c3 ♛c7 6 ♝e2 b5 6...♘c6 7 0-0 ♘f6 8 ♗e3 ♗b4 **7 0-0 ♝b7 8 ♝f3 ♞c6 9 ♜e1 ♞e5 10 ♝f4 d6** 10...0-0-0 11 ♘dxb5 axb5 12 ♘xb5 ♕b6 13 a4 f6 14 ♗e2 ♗c5 15 a5; 10...♘xf3+ 11 ♕xf3 d6 **11 a4 bxa4** 11...♘xf3+ 12 ♘xf3 bxa4 13 ♖xa4 Δ ♕d3, ♖d1; 11...b4? 12 ♘a2 **12 ♝h5! g6** 12...♘g6 13 ♗xg6! hxg6 14 e5 dxe5 15 ♘xa4 ♘e7 16 ♖e3!; 14...♖d8 15 exd6 ♗xd6 16 ♘xe6; 12...♗c8 **13 ♝e2 ♞f6 14 ♜xa4 ♞fd7** 14...♗g7 15 ♘db5 axb5 16 ♘xb5; 15 ♕a1 **15 ♞b3 ♞b6 16 ♜a2 ♝g7 17 ♞a5 ♝c8**

18 ♞a4 18 ♕d2 0-0 19 ♖d1 ♖d8 20 ♗g5 **♞xa4 19 ♜xa4 ♝d7 20 ♜a2 0-0 21 ♛d2 ♜fd8 22 ♜d1 ♝e8 23 c4 ♜ac8** 23...♖ab8 **24 h3 f5?!** 24...♖b8 25 ♗g5 ♖d7 26 b4; 25...f6 26 ♗e3 **25 exf5 gxf5 26 b4 ♞f7** 26...♖b8 27 ♗g5 ♖d7 28 b5 **27 ♝h5 e5 28 ♝g5** 28 ♗g3 Δ ♗h4 **♜d7?** 28...♘xg5 29 ♕xg5 ♗xh5 30 ♕xh5 ♖f8 31 ♖ad2 ♖cd8 32 ♕g5 h6 33 ♕g6 ♖f6 34 ♕g3; 29... ♗d7 30 ♕e7 **29 ♝h4 ♚h8** 29...♖b8 **30 ♛d5 ♛b6** 30...♖b8 31 b5 axb5 32 cxb5 ♖b6 33 ♘c6 ♕b7 34 ♕e6! **31 ♛e6 ♜dc7 32 ♜b2 ♛a7 33 c5 dxc5 34 ♝d8! ♞d6** 34...♗d7 35 ♖xd7 ♖xd7 36 ♕e8+ **35 ♝xc7 ♝xh5 36 ♜xd6 ♛xc7 37 ♜c6 ♝f7 38 ♛xc8+ 1-0**

227 Borngasser-Miles England 78

1 e4 c5 2 ♞f3 e6 3 d4 cxd4 4 ♞xd4 a6 5 ♝d3 ♞c6 6 ♞xc6 dxc6 7 f4 e5 8 f5 ♞f6 9 ♛e2 N 9 ♕f3 **b5 10 a4!? ♝b7 11 0-0 ♝e7 12 ♚h1 0-0 13 ♞d2 ♞d7 14 ♞b3!?** Δ ♗d2± **♝g5! 15 ♝xg5** 15 ♗e3!? **♛xg5 16 ♛f2** 16 ♘a5 ♖ab8≈ **♛e7 17 ♜fd1** 17 ♘a5 ♖fb8≈ **♜fc8 18 ♞a5 ♜c7** Δ ♖ac8, ♗a8 **19 c3 ♜ac8 20 ♛e3** 20 axb5!? **♝a8! =+ 21 ♝e2 ♜b8!** Δ c5 **22 axb5 cxb5** 22... axb5 23 ♘b3! (Δ ♖a7, ♘c5) c5? 24 ♗xb5 +− **23 b4?** 23 ♘b3! =+ **♜bc8 24 ♜d3**

24...♛h4!∓ 25 ♝f3 ♞f6 26 ♜e1 26 g3 ♕h6! **h6 27 g3 ♛g5 28 ♞b3 ♞d7 29 ♛xg5? hxg5 30 ♜c1 g4 31 ♝g2 ♚f8∓ 32 ♚g1 ♚e7 33 ♚f2 ♜h8 34 ♚g1 ♜h6 35 ♝h1 ♜d6 36 ♜cd1?** 36 ♖xd6∓ **♜dc6! 37 ♜c1 ♜c4! 38 ♜e3** 38 ♘a5!? ♗xe4 39 ♖e3!; 38...♖xb4? 39 ♖xd7+! +−; 38...♖d4! −+ **♞f6 39 ♞c5** 39 ♘d2 ♖xb4 −+ **a5! −+ 40 ♜b1 axb4 41 cxb4 ♞d7 42 ♞d3 ♜a7 43 ♜e2 ♜a3 44 ♜d1 ♜d4 45 ♜ed2 ♞f6 46 ♝g2** 46 ♘xe5? ♖xd2 47 ♖xd2 ♖a1+ −+ **♞xe4 47 ♝xe4 ♝xe4 48 ♞xe5 ♜xd2 49 ♜xd2 ♝xf5 50 ♜d5 ♜a1+ 51 ♚f2 ♜a2+ 52 ♚e3 ♝e6 53 ♞c6+** 53 ♖xb5 ♖xh2 −+ **♚f6 54 ♜d2 ♜xd2 55 ♚xd2 ♝d7 56 ♞d4 ♚e5 57 ♚e3 ♚d5 58 ♚d3 g5 0-1 Miles**

228 Hardicsay-Piasetski
Zamardi 78

1 e4 c5 2 ♞f3 e6 3 d4 cxd4 4 ♞xd4 a6 5 ♝d3 ♞e7!? 6 f4 ♞bc6 7 ♞f3 d5 7...b5 **8 e5 ♛b6 9 ♞bd2! ♞f5** 9...♕e3+ 10 ♗e2 ♕xf4 11 ♘c4 **10 ♞b3 a5 11 a4 ♝d7 12 ♛e2 ♝e7** 12... ♗b4+ 13 ♔f1!? Δ g3, ♔g2 **13 ♝xf5 exf5 14 ♝e3 ♛b4+** 14...♕c7 15 ♘fd4 **15 ♚f2 ♛c4 16 ♜hd1 ♞b4 17 ♞fd4! ♝d8 18 c3 ♞a6 19 ♞d2 ♛xe2+ 20 ♚xe2 ♞c5 21 ♞xf5 ♞xa4 22 ♞d6+ ♚f8 23 ♜a2 b5 24 ♝d4! ♞b6 25 ♞b7 ♞c4 26 ♞f3 ♝c7 27 ♝c5+ ♚e8 28 b3 ♞b6 29 ♞d6+ ♝xd6 30 ♝xb6 ♝e7 31 ♜xa5 ♜c8 32 ♝d4 ♝c6 33 ♜a7 h5 34 b4! ♝d7 35 ♜da1 ♜h6 36 ♜b7 ♝c6 37 ♜b6 ♝d8 38 ♜ba6 ♜g6 39 ♚f2 h4 40 ♝c5 ♜g4 41 ♝e3 ♝d7 42 ♜1a3 ♝f5 43 ♜a8 ♜xa8 44 ♜xa8 ♚d7 45 g3** 45 e6+! +− **hxg3 46 hxg3 ♝c7 47 ♞d4 ♝d3 48 ♜a7 ♚c8 49 ♞c6 f6 1-0**

229 A.Rodriguez-Kochiev
Mexico 78

1 e4 c5 2 ♘f3 e6 3 d4 cxd4 4 ♘xd4 a6 5 ♗d3 ♘e7!? 6 0-0 ♘ec6!? 6...♘bc6 7 ♘xc6 ♘xc6 8 ♕g4!? ♘e5 9 ♕g3 ♘xd3 10 cxd3 += Bednarski-Banas, CSSR 72; 7 ♗e3 **7 ♘b3** 7 ♘xc6!? **♗e7 8 ♘c3** 8 f4 d6 9 ♘1d2 ♘d7 10 ♘f3± Kurajica-Popov, Butumi 66 **0-0 9 f4 d6 10 ♗e3 ♘d7 11 ♕e2** 11 ♕f3 **b6 12 ♖ad1** 12 a3!? **♘b4 13 e5!?** 13 ♘d4 ♗b7 14 a3!? ♘xd3 15 cxd3 Δ f5 **♘xd3 14 ♖xd3?!** 14 exd6 ♗xd6!? 15 ♕xd3 ♗e7; 15...♗c7; 14 ♘3c5!? **dxe5 15 fxe5 ♕c7 16 ♗f4 ♗b7 17 ♖h3!? ♖fd8 18 ♘d2 ♘f8 19 ♘de4 ♖d4 20 ♗g5** 20 ♘d6!? **♗xe4! 21 ♗xe7** 21 ♘xe4? ♖xe4 **♗f5 22 ♗d6 ♕c6 23 ♖g3 ♖c4 =+ 24 ♕d2 ♖c8 25 h3 ♘g6 26 ♖gf3** Δ g4 **h5 27 ♕f2 ♘h4 28 ♖e3** 28 ♖g3 ♗g6 Δ ♘f5 **♖f4!∓ 29 ♕e2 ♖xf1+ 30 ♕xf1 ♗xc2 31 g4?! hxg4 32 hxg4 ♕c4 33 ♕e2 ♕f4 34 ♖h3 ♖c4 −+ 35 ♔h1** 35 ♕xc2 ♕xg4+ 36 ♔h2 ♘f3+ 37 ♖xf3 ♕xf3 Δ ♖h4+; 35 ♖xh4 ♕g3+ **♗e4+! 36 ♔g1 ♘f3+ 0-1 Speelman**

230 Honfi-Diesen Stip 78

1 e4 c5 2 ♘f3 e6 3 d4 cxd4 4 ♘xd4 a6 5 ♗d3 ♘f6 6 0-0 d6 7 c4 ♕c7 8 b3 g6 9 ♗b2 ♗g7 10 ♕e2 ♘bd7 11 ♘c3 0-0 12 ♖ad1 b6 13 ♗b1 ♗b7 14 ♔h1 ♖ad8 15 f4 ♕b8? 15...e5 16 fxe5 ♘xe5 17 ♘d5+ = **16 ♘f3 ♘h5 17 f5**

Diagram

17...♖fe8?! 18 ♕f2 ♘hf6 19 ♕h4 ♖e7?! 20 fxg6 fxg6 21 e5! dxe5 21...♘xe5 22 ♘xe5 dxe5 23 ♖xf6! ♗xf6 24 ♕xf6 ♖xd1+ 25 ♘xd1 ♖f7 26 ♕xe6 ♗c8 27 ♕d5 ♗b7 28 ♕d3 +− **22 ♘e4 ♖f8? 23 ♗a3 ♗xe4 24 ♗xe7 ♗xb1 25 ♗xf8 ♕xf8 26 ♖xb1 1-0 Honfi**

2...e6, 4...♘c6

231 Jansa-Janosevic
Smed Palanka 78

1 e4 c5 2 ♘f3 ♘c6 3 d4 cxd4 4 ♘xd4 ♕c7 5 ♘c3 e6 6 ♗e2 a6 7 0-0 ♘f6 8 ♔h1 d6 9 f4 ♗d7 10 ♗e3 ♗e7 11 ♕e1 b5 12 a3 0-0 13 ♕g3 ♘xd4 14 ♗xd4 ♗c6 15 ♖ae1 ♕b7 16 ♗d3 ♖ad8?! 16...b4 17 axb4 ♕xb4 18 ♘e2 ♕b7 19 e5 ♘h5 20 ♕h3 g6 21 ♘g3 dxe5 22 ♗xe5 ♘g7 23 ♗c3 f6?! 24 ♗c4 Sax-Jansa, Budapest 76; 17 ♘d1!? g6 18 ♘f2 bxa3 19 bxa3 d5 20 e5 ♘e4 21 ♗xe4 dxe4 22 ♘g4 ♖fd8 23 ♘h6 Sznapik-Smejkal, Sandomierz 76; 16...g6 **17 ♕h3 ♘e8? 18 ♘d5! g6** 18...exd5 **19 ♖e3! e5** 19...exd5 20 ♕xh7+ +− **20 fxe5 ♗xd5 21 exd5 ♕xd5 22 ♗c3 dxe5 23 ♖xe5 ♕d7 24 ♕xh7+ 1-0**

232 Hardicsay-Regan
Budapest 78

1 e4 c5 2 ♘f3 e6 3 d4 cxd4 4 ♘xd4 ♘f6 5 ♘c3 ♘c6 6 ♘db5 ♗b4 6...d6 **7 a3 ♗xc3+ 8 ♘xc3 d5 9 exd5 ♘xd5** 9...exd5± **10 ♗d2 ♕h4 11 ♕f3! ♘d4 12 ♕d3 e5?!** 12...♘f4 13 ♕e4 +−

13 ♘xd5 ♗f5 14 ♕c3! 14 ♕c4? ♘xc2+ −+; 14 ♘c7+ ♔d7!∓ **♕e4+** 14...♖c8 15 ♗b5+!! ♔d8 16 ♕a5+ b6 17 ♕xa7 +−; 15...♘xb5 16 ♕xe5+ +−; 14... 0-0! 15 ♘e3 ♖fe8 16 ♕b4 a5!≈ **15 ♘e3 ♖c8 16 ♗d3 ♖xc3** 16...♘f3+ 17 ♔d1 +− **17 ♗xe4 ♖xe3+ 18 fxe3 ♗xe4 19 exd4 1-0 Hardicsay**

233 Nunn-Zapata
Buenos Aires 78

1 e4 c5 2 ♘f3 e6 3 d4 cxd4 4 ♘xd4 d6!? 5 c4 ♘c6 6 ♘c3 ♘f6 7 ♗e2 ♗e7 8 0-0 0-0 9 ♗e3 ♗d7 10 f4 += ♘xd4 10...a6 11 ♕e1 ♕b8 12 ♕g3 ♖c8 13 ♖ad1 ♘xd4 14 ♗xd4 ♗c6 15 ♔h1 g6 16 e5 += Nunn-Zapata, Mexico 77; 13 ♘f3! **11 ♗xd4 ♗c6 12 ♗d3 ♕d7** Δ 13...e5 14 fxe5 dxe5 15 ♗xe5 ♘g4 **13 f5! a6** 13...exf5 14 ♖xf5; 13...e5 14 ♗e3 Δ g4-g5 **14 a4 ♖fe8 15 b4!± exf5 16 ♖xf5 ♗d8 17 ♕f3 ♕e6 18 ♖f1?!** 18 ♖e1! (Δ b5) b6 19 ♘d5± **♘xe4?** 18...♗xe4! 19 ♘xe4 ♘xe4 20 ♖xf7? ♗f6 21 ♗xf6 ♕xf7 22 ♗xe4 ♕xf6 23 ♕xf6 gxf6 24 ♗xb7 ♖a7 25 ♗d5+ ♔g7 =+; 21 ♖xf6 ♘xf6! 22 ♗xf6 gxf6 Δ ♕e3+∓; 20 ♗xg7? ♘g5! 21 ♕h5 ♔xg7 22 ♖xg5+∓; 20 ♖e1? ♘g5 −+; 20 ♖f4! ♘d2 21 ♕xb7 ∝/+=?

19 b5! 19 ♘xe4 ♗xe4 20 ♖xf7? ♗xf3? 21 ♖xg7+ ♔h8 22 ♖xh7+ ♔g8 23 ♖h8+ ♔f7 24 ♖xf3+ ♗f6 25 ♖h7+ ♔g8 26 ♖xf6 +−; 21...♔f8 22 ♖xf3+ ♗f6 23 ♖xf6+ +−; 20...♗f6! 21 ♖xf6 ♕xf6! 22 ♕xe4 ♖xe4 23 ♗xf6 ♖e3! =+ **axb5 20 cxb5 ♘xc3?** 20...♘d2 21 ♕g3 f6 22 bxc6 ♘xf1 23 cxb7? ♘xg3 24 bxa8♕ ♘xf5 −+; 23 ♖xf1! bxc6 24 ♕h4±; 21 ♕h5?! ♘xf1 22 ♖xf1 h6 23 bxc6 bxc6 24 ♗f5 ♕c4 25 ♕g4 ♗g5!∝ **21 bxc6 ♘e4** 21...♘e2+ 22 ♗xe2 ♕xe2 23 ♕xe2 ♖xe2 24 cxb7 ♖b8 25 ♖b1 +− **22 cxb7 ♖b8 23 ♖b5 +− ♘c5? 24 ♕g3!** Δ ♗xc5 **♗f6 25 ♗xf6 ♕e3+ 26 ♕xe3 ♖xe3 27 ♗d4 ♖xd3 28 ♗xc5 dxc5 29 ♖xc5 ♔f8 30 ♖c8+ ♖d8 31 ♖xd8+ ♖xd8 32 a5 1-0 Nunn**

2...e6, 4...♘f6

234 Mednis-Malich
Budapest 78

1 e4 c5 2 ♘f3 e6 3 d4 cxd4 4 ♘xd4 ♘f6 5 ♘c3 d6 6 ♗e2 ♗e7 7 0-0 0-0 8 f4 ♘c6 9 ♗e3 ♘xd4 10 ♗xd4 10 ♕xd4 b6 11 e5 dxe5 12 fxe5 ♕xd4 13 ♗xd4 ♘fd7 14 ♗f3 ♖b8 15 ♘b5 ♗c5! N = Neikirch-Malich, DDR 77 **b6 11 ♕d3!?** 11 ♕e1 Δ ♕g3 += **♗b7 12 ♖ad1 ♕c8!?** N 12...♖c8 Δ ♖xc3!?≈ **13 ♕g3 ♖d8 14 ♔h1 ♗c6** Δ b5/♕b7 **15 f5! e5 16 ♗e3 b5!? 17 ♗h6 ♗f8 18 ♗g5! ♗e7 19 ♗h6?!** 19 a3! ♖b8! 20 ♗xf6 ♗xf6 21 b4! a6 22 ♖d2 h6 23 ♖fd1 ♕c7 += **♗f8 20 ♗g5 ♗e7 ½-½ Malich**

235 Emerson-Nicholson
England 78

1 e4 c5 2 ♘f3 e6 3 d4 cxd4 4 ♘xd4 ♘f6 5 ♘c3 d6 6 g4 a6 7 g5 ♘fd7 8 ♗e3 b5 9 a3 9 ♗g2 **♘b6 10 h4 ♘8d7 11 h5 ♗b7** 11...♘e5!? **12 ♖h3! ♘c5?!**

12...♕e7 13 g6 0-0-0 14 gxf7 ♕xf7 15 ♕g4 ♖e8 16 ♖f3 ♘e5 17 ♖xf7 ♘xg4 18 ♗h3 ♘xe3 19 fxe3 ♔b8 20 ♗xe6± Emerson-Pritchett, England 77; 12...♘e5 13 g6 hxg6 14 hxg6 ♖xh3 15 gxf7+ ♘xf7 16 ♗xh3 ♘c4? 17 ♗xe6± Torre-Vogt 77; 16...♕h4 17 ♕g4 ♕xg4 18 ♗xg4 ♘c4 += **13 g6 hxg6 14 hxg6 ♖xh3 15 gxf7+ ♔xf7 16 ♗xh3 ♘c4?!** 16...♕h4!? **17 ♕h5+ g6 18 ♕h7+ ♗g7 19 ♘xe6± ♘xe6 20 ♗xe6+ ♔xe6 21 ♕xg7 ♘xe3 22 ♕xg6+ ♕f6 23 ♕xf6+ ♔xf6 24 fxe3 ♔e5 25 0-0-0 ♗xe4** 25...♖h8 26 ♖g1 +− **26 ♘xe4 ♔xe4 27 ♖xd6 ♔xe3 28 b4! ♔e4** 28...a5 29 bxa5 [29 ♖b6? axb4 30 axb4 ♔d4 31 ♖xb5 ♔c3=] ♖xa5 30 ♔b2 ♔e4 31 ♔b3 ♔d5 32 ♖d8 ♖a4 33 ♖b8 ♖a5 34 ♔b4 ♖a4+ 35 ♔xb5 ♖xa3 36 ♔b4 ♖a2 37 ♔b3 ♖a1 38 ♖d8 +− **29 ♔b2 ♔e5 30 ♖b6 ♔d5 31 ♔b3 ♖a7 32 a4 bxa4+ 33 ♔xa4 ♖a8 34 ♔a5 ♖c8 35 ♔xa6 ♖xc2 36 ♖b7 ♖a2+ 37 ♔b6 ♔d6 38 b5 ♖a1 39 ♖b8 ♔d7 40 ♔b7 ♖h1 41 ♖c8 ♖b1 42 ♖c7+ ♔d6 43 b6 ♖b2 44 ♖c1 ♖h2 45 ♔a7 ♖a2+ 46 ♔b8 1-0 Povah**

236 Pokojowczyk-Sznapik Lodz 78

1 e4 c5 2 ♘f3 d6 3 d4 cxd4 4 ♘xd4 ♘f6 5 ♘c3 e6 6 g4 a6 7 g5 ♘fd7 8 ♗e3 b5 9 a3 9 a4!? b4 10 ♘a2 ♗b7 11 ♗g2 ♘c5 12 ♘xb4 ♘xe4 13 ♕g4 += Smyslov-Vogt, Leningrad 77 **♗b7?!** 9...♘b6 **10 h4 ♘b6 11 h5 ♘8d7 12 ♖h3!** 12 ♖g1 g6 =+ **♗e7?!** 12...♘e5 13 g6 hxg6 14 hxg6 ♖xh3 15 gxf7+ ♘xf7 16 ♗xh3 Torre-Vogt, Polanica Zdroj 77 ♕h4 17 ♕g4 ♕xg4 18 ♗xg4 ♘c4 += **13 g6 ♗f6 14 ♕g4 ♕e7 15 gxf7+ ♔xf7 16 0-0-0± ♖hc8** 16...♘e5? 17 ♕xe6+ **17 f4 ♖xc3!? 18 bxc3 ♖c8 19 f5 e5 20 ♘e6 d5 21 ♗g5 ♕xa3+ 22 ♔d2 ♖g8 23 h6 g6 24 ♗xf6 ♘xf6 25 ♘g5+ ♔e7?** 25...♔e8 26 ♕h4± **26 ♕h4 ♔e8**

27 ♘xh7!! ♘xh7 27...♘xe4+ 28 ♔e1 ♕e7 29 ♕xe7+ ♔xe7 30 fxg6 ♖xg6 31 ♘f8 +− **28 fxg6 ♖xg6 29 ♕h5 ♕d6 30 ♖g3 ♔f7 31 ♕f5+ ♖f6 32 ♕xh7+ 1-0 Webb**

237 Westerinen-Sigurjonsson
Skien 78

1 e4 c5 2 ♘f3 d6 3 d4 cxd4 4 ♘xd4 ♘f6 5 ♘c3 e6 6 g4 ♘c6 7 g5 ♘d7 8 ♗g2 a6 9 0-0 ♗e7 10 f4 0-0 11 ♘f3!? b5 12 b3 ♗b7 13 ♕e2 ♖e8 14 ♗b2 ♖c8 15 ♖ae1 ♘c5∝ 16 ♕f2 b4 17 ♘d1 d5 18 exd5 exd5 19 ♕h4 ♘e4 =+ 20 ♔h1 ♗c5 21 f5 ♕d6 22 ♕g4 a5 23 ♘h4 ♗a6? 23...♘e5!∓ **24 g6! hxg6?** 24...♘e5!∝ **25 fxg6 fxg6 26 ♗xe4??** 26 ♘xg6! (Δ ♕h5) ♗xf1 27 ♖xf1 ♘e7 28 ♗xe4 dxe4 29 ♘f8!! ♕h6 30 ♖f6!! +− **♗xf1! 27 ♗xg6 ♖xe1!! −+ 28 ♗h7+ ♔f8 29 ♕xc8+ ♘d8 30 ♕f5+ ♕f6! 0-1 Pytel**

238 Bordonada-Adamski
Buenos Aires 78

1 e4 c5 2 ♘f3 d6 3 d4 cxd4 4 ♘xd4 ♘f6 5 ♘c3 e6 6 g4 h6! 6...♘c6 7 g5 ♘d7 8 ♗e3 a6 9 ♖g1 ♕c7 10 f4 b5 11 a3 ♖b8 12 ♕d2 ♘c5 13 b4? (13

♘xc6 ♕xc6 14 ♗g2) 13...♘xd4 14 ♕xd4 ♘d7 15 ♖d1 ♗b7 16 ♗h3 ♖c8 17 ♖d3 ♕b8!∓ Sax-Tringov, Osijek 78 **7 ♖g1** 7 g5 hxg5 8 ♗xg5 ♘c6 9 ♕d2 ♕b6 10 ♘b3 a6 11 0-0-0 ♗d7 12 f4 ♗e7 13 h4 ♕c7 14 ♗e2 0-0-0 15 h5 ♔b8 16 ♕e3!± Spassky-Ribli, Manila 76 **♘c6 8 ♗e3 a6 9 f4!?** 9 ♗e2 ♗d7 10 h4 ♘xd4 11 ♗xd4!? Gipslis **♘xd4 10 ♕xd4 e5! 11 ♕d1** 11 fxe5 ♘xg4∓ **exf4 12 ♗xf4 ♗e6 13 h3 ♕a5 14 ♕d4 d5! 15 exd5 ♗c5**

16 ♗b5+! ♕xb5! 17 ♘xb5 ♗xd4 18 ♘xd4 ♘xd5 19 ♗e5 0-0 20 0-0-0 += ♔h7 21 ♖g3 ♖ad8 22 g5 ♗c8 23 gxh6 g6 24 ♗g7 ♖fe8 25 ♖f1 f6 26 ♖fg1 ♘f4 27 ♗xf6 ♖xd4 28 ♗xd4 ♘e2+ 29 ♔d1 ♘xd4? 29...♘xg1 30 ♗xg1 ♔xh6 += **30 c3 ♘f5 31 ♖xg6 ♗e6 32 ♖f6 ♘e3+ 33 ♔c1 ♗xa2 34 ♖g7+ ♔h8 35 ♖xb7 ♖d8?** Zeitnot 35...♗c4± **36 b3 +− ♗xb3 37 ♖xb3 ♖d1+ 38 ♔b2 ♘c4+ 39 ♔c2 ♘e3+ 40 ♔b2 ♘c4+ 41 ♔a2 ♖d2+ 42 ♔a1 ♖d1+ 43 ♖b1 ♖d5 44 ♖b8+ ♔h7 45 ♖b7+ ♔g8 46 ♖g7+ ♔h8 47 ♖f8 mate 1-0 Filipowicz**

239 Mednis-J.Fernandez
Budapest 78

1 e4 c5 2 ♘f3 d6 3 d4 cxd4 4 ♘xd4 ♘f6 5 ♘c3 e6 6 g4 h6 7 g5 hxg5 8 ♗xg5 ♘c6 9 ♕d2 ♕b6 10 ♘b3 a6 11 0-0-0 ♕c7 11...♗d7 12 f4?! (12 h4! +=) 0-0-0 13 ♗g2 ♗e7 14 ♔b1 ♘g4! 15 ♗xe7 ♘xe7 16 ♕xd6 ♕xd6 17 ♖xd6 ♘g6 18 f5 ♘6e5 =+ Mednis-Jansa, Kragujevac 77 **12 ♗g2!?** N 12 f4 += **♗d7** 12...b5? 13 e5! +−; 12...♘e5 13 f4 ♘c4 14 ♕e2 ♗d7 15 ♖d3 ♖c8 16 h4 += **13 f4 0-0-0 14 h4 ♗e7 15 ♗f3 += g6** 15...♔b8 16 h5 +=; 15...♘h5 16 f5! += **16 ♕f2 ♘g8** 16...♘h5 17 f5! += **17 ♗xe7 ♘gxe7 18 ♔b1 ♔b8 19 ♕g3! += ♗c8 20 ♕g5 ♖h7 21 ♖d2 ♕b6?!** 21...♖dh8 22 ♖hd1 ♖xh4 23 ♖xd6 +=; 21...b5!? += **22 ♖hd1 ♕e3?!** 22...♕c7 += **23 ♕g3! e5?** 23...♔c7∓ **24 fxe5! ♘xe5 25 ♖xd6! +− ♖xd6 26 ♖xd6!** 26 ♕xe5?! ♘f5! 27 ♖xd6 ♘xd6 28 ♕xd6+± **♘7c6** 26...♕xf3 27 ♕xe5; 26...♘f5 27 exf5 ♗xf5 28 ♘d1 **27 ♖xc6 ♖h5** 27...bxc6 28 ♕xe5+ +− **28 ♖f6 1-0** 28...♗g4 29 ♘d1 **Mednis**

240 Chiburdanidze-Erenska
Buenos Aires 78

1 e4 c5 2 ♘f3 e6 3 d4 cxd4 4 ♘xd4 ♘f6 5 ♘c3 d6 6 g4 h6 7 g5 hxg5 8 ♗xg5 ♘c6 9 ♕d2 ♕b6 10 ♘b3 ♘e5 11 ♕e2 11 ♗e2 **♗d7 12 0-0-0 ♖c8 13 f4 ♘c4 14 ♖d4 ♘a5 15 ♕d2 ♘xb3+ 16 axb3± ♘g4!?** Δ f6 **17 ♗e2 ♘f2 18 ♖f1 ♖xh2?** 18...♘h3!∝ **19 f5! e5 20 ♖c4 ♖xc4 21 ♗xc4 ♗c6** 21...♕d4 22 ♕e2; 21...♘g4 22 ♕d5 **22 ♘d5 ♘xe4** 22...♕d4 23 ♕a5! **23 ♕xh2 ♗xd5 24 ♗xd5 ♘xg5 25 ♔b1 ♕c7 26 ♕g1 ♕c5 27 ♕xc5 dxc5 28 ♗xb7 +− ♔d7 29 c3 ♔c7 30 ♗d5 ♗e7 31 ♔c2 f6 32 ♖a1 ♔b6 33 ♖h1 ♔c7 34 ♖h8 ♔d6 35 c4 e4 36 ♔d2 ♘f3+ 37 ♔e3 ♘d4 38 ♔xe4 ♘xb3 39 ♖b8 ♘d2+ 40 ♔d3 ♘f1 41 ♖b7 ♘g3 42 ♗e6 ♗f8 43 ♖f7 ♗e7 44 ♖xg7 ♘h5**

45 Rg4 Bf8 46 Ke4 Kc6 47 Bf7 Ng7 48 Rg6 Kd6 49 Rg1 Kc6 50 Ra1 Kb6 51 Rh1 1-0 Gipslis

241 Ciocaltea-Giffard
Buenos Aires 78
1 e4 c5 2 Nf3 e6 3 d4 cxd4 4 Nxd4 Nf6 5 Bd3 5 Nc3 Bb4?! 6 e5 Nd5 (6...Ne4 7 Qg4±) 7 Bd2 Nxc3 8 bxc3 Bf8 (8...Ba5) 9 Rb1!? a6 10 Bd3 Qc7 11 f4 Nc6 12 0-0 b5 13 a4!± Westerinen-Gruchacz, Lone Pine 78 **Nc6 6 Nxc6?!** 6 Be3 d5 **dxc6** 6...bxc6 7 c4 d5 8 cxd5 cxd5 9 Nc3 dxe4 10 Bb5+! Krudsen-Ligterink, Haifa 76; 7 0-0 d5 8 Nd2 Be7 **7 f4?!** 7 0-0; 7 Nc3 **e5 8 f5?** 8 0-0 Bc5+ 9 Kh1 Ng4∓; 8 Nc3 **Nxe4! 9 Qf3** 9 Bxe4 Qh4+ −+ **Nf6 10 Nc3 Qb6 11 Qg3**

11...Be7! 12 a3 0-0 13 Bh6 Nh5 14 Qg4 Qxb2 15 Kd2 Qb6 16 Rhf1 16 Qxh5 gxh6 17 Qxh6 Qf2+ −+ **Rd8 17 Rab1 Qd4 18 Qxh5 gxh6 19 f6 Bf8 20 Rf3 Bg4 0-1** 21 Rg3 Qf4+ 22 Ke1 Qxg3+ 23 hxg3 Bxh5 −+ **Ciocaltea**

2...Nf6

242 Pritchett-E.Gonzalez
Buenos Aires 78
1 e4 c5 2 Nf3 Nf6 3 e5 Nd5 4 Nc3 e6 5 Nxd5 exd5 6 d4 Nc6 7 dxc5 Bxc5 8 Qxd5 Qb6 9 Bc4 Bxf2+ 10 Ke2 0-0 11 Rf1 Bc5 12 Ng5 Nd4+ 13 Kd1 Ne6 14 Ne4 d6 15 exd6 Rd8 15...Bxd6? 16 Nxd6 Rd8 17 Bf4! Nxf4 18 Qxf7+ Kh8 19 Qg8+ +− **16 Bd3 Bxd6 17 Qh5** 17 Nxd6 Qxd6 18 Qxd6 Rxd6 19 Be3 b6 =/+= **f5 18 Nxd6 Qxd6** 18...Rxd6 19 Qxf5! Rxd3+ 20 cxd3 +− Levy, Unzicker; 18...g6? 19 Nxc8 +− **19 Qxf5!** ±/+− **Qxh2 20 Qf7+ Kh8 21 Bg5! Rg8 22 Be3!** Δ Kd2, Rae1 **Rd8** 22...Qxg2 23 Rf2! Qg1+ 24 Kd2 Qxa1 Rh2 h6 26 Rxh6+ +−; 23...Qg4+ 24 Kd2 Ng5 25 Rh1! h6 26 Rxh6+ gxh6 27 Qf6+ Rg7 28 Qf8+ +−; 22...Nd8 23 Qf2 ±/+− **23 Kd2 Qxg2+** 23...Bd7 24 Rae1 ±/+− **24 Rf2 Ng5** 24...Qg6 25 Qf3 ±/+− **25 Qxg7+** 25 Qe7? Ne4+ 26 Ke1 Qg1+ 27 Bf1 **1-0** 25...Kxg7 26 Rxg2 h6 27 Bxg5 hxg5 28 Rxg5+ Kf6 29 Rg6+ Kf7 30 Rf1+ Ke7 31 Rh1 +− **Pritchett**

Caro-Kann

243 Pytel-Amram
Val Thorens 78
1 e4 c6 2 Nc3 d5 3 Nf3 dxe4 4 Nxe4 Bg4 5 Bc4 e6 6 h3 Bxf3 7 Qxf3 Nf6 8 Nxf6+ Qxf6 9 Qxf6 gxf6 10 b3! += Nd7 11 Bb2 Bg7? 11...Rg8 **12 f4!± Nb6 13 Be2 h5 14 f5 0-0-0 15 0-0-0 h4 16 fxe6 fxe6 17 Rhf1 Rdg8?! 18 Bxf6 Bxf6 19 Rxf6 Nd5?** 19...Rxg2 **20 Rf2! +− e5 21 Re1 Kb8 22 Bg4 Re8 23 Re4 Rh6 24 d4 Nf6 25 Rxe5 Rxe5 26 dxe5 Nxg4 27 hxg4 Rg6 28 Rf4 Kc7 29 Kd2 Kd7 30 Ke3 Ke6 31 Rf6+ 1-0 Pytel**

244 Eperjesi-Mihalchishin
Pazardjik 78
1 e4 c6 2 d4 d5 3 ♘c3 uxe4 4 ♘xe4 ♘d7 5 ♗c4 ♘gf6 6 ♘xf6+ ♘xf6 7 ♘f3 ♗f5 8 ♘e5 e6 9 g4 ♗g6 10 h4 10 c3 ♗d6 11 ♕e2 ♗e4 12 ♖g1 ♗d5 13 ♗d3 b5 14 b3 ♕a5 15 ♗d2 ♕b6 16 ♖c1 b4 17 ♘c4 ♗xc4 18 bxc4 bxc3 19 ♗xc3 ♗b4! 20 ♗xb4 ♕xb4+ 21 ♔f1! ♕d6 22 g5 ♘d7 23 ♗e4 Tabakov-Inkiov, Sofia 78 **♘d7 11 ♗f4 ♘xe5 12 ♗xe5 h5 13 g5 ♕b6 14 ♗b3 a5 15 a4 c5 16 ♕d2 cxd4 17 ♗xd4 ♕c6! 18 0-0-0 ♗b4 19 ♕e3 ♖c8 20 c3 ♗c5**

21 ♗xe6? 21 ♗xc5! ♕xc5 22 ♕xc5 ♖xc5 23 ♖d6 ♔e7= **0-0!∓ 22 ♗xc5 ♕xa4! 23 ♔d2 ♖xc5 24 ♕xc5 ♖d8+ 25 ♗d5 ♕e4! 26 ♕e3 ♖xd5+ 27 ♔e2 ♕c2+ 0-1** 28 ♖d2 ♖xd2+ 29 ♕xd2 ♕e4+ +− **Mechkarov**

245 Chiburdanidze-J.Miles
Buenos Aires 78
1 e4 c6 2 d4 d5 3 ♘d2 dxe4 4 ♘xe4 ♗f5 5 ♘g3 ♗g6 6 ♘f3 ♘d7 7 h4 h6 8 h5 ♗h7 9 ♗d3 ♗xd3 10 ♕xd3 ♘gf6 11 ♗d2 ♕c7 12 0-0-0 12 c4 e6 13 ♕e2 ♗d6 14 ♘f5 ♗f4∝; 12 ♕e2 e6 13 c4 ♗d6 14 ♘f5 0-0-0 15 ♘xd6+ ♕xd6 16 ♗a5± **e6 13 c4** 13 ♕e2 c5!? 14 ♖h4 c4 15 d5! ♘xd5 16 ♖xc4; 14...♖c8∝ **0-0-0 14 ♕e2 c5 15 ♗c3 ♗d6 16 ♘e4 ♘xe4 17 ♕xe4 ♘f6 18 ♕e2 += cxd4 19 ♘xd4 ♗c5** 19...a6 **20 g3 ♕b6?! 21 ♘b3! ♕c6** 21...♗xf2? 22 c5! ♗xc5 23 ♕c4 +− **22 f3± ♖xd1+ 23 ♖xd1 ♖d8 24 ♖xd8+ ♔xd8 25 ♘xc5 ♕xc5 26 g4 ♔e7 27 ♔c2 g6?** 27...♘e8! Δ f6, e5 **28 b4 ♕c6 29 b5 ♕c5 30 ♔b3 +− ♕c7 31 ♗b4+ ♔d7 32 ♕d2+ ♔c8 33 hxg6 fxg6 34 ♕xh6 ♕d7 35 ♕e3 b6 36 ♔c2 1-0 Gipslis**

246 Radulov-Makropoulos
Balkaniad 78
1 e4 c6 2 d4 d5 3 ♘c3 dxe4 4 ♘xe4 ♘f6 5 ♘xf6+ exf6 6 c3 6 ♗c4 ♕e7+ 7 ♕e2 ♗e6 8 ♗b3! += **♗d6 7 ♗d3 0-0 8 ♘e2 ♖e8 9 ♕c2 g6 10 0-0** 10 ♗h6! Δ 0-0-0 Maric; 10 h4!∝ **♕c7 11 h3 ♘d7 12 ♗e3?!** 12 ♗h6 Maric **f5! 13 ♕d2 ♘f6 14 c4 ♘h5!=** Maric **15 f4?** 15 c5? ♗h2+! 16 ♔h1 f4!∓; 15 ♗h6!∝ **♗d7 16 g3 c5 =+** Maric **17 d5 b5! 18 b3** 18 cxb5? c4 19 ♖ac1 ♖xe3! 20 ♕xe3 ♗c5 21 ♘d4 cxd3 −+ Maric **b4 19 ♖ae1 ♘f6∓ 20 ♔g2 h5 21 ♘g1?** 21 h4 ♘g4 22 ♘g1 ♗f8 (Δ ♗g7-d4∓ Maric) 23 ♗f2! ♗g7 24 ♖xe8+ ♖xe8 25 ♖e1 =+ **h4!∓ 22 gxh4 ♘h5 23 ♗e2** 23 ♘e2 ♖e7 Δ ♖ae8∓

23...♖xe3!! 24 ♕xe3 ♖e8 25 ♕f2 ♘xf4+ 26 ♔h1 ♔g7 27 h5 ♖h8 28 ♕e3 28 hxg6 ♘xh3 **♘xh5 29 ♗xh5 ♖xh5 30 ♖e2 g5! 31 ♕d2 ♕c8 32 ♕b2+ f6 33 ♖fe1 f4! −+ 34 ♖e6 ♗xe6 35 ♖xe6** 35 dxe6 ♗e5 Maric **♗e5 36 ♕e2 ♖h8 37 ♘f3 ♖xh3+ 38 ♔g2 g4!! 0-1** 39 ♘xe5 f3+ −+ **Gheorghiu**

247 Liu Wen Che-Ciocaltea
Buenos Aires 78

1 e4 g6 2 d4 c6 3 ♘c3 ♗g7 4 f4 d5 5 e5 h5 6 ♘f3 ♗g4 7 ♗e2 e6 8 0-0 8 ♗e3 ♘h6 9 ♕d2 (9 g3!?) ♘f5 10 ♗f2 ♘d7 11 0-0 c5?! 12 dxc5 ♘xc5? 13 ♗b5+ ♘d7 14 ♘g5!± Suetin-Timman, 75; 9...♘d7 10 g3 ♗f8 11 ♗f2? ♗b4!= Gipslis-Ubilava, Tbilisi 74 **♘h6 9 ♗e3 ♘f5** 9...♗f8 10 h3 ♘f5 11 ♗f2 ♗xf3 12 ♗xf3 h4 13 ♘e2 += ♘d7?!± Klovan-Podgaets, USSR 74 **10 ♗f2** 10 ♕d2 ♘d7 11 h3?! ♗xf3 12 ♗xf3 ♕a5! 13 a3 ♗f8 14 b4 ♕d8 15 ♗f2 ♘b6 =+ Rossman-Uhlmann, DDR Final 74 **♗h6** N **11 ♕d2 ♘d7 12 b4?** 12 ♘g5!= **♘b6!** Δ ♗xf3, ♘c4 **13 ♘d1 ♗xf3 14 ♗xf3 ♘c4∓ 15 ♕c1 g5** 15...a5!? **16 ♘e3!** 16 ♗xh5 gxf4∓ **♘cxe3!** 16...gxf4 17 ♘xc4 dxc4 **17 ♗xe3 gxf4 18 ♗xf4 ♕b6! 19 c3** 19 ♗xh6 ♕xd4+ **♘xd4! 20 ♔h1** 20 ♗xh6? ♘e2+ −+ **♗xf4 21 ♕xf4 ♘f5 22 ♖ae1 0-0-0 23 a4 a5! 24 ♖b1 ♕e3 25 ♕xe3 ♘xe3 26 ♖fe1 ♘c2 27 ♖e2 ♘a3 28 ♖a1 ♘c4 29 bxa5 ♘xa5 30 ♔g1 ♔c7 31 ♔f2 ♘c4** Zeitnot **32 h4 ♖a8 33 ♔g3 ♘b6 34 ♔f4 ♘d7 35 a5 ♘c5 36 ♖a3 ♖af8 37 ♖d2 f6! 38 exf6 ♖xf6+ 39 ♔e5 ♖f5+ 40 ♔d4 ♖f4+! 41 ♔e3** 41 ♔xc5? ♖c4 mate **♖xh4 42 ♖d4 ♖h1! 43 ♖f4** 43 g4 ♖h3! 44 gxh5 e5! Δ e4 −+ **♖h7 44 ♖f8 h4 45 c4 h3! 46 gxh3 ♖1xh3 47 cxd5 exd5 48 ♔f2 ♖g7! 49 ♖e3 ♖h2+ 50 ♔f1 ♖a2 51 ♖a8 ♖f7 52 ♔g1 d4 53 ♖e2 ♖xe2 54 ♗xe2 d3 55 ♗d1 ♖e7 56 ♔f2 d2 57 ♗g4 ♘e4+ 0-1** 58 ♔f1 ♖d7! 59 ♗d1 ♘c3 −+ **Ciocaltea**

248 Gaprindashvili-Chiburdanidze (6) 78

1 e4 c6 2 d4 d5 3 exd5 cxd5 4 c4 ♘f6 5 ♘c3 ♘c6 6 cxd5 ♘xd5 7 ♘f3 ♗g4 8 ♕b3 8 ♗b5 ♕a5 9 ♕b3 ♗xf3 10 gxf3 ♘xc3 11 ♗xc6+ bxc6 12 ♕b7? ♘d5+! 13 ♗d2 ♕b6 14 ♕xa8+ ♔d7 15 0-0 ♘c7 Nimzovich-Alekhine 31; 11 bxc3 e6 12 d5! exd5 13 0-0 **♗xf3 9 gxf3 e6 10 ♕xb7 ♘xd4 11 ♗b5+ ♘xb5 12 ♕c6+ ♔e7 13 ♕xb5 ♕d7** 13...♘xc3 14 bxc3 ♕d5 15 ♖b1 ♖d8 16 ♗e3 ♕xb5 17 ♖xb5± Cortlever-Karaklaic, Wijk aan Zee 72; 14...♕d7 15 ♖b1!± Fischer-Euwe, Leipzig 60 **14 ♕a5** 14 ♘xd5+ ♕xd5 15 ♕xd5 exd5 16 0-0 ♔e6 17 ♖e1+ ♔f5 18 ♗e3 ♗e7= Smejkal-Filip, CSSR 68 **♘xc3 15 bxc3 f6 16 ♖b1 ♔f7 17 ♕a6 ♗e7 18 ♖b7 ♕d5 19 ♗a3 ♖he8 20 0-0 ♕xf3 21 ♖fb1 ♖ad8 22 ♕xa7 ♕g4+ 23 ♔f1 ♕h3+ 24 ♔g1 ½-½**

249 Gheorghiu-Onat Balkaniad 78

1 e4 c6 2 d4 d5 3 exd5 cxd5 4 c4 ♘f6 5 ♘c3 ♘c6 5...e6 6 ♘f3 ♗e7 7 cxd5 +=; 6...♘c6 7 c5! += **6 ♗g5! += ♕a5** 6...dxc4 7 d5± Bronstein **7 ♕d2!± e5! 8 dxe5 ♘e4!** 8...d4 9 exf6 dxc3 10 bxc3± **9 ♘xe4 ♗b4 10 ♘c3 d4 11 ♘ge2 dxc3 12 bxc3!** 12 ♘xc3? ♕xe5+ 13 ♗e2 ♘d4!∓ **♗c5 13 ♘c1!** Δ ♘b3 **♗b6** 13...♘xe5?? 14 ♘b3 ♕b6 15 ♘xc5 ♕xc5 16 ♕d8 mate **14 ♗e2 ♗e6 15 0-0 ♕xe5 16 ♘d3! ♕d6 17 c5!±** 17 ♘b4± **♗xc5**

18 ♞xc5 ♛xc5 19 ♜ab1! f6! 19...b6? 20 ♖b5 Δ ♗f3 +− **20 ♝e3! ♛e7 21 ♝h5+! ♝f7** 21...g6! 22 ♗f3± **22 ♝xf7+ ♚xf7** 22...♕xf7 23 ♗c5!± Δ ♖fe1+ **24 ♛d5+ ♚g6** 23...♕e6 24 ♖xb7+ +− **25 ♜b5! h5 25 ♜fb1 ♞d8! 26 ♛d3+ ♚f7 27 ♜d5 +− ♚g8 28 ♜d7 ♛e8 29 ♜bd1**

29...♞c6 30 ♜xb7 ♞e5 31 ♛d6 a5 32 ♜e7 ♛c6! 33 ♛xc6 ♞xc6 34 ♜c7! ♞e5 35 ♝d4! +− Δ f4/♗xe5 **♚h7? 36 f4! ♞g4 37 h3 ♞h6 38 ♝xf6 ♜hg8 39 ♜dd7 ♞f5 40 g4! +− hxg4 41 hxg4 ♜a6 42 ♜f7! 1-0** 42...♔h6 43 ♗g5+ **Gheorghiu**

250 Honfi-Djantar
Bajmok 78

1 e4 c6 2 d4 d5 3 exd5 cxd5 4 c4 ♞f6 5 ♞c3 e6 6 ♞f3 ♝e7 7 cxd5 ♞xd5 8 ♝d3 0-0?! 9 ♞e5 ♞f6 10 0-0 ♞bd7 11 ♛c2 ♞b6 12 ♜d1 h6?! 12...g6!? **13 ♛e2 ♝d7 14 ♝f4 ♜c8 15 ♜ac1 ♝c6 16 ♝b1 ♞bd5 17 ♝g3 ♜e8 18 ♞xc6 ♜xc6 19 ♝e5 ♛d7 20 ♜d3 ♜ec8 21 ♜g3 b5 22 ♛d2 ♚f8 23 a3 a5?!** 23...b4!? 24 axb4 ♗xb4 25 ♗a2!? ♘e4?! 26 ♗xg7+ ♔e7 27 ♕xh6 ♘xg3 28 hxg3∝ **24 ♜d1 b4 25 ♞e4 bxa3 26 bxa3 ♛a7 27 h3 a4 28 ♚h2 ♛b6?!** 28...♘e8? 29 ♗xg7+ ♘xg7 30 ♕xh6 +−; 28...♖a8!? Δ ♕a5 += **29 ♝d3 ♞c3?** 29...♕d8± **30 ♝xf6! ♝xf6 31 ♞xf6 gxf6 32 ♛xh6+ ♚e7 33 ♜d2 ♞d5 34 ♝e4 ♜d6 35 ♜g7 ♛b8 36 ♝g6 ♜f8 37 g3 ♜b6 38 ♛h5 ♛e8** 38...♘f4? 39 ♕c5+ ♔e8 40 ♗xf7+ ♖xf7 41 ♖g8+ +− **39 ♜e2 ♜b5 40 ♝d3 ♜a5 41 ♜b2 ♛c6 42 ♛h7 ♜aa8 43 ♝e4!** 43 ♗g6?? ♖h8 44 ♖xf7+ ♔d6 45 ♕g7 ♖ag8 −+ **♜a7 44 ♜c2 ♛d6 45 ♜c8! ♜xc8 46 ♜xf7+ ♚d8 47 ♛g8+ 1-0 Honfi**

251 Larsen-Pomar Spain 78

1 e4 c6 2 d4 d5 3 exd5 cxd5 4 c4 ♞f6 5 ♞c3 e6 6 ♞f3 ♝e7 7 cxd5 ♞xd5 8 ♝d3 0-0 9 0-0 b6?! 10 ♞xd5 exd5 11 ♞e5 ♝a6 12 ♝xa6 ♞xa6 13 ♛a4 ♛c8? 13...♘c7 += **14 ♝f4 ♛b7 15 ♛c6!± ♜ab8** 15...♕xc6 16 ♘xc6 ♖fe8 17 ♖fc1 ♗f8 18 a3 **16 ♜fc1 ♞b4?!** 16...♖fe8 17 a3 **17 ♛d7! ♞a6** 17...♖fd8 18 ♕f5! **18 ♜c3 ♝f6 19 ♛f5! +− ♜fe8** 19...♗xe5 20 ♗xe5 ♖bc8 21 ♕f6! **20 ♜h3 h6 21 ♝xh6 ♛c8** 21...♗xe5 22 ♗g5 f6 23 dxe5 fxg5 24 ♕h7+ ♔f8 25 ♖f3+ ♔e7 26 ♕xg7+ ♔d8 27 ♖f7 ♕c6 28 ♕xg5+ ♔c8 29 ♖c1 ♘c5 30 b4 **22 ♞d7 ♜e6 23 ♝xg7 1-0 Larsen**

1 e4 e5 2 ♞c3

252 Honfi-Smejkal Stip 78

1 e4 e5 2 ♝c4 ♞f6 3 d3 ♞c6 4 ♞c3 ♝c5 5 f4 d6 6 ♞f3 a6 7 fxe5 dxe5 8 ♝g5 h6 9 ♝xf6 ♛xf6 10 ♞d5 ♛d6 11 ♛d2 ♝e6 12 ♜f1 0-0-0! 12...f5? 13 ♘xc7+ +−; 12...♘a5? 13 b4 ♘xc4 14 dxc4 ♗a7 15 c5± **13 ♞h4 ♞e7 14 ♞xe7+ ♛xe7 15 ♞f5 ♝xf5 16 ♜xf5 ♜df8 17 0-0-0 g6 18 ♜f3 f5 19 exf5 gxf5 20 ♜e1! ♝d6** 20...f4? 21 d4! +−; 20...♕d6!? 21 ♕e2 f4! 22 ♕xe5 ♗e3+ 23 ♖exe3 fxe3 24 ♕xd6 cxd6

25 ♖xe3= **21 ♕f2 ♗c5 22 ♕f1** 22 ♕d2= **f4 23 ♖e4!?** 23 ♗d5!? **♗e3+ 24 ♔b1 ♖f6! 25 ♖h3?!** 25 ♖exe3?? fxe3 26 ♖xf6 e2 −+; 25 c3! += **♕g7! 26 c3 ♖g6 27 g3 ♖f8 28 ♕e2 ♔b8 29 a3 b5 30 ♗b3 f3 31 ♕f1 ♗b6 32 ♗d1 f2 33 ♗e2 ♖f5 34 ♖hh4∝ 1-0** time **Honfi**

Spanish

253 Maric-Weill
Il Ciocco 78
1 e4 e5 2 ♘f3 ♘c6 3 ♗b5 a6 4 ♗a4 d6 5 ♗xc6+ bxc6 6 d4 f6 7 ♗e3 ♘e7 8 ♘c3 ♘g6 8...♗g4?! 9 h3 ♗h5 10 ♕d3 ♗f7 11 0-0-0 ♘g6 12 h4 h5 13 ♘d2!± Maric-Gereken, Strasburg 71 **9 h4 h5 10 ♕d3 ♗e6?!** 10...♗e7 **11 d5! N cxd5 12 ♘xd5 ♕d7 13 0-0-0!?** 13 ♕c4 ♔d8! Δ ♘e7 **♗e7 14 ♘d2** Δ g3, f4 **0-0 15 b3 ♗d8 16 ♘b1! f5?! 17 f3 fxe4 18 ♕xe4!? ♗f5**

19 ♘b6! ♕f7?! 19...♗xe4 20 ♘xd7 ♗xf3! 21 ♘xf8 ♗xd1 22 ♘xg6 ♗g4 23 ♖f1 ♗f6 24 ♗g5! ♔f7 25 ♘xe5+ dxe5 26 ♘c3 ♔e6 27 ♘e4 += **20 ♕xa8 ♗g5 21 ♗xg5 ♖xa8 22 ♘xa8 ♕e8 23 ♘b6!** 23 ♘xc7 ♕c6 −+ **cxb6 24 ♖xd6 ♕b5 25 ♖hd1 +− ♕c5** 25...♗xc2? 26 ♖d8+ Δ ♔xc2 +− **26 ♖1d2 a5 27 a4 b5 28 axb5 ♕xb5 29 ♘c3 ♕b4 30 ♔b2 ♘f4 31 g3 ♘e6 32 ♘d5 ♕c5 33 ♘e7+ 1-0 Maric**

254 Petronic-Lemachko
Buenos Aires 78
1 e4 e5 2 ♘f3 ♘c6 3 ♗b5 a6 4 ♗a4 ♘f6 5 d4 exd4 6 0-0 ♗e7 7 ♖e1 b5 8 e5 ♘xe5 9 ♖xe5 bxa4?! 9...d6! **10 ♘xd4 0-0 11 ♘f5** 11 ♘c3! **♖e8 12 ♗g5 d6 13 ♘xe7+ ♖xe7 14 ♗xf6 gxf6 15 ♖e1** 15 ♖h5 ♖e5∝ **♗b7!** Δ ♕d7, ♔h8, ♖g8; 15...♗f5!? **16 ♘c3 ♖xe1+! 17 ♕xe1 ♕d7 =+ 18 ♕d2 ♕g4 19 f3** 19 ♘d5 ♕g5 20 ♘e3 ♖e8! Δ ♔h8, ♗xg2∓ **♕g6?** 19...♗xf3! 20 ♖f1 ♗c6 21 ♖xf6 ♖e8!∓ **20 ♔h1 ♗c6 21 ♖e1 ♕g5! 22 ♕d4** 22 ♕xg5 fxg5 23 ♖e7 ♖c8!∓ **♖e8! 23 ♖xe8+ ♗xe8 24 h4 ♕e5! 25 ♕g4+** 25 ♕xe5 fxe5 26 ♘d5 c6! 27 ♘f6+ ♔f8 28 ♘xh7+ ♔g7 29 ♘g5 d5 30 g4 ♗d7 31 ♘h3 f5 32 ♘f2 e4 −+; 30 ♔g2 f6 31 ♘h3 f5 32 gxf5 exf5+ 33 ♔f3 ♗f5 −+; 30 c3 ♗d7 31 g4 f5 −+; 26 ♘d5 c6! 27 ♘c7 ♔f8 28 ♘xa6 c5 29 b4 axb3 30 cxb3 ♔e7 −+ **♔f8∓ 26 ♕c4 a3 27 bxa3 c5 28 a4 ♕e6! 29 ♕e4 f5 30 ♕d3 ♕e1+ 31 ♔h2 ♕xh4+ 32 ♔g1 ♕e1+ 33 ♔h2 ♕e5+ 34 ♔g1 ♗d7 35 ♔f2 f4! 36 ♘e4 ♔e7 37 c3 a5 38 ♘d2 d5 39 c4 d4?** 39...♗f5! −+ **40 ♕e4 ♕xe4 41 ♘xe4 ♗e6!! 42 ♘d2** 42 ♘xc5 ♗xc4 43 ♘b7 ♗xa2 44 ♘xa5 ♗d5 45 ♔e2 ♔d6 46 ♔d3 ♔c5 −+; 43 ♘b3 ♗xb3 44 axb3 ♔d6 45 ♔e2 ♔c5 46 ♔d3 ♔b4 −+ **♔d6 43 ♔e2 ♔c6 44 ♔d1 ♗f5! 45 ♔c1 ♗d3 46 ♔d1 ♔d6 47 ♔e1 h6 48 ♔d1 ♗f5 49 ♔c1 ♗d3** 49...♗d7? 50 ♘b3! ♗xa4 51 ♘xa5 ♔c7 52 ♔b2! ♔b6 53 ♘b3 ♗xb3 54 ♔xb3!= **50 ♔d1 ♔e5 51 ♔c1 h5 52 ♔d1 f6 53 ♔c1** 53 ♔e1 ♗c2 54 ♘b3 ♗xb3! 55 axb3 d3! −+ **♔f5 54 ♔d1 ♔g5 55 ♔e1 ♔h4 56 ♔f2 f5** Zugzwang

57 ♞b3 ♝xc4 58 ♞xa5 ♝xa2 59 ♞b7 c4 60 a5 c3 61 ♚e2 ♝c4+ 62 ♚d1 d3 63 ♞d6 ♝b3+ 0-1 Lemachko

255 Gaprindashvili-Chiburdanidze (10) 78
1 e4 e5 2 ♞f3 ♞c6 3 ♝b5 a6 4 ♝a4 ♞f6 5 d4 exd4 6 0-0 ♝e7 7 ♜e1 0-0 7...b5 8 e5 ♘xe5 9 ♖xe5 d6 10 ♖g5 bxa4 11 ♖xg7 ♘h5 Reshevsky-Euwe 50; 9 ♘xe5 bxa4 10 ♕xd4 0-0 11 ♗g5 ♖e8 Krause-Tarrash, 27 **8 e5 ♞e8 9 c3 dxc3 10 ♞xc3 d6 11 exd6 cxd6 12 ♞d5 ♝e6 13 ♞xe7+ ♛xe7 14 ♝g5 ♛d7 15 ♞d4 b5 16 ♝c2 ♞xd4 17 ♛xd4 ♞c7 18 ♛d3 f5 19 ♜ad1 ♜ae8 20 ♝f4 d5 21 ♛g3 ♜c8 22 ♝b3 ♝f7 23 ♝e5 ♞e8 24 ♜d4 ♜c6 25 ♜ed1 ♞f6 26 ♝xf6 ♜xf6 27 ♝xd5 f4 28 ♛f3 ♝xd5 29 ♜xd5 ♛c6 30 h4 ♜e6 31 ♚h2 ♛c4 32 ♜d8 ♜ee8 33 ♜xe8 ♜xe8 34 ♜d7 ♛e6 35 ♜d4 ♛xa2 36 b3 ♛e2 37 ♛c6 ♛e5 38 ♜d5 ♛e7 39 ♜g5 ♛e6 40 ♛b7 ♛f6 41 ♛d7 ♜f8 42 ♚h3 f3 ½-½**

256 Chiburdanidze-Kaiszauri Vilnius 78
1 e4 e5 2 ♞f3 ♞c6 3 ♝b5 a6 4 ♝a4 ♞f6 5 0-0 b5 6 ♝b3 ♝b7 7 ♜e1 ♝c5 8 c3 d6 9 d4 ♝b6 10 ♝g5 h6 11 ♝h4 ♛d7!? 12 a4 0-0-0 13 axb5 axb5 14 ♞a3 14 ♗xf6 **g5 15 ♝g3 h5 16 h4 ♜dg8** 16...g4!? 17 ♘g5 ♖dg8 **17 ♞xg5 exd4 18 ♝xf7 ♜xg5 19 hxg5 h4 20 ♝h2**

Diagram

20...dxc3 20...♕xf7 21 gxf6 (21 ♕f3) dxc3 (21...♕xf6) 22 ♕g4+! ♔b8 (22...♔d8) 23 ♕g7! **21 ♝g6** 21 gxf6 cxb2!? (21...♕xf7 22 ♕g4+ +−) 22 ♗g6 bxa1♕ 23 ♕xa1∝ **♞e7 22 gxf6 ♞xg6 23 bxc3 ♜f8 24 ♞xb5! h3** 24...♕xb5 25 ♕g4+ **25 ♞d4 hxg2 26 ♛f3± ♞h4 27 ♛g3 ♛h7 28 ♛g7 ♛xg7 29 fxg7 ♜g8 30 ♜e3** 30 ♗g3? ♗xd4! **♜xg7 31 ♝g3 ♜h7 32 ♝xh4 ♜xh4 33 ♚xg2 d5** 33...♗xe4+? 34 ♔g3; 33...♖xe4 34 ♖xe4 **34 exd5 ♝xd4!? 35 cxd4 ♜xd4 36 ♜a5 ♝xd5+ 37 ♚g3 ♚d7 38 f4 ♚d6 39 ♚g4 ♜d1 40 ♚f5 ♜f1 41 ♚g5 ♝c4 42 f5 c5 43 ♚f6 ♜c1 44 ♜e8 ♝b3 45 ♜a6+ ♚d5 46 ♜e5+ ♚d4 47 ♜d6+ ♚c4 48 ♚e7 ♚b4 49 ♜b6+ ♚a3 50 f6 1-0 Speelman**

257 M.Tseitlin-Lak USSR 78
1 e4 e5 2 ♞f3 ♞c6 3 ♝b5 a6 4 ♝a4 ♞f6 5 0-0 d6 6 c3 ♝d7 6...♗g4 7 d4 b5 8 ♗b3 ♗e7; 6...b5 7 ♗c2 ♗e7 8 d4 0-0 9 a4 ♗g4 10 d5 ♘a5 Reti-Rubinstein 22 **7 ♜e1 ♝e7 8 d4 0-0 9 ♞bd2 ♜e8 10 ♝xc6 ♝xc6 11 dxe5 dxe5 12 ♞xe5 ♝xe4 13 ♛b3! ♝c5 14 ♛xf7+ ♚h8 15 ♞xe4 ♞xe4 16 ♝h6! gxh6 17 ♜xe4 ♜f8 18 ♜g4! ♛e7 19 ♛xe7 ♝xe7 20 ♜d1 ♜f5 21 ♞f3 ♝d6 22 ♜e1 ♜af8 23 ♜e6 ♝f4 24 ♜e7 ♝d6 25 ♜d7 ♜d5 26 ♜d4 ♜a5 27 a3 ♜af5 28 ♚f1 h5 29 ♜e4 a5 30 a4 b5 31 b3 ♜c5 32 axb5 ♜xb5 33 ♞d4 ♜bb8 34 ♜h4 1-0 Tseitlin**

258 Karpov-Korchnoi (28) 78

1 e4 e5 2 ♘f3 ♘c6 3 ♗b5 a6 4 ♗a4 ♘f6 5 0-0 ♘xe4 6 d4 b5 7 ♗b3 d5 8 dxe5 ♗e6 9 c3 ♘c5 10 ♗c2 ♗g4 11 ♖e1 11 ♕e2 Δ ♖d1, b4, ♗b3/♗e4 **♗e7 12 ♘bd2** 12 b4 ♘e6 13 a4 **♕d7** 12...d4 **13 ♘b3** 13 ♘f1 ♖d8 14 ♘e3 ♗h5 15 ♘f5 0-0 **♘e6 14 h3 ♗h5 15 ♗f5 ♘cd8 16 ♗e3 a5 17 ♗c5 a4 18 ♗xe7 ♕xe7 19 ♘bd2?** 19 ♕xd5 c6; 19 ♘bd4 **c6 20 b4 ♘g5 21 ♕e2 g6 22 ♗g4** 22 ♗c2 ♘xf3+ 23 ♘xf3 ♘e6 24 ♕e3 ♗xf3 25 ♕xf3 ♕h4 **♗xg4 23 hxg4 ♘de6 24 ♕e3 h5 25 ♘xg5 ♕xg5 26 ♕xg5 ♘xg5 27 gxh5 ♖xh5 28 ♘f1 ♖h4 29 ♖ad1 ♔e7 30 f3 ♘e6 31 ♘e3 ♖d8 32 ♘g4 ♘g7 33 ♘e3 ♘e6 34 ♘g4 ♘g7 35 ♘e3 ♘f5 36 ♘c2? ♖c4 37 ♖d3 d4! 38 g4 ♘g7 39 ♘xd4 ♘e6! 40 ♖ed1 ♘xd4 41 cxd4 ♖xb4 42 ♔f2 c5?** 42...♖b2+ 43 ♖1d2 ♖xd2+ 44 ♖xd2 b4; 42...♔e6

43 d5 43 ♔e3 ♖dxd4? 44 ♖xd4 cxd4+ 45 ♖xd4 ♖b2 46 ♔e4 a3 47 ♖d5 b4 48 ♖b5 ♔d7 49 ♔d5 ♖xa2 50 ♖b7+ ♔d8 51 ♖xb4 ♖a1 52 ♖d4 a2 53 ♖d2 g5 54 e6 ♔e7 55 exf7 ♔xf7 56 ♔d6; 43...c4! 44 ♖c3 ♖b2 +−; 44 ♖3d2 a3 Δ ♖b2; 43 dxc5 ♖xd3 44 ♖xd3 ♖b2+ Δ ♖xa2 +− **♖b2+ 44 ♔g3 ♖xa2?** 44...b4! (Δ ♖h8, ♖bh2, ♖8h3 mate) 45 e6 fxe6 46 ♖e3 ♖d6 −+ **45 ♖e3 b4 46 e6= ♖a3 47 ♖e2?** 47 d6+? ♖xd6 48 ♖xd6 ♖xe3 −+; 47 ♖xa3! bxa3 48 exf7 ♔xf7 **fxe6 48 ♖xe6+ ♔f7 49 ♖de1** 49 g5 Δ ♖f6+ **♖d7 50 ♖b6 ♖d3 51 ♖ee6 ♖3xd5 52 ♖xg6 a3 53 ♖gf6+ ♔e7 54 ♖fe6+ ♔f8 55 ♖f6+ ♔e7 56 ♖be6+ ♔d8 57 ♖a6 ♖b7 58 ♖f8+ ♔c7 59 ♖f7+ ♖d7 60 ♖f5 b3 61 ♖xc5+ ♔b8 0-1**

259 Karpov-Korchnoi (2) 78

1 e4 e5 2 ♘f3 ♘c6 3 ♗b5 a6 4 ♗a4 ♘f6 5 0-0 ♘xe4 6 d4 b5 7 ♗b3 d5 8 dxe5 ♗e6 9 c3 ♗c5 10 ♘bd2 0-0 11 ♗c2 ♗f5 12 ♘b3 ♗g4 13 ♘xc5 ♘xc5 14 ♖e1 d4 14...♖e8 15 ♗e3 ♘e6 16 ♕d3 g6 17 ♗h6 ♘e7 18 ♘d4 ♗f5 19 ♘xf5 ♘xf5 20 ♗d2 ♕h4 Fischer-Larsen, Santa Monica 66 **15 h3 ♗h5 16 cxd4 ♗xf3 17 ♕xf3 ♘xd4 18 ♕c3 ♕d5** 18...♘xc2 19 ♕xc2 ♘e6 20 ♗e3 ♘d4 21 ♕e4 c5 22 ♖ad1 **19 ♗e3 ♘xc2 20 ♕xc2 ♘d3 21 ♖ed1 ♖fd8 22 ♕xc7** 22 e6 fxe6 23 ♕xc7 e5; 22...c5? 23 e7 ♖d7 24 ♗xc5! ♕xc5 25 ♕xc5 ♘xc5 26 ♖xd7 ♘xd7 26 ♖d1; 22 ♖ac1 **♕xe5 23 ♕xe5 ♘xe5 24 b3 f6 25 ♗b6 ♖xd1+ 26 ♖xd1 ♖c8 27 ♖d2 h5! 28 ♗e3** 28 f4 ♘g6 29 g3 **♔f7 29 f4 ½-½** 29...♖c3 30 fxe5 ♖xe3 31 exf6 ♔xf6; 30 ♔f2 ♘d3+ 31 ♔f3 f5!

260 Karpov-Korchnoi (4) 78

1 e4 e5 2 ♘f3 ♘c6 3 ♗b5 a6 4 ♗a4 ♘f6 5 0-0 ♘xe4 6 d4 b5 7 ♗b3 d5 8 dxe5 ♗e6 9 c3 ♗c5 10 ♘bd2 0-0 11 ♗c2 ♗f5 12 ♘b3 ♗g4 13 ♘xc5 ♘xc5 14 ♖e1 ♗h5 14...d4 **15 h3** 15 ♗g5 ♗xf3 16 ♕xf3 ♕xg5 17 ♕xd5 ♖ad8!=; 15...♕d7 16 ♗e3 ♘e6 17 ♗xh7+! **♖e8 16 ♗f4 ♘e6 17 ♗d2 ♘c5 18 ♗f4 ♘e6 19 ♗d2 ½-½**

261 Karpov-Korchnoi (14) 78
1 e4 e5 2 ♘f3 ♘c6 3 ♗b5 a6 4 ♗a4 ♘f6 5 0-0 ♘xe4 6 d4 b5 7 ♗b3 d5 8 dxe5 ♗e6 9 c3 ♗c5 10 ♘bd2 0-0 11 ♗c2 ♗f5 12 ♘b3 ♗g4 13 h3 ♗h5 13...♗xf3 14 gxf3 ♘xf2 15 ♖xf2 ♗xf2+ 16 ♔xf2 ♘xe5 17 ♕g1! ♖e8 18 ♗g5 ♕d6 19 ♕g3 ♘g4+ 20 fxg4 ♖e2+ 21 ♔f3 ♕xg3+ 22 ♔xg3 ♖xc2 23 ♘d4 ♖xb2 24 ♗c1! +− **14 g4 ♗g6 15 ♗xe4** N **dxe4 16 ♘xc5 exf3 17 ♗f4 ♕xd1** 17...♕e7 18 ♕d5 ♘a5 19 b4 Δ ♕xf3 **18 ♖axd1**

18...♘d8! 18...♖fd8 19 ♔h2-g3xf3 **19 ♖d7 ♘e6 20 ♘xe6** 20 ♗e3 ♖fe8 **fxe6 21 ♗e3 ♖ac8!** 21...♖f7 22 ♖fd1 ♖af8 23 ♗c5 **22 ♖fd1** 22 ♗c5 ♖fe8 23 ♖e1 **♗e4 23 ♗c5 ♖fe8 24 ♖7d4 ♗d5 25 b3 a5 26 ♔h2 ♖a8 27 ♔g3 ♖a6?** 27...♗c6 Δ a4 **28 h4 ♖c6 29 ♖xd5 exd5 30 ♖xd5 ♖ce6 31 ♗d4 c6 32 ♖c5 ♖f8?** 32...♖d8 33 ♔xf3 ♖d5 34 ♔e4? ♖exe5+; 34 ♖xd5 cxd5 35 ♔e3? ♖h6 36 h5 g6!; 35 ♔g3 b4; 35 ♔e2 h5! =+; 35 a3 g6 36 h5! ♔f7 37 ♔f4 +− **33 a4 bxa4 34 bxa4 g6 35 ♖xa5 ♖ee8 36 ♖a7 ♖f7 37 ♖a6 ♖c7** 37...c5? 38 ♗xc5 ♖xe5 39 ♗d6 **38 ♗c5 ♖cc8 39 ♗d6 ♖a8 40 ♖xc6 ♖xa4 41 ♔xf3 h5 42 gxh5 gxh5 43 c4 ♖a2 44 ♖b6 ♔f7 45 c5 ♖a4 46 c6 ♔e6 47 c7 ♔d7 48 ♖b8 ♖c8 49 ♔e3 ♖xh4 50 e6+! 1-0** 50...♔xe6 51 ♗g3!; 50...♔xd6 51 ♖xc8 ♖c4 52 ♖d8+ ♔xc7 53 e7

262 Karpov-Korchnoi (24) 78
1 e4 e5 2 ♘f3 ♘c6 3 ♗b5 a6 4 ♗a4 ♘f6 5 0-0 ♘xe4 6 d4 b5 7 ♗b3 d5 8 dxe5 ♗e6 9 c3 ♗e7 10 ♗c2 ♘c5 11 h3 11 ♘d4 ♘xe5 12 f4 **0-0 12 ♖e1** 12 ♘d4 ♘xe5 13 f4; 12...♕d7 **♕d7 13 ♘d4 ♘xd4 14 cxd4 ♘b7 15 ♘d2** 15 ♘c3 c5 16 dxc5 ♘xc5 17 ♗e3 Δ ♗d4 **c5 16 dxc5 ♘xc5 17 ♘f3 ♗f5 18 ♗e3** 18 ♗xf5 ♕xf5 19 ♕xd5 ♖fd8 20 ♕c6 ♖ac8 21 ♕b6 ♘d3 22 ♖f1 ♘xf2 23 ♖xf2 ♖d1+ +− **♖ac8 19 ♖c1 ♗xc2 20 ♖xc2 ♘e6 21 ♖d2 ♖fd8 22 ♕b3?** 22 ♗b6 ♗b4 23 ♖d3 **♖c4 23 ♖ed1 ♕b7 24 a3 g6 25 ♕a2 a5 26 b3 ♖c3 27 a4 bxa4** 27...b4 28 ♗d4? ♖xf3! 29 gxf3 ♗g5 30 ♗e3 d4; 27...♗b4 28 ♕b2 d4 29 ♘xd4 ♕e4!; 28 ♖d3! ♖xd3 29 ♖xd3 d4 30 ♘xd4! ♗c5? ♘xe6! **28 bxa4** 28 ♕xa4 ♖xb3 29 ♕xa5 ♖a8 **♖c4 29 ♖d3 ♔g7 30 ♕d2 ♖xa4 31 ♗h6+ ♔g8 32 ♖xd5 ♖xd5 33 ♕xd5 ♕xd5 34 ♖xd5 ♗f8 35 ♗xf8 ♔xf8 36 g3 ♔e7 37 ♖b5 ♘c7 38 ♖c5 ♘e6 39 ♖b5 ♘d8 40 ♔g2 h6 41 ♘d2 ♖a1 42 ♘c4 ♘c6 43 ♖c5 ♔d7 44 ♘b6+ ♔c7 50 ♘c8 ♔xc8 ½-½**

263 Karpov-Korchnoi (10) 78
1 e4 e5 2 ♘f3 ♘c6 3 ♗b5 a6 4 ♗a4 ♘f6 5 0-0 ♘xe4 6 d4 b5 7 ♗b3 d5 8 dxe5 ♗e6 9 ♘bd2 ♘c5 10 c3 d4 11 ♘g5! N

Diagram

11...dxc3 (1) 11...♕xg5 12 ♕f3 ♗d7 13 ♗xf7+ ♔e7 14 ♗d5 ♘xe5 15 ♕e2 (15 ♖e1 ♔d8 16 ♖xe5 ♕xe5

17 ♗xa8 ♗d6 18 ♘f1 dxc3 19 bxc3 ♖f8 =+) 15...d3 16 ♕e1 c6 17 f4 (17 ♘f3 ♕f5 [17...♕h5? 18 ♗g5+ Δ ♕xe5] 18 ♗b3 ♔d6) 17...♕h6 18 ♕xe5+ ♔d8 Δ ♗d6, ♔c7!?; 12...♔d7 13 ♗d5 ♗xd5 14 ♕xd5+ ♗d6 15 ♘c4 ♕g6 16 exd6 bxc4 17 ♕xc5 +=; 15...♕f5 16 ♘b6+; (2) 11...♘xb3 12 ♘xe6 fxe6 13 axb3 +=; (3) 11... ♗d5 12 ♘xf7 ♔xf7 13 ♕f3+ ♔e6 14 ♕g4+ ♔e7 (14...♔f7 15 ♕f5+ Δ e6) 15 ♘f3 ♘e6 16 ♗g5+ ♘xg5 17 ♘xg5 ♗xb3 18 axb3 ♕d5 19 c4 bxc4 20 bxc4 ♕xc4 21 ♖ac1 ♕d5 22 ♖c5 ♘xe5 23 ♖e1 ♕xc5 24 ♕e6+ ♔d8 25 ♘f7+ ♘xf7 26 ♕e8 mate **12 ♘xe6 fxe6 13 bxc3 ♕d3 14 ♘f3** 14 c4 **♕xd1** 14...♕xc3 15 ♗d5 (15 ♗g5 ♗e7 16 ♖c1 ♕b4 17 ♕c2 +−; 15...♘xe5 16 ♘d4) (1) 15...0-0-0 16 ♗d2 Δ ♗xc6; (2) 15...♕xa1? 16 ♗xc6+ ♔f7 17 ♘g5+ ♔e7 18 ♗a3 ♕xe5 (18...♕xd1 19 ♖xd1 Δ ♗xc5+) 19 ♗xc5+ ♕xc5 20 ♕d7+ ♔f6 21 ♘e4+ +−; (3) 15...exd5 16 ♕xd5 ♘d7 (16...♘a4 17 ♘d4 ♘xd4 18 ♕xa8+ ♔f7 19 ♗e3 ♕xe5; 17...♖d8 18 ♕xc6+) 17 ♖d1 0-0-0 18 ♗g5 ♗e7 19 ♖ac1 ♕a5 20 ♕xc6 ♗xg5 21 ♘xg5 Δ ♖xd7/♘f7 **15 ♗xd1** 15 ♖xd1 ♘xb3 16 axb3 **♗e7** 15...♘d3 16 ♗g5 ♘dxe5 17 ♘xe5 ♘xe5 18 ♖e1 **16 ♗e3** Δ ♗xc5, ♗b3 **♘d3 17 ♗b3** 17 ♘d4 ♘xd4 18 cxd4 c5 **♔f7 18 ♖ad1 ♘dxe5 19 ♘xe5 ♘xe5 20 ♗f4 ♘c4** 20...♗d6 21 ♗xe5 ♗xe5 22 f4 ♗xc3 23 f5; 22 ♖fe1 ♗xc3 23 ♖xe6 ♔f8 24 ♖d7 **21 ♗xc4?** 21 ♖d7 c5 22 ♖e1 ♖ad8 23 ♖b7 ♖d3 24 ♗g5 ♖e8 25 ♖e4 ♖xc3 26 h3 **bxc4 22 ♖d4 ♗d6 23 ♗e3** 23 ♗xd6 **♖hb8 24 ♖xc4 ♖b2 25 a4 ♖a2 26 g3** 26 ♖b1? ♖b8! **♖b8 27 ♖d1 ♖bb2 28 ♖dd4 ♖b1+ 29 ♔g2 ♖ba1 30 ♖h4 h6 31 ♗c5** 31 ♗a7 (Δ ♗b8) ♖b1 32 ♖c6 ♔e7 **e5 32 ♗a7 ♔e6 33 ♖cg4 ♗e7** 33... ♗f8? 34 ♖g6+ **34 ♖h5 ♗f6** 34... ♗g5? 35 h4 g6 36 hxg5 gxh5 37 gxh6!; 35...♔f5 36 hxg5 ♔xg4 37 gxh6 gxh6 38 ♖xe5 **35 ♖c4 ♔d7 36 ♗b8 c6 37 ♖e4** 37 ♗xe5 g6 38 ♖d4+ ♔c8 39 ♖d6 gxh5; 37...♗xe5 38 ♖xe5 ♖xa4 **♖xa4 38 c4 ♖a5 39 ♗xe5 ♗xe5 40 ♖hxe5 ♖xe5 41 ♖xe5 ♖a4 42 ♖e4 ♖a5 43 h4 h5 44 ♖f4 ½-½**

264 Karpov-Korchnoi (8) 78

1 e4 e5 2 ♘f3 ♘c6 3 ♗b5 a6 4 ♗a4 ♘f6 5 0-0 ♘xe4 6 d4 b5 7 ♗b3 d5 8 dxe5 ♗e6 9 ♘bd2 ♘c5 10 c3 g6?! 11 ♕e2 11 ♗c2 ♗g7 12 ♘d4 ♘xe5 13 f4 ♘c4 14 f5 ♘e3 15 ♕f3 ♘xf1 16 fxe6 ♗xd4+ 17 cxd4 ♘xe6 18 ♔xf1 ♘xd4 19 ♕c3 ♕h4 20 ♘f3 ♘xf3 21 ♕e3+ ♕e7 22 ♕xf3 0-0 **♗g7 12 ♘d4 ♘xe5?** 12...♕d7 13 ♘xc6 ♕xc6 14 ♘f3; 12...♘xd4 13 cxd4 ♘xb3; 12...♘xb3 13 ♘2xb3; 12...♘e7 **13 f4 ♘c4** 13...♘ed3 14 f5 ♘xc1 15 ♖axc1 gxf5 16 ♘xf5 0-0 17 ♗c2± **14 f5 gxf5 15 ♘xf5 ♖g8 16 ♘xc4** 16 ♗c2 **dxc4** 16...bxc4 17 ♗c2 ♔d7 18 ♘xg7 ♖xg7 19 ♕e5 ♕g8 20 ♖f2 f6 21 ♕xf6 ♖f7 22 ♕d4 ♖xf2 23 ♕xf2 ♖f8 24 ♕c5 ♗h3 25 ♗e4 dxe4 26 ♗g5 +−; 16...♘xb3 17 axb3 dxc4

18 bxc4 bxc4 19 ♗h6± **17 ♝c2!** 17 ♘xg7+ ♖xg7 18 ♕e5 ♖xg2+ 19 ♔xg2 ♕d5+ 20 ♕xd5 ♗xd5+ Δ cxb3; 18...♖g6! 19 ♗xc4 bxc4 20 ♕xc5 ♕d5= **♞d3?** 17...♕d5 18 ♗h6 (1) 18...♗xh6 19 ♘xh6 ♖f8; (2) 18...♗f6 19 ♘e3! ♕e5 20 ♗f4! +−; (3) 18...♗e5 19 ♖ad1 ♘d3 20 ♗xd3 cxd3 21 ♖xd3 ♕c5+ 22 ♔h1 ♖d8 (22...♗c4 23 ♕f3) 23 ♖fd1! ♖xd3 24 ♕xd3 **18 ♝h6 ♝f8?** 18...♗xh6 19 ♘xh6 ♖g6 20 ♘xf7 ♕e7 **19 ♜ad1 ♛d5 20 ♝xd3 cxd3 21 ♜xd3 ♛c6** 21...♗c5+ 22 ♔h1 ♖xg2 23 ♖xd5 ♖xe2 24 ♖xc5 +−; 23 ♕xg2? ♕xd3 24 ♕xa8+ ♔d7 −+ **22 ♝xf8 ♛b6+** 22...♔xf8 23 ♘d4 +− **23 ♚h1 ♚xf8 24 ♛f3 ♜e8 25 ♞h6 ♜g7**

26 ♜d7! ♜b8 26...♗xd7? 27 ♕xf7+ ♖xf7 28 ♖xf7 mate **27 ♞xf7 ♝xd7 28 ♞d8+ 1-0**

265 Karpov-Korchnoi (12) 78

1 e4 e5 2 ♞f3 ♞c6 3 ♝b5 a6 4 ♝a4 ♞f6 5 0-0 ♞xe4 6 d4 b5 7 ♝b3 d5 8 dxe5 ♝e6 9 ♛e2 ♝e7 10 ♜d1 0-0 11 c4 bxc4 12 ♝xc4 ♝c5 12...♕d7 13 ♘c3 ♘xc3 14 bxc3 f6!? 15 exf6 ♗xf6 16 ♘g5 ♗xg5 17 ♗xg5 h6 18 ♗e3 ♕d6 19 ♗b3 ♘e5 20 ♖d4 c5 21 ♖f4 ♘d7 22 ♖d1 ♕c6 23 ♕d2 ♘f6 24 ♖h4 ♖a7 **13 ♝e3 ♝xe3 14 ♛xe3 ♛b8 15 ♝b3 ♞a5 16 ♞e1** 16 ♘bd2 ♕a7! 17 ♕xa7 ♖xa7 18 ♖ac1 c5 19 ♘xe4 ♘xb3 20 axb3 dxe4 21 ♘d2 e3! 22 fxe3 ♗b7 Matanovic-Korchnoi, Suhumi 66 **♛b6** 16...♘xb3 17 axb3 ♕b6 18 ♕xb6 cxb6 19 b4! Δ f3 +− Hubner-Demarre, Dresden 69 **17 ♛xb6 cxb6 18 f3 ♞xb3 19 axb3 ♞c5 20 b4 ♞d7 21 ♞d3** Δ f4 **g5!?** 21...a5 22 ♘c3 axb4 23 ♖xa8 ♖xa8 24 ♘xb4 ♘xe5 25 ♘bxd5 ♗xd5 26 ♘xd5 Δ ♘xb6; 21...♖fc8= **22 ♞c3 ♜fc8 23 ♞f2 d4** 23...♘xe5 24 ♘xd5 ♗xd5 25 ♖xd5 f6 26 ♘e4; 23...a5 **24 ♞e2! d3** 24...♘xe5 25 ♘xd4, 26 ♘e4 **25 ♞xd3 ♝c4** 25...♗b3 26 ♖d2 ♖c2; 26 ♖e1 ♗c4 27 ♘ec1 ♖e8 Δ ♖ad8, ♘b8-c6

26 ♞g3?! 26 ♘ec1 ♖e8 27 ♖e1 ♖e7 Δ ♖ae8; 26 ♘c3 ♗xd3 27 ♖xd3 ♘xe5 28 ♖d5 f6 29 ♖d6 ♖c6 30 ♖xc6 ♘xc6 31 b5 **♝xd3 27 ♜xd3 ♞xe5 28 ♜d5 ♞g6** 28...f6 29 ♘e4 ♔g7 30 ♘xg5 +− **29 ♜xg5 ♜c2 30 b3 ♜b2 31 ♞f5** 31 f4 **♜xb3 32 h4 ♚f8 33 h5 ♞e7 34 ♞xe7 ♚xe7 35 ♜e1+ ♚f8 36 ♜e4 a5 37 ♜eg4 ♚e7 38 bxa5 ♜xa5** 38...bxa5? 39 ♖a4 **39 h6 ♜xg5 40 ♜xg5 b5 41 ♜g7 ♜b1+ 42 ♚h2 ♜d1** 42...b4 43 ♖xh7 b3 44 ♖h8 b2 45 ♖b8 +− **43 ♜xh7 ♜d8 44 ♜g7 ½-½**

266 Padevsky-Honfi Bajmok 78
1 e4 e5 2 ♞f3 ♞c6 3 ♝b5 a6 4 ♝a4 ♞f6 5 0-0 ♝e7 6 ♝xc6 dxc6 7 d3 ♞d7 8 ♞bd2 0-0 9 ♞c4 f6 10 ♞h4 ♞c5 11 ♞f5 ♝xf5 12 exf5 ♛d5 13 ♛g4 13 b3!? **♜ad8!** N 13...e4 14 ♘e3 ♕e5 15 ♘c4 ♕d5= Gipslis-Geller, USSR 70 **14 ♜e1 ♜fe8 15 ♝e3** 15 b3 e4! 16 dxe4 ♘xe4 =+ **e4! 16 ♝xc5 ♝xc5 17 ♜xe4 ♜xe4 18 ♛xe4 ♛xe4 19 dxe4 b5 20 ♞e3** 20 ♘a5 ♖d2 −+ **♝xe3 21 fxe3 ♜d2 22 ♜c1 ♚f7 −+ 23 a3 c5 24 b3 ♚e7 25 c4 b4 26 axb4 cxb4 27 ♜a1 ♜b2 28 ♜xa6 ♜xb3 29 ♚f2 ♜c3 30 ♜c6 ♚d7 31 ♜c5 c6 32 ♜a5 ♜xc4 33 ♜a7+ ♚c8 34 e5 ♜c5?** 34...b3! 35 ♖a8+ ♔b7 36 ♖a3 ♖b4 37 e6 b2 38 e7 b1♕ 39 e8♕ ♕xf5+ −+ **35 e6 ♜xf5+ 36 ♚e2 ♚d8 37 ♜xg7 b3?** 37...♖a5∓ **38 ♜xh7! b2 39 ♜d7+ ♚e8 40 ♜d1 ♜c5 41 ♜b1 ♜c2+ 42 ♚d3 ♜xg2 43 h4= ♚e7 44 ♚c3 ♜e2 45 ♚d3! ♜h2 46 ♚c3 ♚xe6 47 ♜xb2 ♜xh4 48 ♜b8 ♜h1 49 ♜e8+ ♚d5 50 ♜f8 ♚e5 51 ♜e8+ ♚d6 52 ♜d8+ ♚e7 53 ♜c8 ♜d1 54 ♚c4 ♚d7 55 ♜f8 ♚e6 56 ♜c8 ♚e5 57 ♜e8+!** 57 ♖xc6? ♖c1+ 58 ♔b5 ♖e1! −+ **♚f5 58 e4+ ♚f4 59 ♜e6 ♜c1+ 60 ♚d3 ♚g5 61 ♚d4 ½-½ Honfi**

267 Arsenjev-Shirmin USSR 78
1 e4 e5 2 ♞f3 ♞c6 3 ♝b5 a6 4 ♝a4 ♞f6 5 0-0 ♝e7 6 ♜e1 b5 7 ♝b3 d6 8 c3 0-0 9 d4 ♝g4 10 ♝e3 exd4 11 cxd4 ♞a5 11...d5! 12 e5 ♘e4≈ **12 ♝c2 c5 13 ♞bd2 cxd4 14 ♝xd4 ♞c6 15 ♝e3 d5 16 h3 dxe4?** 16...♗h5 17 g4!≈ **17 hxg4 exf3 18 ♛xf3 ♞e5 19 ♛h3 ♞exg4 20 ♞e4± g6** 20...h6 21 ♘xf6+ ♘xf6 22 ♗xh6! gxh6 23 ♕xh6± **21 ♞xf6+ ♞xf6 22 ♝g5 ♞d5 23 ♝h6 ♜e8 24 ♜ad1 ♛a5 25 ♝b3 ♜ad8 26 ♜e5 ♝d6 27 ♝d2 ♝b4 28 ♜xe8+ ♜xe8 29 ♛d7! 1-0 Suetin**

268 Adorjan-Radio Listeners Hungary 78
1 e4 e5 2 ♞f3 ♞c6 3 ♝b5 a6 4 ♝a4 ♞f6 5 0-0 ♝e7 6 ♜e1 b5 7 ♝b3 d6 8 c3 0-0 9 h3 ♞a5 10 ♝c2 c5 11 d4 ♛c7 12 ♞bd2 cxd4 13 cxd4 ♞c6 14 ♞b3 a5 15 ♝e3 a4 16 ♞bd2 ♝e6 17 a3 ♞a5 18 ♝d3 ♛b8 19 ♛e2! ♝d7!? 19...b4 20 axb4 ♕xb4 21 ♖eb1 exd4 22 ♗xd4 ♘b3 23 ♘xb3 axb3 24 ♗c3± **20 ♜ec1!?** N 20 ♖ac1 Tal-Kuzmin, Leningrad 77 **♜e8 21 ♜ab1 h6** 21...♗f8 22 ♗g5!; 21...♗d8!? **22 b4! axb3 23 ♞xb3 d5?** 23...♘xb3! 24 ♖xb3 ♖a4! +=/= **24 ♞xe5! ♝xa3** 24...dxe4 25 ♗xe4 ♘xb3 26 ♖xb3 ♘xe4 27 ♘xd7 ♕d6 28 ♘c5 +−

25 ♞c5!! ♜xe5 25...dxe4 26 ♗xb5 ♗xb5 27 ♖xb5 ♕d8 28 ♖c3! ♗xc5 29 ♖cxc5! ♖e7 30 ♕e1 ♖ea7 31 ♕b4 Δ ♗d2 +−; 25...♗xc1 26 ♘cxd7 ♘xd7 27 ♘xd7 ♕d6 28 ♖xc1 ♕xd7 29 ♗xb5 ♕e6 30 ♗xe8 ♖xe8 31 ♕b5 +−; 25...♗xc5 26 ♘xd7! ♘xd7 27 ♗xb5 ♕d8 28 dxc5 ♖xe4 29 c6 ♘f6 30 c7 ♕c8 31 ♗a6! +− **26 dxe5 ♛xe5** 26...♗xc1 27 exf6 +− **27 ♞xd7 ♞xd7 28 ♜d1! dxe4 29 ♜xb5 exd3 30 ♛xd3 ♛e7 31 ♛d5 ♛e8 32 ♛xd7?** +− 32...♖xa5! +− **♞c4 33 ♝f4 ♛e2**

34 ♕d3 ♕e6 35 ♕d5 ♖e8 36 ♕xe6 ♖xe6 37 ♖d4 ♖c6 38 ♖d7 ♗d6? 39 ♗xd6 ♘xd6 40 ♖b8+ ♔h7 41 ♖bd8 ♘e4 42 ♖xf7 ♖g6 43 ♖d4? ♘g5 44 ♖f5!! ♘xh3+ 45 ♔h2 ♘g5 46 f4 ♘e6 47 ♖d7! Zugzwang **♖g4 48 g3 ♖g6 49 ♔g2 ♔g8 50 ♔f3 ♔h7 51 g4** Δ ♔g3-h4-h5 **♔g8 52 ♔g3 ♘f8 53 ♖d8 ♖f6 54 ♖xf6 gxf6 55 ♔h4 ♔f7 56 ♖d4 ♘e6 57 ♖c4 ♘g7 58 ♖c7+ ♔g8 59 ♖c8+ ♔h7 60 ♖f8 1-0 Adorjan**

269 Kapengut-Beljavsky
Ashkhabad 78

1 e4 e5 2 ♘f3 ♘c6 3 ♗b5 a6 4 ♗a4 ♘f6 5 0-0 ♗e7 6 ♖e1 b5 7 ♗b3 d6 8 c3 0-0 9 h3 ♗b7!? 10 d4 ♖e8 11 ♗g5!? h6 12 ♗h4 ♘d7! N 12...♘h7 13 ♗g3 ♗f6 14 ♗d5 ♖b8 15 ♘a3 ♘g5 16 ♘xg5 hxg5 17 ♘c2 exd4 Kapengut-Podgaets, Beltsi 77, 18 cxd4! ♘xd4 19 ♗xf7+!± **13 ♗g3** 13 ♗xe7 ♘xe7 14 a4 c5= **♗f6 14 ♕d3! ♘a5 15 ♗c2 c5 16 ♘bd2?!** 16 d5 ♘c4 17 b3 ♘b6 18 c4 +=; 16...c4 17 ♕e2 Δ b4 += **cxd4 17 cxd4 ♘c6 18 a3?** 18 d5 ♘b4 =+ **♘xd4! 19 ♘xd4 ♘c5!** 19...exd4 20 ♗xd6; 20 e5∞ **20 ♕f3 exd4∓ 21 ♖ad1 ♖c8 22 ♗b3 ♕e7** 22...d3!∓ **23 ♗d5 ♗e5** 23... ♗xd5!± **24 ♘f1 ♘e6 25 ♕g4 ♖c2 26 f4 ♗f6 =+ 27 ♖d2 ♖xd2 28 ♘xd2 ♕c7 29 ♕f3 ♘c5 30 b4?!** 30 ♗xb7! ♕xb7 31 b4 ♘d7 32 e5 ♕xf3 33 ♘xf3 dxe5 34 fxe5 ♗d8! =+; 30...♘xb7 31 e5 dxe5 32 fxe5 ♗g5 33 ♘e4∞ **♗xd5! 31 exd5** 31 bxc5 ♗b7 −+ **♖xe1+ 32 ♗xe1 ♘d7 −+ 33 ♕e4 ♔f8 34 ♔f2 ♘b6 35 ♔e2 ♕c3 36 ♗f2 ♘c4 37 ♕d3 ♕b2 38 ♔d1 ♘xa3! 39 ♘e4 ♘b1 40 ♘xf6 ♘c3+! 0-1 Kapengut**

270 Matanovic-Ivkov (5) 78

1 e4 e5 2 ♘f3 ♘c6 3 ♗b5 a6 4 ♗a4 ♘f6 5 0-0 ♗e7 6 ♖e1 b5 7 ♗b3 d6 8 c3 0-0 9 h3 ♘b8 10 d4 ♘bd7 11 ♘bd2 ♗b7 12 ♗c2 ♖e8 13 a4 ♗f8 14 b3 g6 15 ♗b2 ♗g7 16 ♗d3 c6 17 ♕c2 ♘h5!? 17...♖c8 18 dxe5? dxe5 19 b4 ♗f8 20 ♖ed1 ♕b6 21 ♕b3 c5∓ Korchnoi-Portisch, Belgrade 70; 18 ♗f1!? Portisch **18 ♗f1 ♕b6 19 ♖ad1 ♖ad8 20 b4 ♘f4?! 21 g3 ♘h5 22 ♕b3 += d5?!** 22...c5!? **23 a5 ♕c7 24 ♗g2 ♘hf6 25 exd5! cxd5 26 ♘xe5 ♘xe5 27 dxe5 ♖xe5 28 ♖xe5 ♕xe5**

29 c4!± ♕e2 30 cxb5 ♕xb5 31 ♘c4! ♘e8 32 ♘b6 32 ♘e5!? (Δ ♗f1) ♘c7 33 ♘g4 ♘e6 34 ♗xg7 ♔xg7 35 ♕e3 d4 36 ♕h6+ ♔h8 37 ♘f6 ♘f8 38 ♖xd4! +− (Δ ♖h4) **♗xb2** Zeitnot **33 ♕xb2 ♘c7 34 ♕f6 ♘e6 35 ♕e7! ♗c6?** 35...♗a8 36 ♗f1 ♕c6 27 ♗xa6 d4 28 ♘xa8 ♕xa6 29 ♘b6± **36 ♗f1 1-0 Maric**

271 Astapov-Kolker USSR 78

1 e4 e5 2 ♘f3 ♘c6 3 ♗b5 a6 4 ♗a4 ♘f6 5 0-0 ♗e7 6 ♖e1 b5 7 ♗b3 0-0 8 c3 d5 9 exd5 ♘xd5 10 ♘xe5 ♘xe5 11 ♖xe5 c6 12 d4 ♗d6 13 ♖e1 ♕h4 14 g3 ♕h3 15 ♗xd5? 15 ♗e3! **cxd5 16 ♕f3 ♗f5 17 ♕g2** 17 ♕xd5? ♖ae8! 18 ♗d2 ♗f4!! 19 gxf4 ♕g4+ 20 ♕g2

♖xe1+ 21 ♗xe1 ♕d1 −+ **♕h5 18 ♕xd5 ♖ad8 19 ♕c6**

19...♖de8!? N 19...♗e6 20 ♕e4 ♗d5 21 ♕e2 ♗f3 22 ♕f1 f5 Keres **20 ♖xe8?!** 20 ♕xe8! ♖xe8 21 ♖xe8+ ♗f8 22 ♖e1 ♗e4 23 ♘d2 ♗c6 24 a4!∞ Δ axb5 **♕d1+ 21 ♔g2 ♕xc1!∓ 22 ♖e2** 22 ♖xf8+ ♗xf8 23 ♕f3 ♗xb1 −+ **♗d3 23 ♕f3 ♕d1 24 ♖e1! ♕xe1 25 ♕xd3 ♖e8 26 ♕f1?** 26 a4 b4 27 c4 ♖e2 28 ♕f3 ♖xb2 **♕e4+ 27 ♔g1 ♕c2 28 a4 ♕xb2 29 ♘d2 ♕xd2 0-1 Maric**

272 Seret-Peters Bagneux 78

1 e4 c5 2 ♘f3 ♘c6 3 ♗b5 d6 4 0-0 ♗d7 5 c3 ♘f6 6 ♖e1 a6 7 ♗a4 b5 8 ♗c2 e5 9 h3 ♗e7 10 d4 ♕c7 11 d5 ♘a5 11...♘d8 12 ♘h2 0-0 13 f4 exf4 14 ♗xf4 ♘e8 15 ♘d2 f6 16 a4 ♖b8 += Peters-Pytel, Bagneux 78 **12 b3! 0-0 13 ♘bd2 ♖fc8?! 14 ♘f1 g6 15 ♗g5 ♕d8 16 ♘g3 ♘b7 17 ♕d2 a5 18 ♗h6 ♘e8 19 ♘g5!± ♘c7 20 f4 f6 21 ♘f3 exf4 22 ♗xf4 b4 23 c4 a4 24 ♖ac1 ♘e8 25 h4 ♘g7 26 ♗h6 ♗f8 27 h5 ♘xh5** 27...♕e7 28 hxg6 hxg6 29 e5! **28 ♘xh5 gxh5 29 e5! dxe5 30 ♘xe5 axb3** 30...fxe5 31 ♕d3 ♕e7 32 ♖xe5! +− **31 axb3 ♖c7 32 d6 ♘xd6 33 ♕d5+ ♔h8 34 ♗xf8 ♕xf8 35 ♕xd6! ♕xd6 36 ♘f7+ ♔g8 37 ♘xd6 ♖a6 38 ♖cd1 ♗g4 39 ♖d5 ♖a2 40 ♗f5 ♖b2 41 ♘b5 1-0 Pytel**

273 Chiburdanidze-Gaprindashvili (1) 78

1 e4 e5 2 ♘f3 ♘c6 3 ♗b5 f5 4 d3 4 ♘c3; 4 d4 **fxe4** 4...♘f6 5 0-0 **5 dxe4 ♘f6 6 0-0** 6 ♘c3 ♗b4! 7 ♕d3 d6 8 ♗d2 ♗xc3 9 ♗xc3 0-0 10 0-0-0 ♕e8 11 h3 a6 12 ♗c4+ ♗e6 13 ♖he1 ♗xc4 14 ♕xc4+ ♔h8 15 ♕e2 ♘d7 16 ♔b1 b5 Nezmetdinov-Bronstein, Tbilisi 59; 6 ♗c4 ♗c5 7 0-0 d6 8 c3 ♗g4 9 b4 ♗b6 10 a4 a5 11 b5 ♘e7 12 ♕b3 ♗xf3 13 ♗f7+ ♔f8 14 gxf3 ♘g6 Szabo-Bronstein, Moscow 56 **d6 7 ♘c3 ♗e7 8 a3!** 8 ♕d3 ♗g4 9 h3 ♗xf3 10 ♕xf3 0-0 11 ♕d1 ♔h8 12 ♗e3 ♕e8; 8 ♘d5; 8 ♗c4 **♗g4 9 h3 ♗xf3 10 ♕xf3 0-0 11 ♕d3 ♔h8 12 ♗e3 ♘h5 13 ♖ad1 ♗g5** 13...♘f4 14 ♗xf4 exf4 15 ♗xc6 bxc6 **14 ♘d5 ♗xe3** 14...♖c8 **15 fxe3! ♘f6 16 ♕c4 ♘e7** 16...♘xd5 17 ♖xf8+ ♕xf8 18 exd5 Δ ♕xc7 **17 ♘xc7!** 17 ♕xc7 ♘exd5 18 ♕xd8 ♖fxd8 19 exd5 ♖ac8 20 c3 ♖c5 21 ♗e2 ♖xd5 22 ♖xd5 ♘xd5 23 ♖f7; 17...♕xc7 18 ♘xc7 ♖fc8 19 ♘e6 ♖xc2 **♖c8** 17...a6 18 ♘xa8 axb5 19 ♕e6 **18 ♘e6 ♖xc4 19 ♘xd8 ♖xc2 20 ♖xd6** 20 ♘xb7 ♖xb2 21 ♘xd6; 20...♖xb2 21 ♗c4 **a6! 21 ♗d3 ♖d2! 22 ♘xb7 ♘c8 23 ♖d5 ♘b6 24 ♖d6 ♘c8 25 ♖d5 ♘b6 26 ♖d6 ½-½**

274 Bohosian-Marszalek Pazardjik 78

1 e4 e5 2 ♘f3 ♘c6 3 ♗b5 f5 4 d3 fxe4 5 dxe4 ♘f6 6 0-0 d6 7 ♘c3 ♗e7 7...♗g4 8 h3 ♗h5 9 g4 ♗g6 10 ♘g5! ♕d7 11 ♘d5! ♘xe4?! 12 ♘e6!± Tseitlin-Krivoshtuk, USSR 68; 7...♗e6 8 ♘g5 ♗g8 9 f4! **8 ♕d3** 8 a3 0-0 9 ♗c4+ ♔h8 10 ♘g5 ♕e8 **♗g4 9 h3 ♗xf3**

10 ♕xf3 0-0 11 ♕d3 11 ♕d1 ♔h8 += Pilnik-Rubinetti, Mar-del-Plata 71 **♔h8 12 ♘d5 ♘d4?** 12...♘xd5!= **13 ♘xf6 ♗xf6 14 ♗c4 ♘c6** 14...♗g5? 15 f4! **15 ♕g3 ♕d7 16 c3 ♘e7 17 ♕g4! ♕e8 18 g3 c6 19 ♗e3 d5 20 ♗d3 ♕c8 21 ♔g2 ♘g6 22 exd5 ♕xg4 23 hxg4 cxd5 24 g5! ♗e7 25 ♗c2 ♖fd8 26 ♖ad1 d4 27 cxd4 exd4 28 ♖xd4 ♖xd4 29 ♗xd4 ♗xg5 30 ♗e4 ♗f6 31 ♗xf6! gxf6 32 ♖c1± ♖e8 33 ♗xg6! hxg6 34 ♖c7!±**

34...♖e2 35 ♖xb7 ♔g8 36 ♔f3 ♖c2 37 ♔e3 a5 38 f3 a4 39 a3! ♖g2 40 g4 ♔f8 41 ♔e4 ♖e2+ 42 ♔d5 ♖e3 43 f4 ♖e2 44 ♖b4 ♔f7 45 ♖xa4 ♖d2+ 46 ♔c6 ♖xb2 47 ♖b4 ♖a2 48 a4 ♔e6 49 ♖e4+ ♔f7 50 ♔b5 f5 51 gxf5 gxf5 52 ♖d4 ♔e7 53 a5 ♖b2+ 54 ♖b4 ♖a2 55 a6 ♔d7 56 ♖a4 ♖b2+ 57 ♔c5 ♖c2+ 58 ♔d5 ♖c8 59 a7 ♖a8 60 ♔e5 ♔e7 61 ♔xf5 ♔f7 62 ♔e5 ♔e7 1-0 Mechkarov

275 Romanishin-Barbero
Buenos Aires 78

1 e4 e5 2 ♘f3 ♘c6 3 ♗b5 ♘f6 4 0-0 d6 5 d4 ♗d7 6 ♘c3 ♗e7 7 ♗xc6 7 ♖e1 exd4 8 ♘xd4 0-0 += **♗xc6 8 ♕d3 ♘d7** 8...exd4 9 ♘xd4 0-0 10 ♘f5 += **9 ♗e3** 9 d5 ♘c5 10 ♕c4 ♗d7 11 b4 ♘a6 12 ♗e3 += **exd4 10 ♘xd4 ♘e5** 10...0-0! **11 ♘xc6 bxc6** 11...♘xc6 12 ♘d5 0-0 13 c4 += **12 ♕e2 0-0 13 f4 ♘g6 14 ♖ad1 ♕e8?! 15 ♕d3 ♗f6? 16 e5!± dxe5 17 f5! ♘f4** 17...♘e7 18 ♗c5 Δ ♘e4 **18 ♕c4 ♗g5 19 ♖de1 ♕d7 20 g3 +− ♘h3+ 21 ♔g2 ♗xe3 22 ♖xe3 ♕d4 23 ♖e4 ♕d2+** 23...♕xc4 24 ♖xc4 ♘g5 25 h4 **24 ♕e2 ♕h6 25 ♖h4 ♕xh4 26 gxh4 ♘f4+ 27 ♖xf4 exf4 28 f6 gxf6 29 ♘e4 ♔g7 30 ♕g4+ ♔h8 31 ♕xf4 ♖g8+ 32 ♔f3 1-0 Gipslis**

276 Honfi-Magyar Budapest 78

1 e4 e5 2 ♘f3 ♘c6 3 ♗b5 ♘f6 4 0-0 ♘xe4 5 d4 a6?! 6 ♗xc6 dxc6 7 ♕e2 ♘d6 7...♗f5 8 ♖d1 ♗e7 9 dxe5 ♕c8 10 ♘d4 += **8 dxe5 ♘f5 9 ♖d1 ♕e7?!** 9...♗d7 **10 ♘c3 ♗d7** 10...h6 11 b3 += **11 ♗g5 ♕e6 12 ♘e4 h6?** 12...♗e7 **13 ♗f6! ♗e7 14 ♖xd7 ♕xd7?!** 14...♔xd7! 15 g4 ♘g3 16 hxg3 gxf6 17 exf6 ♗d6 18 ♖d1∝ **15 ♖d1 ♕e6 16 g4 ♘g3** 16...gxf6 17 gxf5 ♕xf5 18 exf6 +−; 16...♘d6 17 ♘d4 ♕xa2 18 exd6 +− **17 hxg3 gxf6 18 ♘d4 ♕xa2** 18...♕xe5 19 f4 ♕a5 20 ♘xf6+ ♔f8 21 ♘d7+ ♔e8 22 ♘f5 +− **19 exf6 1-0 Honfi**

1 e4 e5 2 ♘f3 ♘c6 3 ♗c4

277 Ivkov-Matanovic (6) 78

1 e4 e5 2 ♘f3 ♘c6 3 ♗c4 ♗c5 4 b4 ♗xb4 5 c3 ♗a5 6 d4 d6!? 7 ♕b3 ♕d7 7...♕e7!? **8 dxe5 dxe5 9 0-0 ♗b6 10 ♗b5?!** 10 ♖d1!? ♕e7 11 a4! a5 12 ♗d5 ♗g4 13 ♖d3 ♗e6 14 ♗a3 ♕f6 15 ♘bd2 ♘ge7 16 ♘c4 Shaposhnikov-Veltmander, USSR 58; 11...♘h6 **♘ge7 11 ♘xe5 ♕e6 12 ♘xc6 ♘xc6 13 ♗a3 ♗d7 14 ♘d2 0-0-0 15 ♘c4 ♘e5=**

Diagram

16 ♞xb6+ ♛xb6 17 ♝e2 ♝e6 18 ♛a4 a6 19 ♝c1 ♜d6!? 20 ♝e3 ♛b2 20... ♕c6 **21 ♜fe1 f6 22 ♜ab1 ♛xa2** Zeitnot **23 ♛b4 b5** 23...b6 24 ♖a1 **24 ♜a1?** 24 ♗xb5! axb5 25 ♖a1 ♕c4 26 ♖a8+ ♔b7 27 ♖xh8 ♕xb4 28 cxb4 ♘d3 29 ♖b1 ♘xb4? 30 ♗c5 +− **♛b3 25 ♛c5 ♝c4 26 ♛a7 ♚d7 27 ♝c5 ♜c6 28 ♜ab1 ♛a2** 28...♕xc3? 29 ♖ec1 +− **29 ♜a1 ♛b3 30 ♜ab1** Zeitnot **♛a2 31 ♜a1 ♛b3 ½-½ Maric**

278 Gaprindashvili-Chiburdanidze (2) 78

1 e4 e5 2 ♞f3 ♞c6 3 ♝c4 ♝e7 4 d3 ♞f6 5 ♝b3 d5 6 ♞bd2 0-0 7 0-0 dxe4 8 dxe4 ♝c5! 9 c3 ♛e7 10 ♝c2 10 ♗c4 a5 11 a4 **a5 11 ♞h4** 11 ♕e2 b6 Δ ♗a6 **g6 12 ♞b3 ♝b6 13 ♛f3 ♝g4** 13...♘e8 14 g3 ♘g7 **14 ♛g3 ♛e6** Δ ♘h5 **15 ♞f5! ♚h8** 15...gxf5 16 exf5 **16 ♞h6** 16 ♗h6 gxf5 17 exf5 ♕e7 18 h3 ♖g8 19 hxg4 ♖xg4 20 ♕h3 ♖ag8; 16 ♘e3 ♗e2 17 ♖e1 ♗a6 18 ♘d5?!; 18 ♘d2 **♝e2 17 ♜e1 ♞h5 18 ♛h4 ♝a6 19 ♞d2 f6 20 ♞f1 ♜ad8 21 ♞g3** 21 ♗e3 ♗xe3 22 ♘xe3 Δ ♗b3 **♞g7 22 ♞f1 ♞h5 23 ♞g3 ♞g7 24 ♞f1 ♞b8 25 ♝e3 ♞d7 26 ♝xb6 ♞xb6 27 ♞e3 a4 28 f4 exf4 29 ♛xf4 ♜d7 30 ♜ed1 ♜fd8 31 ♜xd7 ♜xd7 32 ♜d1 ♞h5! 33 ♛f2 ♚g7 34 g4 ♚xh6 35 gxh5 ♚g7 36 ♛f4 c6 37 ♜xd7+ ♞xd7 38 ♝xa4 ♛xa2! 39 h6+ ♚f7 40 ♛d6 ♚e8 41 ♝d1 ♛b1 42 ♞g4! ♝c4 43 e5 ♝d5 44 ♞xf6+ ♞xf6 45 ♛b8+ ♚f7 46 ♛c7+ ♚e6 47 ♛d6+ ♚f5 48 ♛xf6+ ♚e4 49 ♛f3+ ♚xe5 50 ♛e3+ ♚f5 51 ♛f2+ ♚e5 52 ♛d4+ ½-½**

279 Hug-R.Rodriguez
Buenos Aires 78

1 e4 e5 2 ♞f3 ♞c6 3 ♝c4 ♞f6 4 d3 ♝c5 5 ♞c3 d6 6 ♝g5 h6 7 ♝xf6 ♛xf6 8 ♞d5 ♛d8 8...♕g6!? 9 ♕e2! ♗g4 10 c3 += **9 c3 a6** 9...♘e7 **10 d4 exd4 11 cxd4 ♝a7 12 h3 0-0 13 0-0 ♝e6 14 ♛d2!** 14 ♖c1 ♘a5!∓ **♞e7 15 ♜fe1 ♞g6 16 ♝b3 c5 17 ♜ad1 b5 18 ♞f4! += ♝xb3 19 axb3 ♞h4** 19...♘xf4 20 ♕xf4± **20 ♞xh4 ♛xh4 21 g3 ♛g5 22 h4 ♛g4 23 dxc5 dxc5 24 ♚g2 ♝b8 25 ♞d5± ♛e6 26 ♛e3 ♜c8 27 e5! ♜a7 28 ♛e4 ♜e8 29 f4 f6 +− 30 ♛g6 ♛c6 31 ♚h2 1-0 Samarian**

Scotch

280 M.Tseitlin-Vladimirov
Suhumi 78

1 e4 e5 2 ♞f3 ♞c6 3 d4 exd4 4 c3 d5! 5 exd5 ♛xd5 6 cxd4 ♝g4 7 ♝e2 0-0-0?! 7...♗b4+ 8 ♘c3 ♗xf3 9 ♗xf3 ♕c4= **8 ♞c3 ♛a5 9 ♝e3 ♞f6** 9...♗b4 10 0-0! **10 h3 ♝xf3** 10...♗h5 11 0-0± **11 ♝xf3 ♝b4 12 0-0 ♝xc3 13 bxc3 ♜he8** 13...♕xc3? 14 ♖c1 **14 ♛b3± ♛a6 15 ♛xf7 ♜e7 16 ♛b3 ♜de8 17 ♜ab1 ♞e4 18 ♜fc1 ♞d6 19 ♝g4+ ♚b8 20 c4 ♞e4** 20...♘a5? 21 ♕a4 ♘dxc4 22 ♖xc4 ♘xc4 23 ♕xa6 +− **21 c5 ♞xd4 22 ♝xd4 ♞d2 23 ♛d5 ♞xb1 24 ♜xb1 c6 25 ♛d6+ ♚a8 26 ♝d7 ♛d3**

27 ♖xb7 ♔xb7 28 ♕xc6+ ♔b8 29 ♕d6+ ♔b7 30 ♕d5+ 1-0 30...♔b8 31 ♗e5+; 30...♔a6 31 ♕c6+ ♔a5 32 ♗c3+ ♕xc3 33 ♕b5 mate **Tseitlin**

281 Trabattoni-Honfi Bajmok 78
1 e4 e5 2 ♘f3 ♘c6 3 d4 exd4 4 ♘xd4 ♘f6 5 ♘xc6 bxc6 6 e5 ♕e7 7 ♕e2 ♘d5 8 c4 ♘b6 9 b3? 9 ♘d2 **g6! 10 ♗b2** 10 ♗a3? d6 11 exd6? ♕xe2+ 12 ♗xe2 ♗g7 −+ **♗g7 11 ♘d2 0-0 12 0-0-0 ♖e8 13 f4 d6 14 ♕f3?! dxe5 15 ♕xc6 exf4 16 ♗d3 ♗g4 17 ♖de1?? ♕xe1+ 0-1 Honfi**

French

282 Ljubojevic-Hubner
Buenos Aires 78
1 e4 e6 2 d3 c5 3 ♘f3 ♘c6 4 g3 g6 5 ♗g2 ♗g7 6 0-0 ♘ge7 7 ♖e1 0-0 8 c3 d6 9 d4?! 9 ♘a3 e5; 9 ♗e3 f5; 9 ♘bd2 **cxd4 10 cxd4 ♕b6 11 d5** 11 ♗e3 ♕xb2 12 ♘bd2 d5∓; 11 ♘c3 ♘xd4∓ **♗xb2 12 ♗xb2 ♕xb2**

Diagram

13 dxc6 13 ♘bd2 1) 13...exd5 14 exd5 ♘xd5 15 ♘c4 ♕b5 16 ♘xd6 ♕a5 17 ♘e5 +=; 2) 13...♘a5 14 ♕a4 ♕b6 15 e5 ♘d5 16 exd6 ♕d8 17 ♘e5 b6 18 d7 ♗b7; 14...b6 15 ♖ab1 ♕f6 16 e5∝ **♕xa1 14 ♕b3** 14 cxb7 ♗xb7 15 ♕b3 ♗d5 16 exd5 ♖ab8 17 ♕d3 ♘xd5∓; 15...♖fc8? 16 ♕xb7 ♖ab8 17 ♕xe7 ♖xb1 18 ♖xb1 ♕xb1+ 19 ♗f1 ♕xe4 20 ♘g5 ♕f5 21 ♗d3 +− **♘xc6 15 ♘c3 ♘d4 16 ♖xa1 ♘xb3 17 axb3 ♗d7 =+ 18 e5!** 18 ♖d1 ♖fc8 19 ♖xd6 ♖xc3 20 ♖xd7 ♖xb3 21 ♘e5 ♖b1+ 22 ♗f1 ♖f8∓; 19 ♘e2 ♗c6∓ **d5** 18...♖fc8? 19 ♘e4 +− **19 ♘d4 ♖fc8 20 ♘cb5 ♗xb5 21 ♘xb5 a6** 21...a5 22 ♘d6 ♖c7 23 ♗f1 b6 24 ♗b5 ♖c3 25 ♗a4 ♖a7 26 ♖d1 ♖ac7 27 ♔g2 +=; 22...♖c3 23 ♘xb7 ♖xb3 24 ♖xa5 ♖c8 25 ♘c5 ♖c3 26 ♘d7 d4? 27 ♖a6 Δ ♖d6; 21...♖c2 22 ♗f1 a5 23 ♘d6 b6 24 ♗b5 += **22 ♘d6 ♖c3 23 ♘xb7** 23 b4 ♖b3 24 ♖c1 ♖xb4 25 ♖c7 ♖b1+ 26 ♗f1 a5 27 ♘xf7 a4 28 ♘g5 a3 29 ♘xh7 ♖xf1+ 30 ♔g2 ♖g1+ 31 ♔h3 ♖f8 −+; 28 ♘h6+ ♔f8 29 ♖xh7 ♖a5 −+ **♖xb3 24 ♘c5 ♖b6** 24...♖b5 25 ♘a6 ♖b6 26 ♗f1 **25 ♖a5** 25 ♗f1 a5 26 ♗d3 ♖c6 27 ♘a4 ♖b8 28 ♖a3 f6 29 exf6 e5∓ **♖b5 26 ♖xa6 ♖xa6** 26...♖c8 27 ♘d7 ♖c1+ 28 ♗f1 ♖bb1 29 ♘f6+ ♔g7 30 ♖a8 ♖xf1+ 31 ♔g2 ♖g1+ 32 ♔h3= ♔h6 33 f4 g5 34 ♖g8; 27 ♘d3? ♖b1+ 28 ♗f1 ♖c3 29 ♔g2 ♖xf1 −+ **27 ♘xa6 d4 28 ♗f1** 28 f4? d3 29 ♔f2 d2 30 ♔e2 ♖b1 31 ♔xd2 ♖b2+ −+ **♖xe5 29 ♘b4 ♖c5 30 f4**

f6 ½-½ 31 ♔f2 ♖c3 32 ♘d3 ♖c2+ 33 ♗e2 ♔f7 34 ♔f3 ♔e7 35 h4 ♔d6 36 ♗f1 e5 37 fxe5 fxe5 38 ♔e4=; 31...g5 32 ♔f3 gxf4 33 gxf4 f5 34 ♘d3 ♖c3 35 ♔f2 ♔f8 36 ♘e5 ♔e7 37 ♗c4= **Hubner**

283 Szmetan-Keene
Buenos Aires 2 78

1 e4 e6 2 d3 d5 3 ♞d2 c5 4 ♞gf3 ♞c6 5 g3 ♞ge7 5...♘f6 6 ♗g2 ♗e7∝ **6 ♝g2 g6 7 0-0 ♝g7 8 ♞h4! += 0-0 9 f4 b6 10 ♚h1 a5 11 e5 ♝a6 12 ♞df3 ♛d7** 12...c4!? 13 d4 c2 **13 c3! d4 14 c4± ♞f5 15 ♛e2** 15 ♘xf5 exf5! =+ **♜ad8 16 ♝d2 ♝b7 17 b3 ♜a8 18 ♜ab1 ♜a7** 18...a4 19 b4± **19 a3 ♜fa8 20 g4 ♞xh4 21 ♞xh4 ♜e8 22 ♝e4! ♞d8 23 ♞f3 ♞c6** 23...♗xe4 24 ♕xe4 ♕c6 25 ♘g5!± **24 ♛g2 a4!? 25 bxa4!** 25 b4 cxb4 26 axb4 a3∝ **♛c7 26 a5! ♞xa5 27 ♝xa5 ♜xa5 28 ♞g5! ♝xe4 29 ♞xe4 ♜xa3??** 29...♖ea8 30 ♘d6± **30 ♞d6** +− Δ ♘b5

♜ea8 31 ♞b5 ♛d8 32 ♞xa3 ♜xa3 33 ♜a1! ♜xa1 33...♖xd3?? 34 ♖a8 **34 ♜xa1 ♛h4 35 ♛f3 g5 36 ♚g2 h5 37 ♜a8+! ♝f8** 37...♔h7 38 ♕e4+ **38 gxh5 gxf4 39 h3 ♛e1 40 ♛g4+ ♚h7 1-0 Gheorghiu**

284 Letzelter-Huss
Buenos Aires 78

1 e4 e6 2 d4 d5 3 ♞c3 ♝b4 4 ♞e2 dxe4 5 a3 ♝xc3+ 6 ♞xc3 e5?! 6...♘c6 7 ♗b5 ♘e7 8 ♗g5 f6 9 ♗e3 0-0 10 ♕d2 f5 11 f3∝ **7 dxe5 ♛xd1+ 8 ♚xd1! ♝f5** 8...♗g4+ 9 ♗e2 ♗xe2+ 10 ♔xe2 ♘c6 11 ♘xe4 ♘xe5 12 ♗f4 f6 13 ♘c5 0-0-0 14 ♘e6 ♖d7 15 ♖d1± **9 ♞d5! ♞a6 10 ♝g5!** 10 ♗xa6? 0-0-0!∓ **♝e6** 10...h6? 11 ♗xa6 hxg5 12 ♗xb7± **11 ♝b5+! c6 12 ♝xa6 ♝xd5 13 ♝xb7 ♜b8 14 ♝a6 ♜b6 15 ♝e2 ♜xb2 16 ♚d2 ♞e7 17 ♚c3!** 17 ♖hb1 ♖xb1 18 ♖xb1 ♘g6! 19 ♖b8+ ♔d7 20 ♖b7+ ♔c8 21 ♖xa7 ♔b8 22 ♖a6 ♘xe5≈ **♜b7 18 ♜hb1 ♜c7** 18...♖xb1 19 ♖xb1 ♘g6 20 ♔d4 Δ c4± **19 ♜b8+ ♞c8** 19...♖c8? 20 ♖b7 +− **20 ♝e3!** Δ ♗xa7; 20 ♔d4?! ♗e6 **0-0** 20...♔e7? 21 ♗g4 (Δ ♗c5+ +−) ♖d8 (21...♖e8 22 ♗c5+ ♔d8 23 ♗d6 +−) 22 ♗c5+ ♔e8 23 ♗d6! ♘xd6 24 exd6 ♖xb8 25 dxc7 +− **21 ♝c5! ♜e8 22 ♝a6 1-0 Letzelter** 22...f6 23 ♗d6 ♘xd6 24 exd6 ♖ce7 25 ♖ab1 ♖e5 26 d7! +−

285 Spassky-Portisch
Buenos Aires 78

1 e4 e6 2 d4 d5 3 ♞c3 ♝b4 4 e5 c5 5 a3 ♝xc3+ 6 bxc3 ♛c7 7 ♞f3 7 ♕g4 f5 8 ♕g3 ♘e7 9 ♕xg7 ♖g8 10 ♕xh7 cxd4 11 ♔d1∝ **♞e7 8 a4 b6** 8...♘bc6 9 ♕d2 f6 10 exf6 gxf6 11 ♗e2∝ **9 ♝b5+!** 9 ♗d3 ♗a6= **♝d7 10 ♝d3 ♞bc6 11 0-0 h6 12 ♜e1 0-0 13 ♝d2 c4 14 ♝f1 += f6 15 g3 ♞g6 16 ♝h3 fxe5 17 dxe5 ♜f7?!** 17...♘cxe5!? 18 ♘xe5 ♘xe5 19 ♗f4 ♖xf4 20 gxf4 ♘g6∝; 19 f4 ♘f7 20 ♗e3 e5! **18 ♝g4± ♞ge7 19 ♞d4! ♞xd4 20 cxd4 c3 21 ♝c1 ♞f5 22 ♝h5 ♜ff8 23 ♝a3 ♛c4** 23...♖fc8 24 g4 ♘h4 25 ♗d6 ♕c6 26 ♗e7 g5 (26...g6 27 ♗xh4 gxh5

28 gxh5 +−) 27 f4 +− **24 Bxf8 Rxf8 25 Ra3 Bxa4 26 Qa1 b5 27 Rxc3 Qxd4 28 Rc6 +− Qxa1 29 Rxa1 Nd4 30 Rc7 a5** 30...Nxc2? 31 Rxa4 **31 f4 Kh7 32 Bd1 Ra8 33 Kf2 Kg6 34 g4 h5 35 Ke3 1-0 Gipslis**

286 Diez del Corral-Portisch
Buenos Aires 78

1 e4 e6 2 d4 d5 3 Nc3 Bb4 4 e5 c5 5 a3 Bxc3+ 6 bxc3 Qc7 7 Qg4 f5 7...f6!? 8 Bb5+! Nc6 9 Nf3+ **8 Qg3 cxd4** 8...Nc6 9 Nf3 cxd4 10 cxd4 Nge7 11 Qxg7 Rg8 12 Qh6 Bd7 13 Qd2 += Dely-Bondarevsky 59 **9 cxd4 Ne7 10 Bd2 0-0 11 Bd3 b6 12 Ne2 Ba6** 12...Rf7 Diez del Corral-Petrosian, Palma de Mallorca 69, 13 h4! += **13 Bb4! N** 13 Qf3 Qd7 14 0-0 Bxd3 15 cxd3 Nbc6 16 Be3 Kh8 17 Rac1 += Mednis-Foldi, 58; 14 Bb4 Rf7 15 h4 Bxd3 16 Qxd3 Nbc6 17 h5 Rc8 18 Rh3 Nd8 19 Rg3 Rc4 20 h6 Ndc6!≈ Hort-Petrosian, Kapfenberg 70 **Bxd3 14 cxd3 Nbc6 15 Bd6 Qd7 16 0-0 Rfc8 17 h4 Ng6?!** 17...Kh8!? Δ Ng8 **18 h5 Nh8 19 h6 g6 20 Nf4!** Δ Nh5

20...Nxd4 21 Ra2 Qb7 21...Nb5 22 Nh5 **22 a4!** 22 Nh5 Nf7 **Rc6 23 Qe3 Nc2 24 Rxc2! Rxc2 25 Nxe6 Nf7 26 Nd4 Ra2 27 Nxf5! +− Nxd6 28 exd6 gxf5 29 Qg5+ Kf8 30 Re1 Qf7 31 Re7 1-0 Samarian**

287 Arzumanjan-Svenningsson
Corr 78

1 e4 e6 2 d4 d5 3 Nc3 Bb4 4 e5 c5 5 a3 Bxc3+ 6 bxc3 Ne7 7 a4 Nbc6 8 Nf3 Qa5 9 Bd2 Bd7 10 Be2 c4 11 0-0 f6 12 Re1 0-0-0 13 exf6? gxf6 14 Bf1 Nf5 16 Qc1 h5 16 Qa3 Rdg8 17 Rab1 Rh7 18 Rb5 Qc7 19 Reb1 b6 20 Qc1 Nd6 21 R5b2 Ne4 22 Qe1 Na5 23 Rb4 h4 24 Qe3 Be8 25 Be1 f5 26 Ne5 Nc6 27 f3 Nxe5! 27...Nxb4 28 Rxb4 Nd6 29 Nxc4! **28 dxe5 f4 29 Qd4** 29 Qxf4 Qc5+ 30 Kh1 Ng3+! 31 Bxg3 hxg3 32 h3 Qf2 Δ Rxh3+, Qh2 mate **Ng5 30 Kh1 Nxf3! 31 gxf3 Bh5 32 Be2 Qg7 33 Qf2 h3 34 a5 Qg2+ 35 Qxg2 Rxg2 36 axb6** 36 Bxc4 Bxf3 37 Ba6+ Kc7 38 Rxf4 Rhg7 39 Bg3 R2xg3+ **Rxe2 37 Kg1 a5! 38 Rb5 Rg7+ 39 Kf1 Rxh2 40 b7+ Kb8 41 Bf2 Rxf2+ 42 Kxf2 Rg2+ 43 Kf1 Bxf3 0-1** 44 Rxa5 Be2+ 45 Ke1 Rg1+ 46 Kxe2 Rxb1 47 Ra8+ Kxb7 48 Rh8 Rh1

288 Sigurjonsson-Matsumado
Buenos Aires 1 78

1 e4 e6 2 d4 d5 3 Nc3 Bb4 4 e5 Qd7 5 Bd2 b6 6 Nf3 Ne7 6...Ba6 7 Bxa6 Nxa6 8 Ne2 += **7 h4!?** 7 a3!? Bxc3 8 Bxc3 Ba6 9 Bxa6 Nxa6 10 Qd3 Nb8 11 0-0 +=; 7 Bd3?! Ba6 **Ba6** 7...h5 **8 Bxa6 Nxa6 9 h5 h6 10 Qe2 Nb8 11 0-0-0 c5?** 11...Nc6 **12 Nb5!± c4** 12...Bxd2+ 13 Rxd2 Nc8 14 g4±; 14 c4!?± **13 Bxb4 Qxb5 14 Bxe7 Kxe7 15 Nh4!** Δ f4-f5 **Qa4?! 16 Rh3 Nc6** 16...Qxa2?? 17 Ra3 +− **17 Ra3 Qb5 18 f4 Nb4 19 f5 Rhc8** Δ Nd3+ **20 Kb1 a6 21 fxe6 fxe6**

22 ♖f1 Δ ♘g6+ +− **c3? 23 ♘g6+ ♔d7 24 ♖f7+ ♔e8 25 ♖f8+ ♔d7 26 ♕xb5+ 1-0** 26...axb5 27 ♖xa8 +−

289 Szalancy-Sinkovits
Budapest 2 78

1 e4 e6 2 d4 d5 3 ♘c3 ♗b4 4 e5 ♘e7 5 a3 ♗xc3+ 6 bxc3 c5 7 ♘f3 ♗d7 8 a4 ♘bc6 9 ♗e2 9 ♗d3 **♕a5 10 ♗d2** 10 0-0 ♕xc3 11 ♗d2 ♕b2 12 ♖b1 ♕a3 13 ♖b3 ♕a2 14 ♕c1! Δ ♖a3 **c4 11 0-0 f6 12 ♖e1 fxe5 13 ♘xe5** 13 dxe5 h6 14 ♗f1 0-0 15 g3 ♘g6= **♘xe5 14 dxe5 0-0 15 ♗f1 ♗xa4 16 ♖e3 ♗xc2! 17 ♕c1 ♗a4 18 ♕a3 ♘f5! 19 ♕xa4 ♕xa4 20 ♖xa4 ♘xe3 21 ♗xe3 a5! 22 f4 b5 23 ♖a1 ♖fc8 24 g4! b4 25 f5 b3 26 fxe6 b2 27 ♖b1 ♖ab8 28 ♗g2 a4 29 ♗xd5 a3 30 e7+ ♔h8 31 e8♕+! ♖xe8 32 ♗xc4 ♖ec8?** 32...♖xe5 33 ♗f4? ♖e4 34 ♗xb8 35 ♖xc4 −+; 33 ♗d4 ♖e2! **33 ♗a2 ♖xc3 34 ♔f2 ♖bb3!? 35 e6?!** 35 ♖d1! h6 36 e6! **h5** 35...♖xe3 36 ♗xb3? ♖xb3 37 e7 ♖b8 38 ♖d1 ♖e8!! 39 ♖d8 ♔g8!! 40 ♖xe8+ ♔f7 −+; 36 ♖d1! h6 37 ♗xb3 ♖xb3 38 e7 ♖b8 39 ♖d8+ ♔h7 40 ♖xb8 a2 41 ♖h8+ ♔xh8 42 e8♕+ ♔h7 43 ♕e4+ +− **36 e7 ♖c2+** 36...♖xe3 37 ♗xb3 ♖xe7 **37 ♔f3 hxg4+ 38 ♔e4 ♖b8 39 ♖f1 ♖cc8 40 ♗c5! ♖e8 41 ♖f8+ ♔h7 42 ♖xe8 ♖xe8 43 ♔f5 ♔h6 44 ♗d6 ♔h5 45 ♔e6 ♔h4 46 ♔f7 ♖a8 47 e8♕ ♖xe8 48 ♔xe8 ♔h3 49 ♔f7 g5 50 ♔f6 ♔h4 51 ♔g6 1-0**

290 Groszpeter-Dr.Vigh
Budapest 1 78

1 e4 e6 2 d4 d5 3 ♘c3 ♘f6 4 ♗g5 ♗e7 5 e5 ♘fd7 6 ♗xe7 ♕xe7 7 f4 a6 8 ♘f3 c5 9 ♕d2 ♘c6 10 0-0-0 c4 11 f5 b5 12 ♕g5 ♕xg5 13 ♘xg5 ♘b6 14 fxe6 fxe6 15 g3 h6 16 ♘h3 0-0 17 ♘f4 b4 18 ♘ce2 a5 19 ♗h3 ♖e8 20 ♖hf1 a4 21 ♖f3 ♖b8 22 ♖df1 c3! 23 bxc3 bxc3 24 a3 24 ♖xc3 ♘b4 25 ♖a3 ♗d7! Δ ♘c4 −+; 25 ♔b1 ♘c4 26 ♔a1 a3 **♘c4 25 ♖xc3 ♖e7?** 25...♘a7! Δ ♘b5, ♘xa3 **26 ♘g6! ♖eb7 27 ♖f8+ ♔h7**

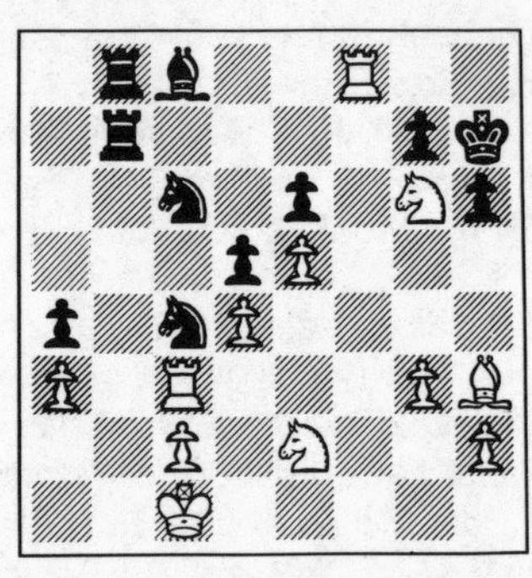

28 ♖xc4! dxc4 29 ♗g2!! ♖b1+ 29...♔xg6 30 ♗e4+ ♔g5 31 ♗xc6 ♖b1+ 32 ♔d2; 29...♗d7 30 ♗e4! ♖xf8 31 ♘xf8+ ♔g8 32 ♘xd7 ♖xd7 33 ♗xc6 +− **30 ♔d2 ♗b7** 30...♔xg6 **31 ♗e4 ♖xf8 32 ♘xf8+ ♔g8 33 ♘xe6 ♘a5 34 ♘c3 ♖f1 35 d5 ♖f2+ 36 ♔e3 ♖xh2 37 ♘c7 ♔f8 38 e6 ♔e7 39 ♔d4 ♗c8 40 ♘3b5 ♘b7 41 ♔e5 ♖d2 42 ♘a7! ♔d8 43 ♘xc8 ♔xc7 44 e7 ♔d7 45 ♗f5+ 1-0**

291 Letzelter-Asmundsson
Buenos Aires 78

1 e4 e6 2 d4 d5 3 ♘c3 ♘f6 4 ♗g5 ♗e7 5 e5 ♘fd7 6 h4 a6 7 ♕g4 ♗xg5 8 hxg5 c5 9 g6! f5 10 ♕f4 h6 11 ♘f3 Δ ♘g5 +− **0-0 12 dxc5 ♘c6**

Diagram

13 0-0-0!? 13 ♖d1! (1) 13...♕e8 14 ♖xd5!! exd5 15 ♖xh6! gxh6 16 ♕xh6 ♕e7 17 ♘xd5 ♕g7 18 ♘e7+! ♘xe7 19 ♗c4+ ♖f7 (19...♘d5? 20

♗xd5+ ♖f7 21 gxf7+ ♔f8 22 ♕d6 mate) 20 ♗xf7+ ♔f8 21 ♘g5!! ♘f6 (21...♕xh6 22 ♘e6 mate) 22 exf6! ♕xh6 23 ♘h7+ ♕xh7 24 gxh7 +− (2) 13...♕c7 14 ♖xd5! exd5 15 ♘xd5 ♕a5+ 16 b4! ♘xb4 (16...♕xa2 17 ♘e7+! ♘xe7 18 ♗c4+ +−) 17 ♘e7+ ♔h8 18 ♖xh6+! +− **♛e8 14 ♜xh6!? gxh6 15 ♛xh6 ♛e7 16 g7! ♜e8?** 16...♕xg7 17 ♕xe6+ ♖f7 (17...♕f7 18 ♕d6! +=) 18 ♕xd5 ♘dxe5 19 ♘xe5 ♕xe5 20 ♗c4∝ **17 ♛h8+ ♚f7 18 ♞xd5!! exd5 19 e6+! ♚xe6** 19...♕xe6 20 ♘g5+ +− **20 ♜e1+ ♞de5 21 ♞xe5 ♞xe5 22 ♜xe5+! 1-0 Letzelter**

292 Ostojic-F.Portisch
Virovitica 78

1 e4 e6 2 d4 d5 3 ♞d2 c5 4 exd5 exd5 5 ♝b5+ ♞c6 6 ♛e2+ ♝e7 7 dxc5 ♞f6 8 ♞b3 0-0 9 ♝e3 a6!? 10 ♝a4?! 10 ♗d3 d4 11 ♗g5 a5 12 a4∝ Hubner-Uhlmann, Palma de Mallorca 70; 10 ♗xc6+!? **♞e4 11 0-0-0 ♞b4! 12 ♚b1** 12 a3?? ♘a2+ 13 ♔b1 ♘ac3+ −+ **♝f5 13 ♜c1 ♜c8! 14 g4** 14 a3? ♘xc2! 15 ♖xc2 b5 16 cxb6 ♖xc2 −+ **♝g6 15 f4 h5 16 a3?** 16 f5! ♗h7 17 ♘f3 hxg4 18 ♘fd4∝

Diagram

16...♞xc2! 17 f5 ♞xe3 18 fxg6 b5!! 19 cxb6 ♜xc1+∓ 20 ♚xc1 20 ♘xc1 ♕xb6∓ **fxg6 21 ♞f3** 21 ♕xe3?? ♗g5 −+ **♛xb6 22 ♞fd4 ♜f2 −+ 23 ♛d3 ♝f6 24 gxh5 gxh5 25 h3 ♚h8 26 ♜e1 ♞g2 27 ♜xe4** 27 ♖d1 ♗xd4! 28 ♕xd4 ♕c7+ Δ ♕c2+ −+ **dxe4 28 ♛xe4 ♞f4 29 ♞f3 ♛c7+ 30 ♚d1 ♜f1+ 31 ♚d2 ♛d6+ 32 ♞bd4 ♜xf3 0-1 Maric**

293 Larsen-Portisch Tilburg 78

1 e4 e6 2 d4 d5 3 ♞d2 c5 4 exd5 exd5 5 ♝b5+ ♝d7 6 ♛e2+ ♝e7 7 dxc5 ♞f6 8 ♞b3 0-0 9 ♝e3 ♜e8 10 ♞f3 a6 10...♗xc5!? 11 ♗xd7 ♘bxd7 12 0-0 ♘xc5 13 ♖fe1?!= Parma-Korchnoi, Moscow 71; 13 ♘fd4!? **11 ♝d3 ♝a4 12 ♞fd4!?** 12 0-0 ♗xb3 13 axb3 ♗xc5 =+ **♞bd7 13 0-0 ♞xc5 14 ♞xc5** 14 c3!? **♝xc5 15 ♛f3** 15 c3!? **♛b6 16 ♞f5 ♝xe3 17 fxe3!?** 17 ♘xe3 **♝d7 18 ♞d4 ♜e7 19 ♝f5 ♝b5** 19...♕xb2!? **20 ♜fe1 ♜ae8 21 c3 ♛c7= 22 ♜ad1 ♝a4 23 ♜d2 ♜e5 24 ♝d3 ♝d7 25 ♜f2 ♜h5 26 ♛f4** 26 h3?! ♖g5 **♛xf4 27 ♜xf4 ♜he5 28 ♞c2 ♞g4 29 ♜b4 ♝c8** 29...b5? 30 a4 a5? 31 ♗xb5! **30 ♜d4 ♚f8 31 a4!** 31 h3?! ♘xe3 32 ♘xe3 ♖xe3 33 ♖xe3 ♖xe3 34 ♖xd5 ♗e6 35 ♖d4 ♗xa2 36 ♗e4 (Δ ♔f2) ♖e2; 35 ♖d8+? ♔e7 36 ♔f2? ♖xh3!; 36 ♖d4 **a5!?** 31...♘xe3!? 32 ♘xe3 ♖xe3 33 ♖xe3 ♖xe3 34 ♖xd5 ♗e6

35 Rd4 += **32 Bb5 += Rd8 33 h3** 33 e4?! Nf6!? 34 c4 Rxe4 35 R1xe4 Nxe4 36 cxd5 Nd6 **Nf6 34 b4!? Bf5 35 Bd3 Rc8 36 Bxf5 Rxf5 37 Rd3 axb4 38 Nd4! Re5 39 cxb4 Rc4 40 Rb1 Re8 41 a5 Rec8 42 Kh2 g6 43 b5 Ra4 44 a6! bxa6 45 b6 Rac4 46 Ra3 Rb8 47 Rxa6 Nd7 48 b7 Rc7 49 Ra8 Ke7 50 Rxb8 Nxb8 51 Kg3 Rc3 52 Kf4 Kd7 53 g4 h6 54 Rb6 Rc1 55 Ke5 Kc7 56 Rb3** 56 Rf6?? Nd7+ **Nd7+ 57 Kxd5 h5 58 Nb5+** 58 gxh5?! Rc5+! 59 Ke4 Rxh5 **Kxb7 59 Nd6+ Ka6** 59...Kc7? 60 Rb7+ Kd8 61 Nxf7+! Ke8 ½-½ 60 Nxf7 hxg4 61 hxg4 Nf6+ Δ Nxg4 += **Speelman**

294 Karpov-Korchnoi (22) 78
1 e4 e6 2 d4 d5 3 Nd2 c5 4 exd5 exd5 5 Bb5+ Bd7 6 Qe2+ Be7 6...Qe7 **7 dxc5 Nf6 8 Nb3 0-0 9 Be3 Re8 10 Nf3 Bxc5 11 Nxc5 Qa5+ 12 Qd2 Qxb5 13 0-0-0 b6** 13...Bg4 14 Bd4 Ne4 15 Qf4 Bxf3 16 gxf3 Nxc5 17 Bxg7 Kxg7 18 Rhg1+ Kf8 19 Qd6+! Re7 20 Qh6+ Ke8 21 Rg8+ Kd7 22 Rxd5+ Kc7 23 Qd6 mate; 15...Nxc5 16 Qxg4 **14 Nxd7 Nbxd7 15 Kb1 Ne4 16 Qd3 Qxd3 17 Rxd3 Ndf6 18 h3 Nc5 19 Rdd1 Ne6 20 c3 b5 21 Nd4 a6 22 Nc2 a5 23 Rd3 Rab8 24 Rhd1 h6 25 f4 Rbc8 26 g4 d4! 27 cxd4** 27 Nxd4 Nc5 Δ Nxd3 **Nd5 28 Rf1 b4 29 Bd2 Re7?** 29...Nec7 **30 f5 Ng5 31 Ne3 Nf6 32 d5 Nxh3** 32...Nge4 **33 d6 Rd7 34 Nd5 Nxd5 35 Rxd5 Ra8 36 Be3 Ng5** Zeitnot 36...Ra6 **37 Bb6 Ne4 38 Rfd1** 38 Bxa5? Rxa5 39 Rxa5 Nd2+ **a4 39 R5d4 Re8 40 Rxb4 Rxd6 41 Rxd6 Nxd6 42 Bc7?!** 42 Rxa4 +− **Re1+ 43 Kc2 Ne8 44 Ba5 a3 45 Rb8 Re7 46 Bb4?** 46 bxa3 +−; 46 b4 +− **Re2+ 47 Kd3 axb2 48 Bd2** 48 Bc3 b1Q+! 49 Rxb1 Rxa2 50 Rb8 Rg2 51 Rxe8+ Kh7= 52 Re4 h5 53 gxh5 Rh2 54 Rg4 f6 55 Ke4 Rxh5= **Re7 49 a4 Rd7+ 50 Kc2 Kh7 51 Rxb2 h5! 52 gxh5 Nd6!** Δ Nc4 **53 Ra2 Nxf5 54 a5 Nd4+ 55 Kc3** 55 Kb1 Nb3 56 Be3 Nxa5 57 Rxa5 g6 58 h6 f6 59 Ra2 g5 60 Rh2 Kg6 61 Bc5 Rd8 Δ Rh8 **Nc6 56 a6 Rd5 57 Bf4 Rf5** 57...Rxh5 58 Rh2! **58 Bd6 Rd5 59 Bg3 Rg5 60 Bf2** 60 Bc7 Rc5+ **Rxh5 61 Kc4 Na5+ 62 Kc3 Nc6 63 Kc4 Na5+ 64 Kc3 ½-½**

295 Karpov-Korchnoi (16) 78
1 e4 e6 2 d4 d5 3 Nd2 c5 4 exd5 exd5 5 Bb5+ Bd7 5...Nc6 **6 Qe2+ Qe7** 6...Be7 **7 Bxd7+ Nxd7 8 dxc5 Nxc5 9 Nb3 Qxe2+ 10 Nxe2 Nxb3 11 axb3 Bc5 12 Bd2** 12 Nc3 Nf6 13 Na4; 12...0-0-0? 13 Ra5! Hort-Ivkov, Wijk aan Zee 70 **Ne7 13 Nf4** 13 Bc3 Nc6?! 14 Rd1 Botvinnik-Euwe 48 **0-0 14 0-0** 14 Nd3 Bb6 15 Ba5; 15 Bb4 Δ Kd2 **Rfd8 15 Nd3 Bb6 16 c3 f6** 16...d4 17 c4 **17 Rfd1 Kf7 18 Kf1 Nf5?** 18...Nc6 **19 Be1 Ne7 20 Nb4 Rd7 21 Rd3 Rad8 22 Rad1 Ke6 23 Bd2** Δ Be3 **Nc6 24 Nxc6 bxc6 25 b4 Kf7 26 Be3 Bxe3 27 Rxe3 Rb8 28 Re2 Rb5 29 Ra1 Rdb7** Δ a5/c5 **30 Rd2 Ke6 31 Ra6 R5b6 32 Ra2 Kd6 33 Ke2 Re7+ 34 Kd3 a6 35 Rd1** 35 Re2 Rxe2 36 Kxe2 c5 37 bxc5+ Kxc5 38 Kd3 Rb3 39 Kc2 Rb6 40 Ra5+ Δ b4± **Kc7 36 Raa1** 36 Rda1 Δ Ra4, b3 **Kd8 37 f3**

Diagram

37...Re5! 38 Kd4 Kc7 38...Re2?

39 ♖e1 ♖xg2 40 ♔c5 ♔c7 41 ♖e7+ ♔d8 42 ♖a7; 42 ♖f7; 40...♖b8 41 ♖xa6 **39 ♜e1 ♚d6 40 f4?** 40 h4 **♜xe1 41 ♜xe1 a5! 42 bxa5 ½-½** 42... ♖xb2 43 ♖a1 c5+ 44 ♔e3 ♔c7 45 a6 ♔b8 46 ♖a5 ♖xg2 47 a7+ ♔a8 48 ♖xc5 ♖xh2 49 ♖xd5

296 Dahl-Wurtz Corr 78

1 e4 e6 2 d4 d5 3 ♞d2 c5 4 exd5 exd5 5 ♞gf3 a6 6 ♝e2 ♞c6 7 0-0 c4 8 a4 ♜b8 9 ♜e1 ♝e7 10 ♞f1 b5 11 ♝f4 ♜b7 12 axb5 axb5 13 ♞e5 ♞xe5 14 ♝xe5 f6 15 ♝f4 g5? 15...♔f7 Δ ♗d6, ♘e7 **16 ♝d2 ♝f5 17 ♝h5+ ♚f8 18 ♞g3 ♝g6 19 ♛f3 ♚g7 20 ♜a6 ♞h6 21 ♜ee6 ♜f8 22 ♝xg6 hxg6 23 ♝xg5! ♞g8** 23...fxg5 24 ♖xg6+ +− **24 ♝d2 b4 25 h4 ♜b5 26 h5 ♛e8 27 ♛g4 ♚h7 28 hxg6+ ♛xg6 29 ♛h3+ ♚g7 30 ♞f5+ ♚f7 31 ♞xe7 1-0** 31...♘xe7 32 ♖xe7+

297 Hort-Spassky Tilburg 78

1 e4 e6 2 d4 d5 3 ♞d2 c5 4 exd5 ♛xd5 5 ♞gf3 cxd4 6 ♝c4 ♛d6 7 0-0 ♞f6 8 ♞b3 ♞c6 9 ♞bxd4 ♞xd4 10 ♞xd4 ♝e7 10...a6 **11 c3** 11 b3!? **♝d7 12 ♛f3 ♛c7 13 ♝b3 ♝d6 14 h3 ♝e5 15 ♝g5** 15 ♖e1 ♗xd4?! 16 cxd4 ♗c6? 17 d5!; 15...0-0 16 ♗g5 ♗xd4!? 17 cxd4 ♗c6 18 ♕d3 +=; 18 ♕c3 +=; 16...h6; 16...♖ad8 **♝xd4!? 16 cxd4 ♝c6 17 ♛e3** 17 ♕c3? ♘e4! **♞d5 18 ♛e5 ½-½ Speelman**

298 Nunn-Piasetski
Buenos Aires 78

1 e4 e6 2 d4 d5 3 ♞d2 ♞c6 4 ♞gf3 ♞f6 5 e5 ♞fd7 6 ♞b3 ♝e7 7 ♝b5 a5 8 0-0!? 8 a4 ♘cb8 Δ b6, ♗a6 **a4 9 ♞bd2 ♞b6** 9...a3 10 b3 ♗b4 11 ♘b1! Δ c3, b4, ♘xa3 **10 c3 0-0?** 10...♗d7 11 ♗d3 ♘a7 12 ♖e1 ♗b5 13 ♗b1 += **11 ♜e1 ♝d7 12 ♝d3 ♞a7 13 ♞f1 ♝b5 14 ♝b1± ♞d7 15 ♛c2 g6 16 ♝h6** 16 ♕d2 ♖e8 17 ♕h6 ♗f8 18 ♕h3± **♜e8 17 ♛d2 c5 18 ♛f4** 18 ♘e3 Δ ♘g4, ♗g5 **♞c6 19 ♞g5 ♜f8 20 h4?** 20 ♘e3! ± **cxd4 = 21 ♝xf8?** 21 cxd4 ♕b6 22 ♗xf8 ♖xf8 23 ♘f3 ♗xf1 24 ♖xf1 ♕xb2 25 ♗d3 ♘b4=; 22...♗xg5 23 ♕xg5 ♖xf8 24 h5∝ **♝xg5** 21...♕xf8!? 22 ♘f3? a3 **22 hxg5 ♛xf8∓** 22...dxc3 23 ♗a3 **23 ♞h2** 23 cxd4 ♕b4 24 ♕d2 ♕xd2 25 ♘xd2 ♘xd4∓; 23 a3 dxc3 24 bxc3 ♗xf1 25 ♔xf1 ♕g7∓; 23 ♕d2 ♗xf1 24 ♔xf1 ♘dxe5 25 cxd4 ♘c4 26 ♕c3 b5∓ **a3 24 b3 dxc3 25 ♞g4**

25...♜d8? 25...♘b4! 26 ♖c1 ♖c8 27 ♗c2 ♗d3 −+; 25...d4 26 ♗e4 d3 =+ **26 ♜c1! d4 27 ♝e4∝ ♞b4 28 g3! ♛e7 29 ♚g2 ♞c5!** 29...♘f8 30 ♘f6+ ♔g7 31 ♖h1 h5 (31...d3 32

♖h6! Δ ♕h4) 32 gxh6+ ♔h8 33 h7 d3 34 ♕h6 ♘d7 35 ♘xd7 ♕xd7 36 ♕g5 +−; 30...♔h8 31 ♖h1 h5 32 ♘xh5 +− **30 ♘f6+ ♔g7 31 ♖h1 h5** 31...♖h8 32 ♖h6 **32 ♖xh5! gxh5 33 ♘xh5+ ♔f8** 33...♔g8 34 ♖h1 ♘xe4 35 ♘f6+ ♘xf6 36 exf6 +−; 34...♔f8 35 g6 +− **34 g6 ♘xe4** 34...♕c7 35 ♕f6 ♔e8 36 ♘g7+ ♔d7 37 gxf7 ♕c8 38 ♗f5∞; 36 gxf7+ ♔d7 37 ♕g7! ♔c8 38 f8♕ ♖xf8 39 ♕xf8+ ♔d7 40 ♘f6 mate **35 g7+ ♔g8?** 35...♔e8 36 ♘f6+ ♕xf6! 37 exf6 ♔d7 38 f3±; 36 g8♕+ ♔d7 37 ♕gxf7 ±/+− **36 ♘f6+ +− ♘xf6 37 exf6 ♘d5 38 ♕h6 1-0 Nunn**

299 Skrobek-Lechtynsky Decin 78

1 e4 e6 2 d4 d5 3 ♘d2 ♘f6 4 e5 ♘fd7 5 f4 c5 6 c3 ♘c6 7 ♘df3 ♕b6 8 ♘e2!? 8 g3! cxd4 9 cxd4 ♗b4+ 10 ♔f2 f6 11 ♔g2!; 8...f6 9 ♗h3! cxd4 10 cxd4 ♗b4+ 11 ♔f1 **f6 9 g3?** 9 exf6!? **cxd4 10 cxd4 fxe5 11 dxe5** 11 fxe5 ♗b4+ 12 ♔f2 ♘dxe5 −+; 12 ♗d2 0-0 13 ♗g2 ♖xf3 14 ♗xf3 ♘xd4 −+ **♗b4+ 12 ♗d2 ♕e3! ∓/−+ 13 ♕b3?** 13 ♗g2 0-0 **♕e4! −+ 14 ♗xb4** 14 ♗g2 ♘c5 −+ **♘xb4 15 ♘g5 ♘c2+ 16 ♔f2 ♘xa1 17 ♕a3 ♕xh1 18 ♕d6 ♕xh2+ 19 ♗g2 ♘xe5! 20 ♘xe6 ♘g4+ 21 ♔f3 ♘f6 22 ♘2d4 ♔f7! 23 ♘g5+ ♔g6! 24 ♔f2 ♖e8 25 ♘gf3 ♕h5 26 ♘e5+ ♖xe5 27 fxe5 ♕xe5 0-1 Pritchett**

300 Nicevski-Vilela Decin 78

1 e4 c5 2 ♘f3 e6 3 c3 d5 4 e5 ♘c6 5 d4 ♕b6 6 a3 c4 7 ♘bd2 ♘a5 8 g3 ♗d7 9 ♗h3 h6 9...♗e7 10 0-0 h5 11 ♘e1 g5! 12 ♘c2?! ♗a4 13 ♖b1 g4 14 ♗g2 ♘h6 15 b4 cxb3 16 ♘e3 ♗b5 17 ♖e1 ♗d3 18 ♖b2 ♗xa3 −+ Blatny-Drvota, Decin 2 78 **10 0-0 0-0-0 11 ♖b1 ♔b8 12 ♘e1 ♘e7 13 ♘g2 ♕c7 14 ♕f3!?** 14 ♘e3, Δ f4 **♗e8 15 ♘f4?** 15 ♘e3 ♗a4!∓ **16 ♗g4** 16 ♗xe6 fxe6 17 ♘xe6 ♕c8∓ **♗c2 17 ♖a1 g6 18 ♕g2 h5 19 ♗d1 ♗xd1 20 ♖xd1 g5 21 ♘e2 g4 22 ♘f1 ♘ac6 23 ♗g5 ♖g8 24 ♗f6 ♗h6 25 f4 ♖c8 26 ♘e3 ♘g6 27 ♔f2 ♘f8 28 h3!?** 28 h4 ♘d7 29 ♗g5 ♗f8∓; 29 ♗g5 ♗f8∓ **♘d7 29 hxg4?** 29 ♗h4 ♕b6 30 ♖ab1 ♔a8∓ **♘xf6! 30 exf6 hxg4 31 ♖h1 ♗f8 32 ♕h2**

32...♖g6! 33 ♕h4 ♕b6 −+ 34 ♘xg4 34 ♖ab1 ♖h6 35 ♕xg4 ♖xh1 36 ♖xh1 ♕xb2 −+; 34 ♖hb1!? ♘a5 35 ♘xg4 ♘b3 36 ♖a2 ♘d2 37 ♖ba1 ♘e4+ 38 ♔f3 ♗d6, Δ ♖cg8 −+ **♕xb2 35 ♘e5 ♘xe5 36 fxe5 ♗h6 37 ♕h5 ♕d2 38 ♕f3 ♖cg8 39 ♖ad1 ♕c2 40 ♖dg1 ♕b2 41 ♖h3 ♕xa3 42 ♖gh1 ♕f8 43 ♖1h2 ♗d2 44 ♖h7 ♖g5 45 ♖2h5 a6 46 ♕h1 ♔a7 47 ♕d1 ♖xh5 48 ♖xh5 ♖g5 49 ♖h7 ♖f5+ 50 ♔g2 ♗e3 51 ♘f4 ♗xf4 52 gxf4 ♖xf4 53 ♔g3 ♖e4 54 ♕h5 ♕a3 55 ♕f3 ♕c1 56 ♖xf7 ♕g1+ 57 ♔h3 ♖e3 58 ♕xe3 ♕xe3+ 59 ♔g4 ♕xc3 60 ♔g5 0-1 Pritchett**

301 Honfi-Raicevic Bajmok 78

1 e4 e6 2 d4 d5 3 e5 c5 4 c3 ♕b6 5 ♘f3 ♗d7 6 a3!? a5 7 ♗d3 ♘c6 8 dxc5 ♗xc5 9 0-0 ♘ge7 10 ♘bd2

♞g6 10...a4 11 b4 axb3 12 ♘xb3 += **11 ♝xg6 hxg6 12 ♞b3 ♝e7 13 a4 ♜h5 14 ♜e1 0-0-0 15 ♝e3 ♛c7 16 ♝f4 ♜dh8 17 ♞bd4 g5?! 18 ♞b5 ♛b6 19 ♝e3 ♛d8 20 g4! ♜h3 21 ♝xg5! f6** 21...♗xg5 22 ♘d6+ ♔b8 23 ♘xf7 +− **22 ♝f4 ♛f8 23 ♝g3 fxe5 24 ♞xe5 ♞xe5 25 ♜xe5 ♝h4 26 ♜h5 ♝xg3 27 hxg3 g6 28 ♜xh3 ♜xh3 29 ♛e2 ♛h8 30 ♛f3 ♚b8 31 ♜e1 e5! 32 ♚f1** 32 ♕xd5?? ♗c6 −+ **e4 33 ♛f4+ ♚a8 34 ♚e2 ♝xb5+ 35 axb5 ♛e8 36 c4! dxc4 37 ♜d1 ♜h8 38 ♛g5?** 38 ♖d5 +− **♛f8! 39 ♛e3 ♛b4?** 39...♕f6! += **40 ♛d4! +− ♜c8 41 b6 ♛b3 42 ♛f6 c3 43 bxc3 ♛c4+ 44 ♚e1 e3** 44...♕c6 45 ♖d8 +− **45 fxe3 ♛e4 46 ♜d8 ♛xe3+ 47 ♚f1 ♛c5 48 ♜xc8+ ♛xc8 49 ♛e5 ♛d8 50 ♛xa5+ ♚b8 51 ♛a7+ ♚c8 52 ♛a8+ ♚d7 53 ♛xb7+ ♚e6 54 ♛c6+ 1-0 Honfi**

302 Enders-Casper
DDR 78
1 e4 e6 2 d4 d5 3 e5 c5 4 c3 ♞c6 5 a3 ♛b6 6 ♞f3 c4 7 ♞bd2 ♞a5 8 g3 ♝d7 9 ♝h3 ♝e7!? 10 0-0 h5 11 ♞e1 g5 12 ♝g2 0-0-0 13 ♞df3!? ♞b3 14 ♜b1 ♞xc1 15 ♛xc1 g4 16 ♞g5 ♞h6 17 h4 gxh3 18 ♝xh3 f6 18...♖dg8 19 f4± **19 exf6 ♝xf6 20 ♞ef3** 20 f4 **♜df8 21 ♜e1?** 21 ♕d2∝ **♞g4** △ 22...e5 23 ♗xg4 hxg4 24 ♘xe5 ♗xe5 25 ♖xe5 ♕h6; 24 dxe5 ♗xg5 **22 ♝xg4 hxg4 23 ♞e5 ♜h5!**

Diagram

24 ♞xd7? 24 f4 **♚xd7 25 f4 ♜fh8 26 ♜f1?** 26 ♕d1 ♗xg5 27 fxg5 ♖h1+ 28 ♔f2 ♖8h2+ 29 ♔e3 ♖xe1+ 30 ♕xe1 ♕d8 31 ♕f1 ♕xg5+ 32 ♕f4 ♕g6 −+ **♝xd4+ 0-1**

303 Gliksman-Gereken
Budapest 2 78
1 e4 c5 2 c3 e6 3 d4 d5 4 e5 ♞c6 5 ♞f3 ♞ge7 5...♕b6 **6 ♝d3** 6 ♘a3 ♘f5 7 ♘c2 cxd4 8 cxd4 ♗e7 9 ♗d3 0-0 10 0-0 f6 11 ♗xf5 exf5 12 ♖e1 fxe5 13 dxe5 f4!= **cxd4 7 cxd4 ♞f5 8 ♝xf5 exf5 9 0-0 ♝e7 10 b3 0-0 11 ♝a3 ♝e6?** 11...f4 12 ♗xe7 ♘xe7 13 ♕d2 ♘g6 17 ♘c3 ♗f5 += **12 ♝xe7 ♛xe7 13 ♞c3 ♚h8!? 14 ♛d2 ♜g8 15 h4 h6 16 h5 ♛d7?** 16...♔h7 17 g3 g5 18 hxg6+ fxg6 (18...♖xg6) 19 ♔g2 ♖af8 20 ♖h1 g5∝ **17 ♞e2 ♜gc8 18 ♜fc1 ♞e7 19 ♞f4 ♜xc1+ 20 ♜xc1 ♜c8 21 g3± ♚g8 22 ♜xc8+ ♞xc8 23 ♛c3 ♚f8 24 ♞e1 ♛c6 25 ♛xc6 bxc6 26 ♚f1 ♚e7 27 ♞ed3 ♝d7 28 ♞c5 ♝e8 29 ♚e2 g5 30 hxg6 fxg6 31 ♞g2 g5 32 f4 ♞b6 33 ♞e3 ♝g6 34 g4! fxg4** 34...gxf4 35 ♘xf5+ ♗xf5 36 gxf5 h5 37 ♔f3 +− **35 f5 ♝h7** 35...♗h5 36 f6+ ♔f7 37 ♘f5 +− ♔g6 38 ♘d6 g3 39 ♔f1 ♗f3 40 f7 **36 f6+ ♚f7 37 ♞xg4 h5 38 ♞h6+ ♚e8 39 ♞e6 ♞d7 40 ♞xg5 ♝g6 41 ♞g8 1-0 B.Balogh**

Alekhine

304 Honfi-Vukic Bajmok 78
1 e4 ♞f6 2 e5 ♞d5 3 d4 d6 4 c4 ♞b6 5 f4 dxe5 6 fxe5 ♞c6 7 ♝e3 ♝f5 8 ♞c3 e6 9 ♞f3 ♝e7 10 ♝e2 0-0 11 0-0 f6 12 exf6 ♝xf6 13 ♛d2 ♛e7 14 ♜ad1 ♜ad8 15 ♛c1 ♜fe8 16 ♚h1 16 ♖f2 **♚h8 17 h3 ♝g6?!** 17...h6!? **18 ♜fe1 ♛f7 19 c5! ♞d5 20 ♝g5 ♞ce7 21 ♝c4 c6 22 ♞e5 ♛g8 23 ♞xg6+ ♞xg6 24 ♞e4 ♜f8 25 ♜f1 ♞ge7 26 ♜f3?!** 26 ♗xf6 gxf6 27 ♖d3± **♝xg5 27 ♞xg5 h6 28 ♜xf8 ♜xf8 29 ♞f3 ♞f4 30 ♜f1 g5?!** 30...♕h7!∝ **31 ♞e5 ♞f5 32 ♛c3 ♛g7 33 ♚h2 ♜f6 34 g3 ♞d5 35 ♝xd5 exd5?!** 35...cxd5 36 ♕a5 b6 37 cxb6 ♘xg3 38 bxa7 ♘xf1+ 39 ♔g1 +− **36 ♛f3!** Δ g4 **h5 37 ♛xh5+ ♚g8** 37...♘h6 38 ♖xf6 ♕xf6 39 ♕xh6+ ♕xh6 40 ♘f7+ +− **38 ♞g4 1-0** 38...♖f8 39 ♖xf5 **Honfi**

305 Rivas-Ochoa
Spain Final 78
1 e4 ♞f6 2 e5 ♞d5 3 d4 d6 4 ♞f3 ♝f5?! 5 ♝d3 ♛d7 6 0-0 ♞c6 6...♘b4 7 ♗xf5 ♕xf5 8 c3 ♘c2 9 ♘h4 ♕e4 10 ♘d2 ♕d3 11 ♖b1 dxe5 12 ♘df3 ♘b4 13 ♕a4+ ♘4c6 14 ♘xe5± Kavalek-Ljubojevic **7 c4 ♞b6 8 exd6 cxd6** 8...♗xd3 9 ♕xd3 exd6 10 ♖e1+ ♗e7 11 d5 ♘b8 12 ♕e2± **9 b3 ♝xd3 10 ♛xd3 e6 11 ♝a3! ♝e7 12 ♞c3 0-0 13 d5! ♞e5** 13...exd5 14 ♘xd5 ♘xd5 15 ♕xd5± **14 ♞xe5 dxe5 15 d6 ♜fd8 16 c5 ♞c8 17 ♛e2 ♝f8 18 ♜fd1** 18 ♕xe5?! b6 19 ♕e4 ♖b8 20 c6 ♘xd6; 19 b4 a5 **f6 19 ♜ac1 ♜b8 20 ♞a4 a6 21 ♝b4! +− ♛b5 22 ♛xb5 axb5 23 ♝a5 ♜d7 24 ♝c7 ♜a8 25 ♞c3 ♞a7 26 a4 b4 27 ♞a2 ♞c6 28 ♜c4 ♜c8 29 ♝b6 ♞d4 30 ♜xb4 g5 31 ♚f1 h5 32 a5 g4 33 ♜b1 ♚f7 34 ♜a4 ♜a8 35 ♞c3 ♚e8 36 b4 ♜f7 37 b5 ♚d7 38 a6 bxa6 39 ♜xa6 ♜xa6 40 bxa6 ♝h6 41 a7 ♜f8 42 ♝d8 1-0**

306 Martin-J.Fernandez
Spain Final 78
1 e4 ♞f6 2 e5 ♞d5 3 d4 d6 4 ♞f3 ♝g4 5 ♝e2 c6?! 6 c4 6 ♘g5 ♗f5! 7 e6 ♗xe6 8 ♘xe6 fxe6 9 ♗g4 ♘c7 10 0-0 ♘d7 11 ♖e1 e5 12 ♗xd7+ ♕xd7 13 dxe5 d5! **♞b6 7 ♞bd2 ♞bd7!** 7...dxe5 8 ♘xe5 ♗xe2 9 ♕xe2 ♕xd4 10 ♘df3± **8 ♞g5 ♝f5! N** 8... ♗xe2 9 e6! f6 10 ♕xe2 fxg5 11 ♘e4! ♘f6 12 ♘xg5 ♕c7 13 ♘f7 ♖g8 14 g4 +− **9 ♝g4?! e6! 10 f4 dxe5 11 ♝xf5 exf5 12 dxe5 h6 13 ♞gf3** 13 ♕h5?! g6 14 ♕h3 ♘c5 15 0-0 ♘d3 **♞c5 14 0-0 ♛d3!** 14...♘d3? 15 ♘b3 ♘xc4?? 16 ♕c2 **15 ♛e1 ♞e6 16 ♚h1 0-0-0 17 g3 g5! 18 fxg5 hxg5 19 ♞b3 f4! 20 gxf4 g4! 21 f5 gxf3 22 fxe6 ♝b4 23 ♛f2**

23...♜xh2+! 24 ♚xh2 ♜h8+ 25 ♚g3 ♜g8+ 26 ♚f4 fxe6! 27 ♛xf3 ♜f8+ 28 ♚g3 ♝e1+ 29 ♚g2 ♜xf3 30 ♜xe1 30 ♖xf3 ♕e2+ **♜g3+ 31 ♚h2 ♜h3+ 0-1** 32 ♔g1 ♕g3+ 33 ♔f1 ♕f3+ 34 ♔g1 ♖h1 mate

307 Dobsa-Bullockus Corr 78
1 e4 ♞f6 2 e5 ♞d5 3 d4 d6 4 ♞f3 ♝g4 5 ♝e2 c6 6 ♞g5 ♝f5 6...♗xe2

7 Qxe2 dxe5 8 dxe5 e6 9 0-0 Nd7 10 f4 += **7 Bd3** 7 Bg4 Bxg4 8 Qxg4 dxe5 9 dxe5 e6 10 0-0 Nd7 11 c4 Nb4 12 Qe2! Ciocaltea-Westerinen, Bucharest 74; 7 e6 Bxe6 8 Nxe6 fxe6 9 Bg4 Nc7 10 0-0 Nd7 11 Re1 e5 12 Bxd7+ Qxd7 13 dxe5 d5! **Bxd3 8 Qxd3 dxe5 9 Qf5 f6 10 Nxh7 exd4 11 0-0 Qd6** 11...Qd7 **12 c4 dxc3 13 bxc3! Nd7 14 Qg6+ Kd8 15 Rd1 Ne5 16 Qc2** 16 Qe4? f5 17 Qxf5 g6! **g6 17 Nxf8 Rxf8 18 Ba3 Qc7 19 c4 Nf3+ 20 gxf3 Rh8 21 cxd5 Qxh2+ 22 Kf1 Qe5** Δ Rh1+, Qh2 mate **23 dxc6+ Ke8** 23...Kc8 24 cxb7+ Kxb7 25 Qb2+ **24 Qxg6+ Kf8 25 Bxe7+! 1-0**

308 Pavlov-Jansson Sweden 78

1 e4 Nf6 2 e5 Nd5 3 d4 d6 4 Nf3 Bg4 5 Be2 c6 6 Ng5 6 0-0 Bxf3 7 Bxf3 dxe5 8 dxe5 e6 9 Qe2 Nd7 10 Re1 Qc7 11 Bd2 Bc5 12 c4 Ne7 13 Bc3 a5 Matanovic-Knezevic 73; 9 c4 Ne7 **Bf5 7 Bg4** 7 e6 fxe6 8 g4 Bg6 9 Bd3 Bxd3 10 Qxd3 g6 11 0-0 Bh6 12 Nxe6 Qd7 13 Qe2; 10... Na6 11 Nxh7 Qa5+ 12 c3 (12 Bd2 Nf4) Nf6 13 Ng5 Nc7 (13...Qd5) 14 f3 c5 15 0-0 **Bxg4 8 Qxg4 dxe5 9 dxe5** 9 Qf5 f6 10 Nxh7 exd4 11 0-0 e5 12 c4 Nc7 13 f4 Qd7 14 Qh5 Kd8 15 fxe5 Qe8; 11...e6 12 Qxe6+ Be7 **e6 10 0-0 Qc7 11 Re1?!** 11 f4 **h6 12 Nf3 Nd7 13 b3 0-0-0 14 Bb2 g5! 15 Nbd2 Rg8 16 Ne4 Kb8 17 Rad1?** 17 a3 **Bb4! 18 c3 Be7 19 c4 Nf4 20 Bc3** 20 h4 Nxg2! **Nc5 21 Rxd8+ Rxd8 22 Nxc5 Bxc5 23 h4 Qb6 24 Kh2 Bxf2 25 Rf1 Qe3 26 Bd4** 26 Ba1 Qe2 Δ Rg8 **Rxd4 27 Nxd4 Qxd4 28 hxg5 hxg5 29 g3 Ng6 30 Qxd4 Bxd4 31 Rxf7 Nxe5 32 Re7 Ng4+ 33 Kg2 e5 34 Kf3 Nf6 35 g4 a5 36 Rf7 e4+ 37 Kg3 0-1**

309 Kasparov-Palatnik
Daugavpils 78

1 e4 Nf6 2 e5 Nd5 3 d4 d6 4 Nf3 g6 5 Bc4 Nb6 6 Bb3 a5 7 a4 7 e6 Bxe6 8 Bxe6 fxe6 9 Ng5 Qd7 10 Qe2 +=; 7...f6? 8 Ng5!± **Bg7 8 Ng5 e6** 8...d5 9 f4 += **9 f4 dxe5 10 fxe5 c5 11 0-0 0-0 12 c3 Nc6?** 12...cxd4 13 cxd4 Nc6 14 Nf3 f6 15 Nc3 fxe5 16 Bg5 += **13 Ne4! Nd7** 13...cxd4? 14 Bg5± **14 Be3 Ne7** 14...cxd4 15 cxd4 Qb6 16 Bf2± **15 Bg5 cxd4** 15...h6 16 Bh4 g5 17 Bxg5! hxg5 18 Qh5 +− **16 cxd4 h6 17 Bh4 g5 18 Bf2** 18 Bxg5? hxg5 19 Qh5 Nxe5! 20 Nxg5 Qxd4+ 21 Kh1 Qd3 −+ **Ng6 19 Nbc3 Qe7 20 Bc2 b6 21 Be3 Ba6 22 Rf2 Nh8 23 Bxg5!** 23 h4± **hxg5 24 Qh5 f5 25 Nxg5 Rf7** 25...Rfd8 26 Rxf5! exf5 27 Bb3+ +−; 25...Rfc8 26 Qh7+ Kf8 27 Nxe6+! Qxe6 28 Bxf5 +−

26 Bxf5!! Rxf5 26...exf5 27 Nd5 Qe8 28 e6 +− **27 Rxf5 exf5 28 Nd5 Qe8 29 Qh7+ Kf8 30 Qxf5+ Kg8 31 Qh7+ Kf8 32 Ra3** 32 Nc7 +− **Rc8** 32...Qg6 33 Rf3+ Ke8 34 Qg8+ Nf8 35 Rxf8+ Bxf8 36 Nf6+ Kd8 37 Qxf8+ Kc7 38 Ne6+ **33 Rf3+**

♘f6 33...♘f7 34 ♖xf7+ ♕xf7 35 ♘xf7 ♖c1+ 36 ♔f2 ♖f1+ 37 ♔g3 ♖xf7 38 ♕h4! +− **34 h3! ♕g6 35 ♖xf6+ ♗xf6 36 ♘e6+ ♔e8 37 ♘xf6+ 1-0 Kasparov**

310 Vaisman-Szmetan Iasi 78
1 e4 ♘f6 2 e5 ♘d5 3 d4 d6 4 ♘f3 g6 4...♗g4!? **5 ♗c4 ♘b6** 5...c6 **6 ♗b3 ♗g7** 6...a5 7 a4 d5 8 0-0 ♗g7 9 ♗f4 0-0 10 ♘bd2 += Ciocaltea-Ogaard, Reykjavik 74; 7 e6!? ♗xe6 8 ♗xe6 fxe6 9 ♘g5 Kapengut-Palatnik, Biel 77 **7 ♘g5 d5 8 0-0** 8 f4 f6 9 ♘f3 ♗g4 10 ♘bd2 ♘c6 11 c3 0-0 12 h3 ♗xf3 13 ♘xf3 e6?!; 13...♕d7!? 14 ♗c2 += **0-0 9 f4 f6 10 ♘f3 ♗g4 11 ♘bd2 ♘c6 12 c3 ♕d7 13 h3 ♗xf3 14 ♘xf3 ♖ad8?** 14...♘d8! **15 ♗c2 ♘a5 16 ♕e1! ♘ac4?! 17 b3 ♘a5 18 e6! ♕e8 19 f5 g5 20 h4 h6 21 ♕g3 +− ♖c8 22 ♗d2 ♘c6 23 ♕h3! ♘d8 24 ♖ae1 c5 25 hxg5 fxg5 26 ♘xg5! cxd4** 26...hxg5 27 f6 ♖xf6 28 ♕h7+ ♔f8 29 ♗xg5 +− **27 ♘h7! dxc3** 27...♔xh7 28 f6+ **28 ♗xh6 1-0 Ciocaltea**

311 Nicevski-Ozsvath
Budapest 2 78
1 e4 d6 2 d4 g6 3 ♘f3 ♗g7 4 ♗c4 ♘f6 5 ♕e2 0-0 5...♘c6 6 e5 dxe5 7 dxe5 ♘g4 8 ♗b5 ♗d7 9 ♗f4 0-0 10 ♘c3 a6 11 ♗c4 += **6 0-0 ♗g4 7 e5 ♘e8!** 7...dxe5 8 dxe5 ♘d7 9 e6 ♘e5 10 exf7+ ♔h8 11 ♕xe5! ♗xe5 12 ♘xe5 ♕d4 13 ♗d2∝ **8 ♘bd2** 8 ♖d1 ♘c6 9 ♗d5 ♕d7 10 ♗f4 ♕f5= **♘c6 9 ♕e3 d5! 10 ♗b5 ♗d7 11 a4 a6 12 ♗e2 a5 13 c3 ♕c8 14 ♘h4 ♘d8 15 b3 ♘e6 16 ♗a3 ♕d8 17 ♗g4** 17 f4 ♗h6 **c6 18 ♖ad1 b5!= 19 f4 ♗h6 20 ♕g3 b4 21 ♗xe6 fxe6 22 cxb4 ♕b6 23 ♕c3 axb4 24 ♗xb4 ♖xf4 25 ♖xf4 ♗xf4 26 ♗xe7 ♘g7 27 g3 ♗h6 28 ♗c5 ♕a6 29 ♕f3 ♘f5 30 ♘xf5 exf5! 31 ♘b1 ♖b8 32 ♖d3 ♗e6 33 h4 ♖b7 34 ♕f1 ♖f7 35 ♖f3 ♕a5 36 ♘c3 f4 =+ 37 b4 ♕d8 38 a5 ♗g4 39 ♖f2 ♗f5 40 a6** 40 ♖xf4 ♗xf4 41 ♕xf4 ♗d3 42 ♕e3 ♖f1+ 43 ♔h2 ♕f8∓ **fxg3 41 ♖xf5 gxf5! 42 a7 ♗e3+ 43 ♔g2 f4 −+ 44 ♘e2 f3+ 45 ♔xg3 fxe2 46 ♕a1 ♗d2 47 a8♕ e1♕+ 48 ♔g4 ♕e2+ 49 ♔h3 ♕f3+ 50 ♔h2 ♗f4+ 51 ♔g1 ♗e3+ 52 ♔h2 ♕f2+ 0-1 B.Balogh**

Pirc

312 Rivas-Palacios
Spain Final 78
1 e4 d6 2 d4 g6 3 ♘c3 ♗g7 4 ♘ge2 ♘d7 4...c6 5 a4 e5 6 ♗e3 ♘f6 7 dxe5 dxe5 8 ♕xd8+ ♔xd8 9 h3 Gulko-Petrosian **5 g3 e5 6 dxe5 ♘xe5 7 ♗g2 h5 8 f4 ♘c6 9 h3 ♘f6 10 ♗e3 ♗e6 11 ♕d2 ♕d7 12 0-0-0 0-0-0 13 ♘d4 ♘e7 14 ♘xe6 fxe6 15 ♖he1 ♔b8 16 ♕f2 ♘c8 17 e5 ♘g8** 17...♘e8 18 ♗e4 ♕f7 19 ♕f3 d5 20 ♘xd5 exd5 21 ♗xd5 **18 ♘e4 d5 19 ♘c5 ♕e8 20 c4 c6** 20...b6 21 ♘xe6 ♕xe6 22 cxd5 **21 cxd5 cxd5 22 ♔b1 ♗f8 23 ♖c1 ♖h7 24 ♖c3 ♗xc5 25 ♗xc5 b6 26 ♗d4 ♖dd7 27 ♖ec1 ♖c7 28 ♕c2 ♖xc3 29 ♕xc3 ♕d8 30 ♕c2 ♘ge7 31 g4 hxg4 32 hxg4 ♕d7 33 ♗f1 ♖h1 34 ♕g2 ♖h8 35 b3! ♘c6 36 ♗b5 ♘8e7 37 f5 gxf5 38 gxf5 ♕b7 39 ♗b2 exf5 40 ♗xc6 ♘xc6 41 ♕xd5 ♖c8 42 ♕d6+ ♔a8 43 ♕e6 ♘e7 44 ♖xc8+ ♘xc8 45 ♕xf5 a5 46 e6 ♔a7 47 ♗d4 ♔a6 48 ♕d3+ ♔a7 49 ♕f5 ♔a6 50 ♕d3+ ♔a7 51 ♗e5 ♘e7 52 ♔b2 ♕d5 53 ♕xd5 ♘xd5 54 ♔c2 ♔b7 55 ♔d3 ♔c6 56 ♔e4 b5 57 a3! ♘e7 58 ♗g7 ♘d5 59 ♔e5 ♘c7 60 ♗f8 ♘e8 61 ♗e7 a4 62 b4 ♘c7 63 ♗d6 ♘e8 64 ♗c5 ♘c7 65 ♔f6 ♔d5 66 e7 1-0** 66...♔c4 67 ♔f7 ♔b3 68 ♗d6; 66...♔c6 67

♔f7 ♔d7 68 ♗d4 ♘e8 69 ♗e5

313 Liu Wen Che-Donner
Buenos Aires 78

1 e4 d6 2 d4 ♞f6 3 ♞c3 g6 4 ♝e2!? 4 ♘f3 ♗g7 5 ♗e2 0-0 6 0-0 ♘c6 7 d5 ♘b8 8 ♗g5!? Christiansen-Seirawan, USA 78; 4 f4 **♝g7 5 g4!?** N **h6 6 h3 c5** 6...♘bd7 Δ c6, ♕c7, e5; 6...♘a6 **7 d5 0-0?! 8 h4 e6 9 g5 hxg5 10 hxg5 ♞e8 11 ♛d3± exd5 12 ♞xd5 ♞c6?** 12...♗e6 13 ♕g3 ♗xd5 14 exd5 f5 15 ♘h3±; 15 exf6 ♕xf6∞ **13 ♛g3 ♝e6 14 ♛h4 +− f5 15 ♛h7+ ♚f7**

16 ♛xg6+!! ♚xg6 17 ♝h5+ ♚h7 18 ♝f7+ ♝h6 19 g6+! ♚g7 20 ♝xh6+ 1-0 Filipowicz

314 Chiburdanidze-Gaprindashivli (13) 78

1 e4 d6 2 d4 ♞f6 3 ♞c3 g6 4 ♝e3 c6 5 ♛d2 ♞bd7 6 h3 ♛c7 7 g3 b5 8 ♝g2 b4 9 ♞d1 ♜b8 9...c5 10 e5 ♗b7 **10 ♞e2 ♝g7 11 0-0 0-0 12 b3** 12 a3 b3 13 ♘dc3 **e5 13 c3 d5?! 14 exd5 ♞xd5 15 cxb4 ♝a6 16 ♝xd5! cxd5 17 ♞dc3 ♛d6 18 b5! ♜xb5!** 18...♗xb5 19 ♘xb5 ♖xb5 20 ♖ad1; 18...♗c8 19 ♔h2 **19 ♞xb5 ♝xb5 20 ♜fe1 ♛e6 21 ♚h2 ♞f6 22 ♞g1** 22 dxe5 ♘e4 23 ♕b4 **♞e4 23 ♛b4?** 23 ♕b2 **exd4! 24 ♝f4 ♛a6 25 f3 ♞f2 26 a4 ♝c6 27 ♛d2 ♞d3 28 ♛e2 ♝b7 29 ♜ed1 ♞xf4 30 ♛xa6 ♝xa6 31 gxf4**

31...d3? 31...♖c8! 32 ♖ac1 ♖c3 33 ♖xc3 dxc3 34 ♖xd5 ♗f8; 33 ♘e2 ♖xf3 34 ♘xd4 ♖xf4; 33...♖xb3 34 ♘xd4 ♖b4 **32 ♜ac1 ♜e8 33 ♜c5 ♜e2+! 34 ♞xe2 dxe2 35 ♜cxd5 exd1♛ 36 ♜xd1 ♝e2** 36...♗f8 37 ♖d8 ♔g7 **37 ♜d7 a6 38 ♚g2 a5 39 ♚f2 ♝a6 40 ♜d8+ ♝f8 41 ♜a8 ♝b7 42 ♜xa5 ♝d6? 43 ♚g3 ♚f8 44 ♜a7 ♝d5 45 ♜d7 ♝xb3 46 ♜xd6 ♝xa4 47 f5! ♚g7** 47...gxf5 48 ♔f4 ♗c2 49 ♔g5 ♔g7 50 f4 **48 f6+ ♚h6 49 ♚f4 g5+! 50 ♚e5 ♚h5 51 ♜d8 ♝c2 52 ♜f8 ♝b3 53 ♜h8 h6 54 ♚d6 ♚g6 55 ♚e7 h5 56 ♜g8+ ♚f5 57 ♜g7 ♚f4 58 ♜xf7 ♚xf3 59 ♜h7! h4 60 ♜g7 ♚g3 61 ♜xg5+ ♚xh3 62 ♚d6! ♚h2 63 ♚e5 h3 64 ♚f4 ♝f7 65 ♚f3 ♝c4 66 ♚f2 ♝e6 67 ♜g7 ♚h1 68 ♜h7 1-0**

315 Chiburdanidze-Gaprindashvili (5) 78

1 e4 d6 2 d4 ♞f6 3 ♞c3 g6 4 ♞f3 ♝g7 5 ♝e2 c6 6 a4 6 0-0 0-0 7 h3 b5 8 e5 ♘e8 9 a4 b4 10 ♘e4 ♗f5 11 ♘g3 ♗e6 12 c4 bxc3 13 bxc3 ♗d5 14 ♖e1 Karpov-Hort, Nice 74 **a5 7 0-0 0-0 8 h3 ♞a6 9 ♜e1** 9 ♗e3 ♘b4 10 ♕d2 ♕c7 11 ♖ad1 ♖e8 12

♖fe1 Spassky-Hort (7) 78; 9 ♗f4 ♘c7 10 ♖e1 ♘e6 11 ♗e3 ♕c7 12 ♗f1 Spassky-Hort (9) 78 **♕c7 10 ♗g5 h6 11 ♗e3 ♔h7 12 ♕d2 ♘b4 13 ♖ad1 ♗d7 14 ♘h2!** 14 e5 ♘fd5 15 ♘xd5 cxd5 16 exd5 **b5 15 ♗f3 bxa4 16 ♘g4 h5** 16...♘g8 **17 ♘xf6+ exf6** 17...♗xf6 18 g4; 18 ♗g5 **18 ♗f4! ♖fe8 19 ♘xa4 g5** 19...c5 20 ♘xc5 **20 ♗g3 g4 21 hxg4 hxg4 22 ♗e2 f5** 22...♖xe4 23 ♗d3 ♘xd3 24 ♖xe4 **23 exf5 ♗xf5 24 c3 ♘d5 25 ♗d3! ♗xd3** 25...♕d7? 26 c4 Δ ♘b6; 26 ♗xd6 **26 ♕xd3+ ♔g8 27 ♕f5 ♘f6 28 ♕f4 ♕b7 29 ♕xd6** 29 ♗h4!? **♘e4 30 ♖xe4 ♖xe4 31 ♘c5 ♕e7?** 31...♕xb2 32 ♘xe4 ♕e2 **32 ♘xe4 ♕xe4 33 ♖a1 a4 34 b3?** 34 ♕f4 **♗f8? 35 ♕f4 ♕g6 36 bxa4 ♖xa4 37 ♖xa4 ♕b1+ 38 ♔h2 ♕h7+ 39 ♗h4 ♕xh4+ 40 ♔g1 ♕h5 41 ♖a8 1-0**

316 Chiburdanidze-Gaprindashvili (15) 78

1 e4 d6 2 d4 ♘f6 3 ♘c3 g6 4 ♘f3 ♗g7 5 ♗e2 c6 6 0-0 0-0 7 a4 ♘bd7 7...a5 **8 a5 ♕c7 9 h3 ♖d8** 9...e5 **10 ♗e3** 10 ♗f4 e5 11 ♗h2 **♘f8 11 ♕d2 ♗d7 12 ♖fd1 ♗e8 13 b4?** 13 ♗h6; 13 ♕e1 **e5 14 dxe5 dxe5 15 ♕e1 ♖xd1** 15...♘e6 16 ♖xd8 ♖xd8 **16 ♖xd1 ♘e6 17 ♗c4 ♕e7! 18 ♗xe6** 18 ♘xe5 ♕xb4 19 ♗xe6 fxe6; 18...♘xe4 19 ♘xg6; 18 ♖b1 **♕xe6 19 ♗c5 ♘d7 20 ♗d6** 20 ♖d6 ♕c4 **f6 21 ♕e2** 21 ♕e3 ♕c4 22 ♘d2 **♗f8 22 ♗xf8 ♘xf8 23 ♘d2?** 23 ♕d3; 23 ♘a4 **♕e7! 24 ♕c4+** 24 ♖b1 ♘e6 **♗f7 25 ♕c5 ♕xc5 26 bxc5 ♖d8 27 ♔f1 ♖d4 28 ♔e1 ♘e6?** 28...♘d7 29 ♘b3 ♗xb3 **29 ♘b3 ♖c4 30 ♔d2 ♘f4** 30...♘xc5 31 ♘xc5 ♖xc5 32 ♖b1 **31 a6! bxa6 32 ♖a1 ♘xg2 33 ♖xa6 ♗e8 34 ♖xa7 h5 35 ♖b7 ♘f4 36 f3 ♔f8** 36...♘xh3? 37 ♖b8! Δ ♔d3 **37 h4 ♘e6 38 ♘d1 ♘xc5 39 ♘xc5 ♖xc5 40 ♘e3 ♖a5 41 ♖c7** 41 ♘c4 ♖a4 **♖a8 42 ♘c4 ♖d8+ 43 ♔e2 ♖d4 44 ♘e3 ♖d6 45 c4 ♖d8 46 c5 ♖d4 47 ♔e1 ♖d7 48 ♖xd7** 48 ♖c8 ♔e7 49 ♘c4 ♖d3 50 ♘d6 ♗d7 51 ♖g8 ♖c3; 48 ♖xc6? ♖d3 −+ **♗xd7 49 ♘c4 ♔e7 50 ♔f2 ♗e6 51 ♘d6 g5 52 ♔g3 ♔d7 53 ♘b7 ♗b3 54 hxg5! fxg5 55 ♘a5 ♗d1 56 ♘c4 ♔e6 57 ♔f2 ♔f6 58 ♘a5 ♗a4 59 ♘c4 ♗b5 60 ♘d6 ♗a6 61 ♘e8+ ♔g6 62 ♘d6 ♗d3 63 ♔e3 ♗c2 64 ♘c4 ♔f6 65 ♔f2 ♗a4** 65...g4 66 ♘e3 ♗d3 67 fxg4 h4! **66 ♘b6 ♗d1 67 ♘d7+ ♔e6 68 ♘b8 ♗a4 69 ♘a6 ♗b5** 69...g4 **70 ♘b4 ♔f6 71 ♔g3 ♔g6 72 ♘c2 h4+** 72...g4 73 fxg4 ♗d3 74 gxh5+ ♔xh5 75 ♘e3 ♗xe4 76 ♘g4 **73 ♔g2 g4! 74 ♘e3 gxf3+?** 74...g3 75 ♘g4 ♔g5 76 ♘xe5 ♗e2 77 ♘xc6 ♔f4 Δ h3+ **75 ♔xf3 ♔g5 76 ♘d1! ♗c4** 76...h3 77 ♔g3 h2 78 ♘f2 ♗f1 79 ♘h1! ♗d3 80 ♘f2 ♗c2 81 ♔f3 ♔h4 82 ♔g2 **77 ♘f2 ♗f1 78 ♘h1 ♗h3 79 ♘f2 ♗e6 80 ♘d3! ♗g4+ 81 ♔f2 ♔f6 82 ♘b4 ♗d7 83 ♔f3 h3 84 ♔g3 ♔e7 85 ♘d3 ♔f6 86 ♘b4 ♔e7 87 ♘d3 ♔e6 88 ♔xh3 ♗e8 89 ♔g3 ♗g6 90 ♔f3 ♗h5+ 91 ♔e3 ♗d1 92 ♘b4 ♗a4 93 ♘d3 ♗b5 94 ♘e1 ½-½**

317 Matanovic-Ciocaltea
Buenos Aires 78

1 e4 g6 2 d4 ♗g7 3 ♘c3 c6 4 ♘f3 d6 4...d5 5 h3! += Gheorghiu **5 ♗e2 ♘f6 6 0-0 0-0 7 ♖e1!?** 7 a4 a5 8 h3 Δ ♗e3 += Gheorghiu **a5?!** 7...♕c7 8 e5! dxe5 9 ♘xe5 ♖d8? 10 ♗c4!± Diesen-Shamkovich, New York 76; 7...b5 8 e5! ♘e8 9 exd6 ♘xd6 10 ♘e5 += Tompa-Schoneberg, Leipzig 77 **8 ♗f1 ♘a6 9 h3 d5?** 9...♘c7!? += **10 exd5!** 10 e5 ♘e8 (Δ ♘c7

∝ Gheorghiu) 11 ♗e3 ♘ac7 12 ♕d2 f6≈ **♞xd5 11 ♞xd5 cxd5 12 ♝f4± ♞c7 13 ♛d2 ♞e8** 13...♘e6 14 ♗h6± Gheorghiu **14 ♛e2 ♞d6?** 14...e6!?± **15 ♛xe7 ♛xe7 16 ♜xe7 ♞f5 17 ♜ee1 ♞xd4 18 ♞xd4 ♝xd4 19 ♝d6! ♝xb2** 19...♖d8 20 ♗e7 ♖d7 21 ♗b5! ♖c7 22 c3! +− **20 ♝xf8 ♚xf8** 20... ♗xa1 21 ♗h6! **21 ♜ab1 ♝c3 22 ♜ed1 d4 23 a3! ♚e7 24 ♜b6 ♜a7 25 ♜db1 a4 26 ♝d3** 26 ♗c4!? **♝a5 27 ♜6b5 b6 28 ♜d5 ♜d7 29 ♜e5+ ♚f6** 29... ♔d6 30 ♖e4! ♔c7 31 ♗b5 Δ ♖e7+ **30 ♜e8 ♜c7 31 ♜e4 ♜d7 32 ♝b5 ♜d6 33 ♝xa4 ♝f5 34 ♜f4 d3 35 cxd3 ♜xd3 1-0 Ciocaltea**

318 Chiburdanidze-Gaprindashvili (7) 78

1 e4 d6 2 d4 ♞f6 3 ♞c3 g6 4 ♞f3 ♝g7 5 ♝e2 0-0 6 0-0 c6 6...♗g4 7 h3 ♗xf3 8 ♗xf3 ♘c6 9 ♘e2 e5 10 c3 ♖e8 11 d5 ♘e7 12 c4 ♘d7 13 ♖e1 f5 Alexandria-Gaprindashvili (2) 75 **7 h3** 7 a4 **♞bd7 8 ♝f4 ♛a5** 8...e5?! 9 dxe5 dxe5 10 ♘xe5 ♘xe4 11 ♘xe4 ♗xe5 12 ♗xe5 ♘xe5 13 ♕xd8 ♖xd8 14 f4 ♘d7 15 ♖ad1 ♔g7 16 ♗f3 ♖c8 ♘d6 Faibisovich-Polovents, Leningrad 75 **9 ♛d2 e5 10 ♝e3 ♜e8 11 ♜fe1 ♛c7!** 11...exd4 12 ♘xd4 d5? 13 ♘b3! **12 dxe5 dxe5 13 a4 ♝f8 14 ♝c4** 14 a5 ♗b4 15 ♘b5! cxb5 (15...b5!) 16 ♕xb4 ♕xc2 17 ♘d2; 14...a6 15 ♖a4 ♘c5 16 ♖c4 **♞b6 15 ♝b3 ♝e6 16 ♝xe6 ♜xe6 17 ♛e2 a5 18 ♜ed1 ♞fd7** 18...♗b4 19 ♘a2 ♘xa4 20 ♘xb4 axb4 21 b3 ♘xe4 22 ♕c4! ♘ec3 23 ♖e1 b5 24 ♕xb4 c5 25 ♕h4 **19 b3 ♜ee8 20 ♞d2 ♝b4 21 ♞a2 ♝c5 22 ♞c1 ♝d4 23 ♜b1!** 23 ♗xd4? **♞c5 24 c3 ♝xe3 25 ♛xe3 ♞e6 26 ♞d3 ♜ad8 27 ♞xe5** 27 ♘b2 ♖d7 28 ♘dc4 ♘xc4 29 ♘xc4 ♖ed8 30 ♖xd7 ♖xd7 31 ♕a7 b5! **♛xe5 28 ♛xb6 ♞f4 29 ♞f3** 29 ♕xb7? ♖xd2! 30 ♖xd2 ♕xe4 −+ **♜xd1+ 30 ♜xd1 ♛xc3** 30...♕xe4? 31 ♖e1 ♘e2+ 32 ♔h1 ♕c2 33 c4! **31 ♜d8?** 31 ♕xb7 ♘xh3+; 31 ♔h2 ♖xe4 32 ♕xb7 ♕c2 33 ♖d8+! ♔g7 34 ♖d7; 32...♖b4 33 ♖d8+ ♔g7 34 ♕e7 **♜xd8 32 ♛xd8+ ♚g7 33 e5 ♞e6**

34 ♛f6+? 34 ♕d1! ♘c5 1) 35 ♕d4 ♕xd4 36 ♘xd4 f6 37 exf6+ ♔xf6 38 f4 g5!; 35...♕c1+? 36 ♔h2 ♘xb3 37 ♕h4!; 2) 35 ♕d6 ♕c1+ 36 ♔h2 ♕f4+ 37 g3 ♕xf3 38 ♕xc5 ♕xb3 39 ♕xa5; 35...♘e4 36 ♕d4 ♕xd4 37 ♘xd4 ♘d2 38 f4 c5 39 ♘b5 ♘xb3 40 ♘d6 b6 41 ♘c4 ♘c1 42 ♔f2 **♚g8 35 ♚h2** 35 h4 ♕xb3 36 ♘g5 ♕d1+! 37 ♔h2 ♘xg5 **♛xb3 36 ♞g5 ♞xg5 37 ♛d8+ ♚g7 38 ♛xg5** 38 ♕f6+ ♔h6 39 h4 ♘e4! 40 ♕f4+ ♔g7 41 ♕xe4 ♕b4! **♛e6 39 ♛e3 ♛d5 40 g3 b5 0-1**

319 Thormann-Syre DDR 78

1 e4 g6 2 d4 d6 3 ♞f3 ♞f6 4 ♞c3 ♝g7 5 ♝e2 0-0 6 0-0 ♝g4 7 ♝e3 ♞c6 8 ♛d2 e5 9 d5 ♞e7 10 ♜ad1 ♝xf3 10...♗d7 **11 ♝xf3 ♞d7 12 g3** 12 ♗e2 f5 13 g3 ♘f6 14 f3 ♕d7 15 ♗b5 ♕c8 16 ♖f2 a5 17 ♗f1 ♘h5 18 ♗h3 += Spassky-Parma 69 **f5 13 ♝g2 ♞f6 14 ♝g5 a6 15 f4 exf4?** 15...♘e4! **16 ♛xf4 ♚h8 17 ♛h4 ♛d7 18 ♝h3**

♜ae8 19 ♜d2 ♞fg8 20 ♚h1 b5 21 ♞e2 c5 22 ♞f4 22 c3 **♝xb2 23 exf5 gxf5 24 g4 fxg4 25 ♝xg4 ♛b7 26 ♜d3 ♜xf4!? 27 ♝xf4 ♞g6 28 ♛g3 ♜f8 29 c3 c4 30 ♜dd1 ♞xf4 31 ♜xf4 ♜xf4 32 ♛xf4 ♝xc3 33 ♛xd6 ♛g7 34 ♝e6** Δ ♖g1 **♛f6 35 ♛g3 ♞e7 36 d6 ♞g6 37 d7 ♝a5 38 d8♛+ ♝xd8 39 ♜xd8+ 1-0** 39...♕xd8 40 ♕c3+

320 Faibisovich-Karasev USSR 78

1 e4 d6 2 d4 ♞f6 3 ♞c3 g6 4 ♞f3 ♝g7 5 ♝e2 0-0 6 0-0 ♝g4 7 h3 7 ♗e3 **♝xf3 8 ♝xf3 ♞c6 9 ♝g5?!** 9 ♘e2 e5 10 c3 ♖e8 11 d5 ♘e7 12 c4 Alexandria-Holmov, Suhumi 77 **h6?!** 9...e5 10 dxe5 dxe5 11 ♘d5 ♘d4 12 c3 ♘e6; 9...♘d7 10 ♘e2 h6 11 ♗e3 e5 **10 ♝e3 e5 11 d5 ♞e7 12 ♛d2 ♚h7 13 ♜ad1** 13 ♗e2 c6 14 dxc6 bxc6 15 f4 **♞d7 14 ♝e2** 14 g4 ♘g8! Δ ♗f6-g5 **f5 15 f3 f4 16 ♝f2 ♞f6 17 ♝d3 g5 18 ♞e2 h5 19 c4 ♞g6 20 c5 g4 21 cxd6 cxd6 22 ♚h1 ♝h6 23 ♜c1 gxf3 24 gxf3**

24...♞g4!? 25 hxg4 hxg4 26 ♚g2! g3 27 ♜h1 gxf2 28 ♛b4! 28 ♔xf2? ♕b6+ **f1♛+ 29 ♚xf1 ♛e7 30 ♚f2 ♜g8 31 ♜h2 ♞h8?** 31...♘h4 32 ♖ch1 ♗g5 33 ♘c3 **32 ♞d4** 32 ♘xf4! **exd4** 32...♘f7 33 ♘f5 ♕d7 34 ♗b5 ♕d8 35 ♗f1 ♖b8 36 ♗h3 **33 e5+ ♜g6** 33...♔g7 34 ♖g1+ ♔f8 35 ♖xg8+ ♔xg8 36 ♖xh6; 33...♘g6 34 ♖ch1 **34 ♛xd6! ♛xd6** 34...♕g5 35 ♗xg6+ ♘xg6 36 ♖g1 ♕f5 37 ♕c7 **35 exd6 ♚g7** 35...♖g8 36 ♖c7+ ♖g7 37 d7 ♘f7 38 ♖c8; 35...♖f8 36 ♖c7+ ♘f7 37 ♖g2 **36 ♜c7+ ♞f7** 36...♔f6 37 ♖e7! ♗g5 38 ♖hh7 ♗h6 39 ♖e6+ ♔g5 40 ♖e5 +− **37 ♝xg6 ♚xg6 38 ♜xf7 ♚xf7 39 ♜xh6 d3 40 ♚e1 ♜e8+ 41 ♚d2 ♜e5 42 ♜h8 1-0** 42...♖xd5 43 d7 ♖xd7 44 ♖h7+ ♔e6 45 ♖xd7 ♔xd7 46 ♔xd3 ♔e6 47 ♔e4

321 Karpov-Korchnoi (32) 78

1 e4 d6 2 d4 ♞f6 3 ♞c3 g6 4 ♞f3 ♝g7 5 ♝e2 0-0 6 0-0 c5 7 d5 7 dxc5 dxc5 8 ♕xd8 ♖xd8 9 ♗e3 b6 10 ♖fd1 ♗d7 11 ♘e5 ♘e8; 10...♘c6 **♞a6 8 ♝f4 ♞c7 9 a4 b6 10 ♜e1 ♝b7 11 ♝c4 ♞h5?!** 11...a6 **12 ♝g5 ♞f6 13 ♛d3 a6 14 ♜ad1 ♜b8 15 h3 ♞d7 16 ♛e3 ♝a8 17 ♝h6 b5 18 ♝xg7 ♚xg7 19 ♝f1 ♞f6 20 axb5 axb5 21 ♞e2 ♝b7 22 ♞g3 ♜a8 23 c3 ♜a4 24 ♝d3 ♛a8?! 25 e5! dxe5** 25...♘fxd5 26 ♘h5+ gxh5 27 ♕g5+ ♔h8 28 ♕h6 f5 29 exf6 ♘xf6 30 ♖xe7 +− **26 ♛xe5 ♞cxd5 27 ♝xb5 ♜a7 28 ♞h4 ♝c8 29 ♝e2 ♝e6** Δ ♕b8 **30 c4 ♞b4 31 ♛xc5 ♛b8?** 31...♘c2 **32 ♝f1 ♜c8 33 ♛g5 ♚h8 34 ♜d2 ♞c6** 34...♗xc4 35 ♗xc4 ♖xc4 36 ♖xe7! **35 ♛h6 ♜g8 36 ♞f3 ♛f8 37 ♛e3 ♚g7?** 37...♖b7 **38 ♞g5 ♝d7 39 b4! ♛a8 40 b5 ♞a5 41 b6 ♜b7 1-0**

322 Karpov-Korchnoi (18) 78

1 e4 d6 2 d4 ♞f6 3 ♞c3 g6 4 ♞f3 ♝g7 5 ♝e2 0-0 6 0-0 ♝g4 7 ♝e3 ♞c6 8 ♛d3!? Δ ♘d2 **e5 9 d5 ♞b4** 9...♘e7 10 ♘d2 ♗d7 11 ♘c4 ♘e8 12 f4 ±/+= **10 ♛d2 a5 11 h3** 11 ♘e1 ♗d7 12 a3 ♘a6 13 ♘d3 **♝d7 12 ♝g5** 12 a3

Na6 13 Rab1 (Δ b4) Nc5 14 Bxc5 dxc5 15 Nxe5 **Qe8 13 Nh2** 13 Ne1 **Kh8 14 a3 Na6 15 Bh6 Bxh6 16 Qxh6 Ng8?** 16...Nc5 17 Qe3 c6 18 b4 cxd5 19 bxc5 d4 20 Qd3 dxc3 21 cxd6 Bc6= **17 Qe3 f5** 17...a4 18 f4 exf4 19 Rxf4 Nc5 20 Raf1 f6 **18 exf5 Bxf5 19 Rac1 Nf6?** 19...Nc5 20 b4 axb4 21 axb4 Na4 22 Nb5; 19...Qe7; 19...Bd7; 19...a4 **20 g4! Bd7 21 f4 exf4 22 Qxf4 Nc5 23 Rce1** 23 Qd4 Qe5 24 Qxe5 dxe5 25 Nf3; 23...Nce4 24 Rxf6! Rxf6 25 g5 +− **Nfe4 24 Qe3 Qe5 25 Nxe4 Nxe4 26 Bf3 Ng5** 26...Qg3+ **27 Qxe5+ dxe5 28 Bg2 Rxf1+ 29 Nxf1 Re8 30 Nd2?** 30 b3! **a4! 31 Re3 Kg7 32 Kf2?** 32 Rc3 Rc8 33 Kf2 **Re7 33 c4 b6 34 Rc3 h5! 35 Kg3** 35 gxh5 gxh5 36 Kg3 **hxg4 36 hxg4 Be8 37 c5 bxc5 38 Ne4 Nxe4+ 39 Bxe4 Kf6 40 Rxc5 Kg5 41 Bd3 Rf7 42 Be2 Rh7 43 Bf3 Rf7 44 Rc4 Rh7 45 Rb4 Re7 46 Kf2 Bd7 47 Kg3 Be8 48 Kf2 Bd7 49 Ke3 e4! 50 Bxe4 Kxg4 51 Kf2 Kg5 52 Bc2 Re5 53 Bxa4 Bxa4 54 Rxa4 Rxd5 55 Ke3 Rb5 56 b4 Re5+ 57 Kd4 Kf4 58 Ra8 g5 69 Rc8 Re4+ 60 Kd5 Re5+ 61 Kc6 g4 62 Rxc7 g3 63 Kb6 g2 64 Rc1 Kf3**

½-½ 65 a4 Kf2 66 a5 Re1 67 Rc2+ Re2 68 Rc1 Re1 69 Rc2+; 67...Kf1 68 Rxg2 Kxg2 69 a6 Ra1 70 a7 Kf3 71 Kb7 Ke4 72 a8Q Rxa8 73 Kxa8 Kd5=

323 Ljubojevic-Sznapik
Buenos Aires 78

1 e4 g6 2 d4 Bg7 3 Nc3 d6 4 f4 a6?! 4...Nf6 5 Nf3 0-0 6 Bd3 Na6; **5 Nf3 b5 6 Bd3** 6 a4 b4 7 Ne2?! Bb7 8 Ng3 Nbd7 9 a5 c5? (9...e6!) 10 d5!± Karasev-Sznapik, Polanica 74 **Bb7 7 a4** 7 Qe2! Nd7 8 e5 c5 9 Be4!± Filipowicz-Sznapik, Mielec 74; 7 0-0 Nd7 8 e5! c5 9 Be4! Bxe4 10 Nxe4 cxd4 11 e6! += Bataszow-Sznapik, Bath 76 **b4 8 Ne2 Nd7 9 c3 bxc3 10 bxc3 c5 11 Rb1 Rb8 12 0-0 cxd4 13 cxd4 Ngf6 14 e5 Nd5 15 Ng5!±** Δ e6 **e6** 15...0-0 16 e6 Gheorghiu **16 Ne4! 0-0** 16...dxe5 17 Nd6+ Gheorghiu **17 Nxd6 Ba8 18 Bd2 Rb6 19 Qc2** 19 Rxb6 Qxb6 20 Qb1±; 19...Nxb6 20 a5 Δ Bxa6 +− **Rc6 20 Qa2 Rxd6! 21 exd6 Ndf6 22 Qa3 Ne8 23 Bxa6! +−** Gheorghiu **Nxd6 24 Rfc1 Qd7 25 a5 Nc7 26 Bd3 Ndb5 27 Qc5 Nxd4 28 Bc3! e5!** 28...Nxe2+ 29 Bxe2 +− Gheorghiu; 28...Nf3+ 29 gxf3 Qxd3 30 Bxg7! (Δ Qxf8 mate) Kxg7 31 Qc3+ Qxc3 32 Rxc3 +− **29 Nxd4! exd4 30 Bd2 Nd5 31 Bb5!** Δ Bc6 Gheorghiu **Qg4 32 Bc6 Bxc6 33 Qxc6 Nc3 34 Bxc3 dxc3 35 Qd6! Qe2 36 h3! c2 37 Rb3 Bb2 38 Rb8! +−** 38 Rxb2? Qe3+ **Bg7** 38...Bd4+ 39 Kh2 Rxb8 40 Qxb8+ Kg7 41 Qc7 +− **39 Kh2! h5 40 a6 Qf2 41 Rxc2! Qxc2 42 a7 Qa4 43 Rxf8+ Bxf8 44 Qb8 1-0 Filipowicz**

324 Raitza-Thormann DDR 78

1 e4 g6 2 d4 Bg7 3 Nc3 d6 4 f4 Nc6 5 Be3 Nf6 5...Nh6 **6 h3 0-0 7 g4 e5**

8 dxe5 dxe5 9 f5 h6?! 9...gxf5! 10 gxf5 Nd4 11 Nf3 Fischer-Udovic 70 **10 Bd3 Nd4 11 Qd2 c5 12 0-0-0 Kh7 13 Nce2** 13 Nge2?? Nf3 **c4! 14 Bxc4 Nxe4 15 Qd3 gxf5 16 Nxd4 exd4 17 Ne2**

17...dxe3! 18 Qxd8 Rxd8 19 Rxd8 Bf6 20 Rf8 20 Rdd1 Nf2; 21 Rhd1 Nd2 22 Rd6 Be7; 20 Re8 Nd6 **Nd6 21 Bxf7 Kg7?** 21...Be7! **22 Rxc8 Nxc8 23 Bd5 fxg4 24 Rg1! h5 25 hxg4 h4 26 c3?** 26 g5 Be5 27 Rg4 ½-½

325 Skrobek-Pribyl Decin 78
1 e4 g6 2 d4 Bg7 3 Nc3 d6 4 f4 Nf6 5 Nf3 c5 6 Bb5+ Bd7 7 e5 Ng4 8 e6 Bxb5 9 exf7+ Kd7 10 Nxb5 Qa5+ 11 Nc3 cxd4 12 Nxd4 Bxd4 13 Qxd4 Nc6 14 Qc4 Qa6? 14...Rhf8 **15 Nb5!±** 15 Qxa6 bxa6 16 h3 += **Rhf8 16 Bd2 Rac8 17 Qe2! Nf6 18 0-0 Rxf7 19 Rfe1 Nd8 20 c4! Ke8 21 Bc3 Ng8 22 Rad1 +− Rc6 23 c5** 23 Rxd6 **Rxf4 24 cxd6 Qb6+ 25 Kh1 Rf2 26 Qe5 Rxc3 27 Nc7+ Kf7 28 dxe7 Nf6 29 exd8Q 1-0 Pritchett**

326 Buzbuchi-Prudeanu
Poiana Brasov 78
1 e4 d6 2 d4 g6 3 Nc3 Nf6 4 f4 Bg7 5 Nf3 0-0 6 Bd3 6 e5 **Nc6** 6...Na6 **7 e5** 7 h3?!; 7 Be3; 7 0-0 e5 **dxe5 8 dxe5** 8 fxe5 **Nd5 9 Bd2 f6?!** 9...Be6!? **10 Qe2 Kh8 11 0-0-0 Bg4 12 Be4! e6 13 Nxd5 exd5 14 Bc3 fxe5 15 Rxd5 Qe7 16 fxe5 Nxe5?** 16...Rae8 **17 Rxe5! +− Bxe5 18 Nxe5!** 18 Bxe5+ Qxe5! **1-0** 18...Bxe2 19 Nf7+ Kg8 20 Nh6 mate **Ciocaltea**

327 Sax-Donner
Buenos Aires 78
1 e4 d6 2 d4 Nf6 3 Nc3 g6 4 f4 Bg7 5 Nf3 0-0 6 Bd3 Nc6 7 0-0 e5 7...Bg4 **8 dxe5** 8 fxe5!? dxe5 9 d5 Ne7 10 Nxe5 Nfxd5 11 Nxf7 Nxc3 12 Nxd8 Nxd1 13 Bc4+ Kh8 14 Rxf8+ Bxf8 15 Nf7+ Kg8 16 Ng5+ Kh8! 17 Nf7+ ½-½ Judovich-Luik, Corr. 67-68 **dxe5 9 f5 Nb4 10 fxg6 hxg6 11 Bg5 += c6** 11...Nxd3 12 cxd3± Padevsky-Udovcic, Zagreb 65 **12 Kh1 Nxd3 13 cxd3 Qd6 14 d4± Nh7 15 d5! Nxg5 16 Nxg5 Qe7 17 Nf3 Bd7 18 Qb3 b6 19 Rad1 Rfd8 20 Rd2 c5**

21 d6! Qe6 22 Nd5! Qxd6 23 Ng5 Be6 24 Qg3 1-0 Samarian

328 Unzicker-Chandler
Buenos Aires 78
1 e4 d6 2 d4 Nf6 3 Nc3 g6 4 f4 Bg7 5 Nf3 0-0 6 e5 dxe5 7 fxe5 Nd5 8 Bc4 Be6 8...c6?! 9 0-0 a5 10 Bg5 h6 11 Bd2 Be6 12 Nxd5 Bxd5 13 Bxd5

cxd5 14 c3 Ra6 15 Ne1± Unzicker-Matanovic, Berlin 71 **9 Nxd5** 9 Qe2 c5 10 Bxd5 Bxd5 11 Nxd5 Qxd5 12 c4 Qd7 13 d5 e6 14 d6 f6≈ Koch-Rittner, Corr. 56 **Bxd5 10 Bxd5 Qxd5 11 Qe2 b5** 11...c5 12 c4 Qd7 13 d5 e6 14 d6 Nc6 15 Bf4 f6 16 0-0-0≈ **12 0-0 Nd7 13 c3 Nb6** 13...a6 Δ c5 **14 b3 a5 15 Ba3 Qd7 16 Bc5 Nd5 17 Qd2** 17 c4 bxc4 18 bxc4 Nf4 Δ Ne6 **Rfb8?!** 17...c6 **18 Rac1 b4?!** 18...c6 **19 c4 Nc3 20 Rfe1 a4 21 Rc2** 21 Bxb4? Nxa2! **axb3 22 axb3 f5! 23 exf6** 23 Bxb4? Ne4 **Bxf6 24 Bxb4 Rxb4 25 Rxc3 Rab8 26 Ree3 c5?!** 26...Bg7 **27 Rcd3 cxd4 28 Nxd4 Bxd4** 28...Bg5 29 Nc2! **29 Rxd4 Qa7 30 Rd7?!** 30 Rd8+! Rxd8 31 Qxd8+ Kf7 32 Qd5+ Kg7 33 c5± **Qc5 31 Qd5+ Qxd5 32 cxd5 Rd4?** 32...Rxb3 33 Rexe7 Rb1+ 34 Kf2 R1b2+ 35 Kg3 R8b3+ 36 Kh4 +−; 32...R8b7! 33 Rdxe7 Rxe7 34 Rxe7 Rxb3 35 d6 +−; 33 Rdxe7 Rxb3=; 33 Rxb7! Rxb7 34 Kf2± **33 Rexe7 Rd2 34 Rg7+ Kf8 35 Rxh7 Ke8 36 Ra7 1-0 Samarian**

329 Gaprindashvili-Chiburdanidze (9) 78

1 e4 d6 2 d4 Nf6 3 Nc3 g6 4 g3 Bg7 5 Bg2 0-0 6 Nge2 Nbd7 7 0-0 c5 8 h3 a6 9 Be3 Qc7 10 Qd2! 10 f4 cxd4 11 Bxd4 e5 12 Be3 b5 13 a3 Bb7 14 f5 Nb6 15 Rb1 Nc4 16 Qd3 d5! **cxd4** 10...Rb8 11 g4 b5 12 g5 b4 13 gxf6 bxc3 14 Nxc3 Nxf6 15 dxc5 Rxb2! **11 Nxd4 Ne5 12 b3 Nc6 13 Nxc6** 13 Rfd1 **bxc6 14 Rad1 Bb7 15 Na4 c5?** 15...Nd7 **16 e5! dxe5** 16...Ne8 17 Bxb7 Qxb7 18 exd6 exd6 19 Qa5 **17 Bxb7 Qxb7 18 Nxc5 Qc8** 18...Qf3 19 Rfe1 h5 **19 Kh2 Ra7** 19...h5 20 c4 Qf5 21 f3 Rfd8 22 Qxd8+ Rxd8 23 Rxd8+ Kh7 24 Nxa6 e4!; 22 Qe2 Rxd1 23 Rxd1 g5 **20 c4** 20 Ne6? Rd7! **Rc7 21 Na4 Ne4 22 Qd3 Nd6** 22...f5 23 Nb6 Qe8 **23 Nb6 Qb7 24 Nd5 Rc6** 24...Rd7 25 Nxe7+! **25 c5 Nc8** 25...Nf5 26 b4 e6 27 Nb6 Nd4 28 f4 e4! **26 b4 e6 27 Nb6 e4 28 Qd2!** 28 Qxe4? Rxb6! **Nxb6 29 cxb6 Bc3 30 Qd7 Rxb6** 30...Qxd7 31 Rxd7 Bxb4 32 b7 Bd6 33 Rd1! Bc7 34 Ba7 **31 Bxb6 Qxb6 32 a3 Be5** 32...Bb2 33 Qa4 **33 Kg2 e3 34 fxe3 Qxe3 35 Qd3 Qg5 36 Rf3 Rc8 37 Rd2** 37 Qxa6 Rc2+ 38 Kf1 Bxg3 39 Qa8+ Kg7 40 Rxf7+ Kxf7 41 Rd7+ Kf6 42 Qd8+ **Kg7** 37...h5 38 h4 Qh6 39 Rdf2 f5 40 Qd7; 38...Qg4 39 Qxa6 **38 Rxf7+ Kh6 39 h4! 1-0**

330 Peresipkin-Ftacnik Kiev 78

1 e4 d6 2 d4 Nf6 3 Nc3 g6 4 Bg5 Bg7 4...c6 5 Qd2 Nbd7 6 f4 Bg7 7 e5 Nd5∞ Ree-Quinteros, Haifa 76; 5 Qe2 h6 6 Bxf6 exf6 7 0-0-0 Bg7= **5 Qd2 h6** 5...c6 6 f4 h6 7 Bh4 d5 8 e5 Nh7 9 Nf3 += **6 Bh4 g5?!** 6...c6 7 f4 0-0 8 Nf3 Na6?! 9 e5 += Savon-Kuzmin, USSR 75; 8...Bg4!? **7 Bg3 Nh5 8 0-0-0 += Nc6 9 Bb5! Bd7 10 Nge2 e5** 10...e6 **11 dxe5 Nxe5 12 Nd4! c6** 12...a6 13 Bxd7+ Δ Nf5± **13 Be2 Nxg3** 13...Nf4?! **14 hxg3 Qf6!? 15 f4! gxf4 16 gxf4 Ng6 17 g3 0-0-0 18 Rh5! +=** Δ Ra5 **Ne7 19 Qe3 Kb8 20 Ra5 Nc8! 21 Rh5** 21 e5? dxe5 22 fxe5 Qg5 **Rde8** 21...Ne7 **22 Qf2 Rhg8 23 Bf3 Qg6 24 Rg1 Nb6 25 Qd2 Nc4 26 Qd3 d5?! 27 e5± Bf8 28 Qxg6 Rxg6 29 b3 Ne3** 29...Na3 **30 Kd2 Ng4 31 Rh4 Bc5 32 Nce2 Reg8 33 c3 Bf8 34 b4 Kc7** 34...c5?! **35 Rh5 Kd8 36 Nf5 Bxf5 37 Rxf5 Ke7 38 Rh5** Δ

♘d4 +– **f6 39 e6! f5 40 ♝xg4 fxg4 41 ♞d4 ♝g7 42 ♞f5+ ♚xe6 43 ♜e1+ ♚f7 44 ♜e7+ ♚f6 45 ♜xb7 +– ♝f8 46 ♞h4 ♜8g7 47 ♜f5+ ♚e6 48 ♜xf8 ♜xb7 49 ♞xg6 1-0 Gufeld**

331 Pribyl-Swic Lodz 78

1 e4 d6 2 d4 ♞f6 3 ♞c3 g6 4 ♝g5 h6?! 4...♗g7; 4...c6 **5 ♝e3 c6 6 ♝e2 ♝g7 7 ♞f3 ♛b6?! 8 0-0! ♛xb2 9 ♛d2 ♛a3** 9...♘g4? 10 ♖fb1 ♕a3 11 ♘b5! cxb5 12 ♖b3 +– **10 h3 ♛a5 11 a4 ♞bd7 12 ♝c4 0-0**

13 ♝xh6!! ♝xh6 13...d5? 14 ♘xd5!; 13...♕h5± **14 ♛xh6 d5?!** 14...♕xc3? 15 ♕xg6+ ♔h8 16 ♗xf7 ♘h7 17 e5 dxe5 18 ♖ae1 +–; 14...♕h5± **15 ♝d3! ♛xc3?** 15...dxe4 16 ♘xe4 ♕h5± **16 e5 +– ♞h7 17 ♜ae1! c5 18 ♜e3 ♛a5 19 ♞h4 cxd4 20 ♞f5 1-0 Webb**

332 Ermenkov-Kirpichnikov Jurmala 78

1 e4 d6 2 d4 ♞f6 3 ♞c3 g6 4 h3 c6 5 ♞f3 ♝g7 6 a4 0-0 7 ♝e3 e5?! 7...♘bd7 8 ♕d2 ♕c7 9 ♗e2 b6 10 0-0 a6∝ **8 dxe5 dxe5 9 ♛xd8 ♜xd8 10 ♝c4! ♞bd7 11 0-0-0** 11 ♖d1 ♖e8 12 0-0 Δ ♘g5; f4; 11 a5 += **♜e8 12 ♜d2 ♝f8! 13 ♞g5 ♜e7 14 ♜hd1 h6 15 ♞f3 ♜e8 16 ♞e1 ♞c5 17 f3 ♚g7 18 ♚b1 a5! 19 ♞d3 ♞fd7 20 ♞xc5 ♞xc5 21 b3 ♝e6 22 ♝xc5 ♝xc5 23 ♝xe6 ♜xe6 24 ♜d7 ♜b8** 24...♖e7 25 ♖xe7 ♗xe7 26 ♖d7 **25 ♚a2 ♚f8 26 ♜7d3 ♚e7 27 ♞b1 ♜d6 28 ♜xd6 ♝xd6 29 ♞d2 ♝c7 30 ♞c4 ♚e6** 30...b5?! 31 axb5 Δ ♘e3 **31 ♚b2 f5 32 ♜e1 ♜d8 33 ♚c3 ♜d4 34 ♜e2 b5?!** Zeitnot **35 axb5 cxb5 36 ♞d2 a4?! 37 ♚b2! ♝a5 36 c3 ♜d3 37 b4 ♝b6 38 ♚c2± 1-0 Gufeld**

333 Mariotti-Pribyl Italy 78

1 e4 d6 2 d4 ♞f6 3 ♞c3 g6 4 h4 ♝g7 5 f3 5 ♗e2 Δ h5 **h5 6 ♝c4 c6 7 ♝b3 ♛c7 8 ♝e3 e5** 8...♘bd7 **9 ♛d2 b5?!** 9...b6 Δ ♗a6 **10 dxe5! dxe5 11 ♞h3 ♝xh3 12 ♜xh3 += ♞bd7 13 0-0-0 a5 14 a4! b4 15 ♞b1!** Δ ♘d2-c4± **0-0 16 ♛f2 ♜fd8 17 ♞d2± ♝f8 18 g4! c5** 18...hxg4 19 hxg4 ♘xg4? 20 ♕xf7+ +– **19 ♝g5 ♜e8 20 ♜g3 ♚g7 21 ♛e3 ♜a6 22 ♞c4 ♜ae6 23 ♛d3 ♝e7 24 ♜gg1 ♜d8 25 ♞e3 ♞f8 26 ♛b5 +– ♜ed6 27 ♜xd6 ♜xd6 28 gxh5 ♛d8** 28...♘xh5? 29 ♗xe7 ♕xe7 30 ♘f5+ +– **29 hxg6 fxg6 30 ♛c4! ♜e6 31 h5 gxh5 32 ♞f5+ ♚h7 33 ♝h6 1-0 Maric**

334 Sveshnikov-Romanishin Lvov 78

1 e4 g6 2 d4 ♝g7 3 ♞c3 c6 4 f4 b5 5 ♞f3 d5 6 e5!? 6 a3; 6 ♗e3; 6 exd5 **♝g4!? 7 h3 ♝f5 8 g4 ♝c8! 9 ♝e3 ♞d7 10 ♝d3** 10 ♗g2 **♞b6 11 ♛e2 h5∝ 12 b3?!** 12 ♖g1 Δ f5 **e6** 12...hxg4 13 ♘g5 Δ e6∝ **13 ♛f2 ♞e7 14 ♞e2** Δ ♘g3, f5 **♛c7 15 ♞g3 f5! 16 exf6** 16 gxh5 gxh5 17 ♖g1 **♝xf6 17 0-0 ♝d7 18 ♚g2 ♞bc8! 19 ♝d2 ♞d6 20 ♞e5 0-0 21 ♛e3 ♝c8 22 ♜h1 c5 23 c3** 23 dxc5? d4! 23 cxd6 dxe3 24 dxc7 exd2 =+ Δ ♗b7+ **♝b7 24 ♞f3 ♞e4! 25 ♝xb5 g5!!** –+ **26 ♞xh5**

♞g6! 27 fxg5 ♝h8! Δ ♖xf3 −+ **28 ♜af1 e5! 29 dxc5 ♞xd2 30 ♛xd2 ♛xc5** 30...d4? 31 c6! **31 ♝e2 ♜ac8 32 ♜c1 ♞h4+ 33 ♚g3** 33 ♘xh4 ♕f2 mate **♞xf3 34 ♝xf3 e4** 34...♖xf3!? **35 ♝d1 ♝xc3** Δ d4, e3 **36 ♜xc3 ♛xc3+ 37 ♛xc3 ♜xc3+ 38 ♚h4 d4 39 ♜e1 e3 40 b4 ♝f3 41 ♝a4 0-1 Friedgood**

335 Sveshnikov-Tseshkovsky
Lvov 78
1 e4 g6 2 d4 ♝g7 3 ♞c3 c6 4 g3 d5 5 e5 f6 6 exf6 6 f4?! **♞xf6 7 ♝g2 0-0 8 ♞f3 ♝g4 9 h3 ♝xf3 10 ♝xf3 ♞bd7 11 0-0 e5 12 ♞e2 ♛e7** =+ **13 ♝g2 ♜ae8 14 ♝g5 exd4 15 ♞xd4 ♛f7 16 ♝xf6 ♞xf6 17 ♛f3 ♞e4 18 ♛xf7+ ♜xf7 19 ♜ad1 ♞d6!**∓

20 b3 ♝xd4 21 ♜xd4 ♜e2 22 c4 ♞f5 23 ♜f4 dxc4 24 ♜d1 c3 25 ♜c1 ♜xa2 26 ♜xc3 ♜d2 Δ ♘d4-e2+ **27 ♝f1 ♞d4 28 ♜e4** 28 ♗c4 ♘e2+ −+ **♚f8 29 ♝c4 ♞f3+ 30 ♚g2 ♞g5! 31 ♜f4 ♜xf4 32 gxf4 ♜xf2+ 33 ♚xf2 ♞e4+** −+ **34 ♚f3 ♞xc3 35 f5 gxf5 36 ♚f4 ♞e4 37 ♚e5 ♚e7 38 ♝g8 ♞g5 39 ♚xf5 ♞xh3 40 ♝xh7 ♚d6 0-1 Friedgood**

336 Britton-Nunn
London 78
1 e4 g6 2 d4 ♝g7 3 ♞c3 d6 4 ♞f3 a6 5 ♝e2 5 a4 ♘f6 6 ♗e2 0-0 7 0-0 b6!? 8 e5 ♘fd7 9 exd6 cxd6 10 ♗g5 h6 11 ♗e3 ♘f6 12 d5 ♘bd7 13 ♕d2 ♔h7 14 ♖a3?! ♗b7 15 ♖b3 ♖c8 16 h3 ♖xc3! =+ Matanovic-Nunn, London-Belgrade 76; 9 ♗f4 ♘c6 10 ♕c1 ♗b7 11 ♖d1 ♘b4 12 ♗h6 ♕c8= Johansson-Nunn, England-Iceland 77; 8 ♖e1 ♘c6 9 h3 ♗b7 10 d5! ♘b4 11 ♗f1 c6 12 dxc6 ♘xc6 += **b5 6 0-0 ♞d7** 6...♗b7?! 7 ♖e1 ♘d7 8 ♗f1 c5 9 a4 b4 10 ♘d5 e6 11 ♗f4!± Honfi-Vadasz, Kecskemet 75 **7 ♜e1** 7 ♗g5 ♗b7 8 ♖e1 c5 9 ♗f1 cxd4 10 ♘xd4 ♘gf6 11 ♕d2 h6 12 ♗h4 0-0 += Bennett-Nunn, England 75 **c5 8 d5=** 8 ♗f1; 8 ♗g5 += **♞gf6 9 ♝f1 0-0 10 h3 ♛c7 11 a3 ♝b7 12 ♝f4 ♜ad8 13 ♛d2?!** 13 ♗h2= **♞e5! 14 ♛e3** 14 ♘xe5? dxe5 15 ♗g5 e6 16 ♖ad1 b4∓; 14 ♗xe5 dxe5 Δ e6 **e6 15 ♝xe5** 15 dxe6? ♘xf3+ 16 ♕xf3 fxe6∓ **dxe5 16 dxe6 fxe6 =+ 17 ♞d2** 17 ♖ad1 ♖d4 **♜d4 18 f3** 18 a4 b4 19 ♘e2 ♘xe4 20 ♘xd4 exd4 21 ♕e2 ♖xf2 −+; 18 g3 b4 **♞h5 19 ♞e2 ♞f4! 20 ♞xd4 exd4 21 ♛f2 ♝e5 22 a4** 22 g3 ♘h5 23 f4 g5 24 ♕f3 ♘g7∓; 24 ♕g2 gxf4 25 gxf4 ♗g7∓; 22 ♖ec1 ♘h5 23 g4 ♗g3 24 ♕e2 ♘f4 25 ♕d1 ♕e7 Δ ♕h4 −+ **♞h5** Δ ♗g3-h2+ **23 g4 ♝g3 24 ♛e2** 24 ♕g2 ♘f4 **♞f4 25 ♛d1 c4 26 axb5 axb5 27 ♝g2 ♝xe1 28 ♛xe1 e5**∓ **29 ♞f1 ♛c5 30 ♚h2 d3 31 cxd3 ♞xd3 32 ♛d2 ♛d4 33 ♜b1 ♝xe4!!** −+ **34 fxe4 ♜f2 35 ♛g5** 35 ♕e3 ♘f4 36 ♕xd4 ♖xg2+ −+; 35 ♕a5 ♖xg2+ 36 ♔xg2 ♘f4+ 37 ♔f3 ♕d3+ 38 ♔f2 ♕e2+ 39 ♔g3 ♕g2+ 40 ♔h4 ♕f2+ 41 ♘g3 ♘g2+ 42 ♔g5 ♕f4 mate;

37 ♔g3 ♕g1+ **♜xg2+ 36 ♚xg2 ♞f4+ 0-1** 37 ♔g3 ♕g1+ 38 ♔h4 ♕f2+ 39 ♘g3 ♘g2 mate **Nunn**

337 Browne-Kagan
Buenos Aires 1 78

1 d4 g6 2 e4 ♝g7 3 ♞c3 d6 4 ♞f3 c6 5 a4 a5!? 6 ♝c4! ♞f6 6...e6?! **7 e5! dxe5 8 ♞xe5 0-0** 8...♘d5 9 ♕f3! **9 0-0 ♞bd7 10 ♝g5** 10...♘xe5!? 11 dxe5 ♕xd1 12 ♖axd1 ♘g4 13 e6! ♗xe6 14 ♗xe6 fxe6 15 ♗xe7 ♖f7 16 ♗c5! += **♛c7 11 f4?! ♞b6 12 ♝b3 ♞bd5?** 12...♘fd5! 13 ♘xd5 ♘xd5 14 ♗xd5 =+ **13 ♛f3 ♝e6 14 ♞e2! ♛c8?! 15 h3 ♞b4 16 c4!** 16 ♗xe6 ♕xe6 17 c3 ♘bd5 18 ♘g3!±; 17...♘fd5!! 18 cxb4 f6 **♝f5 17 ♞g3 ♝c2 18 ♝xc2 ♞xc2 19 ♜ad1 h6! 20 ♝h4** 20 ♗xf6? exf6! **♛c7 21 ♛e2 ♞b4 22 ♞e4! ♜ad8**

23 ♞c3! 23 f5? g5 24 ♗g3 ♘xe4 25 ♕xe4 f6; 26 ♗e1? ♘xe4 27 ♕xe4 ♗xe5 −+; 24 ♗f2 ♘xe4 25 ♕xe4 c5! **♛c8 24 g4 ♜fe8 25 ♚g2?!** 25 f5! ♘d7?? 26 ♘xf7! +−; 25...g5 26 ♗g3 e6± **♞d7! 26 ♞e4 ♞xe5 27 dxe5** 27 fxe5 b6! 28 ♕f3 ♕e6 **♝f8 28 ♝f2 ♛c7 29 ♝d4! ♝g7 30 b3** 30 ♕f2? c5! 31 ♘xc5 ♕c6+ 32 ♕f3?? ♖xd4!; 32 ♔g1 b6! **b6 31 ♞g3 c5 32 ♝c3 ♜xd1 33 ♜xd1 ♜d8 34 ♜xd8+ ♛xd8 35 f5!± ♞d3** 35...♕d3?! 36 ♕xd3! ♘xd3 37 f6 exf6 38 exf6 ♗f8 39 ♘e2 ♗d6 40 ♔f3 ♗e5 41 ♗xe5 ♘xe5+ 42 ♔e4 ♘d7 43 ♔d5 ♘xf6+ 44 ♔c6 +− **36 ♛e3 e6?!** 36...♕a8+ **37 f6 ♝f8 38 h4 ♞b4 39 ♛e2 ♞c6 40 ♞e4 ♛c7 41 ♛d2! ♛b8?!** 41...♘d4! 42 ♗xd4 cxd4 43 ♕xd4 ♗c5! += **42 ♛f4 ♛a8 43 ♚f3 ♚h7 44 ♛d2 ♛b7 45 ♛d3 ♚g8 46 ♛e3 ♛b8 47 ♞f2 ♛d8 48 ♛e4 ♛d7 49 ♚e2 ♞b4 50 ♞h3! ♞c6 51 ♞f4** 51 h5 g5 52 ♘g1 Δ ♘f3, ♗d2xg5 +− **♞d4+ 52 ♝xd4 ♛xd4? 53 ♛xd4 cxd4 54 ♚d3 +− h5 55 gxh5 gxh5 56 ♞xh5 ♚h7 57 ♞f4 ♚h6 58 ♚xd4 ♝c5+ 59 ♚e4 ♝a3 60 ♞d3 ♝f8** 60...♔h5 61 b4! axb4 62 c5 bxc5 63 ♘xc5 +− **61 c5! ♝xc5** 61...bxc5 62 ♘b2 Δ ♘c4 **62 ♞xc5 bxc5 63 ♚d3 ♚g6 64 h5+ ♚xh5 65 ♚c4 ♚g5 66 ♚xc5 ♚f5 67 ♚d6 1-0 Browne**

338 Gufeld-Hodes USSR 78

1 e4 c6 2 d4 g6 3 ♞f3 ♝g7 4 c3 d6 5 ♞bd2 ♞f6 6 ♝d3 0-0 7 0-0 ♛c7 8 a4 a5 9 ♞c4 ♞xe4 9...♘bd7 **10 ♝xe4 d5 11 ♝d3 dxc4 12 ♝xc4 += ♞bd7 13 ♜e1 e6** 13...e5? 14 dxe5 ♘xe5 15 ♗f4 +− **14 ♝g5 c5 15 d5** 15 ♖c1± **exd5** 15...♘b6 16 d6 ♕b8 17 ♗b5± **16 ♝xd5 ♞b6 17 ♝b3** 17 ♖e7 ♗d7 18 ♗b3 ♖ae8 **c4 18 ♝c2 ♝e6 19 ♞d4 ♝d5 20 ♛d2** 20 ♕g4!? **♜fe8 21 ♝f4?!** 21 ♖ad1 += **♛d7 22 ♝h6?!** 22 ♘b5 += **♝e5** 22...♗xh6 23 ♕xh6 ♘xa4! 24 ♘f5 gxf5 ♕g5+ =; 22...♕g4?! 23 f3 ♗xd4+ 24 cxd4 ♗xf3 25 h3 +− **23 h3 f6 24 ♝f4 ♜ad8 25 ♜e2 ♝f7 26 ♝xe5** Zeitnot **♜xe5** 26...fxe5 27 ♘f3 **27 ♛f4 ♜de8= 28 ♜d2! ♞d5 29 ♛g3 ♜e1+ 30 ♜xe1 ♜xe1+ 31 ♚h2 ♛e7 32 ♞f3 ♜e2 33 ♜xe2 ♛xe2 34 ♞d4**

+= ♕e7 35 ♘f5 ♕e2 36 ♘d4 ♕e1 37 ♘f3 ♕e7 38 ♘d4 ♗e8 39 ♘f5 ♕e2? 40 ♕d6!± ♗c6 40...♕xc2 41 ♕xd5+ ♔h8 42 ♕d6 +− **41 ♕d8+ ♔f7 42 ♗e4! gxf5 43 ♗xd5+ ♗xd5 44 ♕xd5+ ♔g6 45 ♕g8+ ♔h6 46 ♕f7! ♔g5?!** 46...♕xf2 47 ♕xf6+ ♔h5 48 ♕f7+ ♔h6 49 ♕xb7 **47 ♕xh7?** 47 ♕g7+ ♔f4 48 ♕xh7 ♕xf2 49 ♕c7+ +−; 48...♕xb2 49 ♕c7+ ♔g5 50 f4+ ♔g6 51 ♕xc4± **♕xf2 += 48 ♕g7+ ♔h5 49 ♕h7+ ♔g5 50 ♕g8+** 50 ♕xb7 ♕f4+ 51 g3 ♕d2+ 52 ♕g2 ♕e3 += **♔h6 51 ♕xc4 ♕xb2 52 ♔g3?! ♕b1 53 ♔f4?!** Zeitnot **♕c1+ = 54 ♔g3 ♕e3+ 55 ♔h2 f4 ½-½ Gufeld**

339 Barczay-Pribyl
Decin 78

1 e4 g6 2 d4 ♗g7 3 ♘f3 d6 4 c3 ♘f6 5 ♗d3 0-0 6 0-0 ♘c6!? 7 d5 ♘b8 8 c4 += e6 9 dxe6 ♗xe6 10 ♘c3 ♘a6 11 ♖e1 ♘c5 12 ♗f1 ♖e8 13 ♘d4 ♗d7 14 f3 a5 15 ♗e3 ♘h5!? 15... c6 **16 ♕d2 f5?** 16...c6 17 ♖ad1 ♕c7 += **17 exf5 gxf5 18 ♗f2 ♖xe1** 18...c6 **19 ♖xe1 f4 20 ♘db5 ♘e6 21 c5! +− dxc5** 21...♘xc5 22 ♕d5+ +−; 21...♗xb5 22 ♘xb5 dxc5 23 ♕xd8+ ♘xd8 24 ♘xc7 ♖b8 25 ♖e8+ ♔f7 26 ♗xc5 +−; 24...♖c8 25 ♖e8+ ♔f7 26 ♗c4+ ♔g6 27 ♘e6 +− **22 ♗c4 ♗xc3 23 ♘xc3 ♕e7 24 ♕xd7 1-0 Pritchett**

1 ♘f3

340 Taimanov-Sahovic
Jurmala 78

1 ♘f3 b5 2 e3 a6 2...b4!? **3 c4 bxc4 4 ♗xc4 d5 5 ♗e2! ♘f6 6 b3 += e6 7 0-0 ♗d6 8 ♗a3 ♗xa3 9 ♘xa3 ♕d6 10 ♕c1 0-0 11 ♕b2** 11 d4!? **c5 12 ♖ac1 ♘bd7 13 d4 ♗b7 14 dxc5 ♘xc5 15 ♖fd1 ♕e7 16 ♘b1 ♖fc8 17 ♘c3 ♘cd7 18 ♘a4 ♗c6 19 ♘d4! ♗b7!** 19...♗xa4 20 bxa4± **20 b4 ♘e4 21 a3 ♘d6 22 ♘b3 ♗c6 23 ♘ac5 ♗b5 24 ♘xd7 ♕xd7 25 ♘c5 ♕e8 26 ♗f3 ♗c6 ½-½ Sahovic**

341 Portisch-Djindjihashvili
Buenos Aires 78

1 ♘f3 b6 2 g3 ♗b7 3 ♗g2 e5 4 d3 g6 5 e4 ♗g7 6 h4!? h5 7 c4 ♘e7 7...d6 Δ ♘f6 **8 ♘c3** Δ d4?! **c5 9 a3 ♘bc6 10 ♖b1 ♘d4=** Djindjihashvili; += Portisch **11 ♘xd4 cxd4 12 ♘d5 ♘xd5 13 exd5** 14 cxd5= **d6 14 0-0 0-0 15 b4 ♗c8!? 16 a4 ♗g4 17 ♕c2 ♕d7 18 ♔h2 f5!? 19 f3!±**

19...f4 20 fxg4 fxg3+ 21 ♔g1! 21 ♔xg3 e4∞ **♖xf1+ 22 ♗xf1 ♖f8 23 ♕g2 ♕xg4 24 ♗g5 ♖f2 25 ♕e4 ♕d7 26 ♕xg6 ♕xa4 1-0** 27 ♗h6 Δ ♕xg3 **Gheorghiu**

342 Palatnik-Romanishin
Kiev 78

1 ♘f3 d5 2 c4 dxc4 3 ♕a4+ ♘c6 4 ♘e5 ♕d6 5 ♘xc4 5 ♘xc6 ♗d7 **♕c5** 5...♕b4 **6 d4!? ♕b4+** 6...♕xd4 7 ♗e3 Δ ♘c3, ♖d1 **7 ♕xb4 ♘xb4 8 ♘ba3 ♘f6 9 f3 e6 10 ♔f2 ♗d7 11 e4 c5 12 ♗f4 ♘h5 13 ♘d6+ ♔e7**

14 ♗d2 ♔xd6 15 dxc5+ ♔c7 15... ♔xc5 16 ♖c1+ ♔b6 17 ♗e3+ ♔a5 18 ♘c4+ ♔a6 19 ♘b6+ +− **16 ♗xb4 a5 17 ♗d2 ♗xc5+ 18 ♗e3 ♗xe3+ 19 ♔xe3 f5! 20 ♖c1+ ♗c6 21 e5** 21 ♗b5 fxe4 22 ♗xc6 bxc6 23 ♔xe4 **g5 22 ♗c4 ♖ad8** 22...♘f4 **23 ♖hd1 ♘f4 24 g3 ♘g6 25 f4 gxf4+ 26 gxf4 ♘h4 27 ♖g1 ♖hg8 28 ♖xg8 ♖xg8 29 ♗xe6 ♘g2+ 30 ♔f2 ♖g4 31 ♖c4 ♘h4 32 ♗d5 ♘g6 33 ♔e3 ♖h4 34 ♘b5+ ♔b6 35 ♗xc6 bxc6 36 ♘d4 ♖xf4 37 ♖xc6+ ♔b7 38 ♖f6 ♖e4+ 39 ♔d3 ♘xe5+ 40 ♔c3 f4 41 ♖h6 f3 42 ♖xh7+ ½-½**

343 Langeweg-Romanishin
IBM 78

1 ♘f3 d5 2 c4 dxc4 3 e3 ♗g4 3... ♘f6 4 ♗xc4 e6 **4 ♗xc4 e6 5 ♕b3!?** 5 d4 += **♗xf3 6 gxf3 ♘bd7** 6...♕c8 7 d4 Δ ♘c3±; 6...b6?! 7 d4± **7 ♕xb7 ♘gf6** 7...♖b8 8 ♕a7± **8 ♘c3 ♗e7** 8...♗d6 9 ♘e4 0-0 10 ♘xd6 cxd6 11 ♕b3 += **9 f4 0-0 10 0-0** 10 d4 c5 11 d5 ♘b6 −+; 10 ♕g2 ♘b6 11 ♗e2 ♘bd5 Δ ♘b4 =+ **e5** 10...♘b6 11 ♗e2 ♘fd5 Δ f5, ♖f6 **11 f5** 11 fxe5 ♘xe5 12 ♗e2 ♖b8 13 ♕g2 ♘d3 14 ♗xd3 ♕xd3 =+ **c6! 12 d3** 12 ♕xc6 ♖c8 13 ♕b5 e4∓ Δ ♖c5/♘e5 **♖c8** 12...♘c5 13 ♕xc6 ♖c8 += **13 ♕b3** 13 ♕xa7 ♘c5 Δ ♖a8 −+ **♘b6 14 ♗a6** 14 e4 ♗c5 15 ♗e3 ♗xe3 16 fxe3 ♖b8! =+ **♖b8 15 ♕d1 ♘fd5** 15...♘bd5!? **16 ♘xd5 cxd5** 16...♘xd5 17 a3 **17 e4 ♕d6 18 exd5 ♕xd5** 18...♘xd5! **19 ♗d2 ♖fd8 20 ♕g4 ♗f6 21 ♗c3 ♕d6 22 ♖fe1 ♘d5 23 ♗c4 ♘f4 24 ♖e3 ♘d5 25 ♖ee1 = ½-½ Taulbut**

344 Hubner-Spassky
Tilburg 78

1 ♘f3 d5 2 c4 e6 3 g3 ♘f6 4 ♗g2 ♗e7 5 0-0 0-0 6 d4 c6 7 ♘c3 ♘bd7 8 b3 b6 9 ♘e5!? ♘xe5 10 dxe5 ♘d7 11 ♗b2 ♗a6 11...♘xe5? 12 cxd5 cxd5 13 ♘xd5! exd5 14 ♗xe5 +=/± **12 cxd5 cxd5 13 ♖c1 ♖c8 14 ♕d4** 14 ♖e1!? (Δ e4) ♘c5 15 ♕d4 **b5!?** 14...♗c5!?; 14...♘c5 15 ♖fd1; 14... ♗b7!? **15 ♕xa7 ♖a8?!** 15...♘c5! 16 ♘xd5 exd5 17 ♖xc5 ♗xc5 18 ♕xa6 ♕d7 19 a4 ∞/+=; 17...♖a8? 18 ♕c7 ♗xc5 19 ♕xc5 +=/±; 17...♖xc5 18 ♕xa6 ♖c2 19 ♗d4; 18...♕d7!? **16 ♕e3 ♕b8 17 ♖fd1 ♖a7 18 ♘b1 b4 19 ♗d4 ♖a8 20 ♖c2 ♗b5 21 f4 +=/± ♖a6 22 ♕c1 ♕a8 23 ♕b2 ♘b8 24 ♗f2 ♘c6 25 ♗f1** Δ ♘d2-f3; 25 ♘d2? ♗xe2 **♕b7 26 ♘d2 ♖fa8 27 ♘f3 g6 28 ♘e1** 28 ♘d4!? **♗d8 29 ♘d3 ♗xd3 30 exd3 ♗b6 31 d4± ♖a5 32 ♕c1 ♘e7 33 ♕d2 ♗d8 34 ♖dc1 ♕a7 35 ♖a1 ♕b7 36 ♔g2 ♖8a7**

37 Be1! Nc6 38 Rac1 Ne7 39 Qxb4 Rxa2 40 Qxb7 Rxc2+ 41 Rxc2 Rxb7 42 b4 Bb6 43 Bf2 Ra7 43...Nf5 44 g4! Nxd4 45 Rc8+ Kg7 46 Bh4! Δ Bf6+, Rg8 +− **44 g4 Kg7 45 Bb5 f5?** 45...Ra3 46 Bh4!? (46 Bc6!?; 46 Bd7!?) Ng8 47 Be8 Ra8! 48 Bd7 Ra7 49 Bc8 Bxd4!? 50 Bd8!; 47...Bxd4? 48 Rc7 Ra7 49 Rxa7 Bxa7 50 Bd8!; 46...Kf8!? **46 exf6+ Kxf6 47 Be8 Kg7** 47...Ra8 48 Bh4+! **48 Re2 Bc7 49 Rxe6 Bxf4 50 b5 Ng8 51 Ra6 Re7 52 Bc6 Nf6 53 b6 Ne4 54 Be1! Bb8 55 Ra8 1-0 Speelman**

345 Jansa-Adorjan
Budapest 78

1 Nf3 Nf6 2 g3 b6 3 Bg2 Bb7 4 c4 e6 5 0-0 Be7 6 b3 0-0 7 Bb2 c5 8 Nc3 d5 9 cxd5 Nxd5 10 Nxd5 Bxd5 11 d4! Bf6 12 Qd3 Nd7 13 Rad1 cxd4 14 Bxd4 Rc8?! 15 e4! += Bb7?! 15...Ba8!? **16 Ba1?!** 16 e5 Be7 17 Ng5 Bxg5 18 Bxb7 Nc5 19 Qf3 Nxb7 20 Be3 Qc7 21 Bxg5 += **Rc7 17 e5 Be7= 18 Nd2?** 18 Qe2 Qa8 19 Ne1= **Bxg2 19 Kxg2**

19...Nxe5!∓ 20 Qxd8 Rxd8 21 Bxe5 Rcd7 22 Bc3 22 Bf4 Bb4∓ **Bf6! 23 Rc1** 23 Bxf6 gxf6 Δ Rxd2 **Bxc3 24 Rxc3 Rxd2∓ 25 a4 g5 26 Rc7 R8d7 27 Rfc1 Kg7 28 h3 h6 29 R1c4 R7d5** Δ Rf5, Rxf2+ **30 g4 Rd7 31 b4 R2d4 32 Rc3 Kf6 33 a5 bxa5 34 bxa5 R4d5 35 a6 R5d6 36 Rb7!? Ke7 37 Rcc7 Rxc7 38 Rxc7+ Rd7 39 Rc6 Kd8! 40 Kf3 Rc7 41 Rd6+ Ke7 42 Rd3 Rc6 43 Ra3 Kf6 44 Kg3 Kg6 45 h4 gxh4+ 46 Kxh4 Rc4** Δ f5 −+ **47 Kg3 f6 48 Rd3 Rc6 49 Ra3 h5 50 gxh5+ Kxh5+ 51 Ra5+ Kg6 52 Ra3 Kf5 53 Ra5+ Ke4 54 Kg4 Kd4! 55 Ra2 Kc5 56 Kh5 Kb5 57 Kg6 f5 −+ 58 Kf6 Rxa6! 59 Rb2+** 59 Rxa6 Kxa6 60 Kxe6 Kb5! 61 Kxf5 a5 62 Ke4 Kc4! 63 f4 a4 64 f5 a3 65 f6 a2 66 f7 a1Q 67 d8Q Qe1+ −+ **Kc4 60 Rb7 Kd5 61 Rb5+ Ke4 62 Rb4+ Kf3 63 Rb2 Rb6 64 Ra2 a5 65 Rxa5 Kxf2 66 Kg5 Rb3 67 Ra4 Kg3** Δ f4, Rb5+ −+ **0-1 Maric**

346 Gaprindashvili-Chiburdanidze (4) 78

1 Nf3 Nf6 2 g3 d5 3 c4 c6 4 Bg2 dxc4 5 a4 g6 6 Na3 Qd5 6...Bg7 7 Nxc4 0-0 **7 0-0 Na6 8 Ne1 Qh5 9 Nxc4 Bh3 10 Nf3 Bxg2 11 Kxg2 Bg7 12 d3** 12 Qb3 **0-0 13 h3 Qd5 14 Bd2 Rfd8 15 Qc2** 15 b4 Ne4 16 Ne3 **Rac8 16 Bc3 c5! 17 Rad1?!** 17 Rfd1 **h6 18 Qb3 b6 19 e4 Qe6 20 Nh4**

20...Nb4! Δ Nxd3 **21 Bxb4 cxb4**

22 ♜fe1 22 ♕xb4 ♘xe4 23 ♖fe1 ♕c6 24 dxe4 ♖xd1 25 ♖xd1 ♕xe4+ −+; 24 ♖xe4 f5; 22...♖xd3 23 ♖xd3 ♕xe4+ 24 ♖f3 ♖xc4 **♞d7! 23 ♛c2** 23 ♕xb4 ♘c5 **♞c5 24 b3 a6 25 ♞f3 b5 26 axb5 axb5 27 ♞e3 ♞a4 28 ♛a2 ♞c3 29 ♛a5 ♞xd1 30 ♜xd1 ♛xb3 31 ♛xb5 ♜c3 32 ♛b7 ♜cxd3 33 ♜xd3 ♜xd3 34 ♞d5 ♜xf3 0-1** time

347 Schurade-Thormann
DDR 78
1 ♞f3 ♞f6 2 g3 d5 3 ♝g2 ♝g4 4 c4 c6 5 ♛b3 ♛b6 6 ♞c3 6 ♕xb6 axb6 7 cxd5 Δ ♘e5 **e6 7 d3 ♞bd7 8 0-0 ♝d6 9 ♛xb6 axb6 10 cxd5 exd5! 11 e4 dxe4 12 ♞xe4 ♞xe4 13 dxe4 0-0 14 ♞d4?!** 14 ♖d1 ♗c5 15 h3 **♝e5 15 ♞c2 ♜fd8 16 f3 ♝e6 17 f4 ♝f6 18 e5 ♝e7 19 b3?** 19 a3 **♝f5! 20 ♞e3 ♝c5 21 ♚h1 ♝d3 22 ♜d1**

22...♝d4! 23 ♜xd3 ♝xa1 24 ♞c4? ♞xe5! 0-1 25 ♖xd8+ ♖xd8 Δ ♖d1+

348 Romanishin-Vaganian
Lvov 78
1 ♞f3 d5 2 g3 c5 3 ♝g2 g6 4 d4 cxd4 5 ♞xd4 ♝g7 6 ♞b3 e6 6...♘f6 7 ♘c3 e6 8 e4 **7 0-0 ♞c6 8 e4 ♞ge7 9 exd5 exd5** 9...♘xd5 10 c4 ♘b4 11 ♕xd8+ ♔xd8 12 ♘c3 **10 c3 0-0 11 ♜e1 b6?!** 11...♗e6 12 ♘c5 ♗c8! **12 ♞a3 ♝a6 13 ♞c2 ♛d7 14 ♞bd4 ♜fe8 15 ♝g5** 15 ♘xc6 ♘xc6 16 ♕xd5 ♕xd5 17 ♗xd5 ♖xe1+ 18 ♘xe1 ♖d8 19 ♗b3 **♞e5 16 ♞b4 ♝b7 17 a4?** 17 ♕b3 **♞f5! 18 a5** 18 ♗h3? ♘xd4! 19 ♗xd7 ♘ef3+ **bxa5** 18...♘xd4 19 cxd4 bxa5? 20 ♘xd5! ♗xd5 21 dxe5; 19...♘c6 20 a6 **19 ♞bc2 ♞c4 20 ♜xe8+ ♜xe8 21 ♝h3** 21 b3 **♞xb2 22 ♛b1 ♞c4 23 ♞xf5 gxf5 24 ♞d4 ♞d6 25 ♝f4 ♝e5 26 ♝xe5 ♜xe5 27 ♜xa5 ♛c7 28 ♜a3 a5 29 ♛c1** 29 ♕a1 ♘c4 30 ♖a2 ♕e7 **♛e7 30 ♜a1 f4!?**

31 gxf4 31 ♕xf4 ♖e1+ 32 ♖xe1 ♕xe1+ 33 ♔g2 ♕e4+ **♜h5 32 ♝g2 ♞e4 33 ♛e3 ♛h4 34 ♞f3 ♛f6 35 ♛a7?!** 35 ♘d4 **♛xc3 36 ♛xa5 ♜f5??** 36...♕xa5 **37 ♛xc3 ♞xc3 38 ♜a7 ♝c6 39 ♞d4 ♜f6** 39...♘b5 40 ♘xc6 ♘xa7 41 ♘e7+ +− **40 ♜c7 ♚g7 41 ♞xc6 ♞e2+ 42 ♚f1 ♞xf4 43 ♞d4 ♜a6 44 ♞e2 ♞e6 45 ♜c1 d4 46 ♜d1 d3 47 ♞c1 ♜a1 48 ♚e1 ♞c5 49 ♝f1 ♜a6 50 ♞xd3 ♜e6+ 51 ♝e2 1-0**

349 Gofstein-Buturin
USSR 78
1 ♞f3 d5 2 g3 2 b3 **c6! 3 ♝g2 ♝f5 4 d3 ♞f6 5 0-0 e6 6 ♞bd2** 6 ♗f4 h6 7 ♘bd2 ♘bd7 8 ♕e1 g5!? 9 e4!

dxe4 10 dxe4 ♗g4 11 ♗e3± Powell-Peters, USA 76; 6 b3!? **h6** 6...♗e7 7 b3 0-0 8 ♗b2 a5 9 a3 h6 10 c4 += **7 b3 ♝e7 8 ♝b2 ♞bd7** 8...0-0 9 c4 a5 10 a3 ♘bd7 11 ♖c1 ♗h7 12 ♖c2 += **9 ♛e1 0-0 10 e4 ♝h7 11 ♛e2 a5 12 a4 ♛b6 13 ♞e1!?** N 13 ♔h1 ♕a6! 14 e5 ♘e4 A.Petrosian-Vladimirov, USSR 77 **♛a6 14 e5 += ♞e8 15 f4 b5** 15...♘c7 Δ f5 **16 ♚h1 ♞c7** 16...bxa4!? 17 ♖xa4 ♘b6 18 ♖a1 a4 **17 g4 c5?!** 17...f5!? 18 exf6 ♗xf6 19 ♗xf6 ♖xf6 20 ♗h3 Δ ♘g2, g5 += **18 f5 c4 19 axb5 cxd3 20 ♞xd3 ♛xb5 21 f6!± ♝xd3?! 22 cxd3 ♝b4 23 fxg7 ♚xg7 24 g5! hxg5 25 ♛e3 +− ♜h8 26 ♛xg5+ ♚f8 27 ♛g6 1-0 Gufeld**

350 Ribli-Nikolac IBM 78
1 ♞f3 d5 2 g3 c6 3 ♝g2 ♝g4 4 b3 ♞d7 5 ♝b2 ♞gf6 6 0-0 e6 7 d3 ♝xf3 7...♗d6 8 ♘bd2 0-0 9 h3 ♗h5 += **8 ♝xf3 ♝d6 9 ♞bd2 ♛e7** Δ ♗a3 **10 a3 h5!?** 10...0-0 11 c4 += **11 e4 dxe4 12 ♞xe4** 12 dxe4?! ♗e5= **♞xe4 13 ♝xe4** 13 dxe4 ♗e5= **♞f6 14 ♝g2 h4 15 ♛f3! 0-0-0? 16 ♜fe1 hxg3 17 hxg3 ♝c7 18 b4** Δ b5 **♝b6 19 ♜ad1** Δ d4, c4, b5 **a6** 19...a5 20 ♖b1; 19...♖d7 **20 ♜e2± ♜h6 21 d4 ♛f8 22 c4 ♜h5 23 ♜ed2** Δ d5, ♗xf6 **♛h8 24 a4 ♜f5 25 ♛b3 ♛h5 26 b5 axb5 27 axb5 c5 28 ♛a4 ♚b8 29 dxc5 ♜xd2 30 ♜xd2 ♜xc5 31 ♝xf6 gxf6 32 ♜d7 1-0 Taulbut**

351 Langeweg-Nikolac IBM 78
1 ♞f3 ♞f6 2 c4 b6 3 g3 ♝b7 4 ♝g2 e6 5 0-0 ♝e7 6 b3 0-0 7 ♝b2 d5 8 e3 ♞bd7 9 ♞c3 ♞e4 10 cxd5 ♞xc3 11 dxc3 exd5 11...♗xd5 12 ♕e2 Δ e4/♖fd1 **12 ♛c2 ♝f6 13 ♜fd1 += ♛e7 14 ♜ac1 ♜fd8 15 ♞e1! ♞c5?** 15...♘e5 16 c4±; 15...c6 +=/±

16 ♝a3± c6 17 ♞d3 ♜ac8 18 c4 d4 19 e4 g6 20 ♛d2 ♝g7 21 ♜c2 ♝f8 22 ♝xc5 bxc5 23 ♜e1 ♛c7 24 e5 ♜e8 25 f4 ♜cd8 26 ♝e4 ♝c8 27 ♛g2 ♝d7 28 g4 ♚h8 29 ♛f3 ♜e6 30 ♜ce2 ♝e7 31 ♚h1 ♜g8 32 f5 gxf5 33 gxf5 ♜h6 33...♖xe5 34 ♘xe5 ♕xe5 35 ♗d3 +− **34 ♜g2 ♛c8 35 ♜eg1 ♜xg2 36 ♜xg2 f6 37 e6 ♝e8 38 ♛g4 1-0 Taulbut**

352 Kasparov-Sideifzade USSR 78
1 ♞f3 ♞f6 2 c4 g6 3 ♞c3 d5 4 cxd5 ♞xd5 5 ♛a4+ ♝d7 6 ♛h4 e6?! 6...♗c6 7 ♕d4 += **7 ♞xd5 exd5 8 ♛d4 f6 9 ♛xd5 ♞c6** ∝/+= **10 ♛b3** 10 ♕e4+ ♕e7 11 ♕xe7+ ♗xe7 12 a3! ♘a5 13 d3±; 10...♗e7 **♛e7 11 d3** 11 ♕xb7? ♖b8 12 ♕xc7 ♖c8 13 ♕g3 ♘b4 14 ♘d4 ♘xa2∓; 11 e3!? 0-0-0 12 ♗e2 g5 13 0-0 g4 14 ♘e1 ♘d4 15 ♕d1 ♘xe2+ 16 ♕xe2 h5 += **0-0-0 12 ♝d2 ♝g4 13 0-0-0 ♝xf3 14 gxf3 ♞d4 15 ♛a4 ♞xe2+ 16 ♚b1 ♞d4!** 16...♖xd3? 17 ♕c4 ♕d7 18 ♗xe2 ♖xd2 19 ♖xd2 ♕xd2 20 ♖d1 +− **17 ♛xa7 ♛c5 18 ♛a8+??** 18 ♕xc5 ♗xc5 19 ♗e3 f5 20 f4 +=/= **♚d7 19 ♝h3+ f5 20 ♛xb7 ♛c2+ 21 ♚a1 ♝d6 −+ 22 ♛d5** 22 ♗c3 ♖b8 23 ♕d5 ♕xc3!

♜a8! 23 ♝a5 ♛a4 24 b4 ♜xa5! 25 bxa5 ♞c2+ 26 ♚b2 ♜b8+ 27 ♚c1 ♞d4 28 ♚d2 ♛b4+ 0-1 Kasparov

353 Gufeld-Alburt
USSR 78

1 ♞f3 ♞f6 2 g3 c5 3 ♝g2 ♞c6 4 0-0 d5 5 d3 e5 6 e4 ♝e7 7 ♞c3 7 exd5 **d4 8 ♞e2 h5?! 9 c4** 9 ♘h4!? **♝g4 10 ♞h4 g6 11 h3** 11 f3!? ♗d7 12 f4 **♝d7 12 f4 exf4 13 ♞xf4** 13 gxf4!? **♞e5** 13...g5? 14 ♘d5 gxh4 15 ♘xe7 ♕xe7 16 ♗g5 +− **14 ♞f3 ♝d6 15 ♞d5?!** 15 b4!? cxb4 16 a3 ∝/+= **♞xd5 16 exd5 ♞xf3+ 17 ♛xf3 ♝f5= 18 ♝f4** 18 ♖e1 ♔f8 **0-0 19 ♝xd6 ♛xd6 20 ♜ae1** 20 g4?! hxg4 21 hxg4 ♗d7 22 ♖ae1 f5 =+ **♛d7 =+**

21 ♜f2! ♜ae8 21...♗xh3 22 ♗xh3 ♕xh3 25 ♖e7≈ **22 ♜fe2 ♜xe2 23 ♜xe2 ♜e8 24 ♚f2 ♜xe2+ 25 ♛xe2 ♛d6 26 h4! ♚f8 27 ♝e4 ♝d7 28 ♛d2 b5 29 b3 ♛f6+ 30 ♚g2 b4 31 ♛f2 ♛a6 32 ♛d2 ♚g7 33 ♚f2 ♝h3 34 ♚e1 ♝g4 35 ♚f2 ♛f6+ 36 ♚e1 ♛e7 37 ♚f2 a5 38 ♛f4 ♛f6 39 ♛xf6+ ♚xf6 40 ♝f3 ♝f5 41 ♝e4 ♝d7 42 ♝f3 a4 43 ♝d1 a3 44 ♝e2 ♝f5 45 ♚g2 ♚e5 46 ♚f2 f6 47 ♚g2 g5 48 ♚f2 ♝g6 49 ♚g2 ♝e8** 49...gxh4 50 gxh4 ♔f4 51 ♔f2 **50 ♚f2 ♚f5 51 ♚f3 ♚e5 50 ♚f2 g4 53 ♝d1 f5 54 ♝c2!= f4 55 ♚g2 fxg3** 55...f3+ = **56 ♚xg3 ♝d7 57 ♝b1 ♝f5 58 ♝c2 ♝g6 59 ♝b1 ½-½ Gufeld**

354 Vladimirov-Agzamov USSR 78

1 ♞f3 ♞f6 2 g3 d5 3 ♝g2 c5 4 0-0 ♞c6 5 d3 e5 6 ♝g5!? ♝e7 7 ♞fd2 7 ♗xf6 ♗xf6 8 ♘fd2 e4!? **♝e6** 7...♘g8! **8 ♝xf6 ♝xf6 9 ♞c3 0-0 10 e4 d4 11 ♞d5 ♞b4! 12 ♞xf6+ ♛xf6 13 f4 += exf4 14 gxf4 ♛h6 15 f5 ♝d7 16 ♜f3 ♞c6 17 ♜h3 ♛f6 18 ♛h5 h6 19 ♚h1** Δ ♖g1, ♘f1-g3-h5 **♚h8 20 ♜g1 ♞b4? 21 ♛d1 ♞xa2 22 ♞f1 a5 23 ♞g3 ♛e5 24 ♝f3 ♜a6 25 ♛d2 ♚h7 26 ♞h5 ♜g8 27 ♞f4!** 27 ♖hg3? g5∝ **♜d6?** Zeitnot 27...♘b4 **28 ♝h5 +− ♝e8 29 ♞e6! ♜xe6 30 fxe6 ♛xe6 31 ♝g4 ♛d6 32 ♝f5+ ♚h8 33 ♜g6! 1-0** 33...fxg6 34 ♖xh6+ gxh6 35 ♕xh6 mate

355 Panno-Djindjihashvili
Buenos Aires 2 78

1 ♞f3 ♞f6 2 g3 g6 3 b3 ♝g7 4 ♝b2 d6 4...d5 5 ♗g2 c5= **5 ♝g2 e5 6 0-0** 6 d4!? e4 =+ **e4! 7 ♞e1 0-0 8 c4 ♜e8 9 d3 e3!∓ 10 f3 d5 11 ♞c2 c5!** Δ d4∓ **12 cxd5 ♞xd5 13 ♝xg7 ♚xg7 14 d4 ♞b4! 15 ♞xb4** 15 ♘ba3!? ♘xc2 16 ♘xc2 ♗f5!∓ **cxb4 16 a3 ♝e6! 17 f4 ♞c6 18 d5 ♛f6! 19 ♜a2 ♜ad8 −+**

20 f5 ♝xd5! 21 ♝xd5 ♛e5 22 fxg6 ♜xd5 23 ♛e1 23 ♖xf7+ ♔xg6 24 ♕f1 ♖ed8 −+ **hxg6 24 axb4 ♜ed8 25 ♛c3 ♞d4! −+ 26 ♛b2 ♜c8 27 ♞a3** 27 ♖xa7 ♖c2 −+ **b5!** Zugzwang **28 ♜f4 g5! 29 ♜f1 f5 30 ♛b1 ♜d6 31 ♛a1 ♚g6** 31...♖h8! −+ **32 ♛b1 ♜dc6 33 ♛a1 ♜c3 34 ♜d1 ♞xb3 35 ♛b1 ♞d2** 35...♘d4! −+ **32 ♛b1 ♜dc6 33 ♛a1 ♜c3 34 ♜d1 ♞xb3 35 ♛b1 ♞d2** 35...♘d4! −+ **36 ♛a1 f4??** 36...♔h5 Δ ♔g4 −+ **37 ♞b1! ♞xb1 38 ♛xb1+ ♚f6 39 ♜a6+ ♜3c6 40 ♜xa7 1-0** time **Gheorghiu**

356 Pomar Ciocaltea
Buenos Aires 78

1 ♞f3 g6 2 d4 ♝g7 3 g3 ♞f6 4 ♝g2 0-0 5 0-0 d6 6 b3 c6?! 6...e5!?; 6... c5!? **7 ♝b2** 7 c4 e5 8 dxe5 dxe5 9 ♗a3 ♕xd1 10 ♖xd1 ♖e8 11 ♘c3 e4?± Romanishin-Geller, USSR Final 76 **a5 8 a4! ♞a6 9 ♞bd2 d5** 9...♗f5 10 ♘h4 Δ e4± **10 ♜e1 ♞b4 11 c3 ♞a6 12 ♝a3 ♜e8 += 13 e4 dxe4 14 ♞xe4 ♞xe4 15 ♜xe4 ♝f5 16 ♜e1 ♝g4! 17 h3 ♝xf3 18 ♛xf3 e6 19 ♛e2** 19 ♖ad1 ♕b6 Δ ♖ad8≈ **e5?** 19...♕b6 Δ ♖ad8 += **20 dxe5± ♜xe5 21 ♛c4 ♛f6** 21...♖xe1+ 22 ♖xe1 ♕d2 23 ♖e7 +− **22 ♜xe5! ♛xe5 23 ♜d1! ♛e8** 23...♕xc3 24 ♕xc3 ♗xc3 25 ♖d7 ♗b4 26 ♗xb4± **24 ♚h2 ♝f8! 25 ♝c1** 25 ♗xf8 ♕xf8 26 ♖d7 ♘c5 27 ♖c7 ♖b8 Δ ♘e6= **♞c5 26 ♝e3 ♞e6? +−** 26...b5!?≈ **27 h4 ♞c7 28 h5 ♜d8 29 ♜xd8 ♛xd8 30 hxg6 hxg6 31 ♝b6! ♛d6 32 ♝xa5 ♞d5 33 ♝xd5 cxd5 34 ♛c8! ♛f6 35 ♚g2** 35 ♗b4? ♕xf2+ = **♚g7 36 ♝d8! ♛e5 37 ♝b6 ♛e4+ 38 ♚h2 ♝d6 39 ♝d4+ ♝e5 40 ♝xe5+ ♛xe5 41 ♛xb7 1-0 Ciocaltea**

1 f4

357 Walter-Schlesinger
Corr 78

1 f4 e5 2 fxe5 d6 3 exd6 ♝xd6 4 ♞f3 ♞f6 5 g3 ♞g4 6 ♝g2 ♞xh2 7 ♞xh2 ♝xg3+ 8 ♚f1 ♛f6+ 8...h5 9 e4 ♘c6 10 d3 ♕d6 11 ♘f3 ♗g4 12 ♗e3 **9 ♞f3** 9 ♗f3 ♗h3+ 10 ♔g1 ♕g6 **g5 10 d4 g4 11 ♜h6 ♛f5 12 e4 ♛b5+** 12...♕xe4 13 ♘h4 ♕e7 14 ♕e2 **13 ♛e2 ♛xe2+ 14 ♚xe2 gxf3+ 15 ♝xf3 ♞c6 16 c3 ♞e7** 16...♗d7 17 ♗g5 ♖g8!? 18 ♖xh7 **17 ♝g5** 17 ♗e3 f5 **♞g8** 17...♖g8 18 ♗xe7 ♔xe7 19 ♘d2 ♗f4 20 ♖xh7 ♗g4 21 ♖f1; 17... f5? 18 ♗f6 ♖f8 19 e5; 17...♘g6 18 ♗f6 ♘f4+ **18 ♜h5 f6 19 ♝e3 ♝d6 20 ♞d2 ♚f8 21 ♜ah1 ♚g7 22 ♜g1+ ♚f7** 22...♔f8 23 e5 fxe5 24 dxe5 ♗e7 25 ♗d5; 23...♗e7 24 ♗d5 Δ ♖xh7, ♖xg8 mate **23 e5 ♝e7** 23...fxe5 24 dxe5 ♗e7 25 ♗d5+ **24 ♝e4 h6** 24...fxe5 25 ♗xh7 **25 ♝g6+ 1-0**

1 g3

358 Larsen-Browne Tilburg 78

1 g3 c5 2 ♝g2 g6 3 c3 3 e4 **d5 4 d4 cxd4 5 cxd4 ♝g7 6 ♞c3 ♞c6 7 ♝xd5** 7 ♘xd5!? e6 8 ♘c3 ♘xd4 **♞xd4** 7...♗xd4!? **8 ♝e3 e5** 8...♘f5?? 9 ♗xf7+!; 8...♕b6!? 9 ♕d2 **9 ♞f3 ♞e7** 9...♘xf3+? 10 ♗xf3 +=/± **10 ♞xe5** 10 ♘xd4?! ♘xd5 11 ♘db5 ♘xe3 12 ♕xd8+ ♔xd8 13 fxe3 **♞xd5 11 ♝xd4 0-0 12 ♞f3** 12 ♘xf7? ♘xc3! **♞xc3 13 bxc3 ♝g4 14 ♝xg7 ♝xf3**

Diagram

15 ♝xf8! 15 ♕xd8 ♖fxd8 16 exf3 ♔xg7= **♝xh1 16 ♛xd8 ♜xd8 17 ♝c5 b6 18 ♝d4 ♝c6 19 g4** 19 f3 f5

f5!? 20 gxf5 gxf5 21 ♚d2 21 f3 Δ ♔f2 **♚f7 22 a3** 22 ♖g1 **♜d6 23 f3 ♜h6 24 ♜h1 ♜g6 25 c4 ♜g2** Δ ♗xf3 **26 ♚e1 ♚e6 27 h3 ♝b7 28 ♚f1 ♜g8 29 ♚f2 ♜c8 30 ♜c1 ♝a6 31 c5 ♚d5!** 31...bxc5? 32 ♗xc5 ♔d5 33 ♗e3 ♖xc1 34 ♗xc1 ♗b5=; 32 ♖xc5! **32 ♝e3 bxc5 33 ♜g1 ♜c7 34 ♜g5 ♜f7 35 ♜h5 ♝b5 36 ♝f4 ♚c4 37 ♝d6! ♚d5 38 ♜h6 a5** 38...c4? 39 ♗b4 **39 ♝f4 ♚c4 40 ♜b6 ♜d7 41 h4** Δ h5-h6 **h5!? 42 ♜h6 ♚b3 43 ♜xh5 ♚xa3** 43...♖f7!? **44 ♜xf5 ♚b4 45 h5 a4 46 h6 a3 47 ♜h5 a2 48 ♝e5 ♜h7 49 ♜h1 c4 50 ♝g7 c3 51 ♜c1 ♜xg7! 52 hxg7 ♝c4 53 ♚e3 ♚b3 54 ♚d4 ♝g8 55 ♜g1 ♚b2 56 ♚d3 ♝b3 57 e4 ♝c2+ 58 ♚d4 ♝b3 59 ♚d3 ½-½ Speelman**

Games Index

ADAMSKI: Bordonada 238; Lerner **14**; Sznapik 196
ADORJAN: Djindjihashvili 44; Jansa 345; Kovacs 174; Mednis **172**; Radio Listeners **268**; Regan 162; Romanishin 152; Timman **22**
AGRAMOV: Panchenko 226
AGZAMOV: Vladimirov 354
ALBURT: Gofstein **85**; Gufeld 353; Kasparov **145**
ALEXANDRIA: Hund 217
AMRAM: Pytel 243
ANDRIANOV: Azmajparashvili **90**
ARSENYEV: Shirmin **267**
ARTISHEVSKY: Fridman **191**
ARZUMANJAN: Sveningsson **287**
ASMUNDSSON: Letzelter 291
ASTAPOV: Kolker **271**
AZMAJPARASHVILI: Andrianov 90; Tabarov 144
BABERO: Romanishin 275
BAGIROV: Rashkovsky **108**
BARCZAY: Lukacs **60**; Pribyl **339**; Trapl 222
BEGUN: Kasparov 59
BELJAVSKY: Kapengut 269; Petrosian **119**
BHEND: Nunn 181
BIGELDIN: Kolker 190
BIRNBOIM: Westerinen **153**
BIYIASAS: Speelman 157
BOHLIG: Filipowicz **89**
BOHOSIAN: Marszalek **274**
BOLL: Smejkal 123
BOTTERILL: Hoi 112; Ligterink **106**; Martin 148; Miles 81, **129**; Povah **182**; Short 110; Whiteley **147**
BORDONADA: Adamski 238
BORNGASSER: Miles 227
BOUAZIZ: Wedberg 187
BRAGA: Ghitescu **224**
BRITTON: Nunn **336**
BRONSTEIN: Nikolaevsky 35
L.BRONSTEIN: Miles 61; Tringov **87**
BROWNE: Kagan **337**; Larsen 359; Miles **36**; Petrosian 113
BUGOR: Hardicsay **178**
BULLOCKUS: Dobsa 307
BUTURIN: Chechelian **120**; Gofstein 349
BUZBUCHI: Prundeanu **326**
BYRNE: Kuligowski 69
CASPER: Enders 302
CHANDLER: Unzicker 328
CHECHELIAN: Buturin 120
CHIBURDANIDZE: Dvoretsky **177**; Erenska **240**; Gaprindashvili **183**, 184, **214**, 248, 255, **273**, 278, 314, **315**, **316**, **318**, 329, 346; Kaiszauri **256**; J.Miles **245**; Tukmakov **195**
CHRISTIANSEN: Kochiev **141**
CIOCALTEA: Giffard **241**; Liu Wen Che 247; Matanovic 317; Panno 356; Petrosian 155; Petursson **170**
COOPER: Petrosian **107**; Speelman 142
CORDEN: Speelman **160**
CSOM: Espig 8; J.Fernandez 210
DANIELSON: Filipowicz **83**
DAY: Polugaevsky 55
DE CORVAHLO: Guil.Garcia 70
DE SILVA: Speelman **192**
DELANEY: Iskov **188**
DIESEN: Honfi 179, 230
DIEZ DEL CORRAL: Portisch **286**; W.Schmidt **128**
DJANTAR: Honfi 250
DJINDJIHASHVILI: Adorjan **44**; Panno 355; Portisch 341; Ribli **3**
DJURIC: Hartmann **111**
DOBSA: Bullockus **307**
DOLMATOV: Ristic 176
DONNER: Liu Wen Che 313; Sax 327
DOROSHKEVICH: Gufeld **136**

DAHL: Wurtz **296**
DVORETSKY: Chiburdanidze 177
EDOCS: Hardicsay **189**
EKSTROM: Hjartarson **165**
EMERSON: Haik 132
ENDERS: Casper **302**
EPERJESI: Mihalchishin 245
ERENSKA: Chiburdanidze 240
ERMENKOV: Kirpichnikov **332**; Polugaevsky **198**
ESPIG: Csom **8**
FAIBISOVICH: Karasev **320**
FARAGO: S.Garcia 13; Swic **130**
J.FERNANDEZ: Csom **210**; Malich 114; Martin 306; Mednis 239
FERREIRA: Silva 225
FILGUTH: Panchenko **169**
FILIPENKO: Gofstein 52
FILIPOWICZ: Bohlig 89; Danielsen 83; Tuck 6
FLECKER: Pytel **135**
FORINTOS: Kristiansen **146**
FORMANEK: Zilber **71**
FRIDMAN: Artishevsky 191
FTACNIK: Peresipkin 320; Romanishin **33**
GALAHOV: Gurevich 12
GAPRINDASHVILI: Chiburdanidze 183, **184**, 214, **248**, **255**, 273, **278**, 314, 315, 316, 318, **329**, **346**
GEREKEN: Gliksman 303
GILD.GARCIA: Guil.Garcia 80
GUIL.GARCIA: De Corvahlo **70**; Gild.Garcia **80**; Rogoff 154
S.GARCIA: Farago **13**
GEDEVANISHVILI: Zaichik 88
GEORGADZE: Vogt 186
GHEORGHIU: Onat 249
GHITESCU: Braga 224; Padevsky 93; Sampouw 194; Schneider **102**; Tabanne 211
GIFFARD: Ciocaltea 241
GIPPOREL: Pytel **104**
GLIGORIC: Timman 57
GLIKSMAN: Gereken **303**
GOFSTEIN: Alburt 85; Buturin **349**; Filipenko **52**; Hodos 10; Platonov 39
GOICHBERG: Iskov 218
GONSIOR: Zichichi 15
GONZALEZ: Miles 109
E.GONZALEZ: Pritchett 242
GRIGORIAN: Kishnev **47**; Sherbakov 100
GROSZPETER: Vigh **290**
GUFELD: Alburt **353**; Doroshkevich 136; Hodos **338**; Kasparov 219; Kozlov 138; Rashkovsky 139; Shereshevsky 41
GULKO: Kuligowski **223**; Mikenas **73**
GUREVICH: Galahov **12**
HAIK: Emerson **132**; Roos **133**
HARDICSAY: Bugor 178; Edocs 189; Malich **37**; Mednis **171**; Piasetski **228**; Regan **232**
HARTMANN: Djuric 111
HAUSNER: Vogt **150**
HAZAI: Honfi **161**; Pribyl 40
HJARTARSSON: Ekstrom 165; Pytel 78
HODOS: Gofstein **10**; Gufeld 338
HOFFMANN: Maric 164
HOI: Botterill **112**
HONFI: Diesen **179**, **230**; Djantar **250**; Hazai 161; Magyar **276**; Nemet **204**; Padevsky 266; Raicevic **301**; Smejkal **252**; Trabattoni 281; Vukic **304**
HORT: Nikolac 126; Romanishin **121**; Spassky **297**; Vogt **143**
HUBNER: Ljubojevic 282; Spassky **344**
HUG: R.Rodriguez **279**
HUND: Alexandria **217**
HUSS: Letzelter 284
INKIOV: Spassov 213
ISKOV: Delaney 188; Goichberg 218;

Niklasson **94**
IVKOV: Matanovic **270**, 277
JANOSEVIC: Jansa **231**
JANSA: Adorjan **345**, Janosevic 231
JANSSON: Pavlov 308
JUFEROV: Kapengut **199**
KAGAN: Browne **337**; Kasparov **45**; Polugaevsky 206; A.Saharov 105
KAIZAURI: Chiburdanidze **256**; Peshina 166
KAPENGUT: Beljavsky 269; Juferov 199; Kim 173; Tseshkovsky 205; Zilberstein 9
KARASEV: Faibisovich 320
KARPOV: Korchnoi **18**, 25, **26**, 27, **30**, 31, **63, 64, 65, 66, 67, 68, 76, 77, 97, 98, 101, 103, 167,** 258, 259, 260, 261, 262, 263, 264, 265, **294, 295, 321, 322**
KASPAROV: Alburt **145**; Begun **59**; Gufeld 219; Kagan 45; Palatnik **309**; Shereshevsky 46; Sideifzade **352**
KEENE: Kuligowski **117**; Szmetan 283
KELLER: Pytel 4
KIM: Kapengut **173**
KIRPICHNIKOV: Ermenkov 332
KISHNEV: Grigorian 47
KOCHIEV: Christiansen **141**; Kuzmin 134; A.Rodriguez **229**
KOIFMAN: Shestoperov 49
KOKKINOSZ: Soos **96**
KOLKER: Astapov **271**; Bigeldin 190
KORCHNOI: Karpov 18, **25**, 26, **27**, 30, **31**, 63, 64, 65, 66, 67, 68, 76, 77, 97, 98, 101, 103, 167, **258, 259, 260, 261, 262, 263, 264, 265,** 294, 295, 321, 322; Panno 95
KOSIKOV: Rashkovsky 50
KOVACS: Adorjan 174
KOZLOV: Gufeld 138; Mischuchkov 127; Sveshnikov 74; Zelnin 140
KRISTIANSEN: Forintos 146
KRUG: Vogt 215
KULIGOWSKI: Byrne 69; Gulko **223**; Keene 117
KUZMIN: Kochiev **134**; Tukmakov 118
LABARTHE: Smejkal **19**
LAIN: Nogueiras **212**
LAK: M.Tseitlin **257**
LANGEWEG: Nikolac **351**; Romanishin **343**
LARSEN: Browne 358; Pomar 251; Portisch **293**; O.Rodriguez 124; Speelman **38**
LEBREDO: Petrosian 2
LECHTYNSKY: Skrobek 299
LEGKY: Shvedchikov 86
LEMACHKO: Petronic **254**
LERNER: Adamski **14**
LETZELTER: Asmundsson **291**; Huss **284**
LIGTERINK: Botterill **106**
P.LITTLEWOOD: Speelman 159
LIU WEN CHE: Ciocaltea **247**; Donner **313**
LJUBOJEVIC: Hubner **282**; Ribli 203; Sosonko 220; Sznapik **323**
LUKACS: Barczay **60**
LUNDIN: Schussler 24
MADENBRINK: Pytel 11
MAGYAR: Honfi **276**
MAKROPOULOS: Radulov **246**
MALICH: J.Fernandez 114; Hardicsay **37**; Mednis **234**; Nunn 84; Regan **163**
MARIC: Hoffmann 164; Weill 253
MARIOTTI: Pribyl **333**
MARSZALEK: Bohosian **274**; Pokojowczyk **221**
MARTIN: Botterill 148; J.Fernandez **306**
MASCARINAS: Sznapik **216**
MATANOVIC: Ciocaltea **318**; Ivkov 270, **277**
MATSUMADO: Sigurjonsson 288

MEDNIS: Adorjan **172**; J.Fernandez 239; Hardicsay **171**; Malich 234
MEDUNA: Vogt **185**
MIHALCHISHIN: Eperjesi **244**
MIHALJCISIN: Raicevic **72**
MIKENAS: Gulko **73**
MILES: Botterill 81, **129**; Borngasser **227**; L.Bronstein 61; Browne **36**; Gonzalez 109; Rivas 48; Spassky **115, 116**
MILES.J: Chiburdanidze **245**
MISHUCHKOV: Kozlov **127**
MORRIS: Rantanen **201**
MURASHKO: Semeniuk 29
NEMET: Honfi **204**
NICEVSKI: Ozsvath **311**; Schinzel **168**; Vilela **300**
NICHOLSON: Emerson **235**
NIKLASSON: Iskov 94
NIKOLAC: Hort 126; Langeweg 351; Pfleger **51**; Ribli 350; Timman **62**
NIKOLAEVSKY: Bronstein 35
NOGUEIRAS: Lain 212
NORDBY: Pytel 202
NUNN: Bhend 181; Britton 336; Malich **84**; Piasetski **298**; F.Portisch 180; Spassov 209; Vadasz **58**; Vaganian **56**; Zapata 233
NURMI: Speelman 1
OCHOA: Rivas 305; Silva **193**
ONAT: Gheorghiu **249**
OSTOJIC: F.Portisch **292**; Pytel **21**
OZSVATH: Nicevski 311
PADEVSKY: Ghitescu 93; Honfi 266
PALACIOS: Rivas 312
PALATNIK: Kasparov 309; Romanishin **342**
PANCHENKO: Agramov 226; Filguth **169**
PANNO: Ciocaltea **356**; Djindjihashvili **355**; Korchnoi **95**
PAVLOV: Jansson **308**
PEEV: Pribyl **42**; Timoshenko 92; Trapl 149
PERESIPKIN: Ftacnik **330**
PESHINA: Kaizauri **166**
PETERS: Seret **272**
PETRONIC: Lemachko 254
PETROSIAN: Beljavsky **119**; Browne 113; Ciocaltea 155; Cooper **107**; Lebredo **2**
PETURRSON: Ciocaltea **170**
PFLEGER: Nikolac 51; Polugaevsky **54**; Timman 34
PIASETSKI: Hardicsay **228**
PLATANOV: Gofstein 39
POKOJOWCZYK: Marszalek 221; Sznapik 236
POLUGAEVSKY: Day 55, Ermenkov **198**; Kagan **206**; Pfleger 54
POMAR: Larsen **251**
PORTISCH: Diez del Corral 286; Djindjihashvili **341**; Larsen 293; Spassky 285
F.PORTISCH: Nunn **180**; Ostojic 292; Ujtelky 156
POVAH: Botterill **182**; Tatai **82**
PRANDSTETTER: Vilela **20**
PRIBYL: Barczay 339; Hazai 40; Mariotti 333; Peev 42; Skrobek 325; Swic **331**
PRIPIS: Rashkovsky **122**
PRITCHETT: E.Gonzalez 242
PRUNDEANU: Buzbuchi 326
PYTEL: Amram 243; Flecker **135**; Gipparel **104**; Hjartarsson 78; Keller 4; Madenbrinck **11**; Nordby **202**; Ostojic 21: Reicher **91**; Seret 16; Tiller 32; Zasche 5
RADULOV: Makropoulos 246
RAICEVIC: Honfi 301; Mihaljcisin **72**
RAITZA: Thormann **324**
RANTANEN: Morris 201
RASHKOVSKY: Bagirov **108**; Gufeld 139; Kosikov 50; Shtukaturkin 158
REE: Speelman **17**

REGAN: Adorjan 162; Hardicsay **232**; Malich 163
REICHER: Pytel 91
RIBLI: Djindjihashvili **3**; Ljubojevic **203**; Nikolac **350**; Romanishin **7**; Timman 131
RISTIC: Dolmatov 176
RIVAS: Miles **48**; Ochoa **305**; Palacios **312**
A.RODRIGUEZ: Kochiev 229
O.RODRIGUEZ: Larsen **124**
R.RODRIGUEZ: Hug **279**
ROGOFF: Guil.Garcia 154; Villareal 151
ROMANISHIN: Adorjan 152; Babero 275; Ftacnik **33**; Hort **121**; Langeweg 343; Palatnik 342; Ribli 7; Sveshnikov 324; Timman **23**; Vaganian **348**
ROOS: Haik **133**
SAHAROV: Kagan **105**
SAHOVIC: Speelman 43; Taimanov 340
SAMPOUW: Ghitescu 194
SAVON: Velikov **28**
SAX: Donner **327**; Tukmakov 197
SCHINZEL: Nicevski **168**
SCHLESINGER: Walter 357
SCHMIDT: Diez del Corral **128**; Spassky 79; Torre 137
SCHNEIDER: Ghitescu **102**; Sosonko **75**
SCHURADE: Thormann **347**
SCHUSSLER: Lundin 24
SEMENIUK: Murashko **29**
SERET: Peters **272**; Pytel **16**
SHERBAKOV: Grigorian 100
SHERESHEVSKY: Gufeld 41; Kasparov 46
SHESTOPEROV: Koifman 49
SHIRMAN: Arsenyev 267
SHORT: Botterill **110**
SHTUKATURKIN: Rashkovsky **158**
SHVEDCHIKOV: Legky **86**
SIDEIF ZADE: Kasparov 352
SIGURJONSSON: Matsumado **288**; Westerinen **237**; Wibe **207**
SILVA: Ferreira 225; Ochoa 193
SINKOVITS: Szalancy 289
SKROBEK: Lechtynsky **299**; Pribyl **325**
SMEJKAL: Boll 123; Honfi **250**; Labarthe 19
SOOS: Kokkinosz 96
SOSONKO: Ljubojevic **220**; Schneider 75
SPASSKY: Hort 297; Hubner 344; Miles 115, 116; Portisch **285**; W.Schmidt **79**
SPASSOV: Inkiov **213**; Nunn **209**
SPEELMAN: Biyiasas 157; Cooper 142; Corden **160**; Larsen 38; P.Littlewood **159**; Nurmi **1**; Ree 17; Sahovic **43**; de Silva 192
SURADIRADJA: Torre **175**
SVENNINGSSON: Arzumanjan 287
SVESHNIKOV: Kozlov **74**; Romanishin **334**; Tseshkovsky **335**; Tukmakov **53**
SWIC: Farago **130**: Pribyl 331
SYRE: Thormann 319
SZALANCY: Sinkovits **289**
SZMETAN: Keene **283**; Vaisman 310
SZNAPIK: Adamski 196; Ljubojevic 323; Mascarinas 216; Pokojowczyk **236**
TABANNE: Ghitescu 211
TABOROV: Azmajparashvili **144**
TAIMANOV: Sahovic **340**
TATAI: Povah 82
THORMANN: Raitza 324; Schurade 347; Syre **319**
TILLER: Pytel **32**
TIMMAN: Adorjan **22**; Gligoric 57; Nikolac 62; Pfleger **34**; Ribli **131**; Romanishin 23
TIMOSHENKO: Peev **92**; Volchikhin **125**

TORRE: W.Schmidt **137**; Suradiradja 175
TRABATTONI: Honfi **281**
TRAPL: Barczay 222, Peev **149**
TRINGOV: L.Bronstein **87**
TSESHKOVSKY: Sveshnikov **335**
M.TSEITLIN: Lak 257; Vladimirov 280
TSESHKOVSKY: Kapengut **205**; Tukmakov 200
TUCK: Filipowicz 6
TUKMAKOV: Chiburdanidze **195**; Kuzmin **118**; Sax **197**; Sveshnikov 53; Tseshkovsky **200**
UJTELKY: F.Portisch **156**
UNZICKER: Chandler **328**
VADASZ: Nunn 58
VAGANIAN: Nunn 56; Romanishin 348
VAISER: Zilberstein 99
VAISMAN: Szmetan **310**
VELIKOV: Savon 28
VILELA: Nicevski 300 Prandstetter 20
VILLAREAL: Rogoff **151**
VITOLINS: Westerinen **208**
VLADIMIROV: Agzamov 354; M. Tseitlin **280**
VOGT: Georgadze 186; Hausner **150**; Hort **143**; Krug **215**; Meduna 185
VOLCHIKHIN: Timoshenko 125
VUKIC: Honfi 304
WALTER: Schlesinger **357**
WEDBERG: Bouaziz 187
WEILL: Maric **253**
WESTERINEN: Birnboim **153**; Sigurjonsson 237; Vitolins 208
WIBE: Sigurjonsson 207
WHITELEY: Botterill **147**
WURTZ: Dahl 296
ZAICHIK: Gedevanishvili 88
ZASCHE: Pytel **5**
ZELNIN: Kozlov **140**
ZICHICHI: Gonsior 15
ZILBERSTEIN: Kapengut 9; Vaiser **99**